EAST ANGLIAN ARCHAEOLOGY

Frontispiece: Oblique aerial photograph looking north-west across Area D, Great Fransham, showing ridge-and-furrow in a narrow field beyond the farm in the foreground, with High Green Farm /Med 112 towards top left (TF 92 14 / A / HST 6, Derek Edwards 8/5/1998)

To the memory of Alan Davison and Trevor Ashwin, two stalwarts of Norfolk archaeology, and Valerie Mary Garland, whose legacy to the Norfolk & Norwich Archaeological Society made publication of this volume possible.

'Houses rise and fall, crumble, are extended,
Are removed, destroyed, restored, or in their place
Is an open field'

From *East Coker* by T.S. Eliot (1940)

FRANSHAM:
people and land in a central Norfolk parish from the Palaeolithic to the eve of Parliamentary Enclosure

by Andrew Rogerson

with illustrations by
Steven Ashley and Jason Gibbons

East Anglian Archaeology
Report No. 176, 2022

Historic Environment Service
Norfolk County Council

EAST ANGLIAN ARCHAEOLOGY
REPORT NO.176

Published by
Historic Environment Service
Norfolk County Council
Union House
Gressenhall
Dereham NR20 4DR

in conjunction with
ALGAO East
www.algao.org.uk/england

Editor: S.E. West
Managing Editor: Jenny Glazebrook

Editorial Board:
James Albone, Historic England
Abby Antrobus, Historic Environment, Suffolk County Council
Brian Ayers, University of East Anglia
Stewart Bryant, Archaeological Consultant
Kasia Gdaniec, Historic Environment, Cambridgeshire County Council
Maria Medlycott, Historic Environment, Essex County Council
Zoe Outram, Historic England Science Adviser
John Percival, Historic Environment, Norfolk County Council
Adrian Tindall, Archaeological Consultant
Alison Tinniswood, Historic Environment, Hertfordshire County Council
Jess Tipper, Historic England

Set in Times New Roman by Jenny Glazebrook using Corel Ventura™
Printed by Henry Ling Limited, The Dorset Press

© HISTORIC ENVIRONMENT SERVICE, NORFOLK COUNTY COUNCIL

ISBN 978 0 905594 57 6

Published with the aid of funding from the Aurelius Charitable Trust, Council for British Archaeology East, Norfolk & Norwich Archaeological Society and Norfolk Historic Environment Service.

East Anglian Archaeology was established in 1975 by the Scole Committee for Archaeology in East Anglia. The scope of the series expanded in 2002 to include all six eastern counties. Responsibility for publication rests with the editorial board in partnership with the Association of Local Government Archaeological Officers, East of England (ALGAO East).

For details of *East Anglian Archaeology*, see last page

Cover illustration
View from the site of Curds Hall, looking east towards All Saints' church, Great Fransham.
Photo: Andrew Rogerson

Contents

List of Plates	vi
List of Figures	vi
List of Tables	viii
Acknowledgements	viii
Abbreviations	ix
Summary/Résumé/Zusammenfassung	ix

Chapter 1 Introduction
The study area	1
The choice of the study area	6
Methods of archaeological survey	7
Site definition	9
The use of documentary sources	11

Chapter 2 Prehistory
Introduction	13
The Palaeolithic	13
The Mesolithic	13
The Neolithic and Early Bronze Age	15
Diagnostic worked flints and pottery	15
General scatters of worked flint	19
Pot-boiler sites	19
Gazetteer of pot-boiler sites	20
The later Bronze Age	21
The Iron Age	23

Chapter 3 The Roman period
Introduction	27
Gazetteer of Roman sites	28
Discussion	32

Chapter 4 Early and Middle Saxon periods
Early Saxon: introduction	37
The local background	37
The Fransham evidence	39
Gazetteer of sites	40
Discussion	43
Middle Saxon introduction	45
The local background	45
The Fransham evidence	47
Discussion	49

Chapter 5 Late Saxon and Early Norman periods
Introduction	53
The local background	53
The archaeological evidence in Fransham	54
Gazetteer of sites	55
The Domesday evidence	62
Discussion	67

Chapter 6 Medieval population and wealth, manorial and tenurial structure
Introduction	70
Population and wealth	70
Manorial structure	72
Great Fransham	74
Rougham / Fransham	76
Ellinghams	76
East Lexham	77
Mascales	77
Blyfords	77
Rougholme	77
De Tosny manors in Little Fransham	78
Kirkhams	78
Wilcoks	80
Demesnes of Kirkhams and Wilcoks	80
Sparhams	81
Cannons	81
West Bradenham	82
Barony of Rye	83
Mileham	83
Bromehill Priory	83
Castle Acre Priory	83
Creake Abbey	84
Hempton Priory	84
Pentney Priory	84
Thetford Priory of the Holy Sepulchre	84
Wendling Abbey	84
Great Fransham rectory	85
Little Fransham rectory	85
The Leet of Milles atte Mor	86

Chapter 7 The Medieval landscape
Introduction	89
The location and definition of settlement sites	89
Pottery distribution between settlements	91
The common pastures	94
The allocation of site numbers	94
Documentary references	94
The spelling of le Strange	94
Land divisions	94
Land types	99
Great Fransham Areas A–O	99
Little Fransham *Quarentinae* 1–29	132

Chapter 8 The Middle Ages, an overview
Settlement numbers and population	165
Settlement distribution	167
The dynamics of settlement	168
The tenemental system	171
The pottery industry	172
Late Medieval decline	173
Agrarian organisation	173

Chapter 9 The Post-medieval period
The archaeological evidence	175
The documentary evidence	175
Population	178
Settlement	179
The common pastures	184
Demesne lands	185
Enclosure	189
The Necton Town estate	190
The end of the study period and the Parliamentary Enclosure of 1807	190

Chapter 10 Postscript
	192

Appendix 1 Translation of the Great Fransham
feodary of c.1279   195
Appendix 2 Gazetteer of medieval settlement sites   197
Appendix 3 Documents relating to 'Rougham
and Fransham' manor   238
Appendix 4 Unlocated medieval place names   239
Appendix 5 References to fald gates up to 1526   240
Appendix 6 Gazetteer of post-medieval settlement sites   241

Bibliography   243
Index, by Sue Vaughan   263

List of Plates

Frontispiece: Oblique aerial photograph looking across Area D, Great Fransham   ii

Plate	Description	Page
Plate 1.1	Enclosure Award map, drawn in 1805 (NRO C/Sca 2/122)	2
Plate 3.1	Detail from 1946 RAF vertical aerial photograph showing 'A', north at top	31
Plate 6.1	Undated quitclaim by Robert son of Roger le Strange of Little Fransham to William de Sapy of a messuage and four acres called *Princescroft*, before 1273 (NRO MC 360/5, 713X6)	75
Plate 6.2	Undated grant by John of Little Fransham, son of Roger le Strange, to his son Henry of Hugh his villein (*rusticus*) with all his tenement and land, along with one piece and 2½ acres of land, before 1273 (NRO MC 360/6, 713X6)	75
Plate 6.3	The earliest extant court roll of Little Fransham (Kirkhams) manor, held on the Saturday after the feast of St Agnes, 20 Edward II (24 January 1327) (NRO MS 13090 40A4)	79
Plate 7.1	Copy of Enclosure Award map, drawn in 1833 (NRO Ca 1/22)	92
Plate 7.2	Detail from Enclosure Award map, Great Fransham rectory in Area B	106
Plate 7.3	Detail from 1946 RAF vertical aerial photograph, part of Area B with West End Moor and Med 22–9	107
Plate 7.4	Pottery sherds from Med 35 and Med 36	111
Plate 7.5	All Saints' church Great Fransham in Area L, from the south-east, July 2018	125
Plate 7.6	Detail from 1946 RAF vertical aerial photograph, centred on St Katherine's meadow in Area N	128
Plate 7.7	Detail from 1988 vertical aerial photograph, centred on St Katherine's meadow in Area N	128
Plate 7.8	Detail from 1946 RAF vertical aerial photograph, showing main village of Little Fransham, *Quarents.* 5, 6, 11 and 12	137
Plate 7.9	Detail from the Enclosure Award map, showing main village of Little Fransham	137
Plate 7.10	Detail from the Enclosure Award map, Little Fransham rectory in *Quarent.* 6	138
Plate 7.11	St Mary's church Little Fransham in *Quarent.* 6, from south-east, July 2018	140
Plate 7.12	Detail from the Enclosure Award map, Kirkhams manor house site (Med 74) in *Quarent.* 9	142
Plate 7.13	Detail from 1946 RAF vertical aerial photograph, Kirkhams manor house site (Med 74) in *Quarent.* 9	143
Plate 7.14	Detail from copy of Enclosure Award map, Cannons grange in *Quarent.* 16	150
Plate 7.15	Looking north-east from the Pack Way across *Quarent.* 19 towards Med 116	155
Plate 7.16	Lower Farm on the western edge of Eastendmoor, Little Fransham, in *Quarent.* 29, July 2018	161
Plate 10.1	Looking south-west from just north of Med 94 along the A47 trunk road, November 2018	194
Plate 10.2	Fransham village sign, November 2018	194

List of Figures

Fig.	Description	Page
Fig. 1.1	Norfolk and Fransham, with edge of Central Norfolk Clay Plateau shown stippled, scale 1:600,000	xii
Fig. 1.2	Fransham, soil types, contours and drainage, scale 1:25,000	4
Fig. 1.3	Fransham and surrounding parishes in c.1923	5
Fig. 1.4	Fransham, major unsurveyed areas, scale 1:25,000	8
Fig. 1.5	Schematic plans showing locations of archaeological sites from the Iron Age to the medieval period	10

Chapter 2

Fig.	Description	Page
Fig. 2.1	Distribution of Palaeolithic and Mesolithic finds, scale 1:25,000	12
Fig. 2.2	Lower Palaeolithic hand-axe and Upper Palaeolithic scraper, scale 1:2	13
Fig. 2.3	Distribution of Neolithic and Bronze Age finds, and 'pot boiler' sites, scale 1:25,000	14

Fig. 2.4	Late Neolithic / Early Bronze Age flint arrowhead, scale 1:1	15
Fig. 2.5	Neolithic flint pick, scale 1:2	16
Fig. 2.6	Fragment of Neolithic stone axe, scale 1:2	17
Fig. 2.7	Early Bronze Age flint dagger, scale 1:1	17
Fig. 2.8	Worked flint densities, scale 1:25,000	18
Fig. 2.9	Middle Bronze Age spearhead and palstave chisel, scale 1:2	21
Fig. 2.10	Late Bronze Age gold pendant, scale 1:1	23
Fig. 2.11	Iron Age sites, scale 1:25,000	22
Fig. 2.12	Late Iron Age scabbard mount and harness fitting, and Iron Age or Romano-British razor, scale 1:1)	25

Chapter 3

Fig. 3.1	Romano-British sites expressed as sherd distributions, scale 1:25,000	26
Fig. 3.2	RB 1, scale 1:5,000	28
Fig. 3.3	Romano-British sites with suggested areas of arable, scale 1:25,000	34

Chapter 4

Fig. 4.1	Early Saxon sites and sherd scatters, scale 1:25,000	38
Fig. 4.2	ES 1, ES 2 and ES 6, scale 1:5,000	41
Fig. 4.3	Early Saxon brooch knob found near ES 5, scale 1:1	41
Fig. 4.4	Late Roman and Early Saxon metal objects, scale 1:1	42
Fig. 4.5	Early Saxon metal objects, scale 1:1	43
Fig. 4.6	Early Saxon Small-long brooch, scale 1:1	43
Fig. 4.7	Middle Saxon site and sherd scatters, scale 1:25,000	46
Fig. 4.8	MS 1, individually plotted sherds, scale 1:5,000	47
Fig. 4.9	Incomplete ninth- and ninth/tenth-century strap-ends, scale 1:1	48
Fig. 4.10	Fransham, Wendling and adjoining parish boundaries, scale 1:200,000	50

Chapter 5

Fig. 5.1	Late Saxon and early Norman sites and sherd scatters, scale 1:25,000	52
Fig. 5.2	LS 20, Fluxgate gradiometer survey results and interpretation, scale 1:1,250	59
Fig. 5.3	LS 20, Fluxgate Gradiometer survey and sherd concentrations in simplified outline, scale 1:2,500	60
Fig. 5.4	Late Saxon copper alloy buckle frames and stirrup terminal, scale 1:1	62

Chapter 7

Fig. 7.1	Medieval settlement sites known from archaeological evidence, scale 1:25,000	88
Fig. 7.2	Distribution of medieval ceramic roof tile, scale 1:25,000	90
Fig. 7.3	Subdivisions of Great Fransham into Areas A–O and Little Fransham in *Quarentinae* 1–29, scale 1:25,000	98
Fig. 7.4	Area A, scale 1:10,560, with key to symbols shown on plans of Areas and *quarentinae*	100
Fig. 7.5	Med 4, distribution of sherds, scale 1:5,000	101
Fig. 7.6	Med 5, distribution of sherds, scale 1:5,000	101
Fig. 7.7	Medieval copper alloy objects from Med 5 and impression taken from seal matrix, scale 1:1	102
Fig. 7.8	Area B, scale 1:10,560	104
Fig. 7.9	Med 15 and 19, distribution of sherds, scale 1:5,000	105
Fig. 7.10	Late medieval buckle frame found near Med 17, scale 1:1	105
Fig. 7.11	Med 24–9, distribution of sherds, scale 1:5,000	107
Fig. 7.12	Area C, scale 1:10,560	108
Fig. 7.13	Med 33–43, distribution of sherds, scale 1:5,000	110
Fig. 7.14	Areas D–G, scale 1:10,560	112
Fig. 7.15	Med 112 and surrounding earthworks, scale 1:5,000	113
Fig. 7.16	Med 113, earthwork site, scale 1:1,250	114
Fig. 7.17	Med 54 and 55, distribution of sherds, scale 1:5,000	115
Fig. 7.18	Med 56, distribution of sherds, scale 1:5,000	116
Fig. 7.19	Areas H and O, scale 1:10,560	119
Fig. 7.20	Med 57, 60 and 69, distribution of sherds, scale 1:5,000	120
Fig. 7.21	Areas J and N, scale 1:10,560	121
Fig. 7.22	Areas K and L, scale 1:10,560	122
Fig. 7.23	Twelfth-century copper alloy sword scabbard chape, scale 1:1	125
Fig. 7.24	Area M, scale 1:10,560	126
Fig. 7.25	Two medieval copper alloy objects, scale 1:1	127
Fig. 7.26	Med 61 and 115, distribution of sherds, scale 1:5,000	129
Fig. 7.27	Med 62 and 93, distribution of sherds, scale 1:5,000	130
Fig. 7.28	*Quarentinae* 1 and 2, scale 1:10,560	132
Fig. 7.29	Med 9–12, distribution of sherds, scale 1:5,000	133
Fig. 7.30	*Quarentinae* 3 and 4, scale 1:10,560	134
Fig. 7.31	*Quarentinae* 5 and 6, scale 1:10,560	136
Fig. 7.32	Med 89 and 90, distribution of sherds, scale 1:5,000	138
Fig. 7.33	Plan of Little Fransham rectory in 1804, scale not given	139
Fig. 7.34	*Quarentinae* 7 and 8, scale 1:10,560	141
Fig. 7.35	*Quarentina* 9, scale 1:10,560	142
Fig. 7.36	*Quarentina* 10, scale 1:10,560	143
Fig. 7.37	Med 98–102, distribution of sherds, scale 1:5,000	144
Fig. 7.38	Med 100 and 101 soilmarks, distribution of sherds, scale 1:5,000	144
Fig. 7.39	*Quarentinae* 11–15, scale 1:10,560	145
Fig. 7.40	Med 86–8, distribution of sherds, scale 1:5,000	147
Fig. 7.41	Med 76–85, distribution of sherds, scale 1:5,000	148
Fig. 7.42	*Quarentinae* 16 and 17, scale 1:10,560	150
Fig. 7.43	Med 65–7, distribution of sherds, scale 1:5,000	151
Fig. 7.44	*Quarentinae* 18–20, scale 1:10,560	153
Fig. 7.45	Med 68 and 97, distribution of sherds, scale 1:5,000	153
Fig. 7.46	*Quarentinae* 21–26, scale 1:10,560	156
Fig. 7.47	*Quarentinae* 27 and 28, scale 1:10,560	158
Fig. 7.48	*Quarentina* 29, scale 1:10,560	159

Fig. 7.49	Med 63 and 64, distribution of sherds, scale 1:5,000	159		Chapter 9		
				Fig. 9.1	Post-medieval houses occupied in the later seventeenth century, scale 1:25,000	176
Fig. 7.50	Med 105–6 and 117 earthworks, scale 1:1,250	160		Fig. 9.2	Little Fransham, houses listed in the 1664 hearth tax, scale 1:25,000	180
Chapter 8				Fig. 9.3	Little Fransham, houses listed in the 1666 hearth tax, scale 1:25,000	181
Fig. 8.1	Schematic plans showing archaeological sites in occupation by century, Late Saxon and medieval	166				

List of Tables

Table 5.1	Summary of Domesday entries for Fransham and surrounding vills	64		Table 9.1	Hearth Tax in Little Fransham, 1664 and 1666	179
Table 6.1	The Lay Subsidies of 1327 and 1332: numbers of taxpayers and total assessments per vill in Launditch Hundred	71		Table 9.2	Acreages of Kirkhams and Wilcocks demesne in Little Fransham, 1605	186
				Table 9.3	Acreages of Kirkhams and Wilcocks demesne outside Little Fransham, 1605	186
Table 6.2	Diagram showing the Great Fransham feodary of *c*.1279	73		Table 9.4	Leases of Sir Arthur Capell's demesne lands 1601–37	187
Table 7.1	Medieval settlement sites	95				

Acknowledgements

Many people have made the production of this book possible. Special thanks go to the following: Julia my wife and my two sons, Bede and Chad, for their outstanding tolerance over many years, my late parents for essential financial help, Tom Williamson for his enormous inspiration, wise instruction and indispensable guidance, the late Hassell Smith and the late Roger Virgoe for teaching me palaeography, the late Paul Rutledge and Elizabeth Rutledge for help in transcriptions and advice on documents, Joan Daniels for producing two complex tables, Steven Ashley for his illustrations and for cajoling me over many years to get on and finish the work, Jason Gibbons for his illustrations, Garry Crace for Plate 7.4, the late Trevor Ashwin for examining a group of animal bones, the late Peter Robins for identifying the worked flints, Adrian Marsden for his numismatic identifications, Christopher Aldridge, John Aldridge, Damian Alger, Stephen Brown, Chris Burks, Vince Butler, John Coggles, Steven Maloney, Frank Rowbury and Derek Woollestone for allowing me access to their metal finds, to friends and colleagues John Davies, the late Alan Davison, the late Tony Gregory, Frances Healy, the late Sarah Jennings, the late Sue Margeson, Bill Milligan and the late John Wymer, for help and advice on many and various matters, Peter Wade-Martins for his persistent encouragement to write this book, Brian Cushion for surveying and drawing earthworks at Hey Green (included here as Fig. 7.15), Michael de Bootman for carrying out geophysical surveys and for providing Figs 5.2 and 5.3, John Simmons for his geophysical work in Great Fransham churchyard, Chris Gardner and the late Norman Salmon for trusting me with documents in their possession, the staff of the Norfolk Record Office — especially Frank Meers and Tom Townsend — for their unfailing civility and assistance, Rebecca Gregory for her invaluable advice on the meaning and significance of field-names, and all the farmers and landowners of Fransham for allowing me access to their properties. Plates 1.1, 6.1 to 6.3 and 7.1 are reproduced courtesy of the Norfolk Record Office. Finally, I wish to thank the Scarfe Charitable Trust for a generous grant enabling me to take time off from my normal archaeological duties in order to shorten the delay in the production of this work.

Abbreviations

BL	British Library, London	NMS		Norfolk Museums Service
CUL	Cambridge University Library	NRO		Norfolk Record Office, Norwich
ERO	Essex Record Office, Chelmsford	SRO		Suffolk Record Office, Bury St Edmunds
HER	Historic Environment Record	TBA		Thetford Borough Archive
HRO	Hertfordshire Record Office, Hertford	TNA		The National Archives (formerly PRO, Public Record Office)

see Chapter 1 (p.11) and Bibliography (primary sources) for further details of documentary references in this report.

Summary

The results presented here concern an intensive fieldwalking survey by the author of one civil parish, Fransham, formerly the two ecclesiastical parishes of Great and Little Fransham, lying near the western edge of the Boulder Clay plateau in rural Norfolk. To set the archaeological evidence for the medieval and post-medieval periods into their agrarian, manorial and tenurial contexts, exhaustive use was made of a fairly rich body of available documentary sources.

The earliest material recovered belongs to the Lower Palaeolithic but great emphasis is placed on the Middle Ages and the early post-medieval periods during which both archaeological material and documentary evidence are most informative. No period has provided results that are in any way exceptional, though a few surprises, especially in the prolificacy of some forms of evidence, were forthcoming. It is hoped, however, that the near-complete coverage of the study area and the consistency of collection methods have furnished a more accurate and fuller account of human activity in this parish than has usually been possible in others.

Such widespread and sometimes quite dense scatters of Neolithic and Early Bronze Age worked flint were unexpected in this zone of predominantly heavy soil, as was the surprisingly large number of probably contemporary ploughed-out burnt mounds or 'pot boiler' sites. By contrast, Iron Age and Roman settlements were unremarkable in both their scale and frequency, and, indeed, far more impressive sites on similar soils have recently been recorded close by in Norfolk, and elsewhere. The Anglo-Saxon period has produced two unforeseen results: an Early Saxon settlement and probable cemetery close to the site of a medieval parish church, and a Middle Saxon settlement at some distance from it. The fission into what were to become the two medieval parishes of Great and Little Fransham probably began in the ninth century, and tentative movements from the two major Late Saxon settlements to the edges of some of the extensive areas of common pasture took place before the end of the eleventh century.

Manorial arrangements were reasonably straightforward at Domesday, when there were three holdings, though one was split with another in Rougham, a geographically quite separate place. By the late thirteenth century matters had become very complex and this intricacy is demonstrated, for Great Fransham at least, by copies of a feodary of *c*.1279. Written sources, most of which post-date the fourteenth century, have proved most useful in elaborating the histories of individual settlements that survived into post-medieval times. Documents have been less helpful in providing an understanding of the organisation of communal agriculture, though they do indicate there was a low level of regulation. They have, however, in the absence of early maps been crucial in locating areas of land-use, common fields, several closes both demesne and tenanted, meadows, common pastures, roads and paths. Therefore, a considerable amount of space is given to a topographical description of the study area.

In the Middle Ages most houses were dispersed around the edges of common pastures, though in some places they were so densely packed that they should best be seen as small nucleations. Archaeological evidence demonstrates a high point in the number of settlements in the thirteenth century followed by a drastic reduction during the fourteenth and then few signs of recovery until the sixteenth. During the following two centuries there was little change in either the pattern or intensity of settlement.

Résumé

L'auteur de la présente étude livre les résultats d'un relevé approfondi de la paroisse civile de Fransham, qui était auparavant formé des deux paroisses ecclésiastiques du Great et du Little Fransham, situées près du côté ouest du plateau du Boulder Clay dans le Norfolk rural. Pour placer les vestiges archéologiques des périodes médiévales et post-médiévales dans leurs contextes agraires, seigneuriaux et fonciers, l'auteur a abondamment utilisé un corpus de sources documentaires assez fournies.

Les vestiges les plus anciens qui ont été découverts appartiennent au paléolithique inférieur. Toutefois, une grande importance est accordée au Moyen Âge et au début de la période post-médiévale qui est particulièrement riche sur le plan des matériaux archéologiques et des preuves documentaires.

Quelle que soit la période envisagée, les résultats obtenus n'ont rien d'exceptionnel. Cependant, on peut s'attendre à quelques surprises, notamment sur l'abondance de certaines formes de preuves. Toutefois, si l'on compare cette paroisse à d'autres, il est permis d'espérer un compte-rendu plus large et plus précis de l'activité humaine en raison d'une part de la couverture quasi-complète de la zone d'étude et d'autre part de la consistance des méthodes de collecte utilisées. Dans cette zone de sols lourds pour l'essentiel, on ne pensait pas trouver en certains endroits des fragments de silex travaillés qui dataient du néolithique et du début de l'âge du Bronze. Ces fragments étaient largement répandus avec une grande densité en certains endroits. De même, on a été surpris de découvrir un grand nombre de sites de monticules brûlés présentant des pierres de chauffe. Datant probablement de la même époque, ces monticules sont considérés comme des sites où l'on « faisait bouillir la marmite ». Par contraste, des implantations de l'âge du Fer et de l'époque romaine n'avaient rien de remarquable, tant sur le plan de leur importance que de leur nombre et, assurément, des sites bien plus impressionnants ont été mis à jour sur des sols similaires situés notamment à proximité dans le Norfolk.

La période anglo-saxonne se caractérise par deux résultats inattendus. Le premier renvoie au début de la période saxonne et concerne une implantation — avec probablement un cimetière — située près du site d'une église paroissiale médiévale ; le second résultat concerne une implantation de la période saxonne moyenne qui se trouve à quelque distance de l'église. C'est probablement au 9ème siècle qu'est apparue la distinction d'entités qui allaient devenir les deux églises médiévales du Great et du Little Fransham et c'est avant la fin du 11ème siècle que les deux grandes implantations de la période saxonne tardive ont légèrement gagné du terrain aux limites de plusieurs vastes zones de pâtures communes.

Les dispositions seigneuriales étaient bien définies dans le Domesday, qui contenait trois propriétés, l'une d'entre elles étant toutefois partagée avec une autre propriété à Rougham, qui était un endroit bien distinct sur le plan géographique. À la fin du 13ème siècle, la situation devient très compliquée et, au moins dans le cas du Great Fransham, cette complexité apparaît à la lecture de copies d'un *feodarium* datant approximativement de 1279. Des sources écrites, dont la plupart sont postérieures au 14ème siècle, se sont révélées d'une grande utilité pour reconstituer l'histoire des différentes implantations qui ont perduré après l'époque médiévale. Ces documents ont été moins utiles lorsqu'il s'est agi de comprendre l'organisation de l'agriculture communale mais il faut reconnaître qu'ils ont indiqué l'existence d'un faible niveau de régulation. Toutefois, en l'absence des premières cartes, ces documents ont joué un rôle crucial dans la localisation des éléments suivants : zones d'occupation des sols, champs communs, enclosures gérées par le seigneur ou louées à des métayers, prairies, pâtures communes, routes et chemins. C'est pourquoi, une part considérable de l'étude est consacrée à une description topographique de la zone étudiée.

Au Moyen Âge, la plupart des maisons étaient dispersées aux abords de pâtures communes, bien qu'elles fussent concentrées, en certains endroits, avec une telle densité qu'il serait préférable de les considérer comme de petites nucléations. Il est prouvé sur le plan archéologique que le nombre d'implantations a atteint un niveau élevé au 13ème siècle, avant de diminuer de façon drastique au 14ème siècle pour manifester par la suite quelques signes de reprise jusqu'au 16ème siècle. Pendant les deux siècles suivants, on a constaté que les implantations avaient peu changé sur le plan de leur structure ou de leur développement.

(Traduction: Didier Don)

Zusammenfassung

Die hier aufgeführten Ergebnisse fußen auf einer intensiven Feldbegehung der Gemeinde Fransham, bestehend aus den ehemaligen Pfarrgemeinden Great und Little Fransham nicht weit vom Westrand des Geschiebelehmplateaus im ländlichen Norfolk, durch den Verfasser. Die archäologischen Befunde aus dem Mittelalter und der frühen Neuzeit sind anhand der zahlreich vorhandenen schriftlichen Quellen, die intensiv studiert wurden, vor dem Hintergrund der Agrar- sowie der Guts- und Lehensverhältnisse beschrieben.

Die ältesten Funde gehen auf die Altsteinzeit zurück, allerdings liegt das Hauptaugenmerk auf dem Mittelalter und der frühen Neuzeit, also den Perioden mit der höchsten Informationsdichte, was die archäologischen Befunde und urkundlichen Belege angeht. Keine der Perioden brachte außerordentliche Ergebnisse zutage, dennoch gab es einige Überraschungen, insbesondere was die Fülle der verschiedenen Befundtypen angeht. Wir hoffen, dass die fast vollständige Erfassung des Untersuchungsgebiets und die einheitlichen Erhebungsmethoden dazu beitragen konnten, ein genaueres und umfassenderes Bild der menschlichen Aktivitäten in der Gemeinde zu zeichnen, als es für viele andere Gemeinden möglich war.

Ein derart großräumiges und bisweilen dichtes Auftreten neolithischer und frühbronzezeitlicher bearbeiteter Feuersteine war in diesem aus überwiegend schweren Böden bestehenden Gebiet ebenso wenig erwartet worden wie die überraschend große Zahl an „Kochhügeln" bzw. Kochsteinstellen, die vermutlich in neuerer Zeit aus dem Boden gepflügt wurden. Im Gegensatz dazu waren Umfang und Häufigkeit der eisen- und römerzeitlichen Siedlungen eher unauffällig. In der Tat wurden in jüngster Zeit ganz in der Nähe auf ähnlichem Untergrund weit eindrucksvollere Stätten in Norfolk sowie andernorts dokumentiert. Zur angelsächsischen Periode gab es zwei unerwartete Ergebnisse: eine frühangelsächsische Siedlung mit einem möglichen Gräberfeld unweit einer mittelalterlichen Pfarrkirche sowie eine mittelangelsächsische Siedlung in einiger Entfernung davon. Die Aufspaltung der Gemeinde in die beiden mittelalterlichen Pfarrbezirke Great und Little Fransham begann wahrscheinlich im 9. Jahrhundert, zudem gab es noch vor Ende des 11. Jahrhunderts erste zaghafte Verlagerungen von den beiden größeren spätangelsächsischen Siedlungen hin zu den Rändern einiger ausgedehnter Gemeinschaftsweiden.

Die Gutsverhältnisse waren zur Zeit des Domesday Book mit drei Lehen ziemlich klar geregelt, auch wenn eins der Lehen zum Teil einem anderen Lehen in Rougham, einem geografisch separaten Ort, zugeordnet war. Gegen Ende des 13. Jahrhunderts hatte sich dann jedoch eine höchst komplexe Situation entwickelt, was sich zumindest für Great Fransham durch Kopien eines Lehensvertrags von ca. 1279 belegen lässt. Die Geschichte einzelner Siedlungen, die bis in die Neuzeit hinein bestanden, konnte vor allem anhand schriftlicher Quellen, zumeist aus der Zeit nach dem 14. Jahrhundert, nachvollzogen werden. Weniger hilfreich waren die Quellen beim Verständnis, wie die gemeinschaftlich betriebene Landwirtschaft organisiert war, obwohl sie aufzeigen, dass die Regelungsdichte gering war. Da kaum frühe Landkarten existieren, waren sie jedoch für die Ermittlung der landwirtschaftlich genutzten Bereiche, des Gemeindelands, mehrerer Höfe sowohl in Land- als auch Lehnsbesitz, von Wiesen und Gemeinschaftsweiden sowie Straßen und Wegen wesentlich. Der topografischen Beschreibung des Untersuchungsgebiets wurde daher relativ viel Raum gewidmet.

Im Mittelalter lagen die meisten Häuser weit um die Ränder der Gemeinschaftsweiden herum verstreut, obgleich sie an einigen Orten so dicht beieinander standen, dass sie am besten als kleine Siedlungskerne verstanden werden können. Die archäologischen Befunde zeigen, dass die Zahl der Siedlungen im 13. Jahrhundert ihren Höchststand erreichte, gefolgt von einem drastischen Rückgang im 14. Jahrhundert und nur wenigen Anzeichen einer Erholung bis zum 16. Jahrhundert. In den nachfolgenden zwei Jahrhunderten gab es kaum Veränderungen bei den Siedlungsmustern und der Siedlungsintensität.

(Übersetzung: Gerlinde Krug)

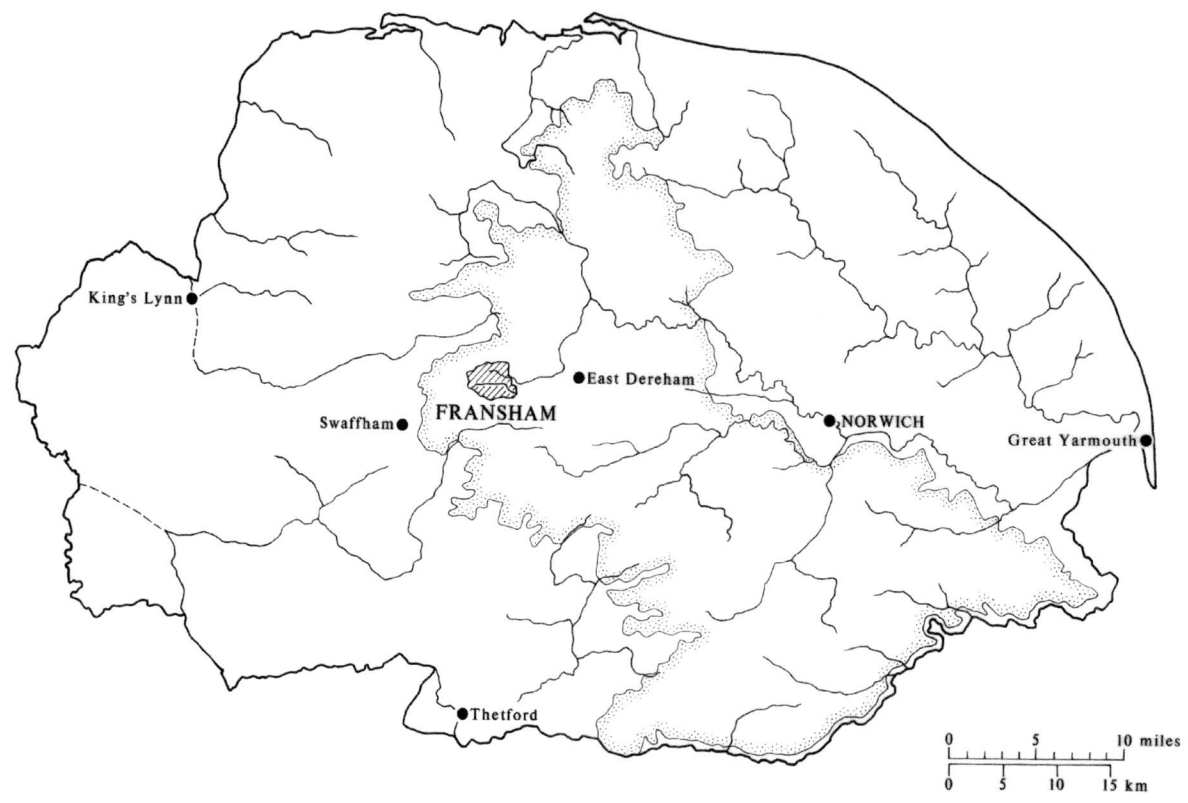

Figure 1.1 Norfolk and Fransham, with the edge of the Central Norfolk Clay Plateau shown stippled, scale 1:600,000

Chapter 1. Introduction

This monograph attempts to illustrate, and where possible explain, the many great changes in settlement pattern and land-use that took place in one mid-Norfolk clayland parish from the Neolithic to the post-medieval period. Archaeological evidence, derived almost entirely from detailed non-invasive fieldwork, will be combined with that drawn from the historical sources beginning with the Domesday Book of 1086. The work is an amplification of a PhD thesis submitted to the University of East Anglia (Rogerson 1995).

Norfolk has a long tradition of the surface collection and recording of archaeological, and particularly prehistoric material (Clarke and Clarke 1937, 57; Lawson 1983), and the county was at the forefront of the historical study of deserted medieval settlement (Allison 1955). In the following pages these two strands, archaeological and documentary, will be woven together with the aim of elucidating the development of a single parish, without, it is hoped, losing sight of the people who were behind the development, for 'the landscape archaeologist preoccupied with the kinks in his parish boundaries can be as obscurantist as the most unrepentant pottery typologist' (Cherry, Gamble and Shennan (eds) 1978, 19).

However, archaeology, as Christopher Taylor has pointed out, 'is useful in explaining what kinds of changes to settlement occurred and when, but not why, how and especially by whom they were carried out' (Taylor 1992, 9). Because documentary evidence, after the first flourish of the Domesday Book, only comes to the fore during the fourteenth century and covers only the final five centuries of this study, it is unavoidable that much more space will be given to 'what and when' than to 'why, how and by whom'.

The Study Area

The civil parish of Fransham contains 1214 hectares, and in 2001 its population amounted to 426 in 177 households. Modern land-use is almost entirely arable farming. In 1935 the two civil parishes of Great and Little Fransham, which corresponded to the two ancient ecclesiastical parishes, were amalgamated by a Review Order (Youngs 1979, 364). A religious rationalisation had already taken place, for Little Fransham rectory had been annexed to that of Great in 1925. The ecclesiastical parish falls within the deanery of Brisley. Until 1834 Fransham lay in Launditch Hundred.

The parish (Fig. 1.1) sits near the western edge of the Boulder Clay Plateau on the central watershed of Norfolk (Williamson 1993, 14–9), within c.2km. of the lighter soils of the Good Sands to the north, c.3.5km. from the loams and sands of the Chalk Scarp to the north-west and c.4km. from Breckland sands to the west (Corbett and Dent 1993). Fransham lies near the western extremes of a region known as the Dissected Clays (Wade Martins and Williamson 1999, 28, fig. 1; Wade-Martins et al. 2005; Whyte 2009 fig. 2) or the Central Norfolk Claylands (Williamson 2005a). Soils here range from rather poorly-draining heavy sandy clay loams on the slopes to medium sandy clay loams on the interfluves, with localised patches of sandier gravelly soils on the latter (Fig. 1.2). The valley-bottom soils are variable but predominantly heavy, and contain much more gravel than is normal on the surrounding upland. There are no definite signs of former peat cover, but soils on former meadow land, virtually all of which is now arable, generally have a higher organic content[i]. The Soil Survey 1:250,000 scale map shows the northern part of the parish covered by soils of the Burlingham 1 Association, clay loams and sandy clay loams mainly found on gentle slopes, and the southern part by heavier soils of the Beccles 1 Association, which, occurring on level and sloping ground, consist of sandy clay loams and clay loams (Soil Survey 1983). These soils are prone to considerable waterlogging, but are much improved by underdraining. They are described in detail by Hodge et al. (1984, 117–9 and 132–5). The Soil Survey 1:100,000 scale map also depicts tongues of typical cambic gley soils in the minor stream valleys. Such soils are not clay-enriched and overlie gravel (Soil Survey 1973).

In common with a very large surrounding area, soils covering most of Fransham are classified as Grade 3 agricultural land by the Ministry of Agriculture (MAFF 1972). This is defined as land with 'moderate limitations' to agricultural use. A small portion in the south-western corner of the parish is of Grade 2, defined as land with some 'minor limitations' to agricultural use (MAFF 1977).

Nowhere in the parish would human settlement have been obviated by hydrological considerations. An adequate water supply would have been available over the whole parish, both from the numerous watercourses, and from shallow wells exploiting water trapped within the Boulder Clay (Williamson 2013, 186–8).

Fransham lies 30km. west of Norwich, midway between the medieval and modern market towns of Swaffham and East Dereham (Fig. 1.3), and is bisected east-west by two major communication routes. The principal present-day feature is the A47 Great Yarmouth to Birmingham trunk road, a widened, straightened and in part realigned descendant of the Swaffham to Norwich turnpike, opened in 1770 (Joby 2005b). A branch of the Midland and Great Northern Joint railway, linking East Dereham with Swaffham and King's Lynn, was completed in 1848 and closed in 1968 (Joby 2005a). Part of this has been ploughed over and part recut to take a section of the trunk road, but most of the remainder survives as embankments, cuttings and tracks.

The present-day boundary of the civil parish follows a course almost identical to that of the outer limits of the ecclesiastical parishes of Great and Little Fransham which appear on the earliest surviving map, that made in 1805 for the Enclosure Award of 1807 (NRO C/Sca 2/122; Pl. 1.1). There is no reason to assume that any major changes have been made to these limits since medieval times, and probably since the Late Saxon period. Indeed, it will be suggested in Chapter 4 that Fransham, along with

Plate 1.1 Enclosure Award map, drawn in 1805 (NRO C/Sca 2/122)

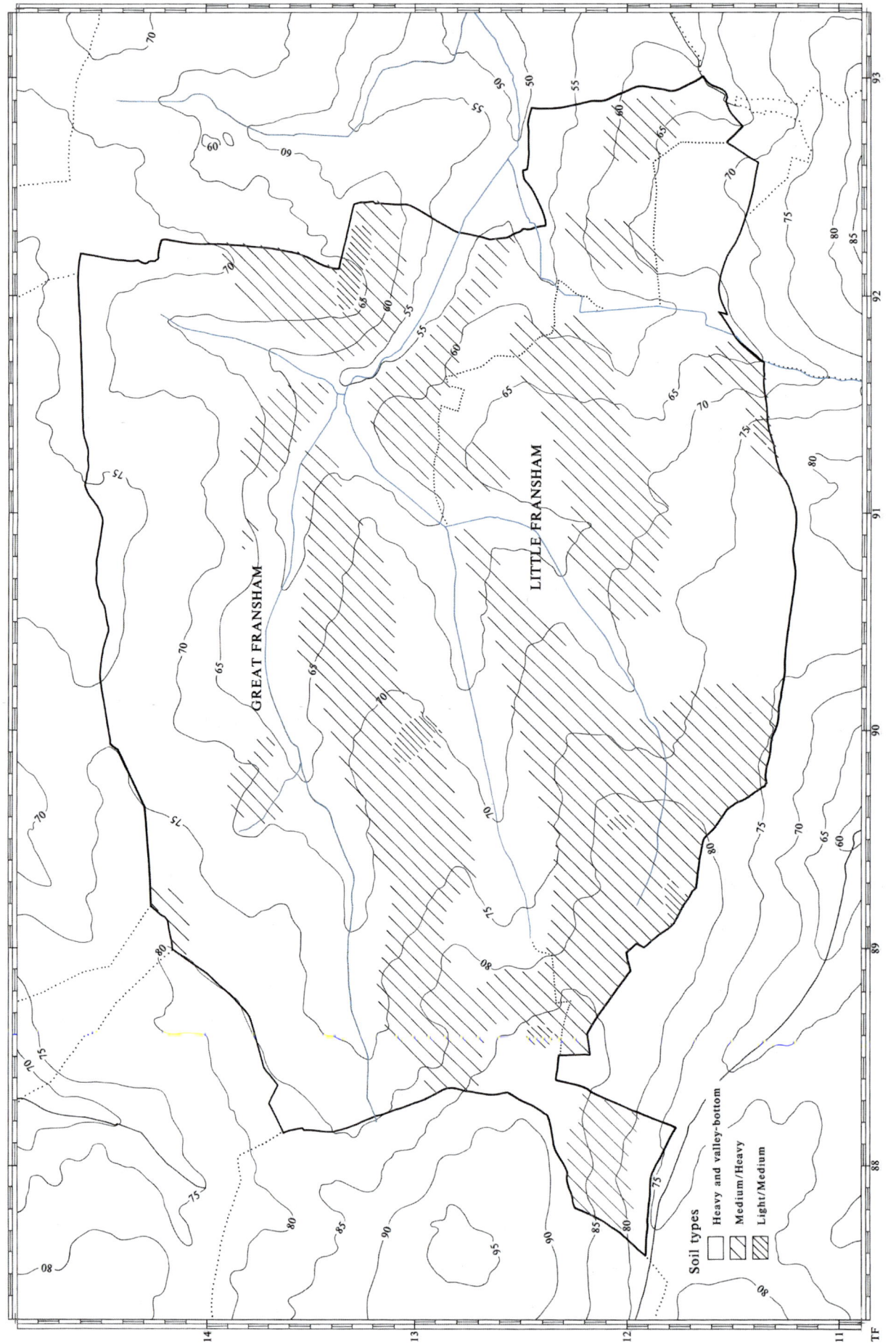

Figure 1.2 Fransham, soil types, contours and drainage, scale 1:25,000

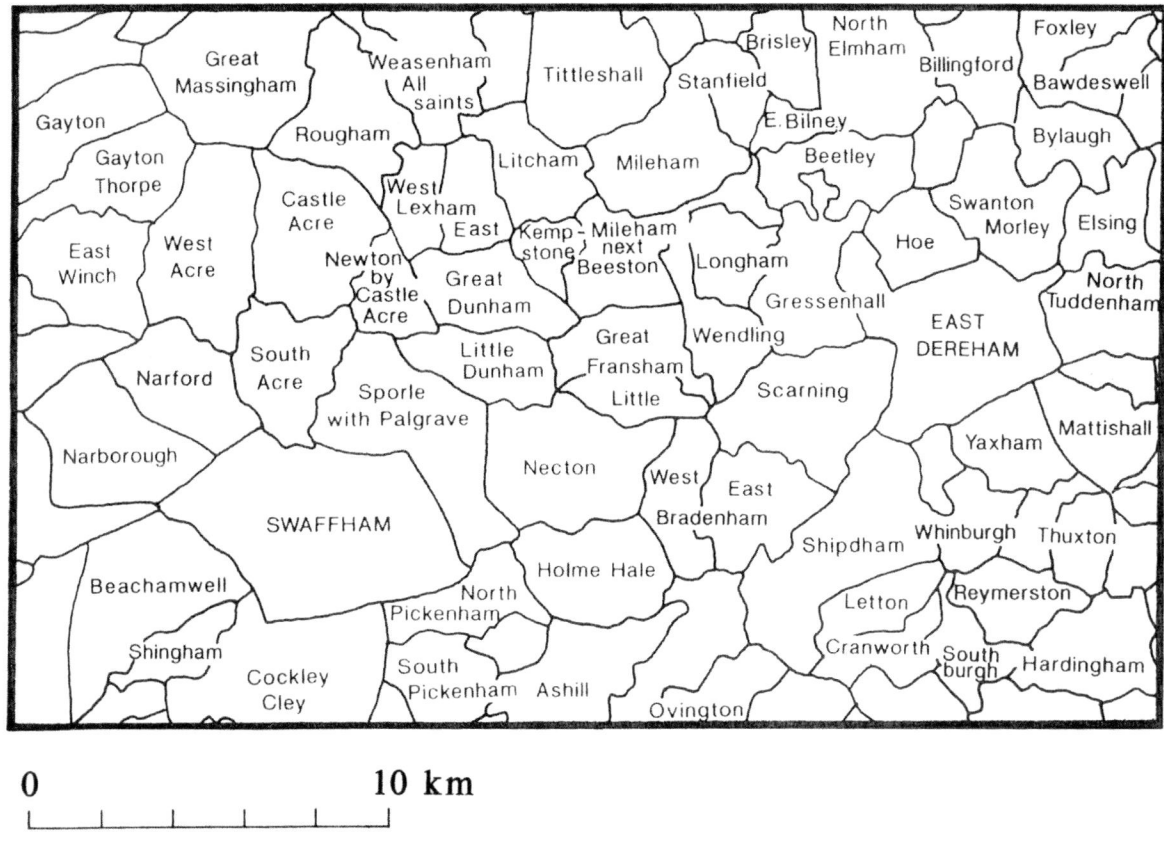

Figure 1.3 Fransham and surrounding parishes in c.1923 (after Wade-Martins 1993)

Wendling parish which lies immediately to the east, may have formed a single land-unit from as early as the seventh century AD. From the tenth century until 1834 the division between Great and Little Fransham on the one hand and Necton and West Bradenham on the other was also the boundary between the Hundreds of Launditch and South Greenhoe (Barringer 2005b).

Fransham's boundary, much of which shows great sensitivity to natural topography, will be described briefly, moving anti-clockwise from the north-eastern corner (Fig.1.2). This point lies on a very flat ground at TF 9220 1460 (73m OD), the surface rising slightly to the north into Wendling and Beeston parishes. To the west the boundary runs in a gently curving line, sometimes along the watershed between the Nar and Wensum drainage systems, but more often just to the south of it, past Beeston and a narrow southern extension of Kempstone parish, for c.4km as far as the north-western corner, a point of junction with Great and Little Dunham parishes at TF 8816 1363 (81m OD).

The western boundary runs over relatively flat terrain draining eastwards into the parish from elevated ground near Dunham Lodge in Little Dunham parish, which achieves a height of 98m OD. The south-western corner, Fransham's highest spot, at 88m OD[ii], lies on the watershed between the Wensum and Wissey drainage systems at TF 8822 1238. However, to the south-west of this point a 23-hectare tongue of Fransham projects down slope to a stream draining south-eastwards to the Wissey. This projection, known as *Pilewude* in 1273/4 and now called Pillwood, is flanked by Little Dunham parish on the west and Necton on the east. It clearly does not belong to the above-mentioned discrete Fransham / Wendling land-unit, and its inclusion in Fransham rather than Necton (a dispute raged in the early fifteenth century) was the result of land tenure.

Excluding Pillwood, the boundary then heads south-eastwards along the Wensum/Wissey watershed for almost 2km as far as Top Farm at TF 8975 1135 (74m OD). Thereafter the southern boundary runs just south of the watershed, roughly following the 75m contour for 0.5km, and then crossing over an ill-defined watershed on a plateau, the highest point of which lies just above 79m OD at TF 9135 1131. To the east of there a stream, forming the boundary between Necton and Bradenham (formerly West Bradenham), flows from the south into Fransham at TF 9170 1135 (65m OD). Beyond this minor valley the boundary runs across a gentle north-facing slope, firstly meeting Scarning parish, and then Wendling in a small north-eastward draining valley at TF 9300 1163.

The Fransham / Wendling boundary, which pays little attention to natural topography, running up and across slopes, and along and across valleys, as well as exhibiting several sharp changes of direction, does not need detailed description. It is worth noting, however, that the remainder of the Wendling boundary, apart from that of its long narrow projection to the north between Beeston and Longham parishes and one other small projection, is similar to that of Fransham. The northern section firstly runs along a watershed and then curves down slope to a stream, while the southern section follows a valley bottom throughout.

The boundary between Great and Little Fransham is of uncertain antiquity, but was probably formalised in the twelfth or early thirteenth centuries. Fifteenth and sixteenth-century documents indicate that it ran along substantially the same lines as are shown on the Enclosure Award map of 1807 (NRO C/Sca 2/122) and the Ordnance Survey County Series 1:2500 scale maps. Apart from a central *c*.2km-long stretch and a much shorter length in the south-east, both running along streams, the boundary does not follow natural features. In some places it coincides with former roads or tracks, and in others it zig-zags, probably around medieval property boundaries.

The topography of Fransham is surprisingly varied, with heights above Ordnance Datum ranging from 88m in the south-west corner down to 50m where the eastward flowing stream enters Wendling. As has been made clear from the above boundary description, almost the whole area lies within the Wensum drainage system. Five streams, three westward, one southward and one northward flowing, eventually converge just outside the parish in Wendling, to form what is now known as the Scarning River or Whitemill Brook. This joins the Wensum at Worthing *c*.10km to the north-west. On the Enclosure Award map all five streams for the most part follow their modern, relatively straight courses. The dates at which canalisation took place are not known. Because of agricultural activity former meanders are no longer visible at ground level. One exception, in pasture at TF 8987 1355, is also clearly discernible on some aerial photographs.

The choice of the Study Area

Four factors influenced the selection of Fransham parish. Firstly, access for carrying out fieldwork was straightforward because I had lived there since 1977. Secondly, a fuller than average series of medieval and post-medieval documents were held at the Norfolk Record Office. Thirdly, the parish lies within the Hundred of Launditch, the whole of which had been subjected to a pioneering study by Wade-Martins (1971; 1980b; 1989, 159–61), and it was considered that the results of a detailed survey could be measured against this previous more extensive work. Fransham, though, was not one of those parishes such as Longham or Mileham, upon which Wade-Martins had concentrated. His results, however, indicated that more was to be found in the way of pre-Norman Conquest settlement on the Norfolk Boulder Clay than had hitherto been suspected. Indeed, until very recently the capacity for clay soils alternately to be waterlogged and dried to a rock-hard consistency has 'over the years, led many to think of clay landscapes as unsuitable places for past settlement and agriculture' (Mills and Palmer 2007, 7). A desire to demonstrate how wrong was this way of thinking was the fourth factor behind the choice of Fransham.

Whatever limitations there may be in the chosen study area, as work progressed, first in the field and later in the study of documentary evidence, I realised that the results might make some small contributions to some of the great debates concerning regional variations in settlement and field systems in post-Roman England. There is no suggestion, however, that the results should act, in any precise sense, as a 'paradigm for a much larger region', for example the Hundred of Launditch or the mid-Norfolk Boulder Clay, because this would be misleading, denying the possible individual peculiarities of both the study area and its surrounding region, and because such a generalisation would not be 'without some risk of substantial error' (Cherry *et al.* (eds) 1978, 24–5).

An additional influence or perhaps challenge was, at the start of the study, the paucity of data concerning the parish contained within the Norfolk Sites and Monuments Record (SMR), now known as the Historic Environment Record (HER). The clay subsoil had inhibited the formation of crop-marks and the overwhelmingly arable exploitation of the area had apparently led to the survival of no upstanding earthwork sites apart from moats, only one of which had been recorded by the Ordnance Survey.

The data available on the HER, no poorer than that for many other parishes, consisted of twenty-one entries, comprising two areas from which Wade-Martins had recovered medieval pot sherds, two churches, five vernacular buildings, three moated sites, one 'pot-boiler' site, two chance finds of medieval metalwork, four finds provenanced only to 'Fransham' (two prehistoric and two medieval), an entirely dubious reference to 'Roman brickworks' in Little Fransham, and a reference to a road-name shown on an Ordnance Survey map.

This motley bag of data would be of little use either to anyone attempting to understand the development of the landscape, or to an individual or body discharging responsibility for what is now called 'the curation of the archaeological resource'. The initiation of this survey was, then, partly inspired by a desire to make Fransham an indicator in the most general terms, rather than a paradigm, of what might lie elsewhere on similar soils, for as John Newman observed, 'Until recently most archaeological research in England has had to rely on a data base that is simply a series of chance reports and casual finds supplemented by pockets of fuller knowledge where a particular individual has been active' (Newman 1994, 10). It was intended that Fransham would become one such pocket.

I am fully aware that many have argued that the parish is an inappropriate unit of study for archaeological fieldwork, particularly for the interpretation of prehistoric and Romano-British settlement and land-use, the parish having been 'imposed in historical times' (Mills 1985, 44) and described as 'little more than a geographically convenient grab sample' (Gaffney *et al.* 1985, 96). The parish, which has been a defined land unit for very much less than the full period of human settlement therein, appears not only restrictive but anachronistic for any period before the Middle or Late Saxon. Indeed, the intensive study of much larger areas by teams rather than individuals has recently become the more acceptable norm (Rippon 2009, 238). There is also no doubt that the study of such a small area offers relatively little in the way of contrasts in geology, soil and topography, upon which many classic fieldwork projects have been based (*e.g.* Shennan 1985; Williamson 1984).

Perhaps, though, non-diversity itself lends some support to the present study. It has been suggested that the Hundred might be a suitable unit for historical examination (Gardiner and Williamson 1993, 177). Such a massive area could not have been subjected to archaeological field survey by a single person in the detail given to this one parish.

Despite the rare coincidence of manors and parishes in Norfolk, the most convenient unit of documentary study is certainly the parish. National government and ecclesiastical records, including wills, generally refer to township and parish. In addition, most manors had most of their lands in one parish. If this study had been based on, for example, a zone defined by National Grid references, then an even documentary coverage would have involved very much more work on more numerous parish and manorial records. A proportion of this effort would have been wasted, as many transcriptions and investigations of documents would have thrown up data on lands, properties and tenements *etc*. lying outside the confining grid lines. It should not be forgotten that the National Grid, as a twentieth-century introduction, has a shorter pedigree than the parish boundary.

Parish-based studies have in recent years told us a great deal about settlement archaeology in Norfolk, and for this we owe much to the late Alan Davison who, as an historical geographer, combined fieldwalking and documentary research to study 'the evolution of human settlement' in many parts of the county. His work on three clayland parishes in south-east Norfolk, Hales, Heckingham and Loddon, has the most relevance here (1990 and 1994a). However, his papers on the Breckland parishes of Harling, Hockham and Illington (1980; 1983; 1987; 1991; 1993), parts of five Breckland parishes in the Stanford Battle Area (1994b), the Mannington and Wolterton estates in north-east Norfolk (1995), the Hargham estate on the edge of the Breckland (Davison with Cushion 1999), West Acre parish (2003; Davison and Cushion 2004), and on a group of deserted and shrunken settlements in the county (1988) have also shown how archaeological and historical research can combine to illuminate and explain much of the history of landscape development. I was privileged to work closely with Davison on Barton Bendish parish (Rogerson with Davison 1997).

Davison worked nearest to Fransham in Sporle with Palgrave, *c.*5km to the south-west, where he discovered and defined the deserted medieval common-edge settlement of Cotes (Davison 1982). His paper ends with words which this present work will show to have been entirely correct, 'The relationship of archaeological and documentary evidence to the margin of the common .... suggests that field-walking the edges of other commons recorded on his [Faden's] map might be productive'. His final piece of published fieldwork partly concerned another Norfolk clayland place, Godwick, some 9km to the north of Fransham (Davison 2007).

Valuable work was also carried by Mike Hardy during the 1980s in a group of clayland parishes on the southern side of the Waveney in north-east Suffolk, Mendham, Metfield and the nine parishes of the Liberty of South Elmham (Hardy 1985; Hardy with Martin 1986; 1987; 1988; 1989; Fairclough and Hardy 2004). Here a profuse series of Romano-British rural and industrial sites sits in a landscape dominated by a complex pattern of commons and greens with associated dispersed medieval settlement and isolated moated sites, while in contrast evidence for occupation in the Anglo-Saxon period was more sparsely distributed (Fairclough and Hardy 2004, fig. 4.7).

Methods of Archaeological Survey

Apart from earthwork surveys the collection and plotting of artefacts on the surface of arable fields, or fieldwalking, was the only technique used. It is regrettable that geophysical methods were not employed (except on two occasions). Hedge counting, now regarded far less reliable as a method of dating hedges than it once was (Barnes and Williamson 2006), was also eschewed. Test-pitting, a relatively new method of 'mini-excavation', might well have filled in gaps left by the presence of private gardens (Jones and Page 2006, 25–6; Gerrard with Aston 2007, 244–61; Lewis 2007), though some success was gained from the collection of pot sherds on flower beds and vegetable patches and from mole-hills in grassland. Another recently proven technique, shovel-testing, whereby the topsoil and its contents are examined in addition to, or in the place of fieldwalking (Gerrard with Aston 2007, 266–78) was also not pursued.

Fieldwalking was begun, in a low-key exploratory fashion, in December 1977, and entered a systematic phase in 1980. This continued until 1994, since when minor unsurveyed areas have been examined as they have become available. Completion was so long in coming because all fieldwork was carried out in my spare time. The project aimed to cover by fieldwalking all arable areas of the parish, to examine all grassland and woodland, and if necessary to record any surviving earthworks. As many gardens as possible were also searched. Approximately 90% of the surface area was surveyed. Permission for access to only one area was withheld for many years: Pillwood, the projection of arable land in the south-west corner of the parish, was eventually examined in April 2016. Figure 1.4 shows all the major parts of the parish which were not subjected to fieldwalking, *i.e.* grassland, woodland, built-up areas, major roads, the line of the railway and larger pits. For clarity, minor roads, tracks, smaller pits and ponds, many of which have been backfilled, are not shown.

Several observations of recently cleaned ditches indicated that the valleys do not contain substantially thick colluvial deposits, the natural gravelly and clayey subsoil often directly underlying the ploughsoil. This low degree of erosion is the result of gentle gradients and soils with a high clay content (Allen 1991, 41–3). Thus, there is little chance that archaeological horizons lie undetected below the reach of the plough on any significant scale (Aston 1985, 24–5; Foard 1980, 40, note 2).

To achieve as much consistency as possible and to avoid distortion caused by differential recovery rates (Hayfield 1980, 27; Foard 1980, 37; Haselgrove 1985, 21–5), I undertook all fieldwalking on my own. On several occasions additional finds were made independently by interested landowners, members of my family and friends. These have not been included in the distribution maps of worked flint and sherd densities presented below.

The work of a number of metal-detector users has made major contributions to the data, through the recovery of artefacts normally elusive to the naked eye. Finds of significance are noted in the text and a selection is illustrated. It should be stressed that the metal-detecting was unregulated, *i.e.* not carried out, in archaeological terms, systematically. Except for three occasions when I accompanied a metal-detectorist for a short period, all the work was conducted independently and without archaeological supervision. The metal-detectorists visited places of their own choice. Finds were handed in for identification and recording along with details of provenance of varying precision. Only the most superficial information on time spent in the field, areas

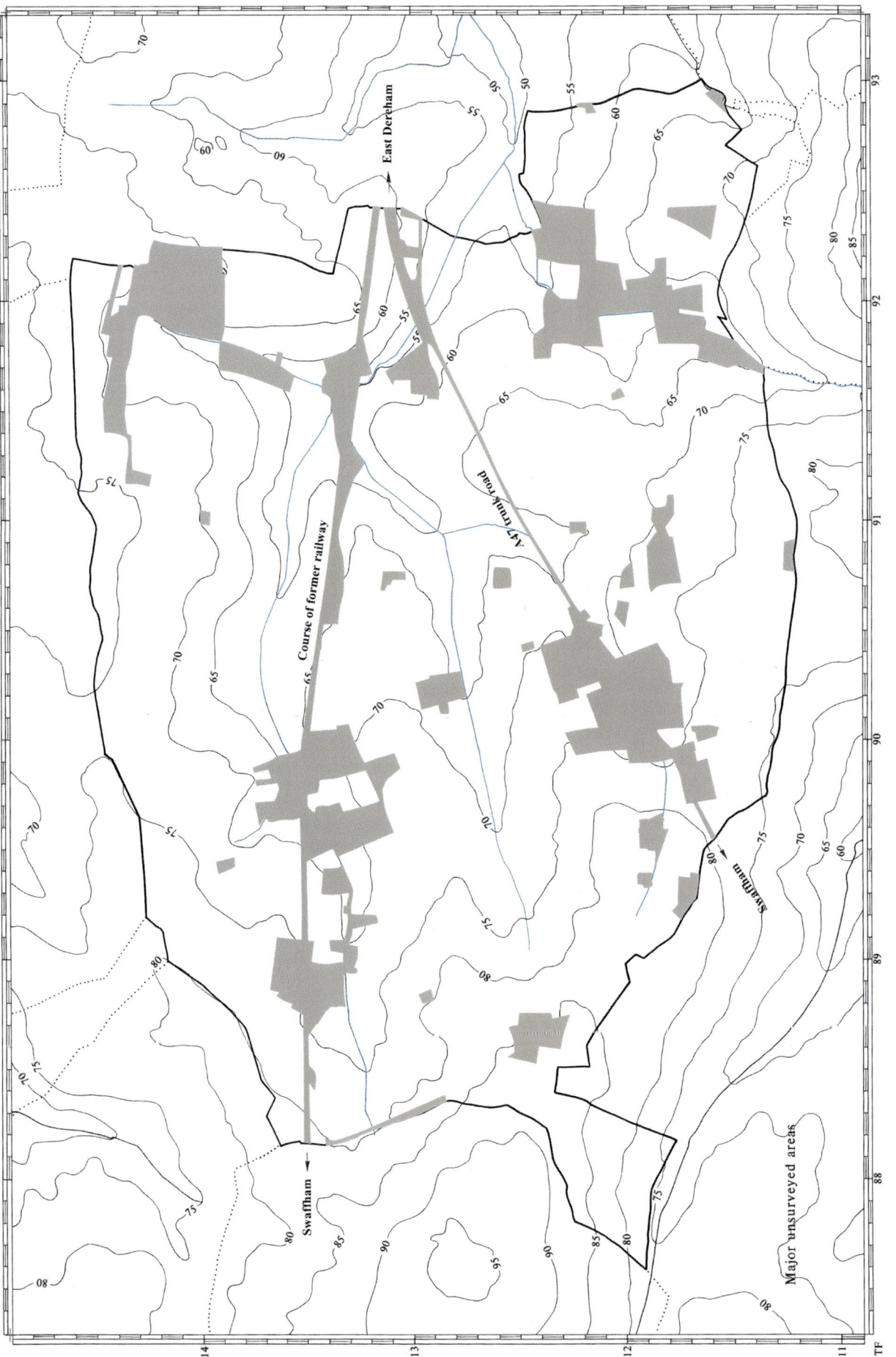

Figure 1.4 Fransham, major areas not subject to fieldwalking shown in black, scale 1:25,000

covered, the spacing and direction of transects, soil and weather conditions and areas of negative results was recorded. Understandably, fields yielding many and/or interesting finds were searched far more frequently than sparse areas. Despite these factors it should be obvious in the pages below that the metal-detected evidence is an important part of the whole. One small statistic may illustrate this point: of 458 recorded numismatic finds, dating from the late Iron Age to the end of the seventeenth century (coins, tokens, jettons, coin weights and coin blanks), only nine were found during fieldwalking and one by a Fransham resident. The remaining 98% was recovered by metal-detecting. A recent study of the use and interpretation of Early Saxon metal-detector finds in Norfolk provides a very useful summary of the quality and quantity of the evidence, which has much relevance to other periods (Chester-Kadwell 2009, especially 59–90). Records of a small selection of objects from Fransham have been entered onto the database of the Portable Antiquities Scheme (https://www.finds.org.uk)[iii].

In the fieldwalking survey the primary units of collection were the individually numbered land parcels shown on the Ordnance Survey County Series 1928 edition 1:2500 scale maps, Norfolk sheets XLVIII 9, 10, 13–5, and LX 1–3. Separate number sequences were used for Great and Little Fransham parishes. Where fields had been amalgamated, which was often the case, vanished boundaries were relocated by taped measurement, and the finds and records kept distinct. Within each field finds were normally collected by 50m x 50m squares, each square being allotted an individual suffix number. On some occasions, normally in areas where closely spaced medieval concentrations were apparent, a grid of units measuring 25m by 25m was employed. Within both sizes of grid, walking was carried out at intervals of 8m along one axis, enabling six transects to be made across squares of 2500 m² and three across those of 625 m². In fields with very few finds the grid system was maintained, and finds were individually plotted. On several occasions subsidiary visits were made to collect additional material as an aid to the firmer dating and the finer definition of finds concentrations. In such cases the next available suffix number was allotted to the finds. Additional material thus collected has not been shown on the various distribution maps shown below.

At first the grid was aligned with one edge of each field. This was soon abandoned when it was realised that so many fields had lost all or some of their boundaries. Thereafter the grid was set up parallel to the direction of the most recent agricultural operations, whether it was the ploughing or the drilling of the crop. The establishment of a reasonably accurate grid was normally quite straightforward because both ploughing and drilling had almost always been carried out with unswerving accuracy. Greater problems in the maintenance of accuracy were encountered while walking fields set with maize, because this crop is drilled in stretches that often follow different, sometimes slightly curving, alignments and thereby overlap.

Finds were marked with a parish letter, G or L (for Great or Little) followed by the OS parcel number and finally the subdivision or find spot suffix number, *e.g.* G228.15 or L21.6. 'Pot boiler' sites and the small series of below-ground observations were similarly numbered. The archaeological survey records, consisting of pro forma sheets for each surveyed field, are held in the Norfolk HER, while the finds have been deposited with Norfolk Museums Service, accession number NWHCM:2022.56. They are stored in parcel number order and divided into the following categories: pottery, brick and tile, worked flint, stone, slag, mammal bone and metalwork. As all archaeological information recovered during the survey has been entered into the HER, relevant HER numbers are cited in the text. Almost all metal-detected finds remain in private hands.

Whenever and wherever possible ground was examined in the best possible soil conditions of weathering. In Great Fransham these were normally in early to mid-March, on land which had been ploughed and furrow-pressed some time between late November and early January in preparation for a spring crop of sugar beet or peas. It was necessary to walk much of the land in Little Fransham in early July after it had been sown with maize in the late spring. In most cases the surface of the soil between the rows of maize (normally $c.15–20$cm high) appeared surprisingly weathered even after a dry early summer. Some later re-examinations in more normal, ploughed, conditions suggested that artefact recovery rates under maize were quite adequate. When necessary, fields sown in autumn with cereal were walked in late October and November. Again, conditions for the visibility of finds were generally good, although as in the case of maize crops it is probable that significant variations in soil colours may have gone unrecorded.

Three meteorological variables, sun, rain and wind, had a debilitating influence on my ability to see objects on the surface of the soil, thereby affecting both the quantity and consistency of artefact recovery. Fieldwork was adjusted or curtailed accordingly. Most importantly, every effort was made to avoid winter and early spring sunshine. If surveying could not be postponed until the onset of an overcast sky, walking pace was slackened to a crawl. Rain was also avoided whenever possible. Finally, walking was abandoned during high winds.

At the start of this survey, Ordnance Survey 1:10560 (6" to 1 mile scale) maps (sheets TF 81SE and 91SW, published 1958) were used as the basis for the small-scale mapping of finds and concentrations, because this map series was then in use by the SMR. These sheets have been used in the production of the parish-wide plans illustrating this work, in preference to their present-day 1:10,000 scale equivalents.

Site definition

From its inception this survey was intended to be complete, a study of the landscape as a whole, not just of 'sites'. Nevertheless, in the following pages much is made of the many pottery concentrations of various periods denoted as sites. It is only with the Iron Age and subsequent periods that sites can be defined with any confidence. Six schematic maps showing locations of archaeologically defined sites from the Iron Age to the medieval period can be seen on Fig. 1.5. The considerable difficulties in assessing how many potsherds should be recorded before a 'site' can be reliably identified and varying views expressed by numerous fieldworkers have been well summarised by Fleming (2016, 23).

Haselgrove (1985) sounded warnings about the over-ready interpretation of ploughsoil assemblages as

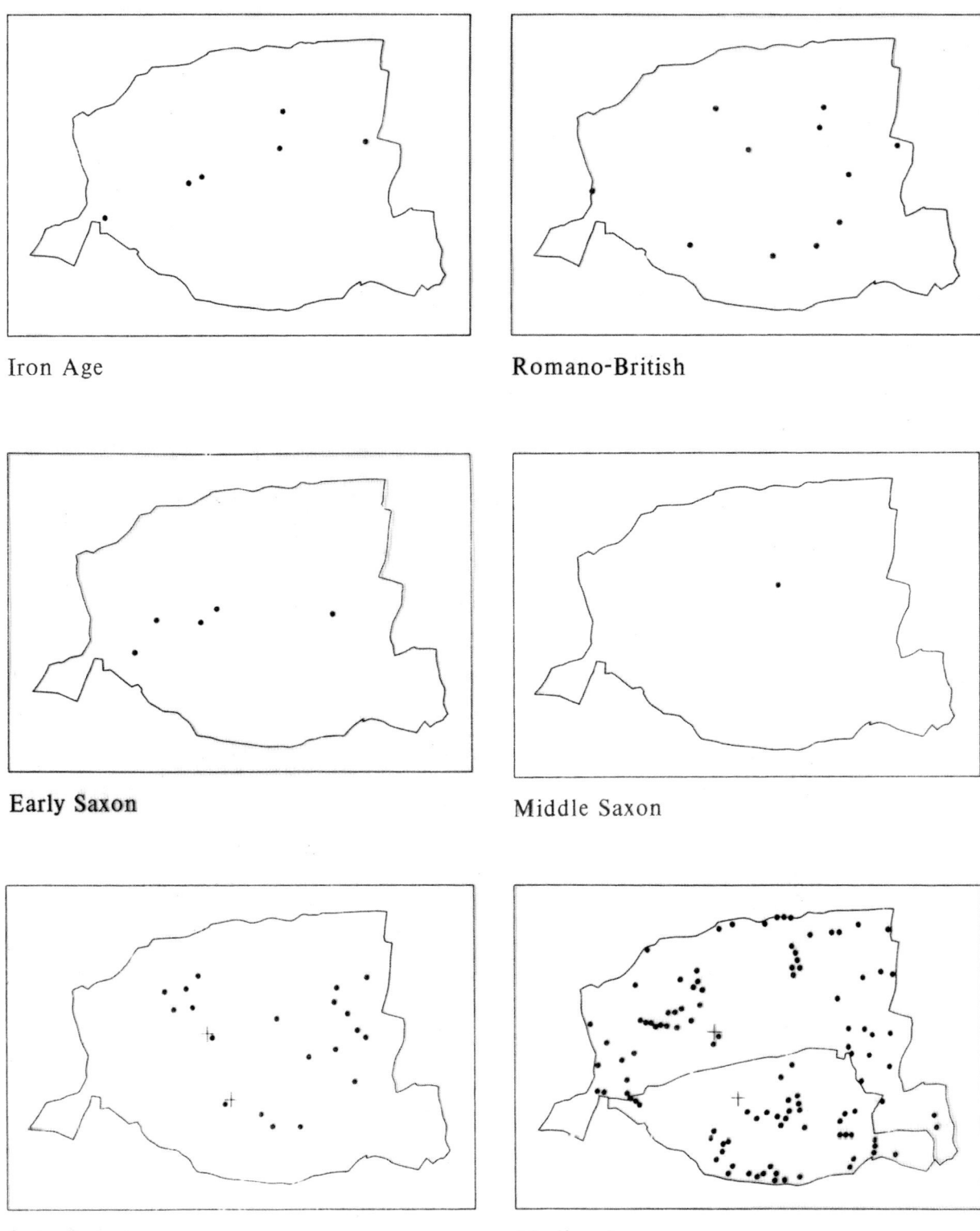

Figure 1.5 Schematic plans showing locations of archaeological sites from the Iron Age to the medieval period

'sites', and has quite rightly stressed that occupation sites, when in use, are three-dimensional and contain many above-ground elements including structures and piles of rubbish. Many objects found on the surface of a flattened, ploughed field will derive not from disturbed buried sub-surface features but from formerly upstanding contexts. In other words, what the fieldworker records is a simplified exposure of a formerly complex situation.

The degree of detail regarding the lay-out of an occupation site which is recoverable from surface artefact collection is therefore very restricted, and no attempt is made here to indicate the uses to which any areas within a site were put, *i.e.* domestic and agricultural buildings, open areas, above and below-ground rubbish disposal zones, and boundaries. There is no doubt, however, that the clear majority of artefact concentrations designated below as 'sites' were indeed places of settlement, rather than off-site dumps of cultural material. Within a place of settlement a surface proliferation of finds may mark not the exact site of a dwelling but an adjacent garden or 'intensive inland cultivation' (Blair 2018, 300).

Such a level of interpretation comes close to what Schofield (1989, 466) described as providing 'a general view of occupation and landscape evolution in which areas that were a focus of attention in specific periods may be outlined'. I consider that the identification of pottery concentrations with the approximate positions of settlement sites is upheld, for the medieval period at least, by the distribution of common-edge 'sites', many of which were located in the field at a stage when no documentary or cartographic research had been carried out, and the former positions of common pastures were unknown. Thus, there is no hesitation in going against the advice of Haselgrove (1985, 14) who urged archaeologists to stop 'sheltering behind an overworked, often almost meaningless, conceptual device — the site'.

Zones producing slight or moderate scatters of normally abraded medieval pot sherds were shown, once the documentary evidence had been consulted, to have been arable fields in the medieval period, the sherds having been accidentally incorporated on middens with farmyard (and ?human) excrement which was then spread on the land as fertiliser (Wilkinson 1982 and 1989; Hayfield 1987). Areas with very sparse scatters of Roman pottery are also interpreted as arable zones (Fig. 3.3), although in the absence of written evidence and with far fewer pot sherds this interpretation is less convincing than for the medieval period. Further confidence in inferences made from the presence and absence of sherd scatters and concentrations was gained from the discovery, again on the evidence of the documents, that many areas in which medieval pot sherds were very scarce or absent had, in the Middle Ages, been either meadow, or enclosed or common pasture (Hayes 1991). However, some areas of arable far from settlement sites might normally have been manured directly by animals, or rarely with domestic debris (Jones and Hooke 2012, 39).

The use of the Documentary Sources

The written evidence was approached with one major purpose, to attempt a reconstruction of the physical lay-out of the study area in the medieval and post-medieval periods, by following the tenurial history of parcels of land, whether they be houses and tofts, arable strips, pasture closes, demesne woodland *etc.*, and by locating the positions of commons, roads and paths from a myriad of abuttals and numerous manor and leet court presentments. It was hoped that this exercise would go some way to explaining the forces behind both the formation of the medieval landscape and the changes that occurred in the late and post-medieval periods. The process was made extremely difficult by the multiplicity of manors, by gaps in the documentary record and by the lack of any parish maps earlier than 1805. As a result the attempted reconstruction is in part tentative and far from complete.

All written sources up to the beginning of the nineteenth century held by the Norfolk Record Office (NRO) were consulted. These are predominantly manorial, and are very much more comprehensive for Little than for Great Fransham. In addition, on the evidence of published sources, of indexes in NRO and of records in the National Manorial Register, documents held in the National Archives at Kew (PRO), the British Library (BL), Essex Record Office at Chelmsford (ERO), Hertfordshire Archives and Local Studies at Hertford (HRO), Suffolk Record Office at Bury St Edmunds (SRO), Cambridge, Chicago and Nottingham University Libraries, the library of Christ Church, Oxford, and Thetford Borough Archives were also consulted. Relevant sources in the muniment rooms at Holkham Hall and Raynham Hall were examined, as was material held in three private collections.

All cited documents are listed and summarised in the Bibliography under *Primary Sources*.

A large body of data relating to individual properties and parcels of land was collected during the examination of documents. This was entered into a computer under files relating to each manor, separate files being maintained for demesne and tenanted lands. Individual properties and parcels were allotted numbers within a sequence for each manor, the order of which was normally based on that in which they had appeared in the earliest detailed rental or extent. Copies of this assembled information have been deposited at the NRO. These include very much more detail than is presented below.

Endnotes

i   Peat extraction took place in Wendling in the medieval period. A 1-acre turbary is specified in an undated (thirteenth-century) charter grant of Philip prior of Castle Acre to Leiffein son of William de Wendling (BL Harley MS 2110). In another deed Ralph Buyt of Wendling conveyed his turbary which lay between the turbary of Peter son of Alverdus and the watercourse running to the pond of *Cuttmere* mill (NRO BL/O/U3/1). A ½-acre turbary was mentioned in *c*.1570 (NRO BL/MA 42).

ii One nineteenth-century writer exaggerated the comparative elevation of the area, 'the highest land I know in Norfolk is that marked two hundred and sixty-seven feet [81.3m] at Little Fransham by the Ordnance Survey.' (Woodward 1884, 439). This may have been the spot height of two hundred and sixty-eight feet marked on the Ordnance Survey first edition 1:2500 scale map next to the Necton parish boundary in the centre of the turnpike road at TF 8930 1169.

iii On 13/2/2019 the database included 394 records of 555 objects found in Fransham. All records are of metal finds including 60 numismatic items, apart from 22 listing 152 pot sherds and fragments of ceramic building material, 7 describing 8 worked flint objects, and 1 concerning 3 pieces of lava quernstones. Since 1/10/2012 all finds recorded for the HER have also been entered on the Portable Antiquities Scheme database. Before that date entry onto that database was both inconsistent and highly selective.

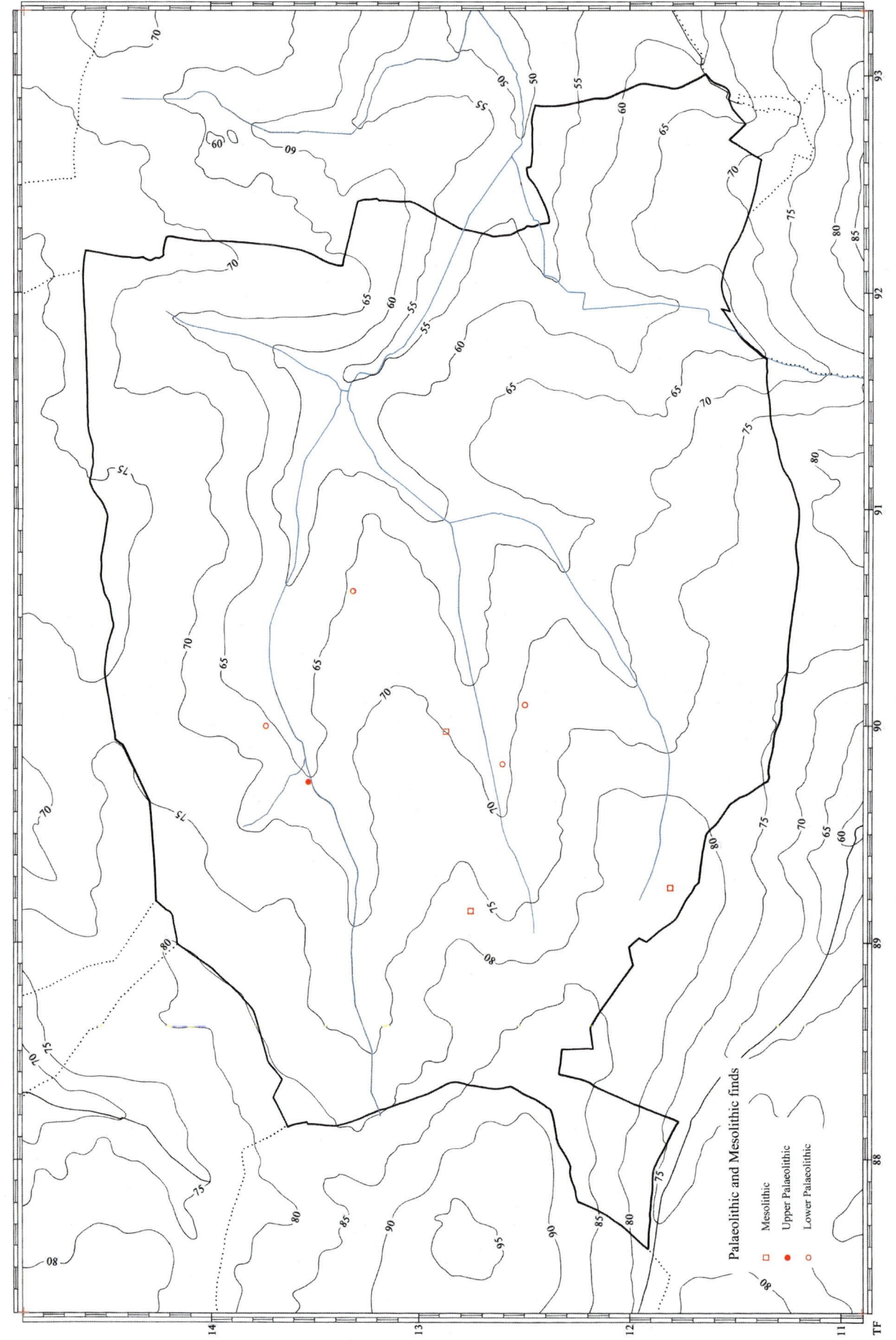

Figure 2.1 Fransham, distribution of Palaeolithic and Mesolithic finds, scale 1:25,000

Chapter 2. Prehistory

Introduction

At the start of this survey no prehistoric field monuments, neither earthworks nor cropmark sites, had been recorded in the study area, and only three HER entries concerned the later stages of prehistory. A squat polished flint axe from Great Fransham was lent by the Tower Armoury to the Pitt Rivers Museum, Oxford, in 1915, and was seen, probably by Rainbird Clarke, in 1934 (HER 4183). According to Bryant (1903) a 'short celt of basalt', presumably a Neolithic or Early Bronze Age stone axe, was found on Mr Parkin's land in Great Fransham in 1825. This land has not been identified (HER 12426), but Parkin may be equated with Henry Perkins, farmer, who appeared in a Norfolk directory twenty years later (White 1845, 333). Norwich Castle Museum records refer to a mound of pot-boilers reported in 1947 by 'Simpson'. The spot was marked at TF 9002 1276 (HER 7288). No trace of such a feature was evident at this reference. It is assumed that a small error was made when the site was marked on the museum map, and that this site is to be identified with one found in the survey, PB 9 which lies 100m to the north east.

The quantity of evidence for prehistoric activity recovered in this survey stands in stark contrast to the above handful of accidental finds, and shows clearly how misleading such evidence is, compared with that recovered by a programme of systematic fieldwork.

The Palaeolithic
(Fig. 2.1)

A small Lower Palaeolithic hand-axe was found at TF 90635 13320 (HER 20651, Fig. 2.2), and a probably Palaeolithic secondary flake at TF 8983 1261 (HER 21631). In addition, Derek Woollestone recovered a retouched flake at TF 9001 1374 (HER 20792) and a scraper at TF 9100 1250 (HER 23080). These four flints can draw little comment. Very few finds have been made in the locality (Wymer 1984, fig. 3.1). Single hand-axes have been recorded from Necton and Holme Hale (Wymer 1985, 46 and 51.

A Late (Final) Upper Palaeolithic double-ended scraper made on a segment of a large blade was casually recovered by Julia Rogerson from a garden in a valley bottom at TF 89754 13538. The chocolate brown flint is peat-stained (HER 20608, Fig. 2.2).

The Mesolithic
(Fig. 2.1)

A prismatic micro-blade core was recovered from an area of light sandy soil at TF 8926 1181 (HER 23906) and a probably Mesolithic truncated microlithic blade on medium soil at TF 8916 1276 (HER 23076). The period is not unequivocally present elsewhere in the study area, although a small, probably Mesolithic blade was recovered during metal-detecting some way to the east in a field centred at TF 8982 1287 (HER 20508). A sprinkling of blades and small blade cores on medium soils may include a Mesolithic element but might equally well belong to the Early Neolithic. Mesolithic exploitation of the Boulder Clay is known from a few parts of Norfolk, for example at Banham in the south of the county (Lawson 1978), but normally in places close to lighter soils. A shaft-hole implement, an axe and a possible digging weight from Wendling parish are evidence of some activity close to the study area in areas of medium soil (TF 9375 1328, HER 7282; TF 9380 1340, HER 18383 and TF 9344 1309, HER 28736). A single blunted blade, probably Mesolithic, was found in Scarning parish at TF 9539 1300 (HER 25436). Jacobi's (1984, 43) reference to an adze found at or near Little Dunham in 1821 is incorrect. Its Norwich Castle Museum Accession Number relates to a Neolithic polished flint axe found there in 1828. Wymer

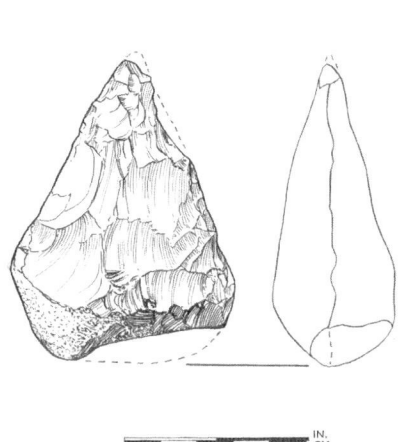
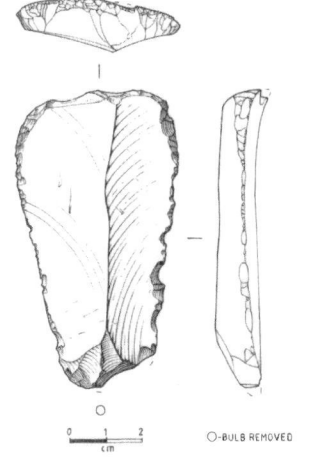

Figure 2.2 Lower Palaeolithic hand-axe (HER 20651) and Upper Palaeolithic scraper (HER 20608), scale 1:2

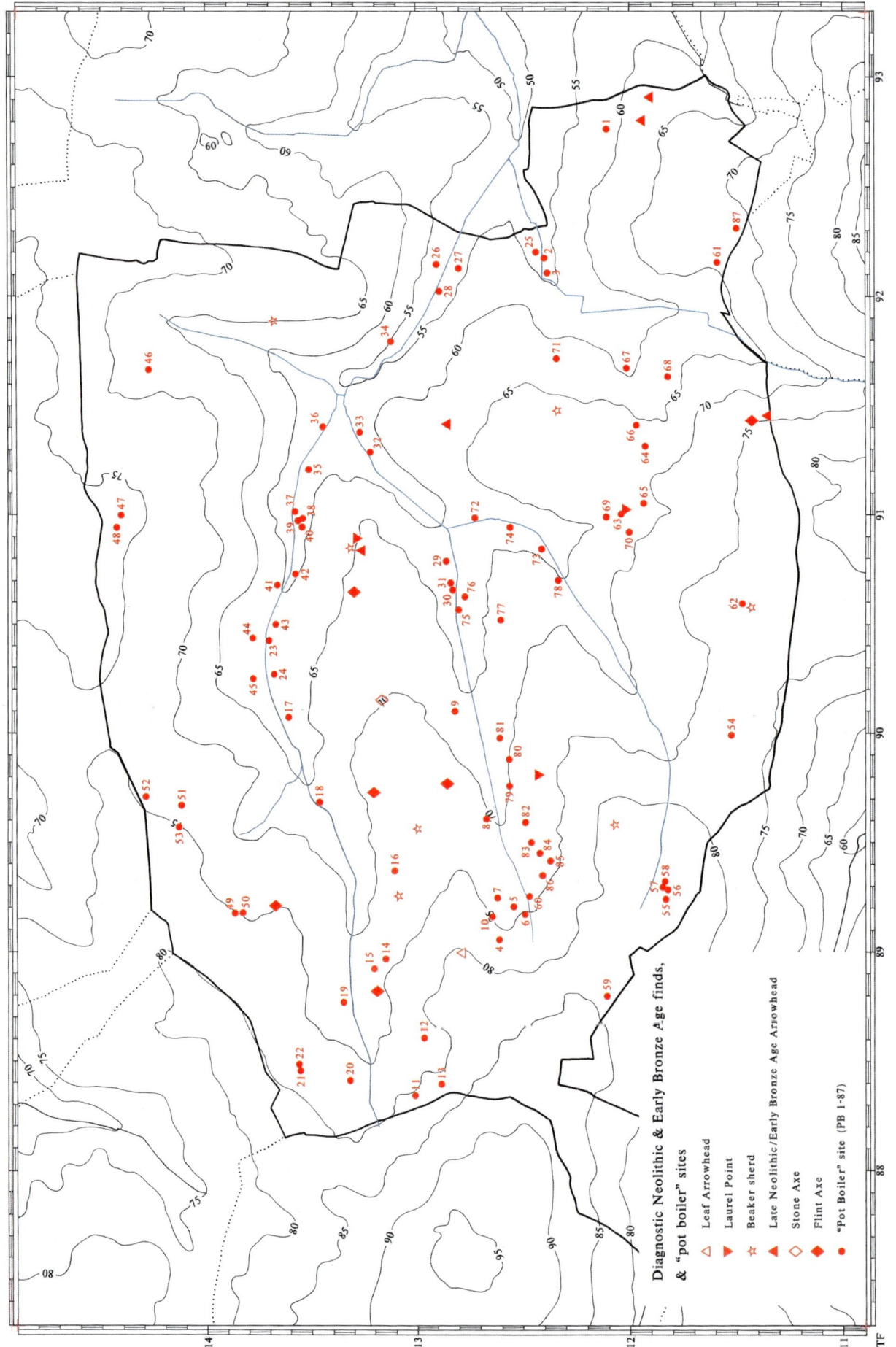

Figure 2.3 Distribution of Neolithic and Bronze Age finds, and 'pot boiler' sites, scale 1:25,000

(1977) did not list any Mesolithic material from Little Dunham.

The Neolithic and Early Bronze Age
(Fig. 2.3)

Scatters of worked flint usually comprise a very large proportion of undiagnostic pieces so that, for most surface collections, only a very broad Neolithic to Bronze Age date-range will be suggested by lithic specialists. Fortunately, certain of the larger groups of flints recovered in this survey were rapidly examined by two specialists, Dr Frances Healy and Dr John Wymer, and all the material has been assessed, with equal rapidity, by Dr Peter Robins. The Early Neolithic is represented by a number of diagnostic tools. In addition to those listed below, a serrated flake (HER 20604), two fabricators and a number of well formed large and medium sized scrapers, of both rounded end and horseshoe forms, are probably of the Early Neolithic. However, the material is predominantly of later Neolithic and Early Bronze Age character. A later Bronze Age and Iron Age element is also probably present. As will be seen below, the earliest datable pot sherds are of Beakers, and an intimate association between Beaker pottery and barbed and tanged arrowheads is well-established (Clarke 1970, 263; Green 1980, 137–41 and 191).

No scholar has made any inference from the available data about the degree and nature of exploitation on the plateau in the Neolithic and Early Bronze Age, although it has been suggested that in the Early Neolithic there was a 'marked apparent avoidance of the heavier boulder clay' (Robinson 1981, 26). A recent assessment of the clays of Leicestershire, Northamptonshire and Rutland has shown the surface evidence is abundant except on the plateaux. The picture is complex, with land-use and intensity of activity changing through time and interacting with variations in clay type, steepness of land form and proximity to water (Clay 2007). The predominantly medium clays of Fransham were clearly not without their attraction to the settlers of the Early Neolithic. Here as elsewhere on the heavier soils of Norfolk, we are clearly dealing with a late Neolithic expansion into a 'previously little-used and in contemporary terms less hospitable area' (Healy 1980, 285–6).

The HER cites one example of a ring-ditch in Fransham (HER 4192). A vague circular mark, *c.*90m in diameter, is visible under grass on two 1946 RAF vertical aerial photographs at TF 8947 1312. It is very likely that the mark is spurious, either natural or the result of animal tethering.

Diagnostic worked flint and pottery
Three *laurel leaves*, flint artefacts characteristic of the Early Neolithic (Clark and Higgs 1960, 221–3) were recovered:
TF 9089 1328 within a moderate flint scatter (HER 20653),
TF 9103 1202 within a profuse flint scatter (HER 24765),
TF 8982 1242 within a profuse flint scatter (HER 23081).

Arrowheads comprised one Early Neolithic *leaf* (Green 1980, 92–6), three *barbed and tanged* (BTA), one

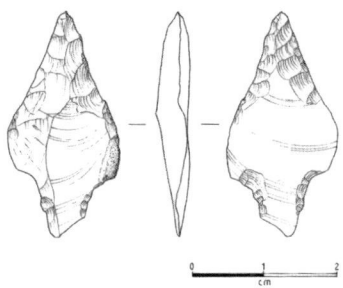

Figure 2.4 Late Neolithic/Early Bronze Age flint arrowhead (HER 24783), scale 1:1

tanged (Green 1980, 117, 138, fig. 45) and two *triangular* of the Later Neolithic/Early Bronze Age (Healy 1980, 206, Green 1980, 142–7):
TF 8900 1278 Leaf arrowhead within a moderate flint scatter (HER 20510).
TF 9084 1327 BTA within a moderate flint scatter and close to a Beaker sherd (HER 20653).
TF 9146 1136 BTA within a profuse flint scatter which also included an axe fragment (HER 24777).
TF 9142 1286 BTA within a sparse flint scatter (HER 21629).
TF 8881 1280 Tanged (but not barbed) arrowhead of Sutton type a, found during metal-detecting within a profuse flint scatter (HER 24783, Fig. 2.4).
TF 9280 1195 and 9291 1191 Two triangular arrowheads within a profuse flint scatter (HER 25541).

It should be noted that arrowheads, although found on settlement sites, may have been lost while hunting far from home and need not be indicative of the proximity of settlement. In Fransham, however, no arrowhead has been recovered from an area devoid of other finds of worked flint.

In addition to one remarkable Neolithic pick recovered by a farmer, fragments of *axes* were found in seven locations. All except one piece were of flint.
TF 900 136. Complete pick found by the late Mr Ted Rivet in *c.*1960 and now in private possession (Fig. 2.5). Of exceptional length (416mm) and of brown stained dark grey/black flint it may have been intended for ceremonial use and was almost certainly found in peaty or wet ground. The field from which it was recovered lies on either side of a stream and survived as meadow at the time of the find. It has yielded only one other worked flint (HER 20594).
TF 9015 1316 Cutting end of polished stone axe of Group I (Cornish), Implement Petrology Committee no. N244, within a moderate flint scatter (HER 15875, Fig. 2.6).
TF 8978 1286 Fragment of re-chipped polished flint axe or adze within a profuse flint scatter, near the find spot of a flake from a Late Neolithic/Early Bronze Age Levalloisoid core (HER 20508).
TF 8973 1320 Fragment of blade end of flaked flint axe within a moderate flint scatter (HER 20604).
TF 8883 1319 Butt end of polished flint axe within a sparse flint scatter (HER 25554).
TF 8921 1367 Flaked flint axe, cutting edge missing, within a sparse flint scatter (HER 20623).
TF 9066 1330 Fragment of cutting edge of flint axe within a moderate flint scatter (HER 20651).
TF 9143 1143 Re-chipped cutting end of polished flint axe, found within a profuse flint scatter, near to a BTA and

very close to a Late Neolithic/Early Bronze Age plano-convex knife (HER 24777).

A flint imitation of an Early Bronze Age hafted metal dagger found during metal-detecting within a moderate flint scatter at TF 8933 1302 (HER 4192, Fig. 2.7), has been identified as Scandinavian and is later than *c*.1950 BC (Frieman 2015, 104, table 9.1).

The dating of axes is unfortunately little tighter than that of less unusual flint tools such as scrapers, and they can be of the earlier or later Neolithic. None is likely to be later than the Early Bronze Age. Axes were put to a variety of uses and their distribution is, therefore, varied: they are found on settlement sites but can also occur in more isolated locations where they may have been lost during

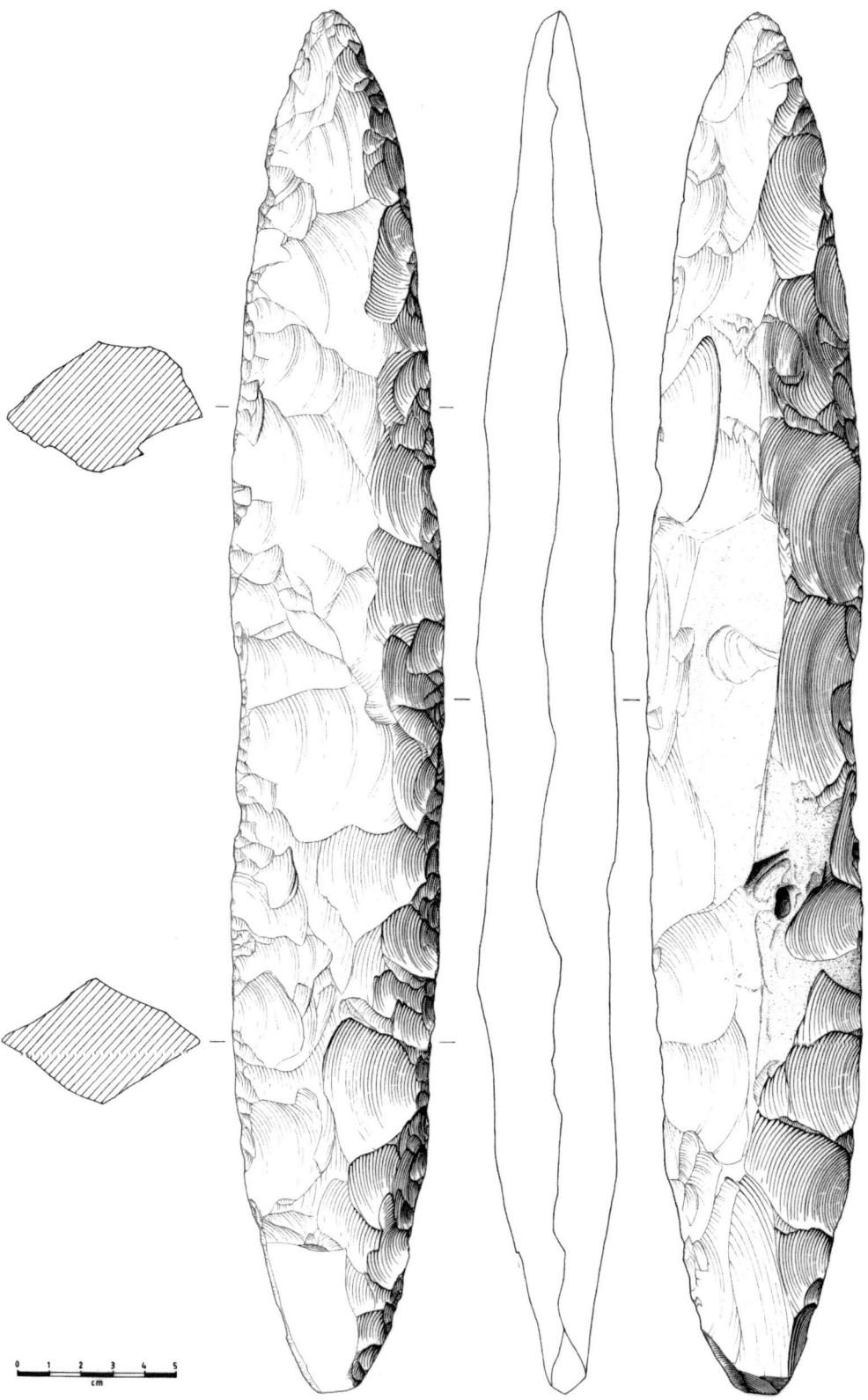

Figure 2.5 Neolithic flint pick (HER 20594), scale 1:2

woodland clearance, woodland management such as coppicing or pollarding (Rackham 1986b, 120), hedging or even cultivation. Complete axes are perhaps more likely to have been lost and then not found in woodland, rather than within settlements (Healy 1980, 123–4). A map of the incidence in Norfolk of flint and stone axes by 10 x 10km grid square shows Fransham falling within a square containing the minimum number of examples, between 1 and 10 (Healy 1980, 126).

'One of the most amorphous types of evidence for [Beaker] domestic activity is the simple scatter of sherds' (Gibson 1982, 42–3). The term scatter seems to be an overstatement in the context of this study during which single Beaker sherds, and in one case a pair, were found in seven locations:

TF 8926 1309 Basal sherd with stick-impressed decoration within a moderate flint scatter (HER 4192),

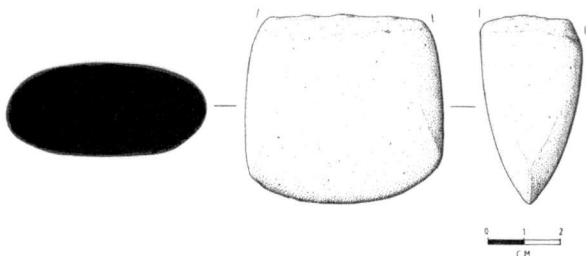

Figure 2.6 Fragment of Neolithic polished stone axe (HER 15875), scale 1:2

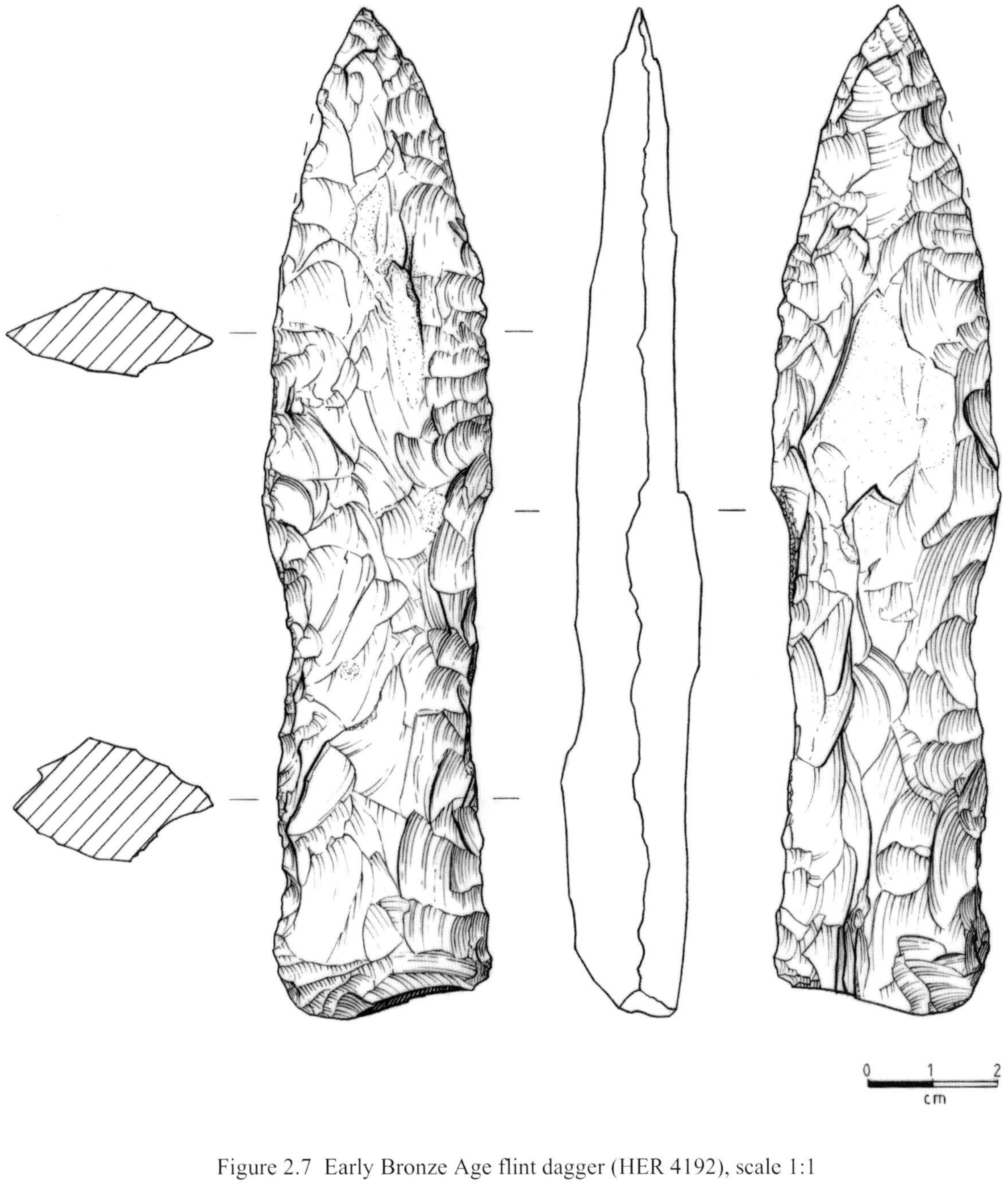

Figure 2.7 Early Bronze Age flint dagger (HER 4192), scale 1:1

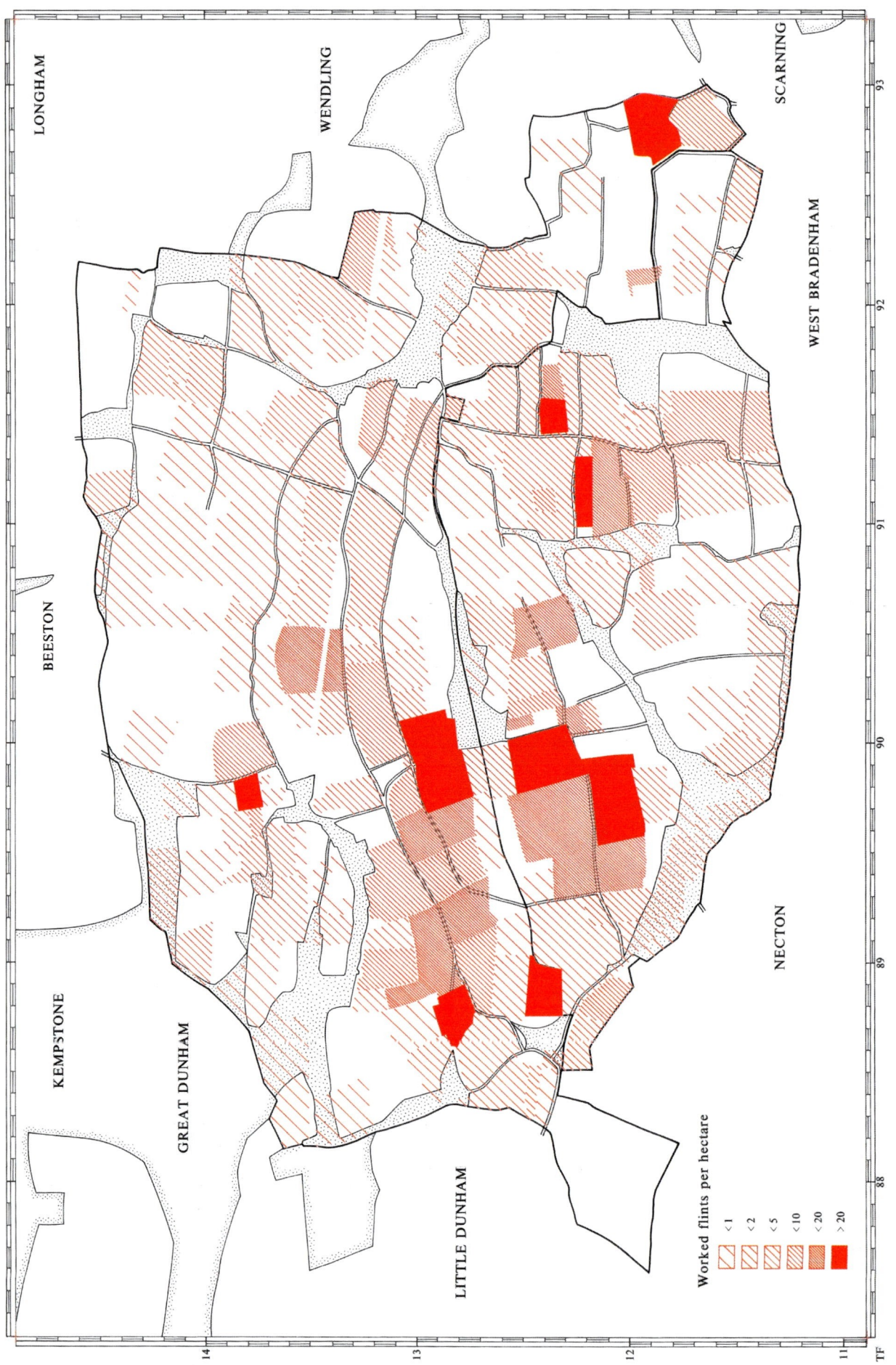

Figure 2.8 Worked flint densities, scale 1:25,000

TF 8956 1300 Sherd with comb-impressed decoration within a considerable flint scatter (HER 20524),

TF 9085 1332 Sherd with comb-impressed decoration within a moderate flint scatter which included a BTA (HER 20653),

TF 9189 1368 Two sherds and a scrap with comb-impressed decoration, probably from the same vessel, within a sparse flint scatter (HER 21627),

TF 8959 1208 Sherd with comb-impressed decoration within a profuse flint scatter (L63, HER 23897),

TF 9058 1144 Sherd with comb-impressed decoration within a sparse flint scatter (HER 25564),

TF 9148 1234 Sherd with incised decoration found close to five plain, probably Bronze Age, grog-tempered sherds within a profuse flint scatter (HER 20824).

General scatters of worked flints
(Fig. 2.8)

Worked flints other than arrowheads and axes were far from ubiquitous in the study area, but they were found with what can only be called surprising frequency in some parts. A total of 4449 pieces was recovered. All appear to have been struck from locally gathered material.

During the course of the fieldwork, considerable problems were encountered in establishing the presence of what might with confidence be called concentrations of worked flints, and in defining the boundaries of scatters. The task proved too difficult and as a result a somewhat schematic method of indicating the densities of flint scatters has been used on Fig. 2.8. This shows the incidence of worked flints in the study area, subdivided by fields appearing on the 1928 edition of the Ordnance Survey 1:2500 scale maps, expressed by numbers of pieces per hectare. The map is to a certain extent misleading, or at least oversimplifying, through its use of recent land parcels as units of measurement. Apparent concentrations of worked flints on restricted patches of lighter soil within wider bands of heavier land do not appear as significant points of density.

Two of the most blatant examples of this 'ironing-out' effect occur at opposite edges of the parish. On the northern boundary at TF 8920 1422 all but three out of 18 flints were recovered from an area of 0.5 hectares in a field of 5.1 hectares (HER 20817). This gave an average of 3.5 flints per hectare, rather than 30 per hectare for the area of the concentration only. This concentration, which included a sherd of flint gritted pottery and produced a further 65 flints on subsequent closely spaced walking, coincided with a patch of more sandy soil within a large area of heavier ground. On a similar island of lighter soil at TF 9141 1140, a total of 64 worked flints including a BTA and a polished axe fragment was recovered from 1 hectare, although the whole field yielded an average of only 8.3 pieces per hectare (HER 24777).

The highest recorded density amounted to a mere 43 pieces per hectare, in a field centred at TF 8984 1287 (HER 20508). This weakness of contrast between dense and thin areas, with extensive and sometimes almost continuous worked flint scatters rendering site definition impractical, has been encountered elsewhere, for example in the Great Ouse Valley, Bedfordshire (Woodward 1978).

Tingle, before analysing surface flint collections from the Vale of the White Horse, felt bound to state that an 'Attempt to reconstruct past activities from a widespread and unstratified flint assemblage must be open to extensive qualification' (Tingle 1991, 21). In the case of Fransham, where examination of worked flints has been only cursory, we can venture no further than to state that both cores, flakes and finished tools such as scrapers were discarded over wide areas of the lighter soils over a vast period of time. Indeed, it would be unwise to attempt a detailed assessment of the nature of Neolithic and Bronze Age occupation.

Experimentation and careful analysis of surface flint collections in southern England has suggested that in that region at least, 'Disturbance under intensive agriculture will make the delimitation of sites as discrete units virtually impossible' (Clark and Schofield 1991, 103). The Fransham situation can hardly vary from this rather depressing conclusion. In the absence of excavation, it is difficult to speculate on the permanence or seasonality of human settlement, and on the relative importance of stock rearing and arable farming. Nevertheless, the broad characteristics of the distribution clearly indicate something about land-use patterns in this remote period.

That mixed agriculture was the norm in East Anglia at the end of the third millennium BC and the first half of the second is well established, and it is no longer acceptable to cast Beaker pottery users as 'nomadic pastoralists' (Healy 1984, 118). It is clear, however, that activities which involved the use and discard of scrapers, to a lesser extent of blades, and of retouched flakes of various forms, as well as the manufacture of tools from local flint sources, were carried out far more frequently in some parts of the study area than in others, and almost entirely on the lighter soils. There seems to be every reason to believe that these activities were carried out most often in and around those places where the flint users and makers lived. That odd worked flints have been recovered from much of the area indicates that some tools were lost or discarded 'off site', *i.e.* away from home, but in what pursuits the associated persons were engaged, we can never know. That some areas have yielded no finds of worked flint suggests only that they were rarely or never frequented by flint discarding people.

All the above surmise on the factors which lie behind variations in the numbers of worked flints leads to a very rough and ready breakdown of the study area into three categories of potential land-use reflected in three rates of occurrence of flints, (1) common, (2) occasional and (3) zero. Such variations in density may correspond to: (1) occupation zones, adjacent arable plots and stock enclosures comprising areas of widely differing size and situated on relatively well-drained soils; (2) large stretches of land, both elevated and low lying, containing a mixture of grassland, open scrubland and managed or at least regularly exploited woodland, along with localities, almost always near a water source, at which were carried out specialised activities resulting in the production of calcined flints (see 'pot-boilers' below); (3) areas, in the main coincident with the heaviest soils, carrying dense and relatively unexploited woodland, along with some valley bottoms which were in part very wet.

Pot-boiler sites
(Fig. 2.3)

Those areas where localised patches of calcined flints usually in a matrix of dark soil occur, are almost the mirror image of those containing the higher densities of worked flints, with flints being most prolific on the well-drained upland whereas calcined flint patches, hereafter called 'pot-boiler' sites, are almost always situated near water. The distribution in Fransham conforms to the norm in that 85% are within 200m of present-day watercourses or of springs at their heads. Many of these must have been closer to open water before streams were canalised in the medieval and post-medieval periods. Only thirteen examples have been recorded on elevated ground at a distance from a stream. Some of these may have been near springs that now feed into field drains and are no longer apparent. Some of the latter (*e.g.* PB 46–8) are far from areas with prolific worked flint scatters, are adjacent to areas of common pasture in historic times and are perhaps not prehistoric.

A total of 87 surface concentrations has been recorded and a further thirteen spreads, too diffuse and ill-defined to be considered 'sites', have also been noted. These 87 appear in the HER as 73 entries under the monument descriptor 'burnt mound'. This should be compared with a total of only 21 HER entries in the area of Broadland District Council in east Norfolk, 259 in Breckland District (including Fransham) and 717 in the county of Norfolk.

One area from which we are fortunate to have reliable data is the Wissey Embayment, the fen and fen skirtland of south-west Norfolk. Here Silvester recorded more than 300 pot-boiler sites and noted that burnt flints were to be found both as concentrations and in areas of worked flints. He was driven to remark that pot-boilers were 'truly ubiquitous along the fen-edge from the Little Ouse to the Wissey'. Although one or two sites may have been Roman, he argued convincingly that most belonged to the Late Neolithic or Early Bronze Age (Silvester 1991, 85–7).

The Fransham examples are consistently smaller than those on fen-edge, where 63.5% covered less than 0.06 hectares and two as much as 0.2 hectares. The 77 measurable Fransham sites average 0.028 hectares, with only three exceeding 0.1 hectares and the largest covering 0.15 hectares.

There can be little doubt that these 87 sites are ploughed down versions of the prehistoric burnt mounds which are found throughout Britain. None can be shown to be Roman, and there is no sound reason why a later date should be considered. Paring and burning, and the spreading of burnt earth, both methods of land improvement recommended by Arthur Young (1804, 416–7 and 434–5) cannot have resulted in such clearly defined and restricted patches of calcined flints, although the thirteen ill-defined areas of sparse 'pot-boilers' could possibly have been the products of such practices. Although one example of a sub-surface 'cut feature' containing pot-boilers was recorded, and despite the probable case of another sub-surface deposit of pot-boilers, it is likely that the surface exposures of burnt flints and dark soil does not normally represent the upper part of a filled pit or hole but are rather horizontal spreads contained entirely within the topsoil. This was confirmed by the observation of the edges of a newly cleaned and widened ditch cut through one site (PB 79). The most popular explanation of the function of such sites has been that the heated flints were used to heat water in which food was cooked (O'Drisceoil 1988). Many flints were required and could of course not be reused. The fires needed to heat the flints produced the ash and the charcoal that darkened the soil. Sauna baths utilising the large amount of steam which must have been emitted when the hot flints were plunged into the water, have also been put forward as a function. Industrial activities such as wood-bending, leather working and the production of grit filler for pottery have also been suggested (Barfield and Hodder 1987). Silvester was surely correct in coming out against any single explanation, but it cannot be claimed that non-invasive fieldwork can go much further towards providing a definite answer. What pot-boiler sites do suggest, however, is the widespread exploitation of low-lying areas where scatters of worked flints are sparse.

Gazetteer of pot-boiler sites
(all dimensions are in metres)

Well-defined surface sites
PB 1 TF 9277 1210 HER 25543 Darkish soil 25 N-S 18 E-W
PB 2 TF 9218 1240 HER 23889 Slightly dark soil 9 N-S, min. 6 E-W. Extends into unexamined area
PB 3 TF 9211 1238 HER 23889 Slightly dark soil 9 N-S 11 E-W
PB 4 TF 8906 1262 HER 23077 Dark soil diam. 15
PB 5 TF 8921 1255 HER 23077 Darkish and dark patches 16 N-S 25 E-W. Unburnt flint flake
PB 6 TF 8918 1249 HER 23077 Slightly dark soil diam. 10
PB 7 TF 8925 1263 HER 20506 Dark soil diam. 14
PB 8 TF 8961 1268 HER 20507 Dark soil 29 N-S 22 E-W. Unburnt flint scraper
PB 9 TF 9011 1282 HER 7288 Dark soil 40 E-W, min. 15 N-S. Slight mound, probably extends under roadway
PB 10 TF 8917 1265 HER 23076 Darkish soil 13 N-S 12 E-W. Extends into formerly separate field to W., G51
PB 11 TF 8835 1301 HER 20520 Dark soil diam. 10
PB 12 TF 8861 1297 HER 20521 Very slightly dark soil with diffuse calcined flints in clearly defined area. 48 N-S 30 E-W
PB 13 TF 8840 1289 HER 20521 Dark soil min. 18 N-S 14 E-W. Extends below former trackway
PB 14 TF 8897 1315 HER 20523 Dark soil, darker to W. 17 N-S 28 E-W
PB 15 TF 8893 1320 HER 20523 Very dark soil 18 E-W 25 N-S
PB 16 TF 8937 1310 HER 4192 Soil indistinguishable from surrounding soil; diffuse calcined flints in clearly defined area 50 N-S 40 E-W
PB 17 TF 9080 1360 HER 20593 Dark soil 7 N-S 12 E-W
PB 18 TF 8969 1347 HER 20604 Dark soil 17 N-S 9 E-W
PB 19 TF 8879 1335 HER 20619 Dark soil 23 N-S, min. 13 E-W, extends beneath trackway
PB 20 TF 8841 1332 HER 20620 Dark soil diam. 15
PB 21 TF 8846 1355 HER 20622 Dark soil 25 N-S 20 E-W
PB 22 TF 8849 1356 HER 20622 Dark soil diam. 5, with adjacent patches brought up by plough
PB 23 9043 1370 HER 20627 Dark soil 6 N-S 12 E-W
PB 24 TF 9027 1367 HER 20627 Dark soil diam. 9
PB 25 TF 9221 1243 HER 23886 Slightly dark soil 10 N-S 14 E-W
PB 26 TF 9215 1290 HER 20634 Slightly dark soil 20 N-S 28 E-W
PB 27 TF 9213 1280 HER 23888 Slightly dark soil with diffuse calcined flints in clearly defined area 15 N-S 17 E-W
PB 28 TF 9203 1289 HER 23887 Slightly dark soil with diffuse calcined flints in clearly defined area 8 N-S 18 E-W
PB 29 TF 9079 1285 HER 20642 Dark soil 7 N-S 11 E-W
PB 30 TF 9066 1282 HER 20643 Dark soil 7 N-S 14 E-W
PB 31 TF 9069 1283 HER 20613 Dark soil diam. 8
PB 32 TF 9129 1321 HER 20740 Dark soil 10 N-S 5 E-W
PB 33 TF 9139 1327 HER 20742 Slightly dark soil 17 N-S 10 E-W
PB 34 TF 9180 1312 HER 20745 Dark soil 40 N-S 25 E-W
PB 35 TF 9121 1351 HER 20754 Dark soil 15 N-S 10 E-W
PB 36 TF 9141 1344 HER 20754 Dark soil 16 N-S 20 E-W
PB 37 TF 9102 1358 HER 20756 Dark soil 7 N-S 11 E-W
PB 38 TF 9099 1354 HER 23074 Dark soil 12 N-S 8 E-W
PB 39 TF 9098 1356 HER 23074 Dark soil 10 N-S 18 E-W
PB 40 TF 9095 1354 HER 23074 Patchy dark soil 6 N-S 9 E-W
PB 41 TF 9067 1367 HER 20758 Dark soil 7 N-S 10 E-W
PB 42 TF 9074 1357 HER 20758 Dark soil 6 N-S 9 E-W
PB 43 TF 9050 1367 HER 20761 Dark soil 10 N-S 28 E-W
PB 44 TF 9044 1378 HER 20769 Dark soil 7 N-S 10 E-W
PB 45 TF 9025 1378 HER 20769 Dark soil 7 N-S 12 E-W
PB 46 TF 9167 1426 HER 20783 Soil indistinguishable from surrounding soil, with clearly defined area of calcined flints 26 N-S 10 E-W

PB 47 TF 9100 1440 HER 20787 Soil indistinguishable from surrounding soil, with clearly defined area of calcined flints diam. 25
PB 48 TF 9095 1442 HER 20788 Soil indistinguishable from surrounding soil, with clearly defined area of calcined flints diam. 12
PB 49 TF 8918 1387 HER 20799 Dark soil diam. 6
PB 50 TF 8918 1384 HER 20799 Dark soil diam. 12
PB 51 TF 8967 1412 HER 20814 Slightly dark soil diam. 16
PB 52 TF 8971 1429 HER 20815 Slightly dark soil diam. 12
PB 53 TF 8958 1413 HER 20816 Dark soil diam. 9
PB 54 TF 8999 1153 HER 24771 Soil indistinguishable from surrounding soil, with clearly defined area of calcined flints 17 N-S 12 E-W
PB 55 TF 8925 1184 HER 23906 Slightly dark soil 27 N-S 12 E-W
PB 56 TF 8929 1183 HER 23906 Dark soil diam. 25
PB 57 TF 8930 1186 HER 23906 Slightly dark soil diam. 20
PB 58 TF 8933 1185 HER 23906 Dark soil diam. 18
PB 59 TF 8881 1211 HER 23079 Soil indistinguishable from surrounding soil, with clearly defined area of calcined flints 28 N-S 14 E-W
PB 60 TF 8926 1248 HER 21630 Dark soil diam. 17 = L95.4
PB 61 TF 9216 1159 HER 25560 Dark soil 12 N-S 20 E-W
PB 62 TF 9060 1148 HER 25565 Dark soil 28 N-S 20 E-W
PB 63 TF 9102 1204 HER 24765 Soil indistinguishable from surrounding soil, diffuse calcined flints within clearly defined area 30 N-S 50 E-W
PB 64 TF 9132 1193 HER 24767 Dark soil diam. 16
PB 65 TF 9106 1194 HER 24767 Dark soil 18 N-S 17 E-W
PB 66 TF 9142 1197 HER 28876 Dark soil diam. 16
PB 67 TF 9168 1201 HER 29221 Dark soil 20 N-S 12 E-W
PB 68 TF 9164 1183 HER 24778 Slightly dark soil diam. 18
PB 69 TF 9100 1210 HER 24768 Dark soil diam. 17
PB 70 TF 9093 1200 HER 29218 Dark soil 28 N-S 18 E-W
PB 71 TF 9172 1234 HER 20823 Dark soil 23 N-S, min.20 E-W = L132.46, visible on both sides of track, extends into uncultivated land
PB 72 TF 9099 1272 HER 23088 Dark soil 12 N-S 7 E-W
PB 73 TF 9085 1240 HER 20829 Dark soil min. 10 N-S 23 E-W. Cut to S by roadside ditch
PB 74 TF 9080 1250 HER 20829 Dark soil diam. 8
PB 75 TF 9052 1280 HER 20830 Dark soil diam. 9
PB 76 TF 9063 1277 HER 20831 Dark soil 20 N-S 16 E-W
PB 77 TF 9053 1260 HER 20831 Soil indistinguishable from surrounding soil, with clearly defined area of calcined flints 11 N-S 13 E-W
PB 78 TF 9071 1233 HER 23895 Dark soil 10 N-S 12 E-W
PB 79 TF 8976 1258 HER 21631 Dark soil 6 N-S 10 E-W
PB 80 TF 8989 1257 HER 21631 Dark soil diam. 16
PB 81 TF 8998 1261 HER 21631 Dark soil diam. 16
PB 82 TF 8960 1250 HER 23082 Dark soil 14 N-S 20 E-W
PB 83 TF 8950 1247 HER 23082 Slightly dark soil 35 N-S 22 E-W
PB 84 TF 8945 1243 HER 23083 Dark soil 6 N-S, min. 4 E-W. Extends beneath trackway
PB 85 TF 8943 1238 HER 24764 Dark soil 19 N-S 13 E-W
PB 86 TF 8935 1242 HER 24764 Slightly dark soil 22 N-S 33 E-W
PB 87 TF 9230 1150 HER 28878 Slightly dark soil 11 N-S 13 E-W

Sub-surface deposits of pot-boilers
TF 8965 1307 HER 20524 Area 2m² containing intermittent lumps of dark soil with profuse calcined flints freshly brought up by ploughing. No other pot-boilers or dark soil in the immediate vicinity, suggesting a deposit previously below depth of ploughing had been very recently been disturbed.

TF 8920 1333 HER 20615 Pit or other feature observed, in one edge of newly-cut ditch, to be 0.80 wide and 0.35 deep, with a lower filling of very dark grey sandy clay with dense pot-boilers.

Ill-defined and diffuse surface pot-boiler spreads
TF 928 123 HER 25545; TF 891 130 HER 24784; TF 885 132 HER 20619; TF 916 132 HER 20742; TF 912 145 HER 23891; TF 902 114 HER 25556; TF 899 116 HER 24771; TF 894 119 HER 24761; TF 893 121 HER 24763; TF 908 116 HER 28886; TF 915 122 HER 20821; TF 908 109 HER 29218; TF 903 127 HER 23896.

The later Bronze Age

Neither Norfolk, nor indeed East Anglia, is abundant in examples of later Bronze Age settlements, and even the funerary evidence is scarce. The vast bulk of the archaeological information in the county comes in the

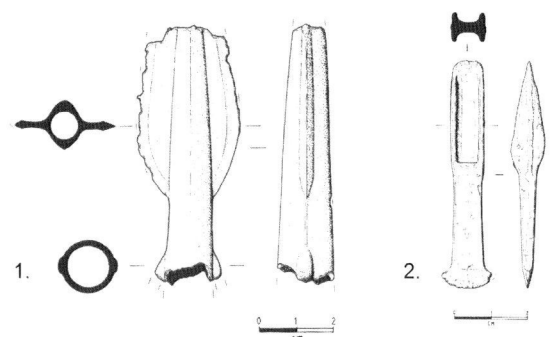

Figure 2.9 Middle Bronze Age spearhead and palstave chisel, scale 1:2

form of hoards and single finds of metalwork (Lawson 1984); no class of enclosure can be securely dated to the period, flintwork must lie unrecognised as 'late' amongst collections of material given a generalised Neolithic/Bronze Age date, and pottery is rare. This rarity is caused partly by difficulties of recognition and definition, and partly by the undoubtedly friable nature of such material as can be securely dated to the period. Most of this pottery is extremely badly fired (Silvester 1991, 87; Healy 1991, 139), and has little more durability than unbaked clay. A gazetteer of Norfolk sites with pottery finds totalled a mere 31 entries (Lawson 1980, 286–9). It cannot be suggested that either the study area or any other area blank on distribution maps, were deserted in the later Bronze Age. However, despite the exhaustive fieldwork undertaken, no pottery certainly assignable to this period was recovered. Other sherds may of course remain unidentified amongst material assigned to the Iron Age.

To emphasise the problem of recognition which attaches to worked flints of this period and of the Iron Age, it would be best to quote from notes kindly supplied by Dr Peter Robins, 'Although Later Bronze Age and Early Iron Age flintwork is not separable from the general background noise of flint debitage and less diagnostic retouched artefacts...., the presence of irregular flakes carrying short lengths of steep retouch and of notched pieces may indicate a late flint working tradition, as may both small irregular cores, often showing signs of shattering, and small, relatively sharp and fresh looking debitage'. A very useful and succinct summary of present knowledge of flintworking in the later Bronze Age and Iron Age was given by Gardiner (1993b, 458).

There is now a large number of recorded find-spots of individual pieces of later Bronze Age metalwork on the Norfolk HER. Many of these have been found on the claylands. It may be that individual losses rather than hoards might give a more accurate picture of the extent and intensity of activity on the various soil types during this obscure period. Eight single finds have been recovered by metal-detecting in Fransham: part of a Middle Bronze Age side-looped spearhead (Fig. 2.9.1) at TF 9222 1151, *c.*100m from PB 61 (HER 25560), a Middle Bronze Age chisel of Rowlands 1976, form iii (Fig 2.9.2) at TF 8922 1381 (HER 20799), a fragment of the mouth of a Late Bronze Age socketed axe at TF 8923 1328 (HER 20612), a fragment of a Middle or Late Bronze Age knife or rapier in an area centred at TF 8935 1301 (HER 4192) and single fragments of cutting edges of Bronze

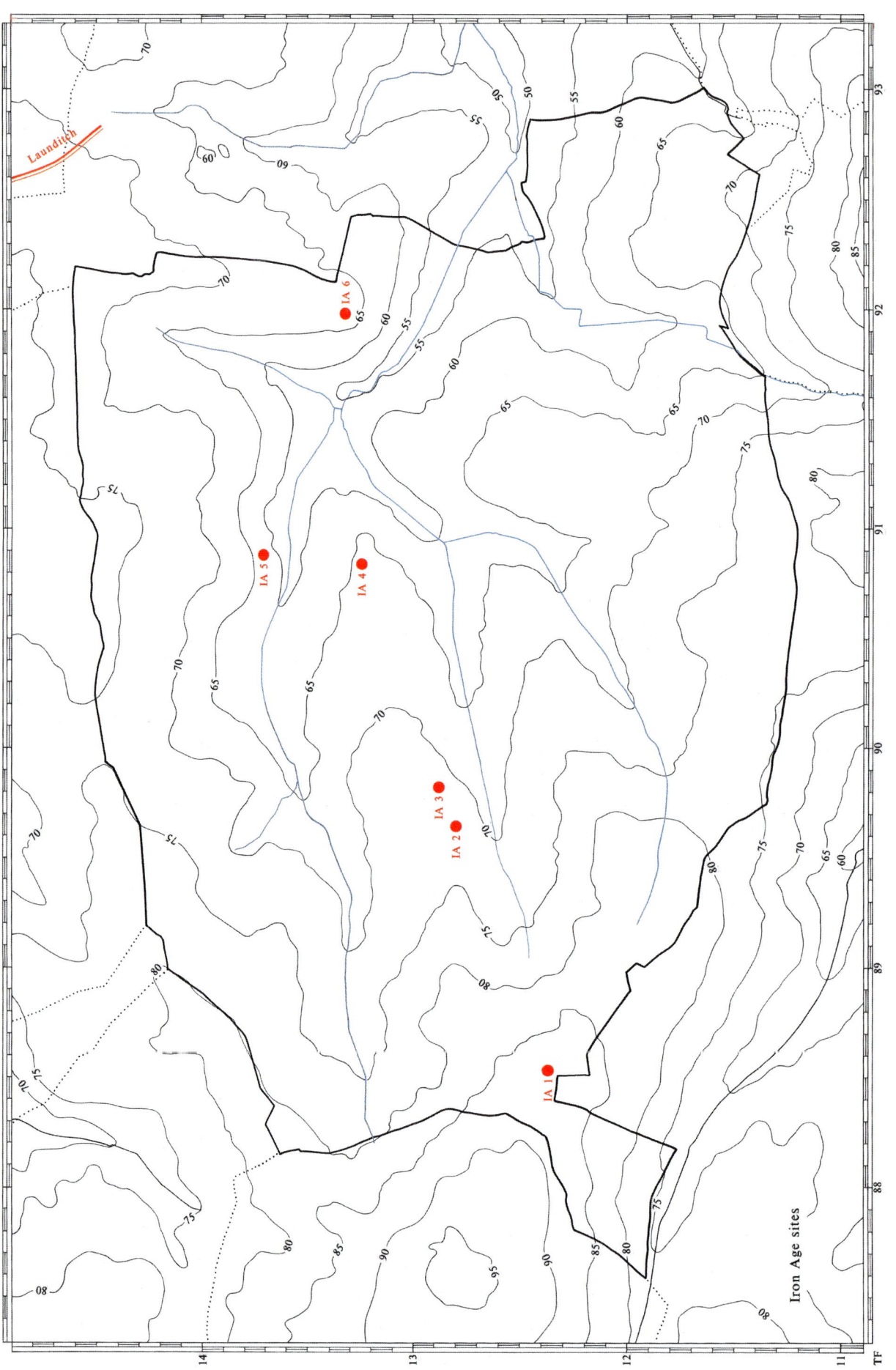

Figure 2.11 Iron Age sites, scale 1:25,000

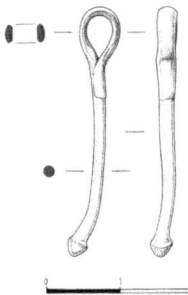

Figure 2.10 Late Bronze Age gold pendant (HER 4192), scale 1:1

Age axes of uncertain form at TF 8937 1285 (HER 23075) and in areas centred at TF 8913 1314 (HER 4192), and TF 8984 1287 (HER 20508). The eighth object is rather remarkable, a Late Bronze Age gold pendant (Fig. 2.10) found at TF 8983 1279 (HER 20508). Dating to the ninth century BC, it is paralleled by a copper alloy example in the Boughton Malherbe (Kent) hoard (www.finds.org.uk/KENT-15A293).

The Iron Age
(Fig. 2.11)

As for earlier periods the quality and amount of evidence for the Iron Age in parishes surrounding the study area are very limited, but one major field monument can be ascribed to the period in question. The Launditch (HER 7235), which gave its name to the Hundred in which Fransham lies, was a linear earthwork, consisting of a bank to the east and a ditch to the west, which ran southwards from low-lying ground in Mileham parish for c.6km to the valley of the Scarning River in Wendling, and formed the parish boundary of Beeston and Wendling with Longham. Now mostly destroyed as a visible feature, it has been considered a post-Roman construction (Wade-Martins 1974), and limited excavation purported to demonstrate this (Lewis 1957). In 1980 I excavated several trenches to the east of the Launditch, immediately north of its intersection with an east-west road which was considered to be Roman (HER 2796). An alignment of post-holes, securely dated by pottery to the Iron Age, ran for at least 200m almost parallel with and set back 20–25m from the monument. In addition, excavations by Kenneth Penn at the intersection of the road and linear earthwork have suggested, although not definitively, that the Launditch was constructed in the Iron Age (Ashwin and Flitcroft 1999). John Davies has lent additional support for a pre-Roman date (Davies 1996). Peter Wade-Martins, however, has recently cast doubt on this by suggesting that construction in the fifth century was 'more likely' (Wade-Martins 2016). This uncertainty has become more opaque as a result of James Albone's calling into question of the east-west road's Roman origin (Albone 2016, 87, 361–2, fig. 10).

The Launditch, whether an Iron Age monument or not, would have formed the western boundary of a territory of c.30km², which included large stretches of well-drained gravel-based soil and which was bounded in other directions by two tributaries of the Wensum, the Scarning River on the south and east, and the Blackwater on the north. The area of the present study lies outside and to the south-west of this putative territory, with the nearest part of Fransham parish falling within 1km of the Launditch.

During the last five centuries BC and the first half of the first century AD, the study area emerges from obscurity with the help of ceramics, hardly prolific yet occurring with sufficient frequency to enable concentrations to be identified. Sherd quantities, though, were small and it was necessary to supplement fieldwalking at normal speed and spacing of the fieldwalking by additional intensive visits, so that sufficient material might be collected for the definition of concentrations and for greater certainty of dating.

A major problem with the Norfolk Iron Age is the extreme imprecision of the pottery dating. At the start of the period there are well-known pottery types such as West Harling (Clark and Fell 1953), while at the end of it new forms and fabrics appear under Belgic influence in the half century leading up to the Roman invasion. The unsatisfactory state of present knowledge was well summarised by Tony Gregory who wrote that Iron Age pottery was 'still dated largely on an intuitive basis between the two supposed fixed points of West Harling, just before the middle of the first millennium, and the 'Belgic' or 'Aylesford-Swarling' horizon....somewhere in the first century BC' (Gregory 1992, 158). Both in personal communication and in his report on the pottery from Thetford Fison Way (Gregory 1992, 158) he identified a tendency in the later Iron Age for gritty fabrics to give way to sandy fabrics. With only small and usually abraded sherds as evidence, few conclusions on chronology can be allowed here, especially when sherd size precludes accurate assessment of forms. An additional drawback is the tendency for confusions of identification to arise with small individual hand-made sherds, particularly those in dark grey reduced sandy fabrics, which might be either Iron Age or Early Saxon (Williamson 1988, 160). There is not the same degree of difficulty with groups of sherds, providing the groups are sufficiently large, containing more than, say, twenty sherds. Fortunately, several groups identified as representing 'sites' were examined by Tony Gregory, and we can be confident that they belong to the pre-Roman period.

Interpretation for an Iron Age presence in the study area is heavily site-based. With the exception of the six concentrations interpreted as sites, the evidence is slight and comes in the form of a small number of pot sherds, normally so sparse that it is difficult to delineate scatters with any confidence ('off-site' sherds have been omitted from Fig. 2.11).

On the Norfolk Boulder clay, only at Park Farm, Wymondham, has there arisen the opportunity to follow up the discovery of an Iron Age sherd concentration in the ploughsoil with excavation. Here beneath a small part of the surface 'site' a complex of Middle Iron Age pits and structural features were cut into the subsoil (Ashwin 1996; Ashwin 1999, 113–6).

Two examples of sub-surface evidence strongly suggest that fieldwalking evidence, probably because of a poor sherd survival rate, must be under-representing the true picture of Iron Age exploitation in Fransham as it has done elsewhere, for example at Maxey (Crowther and Pryor 1985, 46). A small field of c.0.5 hectares (HER

20543) centred at TF 8988 1297 yielded two gritty, probably Iron Age, sherds when walked. The examination of c.150m² of the surface of the natural sandy clay after the stripping of ploughsoil in preparation for building work produced four more sherds. No Iron Age material was collected from the surface of a field of 2.3 hectares centred at TF 9038 1339 (HER 20759). When the ploughsoil was removed from a strip along the western edge of the field for the construction of a farm track, the upper charcoal-bearing filling of a small pit was revealed on the surface of the natural sandy clay at TF 9024 1337. Three pot sherds were recovered, including two in a hard fabric with fine grits. These may be related to the West Harling type.

Gazetteer of Iron Age sites
The six pottery concentrations considered to be sites (IA 1–6) are listed and summarised below in the form of a gazetteer providing the basic details of each.

IA 1 TF 8858 1239 (HER 20447)
True size and shape uncertain, extending north and east beneath uncultivated ground. 40m north-south and 25m east-west. Single sherd in molehill c.50m to the east suggesting much larger. On light to medium soil at 86m OD, almost the highest point in Fransham. Four sherds found initially. Three subsequent slow and closely-spaced examinations increased the total to 250+, an even mixture of gritty and sandy types.

IA 2 TF 8968 1282 (HER 20524)
On medium soil midway down a southern facing slope at 73m OD. Roughly circular, 30–35m diameter. Sandy and gritty sherds with a few also grog tempered. One sherd with finger-nail impressions, part of a tiny ?lug on another. 25 sherds recovered, with 23 more on subsequent visit. Possibly some confusion with Early Saxon finds.

IA 3 TF 8985 1290 (HER 20508)
The least convincing pottery concentration, with only 15 sherds within an area of c.30m diameter. On medium soil on a southern facing slope at 73m OD. Pottery is similar to that from IA 2, with again some possibility of confusion with Early Saxon sherds. Close by Iron Age sherds were found on the surface of the natural subsoil (HER 20543, see above).

IA 4 TF 9086 1326 (HER 20653)
On medium soil close to eastern end of a spur at 65m OD. Thin concentration covering ill-defined area c.40m across. Thirty sherds recovered on two visits, and a further 14 collected subsequently. Pottery distinctly uniform, reduced and fairly hard with strong tendency towards oxidisation of surfaces, sand and profuse angular quartz tempering. Some form of impressed decoration occurs on tops of two rim sherds, probably made with finger-nails.

IA 5 TF 9090 1372 (HER 20766)
Elongated concentration lies 64–65m OD. Lying diagonally across a southern facing slope on medium soil with areas of heavy soil to the east and west. Measures c.55m north-east to south-west but is only c.25m wide. Six sherds on first examination, with c.100 more on two later visits. Predominantly dark grey reduced, sandy with sparse large rounded quartz grains. Two sherds decorated with finger-nail impressions and two with impressed dots. One sherd finely gritted and reminiscent of material from West Harling.

IA 6 TF 9198 1334 (HER 21622)
Subtle concentration, measuring c.30m. across, near southern end of a spur on patch of light to medium gravelly soil at 65m OD. Thirty-six sherds on first visit, with 30 more found subsequently. Even mixture of sandy and gritty fabrics. One sherd with finger-nail impressions.

These six Iron Age sites are nothing more than sherd concentrations covering restricted areas, and it would be rash to guess at what sizes of communities we are dealing with. Some may represent very small groups of dwellings, while others, IA 1 and perhaps IA 5, were larger, and probably populous enough to be called hamlets. A settlement density of just over 0.5 sites per 1 km² is of little help in an assessment of the real population.

Obviously all six sites were not occupied contemporaneously, because the pottery varies considerably between them. Their relative chronology must also remain an open question, and indeed it is doubtful whether non-invasive techniques could ever establish a chronology of Iron Age sites in Norfolk, given the undistinguished nature of the ceramics.

No more for the Iron Age than for the Early Bronze Age can surface artefact scatters help reconstruct activities or yield information on the agricultural economy. Rainbird Clarke was aware that little could be said of Iron Age agriculture in East Anglia (Clarke 1960, 97), and we have moved on a considerable distance over the last five decades (Brudenell 2018). Meagre spreads of sherds around the concentrations are less convincing than the manure scatters of later periods. Only the very thin spread on the central interfluve of Great Fransham approaches such a scatter, and so the importance of arable farming remains uncertain. Sheep and cattle rearing were probably much more important (Harding 1974, 77–88), and much of the medium soil may have been open grassland. A brief note on the meagre results from Fransham contrasted them with the abundant Iron Age surface archaeology of Barton Bendish and suggested a predominantly pastoral regime in the former and a strong arable element in the latter (Rogerson 1999).

In common with their predecessors the Iron Age occupants made little impression on areas of truly heavy soil, perhaps still woodland, although they did live very close to such in several cases, particularly in the case of site IA 5. Two sites were situated on light/medium soil, and four on medium. Three lay on southern facing slopes, and three in elevated positions. One of the latter three (IA 4) lay on the end of a spur but just to the north of a crest which, perhaps significantly, is at this point covered with rather heavy soil. Only one site (IA 1) sits more than 400m from a present-day watercourse, with the remainder located at an average distance of c.240m.

Site IA 1 seems to lie on its own on high ground above the source of a stream and is not surrounded by an outer 'aura' of sherds. The nearest Roman site lies c.450m to the north-west. Sites IA 2 and IA 3, on the other hand, are within a thin but convincing spread of sherds which extends for more than 1km from east to west along the central interfluve. East of this spread there is a reasonably clear gap, which perhaps somewhat coincidently is taken up in part by a large Roman concentration (RB 5). This

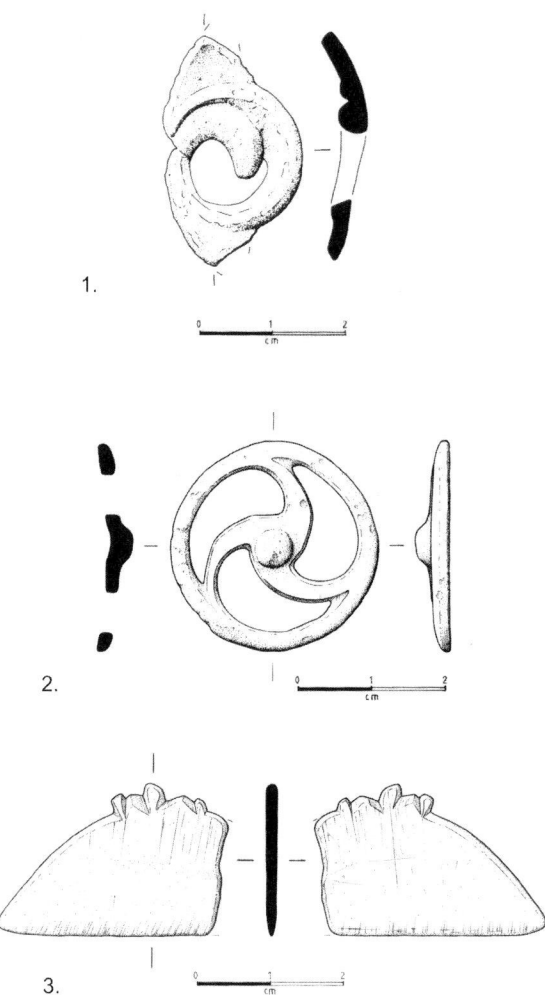

Figure 2.12 Late Iron Age scabbard mount (HER 20792) and harness fitting (HER 4192), and Iron Age or Romano-British razor (HER 20587), scale 1:1

Little Fransham where no certain concentration has been identified. One possible candidate lies at TF 8956 1205 in the area of a Roman site (RB 7). Here only thirteen Iron Age sherds were found over a wide area on a slight hillock. However, the fields in question have not been re-examined, and yet again the total might have been much larger were it not for the blanket of Roman material. It is certain that odd finds of single sherds or very small groups, such as two sherds at TF 9276 1198 (HER 25546), or five sherds in an area centred at TF 911 121 (HER 24765 and 24767–8), do not derive from activities carried out from any of the sites that have been identified. Therefore, it can only be concluded that probably because of the friability of the pottery, an uncertain number of occupation sites failed to reveal themselves with any conviction in this survey, and that the impact of the Iron Age on Fransham was somewhat greater than has been demonstrated by fieldwalking.

This conclusion is supported, at least for the Late Iron Age, by a small number of finds, coins and copper alloy objects, recovered by metal-detecting. The absence of Icenian silver coins from this small group is surprising. A mount, probably from a sword scabbard, was recorded c.40m east of the enclosure surrounding a Roman settlement site, RB 1 (Fig. 2.12 1; Fig. 3.2). Three coins were found within a restricted area on the central interfluve in close proximity to sites IA 2 and IA 3: a Trinovantian cast potin Thurrock type of the mid to late first century BC (TF 8967 1284, HER 20524) and two gold staters of the late first century BC – early first century AD, a Corieltauvian Ferriby type and an Icenian Early Freckenham type (TF 8976 1293 and TF 8978 1282, HER 20508). A spiral-headed pin and a possible harness mount fragment were found nearby at TF 8977 1287 and TF 8977 1292. A fragment of a pendent fitting or fob, recovered from TF 8928 1326, was probably a piece of horse furniture and in the form of an openwork disc or triskele (HER 4192, Fig. 2.12 2). Part of razor of unusual form and perhaps of Iron Age date was metal-detected at TF 9005 1296 (HER 20587, Fig. 2.12 3). A gold disc, whose weight suggests it may have been a coin blank for a 'Norfolk Wolf' type stater of the mid to late first century BC, and a copper alloy button-and-loop fastener of the first century BC/AD were recovered further to the west on the same interfluve at TF 8893 1295 (HER 24784).

The claylands of Norfolk and Suffolk need no longer be seen as almost barren in the second half of the first millennium BC (Clarke 1939, 37), and the large-scale pre-Roman exploitation of at least parts of the plateau is now well attested (Williamson 1987). Pollen evidence from the south of the county, in particular from Hockham Mere (20km south of Fransham), Old Buckenham Mere (30km) and Diss Mere (over 40km) has shown that woodland clearance was most intense from the Later Bronze Age and continued into the Roman period (Bennett 1983; Godwin 1968; Peglar *et al.* 1989; Simms 1978). However, it will be through excavation, and in particular through the environmental evidence thus collected, that we will gain any real understanding of the agriculture and economy that enabled Iron Age people to live in Fransham and places like it.

gap should however be treated with caution for two reasons: firstly, the discovery of an Iron Age feature after ploughsoil stripping shows that it may be more apparent than real; secondly, the presence of Roman pottery may possibly have acted as a 'blanket' or 'decoy', which reduces the visibility of earlier sherds. At the eastern end of the interfluve IA 4, a very isolated site, yielded only two sherds as outliers to the west, despite very careful examination in this area carried out because of the presence there of a substantial Middle and Late Saxon site. Across the valley to the north, site IA 5 lies separated from a Roman site (RB 2) by a minor north-south valley. The odd sherd has been found around IA 5 as well as three at RB 2. Very few occurred outside the concentration of IA 6, the easternmost Iron Age site, which is situated in a commanding position c.150m west of another Roman concentration (RB 4).

Other find spots of Iron Age sherds have not proved on closer and more detailed examination to be concentrations. This is especially true of the area of the former parish of

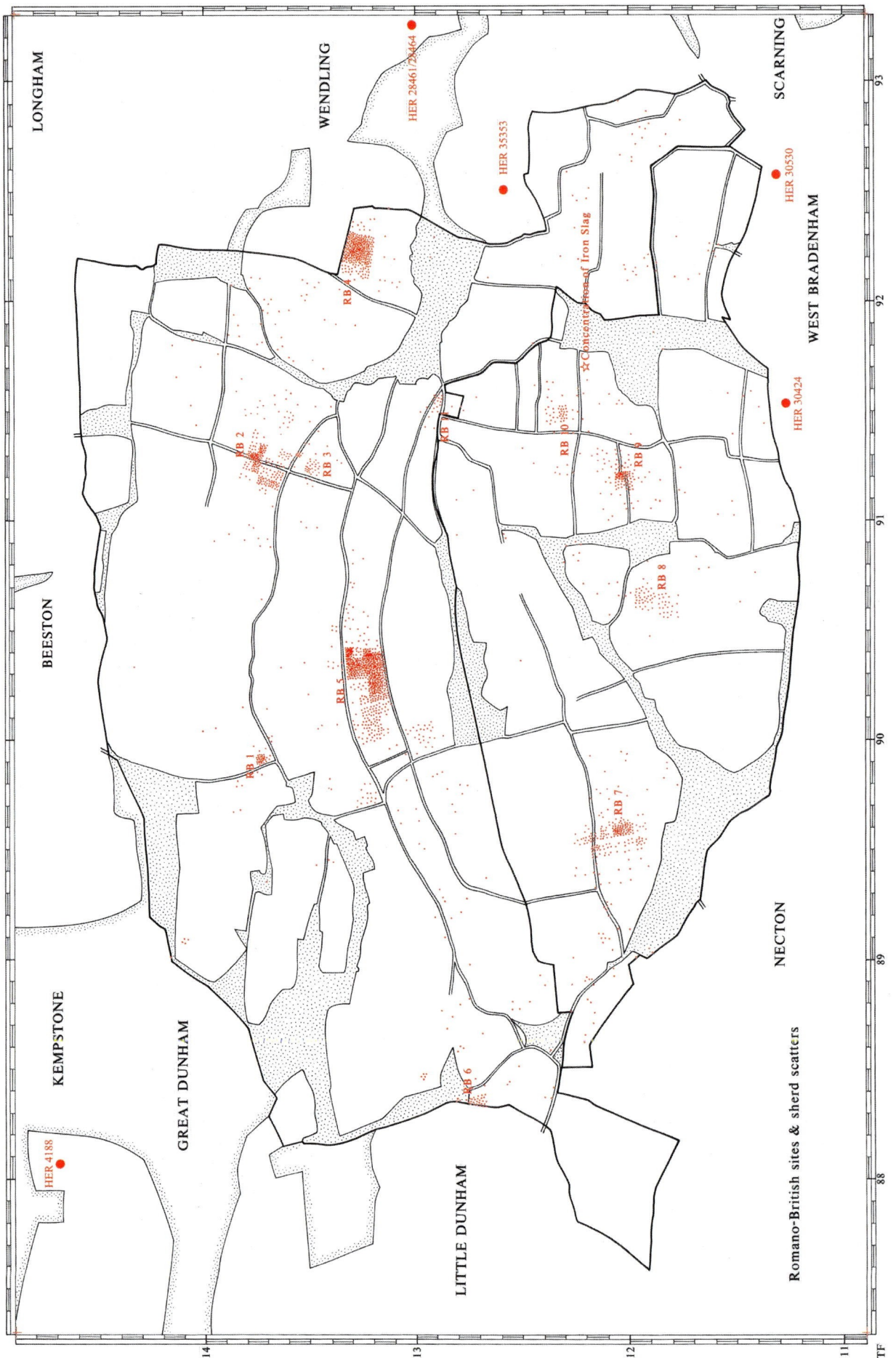

Figure 3.1 Romano-British sites expressed as sherd distributions, areas of medieval common pastures shown stippled, scale 1:25,000

Chapter 3. The Roman Period

Introduction

In common with many places in Norfolk, Fransham appears neglected by Roman roads. All route maps of Roman Norfolk show great signs of incompleteness, and none gives a hint that any road, known or suspected, might have passed through the area of this study. Important roads, however, passed close by (Gurney 2005).

The Peddars Way (Margary 1973, route 33b) lay *c*.5km to the west, on its last great alignment towards to the sea at Holme. South-west of Fransham at a distance of 6.5km, a southern continuation of Margary's route 39 struck north-west from the Peddars Way towards the small town at Dunton (Toftrees), passing at the closest 1.6km from the study area. Until recently the main east-to-west Roman route through the county (Margary 38) was considered to run 3km to the north of Fransham and to cross the southern continuation of Margary route 39 on the southern bank of the Nar adjacent to the Roman settlement in Kempstone parish. A critical assessment of the evidence judges this central part of the road as highly doubtful and omits it from a county map (Albone 2016, 87, 361–2, fig. 10). To the south the nearest east-to-west route ran 7km from Fransham, where it passed through the major settlement at Ashill to join the Peddars Way at Saham Toney. Lastly, it should be noted that Fransham lies 35km west-north-west of the site of the cantonal capital of *Venta Icenorum* (Caistor St Edmund).

'The boundary between casual finds and settlements is most indistinct, particularly since one is a statement of the circumstances of discovery while the other is an interpretation of status.' (Gregory 1982, 352). The Roman settlement pattern in the area surrounding Fransham is not well understood, and at present recorded sites and finds are few in comparison with some areas of the county. The low level is mirrored over a much wider area to the north and east forming a roughly circular zone of few finds over central Norfolk and centred on the small town at Billingford. This zone, with Fransham near its south-western edge, has been clearly demonstrated by Davies and Gregory (1991, 79–80, figs 7 and 8) and Gurney (1993). However, this impression has been modified in the light of recent fieldwork (Gurney 2005).

Within those parishes marching with Fransham only two sites have yielded evidence of masonry structures. In Great Dunham a dense spread of pottery covering *c*.5 hectares surrounds a 0.5-hectare area of mortared flint and tile/brick, including flue tiles. Both pottery and coins are predominantly of the third and fourth centuries. There is some iron slag, and metal finds include a statuette of Mercury. This site, on which there has been no formal survey and no excavation, appears to have included a 'substantial building' and was perhaps a villa (HER 4188). Within another settlement in Great Dunham geophysical survey has recorded the plan of a small masonry building within a spread of rubble, and the site has produced abundant surface finds including fragments of a late first-century military diploma (HER 21441 and 36994).

A settlement that has been considered a 'small town' lies at the northern end of Kempstone parish 3km to the north-west of Fransham. It is unexcavated and known only from cursory fieldwork, one below-ground observation and non-intensive metal-detecting (HER 4079). Settlement debris covers *c*.12ha (Wade-Martins 1971, 157–8; 1980b, 30) on the southern side of the Nar Valley and lies astride the east-west road just to the east of its junction with the southern continuation of Margary route 39. The pottery is predominantly of the third and fourth centuries, as are the coins, which include only four second-century pieces and end with the House of Valentinian. Two pieces of late first-century metalwork have also been recovered. A conspicuous element of this site is the quantity of smelting slag strewn over parts of it. No Roman bricks or tiles are present in Norwich Castle Museum's collections, although Wade-Martins (1980b, 30) noted a spread of tiles. The precise position of Kempstone within the settlement hierarchy of Roman Norfolk is unknown, but it is still regarded as a 'possible' small town (Gurney 1995, fig.6.1). If it was such then it was curiously placed, away from a crossroads, and the absence of evidence for masonry buildings confounds the uncertainty. An unusually large ironworking centre may perhaps be a more apt description. It is hoped that a recent programme of field survey and targeted excavation in the surrounding area by Michael de Bootman and John Shepherd, when published, will provide a much clearer picture of the site's nature and status.

Space precludes the listing of all other known Roman sites and finds in the surrounding parishes, but within the area covered by Fig. 3.1 convincing evidence, in the form of surface finds, for settlement has been recovered in Necton (HER 30424), Scarning (HER 30530) and Wendling (HER 28461 / 28464 and 35353). There is no reason to suspect that this region of Norfolk was any less densely occupied in Roman times than the work of this survey has indicated was the case in Fransham. Indeed, fieldwalking and metal-detecting in Little Dunham and metal-detecting in Bradenham have recently shown that there was a high degree of activity in both parishes.

Before this study was begun, in terms of both quality and quantity of information on the Roman period, the parish of Fransham was worse off than most of its neighbours. The HER contained a single, spurious entry (HER 12424). After a brief description of Little Fransham Old Hall (TF 9027 1186) Bryant stated that 'Near this are foundations of Roman brickworks', but did not elaborate (Bryant 1903). A newspaper article on the hall (Eastern Daily Press, 18 September 1965) must have been following Bryant when it stated, 'Among some mature trees are what are thought to be Roman remains'. Something in the way of brick masonry was presumably once visible near the hall. The only piece of woodland in Little Fransham lies nearby, centred at TF 9031 1195. No foundations can now be seen, and the only archaeological material recovered there was medieval and later (HER 30222).

That no funerary evidence was recovered need cause no surprise given the extreme scarcity of Roman burials throughout Norfolk (Gurney 1998). Evidence for a total of eleven settlement sites, concentrations of occupation debris, primarily potsherds, representing permanently occupied settlements, was recovered during this field survey (Fig. 3.1). The following gazetteer presents the basic details for each site.

Gazetteer of Roman sites
RB 1 (Fig. 3.2) TF 8992 1376 (HER 20792)
Situated on medium soil and on a gentle southern facing slope at 67m OD and c.140m from the base of a valley containing a stream, this site is the sole example for which any below ground evidence has been recovered. The soil rapidly becomes heavier to the north and east.

In 1977 an initial unsystematic collection across the whole field (6.3ha) produced more than 200 sherds of Roman greyware, which were recorded in the field as deriving predominantly from the south-west quarter.

In the following year the field was amalgamated with its neighbours to the north and east, underdrains were laid and a new ditch dug along the inner edge of the surviving western hedge. This latter operation exposed two ditches of Roman date in the edges of the new cut. Both had been dug c.0.5m below the surface of the natural boulder clay, and were c.1.5m wide, with apparently homogenous fills of dark grey sandy clay loam over silty clay loam. Both fills yielded animal bone fragments and oyster shells. The northern ditch (c2 on Fig. 3.2), which was aligned south-west to north-east, produced thirty-two late first and second-century sherds, many in an unabraded condition, as well as two small fragments of brick or tile. The southern ditch (c3), aligned north-west to south-east, produced twenty-five similar sherds. Underdraining operations could not be monitored continuously, but several observations were made.

A patch of dark soil (c4), standing out clearly from a background of yellowish-brown clay in the temporary linear spoil heap of one drain appeared to continue the alignment of c3, while two similar patches (c6 and c7) did the same for c2. An observed absence of dark soil to north-east of c7 suggested that this ditch did not extend much further in this direction, while another patch (c5) may indicate that it had turned into a north-west to south-east alignment. One other patch of dark soil (c8) apparently unrelated to the others, was also recorded. Only two patches (c4 and c5) had associated finds, each producing four Roman sherds. These observations, although incomplete, particularly to the south-east, suggest the presence of a roughly rectangular ditched enclosure of at least 0.8ha.

Systematic walking of the field took place in 1991. Twelve 50m by 50m squares in the south-west part demonstrated that Roman pottery was restricted almost entirely to the area of the putative enclosure. Those squares falling 50% or more within the putative enclosure yielded 79% of the ninety-nine sherds collected. The sherds are shown as dots on Fig. 3.2. No Roman material was found in the northern part of the field, which was as closely walked although not subdivided, while only two sherds were found in the eastern part.

Five indeterminate hand-made sherds are most likely to be of Iron Age date but may belong to the earlier Roman period. A Late Iron Age probable sword scabbard mount

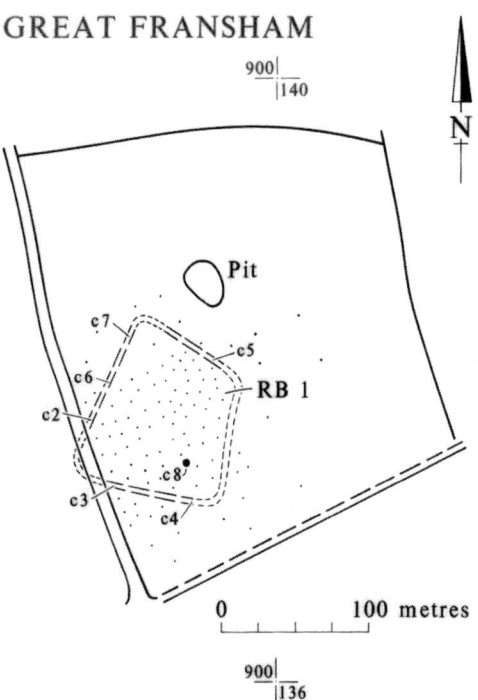

Figure 3.2 RB 1, scale 1:5,000

was recovered by metal-detecting close by, as were two pieces of Roman copper alloy within the enclosure, an indeterminate mount fragment and a furniture knob or boss containing an iron shank.

No very convincing arable area is apparent in sherds scatters around this site. A feeble spread of material stretches away to the north-west for c.200m, and finds to the north and east, where the edge of the pottery concentration is sharply defined, are sparse indeed. Land to the south and south-west of this field, formerly meadow (HER 20592–4), yielded six Roman sherds (including one of samian ware, none of which was found on the site itself). Five of these derived from an area of c.100m² and may have arrived through rubbish dumping rather than manure spreading.

The settlement was probably located to exploit the resources not only of a nearby meadow, its associated stream, a limited zone of medium soil for arable farming, and abundant pasture on medium heavy soils to the north and west, but also woodland to the north and east.

The site's demise before the later Roman period remains unexplained, and no evidence for a later Roman successor has been located in the immediately surrounding area.

RB 2 TF 9126 1372 (HER 20763 and 20754)
This site lies on a southern facing slope between 58m and 68m OD on medium soil with heavy patches and close to a valley containing the stream adjacent to site RB 1. Although walked in rather dry conditions, it was clearly defined as a concentration of c.300 sherds of the second to fourth centuries, with a subsidiary concentration of similar date beyond the stream near the south-east corner (RB 3). The main area forms three sides of an approximate rectangle of c.2.25ha, with a marked scarcity of pottery in

the centre. Although the recording procedure was too coarse to create a clear picture, the plot by incidence in 50m by 50m squares does show bands of density on the north, east and west sides, the relatively blank central area and almost sherd-free southern down slope side.

The pottery concentration at the south-eastern corner lies in former meadow on peaty soil. This is the only example in the parish of a dense Roman scatter in low-lying ground and is best interpreted as a midden. Close to the south-west of this and across the stream lies site RB 3 (see below).

The western edge of the main concentration is crisply defined by an almost complete fall-off of pottery coincident with a band of heavy soil which lies across a shallow valley running north to south. To the west of this a few sherds may mark arable on an area of medium soil (on which lie four medieval sites, Med 40–43, Appendix 2). To the east down the valley edge and uphill to the north-east a slight and intermittent sprinkling of Roman sherds suggests a band of arable on mixed medium and heavy soils as far as $c.700$m from the site, with the extremes of the spread probably merging with material derived from site RB 4.

A medieval road, *Toftgateway*, ran north-south through the centre of the site and crossed the stream at *Baysboll brygge*. Might both road and crossing have Roman origins? There was surely access to RB 3 which lay immediately south of the stream.

The ceramics are an unremarkable mix of micaceous greywares and Nar Valley coarse wares, but single sherds of mortarium, amphora and samian ware, two calcite gritted sherds and a few bead and flange bowl rims were also recovered. Three Iron Age hand-made sandy sherds do not suggest occupation but may derive from site IA 2 to the west. Two tile fragments may possibly be Roman.

Limited metal-detecting has produced two first-century brooches, a steelyard weight, and three Roman coins (Nero, Tetricus I and a clipped *siliqua* of the House of Valentinian).

RB 3 TF 9122 1350 (HER 20754)
A concentration ($c.70$ sherds) lies at 59m OD opposite the south-eastern corner of RB 2 and extends to less than 900m^2 on a slight spur of medium soil flanked on the north, east and west by peat-stained soil. The present course of the stream, 30m to the north, here runs close to the southern edge of the valley.

The occasional sherd along the northern facing slopes to the east and west of the site are the only evidence of associated arable. To the east, the area available for arable was restricted by the confluence of three streams, while to the west the very thin scatter may well merge with that derived from RB 5.

The pottery assemblage is similar to that from RB 2, although five sherds of plain and decorated samian here form a higher proportion of the total. Part of a tegula and three small fragments of probably Roman brick or tile were recovered.

In view of their proximity and the contemporaneity of their pottery, this site and RB 2 should perhaps be regarded as part of the same settlement. No other case of a Roman site situated on both sides of a watercourse has been recorded in the study area.

RB 4 TF 9223 1326 (HER 20749)
Lying at the southern end of a spur on moderately level ground at 64–65m OD, this site has by local standards an elevated aspect, with good visibility in all directions except to the north. It is defined with exceptional clarity by the abrupt manner in which its pottery concentration tails off in all directions (including to the south where an edge was noticeable immediately to the north of a substantial railway cutting). To the north, the concentration itself stops $c.20$m to the south of the (now entirely eradicated) Wendling boundary, and a sprinkling of sherds extends up to the former line, beyond which no walking was carried out. The area of sherd density, $c.1.5$ha, was approximately rectangular, measuring 160m east to west by 120m north to south. The soil, medium with large patches of light/medium very gravelly soil in the central area, is unusual for the parish and was broadly similar to that on which RB 7 is situated.

Over 500 sherds, predominantly of the third and fourth centuries, were recovered from 1.9 hectares. The assemblage consists mainly of Nar Valley coarse ware including bead and flanged bowls with occasional sherds of calcite gritted ware, amphorae, and local colour-coated wares, along with single sherds of samian and Oxfordshire red-slipped ware. No Roman building material was found.

In addition to a ?first-century brooch fragment, six Roman coins have been recovered during metal-detecting (unidentified first/second-century, *sestertius* of Lucius Verus (161–9), irregular cast *dupondius* of Commodus (post-161), two third/fourth-century and Constans or Constantius II).

The extent of arable farming carried out from this site is indicated by a light spread of pottery extending to the north-west for $c.600$m. This probably merges with a similar spread stretching to the north-east from RB 2. A mid- to late first-century brooch was found within this north-western spread at TF 9187 1374. Another thin scatter spills down slope to the south beyond the railway cutting. To the east another extends as far as the Wendling parish boundary.

RB 5 TF 903 132 (HER 15875, 20590 and 20647)
This large site sits on the crest of an east-west interfluve at between 67 and 70m OD. The soil is medium with occasional small lighter patches.

The pottery concentration, covering at least 3.5 hectares, extends for a minimum of 250m east to west, with an abrupt edge to the east and a less clearly defined limit to the west. Here a modern field boundary is coincident with a marked fall-off in the frequency of sherds, but it seems likely that the site continued at least some way into the western field. The maximum width of the concentration is 190m, the northern and southern boundaries being marked with startling definition by roads in use in the medieval period (*Whiteway* to the north an existing route, and *Southgateway* to the south no longer used but marked by a substantial bank, HER 16095). Additional walking in the fields to the north and south of these roads reaffirmed the scarcity of Roman material there, and doubtless therefore the alignments of both, if not the roads themselves, served some purpose in the Roman period[i]. An area of sherd scarcity to the north-west of the densest part of the concentration was also re-walked, and confirmed in its relative barrenness, a probable explanation here being a return to heavier soil.

Over 700 second to fourth-century coarseware sherds, include a higher proportion of calcite-gritted wares than any other site in the study area. Samian and colour-coated wares are feebly represented, and single sherds of late Roman red-slipped ware, amphora and mortarium occur. Only one possible Roman tile fragment was recovered. Other finds made during fieldwalking include a fragmentary jet bead, an illegible probably fourth-century coin and a second-century centre-boss disc brooch. Limited metal-detecting in the central part of the site yielded nine Roman coins ranging from a mid to late second-century *sestertius* to a *siliqua* of Eugenius (AD 392–4).

A fine scatter of sherds continues along the interfluve to the east for up to 450m, while to the west a similar scatter is fairly continuous up the slope along the interfluve as far as RB 6, so that no division between the arable lands of the two can be established. The north facing slope to the north of the site carries a thin scatter for up to *c*.200m from the site's edge, but heavy soil on the slopes to the south are devoid of Roman material. To the south-west this same slope has produced a moderate scatter on lighter soil. This, however, is coincident with a concentration of Early Saxon pottery (ES 1), and some at least of the sherds may have been deposited in the post-Roman period.

A restricted area *c*.150m to the east of the site (TF 9055 1332) carried a moderate concentration of iron smelting slag. This material is probably Roman but may be associated with nearby Middle or Late Saxon occupation.

RB 6 TF 8837 1273 (HER 20519)
This site, on medium to heavy soil at 85m OD adjacent to the boundary with Little Dunham, lies on fairly level ground above the heads of two eastward flowing streams. It amply illustrates a major weakness of the parish-based survey for its western extent, in Little Dunham, was not certainly identified by fieldwalking.

A small total of twenty-seven sherds was collected from *c*.0.25 hectares. An elongated triangle of ground, now in Little Dunham but according to the Enclosure Award map (1807) formerly part of Great Fransham, was examined. The southern apex of this area touched the concentration but produced only one additional sherd.

Such a poor group of material obviates confident dating, but it is probably of the second and third centuries. One samian ware sherd and one fragment of probably Roman tile were recovered. Somewhat curiously, two joining fragments of a sub-rectangular sectioned ceramic bar in an organic and sand tempered fabric resembles a fire-bar from a Roman pottery kiln, but the object may have been used in some other form of oven. No other evidence of pottery production was found. A moderate sprinkling of iron smelting slag coincided with the spread of Roman pottery, rapidly dying away to the north and south.

The extent of manure-spread pottery scatters to the west is unknown. To the east a fairly continuous light scatter merges into a similar scatter emanating from RB 5, while to the south-east a similar merging occurs with material from RB 7.

Metal-detecting in a field immediately to the east (HER 20518) has produced a first to second-century cosmetic mortar, a Trumpet brooch of a similar date, a second-century plate brooch and a coin of Magnentius.

RB 7 TF 8956 1205 (HER 23897, 24763 and 23082)
The greater part of this site lies immediately east of a north-south trackway on the summit of a slight but conspicuous hillock capped by light/medium gravelly soil at 83m OD. This main area measures *c*.100m north-south and *c*.60m east-west, with smaller concentrations occurring to the north-west and south-west beyond the trackway. When a further small concentration to the north is included, the site measures as much as 300m by 120m (3.6 hectares).

Potsherds which are not especially prolific except in the main area of concentration, range in date from the ?late first to fourth centuries. Micaceous greywares and Nar Valley coarse wares predominate, but a few pieces of samian ware, mortarium, amphora and late Roman red-slipped ware were also recovered. Eighteen fragments of probably Roman and Roman tile/brick, although forming the largest group from the parish, cannot be seen as evidence of masonry buildings although, of course, substantial timber structures may have incorporated ceramic material, especially in the roof or hearths. No Roman mortar was identified. Iron Age sherds were sufficiently numerous to suggest that this site may have had pre-Roman origins.

Metal-detecting to the east of the trackway produced a steelyard weight, part of a first-century brooch and four Roman coins (*sestertius* of Commodus, two House of Constantine and unidentified third/fourth-century). Nine Roman coins were found to the west (Claudius II, barbarous radiate, late third-century *antoninianus*, five unidentified third/fourth-century and House of Valentinian).

A light manure-scattered spread of sherds fans out to the north-west and merges with that derived from RB 6. To the east a similar spread extends to *c*.300m. To the north low ground was avoided by the plough, as was a substantial area to the south-west which was common pasture in the medieval period. Somewhat surprisingly, a broad band of medium soil on a gentle northern facing slope to the north-east of the site, and centred at approximately TF 898 123, was almost devoid of Roman sherds.

RB 8 TF 9062 1187 (HER 25566)
Situated on fairly level medium soil at 73m OD, this site was walked in more than usually poor soil conditions. Its sherd total of sixty-five, certainly less than might be expected from a site of 1.4 hectares measuring 200m north-south and 70m east-west, is on the other hand in great contrast to its virtually sherd-free surroundings.

The unsatisfactory pottery assemblage, apparently of the second and third centuries, includes a solitary samian ware sherd. To the east of the site some land was unavailable for fieldwalking. To the north a sparse spread of Roman sherds suggests an area of arable land in what was, by the medieval period, an oval area of *c*.7.5 hectares completely surrounded by commons and roads. To the south and south-east, the occasional sherd occurs as far as the parish boundary. To the south-west a massive area stretching to the parish boundary has failed to yield a single piece of Roman material. This part of the parish was

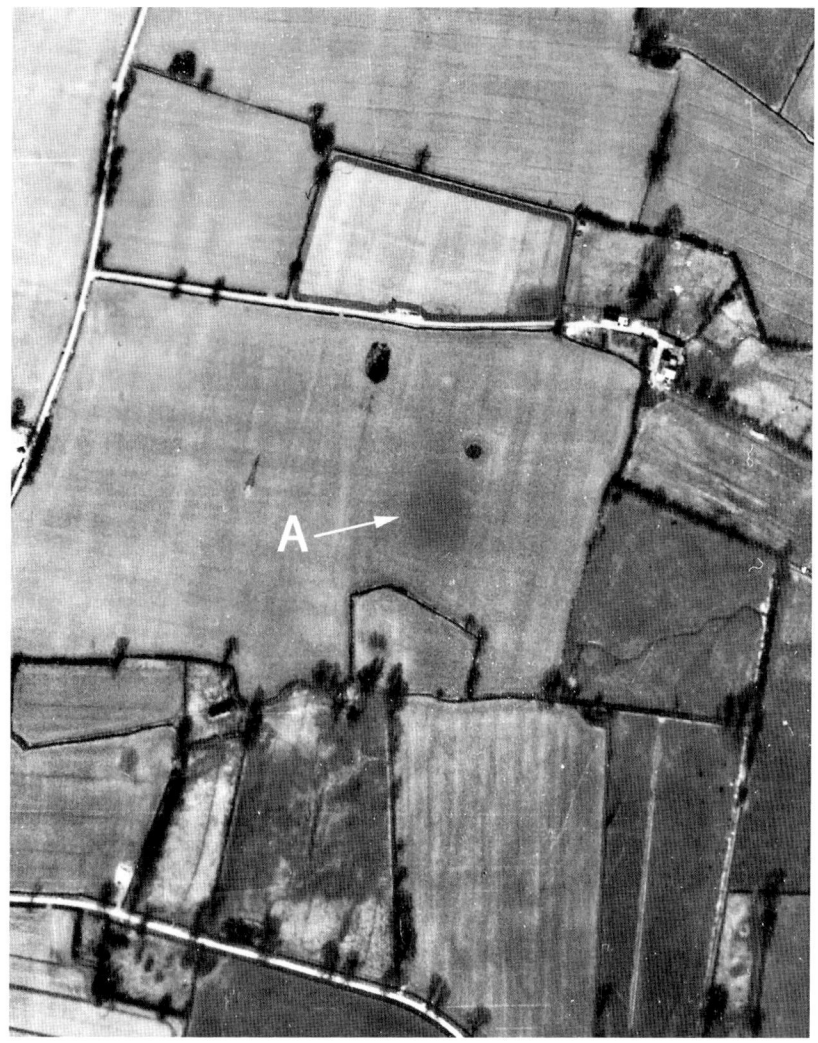

Plate 3.1 Detail from 1946 RAF vertical aerial photograph showing area of dense iron slag 'A' (see RB 10)
(RAF 3GTUD UK 100 Part IV 5291 30 MAR 46)

not exploited as arable until the twelfth century, and until then had probably been woodland.

A Roman rectangular copper alloy mount was found during metal-detecting c.70m to the south-east (HER 25568).

RB 9 TF 9120 1203 (HER 24765–7)
Situated on a low ridge at 68m OD, this minor site commands fine views in all directions except to the south-west. The soil is medium tending to medium heavy. The somewhat weak pottery concentration measures c.80m by 80m (0.6 hectares).

Iron smelting slag, probably of Roman date, is thinly spread over the site. While it spreads a negligible distance from the site to the north, south and west, it is strewn with undiminished frequency over a wide area to the north-east as far as site RB 10, and over a distance of 500m to the east as far as a major concentration of slag at TF 9170 1220 (see RB 10).

Ninety sherds consist entirely of greywares, and the group contains little that is closely datable. A second to fourth-century date is most likely. A few Iron Age sherds were also recovered. Six Roman coins recovered by metal-detecting suggest activity continued into the fourth century (*denarius* of Trajan, unidentified first/second-century *as*, late third-century *antoninianus*, two House of Constantine, unidentified third/fourth-century).

Manure spread sherds occurred up to 600m to the south-west of the site, 300m along the ridge to the north, 150m down slope to the north-west and west, but only 100m down slope to the east. If some or all of the iron slag is derived from this site, then the discrepancy between its distribution and that of the pottery is difficult to explain. It is possible, though, that entirely different disposal practises were at work. It is unlikely that so much iron slag was accidentally incorporated in manure heaps. Perhaps its eventual arrival in the fields was the result of the deliberate spreading of ashy ironworking debris.

RB 10 TF 9148 1231 (HER 20824)
This extremely small site lies on fairly level ground at 65m OD, with a gentle downward slope to the east. The soil is medium, turning heavy to the north and north-west. A meagre total of twenty-five sherds spread over an area of 60m by 60m was recovered in an initial survey. Although this quantity was sufficient to mark out the area from its surroundings, it was too small to indicate a site with any certainty. Excessive dryness of the soil surface probably explains the shortfall. A further examination in moister conditions produced over seventy sherds concentrated in an area measuring 40m north-south and 30m east-west.

The pottery, of the ?second, third and fourth centuries, includes four sherds (a mortarium and a bead and flanged bowl) of red-slipped ware, probably Oxfordshire products. Metal-detecting has produced one Roman coin (a worn *as* of Domitian).

Manure spread sherds cover a very limited area to the north and north-east of the site, but do not extend westwards. To the south a fine sprinkling roughly matches, but is far less intense than, a spread of iron slag (see below).

Iron smelting slag occurs over the area of the pottery concentration and along the southern half of the field (see site RB 9). On the south side of a lane which forms the southern boundary of this field, another 9.8 hectare field produces iron slag in every grid square. Towards its eastern end, at TF 9170 1220, an oval area of dense slag in dark grey-brown soil, 80m north-to-south by 45m east-to-west, appears as a slight mound and is clearly visible as a dark mark on vertical aerial photographs taken by the RAF in 1946 (Pl. 3.1). No Roman pottery was recovered from the mound itself, but Justine Bayley, formerly of the Ancient Monuments Laboratory, examined a large sample and considered it to be smelting slag of the Roman period. No fragments of ore were found during fieldwalking, but a very rapid metal-detector scan produced several fragments of iron-bound conglomerate. The most likely source for this is a valley close to the east, whose present stream lies *c*.220m from the mound.

RB 11 TF 9155 1289 (HER 20639)
The precise site was not located by fieldwork, but one can be inferred to have existed below farm buildings to the east of the above grid reference, on ground gently sloping down to the north-west. Fifteen sherds were recovered on medium soil from an area of 50m by 50m (consisting of four 25m by 25m squares) in the south-east corner of a field, at 60m OD. Twenty sherds were found on a subsequent visit. These amounts contrast with the scarcity of finds from areas to the north, south and west.

Little can be said of the pottery, which is predominantly greyware. It is probably second and third-century, and possibly fourth.

Faint manure-scattered spreads were recorded to the north and south. Part of a fourth-century copper alloy bracelet was found to the south-west at TF 9148 1275 (HER 20827), and a coin of the House of Constantine was recovered during metal-detecting to the south at TF 9155 1283 (HER 21617).

Discussion

The transition from the Iron Age is not easily discerned in the survey results, but there was no sound evidence of continuity of occupation from the pre-Conquest period on any site, a pattern of 'marked discontinuity' noted on other surveys in Norfolk (Taylor 2007, 101). Material dating to the second half of the first century was rarely encountered. Tony Gregory identified late first-century pottery from only two sites, RB 1 and 7, the latter only tentatively. Some finds of this date must have gone unrecognised, both on the six or seven sites that began in the second century, and off-site in manure scatters. Other material may have escaped being found. Conversely, an uncertain but probably small proportion of the pottery identified as Iron Age, particularly of the sandy wares, might well post-date the Roman take-over. This was suggested above in the case of site RB 1. First-century brooches on three sites (RB 2, 4 and 7) and seventeen more found off-site go some way towards filling the chronological gap left by the pottery.

The close dating of surface pottery finds will never be an accurate procedure because they are usually small and undiagnostic. This drawback should be set against the present-day hesitancy on the part of Roman pottery specialists to give dates to coarse wares in general, even to excavated groups including large and fresh sherds. The date-ranges suggested here are therefore tentative.

On the evidence of pottery, a single site (RB 1) failed to survive the second century, two (RB 6 and 9) gave out before the end of the third, and eight (RB 2–5, 7, and 9–11 were still occupied in the fourth.

There is of course no way of knowing how long occupation on the fourth-century sites continued, for with the demise of ceramic and numismatic evidence shortly after *c*.400, an 'archaeologically invisible' continuance of Romano-British occupation into the fifth century is very likely. The latest coin, from RB 5, dates to 392–4. Even on carefully excavated sites there are major problems of chronology at this period (Rodwell and Rodwell 1986, 74–5). The third century appears as the most active period with ten sites (91% of the total) in occupation, while the reduction of activity in the fourth century might perhaps mirror a late Roman shift to the south of Norfolk that has been deduced from the numismatic evidence (Davies and Gregory 1991, 91). The 73% of sites occupied in the fourth century falls somewhat below that of the *c*.86% still in use during the later fourth century in north-west Essex (Williamson 1984, 226).

The abundance of Roman settlement evidence in the study area need not cause any surprise since extensive agricultural exploitation of even the heavier soils of lowland England during the first four centuries AD has long been accepted (Williamson 1984, 225; Taylor 1983, 83). Oliver Rackham might have been exaggerating only a little when he wrote 'By the Roman period, Norfolk was nearly, if not quite, as highly agricultural as it is now. Settlements had filled the upland and spilled over into the Fens' (Rackham 1986a, 162). Locally, the scale of exploitation has best been demonstrated on the mixed soils of Hales, Heckingham and Loddon in south-east Norfolk (Davison 1990), and much unpublished supporting evidence is to be found in the HER, although this is rarely the result of systematic survey.

It should also be noted here that a great proportion of what is known about Roman Norfolk derives from non-intrusive surveys and chance discoveries, and that the number of archaeological excavations within the county falls far short of that in several other areas. This sparsity has been highlighted in recent national overviews (Taylor 2007, fig. 3.5; Smith *et al*. 2016, 212, fig. 6.3). The low density of settlements in Norfolk and Suffolk known from finds scatters, metal detecting and finds groups mapped by Taylor (2007, fig. 3.4) is misleading because both county HERs have been hesitant in identifying concentrations of surface finds, in some cases quite intense and large, as settlements. The enormous quantity of such finds in East Anglia has been clearly expressed in a bar chart by Brindle (2014, fig. 7).

A total of ten sites in the study area, with one other inferred on obscured land, indicate a frequency of 0.9

settlements per 1km², or of 0.82 if RB 3 is assumed to have been part of RB 2. Davison in his study of Hales and its neighbours (1990, 15–6) produced a total of twenty sites giving a frequency of 0.98 per 1km². However, nine of these were so closely clustered that they could be regarded as one substantial loosely strung village. If so, the frequency would fall to 0.59. Barton Bendish, a chalkland parish in south-west Norfolk (Rogerson with Davison 1997, 13–16), yielded a similar figure ranging between 0.59 and 0.93 sites per 1km², the variation again resulting from alternative interpretations on what constitutes a single site. If the lower figure for Fransham, of an average of 0.85 settlements per 1km², is accepted, then the population of the study area must have been close to the national mean, for a breakdown of published intensive and non-intensive field surveys arrived at a national average of 0.8 sites per 1km² (Millett 1990, 183–4).

There is no reason to doubt that the study area was, in the Roman period as in later times, given over almost exclusively to agriculture. Evidence for industry is restricted to the small-scale exploitation of local bog-iron resources in association with three or four sites (RB 6, 9 and 10, and probably RB 5). These activities can only have been in the form of a cottage industry carried out by farmers for themselves and their near neighbours. Such associations between ironworking and Roman rural settlements occur throughout the county and are evidence of production on a scale very different from the intensive industries on the west Norfolk Greensand (Tylecote and Owles 1960).

'Establishing the broad location of arable and pasture in conjunction with settlement may not be too unrealistic a goal' (Fulford 1990, 26). This study has gone some way towards the rough definition of arable areas. Diffuse spreads of potsherds surround or fan out from all the sites except RB 8. Such scatters are often interpreted as resulting from the manuring of arable with material contaminated with inorganic domestic refuse, and there seems no reason to doubt this explanation (Hayfield 1987, 11 and 192–6). A somewhat simplified and 'ironed out' plan of arable as indicated by these scatters is shown on Fig. 3.3. A very basic level of interpretation is all that can be presented: no attempt has been made to suggest phases of expansion or contraction of arable within the Roman period, the small number and the small size of the sherds would not permit it; field arrangements, cropping, rotation and the stinting of animals, all are outside the realms of a field survey and are the province of historical and/or other archaeological methods. It is noticeable that some sites are associated with an inner aura of dense spreads and an outer zone of fewer sherds. This might be interpreted as signs of a form of infield/outfield arrangement, but some at least of the outer spreads could possibly be the result of near off-site dumping or, and perhaps this is more likely, of the dispersing effect of post-Roman agriculture.

If arable farming was a small but significant aspect of the rural economy, then there is little that can be deduced on purely archaeological evidence for the role of pastoralism. Nothing is known of the layout of fields and closes (apart from the probable presence of an enclosure at RB 1) in the absence of aerial photographic evidence, and there is a lack of information from excavated animal bones (the group from RB 1 being insignificantly small).

Those areas on which there is no manure-spread pottery scatter, and which therefore may have been utilised for stock husbandry, include zones which were put to varying uses in post-Roman times. For example, the central northern part of Great Fransham contained extensive woodland in the medieval period as well as arable, on soil which is for the most part heavy. The southern central tract of Little Fransham, of medium and heavy soils, was predominantly arable from the thirteenth century, but place-names suggest the former presence of woodland. The extensive areas of medieval and later common pasture, which are mostly related to valley bottoms and sides, are almost devoid of Roman sherds, as are two great blocks of demesne, both mainly pasture in the late middle ages, which were attached to the two main manors of Great and Little Fransham. Late medieval meadowland was similarly sherd-free, with the exception of two restricted areas both adjacent to Roman sites (RB 1 and 2). There is, of course, no firm proof that medieval woodland had been Roman woodland or that documented commons had similar status in the Roman period. Some medieval woodland, common pasture, several pasture and meadow may have been Roman 'waste', but although the population in the third century was considerably lower than that in the thirteenth, it might be assumed, within the determining constraints of soil type and drainage, that the broad patterns of non-arable land-use were similar at both times. Indeed, long-term persistence of land-use in England and other places, even from prehistory, is no longer considered an impossible claim (Oosthuizen 2013, passim), and relative stability in this region between the Roman and the Late Saxon periods has been attested by a review of pollen analyses (Rippon *et al.* 2015, 170–4).

The economy of Roman Fransham was probably based almost entirely on a non-specialist mixed agriculture, with the arable component being measurable in very broad terms and the extent and intensity of pastoralism being based largely on pollen evidence from the Boulder Clay Plateau and on inference from the evidence of later centuries. In common with the Romano-British norm, agricultural production in the study area was pitched above subsistence level. The vast bulk of the evidence for Roman occupation has come in the form of coarse pottery, and as no evidence for pottery production has been recovered, it is certain that most if not all the vessels used were made elsewhere. Pottery alone can be used to indicate the integration of the study area into a wide system of market and exchange, which involved the acquisition of products of such centres as Brampton, the Shouldham/Pentney area and the Waveney valley. This may seem a statement of the obvious, but the extreme ubiquity and tedious uniformity of Roman ceramics can lead the archaeologist into using them for dating purposes and nothing more. This surplus economy must then have existed, whether the surplus was taken by an estate authority in exchange for commodities such as pots, or whether the peasant farmers were free to dispose of their excess products as they felt fit at a local market centre. It should be remembered, though, that no Fransham site was prolific in coins. In any consideration of the economy the draining effect exerted on any surplus by taxation should also not be forgotten (Robinson and Gregory 1987, 65).

The ten measurable settlements ranged in size between 0.12 and 3.6 hectares, with an average of 1.6 hectares. It is a long leap from measuring sherd concentrations to being

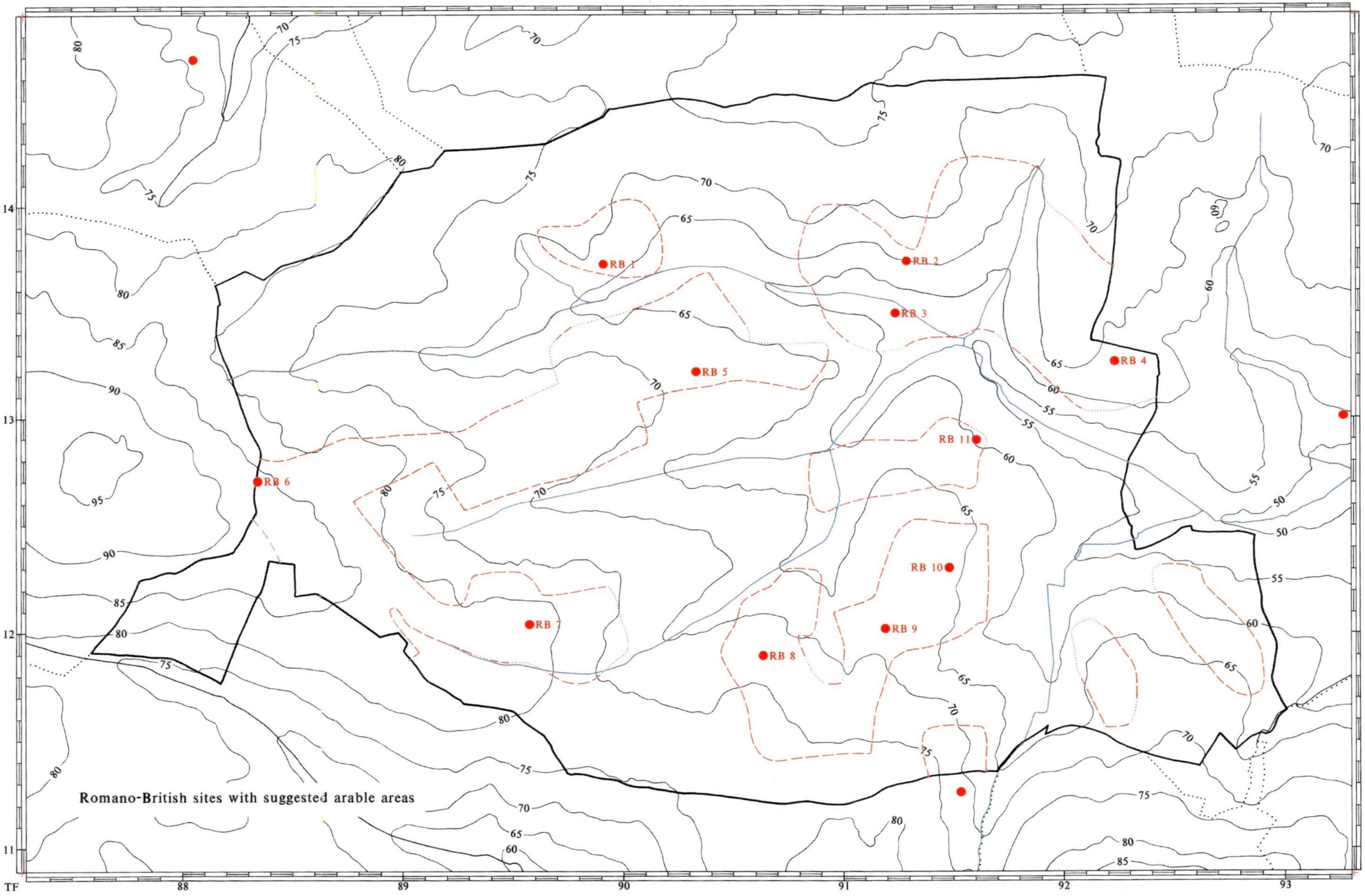

Figure 3.3 Romano-British sites with suggested areas of arable, scale 1:25,000

sure of the number and disposition of houses and other buildings within a settlement. Three sites (RB 2, 5 and 7) give the appearance of hamlets, but the remainder seem to be too small to represent anything more than single or perhaps two dwellings. Neither the lack of sites with areas greater than 4 hectares nor the fact that four of the nine measurable sites had areas smaller than 1 hectare is at all unusual (Taylor 2007 fig. 6.24).

A glance, then, at Fig. 3.1 leaves no doubt that dispersal was the dominant theme of the settlement pattern in Roman Fransham, with nothing approaching the size of the loose agglomeration of settlements which Davison (1990, fig. 6) located in the central part of his study area in south-east Norfolk. It is not possible to estimate the level of outside control or individual initiative in the selection of settlement location. The choice, in this friendly and mild landscape, would have been wide and relatively unrestricted by geographical factors, with a consistently shallow water-table giving ready access to water. However, it should be remembered that before recent underdraining, ground conditions would have reduced the available area of attractive land to a considerable extent, particularly in some low-lying parts and on the flatter regions of the clay uplands. There was a noticeable desire to avoid heavy land, with only two settlements sited on medium to heavy soil, and none occurring on heavy soil. This preference for non-heavy soils is mirrored by that shown in the choice of arable land. Topographical considerations certainly played their part: only one site (RB 3) lay in low ground, two (RB 1 and 2) sat on southern facing slopes, three (RB 8, 10 and 11) on rather flat ground, and the remaining five in elevated positions. Only in the case of RB 7 which lay on the crest of a well-defined hillock, is it possible to suggest why a spot was singled out, while in all other cases one of Taylor's equally 'good' locations could have been selected. Existing land-use and tenures as well as the role of seigniorial authority were probably a major influence on location, but the very obscurity of the pre-Roman and Roman evidence precludes any useful comments on these 'human' factors (Taylor 1983, 84).

It is interesting to note the rare coincidence between Roman and medieval settlement sites, although dispersal was the norm in both periods. A similar pattern has been noted elsewhere, for example in the West Midlands (Hodder 1992, 181). RB 6 was on virtually the same site as Med 3. RB 11, a site inferred from an outer scatter of sherds, may have coincided with a medieval successor (Med 108), and interestingly a minor concentration of Early Saxon material (ES 5) was also present.

The rarity of ceramic building materials and the absence of recognisably Roman mortar indicate that there was no masonry building on any of the sites. Although there is no firm or proven relationship between the use of masonry and the possession of wealth in a Norfolk context, and although major buildings might be constructed of timber and clay, it may be assumed that the lack of Roman masonry in Fransham does indeed indicate a group of peasant communities resident in 'native' or 'relatively poor (or 'un-Roman') settlements' (Hingley 2007, 109). On the other hand, as has been remarked of Roman Essex, 'the predominance of timber [*i.e.* non-masonry] architecture is not an indication of cultural backwardness' (Drury and Rodwell 1980, 70).

The status of the inhabitants, whether free or servile, cannot be estimated, but some attempt could perhaps be made if a systematic metal-detector survey were to be undertaken. The frequency of coin finds on Roman rural settlements is strikingly variable. In Barton Bendish parish sites with very similar appearances to the fieldwalker in terms of their pottery and their size and location, have produced widely divergent coin assemblages, ranging from hundreds of coins to none. A possible explanation may lie in the differing status of the inhabitants (Rogerson with Davison 1997, 17). Might Fransham have been a constituent of an estate attached to one of the two known Roman settlements of high status in Great Dunham (HER 4188 and 21441/36994), and might most of the inhabitants have been of low or servile status? The very small numbers of coins and metal finds recovered do not infer great wealth. Such inferences are dangerous, however, in view of the lack of fieldwork elsewhere in the area and of the silence of material evidence on the question of landownership (Miles 1989, 121). Indeed, as one student of the landscape has remarked, Romano-British archaeology 'hangs in a tenurial limbo' (Williamson 1994, 8).

In contrast to the low numbers of metal objects found in areas defined as settlement sites of the Roman period, finds were surprisingly frequent in some other areas that were subjected to metal-detector searches. In order to make valid comparisons between the quality and quantity of objects found both on and away from such sites, an overall metal-detector survey of constant intensity would be essential. This has not proved practicable. A brief list of off-site metal finds is given below[ii].

Beyond the sites of settlements, the areas of arable farming and the potential areas of woodland, pasture, meadow and waste, all set upon a land form that has hardly changed since the end of the period under discussion, little survives in the present landscape which can be shown with any certainty to have had Roman origins. To the north and south of RB 5 ran east-west roads in the medieval period. The northern one still exists as a road and track, the southern survived as a field boundary until the 1960s. The sharp edges to the pottery concentration coincide with these routes, suggesting their lines at least existed as boundaries in Roman times. They ran in broadly parallel curves along the outer edges of the main central interfluve in the parish, and they are a noticeable feature on the RAF vertical air photographs of 1946. They served as divisions between the three furlongs of the central open field of medieval and post-medieval Great Fransham and their survival into modern times provides some physical link between the Roman and present-day landscape. Were archaeological excavation to have taken place on any large scale within the study area there may well have been more evidence of such continuity, especially in the layout and orientation of fields (Rippon *et al.* 2015, 175–9).

Endnotes

i   For most of their lengths the roads are *c.*200m apart, approximately one furlong (220 yards / 201m).

ii   Roman metal objects found away from defined settlement sites, all found during metal-detecting unless otherwise stated. Objects other than coins are of copper alloy unless otherwise stated.

HER 4192: 4 brooches, Colchester fragment, Colchester Derivative Harlow, Langton Down and Trumpet, 2 possible coin blanks for the production of late third or fourth-century irregular coins, 4 coins, first/second century (2), second century and third/fourth century (TF 8930 1310).

HER 4193: Colchester Derivative Rearhook brooch, 3 coins of Faustina I to Valens (TF 8995 1310).

HER 15875: Colchester Derivative Rearhook brooch (TF 9003 1311).

HER 20508: 4 Colchester Derivative brooches (3 Rearhook and 1 Hinged), finger-ring, 3 hairpins, possible harness mount, lock pin, unidentified object, nail, 12 coins of Vespasian to Valentinian I (TF 8984 1287).

HER 20509: Aesica brooch (TF 8888 1257).

HER 20518: Trumpet brooch, Plate brooch, cosmetic mortar, coin of Magnentius (TF 8856 1272).

HER 20525: Bracelet fragment (TF 8966 1298).

HER 20542: Silver finger-ring fragment (TF 8977 1304).

HER 20587: Colchester Derivative Rearhook brooch, Trumpet brooch, coin of Tetricus I and irregular third-century radiate coin (TF 9000 1294).

HER 20651: Coin of Victorinus (found during fieldwalking at TF 90635 13300).

HER 21617: Coin of House of Constantine (TF 9155 1283).

HER 21627: Colchester Derivative Rearhook brooch (found during fieldwalking at TF 9187 1374).

HER 24771: Colchester Derivative Hinged brooch (centre TF 8989 1153).

HER 24776: Coin of Philip I (centre TF 9167 1152).

HER 24783: Colchester Derivative Hinged brooch, blue glass bead, 6 coins of Vespasian to Constantine I (TF 8876 1282).

HER 24784: Bracelet fragment, coin of Antoninus Pius (TF 8900 1293).

Chapter 4. The Early and Middle Saxon Periods

The terms 'Early Saxon' and 'Middle Saxon' are used here entirely to denote periods, from the early/mid fifth to seventh century, and the eighth and to mid-ninth century respectively. It should be noted that this terminology, here carrying no defined ethnic or cultural implications, has been described as 'traditional' in East Anglia (Rippon 2008, 143), and as having the 'potential for confusion or misinterpretation' (Scull 2009, 3).

Early Saxon: introduction

With a place name in *hâm* perhaps containing a monothematic personal name, Fransham should, according to Cox (1973), have been amongst the core of places settled by the invaders during the Pagan period. However, *ham* names (there are seventy-seven such places in Norfolk) need no longer be seen merely as indicators of early settlement, but also as pointers towards places of particular significance in the Early Saxon times (Williamson 1993, 88; 2005b), within a landscape which was much more extensively cleared and settled than was thought the case until recently. Ekwall suggested that the first element in the place name was likely to derive from the Old English *fræmde, fremede* meaning 'strange' rather than from the Old Danish / Old Swedish *Frændi* (Ekwall 1960, 186). More recently Watts considered the personal name *Frændi* a possibility (Watts 2004, 240) and Mills suggested a personal name of uncertain form followed by either *hâm* or *hamm* meaning 'enclosure' (Mills 2011, 195).

New discoveries of Early Saxon material are nowadays made quite frequently in eastern England. A steadily increasing stock of data relating to sites and finds of the fifth to seventh centuries shows that many parts of East Anglia were exploited in this period (Penn 2005; Scull 1992, fig. 3). Much of this new information is derived from metal-detecting, in addition to that from systematic survey and excavation.

Between the fifth and the seventh centuries both population densities and the nature of agriculture must have changed considerably and in a complex way. This reflected not only the patterns of Roman settlement, but variations in soils, drainage and topography. Similarly, the ethnic make-up of the population, the proportions of the indigenous Celtic-speaking and the incoming Germanic elements, also fluctuated between one area and another, and perhaps between settlement sites of differing status and function. Germanic settlement was not accomplished in one great movement: whatever the true number of incomers, the process of migration and internal population movements between different areas of England continued over as much as a century. There is no doubt, however, that in Norfolk along with Lincolnshire that there was 'significant Germanic influence, reflecting migration, from the early 5th century' (Hills 2017). The immense difficulties involved in understanding the great changes in East Anglian society between the fifth and the seventh centuries cannot be solved with any ease by archaeology, for as one scholar has remarked, 'Any such exercise is bedevilled by familiar problems of differential survival and retrieval of material, differential recognition of site-types, and chronological imprecision.' (Scull 1992, 10).

The local background to the Early Saxon period

Evidence for Early Saxon activity in the immediate surroundings of the study area is somewhat patchy, but there have been important additions to the body of data in recent years in some parishes. The following summary of the available evidence is drawn not only from the seven modern civil parishes which touch upon Fransham, but also from two others, Longham and Gressenhall, which border Wendling Fig. 1.3).

That Fransham and Wendling must have at one time formed a single roughly oval block of land was first noted by Wade-Martins (1971, 219–20, chapter 17 figs 11 and 12). Observing that all these bordering parishes had boundaries which radiated like irregular spokes from the ovoid combination of Fransham and Wendling, he suggested a date for the creation of this estate in the sixth or seventh century and considered that an 'important fifth/sixth century settlement may lie somewhere near the centre of the oval area, and possibly the villages of Wendling and Fransham are offshoots from this'. Of this pair Wade-Martins favoured Wendling as the most likely offshoot, because it was a 'good' *ingas* name.

When considering Launditch Hundred, Wade-Martins (1980b, 82) bemoaned the lack of archaeological evidence for Early Saxon life and death throughout his area of concern, except in North Elmham parish, and made a plea that the situation be improved. As noted in Chapter 2, the sole visible monument which he wished to place in the post-Roman period, the Launditch itself, now seems more likely to have been constructed in the Iron Age (Wade-Martins 1974).

Systematic fieldwalking has not been carried out on a large scale in the surrounding parishes. Metal-detecting, sometimes accompanied by ad hoc collection of pottery and other visible material, has made the greatest contribution, with only one piece of metalwork amongst those listed below having been found by eye. The following brief summary of finds demonstrates that there was a strong Early Saxon presence in this area of the Boulder Clay plateau, while the scarcity of finds from some parishes and the absence of finds from one can only reflect a lack of recorded fieldwork.

No Early Saxon material has been recorded in Necton, while Scarning has produced two brooch fragments (HER 49129). Longham parish has yielded a buckle (HER 35915) and two potsherds (HER 7269), Wendling a wrist-clasp (HER 35105), a possibly Early Saxon glass bead (HER 28461) and a potsherd (HER 30217), and Gressenhall a potsherd (HER 29247). Four fragments of

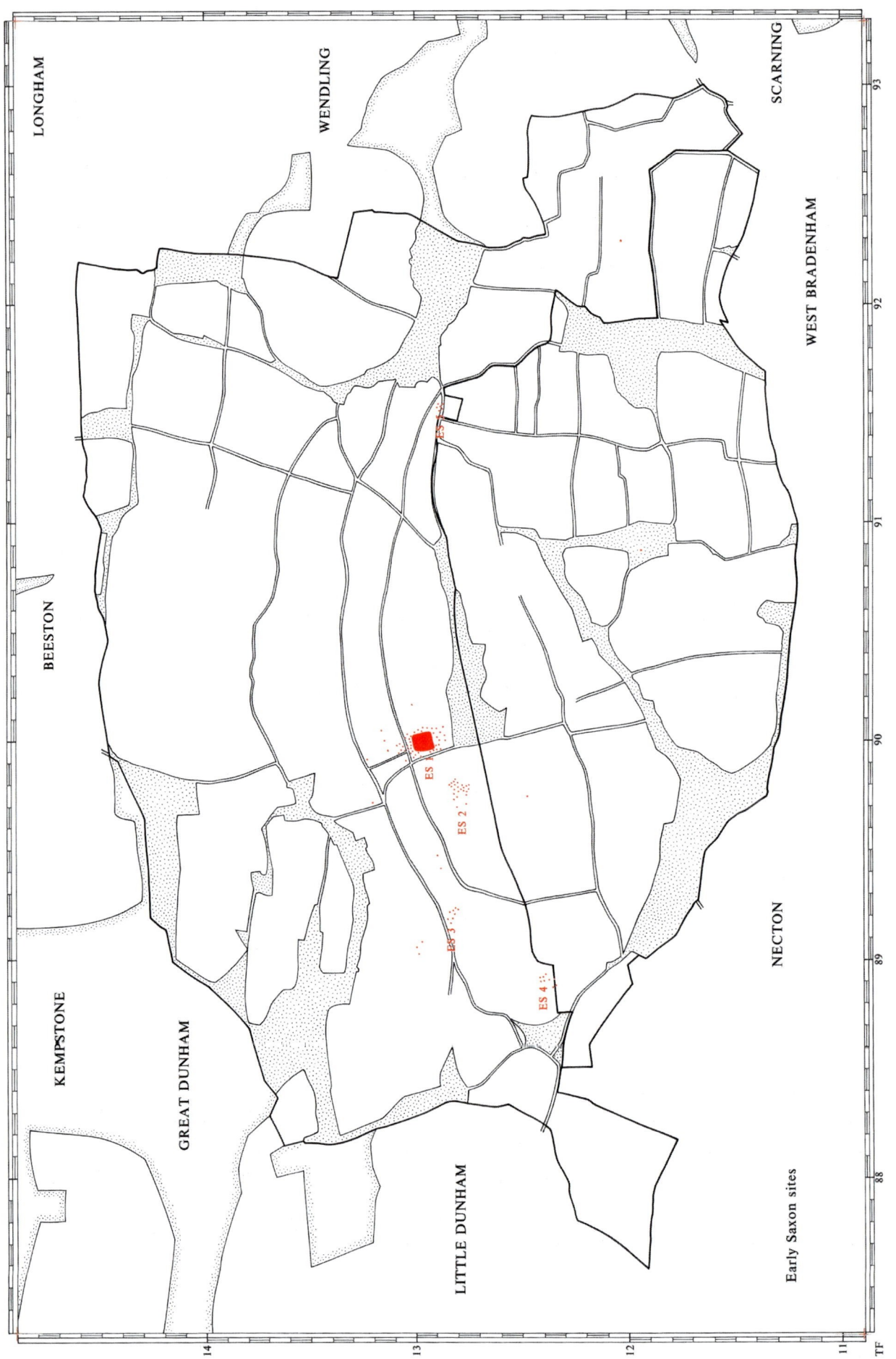

Figure 4.1 Early Saxon sites and sherd scatters, areas of medieval common pastures shown stippled, scale 1:25,000

Cruciform brooches have been recovered from the Roman settlement at Kempstone (HER 4079).

Early Saxon finds have been made on eleven sites in Beeston with Bittering (all in Beeston rather than the former parish of Little Bittering). One, with eleven metal objects and two potsherds, is probably an inhumation cemetery (HER 44099). Four pieces have been recovered from HER 19547, while five sites have yielded single items (HER 4084, 7618, 42585, 42601 and 44450). HER 52788 and 61728 have both produced two pieces, HER 7255 a girdle-hanger and a potsherd, and HER 4077 a glass bead.

Twenty metal finds in two contiguous fields overlooking the Wissey valley in (West) Bradenham suggest one or perhaps two inhumation cemeteries (HER 30636 and 31039). Further contemporary activity in Bradenham is indicated by a single potsherd (HER 37099) and by twelve metal objects from five sites (HER 30984, 31689, 32260, 37653 and 51086). In Great Dunham metal finds from two areas are indicative of inhumation cemeteries, one with sixteen objects (HER 21441 and 36994), the other with twelve (HER 45401 and 45424). Single pieces of metalwork and a potsherd have been recorded from four other locations in the parish (HER 4188, 4196, 49128 and 52585). Seven sites in Little Dunham have produced Early Saxon material, four with one or two potsherds each (HER 4198, 30236, 30992 and 30273), and twelve metal objects have been reported from four locations (HER 4197, 30272, 30277 and 52586).

One long-known inhumation cemetery of this date lies *c*.5km south-west of the parish church of Great Fransham in the parish of Sporle with Palgrave close to the border with Necton. Nine burials, accompanied by sixth-century grave goods were found in 1813 during the clearance of a barrow (HER 4598; Meaney 1964, 181–2; Ashley and Penn 2012). Strong evidence for a second inhumation cemetery in this parish has recently come to light as a result of severe damage from agricultural operations. Amongst just under fifty pieces of metalwork found during detecting within a confined area are large fragments with fresh breaks, some of which are almost complete, including material from the earlier fifth century (HER 60304). Seven pieces of metalwork have also been recovered from the deserted medieval settlement of Great Palgrave (HER 1058). From the rest of Sporle with Palgrave parish, some of which lies on sandy Breckland soils, other Early Saxon finds comprise several potsherds, a hanging bowl escutcheon, two brooch fragments and a Roman coin pierced for suspension (HER 13495, 29380 and 29403).

A small inhumation cemetery with two cremations made use of a prehistoric barrow in Tittleshall parish *c*.7km north of Fransham. Excavation in advance of a gas pipeline also recorded traces, in the form of pits and enclosures, of a broadly contemporary settlement in the immediate vicinity (HER 37617; Walton Rogers 2013). Interestingly another example of secondary burials within a barrow is indicated less than 2km to the south of this site and in Mileham parish where parts of eight Early Saxon brooches and two wrist clasps were found during metal detecting within the cropmark of a ring-ditch (HER 60463).

To set the study area within a wider geographical context in Early Saxon terms, it is worth noting that the great fifth and sixth-century predominantly cremation cemetery at Spong Hill, North Elmham (HER 1012) lies 11km north-east of Fransham (Hills 1977; Hills and Penn 1981; Hills *et al*. 1984; 1987 and 1994). A similarly dated, but apparently smaller, predominantly cremation cemetery straddles the boundary between Castle Acre and West Acre parishes 10km to the west-north-west (HER 3781; Meaney 1964, 172–3). The inhumation cemetery at the Paddocks, Swaffham (HER 1125; Hills and Wade-Martins 1976) is 9km south-west, and a probably mixed cemetery in North Pickenham parish has been identified from surface finds 8km south-south-west (HER 19449). Williamson (1993, 65–6) has argued, on estimated population figures, that Spong Hill was the burial ground for an area of approximately the size of the eastern half of what was later to become the Hundred of Launditch. The final publication of the population statistics did not alter his argument (Mckinley 1994, 66–71). If this is so, then another large fifth and sixth-century cremation cemetery can be expected to lie nearer to Fransham.

Early Saxon: the Fransham evidence
(Fig. 4.1)

Apart from that derived from metal-detecting, information amassed in this survey comes in the form of sparse scatters of pottery fragments concentrated in small areas, best interpreted as marking the sites of domestic settlements, and perhaps of areas of arable exploitation (Wade 1983). It should be stressed that such sherds are almost invariably small and abraded, for Early Saxon pottery was not highly fired and is thus liable to rapid weathering and disintegration when exposed on the surface. In addition, pottery was not used on settlement sites in such great quantities as it had been in the Roman period and was to be in the Middle Ages.

The identification of cemeteries from surface survey is a very different matter. They remain the commonest type of Early Saxon site and the main object of study for scholars of the period. It can be stated with reasonable confidence that no predominantly cremation cemetery exists in the areas walked, for this category of site is easy to locate through the presence of urn fragments (in good soil conditions the site at Spong Hill was still discernible as a pottery scatter some years after thorough and complete excavation). On the other hand, inhumation cemeteries are most unlikely to be located by fieldwalking. Indeed, none has been so found in Norfolk, although since the late 1970s many concentrations of non-ferrous metal female dress accessories found during metal-detecting have been interpreted as such sites. Searching by metal-detector in the study area has been thorough but over restricted areas. It is especially satisfying that late in the preparation of this work (in 2006) metal-detecting enabled the identification of a probable inhumation cemetery or cemeteries in Great Fransham (ES 6). The research value of systematic fieldwork incorporating both traditional collection of visible artefacts and the location of metalwork with the use of metal-detectors, was demonstrated at Playford, Suffolk by Newman (1992, 33–4).

No pottery was recovered which might be dated with confidence to the fifth century only. Most of the material, which consisted of abraded, plain and undiagnostic sherds in sandy, gritty fabrics, could equally well be dated to the fifth as to the sixth and seventh centuries (Newman 1992,

31). Organic tempered ware also occurs. This fabric is unlikely to pre-date *c*.600 (Wade 2009). Sandy, gritty and organic tempered sherds also occur on the one Middle Saxon site located in the survey (MS 1, see below). These might be interpreted as evidence that occupation on MS 1 began in the Early Saxon period. However, it is much more likely that most, if not all, of these sherds belong to the seventh century, and perhaps the eighth. With the almost complete absence from site ES 1 of Ipswich ware, the standard and distinctive Middle Saxon pottery type in East Anglia which began in the early eighth century, there can be no doubt that here we are dealing with occupation substantially of the ?mid fifth, sixth and seventh centuries. Four other, smaller, sites (ES 2–5) could possibly have continued into the seventh century, but again the lack of Ipswich ware suggests that they did not continue far into the eighth. At some time during the seventh century settlement on sites ES 1 and MS 1 probably ran concurrently, before ES 1 and perhaps ES 2–5 were abandoned as MS 1 expanded, but in view of the imprecision of pottery dating there is no way of estimating the length of the overlap.

Gazetteer of Early Saxon sites

ES 1 (Fig. 4.2) TF 9001 1295 (HER 20587)
The main settlement site lies on light to medium soil on a southern facing slope at 70–73m OD. A modern watercourse (the parish boundary between Great and Little Fransham) runs within *c*.160m of the southern end. Just to the north of the northern end a roadway, probably in use during the Roman period and known by the fifteenth century as *Southgateway* or *Greneway*, ran east-west and still survives as a ploughed-over headland bank. The medieval parish church lies on the crest of the hill, 75m north of the roadway. The modern road which runs north-south along the western edge of the field containing this site is of uncertain age, but was in use by the fifteenth century, and probably much earlier.

A total of 240 sherds was collected, on three visits, from the whole field (3.6 hectares). Of this total 199 were found in an area of 1.5 hectares (six 50 x 50m squares). This sherd count is conservative because some pieces which may be either Iron Age or Early Saxon have been excluded. The concentration covers an area of *c*.0.8 hectares, and is roughly rectangular, 100m north-south and 80m east-west. The pottery comprised sandy wares, gritty wares and fabrics containing varying amounts of organic tempering. Only two decorated sherds were identified. Both are in sandy fabrics and carry grooved decoration. One is stamped with double 'V' motifs, and the other has part of a stamped impression, probably a cross-in-circle. Such a low percentage of decorated sherds (0.83%) is to be expected from a settlement site in an assemblage of surface finds. Even from a group of excavated material such as that from Witton in north-east Norfolk (Wade 1983, 66, table 9) the percentage was a mere 1.55%, while at West Stow in north-west Suffolk it achieved 2% (West 1985, 128).

The edges of the concentration are remarkably well-defined. No pottery was recovered from the fields to the south, common pasture in the Middle Ages. Unfortunately, the adjacent field to the east (HER 20588), where again no Early Saxon material was found and where the soil is markedly heavier, was examined in rather poor conditions. A small pottery concentration (ES 2) was located to the west. To the north, an L-shaped field lying immediately to the east and south of the churchyard (HER 4193) was walked on four occasions, with only eleven or twelve sherds being recovered, and one more was found in the next field to the east (HER 15875). Single sherds occurred on a molehill south of the west tower of the parish church (HER 4206) and further afield, *c*.200m to the north-east (HER 20589) and *c*.350m to the north-west (HER 20604).

Immediately after the completion of the field survey, part of a Cruciform brooch was found during metal-detecting just beyond the north-east corner of the site, at TF 9002 1302 (Fig. 4.4 8). More recently many fragments of Early Saxon metalwork, indicative of a probable inhumation cemetery or cemeteries, were recovered over a wide area in and around ES 1 and 2. These are discussed under ES 6.

ES 2 (Fig. 4.2) TF 8980 1280 (HER 20508)
In comparison with ES 1 this is a small and sparse pottery concentration. It lies on medium soil towards the base of a south facing slope at 73m OD, *c*.130m from a watercourse, the boundary between the Franshams, and immediately south-west of a probable inhumation cemetery (ES 6). Apart from several sherds that are more likely to be Iron Age, this field produced only one certainly Early Saxon sherd outside an area of *c*.1 hectare in the south-west corner. Twenty-five sherds were collected, of which fifteen occurred in an area measuring *c*.50m by *c*.25m. Eight more were found on a subsequent visit. A fragment of an Early Saxon brooch was found during metal-detecting in the centre of this site. Just to the west of this site, the south-east corner of the adjacent field yielded two sherds, one of which was in a coarse sandy fabric and stamped with an annular motif (HER 20524).

Found *c*.350m to the south-south-east in Little Fransham, a single sherd of organic tempered ware might have derived from this site, but a sherd in a sandy fabric recovered from the south-west corner of the same field close to a Roman site (RB7) is a conspicuously isolated find (HER 23082).

ES 3 TF 8922 1282 (HER 23076)
This small but ill-defined site, lying on flat ground and medium soil at 75m OD, is represented by a mere seven sherds, in organic tempered and sandy fabrics recovered from an area of *c*.0.3 hectares. The site was examined on one occasion only. Although one other sherd was picked up nearby, the picture was confused by a light sprinkling of Iron Age material. The surrounding field produced two Early Saxon sherds (HER 23075), and two or three more came from a field to the north-west on the opposite side of a trackway (HER 24784). This follows the line of *Whiteway*, a medieval road which may have been in existence in the Roman period. An isolated sherd was found at TF 8886 1287 (HER 24783), a point slightly nearer to this site than to ES 4.

ES 4 TF 8890 1238 (HER 20448)
Only ten sherds in organic tempered and sandy fabrics make up the evidence for this rather nebulous site, and they were recovered on one visit from an area of *c*.0.5 hectares on fairly level medium soil at 80m OD. The site lies immediately to the north of the boundary between

Figure 4.2 ES 1, ES 2 and ES 6, with recorded finds spots of Early Saxon metal objects shown as dots, scale 1:5,000

Great and Little Fransham, which at this point is no longer defined by any visible feature. No other Early Saxon sherds were found in the rest of this field or in either of the two adjacent fields in Little Fransham now part of the same arable plot.

ES 5 TF 9155 1289 (HER 20639)
Six sherds, including one stamped with a cross-in-circle motif, were found in an area of 0.25 hectares on medium soil on ground sloping very gently down to the north-east. If these are not derived from a settlement at this spot, then occupation might be inferred immediately to the east of the above grid reference beneath farm buildings. It has been suggested that a Roman site (RB 11) lies similarly inaccessible in the same area. The southern edge of this field is bounded by a road that to the west formed the boundary between the Franshams. At this point, however, a salient of Great Fransham projected to the south of the road, which was known as *Odeslane* in the fifteenth century. A detachable knob from the head of a Cruciform brooch was found in this salient *c.*30m from the road by metal-detecting (HER 21617, Fig. 4.3).

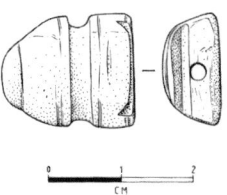

Figure 4.3 Early Saxon brooch knob found near ES 5 (HER 20587), scale 1:1

ES 6 (Fig. 4.2, HER 4193, 7288, 15875, 20508, 20524, 20542–3 and 20587)
Sixty-six fragments of Early Saxon copper alloy objects, predominantly brooches but including girdle hangers, wrist-clasps, strap-ends, tweezers, a suspension ring and part of the binding from a wooden bucket, have been recovered by metal-detecting over a large area that includes ES 1 and ES 2 (a selection is shown on Figs 4.3–6). To these may be added five fragments of Late Roman military metalwork. The find spots of fifty-eight Early Saxon pieces were recorded by the finders. Of these nine fell within the area previously defined as ES1 and one

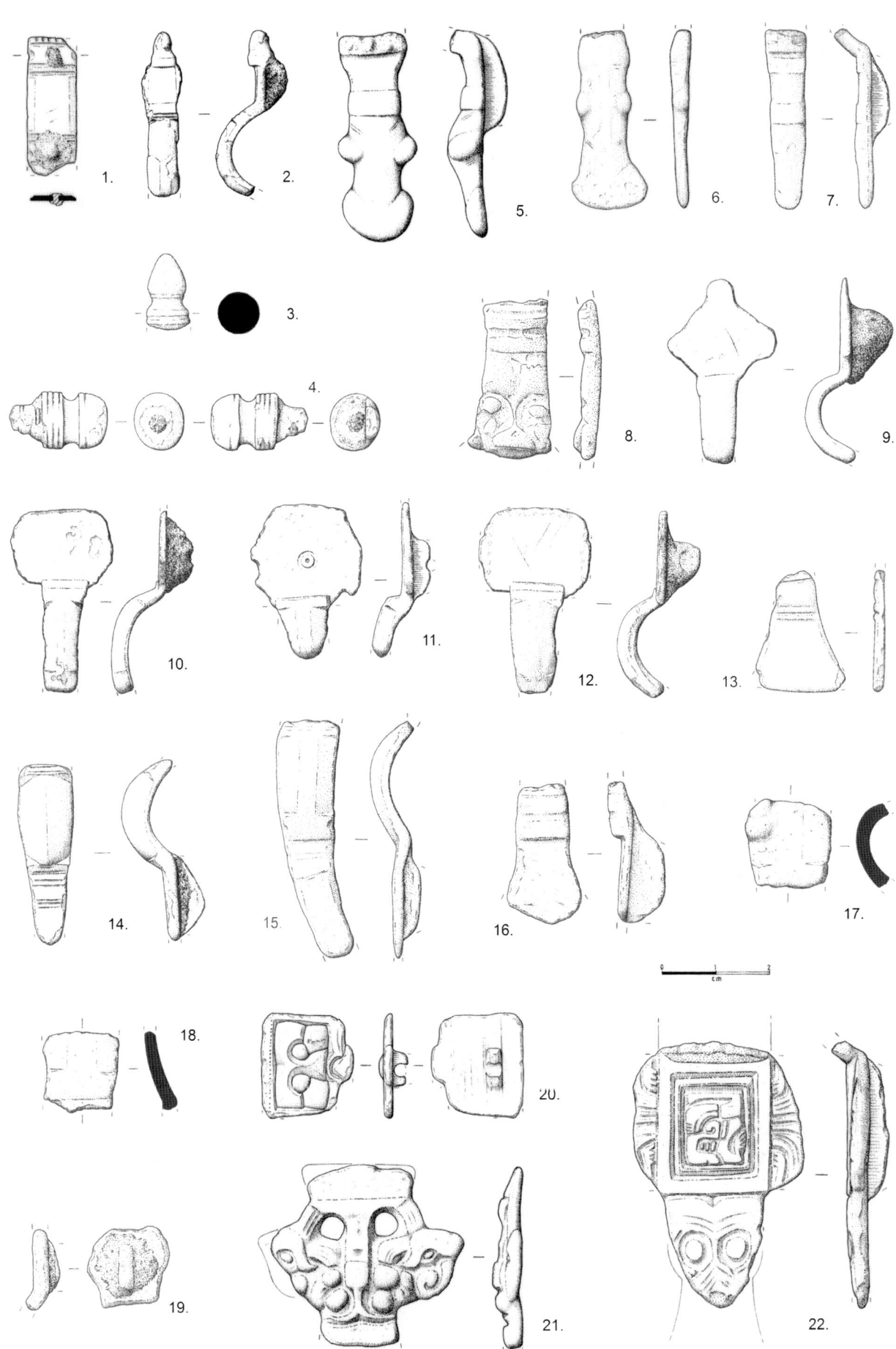

Figure 4.4 Late Roman and Early Saxon copper alloy objects: late Roman belt mount no. 1 (HER 20508); Early Saxon brooch fragments nos 2, 3, 5–7, 10–19 and 21 (HER 20508), nos 4, 8 and 20 (HER 20587), nos 9 and 22 (HER 20524), scale 1:1

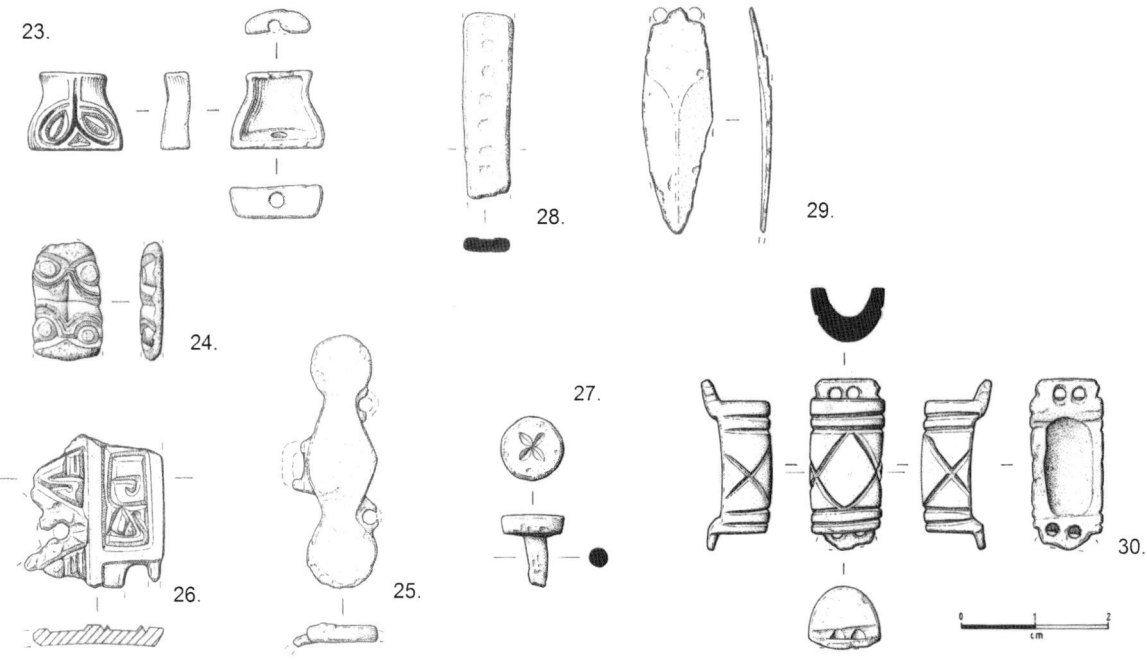

Figure 4.5 Incomplete and fragmentary Early Saxon metal objects:
no. 23 silver Radiate-headed brooch knob (HER 20508), the remainder copper alloy, no. 24 gilt brooch (HER 20508), nos 25–7 wrist-clasp (HER 20508, 20587 and 15875), no. 28 girdle hanger (HER 20508), no. 29 strap-end, no. 30 belt mount (HER 20587), scale 1:1

in the centre of ES 2. This suggests that some material may have been discarded in domestic situations. However, a large proportion of the assemblage, the Early Saxon and possibly the Late Roman, seems likely to derive from an inhumation cemetery or cemeteries. The non-intrusive nature of this survey prevents further useful discussion of the true relationship between these sites of the living and of the dead. Thanks to large-scale excavations a wide variety of relationships are now known in fifth- to seventh-century England (Hamerow 2012, 120–3).

The late Roman military material consists of two buckles of Hawkes and Dunning (1961) Types IIIA and IIIB, a sheet buckle plate with grooved decoration and two large ring-and-dots, an amphora-shaped strap-end and an incomplete rectangular belt stiffener (Fig. 4.4 1). The Early Saxon brooch fragments comprise three Åberg (1926) Cruciform Group I, one Group II, two Leeds and Pocock (1971) Group V Florid Cruciform, three Cruciform of uncertain type, eight Small-long, eight indeterminate bow (*i.e.* Cruciform or Small-long), one Annular, one gilt silver Radiate-headed and one possible Radiate-headed. The most southerly find, a complete Small-long, was recovered from the edge of what was to be common pasture in the Middle Ages (HER 7288, Fig. 4.6). A single bow brooch fragment was found beyond another road with probable Roman origins c.400m to the north-west in a field centred at TF 8940 1313 (HER 4192).

At Mucking only fifteen brooches were found during the excavation of 203 sunken-featured buildings and 53 post-hole structures (Hamerow 1993, 60–2). At West Stow a total of eight brooches was recovered from all excavated Early Saxon features and from layer 2, a sealed deposit overlying the settlement (West 1985). Recent detailed analysis of finds assemblages from excavated

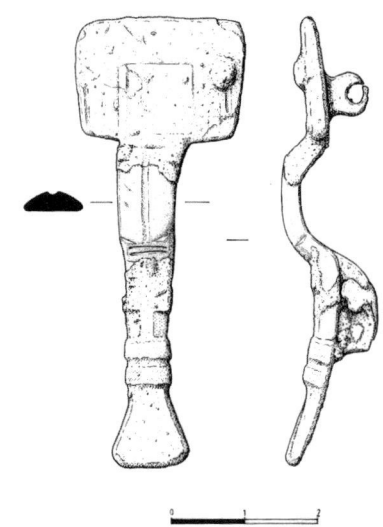

Figure 4.6 Early Saxon Small-long brooch (HER 7288), scale 1:1

settlements, inhumation and cremation cemeteries, and comparison with the range of finds made by metal-detecting suggests that most of the objects under consideration here most likely derive from funerary contexts (Chester-Kadwell 2009, 68–73).

The Early Saxon period: discussion

The evidence presented above gives the most complete picture of an area of Early Saxon settlement in the Hundred of Launditch, fuller even than that of the well-known parish of North Elmham where substantial resources were allocated to excavations at two major sites (Spong Hill and the Middle Saxon settlement in North Elmham Park) and yet where there has been almost no systematic field survey (Rickett 1995). Even in Fransham, however, field survey on its own has given us only the most general picture of the relationship between the settlement sites and their environment, significant details of which can only come from excavation (Arnold 1988, 17–8; Hamerow 2012, 67–72).

With a majority of the study area remaining unexamined, this project would have benefited from a much more extensive metal-detector survey. The example of Colkirk, on the Boulder Clay in the far north of Launditch Hundred, illustrates very clearly the potential of such work. Paul Rutledge, using mainly documentary evidence to produce a masterly review of that parish's settlement history, considered that it was a late pre-Conquest settlement, and noted the absence of earlier finds (Rutledge 1990). Metal-detecting during 1994 in one field close to the present village revealed a substantial concentration of Roman finds near to a group of four pieces of sixth-century metalwork, along with Middle and Late Saxon material (HER 30867). Early settlement in Colkirk has since been reassessed in the light of these and other more recently recorded finds (Rutledge 2003).

Even allowing for the friability of Early Saxon pottery and the difficulties involved in its identification, there is no doubt that the archaeological evidence in Fransham points to a very considerable reduction in settlement between the Late Roman and Early Saxon period, *i.e.* between the fourth and sixth centuries. There is almost no sign of activity in Little Fransham, and within Great Fransham most of the evidence was recovered from the western part of the central interfluve to the west of the largest Roman site (RB 5), in an area which had been well utilised as arable in the Roman period. To the east of RB 5, occupation on the Middle Saxon site (MS 1) probably began in the seventh century. The sparsity of material in Little Fransham is discussed below under a consideration of the Middle Saxon evidence. This situation is similar to that at Witton near North Walsham, where the main Roman site lay in the western part of the survey area (Lawson 1983, 44–9), while the Early Saxon sites lay in the eastern part where Roman sherds occurred but not in concentrations (Wade 1983). The four minor Early Saxon sites in Fransham (ES 2–5) may seem small and very uncertain, but they are more likely to represent elements in a dispersed settlement pattern rather than tiny and far-flung patches of manured arable. Again, there are close similarities with Witton, although here there were also chronological variations, and Wade (1983, 69), aided by diagnostic sherds from excavated groups, was able to postulate three phases, beginning in the fifth century.

But what of the large areas from which no evidence of fifth to seventh-century activity was recovered? There is no question of postulating vast tracts of woodland. Although the extent of arable may have been reduced in some areas during the post-Roman period, this did not lead to any great regeneration of woodland, rather much of the landscape was grass-covered, as a number of pollen analyses in the region have shown (Bennett 1983; Godwin 1968; Peglar *et al.* 1989; Simms 1978; Rippon 2008, 183, f.n.8). In the Upper and Middle Thames Valley region and in East Anglia the proportion of pollen from arable farming increased from the seventh century onwards (McKerracher 2018, 80–3). Recent analysis of all available pollen data has shown that on the East Anglian Boulder Clay as a whole there were no major changes in a largely open landscape between the Roman period and the Norman Conquest. The proportion of woodland pollen remained 'remarkably stable', as did that of pollen from both improved and unimproved pasture. The percentage of arable-derived pollen in fact doubled by the middle of the ninth century and quadrupled by *c.*1066 (Rippon *et al.* 2015, 170–4).

The identification of small Saxon sites, 'many…no more than single farms', from surface artefact scatters is no longer unusual on well-drained soils in Northamptonshire, where much high quality, professional field survey has been conducted. In the Midlands, though, such sites are not found on the claylands, despite their former appeal to the Romano-British population (Brown and Foard 1998, 73; Jones and Page 2006, 85). A similar abandonment of previously occupied clay soils occurred in central Suffolk in the fifth and sixth centuries (West 1999). For example, Walsham le Willows, a parish lying near the edge of the Boulder Clay in the same way as Fransham, was subjected to field survey yet failed to produce any Early Saxon finds (West and McLaughlin 1998, 9). The pattern in central Norfolk is rather different. Retreat from the clay took place but was not complete. The explanation must lie partly in the relatively permeable quality of much of the boulder clay there, but also in better natural drainage aided by gently sloping ground and few completely flat areas (Rippon *et al.* 2015, 337). Indeed, Williamson when considering Suffolk has rightly argued that in assessing Early Saxon settlement 'a more subtle distinction' than the traditional division between 'light' and 'heavy' soils should be made. Clay loams of the Burlingham Associations should be considered alongside some lighter soils as more attractive to settlers than heavy poorly drained clays, various acid sands and waterlogged sands and silts (Williamson 2008, 127–30).

Though set within a dispersed pattern the main Fransham settlement (ES 1) was surely no more than a hamlet. The size of the concentration (0.8 hectares), when superimposed on the plan of West Stow (West 1985, fig. 7), cannot have contained more than two or three buildings, even allowing for the replacement of short-lived structures over 200 years. The area is indeed small when compared with that of four or more concentrations of roughly contemporary pottery at Leckhamstead, Buckinghamshire, that each covered up to 2 hectares (Jones and Page 2006, 85). Considerable caution, however, must be exercised in the interpretation of settlement size on the basis of surface evidence alone. Without excavation the relationship between sherds on the surface of the ploughsoil on the one hand, and the disposition and quantity of buildings as well as other aspects of settlement layout on the other, must remain uncertain (Gaffney and Tingle 1989, 145–64; Schofield 1989, 464–6).

The imprecision of pottery dating has already been stressed. We cannot be certain that any fifth-century ceramics have been recovered, although some of the metal finds are of that date. There remains the possibility that there was a short-lived post-Roman retreat from the study area resulting in desertion, as appears to have been the case from parts of the south-east Suffolk clays (Newman

1992, 32). On the other hand, the two medieval roads which ran along either side of the crest of the central interfluve and which appear to have existed, as boundaries if not routes, in the Roman period, suggest at least some continuity of land-use. It would be unwise, on the evidence of surface survey alone, particularly with the benefit of such slight funerary evidence, to enter too far into the debate, still raging, on the degree of Romano-British survival and the proportion of Germanic immigrants in the fifth to seventh-century population. In the most general terms the Fransham evidence, with its complete change in settlement size and location between the fourth and sixth centuries, points to much disturbance after the end of the Roman period, a situation suggesting a strong degree of replacement in a population which had become overwhelmingly Germanic (Welch 1985, 13–4), rather than a depleted number of inhabitants of Romano-British stock under the cultural, political and economic domination of an elite band of Anglo-Saxon aristocrats (Arnold 1984, 122–33; Hodges 1989, 10–42). Controversies over British survival and Germanic immigration were succinctly summarised by Hills (1993, 14–6) and have been revisited by Williamson (2013, 61–6).

A final question concerning ES 1 and ES 6 and their continuing significance after the seventh century must be addressed. The medieval parish church of All Saints stands on a hill crest c.150m to the north of ES 1 and close to the northern end of ES 6. If any pre-Conquest site is located near a parish church in Launditch Hundred, it is normally of Middle and Late Saxon date (Wade-Martins 1980b; Hoggett 2010, 142–53). Here, though, we have a pre-Christian settlement and cemetery. Might the church overlie a site of pagan significance, and if it does, is this merely coincidental (Hoggett 2010, 144)? Pagan antecedence was one explanation for church isolation postulated by Dymond (1968, 28–9). Such questions cannot be answered without excavation, but the possibility remains (Morris 1983, 49–62; 1989, 46–92). The areas occupied by ES 1 and by much of ES 6 were glebe land of Great Fransham rectory by the early seventeenth century at the latest.

The Middle Saxon period: introduction

Pottery makes East Anglia the envy of fieldworkers studying Anglo-Saxon settlement outside the region (Tingle 1991, 71). This is especially so for the post-Pagan and pre-Danish period on account of a distinctive and durable pottery type, Ipswich ware (Hurst 1957; Hurst 1959; West 1963) which, although never prolific, occurs with sufficient frequency to enable useful conclusions to be drawn on settlement locations and even on arable exploitation through the plotting of manure scatters. The term 'Ipswich ware' is used here, rather than 'Ipswich-type ware'. Almost all this pottery found outside Ipswich itself has been demonstrated to have been made in the town (Vince 2005, 226–7; Blinkhorn 2012).

Although, because of the robustness of the ceramics, Middle Saxon settlement sites are undoubtedly easier to locate than those of the fifth to seventh centuries, the period is of course more obscure in one aspect. During the eighth century easily identifiable funerary evidence rapidly died away as accompanied burial fell out of fashion and cemeteries were established on new sites, many of which may lie beneath churchyards still in use.

The date range of Ipswich ware was first set between c.650 or slightly earlier and c.850, (Hurst 1976, 299–303). This span of two centuries has been reduced as a result of more recent work, with the postulation of a later starting-date of c.720 (Blinkhorn 2012)[i]. It is still indeed a lengthy period, running from the final phase of some Early Saxon sites, such as West Stow (West 1985, 161), to the period before the foundation of new settlements in the ninth century (Newman 1992, 34–5). Yet again, without recourse to excavation, more chronological precision might be forthcoming from the recovery of metalwork and coins (Rogerson 2003; Davies 2010).

The local background to the Middle Saxon period

Apart from part of a ninth-century strap-end (HER 60899) no other Middle Saxon material has been reported from Necton parish. Wendling has produced three fragmentary ninth-century strap-ends, one an isolated find (HER 28463), the others from the same field as an incomplete silver pin of the eighth or ninth century (HER 56937). A single potsherd, probably of Ipswich ware, was found close to the boundary with Gressenhall (HER 53778). The evidence from Gressenhall parish amounts to two potsherds (HER 29247 and 30563). From Kempstone comes another ninth-century strap-end (HER 13042), one potsherd (HER 4083) and two hooked tags that may date as late as the eleventh century (HER 61360). Nine sherds of Ipswich ware were collected during metal-detecting from a field close to the parish church in Scarning (HER 53764) and two others from a more outlying location (HER 53143). A pin, a ninth-century strap-end and a potsherd are recorded from one field (HER 49994) and another strap end from an adjacent one (HER 49993). Ten quite widely distributed sites in Beeston with Bittering parish have yielded Middle Saxon material: a pin, a hooked tag, a strap-end and three potsherds (HER 4084), a brooch and four potsherds (HER 4085), one potsherd (HER 4093), a pair of tweezers, a strap-end and six potsherds (HER 7255), a gilt mount and two potsherds (HER 16576), a pair of tweezers, a strap-end and two potsherds (HER 19547), two pins (HER 30718 and 34835), a coin, a brooch and a potsherd (HER 44099) and a coin of the early ninth-century Mercian king Ludica (HER 61388).

Before 1993 Little Dunham parish had yielded a solitary fragment of Ipswich ware (HER 4199). However, systematic fieldwalking by Ray Ludford has since defined a pottery concentration (fifty-nine sherds) extending to c.3 hectares (HER 30272), along with an outer 'halo' of ten sherds in three surrounding fields (HER 4198, 30236, 30273 and 30277). A pin and a potsherd that may perhaps be Early Saxon were recovered elsewhere (HER 30992). Of nine sites in Great Dunham with recorded Middle Saxon finds, four in contiguous fields have produced over one hundred-and-thirty potsherds during the course of metal-detecting, along with five coins and thirty-six other metal objects (HER 45401, 45424, 49128 and 52585). Sixteen potsherds collected more than 0.5km from this large site indicate a separate focus of activity (HER 13726). Three potsherds have been recovered from the surface of the churchyard (HER 4178). Other finds comprise a pin (HER 4188), a single potsherd (HER

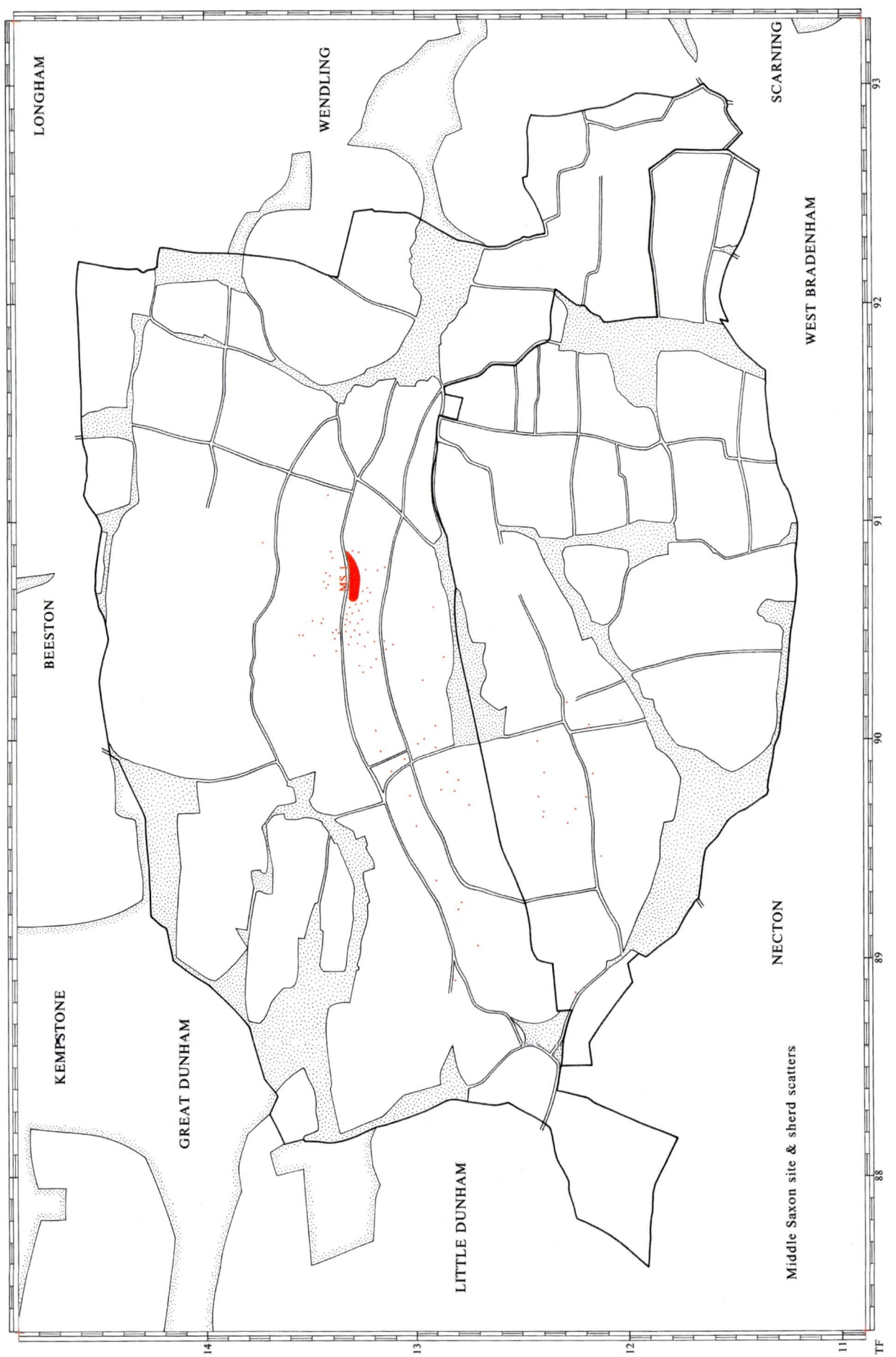

Figure 4.7 Middle Saxon site and sherd scatters, areas of medieval common pastures shown stippled, scale 1:25,000

4196), two belt fittings (HER 31580 and 51235), a sword belt mount (HER 55829) and a coin (HER 61828).

In Longham evidence for a Middle Saxon site (HER 7269) close to the south-east of St Andrew's churchyard, was recorded by Wade-Martins who found eight sherds of Ipswich ware (Wade-Martins 1980b, 37, fig. 15). Closely spaced fieldwalking later refined the extent of this site (Andrews 1992, fig. 5c; Silvester 1993, 27). A total of forty-one sherds was recorded over an area of c.0.25 hectares at the edge of a field. This site may be larger and may extend to the north into an area of pasture. One sherd has been found in the churchyard (HER 7277).

Middle Saxon finds have been made on ten sites in Bradenham. Two contiguous fields in the former parish of West Bradenham have yielded eleven coins (including one of Ludica of Mercia) and eight other metal objects, but only six potsherds (HER 30636 and 30984), while a pin and fourteen potsherds have been recovered from an adjacent field (HER 30422). Two sites have produced two metal objects (HER 31358 and 32260), while single pieces have been recovered from four locations (HER 31039, 31689, 31717 and 51086). Only one potsherd has been recorded from the former parish of East Bradenham (HER 32784).

The great variation in the nature and quantity of recorded data in these surrounding parishes is almost entirely the result of differing intensities and methods of fieldwork, with only Little Dunham and Longham witnessing any controlled archaeological survey. All the parishes must have seen some Middle Saxon settlement, as no doubt future work will demonstrate. Despite this uneven picture, some ranking of sites is discernible: activity in Great Dunham was extensive and there were two settlement foci. The site in Little Dunham was probably much larger than that in Longham, and the metal-detected evidence from West Bradenham indicates a place of high status. The situation in Beeston with Bittering, where all finds come from the Beeston part of the parish (*i.e.* west of the Launditch), is especially interesting. The evidence so far (all recovered during metal-detecting apart from one sherd found casually by a member of the public) indicates that settlement may well have been polyfocal.

Middle Saxon: the Fransham evidence
(Figs 4.7 and 4.8)

Only one site (MS 1) was occupied within the study area during this period. It was founded in the seventh century and was to continue as a settlement until the eleventh. It lies in Great Fransham, at 65m OD c.0.8km east-north-east of the parish church, near the eastern end of the central interfluve, and on medium soil bordering the southern side of a road with probable Roman origins, the medieval *Whiteway*. The ground continues to rise very gently upwards to the south so that the site is very marginally north facing. There is also a very slight rise in ground level from the west to a high point at TF 9076 1330, east of which the land begins to fall towards the confluence of two streams. Unfortunately, a plantation containing 1.9 hectares immediately north of the *Whiteway* and south of a former railway could not be examined. As a result, it is uncertain whether the site flanked this road along one side or both. A track divides the area south of the road into two fields (HER 20651 and 20653).

Each field was examined on a number of occasions. The western one (HER 20651) was first walked in 50m by 50m subdivisions. A strip c.50m wide along the northern edge and a 100m by 100m square in the north-east corner were then walked when the field was planted with daffodils grown for bulbs. This collection was for some reason extremely prolific although the surface was partially obscured. A subsequent attempt to refine records of the distribution of Saxon material by collecting in 25m by 25m squares was abandoned after about one quarter of the field had been walked, because of the excessively dry conditions. The northern half of this field was later walked at 2m intervals and Middle Saxon sherds individually plotted (Fig. 4.8), following a simple method of offsetting

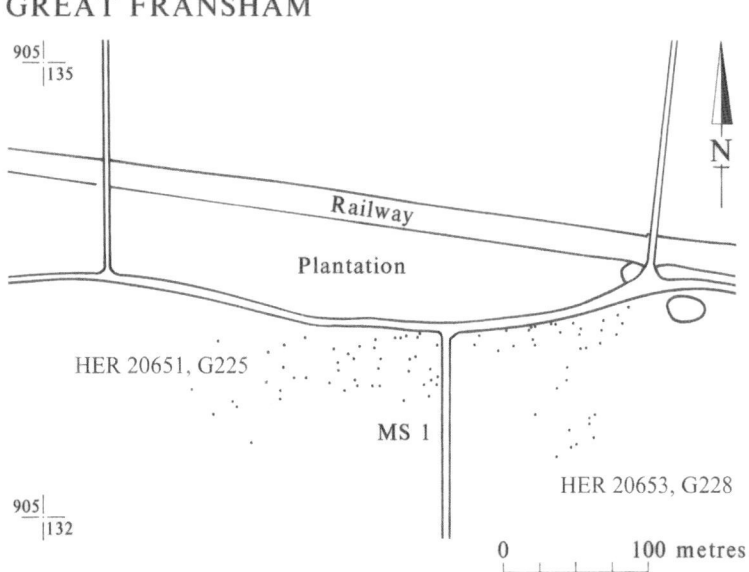

Figure 4.8 MS 1, individually plotted sherds, scale 1:5,000

from a baseline developed in the Fenland Survey (Rogerson and Silvester 1986). Finally, observations were made during excavations for a new farm track near the eastern edge (see below).

The eastern field (HER 20653) was somewhat coarsely subdivided into five areas, and an attempt was made on second and third visits to plot the locations of significant sherds in the north-western part. This field was then subjected to the close-walking 'Fenland method' (Fig. 4.8).

Both fields were subjected to metal-detecting on several occasions. The results were almost negative. Nothing of significance was recovered in the western field, while the eastern produced a lead spindle whorl of uncertain date and an incomplete ninth-century strap-end of Thomas' (2003) Class A Type 5 found at TF 9081 1319 (Fig. 4.9 1). Fieldwalking yielded two Middle or Late Saxon iron objects, part of a whittle-tang knife in the western field and a tooth from a linen heckle in the eastern.

The whole area of this site and its Late Saxon successor is marked by soil that is marginally darker than that to the west, east and south. In the north-east corner of the western field an area c.35m east-west and stretching c.10m south from the road is marked by even darker soil. During the various occasions on which this was walked, numerous fragments of animal bone, very rare over the rest of the site, were noted. In 1993 the ploughsoil was mechanically stripped for the laying of a new north-south farm track. Over most of this strip the base of the ploughsoil was not reached, but at the junction with the road excavation was deeper. Here, at TF 90732 13318, the natural sandy clay was touched at a depth of 0.45m. Immediately above this was a 0.1m thick layer of very dark sandy soil with charcoal flecking, small particles of burnt clay and profuse animal bone. It was not possible to plot the extent of this layer, but an area measuring 2m x 0.4m was excavated with a trowel. A quantity of animal bone was recovered, but no pottery. In such hurried circumstances it was not possible to date this deposit with any confidence, although the absence of pottery and the large amount of animal bone suggests that it is most likely to have been Middle Saxon. Considerable amounts of mammal bones are commonly found on Middle Saxon sites (Wade-Martins 1980a, 41; Silvester 1988, 158), and it is likely that if this deposit were Late Saxon it would have produced some sherds of Thetford-type ware.

The 2.28kg of animal bones recovered in this salvage operation were examined by Trevor Ashwin. The condition of the material suggested that it was medieval or earlier. Cattle bones predominated, and sheep/goat and to a lesser extent pig were present. Because of their size and robustness higher proportions of cattle bones are to be expected in hand-collected rather than sieved assemblages (McKerracher 2018, 52). No obvious butchery marks were identified, but many pieces had been smashed and split for marrow extraction. Little can be made of this small group, but it should be noted that the proportion of sheep here is much smaller than at North Elmham, where they accounted for more than a third of the total (Noddle 1980, 378).

The area of MS 1 amounted to at least 1 hectare, measuring c.200m east-west and 50m or more north-south (nb the unsurveyed plantation north of the road). Because an area at the western end of the eastern field was devoid of Middle Saxon pottery, it might be

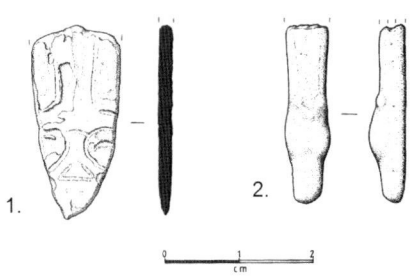

Figure 4.9 Incomplete ninth- and ninth/tenth-century strap-ends (HER 20653 and 24783), scale 1:1

more accurate to see MS 1 as two separate sub-sites. Such a division is born out by differences in the pottery assemblages. An expansion of the settled area eastwards rather a migration from the western to the eastern sub-site is most likely.

The Middle Saxon pottery in the western field consisted of an almost equal match of Ipswich ware and non-Ipswich fabrics (238 and 239 sherds respectively). The latter category was rather miscellaneous, consisting of organic tempered wares, some of which were almost sand-free (unlike those from the Early Saxon site ES 1); hand-made sandy and finely gritted wares; and apparently wheel-turned sandy wares. In the eastern field Ipswich ware was predominant, with 88% of the total of one hundred and thirty sherds.

As discussed above under ES 1, some of the non-Ipswich pottery from this site could well belong to the seventh century. However, it is not possible to know whether we are dealing with a rapid shift from ES 1 to MS 1, or whether there was a period in the seventh century when both sites were occupied. The latter seems more credible. Furthermore, it is even possible that initial settlement on a small scale in the western part of MS 1 might belong to the sixth century. The eastern part of MS 1 might have remained unoccupied until well into the eighth or in the early ninth century. The small number of non-Ipswich sherds here might either be derived from the western area or be contemporary with the occupation. It is reasonable to assume that in the centre of Norfolk products from Ipswich were not always available, and that a surviving local tradition was on hand to supply predominantly hand-made products when there was a shortfall of Ipswich ware. At North Elmham Park there was some indication that late in the Middle Saxon period Ipswich ware became scarce (Wade 1980, 421–3). The evidence, however, was not very clear, being derived entirely from the fillings of cut features, few if any of which had been used for primary rubbish disposal. It should also be noted that the heavy clay soil was not subjected to sieving, and in many cases fillings were removed not by trowelling but with mattocks, forks and shovels. Interestingly, if there really was a period of Ipswich ware shortage at North Elmham, the gap in the market can hardly have been filled by alternative local products. A total of twenty-eight non-Ipswich sherds (sixteen sandy, three gritty and one grass-marked, all hand-made, as well as eight of local slow wheel-turned sandy ware) was recovered from Middle Saxon and later contexts, while one hundred and sixty Ipswich ware sherds were found (Wade 1980, 416–9). At Fishergate,

Norwich, hand-made sherds in sandy and organic tempered fabrics accounted for almost 21% of the Middle Saxon pottery, and in addition a small group of rim sherds, similar to the apparently wheel-turned sandy wares mentioned above, were considered to be either Middle or Late Saxon, or transitional between the two periods (Dallas 1994, 20 and 28). Comparable finds from Tasburgh in south Norfolk, were considered to be transitional (Dallas 1992, 54). A kiln producing pots very similar in form to the Tasburgh material was recorded during archaeological excavation in nearby Wreningham in 2016 (HER 56176).

The south, east and west edges of the pottery concentration in MS 1 are very clearly defined. To the east and south-east there is a complete absence of Middle Saxon material over an area of predominantly heavy soils in two fields stretching down to a stream. To the north-east one isolated sherd was picked up near the confluence of the two streams at TF 9113 1341 (HER 20755). However, a very fine spread of Ipswich ware continues for c.1.8km westwards from MS 1 along the central interfluve. This includes one sherd from the north-west corner of All Saints' churchyard (HER 4206). Two pieces of ninth-century metalwork were recovered during metal-detecting from the vicinity of the church, a hooked tag to the east (HER 4193) and a strap-end to the south (HER 20587). An eighth- to ninth-century Ansate brooch and part of a ninth- or perhaps tenth-century strap-end (Fig. 4.9 2) were found far to the west on the site of a medieval manor house (HER 24783, Med 5).

Beyond a point c.300m west of MS 1 the spread of Ipswich ware is absent from the north-facing slope. However, with such a fine sprinkling of material it is probably spurious, if not misleading, to lay much emphasis on localised gaps in the distribution. On the other hand, large and blank areas are certainly significant, either of permanent pasture, waste or woodland, or of all three. The broad southern facing slope which extends along the northern part of the parish has produced no Middle Saxon pottery apart from one sherd at TF 9091 1373 (HER 20766). To return to the central interfluve, the sparse but fairly consistent spread of Ipswich ware running west from MS 1 can reasonably be interpreted as the result of manure spreading on arable land. The area of this spread amounts to c.50 hectares. It had contained two small Early Saxon sites (ES 2 and ES 3), while another lay just to the west (ES 4).

All the Middle Saxon material described so far was found in Great Fransham. Very few finds of this date were recovered from Little Fransham. One Ipswich ware sherd came from elevated ground close to the source of the stream flanking the south of the central interfluve, on a medieval site at TF 8886 1226 (HER 20818). This may represent a continuation of the central arable zone of Great Fransham. Further east within Little Fransham a roughly rectangular area of c.20 hectares centred on TF 8970 1232 on medium soil with lighter patches in the south-west, carries another very thin sprinkling of eight Ipswich ware sherds (HER 23081, 23082 and 23901). This area is defined to the west and south by an absence of sherds over the reasonably wide stretches of upland subjected to fieldwalking. The lower parts of the northern facing slope on the north are also devoid of finds. The eastern edge of this area is partly obscured by buildings and uncultivated land, particularly to the south of the parish church and rectory. However, four Middle Saxon sherds have been found: one Ipswich ware on a patch of bare soil in St Mary's churchyard immediately north-west of the nave (HER 7297), one hand-made and one Ipswich ware in the south-west corner of the adjoining Late Saxon site (LS 2, HER 23084), and one Ipswich ware in disturbed soil on a building site to the south of LS 2, at TF 9012 1205 (HER 41668).

The remaining areas of Little and Great Fransham to the south and east failed to yield any Middle Saxon finds. As with the northern part of Great Fransham, a lack of manuring debris indicates that these wide stretches of land were probably not exploited as permanent arable, but were instead occupied by areas of woodland, waste and pasture, especially the latter (Rippon *et al.* 2015, 170–2). In the absence of a suggestive 'halo' of sherds, it may seem unlikely that any of the obscured areas of Little Fransham contain a Middle Saxon settlement, but given the four pottery fragments found near the church there remains a possibility that a small site might lie somewhere in the vicinity on land unavailable for fieldwalking.

The Middle Saxon period: discussion

In East Anglia most settlement sites of this period have been found in or near the major valleys, 'Yet some... are known from more remote locations beside the higher reaches of shallow tributary valleys' (Williamson 1988, 171). In Fransham a solitary settlement site (MS 1) was located in just such a position, slightly to the north of a slight rise and to the west of a confluence of two streams. It lay on one or both sides of a road that may have already been ancient, at some distance from its presumed Early Saxon predecessor (ES 1) and from the present site of the parish church, which may or may not have been a place of religious significance at this time. The shift from ES 1 probably took place in the seventh century, before the introduction of Ipswich ware. An occupation site with an attested seventh-century phase is not the norm in East Anglia, most Middle Saxon sites being dated by Ipswich ware alone. Alan Davison, in his study of Hales, Heckingham and Loddon in south-east Norfolk, has claimed a mid seventh-century date for the abandonment of Early Saxon settlements on higher ground and the establishment of new sites near the river Chet (Davison 1990, 66). This dating, however, is based as much on factors such as climactic change as on ceramic developments. One notable exception is the Suffolk site at Bloodmoor Hill, Carlton Colville (Lucy *et al.* 2009).

The move from ES 1 and its smaller contemporary settlements to MS 1 in the seventh century is unsurprising (Rogerson 1996, 60) and is paralleled by many other excavated examples in southern England (Ripon 2007, 119). On the other hand, the shift well away from the site of what was to become the parish church is abnormal, running counter to the normal pattern of a close association between Middle Saxon settlements and many medieval churches (Wade-Martins 1980b; Newman 1992; Rippon 2009, 259; Hoggett 2010, fig. 33; Wright 2015, 138–72). Whatever lay behind the settlement relocation it did not involve a change of soil type, topographical setting or proximity to water, and the cause or purpose of the move remains unexplained.

Extending to at least 1 hectare in the eighth and early ninth centuries, MS 1 is best described as a very small

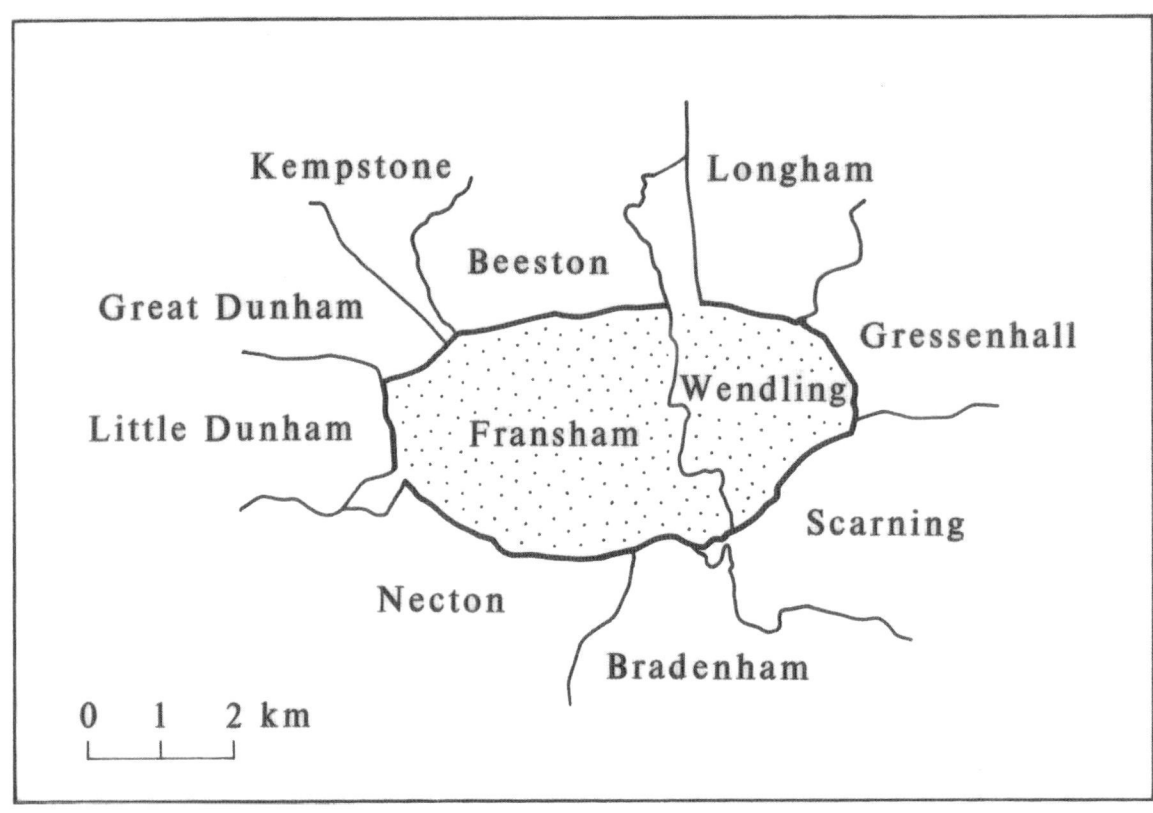

Figure 4.10 Fransham, Wendling and adjoining parish boundaries, scale 1:200,000

nucleated settlement, slightly greater in area than its Early Saxon processor. In terms of the nature of its buildings and its plan nothing can be said on a basis of fieldwalking evidence only. This lack of detail contrasts strongly with what is now known from the excavation of many contemporary sites (Hamerow 2012, 72–83). The place of MS 1 within the landscape is clearer: whereas ES 1 was simply the largest amongst a small group of dispersed settlements, MS 1 either stood alone or was perhaps accompanied by a single and smaller companion site in Little Fransham.

Evidence for Middle Saxon agriculture will always be scant without the benefit of excavation, and this survey has failed to add to the large body of data now available concerning the huge changes in many aspects of farming that took place between the later seventh and earlier ninth centuries, the so-called 'long eighth century' (McKerracher 2018). A fine sprinkling of Ipswich ware sherds demonstrates that a substantial zone of arable was located to the west of MS 1 and that a subsidiary area came under the plough to the south-west, across a stream, in what was to become Little Fransham parish. More extensive signs of arable might have been expected given that pollen analyses in Norfolk and Suffolk have demonstrated an increase in arable in the eighth and ninth centuries (Rippon 2008, 191–2), but it remains quite likely that not all areas subject to tillage were fertilised with manure derived from domestic middens and incorporating potsherds.

Site MS 1 sits not far to the north and west of the centre of the oval land-block (Fig. 4.10) formed by Fransham and Wendling (Wade-Martins 1971, 219–20). Could this ovoid have formed the core of an early multiple estate which was established in the seventh century (Aston 1985, 32–6; Fowler 1976, 36–44; Jones 1979), or even in the fifth or sixth (Carver 1989, 156–8), and might the nine surrounding parishes have made up the periphery? Within this estate, covering an area of $c.$100km^2, there would have been a rich variety of soils and environments: the massive woods in Necton and Bradenham, the pastures and meadows in the Wissey and Scarning river valleys, the dry uplands on the Hungry Hill gravels in Gressenhall, Longham and Beeston, the sands in the south-west of Necton, chalky soil in the west of Great Dunham and heavy land in Scarning and elsewhere. If such an estate did indeed exist it would have been superimposed on the (probably pre-Roman) land division indicated by the Launditch. It would also have to antedate the hundredal system which was established in the early tenth century (Barringer 2005b). However, without any supporting contemporary, or at least pre-Conquest, documentary evidence, it must remain only a remote possibility (Hooke 1989, 9–27), with further doubt being cast by the lack of any finds indicative of high status, which have been recorded in the peripheral parishes of Great Dunham and West Bradenham.

One medieval legal institution which may indicate the former existence of such a territorial unit is the leet [ii]court of Milles at Mor which, by the early fifteenth century, was held in Great Fransham but which by that time pertained to the lord of the main manor of Little Fransham (Chapter 6). Five jurors each from the two Dunhams and Kempstone were expected to attend the court, and the lord of Little Dunham annually paid the lord of this leet a wheat rent for the right to hold his own court leet. However, other evidence for an early connection between these places is lacking. Domesday sokemen may have been descended from freemen of Middle Saxon estates (Williamson 1993,

94), but the sixteen in the Tosny part of Fransham in 1066 were associated with Harold's huge estate centred on Necton which had manors in seven Hundreds. There is nothing else in the Domesday evidence to hint at a former importance in Fransham. If it were ever an estate centre, then evidence apart from the configuration of the parish boundaries and the above-mentioned leet has long since vanished. In addition, MS 1 was entirely unproductive of coins, metal objects or imported pottery which might have hinted at high status, and there is nothing outstanding in the archaeological evidence collected in this survey to point in a similar direction.

Endnotes

i   Radiocarbon dates from an Ipswich ware-producing kiln recently excavated at Stoke Quay on the south side of the River Orwell opposite central Ipswich have indicated that its period of use antedated *c*.700 (Brown *et al.* 2020, 139–40). Perhaps its products were for immediately local consumption and the widespread distribution of Ipswich ware did not commence until *c*.720 (Keith Wade pers. comm.).

ii   A court dealing with minor criminal offences held by a manorial lord with jurisdiction previously exercised by the sheriff of the county.

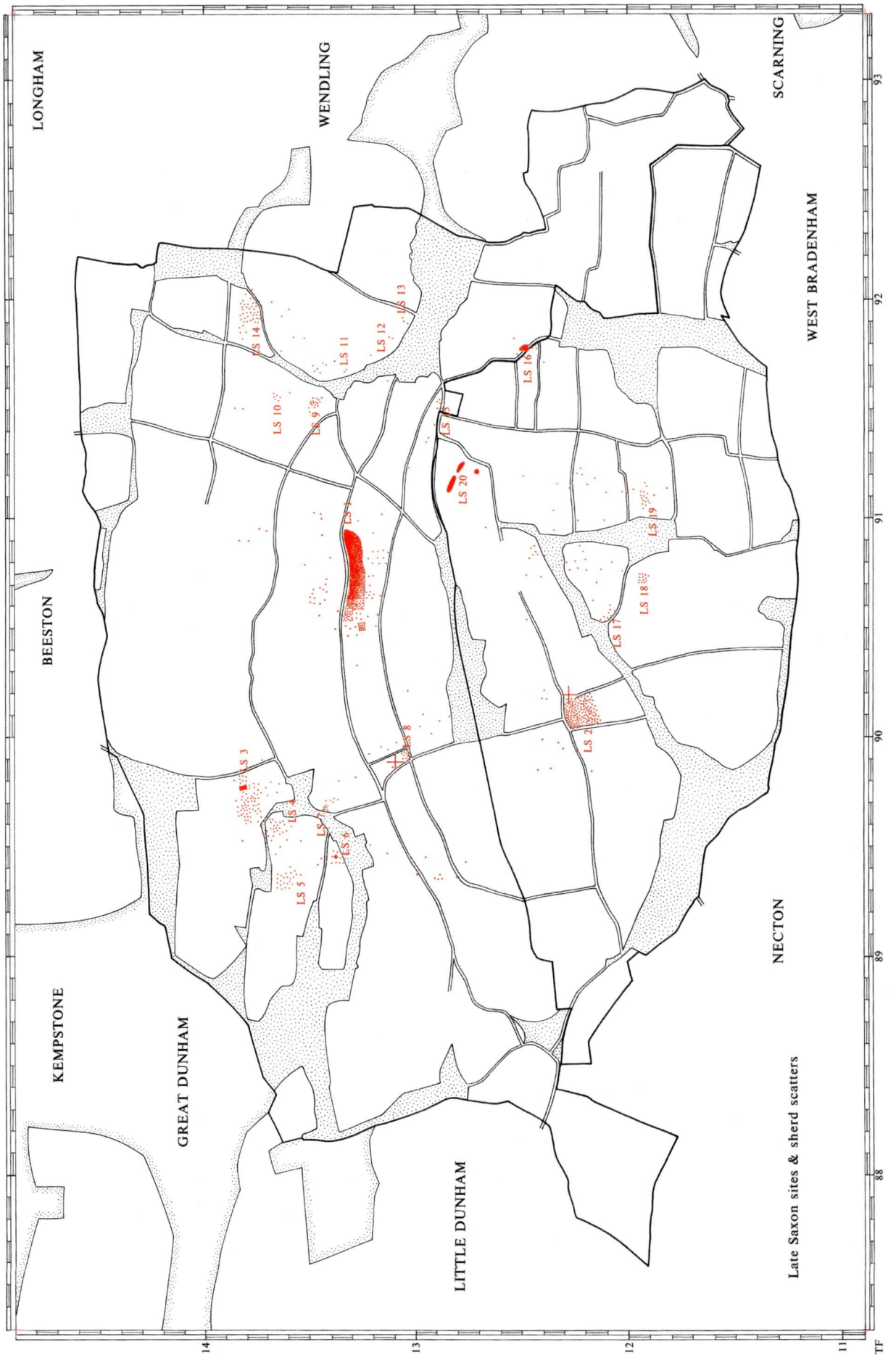

Figure 5.1 Late Saxon and early Norman sites and sherd scatters, areas of medieval common pastures shown stippled, scale 1:25,000

Chapter 5. The Late Saxon and Early Norman Period

Introduction

The period covered by this chapter begins at a point, in the middle or later ninth century, when evidence for settlement and agriculture is still entirely in the form of pottery concentrations and scatters, and it ends with the written evidence of the Domesday Book. The imprecision of pottery dating continues to enforce an unavoidable vagueness on the chronology, although towards the end of the three centuries under review the ceramic evidence becomes sufficiently understood to enable a 'late', *i.e.* eleventh-century, phase to be distinguished.

For the first time since the Roman period there are signs of extensive activity over several parts of the study area. The almost complete concentration of archaeological evidence within Great Fransham parish, so marked a feature of the Early and Middle Saxon periods, comes to an end with the introduction of Thetford-type pottery, although finds in Little Fransham remain comparatively sparse. As will be seen, there were now two major centres of settlement, one on the site of its Middle Saxon antecedent in Great Fransham, the other on a possibly virgin site in Little Fransham. It is suggested that these two were the main settlements associated with the lands of the two tenants-in-chief who held three estates in Fransham at Domesday. One innovation was the pottery industry, which was established on one site in each parish. In addition, a number of small common-edge or near common-edge settlements, mostly single farmsteads, appeared in the course of the eleventh century. These were to mark the end of nucleation and the beginning of what by the twelfth century was a fully fledged pattern of dispersed settlement, a reverse of the process of settlement nucleation now so familiar in the Midland counties (Taylor 1983, 125–30).

To accompany this evidence for more extensive settlement, there are also increased signs of arable farming, in the form of poorly defined and thin scatters of potsherds. This increase, however, is not as great as might have been expected, considering the much more prolific incidence of Thetford-type sherds on settlement sites, compared with that of Ipswich ware. Nevertheless, these scatters suggest that at least by the end of the period an area considerably greater than that of Middle Saxon times had fallen under the plough.

The local background to the Late Saxon period

It would not be appropriate to attempt anything more than the briefest of summaries of the archaeological evidence for this period recorded in the surrounding parishes. This is because the body of such evidence is not only far from large but is also palpably incomplete when set against the record of Domesday. As with other periods the widely differing amounts of fieldwork, both fieldwalking and metal-detecting, explain the great variations in recorded data.

A substantial area of settlement, evidenced by pottery concentrations and metalwork, overlies a Middle Saxon predecessor in the former parish of West Bradenham (HER 30422, 30636 and 30984). Two coins and six metal objects have been recorded in five other locations (HER 30771, 31039, 31689, 32258, 32259 and 45395). East Bradenham has produced two potsherds and a tenth or eleventh-century key (HER 31717, 31781 and 32784).

Nine potsherds have been found on the site of the largely deserted subsidiary settlement of Sparham in Necton parish (HER 4186 and 60952). Three others were picked up in the churchyard (HER 4642) and one more elsewhere (HER 8698). Two pieces of metalwork were recorded close to the present-day village (HER 59689).

Systematic field survey in Little Dunham identified a pottery concentration with five metal objects (HER 30236 and 30272), again an expansion of its Middle Saxon precursor. Seven further sites yielding about forty potsherds, four pieces of metalwork and coin of Cnut suggest that there was more than one focus of settlement in the parish (HER 4197, 11351, 16093, 30277, 30403, 30992 and 52586).

Metal-detecting in Great Dunham has revealed a large settlement, with profuse metalwork and a great deal of pottery (HER 45401, 45424, 49128 and 52585). The area of finds is large and controlled fieldwork might identify discrete foci within it. Four metal objects have been found in and around the site of a Romano-British building (HER 4188). One potsherd has been picked up in the churchyard (HER 4178), and twelve others some way from the main finds area (HER 31201 and 51235). Single metal objects have been recorded on two sites (HER 4194 and 21441).

St Paul's, the parish church of Kempstone (HER 4092), contains late eleventh-century fabric (Batcock 1991, 97–101). Occupation on the south side of the churchyard had extended to a length of 250m by the end of the eleventh century (Wade-Martins 1980b, 30–1; HER 4083 and 61359). A single brooch has been reported from further to the north (HER 61360).

Despite extensive metal-detecting a Late Saxon settlement site has not yet been identified in Beeston with Bittering parish. Ten potsherds and fourteen metal objects have been reported from eleven locations (HER 4084, 4085, 4093, 7255, 16576, 19547, 24180, 44099, 52788, 60364 and 60889). All lie in Beeston rather than in the former parish of Little Bittering.

At Longham the Middle Saxon site located to the south-east of St Andrew's churchyard continued into this period, expanding to an area of more than 3 hectares (Wade-Martins 1980b, 37 and fig. 15; HER 7269). Elsewhere in the parish two objects have been recorded: a stirrup-strap mount (HER 60411), and a harness mount found during an archaeological survey (HER 13025).

Gressenhall, which has seen some fieldwalking, in one case systematic, but very little recorded metal-detecting, has produced twenty potsherds from seven sites (HER 2820, 7292, 12588, 29239, 29240, 29241 and 29246).

In Scarning parish ten potsherds were found during one episode of metal-detecting in a field that also produced Middle Saxon pottery (HER 53764). In addition, eight single finds of metalwork have been recorded (HER 30530, 31081, 34148, 35972, 36096, 49129, 50242 and 51678) along with two coins (HER 53143 and 61454).

Wendling has so far failed to produce a convincing area of Late Saxon settlement. Seventeen potsherds, nine pieces of metalwork and a coin of Edward the Confessor have been found in eight locations (HER 28462, 28463, 30215, 34189, 35105, 40868, 42701 and 56937).

Before leaving the archaeological evidence from the periphery of the survey area, mention must be made of a standing building, Great Dunham St Andrew's (HER 4178). This fine parish church, the surviving one of two in this parish, St Mary's (HER 4200) having been abandoned by the sixteenth century, is in Saxo-Norman style, with an axial tower and formerly an apsidal chancel. The building on its own is indicative of major investment in the area during the eleventh century. It was considered Anglo-Saxon by Clapham (1930, 113–4) and Fisher (1962, 327–9), while it fell into Taylor and Taylor's Period C3, the second half of the eleventh century (1965, 217–21). Fernie (1983, 149 and 178) placed the church in his 'overlap' period which runs from the second quarter of the eleventh to the early twelfth century. Heslop (2014) judged it 'the most sophisticated building extant in west Norfolk from the two decades following the Norman Conquest.'

The archaeological evidence from Fransham
(Fig. 5.1)

Because the earliest Late Saxon archaeology antedates the Norman Conquest by more than two centuries the physical evidence recorded in the study area will be considered before attention is paid to the information given in the Domesday Book on both Fransham and the surrounding parishes.

The archaeological evidence recovered in this survey is almost overwhelmingly ceramic, and all conclusions on the dating of sites are thus completely founded on the dating of the pottery. Therefore, a brief summary of the present state of knowledge follows.

Thetford-type ware, a mass-produced, hard, wheel-thrown sandy fabric retains the broad date-range of 850–1150 (Hurst 1976, 314–20). In view of the fact that here we are dealing not with complete pots or substantial fragments but with mostly small and abraded sherds, a few words of qualification are necessary. Although the rim shapes of the most common form, the jar or cooking pot, are very readily identifiable, sherds from the rest of vessels, even when in the most 'standard' grey reduced fabric, are not easily distinguishable from non-micaceous Roman grey wares. It can be assumed, therefore, that a few sherds have either been misidentified as Roman (and vice-versa) or have been condemned as undatable. Additionally, either late in the production of Thetford-type ware, or amongst some products of rural kilns, or most likely in both cases, a proportion of fabrics failed to be reduced consistently to a grey colour. Such fabrics, when abraded body sherds alone are present, may have been confused with partly oxidised early medieval wares. This problem has probably been kept to a minimum in the analysis of the finds, because Thetford-type cooking pots were invariably wheel-thrown and early medieval wares largely handmade. For the eleventh century the confusion is of less importance anyway, for early medieval wares had appeared by c.1000 (Hurst 1976, 342–3), at a time when later Thetford-type fabrics had probably come into production.

Very little has been published on later Thetford-type wares, but the subject has been covered in discussions on the ceramics of Thetford itself (Rogerson and Dallas 1984, 125–7; Dallas 1993, 124–7; McCarthy and Brooks 1988, 161). A small proportion of the late Thetford-type sherds recovered in this survey have been fired in atmospheres fluctuating between reduction and oxidisation which have resulted in a distinctly 'sandwiched' appearance in fracture. This phenomenon is not met in thin-walled early medieval wares. Some such 'sandwiched' fabrics have been regarded not as Thetford-type ware, but as part of the early medieval tradition, and given the title Early Medieval Sandwich ware and an eleventh to early twelfth-century date-range (Jennings 1981, 23–5). There remains no absolute date for the production of later Thetford-type pottery. Wade placed a rural kiln at Langhale in east Norfolk, which produced such oxidised and 'sandwich' fabrics, sometime in the eleventh century (Wade 1976, 114). The Norwich industry, on the other hand, which turned out a quite consistently reduced range of Thetford-type pottery, is considered to have persevered into the early twelfth century (Atkin et al. 1983, 91). An impossibly late date of 1210–80 based on a Carbon-14 sample obtained from one kiln is best discounted. A reliable chronology for Thetford-type production in Norwich has yet to be established. Very large-scale excavations within Norwich castle have suggested that Thetford-type ware, not all certainly produced within the city, remained in use until the early years of the twelfth century (Goffin, R. in Shepherd Popescu 2009, 156–8 and 336–40).

St Neots-type ware, a shell tempered wheel-thrown fabric with the same date-range as Thetford-type ware (Hurst 1976, 320–3; McCarthy and Brooks 1988, 176), was produced in the East Midlands and imported into west and south-west Norfolk. It is particularly common in Thetford (Rogerson and Dallas 1984, 123; Dallas 1993, 125), but hardly penetrated into the centre of the county. At North Elmham, for example, St Neots-type ware accounted for a mere 1% of the total pottery from Period II (the late ninth and tenth centuries) and was thereafter even scarcer (Wade 1980, 444). In Fransham this material was similarly rare, with a mere five sherds being recovered.

The ceramic products of Stamford, Lincolnshire, form the third class of pottery that occurs in Late Saxon and Early Norman contexts in Norfolk (Kilmurry 1980). It is never common in the county except at Thetford (Rogerson and Dallas 1984, 124–5), and only three sherds from Fransham have been identified.

The potential for confusion in identifications between some Thetford-type sherds and those in Early Medieval ware, the fourth pottery type to be expected, has been noted above. It is a rather loosely defined class, predominantly handmade, well but variably fired in bonfires or clamps rather than in semi-permanent kilns and produced in a very narrow range of forms. Hurst (1963, 155–7; 1976, 342–3) saw it as deriving from earlier Saxon local handmade wares, and he considered that it had developed by *c*.1000. Early Medieval ware should thus be expected on pre-Conquest settlement sites. Apart from its obscure origins, this ware also presents problems of definition when its later history is considered, for during the course of the twelfth century it merged very gently and without any marked phasing into that most common pottery type of all, unglazed medieval sandy ware.

Appended to entries in the following descriptive list of Late Saxon sites are such details as are appropriate concerning what is known of later land tenures and land-use as well as summaries of the sites' locations within the late medieval topography of the parish. Documentary references are not cited because they will appear within more detailed discussions in subsequent chapters.

Gazetteer of Late Saxon and Early Norman sites
(Fig. 5.1)

LS 1 Great Fransham, TF 9075 1330 (HER 20651 and 20653)

The single concentration of Middle Saxon finds located in the survey (MS 1) continued to be occupied into and throughout the Late Saxon period. It lay towards the eastern end of the central interfluve *c*.700m from the parish church and *c*.350m from the nearest area known to have been used as common pasture in later medieval times. In contrast to its apparent continuity from the Middle Saxon period, site LS 1 was not occupied after the eleventh century.

No St Neots or Stamford ware pottery was recovered, with Thetford-type wares comprising the only Late Saxon pottery type to be identified. While the bulk of this material would sit quite happily in the tenth century, the assemblage does include an appreciable proportion of later types in non-standard partly oxidised fabrics, while small quantities of Early Medieval ware, including 'ginger jars' (a distinctive form common in this ware, Jennings 1981, 22 and fig. 8) indicate that activity continued well into the eleventh century. A precise date for the abandonment of this site (or of any other site of this period) cannot be suggested with any confidence. However, the presence of only small quantities of Grimston-Thetford ware (Clarke 1970; Little 1994, 90–1), no more than might have been expected from post-abandonment manuring of arable, suggests that the end probably came in *c*.1100. This ware was in production before *c*.1085 but was not common at Castle Acre Castle, which lies *c*.7km west-north-west of Fransham, until the early twelfth century (Milligan 1982, 224).

Thetford-type ware was recovered in prolific quantities over an area of *c*.1.5 hectares, measuring *c*.300m east-to-west and *c*.50m north-to-south along the southern edge of a road, the medieval *Whiteway*, but its extent on the north side of the road was not traceable because of the presence of a plantation and a former railway line. In any event, the area available for examination, was also marked by slightly darker soil, and was appreciably larger than MS 1. It seems reasonable to assume that this increase in the size of the pottery concentration truly reflects an enlarged settlement containing more people, rather than merely the use of a more freely available and more easily broken pottery type discarded over a wider zone.

The two fields (numbered on Fig. 4.8) were examined on several occasions. As a result, the precise and total number of sherds recovered is of no great significance. When the north-eastern quarter of the western field (G225) was walked under very dry conditions in 25m x 25m squares, only 107 Thetford-type sherds were found, while the total number collected from this field on all visits reaches *c*.700, and from the eastern field (G228) *c*.400. Within the area of the concentration no significant variation in the quantity of sherds recovered was apparent. If they had existed, such fluctuations might have suggested either the distribution of middens or the divisions between properties. They were not detectable, however, probably because of the collection methods employed. On the other hand, the impression gained was of a fairly continuous spread of sherds, which may indicate a closely packed band of house-sites quite unlike the normally looser disposition of later common-edge settlements.

The boundaries of this site were very clearly marked by a fall-off in the frequency of sherds to the east, west and south, so definite that outlying areas carrying slight sherd scatters, which might be interpreted as arable lands, were not especially apparent and very restricted in extent. Westwards along the central interfluve on light to medium soils there was a surprising absence of Thetford-type pottery, although this area had produced a small amount of Ipswich ware. To the east and downhill towards a stream only the odd sherd was recovered on rather heavier soils. To the south a scatter of material stopped on the line of another medieval road, *Southgateway* or *Greneway*, beyond which on a south facing slope of heavy soil no Late Saxon pottery was found. To the north of the railway line a sprinkling of finds occurred over a north facing slope.

This settlement is large enough to be considered as a small nucleation, a village. How then did the land on which it had stood, until a period of fairly rapid abandonment in the years around *c*.1100, fit in with what is known of the medieval landscape? It might be expected that the site of the vanished core of pre-Conquest Fransham would have continued to bear some distinguishing characteristics in terms of location, tenure or nomenclature. Its spatial relationship with the complex of common pastures which were to become the dominant influence on settlement patterns is difficult to interpret, the nearest such being *c*.350m to the south, 400m to the north and 600m to the east, while the parish church of All Saints lies *c*.700m to the west. Valley bottoms to the north and south-east contained the two main complexes of primarily demesne meadows in the late medieval period, *Ellinghams* and *St Katherine's*, and the site itself (or the southern part of it) lay between two east-to-west medieval roads. By *c*.1430 most of this long piece of land, called *Middlefurlong*, was open field, but the area containing this site was largely taken up with a 12-acre close of Great Fransham manor demesne land called *Ladyesmerelond*, the only large close of demesne in the eastern part of *Middlefurlong*. Although its size might possibly have been the result of relatively recent engrossment in the early fifteenth century, it is tempting to see it as a reflection of the substantial 'hole' resulting from the desertion of LS 1.

LS 2 Little Fransham, TF 9012 1222 (HER 23084 and 23085)

This site lies immediately west of the St Mary's parish churchyard, Little Fransham, on level ground and medium soil at 75m OD. The northern edge of an area of common pasture ran within *c*.180m of the recorded southern edge of the site. A 1.95 hectare grass field, formerly two fields, was ploughed up and planted with maize in 1986. This afforded only one short growing season in which fieldwalking could be carried out, before the area was returned to grass (although it had been regularly cultivated in modern times until *c*.1970). Soil and moisture conditions were not particularly good.

One examination produced seventy-four Thetford-type sherds from the former northern field and sixty-two from the southern, with a further thirty-three pieces being found at the west end of the latter on a subsequent visit. The pottery was predominantly standard Thetford-type ware with a small amount of later partly oxidised fabrics. In the circumstances it was not possible to isolate areas of concentrations with any confidence, although fewer sherds were picked up in the north-west and south-east corners. This might suggest two possible concentrations, one to the south-west fronting to the west on a road called *Huberdslane* in the Middle Ages and the other fronting north on another medieval road, the *Packway* or *Church way*. These two routes meet to form a staggered crossroads at the north-west boundary of the site.

The true extent of this site cannot be established because it is partly surrounded by land unavailable for fieldwalking. Fields to the north of the church (the late medieval *Churchfield*) and to the north-west of the site (the late medieval *Bullefield*) have been examined, and in neither was any evidence recovered beyond a very fine scatter of Thetford-type sherds. In addition, no such material was recovered from foundation trenches for a new house and from well weathered spoil heaps immediately north of the site at TF 9011 1232 in the south-west corner of *Churchfield* (HER 24781). Although two Thetford-type sherds were picked up from a flower bed near the western edge of the churchyard (HER 7297), no Late Saxon pottery was found in a field lying to the south-east of this site and to the south of the churchyard at centre TF 9022 1213 (HER 30221). An area of almost 1 hectare fronting on *Huberslane* directly to the south of the site yielded convincing negative evidence for Late Saxon settlement during development works, with only one Thetford-type sherd being recovered (HER 41668). To sum up, this site may possibly extend outside the area examined towards the west, and possibly to the east in the area of the churchyard.

It is very likely that LS 2 formed part, at least, of a pre-Conquest nucleated settlement which began in the late ninth or tenth century as a smaller partner to site LS 1 lying 1.2km to the north-east. It was to become the mother of the many later common-edge settlements that would grow up in what was later known as Little Fransham. Unlike site LS 1, it had no certain Middle Saxon predecessor, and lay immediately adjacent to the site of the medieval parish church as well as in close proximity to an area of common pasture. Like LS 1, it ceased to be occupied as a settlement in *c*. 1100.

It only remains to note the earliest known status of the land containing this site. In the oldest surviving Little Fransham glebe terrier, of 1613), a piece of glebe named *Steeplend Close* was said to contain 4 acres and to butt north on a common footpath leading to *Hall Close*, the *Packway* or *Church Way* mentioned above. Site LS 2, or at least that part of it which has been recorded, was therefore situated entirely on what was to become glebe land.

LS 3 Great Fransham, TF 8978 1383 (HER 20793)

A concentration of Thetford-type sherds, which includes a large proportion of late fabrics, covers *c*.0.3 hectares on a gentle south facing slope on medium soil at 70m OD in the north central part of Great Fransham. More than forty sherds were accompanied by a few of Early Medieval ware, and, unusually, one piece of St Neots ware. Occupation here may have begun in the ?later tenth century and had finished not long after 1100 so the site is also listed as a medieval settlement (Med 20).

Although the concentration is well defined, a fairly dense scatter of similar material was recovered to the south and east in the same field, and west into two other fields (HER 20794 and 20802). There remains the possibility that the scatters to the west represent separate sites, but the re-walking of all these fields bears out the strong definition of this one area. The very marked northern boundary of both this site and the outer scatter was also re-examined, after it was realised that it was coincident over most of its length with a recently removed field boundary, and therefore might have been the result of unequal collecting. This re-examination, however, merely confirmed the previously noted sudden decrease in the number sherds. The north boundary was not ancient (it was absent from the 1805 Enclosure map), but it was roughly coincident with a soil change, with much heavier land to the north.

The site lies 70m west of an unnamed medieval road, *c*.300m north of an easterly flowing stream and 180m north-east of a small tributary which forms the boundary of a common pasture (*West End Moor*). The location falls within *Hallecroft*, a 20-acre close of Great Fransham manor demesne, first recorded in 1330.

LS 4 Great Fransham, TF 8965 1364 (HER 35264)

A spread of about thirty Thetford-type sherds, almost all of which were recovered in the south-east part of a field (HER 20624), does not point to a Late Saxon occupation site in the area examined, because insufficient material was recovered in optimum conditions. Rather the distribution seems to suggest a source immediately outside the field to the east adjacent to where a cottage stands at 68m OD on a gentle southern facing slope and on probably medium soil. The cottage lies close to the site of a customary holding of Great Fransham manor, the tenement Wymers, later Sewles, and the spread of Thetford-type ware lies within the area of *Sewlesclose* which was associated with the tenement. The site, also listed as Med 19, butted south on *West End Moor* and north-east on a road which followed a small stream and led north-west to another common, *Brownesgrene*.

The Thetford-type pottery was almost exclusively of late, eleventh-century, type and was intermingled with much medieval and later material.

LS 5 Great Fransham, TF 8935 1363 (HER 20623)

This rather diffuse site is represented by about thirty Thetford-type sherds recovered from an area of 0.3 hectares on medium soil at 72m OD, which also contained a concentration of medieval material (Med 15A). No evidence was found for an outer pottery scatter indicating associated arable. Immediately north of the site was a common pasture, *Brownesgrene*. The tenurial history of this site is unknown, and the medieval topography to the south and west is obscure. However, archaeological evidence indicates medieval arable land in both directions, with the western boundary being marked by a pronounced headland.

The Thetford-type pottery was all in late, partly-oxidised fabrics. Early Medieval ware occurred in considerable quantities, and some Grimston-Thetford ware was present. A tentative starting date for occupation might be the mid-eleventh century. The medieval pottery suggests that occupation continued into the thirteenth century.

LS 6 Great Fransham, TF 8946 1338 (HER 20613)
In common with LS 5, this site has produced rather sparse evidence for an eleventh-century beginning to an occupation which continued into the medieval period. Only twenty late Thetford-type sherds, one of St Neots ware and much Early Medieval ware were recovered from a dense medieval concentration (Med 22) on a south-facing slope and medium-heavy soil at 69m OD. It is the only site with eleventh-century origins to sit on the northern edge of this (unnamed) area of common pasture. There is no associated outer spread of sherds, probably because pasture fields to the east and west were not available for fieldwalking. The tenurial history of the area is unknown.

LS 7 Great Fransham, TF 8968 1343 (HER 25553)
Seven Thetford-type sherds, including standard grey reduced pieces, and one of St Neots ware, amongst much later material, were found within the curtilage of a dwelling house, Church Farm (also Med 21). A small area, formerly scrub-covered and comprising 0.06 hectares, was cultivated before being immediately seeded with grass. One opportunity for examination was possible, and that under very poor soil conditions. One Thetford-type sherd was found by the owner on the edge of the same area while digging a post-hole and three more were recovered from a minute vegetable patch nearby. A stream, marking a former common edge, runs immediately to the west of the site, while the edge of *West End Moor*, also a former common, was until recently marked by a substantial (3m wide) ditch along the site's northern boundary. A few Thetford-type sherds have been recovered from the field to the east (HER 20604).

LS 8 Great Fransham, TF 8992 1306 (HER 4193)
Lying almost on the crest of the central interfluve on light-medium soil at 73m OD, this site sits near the top of a south facing slope and immediately south of All Saints' churchyard. At least fifteen Thetford-type sherds, predominantly in late fabrics, were intermingled with much medieval material indicating occupation into the thirteenth century (Med 30). A scatter of Late Saxon sherds occurred over fields to the east of the churchyard and to the south of the site, but none was found to the west, beyond a north-to-south road of medieval origin (one piece of Thetford-type ware was recovered from a molehill near the north-east corner of the churchyard). A fragment of a penny of Aethelred II was recovered by metal-detecting in the eastern part. The site lay on land that was glebe in 1613.

LS 9 Great Fransham, TF 9153 1349 (HER 20752)
About twenty-five predominantly late Thetford-type sherds were found in an area of *c.*0.09 hectares on medium-heavy soil close to the base of a south facing slope at 56–7m OD. The site lies just north of land which was meadow in the medieval period. The western edge of former common pasture (medieval *Eastendmoor*) runs more than 100m to the east. A concentration of medieval pottery (Med 53, a Great Fransham manor freehold), located immediately to the west, may have been the immediate successor of this site. Only one or two odd Late Saxon sherds close to the north of the site may possibly indicate arable land, although a weak concentration was recorded in the north-west corner of the former field G272 (see LS 10 below).

LS 10 Great Fransham, TF 9156 1367 (HER 20752)
It is somewhat doubtful whether this should be elevated to the status of a 'site', for the evidence consists of only six sherds of late Thetford-type ware. These were collected on one occasion from an area of *c.*0.06 hectares on a south facing slope. It lay just to the south-east of a backfilled pit on medium soil adjacent to heavy patches, at 61m OD. If this very small assemblage of sherds indicates occupation on this spot, then it must have been short-lived. On the other hand, it may simply have been the result of dumping from LS 9 lying 200m to the south. It is uncertain what parcel of land occupied this spot in the Middle Ages.

LS 11 Great Fransham, TF 9167 1337 (HER 21624)
Occupation in the eleventh century (or perhaps the tenth) is inferred from scattered sherds of predominantly late Thetford-type ware to the north, east and south of a recently demolished house (Home Farm) and its curtilage. Six sherds were found on arable land to the north of the farm (HER 21625), one in the now arable eastern end of the curtilage (HER 21624) and two to the south in the garden of a bungalow which overlies earthworks of a house platform and ditched enclosure (Med 113; Fig. 7.16). All the find-spots lie on the eastern side of a common pasture, *Eastendmoor*, and near the west end of an open field (*Kaulynges* or *Harwyns field* in the fifteenth century). Customary and free messuages held of several manors lay on and to the south of the site of Home Farm in the Middle Ages.

LS 12 Great Fransham, TF 9182 1312 (HER 20745)
Five late Thetford-type sherds picked up within a concentration of medieval material (Med 54, a Great Fransham manor freehold) suggest that this site may perhaps have had late eleventh-century origins. It lies on medium soil at 55m OD near the base of a south-west facing slope on the edge of a common pasture, *Eastendmoor*.

LS 13 Great Fransham, TF 9192 1305 (HER 20745)
This site, like LS 12, is represented by a small handful of late Thetford-type sherds (four) found within a concentration of medieval material (Med 55, a Great Fransham manor freehold). It stands at 55m OD on medium soil, and in a common-edge location. Occupation may have begun here in the late eleventh century.

LS 14 Great Fransham, TF 9192 1375 (HER 21627)
When first examined this site appeared as a fine spread of about forty sherds of reduced Thetford-type ware covering *c.*1 hectare on medium-heavy soil. A subsequent visit involving more closely spaced walking recovered more than two hundred additional sherds and indicated that most were concentrated in an area of *c.*0.5 hectares. Many pieces were clearly overfired, not as 'classic' distorted wasters, but relatively hard and brittle. There were many instances of colour changes, caused by differential firing, which crossed over fractures from one surface of a sherd to the other. Very few pieces were underfired or oxidised. It is certain that this material is debris from pottery production, although no evidence of kiln structures, in the form of fired clay, was recovered. This is not surprising, given that Thetford-type ware was fired in kilns which were constructed largely below the ground surface (Hurst 1976, 345), and that the relative thinness of the spread of sherds suggests only a limited period of production. All identifiable rims were from jars, and the form of a small number of these, with a slightly flaring profile and no internal hollow, was reminiscent of Early Medieval ware. However, it was noteworthy that amongst apparently normally fired pieces there were no 'sandwich fired' or partly oxidised fabrics. Perhaps production took place late in the tenth or early in the eleventh century. A very thin sprinkling of similarly fired sherds was encountered to the south-east, with the furthest being picked up *c.*400m from the centre. This site was located just to the north of the mid-point of a road which, on the Enclosure Award map, ran between the north-east corner of *Fendersmoor* common and the south-east corner of another common (the medieval *Hey Green*). In 1548 the site lay at the eastern end of a 4¼-acre close of customary land held of the manor of Rougholme (see Med 47).

LS 15 Great Fransham, TF 9160 1288 (HER 20639)
Seven late Thetford-type sherds were found amongst Roman, Early Saxon and medieval material in the south-east corner of a field on medium soil at 60m OD (see Med 108, a customary tenement of Great Fransham manor). This small group suggests that an eleventh-century settlement site may lie further to the east under a pair of cottages, farm house and buildings. A few more sherds were recovered further to the west.

LS 16 Great and Little Fransham, TF 9178 1248 (HER 20629 and 20822)
Eight Thetford-type sherds were found on medium soil at 62m OD on a slight south-east facing slope. Pottery indicating occupation into the later twelfth century (Med 60) was spread over an area of *c.*0.1 hectares directly east of the boundary between Great and Little Fransham, which at this point has left no visible sign on the ground. A subsequent visit produced a further twenty sherds. Others were found immediately to the west of the parish boundary, and the odd piece occurred just to the north of the site and as far as 80m to the south-west.

The site is *c.*150m north of the northern edge of *Eastendmoor*, a common pasture entirely within Little Fransham parish. It lies just outside the east end of close called the *Lound,* freehold of the manor of Wilcoks. A freehold messuage of uncertain manorial allegiance (Med 116), is the nearest dwelling, at the north-west corner of *Eastendmoor.* On the Enclosure map the disposition of fields to the north and east of this messuage hint that the northern edge of this common may perhaps have once been further north. If so, this would place the free messuage on the west side of the common and this site at its north-west corner. Perhaps then the site was the predecessor of the free messuage that was established after a major encroachment of the common in the later twelfth century.

LS 17 Little Fransham, TF 9056 1211 (HER 29217)
Fewer than twenty sherds of late Thetford-type ware were included amongst more plentiful Grimston-Thetford and Early Medieval ware sherds on a site which appears to have been abandoned by the end of the twelfth century (Med 102). It is situated within what was to be a demesne close of Kirkhams and Wilcoks manor, on fairly level ground and medium soil with light patches at 70m OD. A thin scatter of similar sherds was found to the north-east and east. A pair of Late Saxon tweezers was recovered during metal-detecting.

LS 18 Little Fransham, TF 9073 1195 (HER 25568)
This site is evidenced by twenty sherds of late Thetford-type ware from an area of *c.*0.25 hectares within a scatter of later material, at 70m OD. The soil is medium, becoming heavier to the east, and the ground almost level. Edges to this slight concentration were clearly discernible in all directions except to the north where there is a house and farm buildings on the site of a customary messuage and 2-acre croft of Cannons Manor (Med 75). No outer aura of sherds suggesting arable land was recorded, apart from a thin spread some distance to the north (see LS 17). The western edge of a common pasture (*Canones Moor* in 1483) lay 30–40m to the east.

LS 19 Little Fransham, TF 9110 1193 (HER 24767)
Fifteen late Thetford-type sherds were recovered from an area of *c.*0.3 hectares at 70m OD on medium soil and on ground which slopes gently downwards to the west. Some Grimston-Thetford and Early Medieval ware sherds were also found. A thin scatter of similar sherds extends north across *Millfield* for a distance of 400m. There was probably no continuity between occupation on this site and that on site Med 92 immediately to the west, with a break in occupation in the late twelfth and early thirteenth century. The medieval site fronted onto a road which formed the eastern edge of a common pasture (*Canones Moor*), while the gap between the Late Saxon site and the common edge was *c.*50m. This area falls within was what was to be demesne of Kirkhams and Wilcoks manor. An eleventh-century copper alloy stirrup-strap mount was recovered close by in the same field.

LS 20 Little Fransham (Fig. 5.2 and 5.3)
This substantial Thetford-type ware production site has been subdivided into three sub-sites, a–c, for the purposes of description. a) TF 9119 1272 (HER 23080), b) TF 9124 1280 and c) TF 9115 1285 (HER 23086). They are shown in simplified form on Fig. 5.3.

Sub-site a) lies on medium soil and level ground at 65m. OD. A total of 230 predominantly overfired sherds, similar in texture and coloration to those from LS 14, was found in an area of *c.*0.09 hectares. The concentration was well-defined, with the quantity of sherds falling off rapidly in all directions. Seventeen jar rims, one bowl rim and seven sherds with applied thumbed strips were

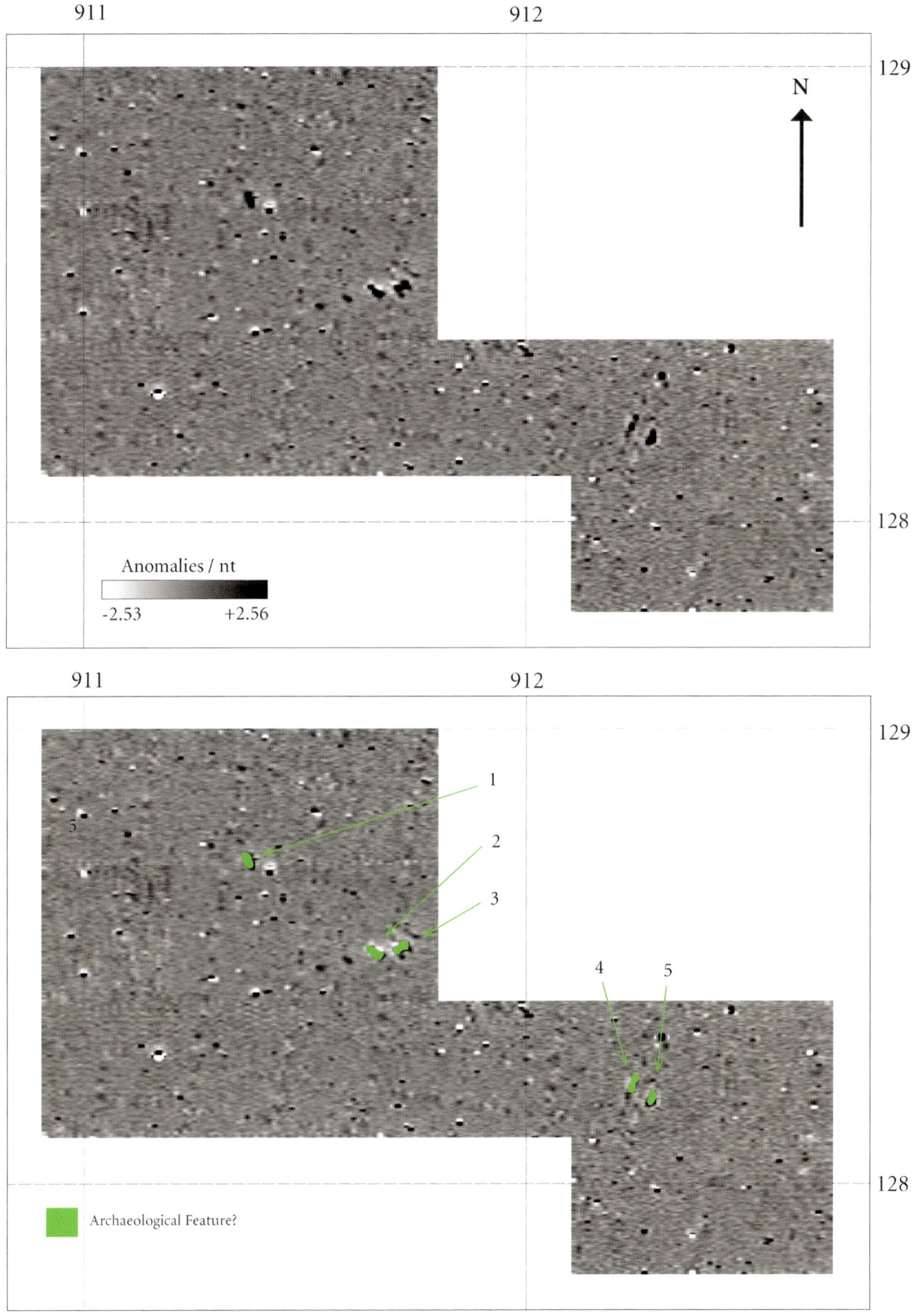

Scale 1:1250

Figure 5.2 LS 20, Fluxgate gradiometer survey results and interpretation, scale 1:1,250

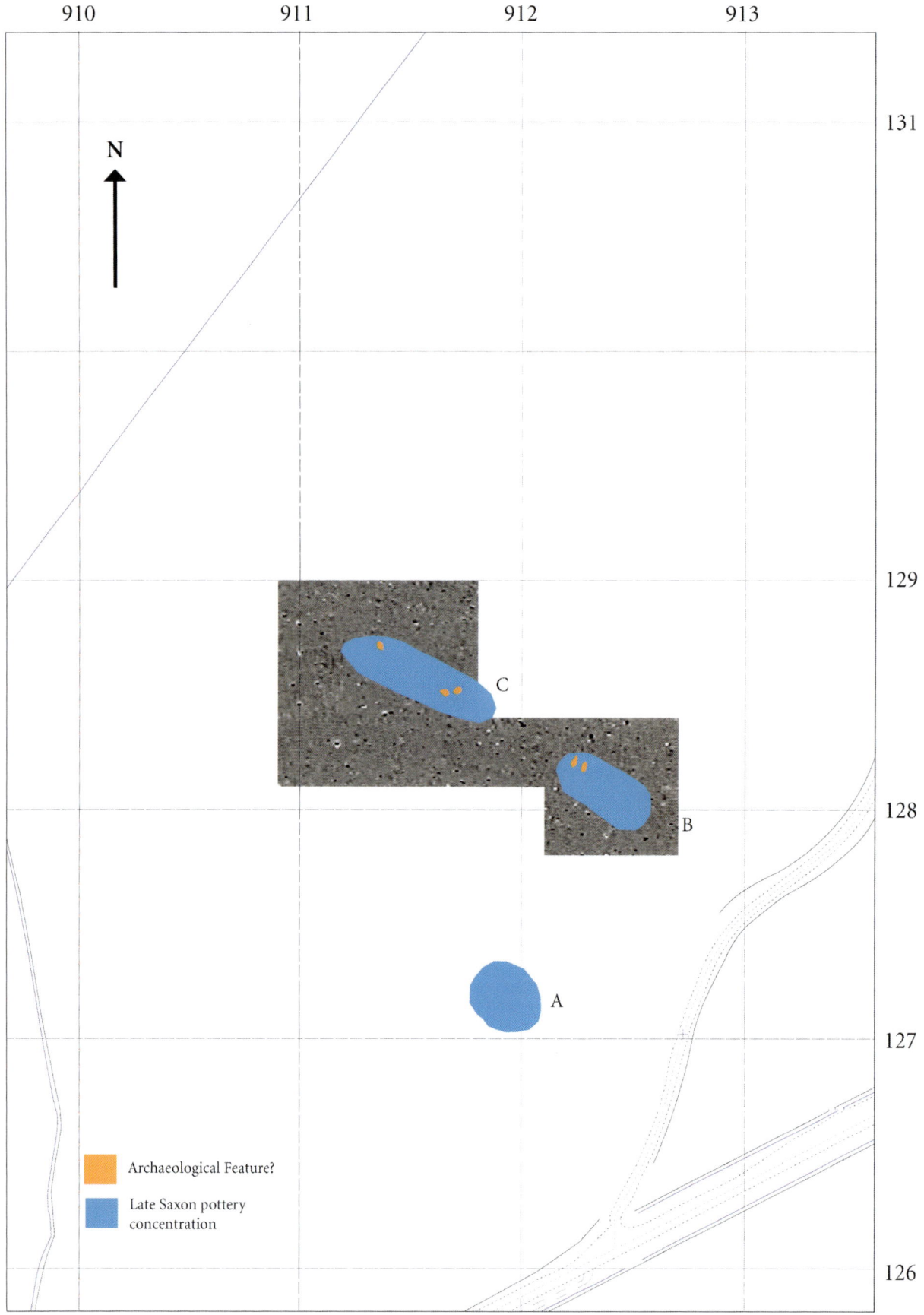

Figure 5.3 LS 20, Fluxgate Gradiometer survey and sherd concentrations in simplified outline, scale 1:2,500

amongst the material collected. Of three bases of identifiable form, two were sagging and one flat. The fabric of many sherds contained fragments of iron ore. Occasional large fragments of quartz and flint were present. Fragments of kiln structure were not found.

Sub-sites b) and c) lie on medium soil which becomes heavier to the north-east and north-west, on ground sloping down to the north-west from 64 to 61m OD. Taken together these two areas are visible as a slightly diffuse zone of darker soil. Sub-site b) was not so easily defined because it was surrounded by a less abrupt fall-off in sherd density. An inner area of profusion covered 0.12 hectares. Sub-site c) was similarly difficult to delineate, but at its most dense covered an elongated area of 0.16 hectares. Although no fragments of kiln structures were evident, several small patches of soft red burnt clay were noted in sub-site b). Between the two sub-sites a circular pit with a diameter of 13m had, to judge from its surface appearance, an ancient filling quite unlike almost all other backfilled and ploughed-over pits (it is not shown on any maps). Perhaps this may have served as a source of clay and (subsequently) water.

A Fluxgate Gradiometer survey was conducted by Michael de Bootman over the area of sub-sites b and c in April 2010. Five anomalies were detected, of which two in sub-site b and one in c displayed figure-of-eight forms suggestive of kiln combustion chambers and stokeholes (Fig. 5.2 nos 2–4). The other two (nos 1 and 5) may be kilns or related features. The report has been lodged in the HER.

The pottery from sub-sites b) and c) is similar in fabric to that from sub-site a) and will be assessed as one group. Over 2200 sherds were recovered from one examination. Of 175 rim sherds from smaller pots, 86% were from jars, the rest from bowls. Ninety-nine sherds, including rims, came from large vessels, mostly storage jars, many with thumbed strips. Amongst 104 basal sherds there was a large majority of unidentifiable form, but the proportion of sagging to flat bases was approximately 2:1. One sherd carried incised linear decoration. Of ten sherds with rectangular rouletted decoration, six were bowl rims. One cylindrical fragment was probably part of the stem of a baluster-shaped cresset lamp.

Dating is, as normal, somewhat problematic, but the density of finds shows that production was clearly carried out much more intensively and for a much longer period than that on LS 14. This period probably falls within the late tenth or early eleventh century. No significant finds of this period were made during metal-detector searches on the whole site.

All three sub-sites lay within a demesne enclosure of Kirkhams manor and called *Magna Mille Cloos* in 1429, part of which may have been called *Potters croft* at an earlier date (see pp156 and 172–3).

Summary of the archaeological evidence

Three categories of site have been recognised, nucleated settlements, small and containing one or two dwellings, and, thirdly, pottery production sites. Firstly, those large and dense enough to be considered as nucleated settlements. One lies in each of the later subdivisions of the Domesday vill (*i.e.* Great and Little Fransham). Only that in Great Fransham certainly had a Middle Saxon predecessor. These two sites were both abandoned by *c.*1100: one was to become a large close of demesne, the other a close of glebe adjacent to the parish church.

Sixteen sites fall into the second category and were, when their size could be defined by fieldwalking, small. They contained single houses, or perhaps in some cases a pair. Most do not seem to have been occupied in the tenth century. Twelve of the sixteen lay dispersed on or very close to the edges of what are known to have been common pastures by later medieval times. Of the remaining four (LS 3, 8, 10 and 16) it is likely in two examples (LS 3 and 16) that the commons have contracted leaving their edges further from the sites. With the exception of LS 8, which may possibly have been the early medieval precursor of Great Fransham rectory, the other fifteen lie within areas, often ovoid and surrounded by roads and common edges, which give the impression of having been created or 'punched' out of much larger areas of waste (Williamson 2014, 169). This process is at its most clear in Great Fransham in the cases of LS 4–7 and LS 11–13 and in Little Fransham of LS 17 and 18.

In the few instances where medieval documents point to the tenurial status of sites in the second category, they are of a roughly even mixture of free and customary tenures and demesne. This pattern of straggly, dispersed and predominantly common-edge settlement was set to become the norm in the twelfth century and later. In Fransham the start-date for this complete change in settlement pattern was unquestionably the eleventh century. This appears to have been a dramatic event which eventually resulted in the total desertion of the two nucleated settlements.

The significance of the third category, pottery production sites, is difficult to assess, for such sites are extremely rare in rural contexts. Fransham is only the fourth rural parish in Norfolk to have furnished evidence of Thetford-type ware production (McCarthy and Brooks 1988, 162 and 164; Clarke 1970; Wade 1976; Rogerson and Adams 1978). The later histories of these two industrial sites were very different. One was to fall within a large close of demesne and the other within a piece of customary land.

At the beginning of this chapter reference was made to the unexpectedly sparse scatters of Thetford-type ware which have been interpreted as evidence for the manuring of arable land. Intensive field survey in another Norfolk parish, Barton Bendish, produced a somewhat more convincing picture of the extent of cultivated land, but even there the density of pot sherds was little greater than that of the Middle Saxon and very weak in comparison with the medieval (Rogerson with Davison 1997, 21–25). It is reassuring that the Whittlewood Project in south-west Northamptonshire and north Buckinghamshire has failed to recover later ninth- to eleventh-century pottery scatters in areas away from settlement and in open fields. A thoughtful assessment of the evidence has suggested that land taken into cultivation at this time was rich in organic material, and that this, coupled with the lack of necessity to crop intensively, obviated the need to cart domestic refuse away from the immediate surroundings of settlements (Jones 2004, 164–169 and 184). A similar dearth of manure scattered material antedating the eleventh century was noted at Shapwick, Somerset, where direct manuring by animals grazing on the fallow was considered to be the chief method of soil fertilisation (Gerrard 1997, 69).

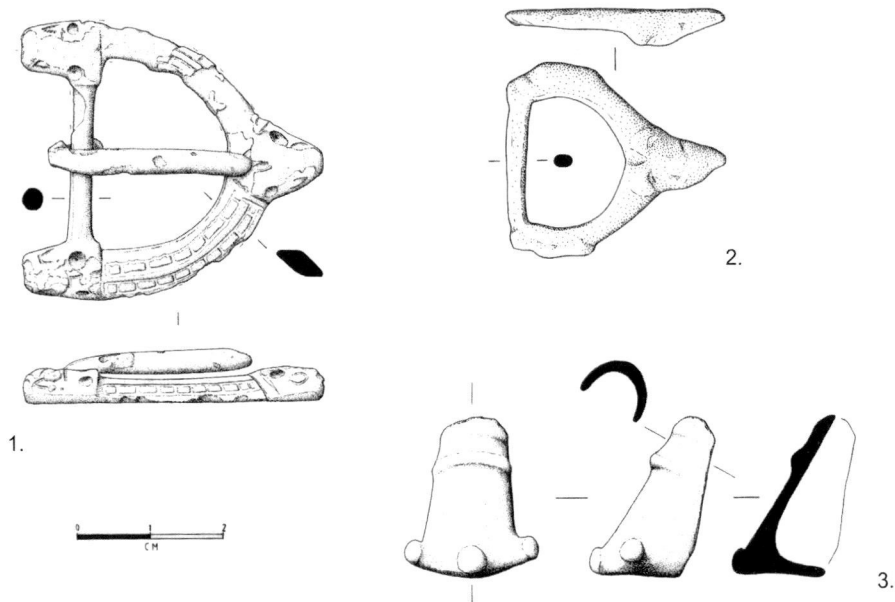

Figure 5.4 Late Saxon copper alloy buckle frames and stirrup terminal (HER 4192, 20818 and 20508), scale 1:1

Manure-spread pot sherd scatters alone cannot answer the question whether any area was once within an open field or a close. They are equally silent on whether strip cultivation or some other method of tillage was employed. In this survey some Late Saxon settlement sites were found to lie on the edge of what were open fields by the high medieval period, *e.g.* LS 11–13 and 18–19, but it cannot be demonstrated that those fields were open in the tenth and eleventh centuries. Other sites, such as LS 3–7, were in areas that were to be predominantly enclosed when first glimpsed in the documentary record. Many, but not all, settlements, lay next to or near edges of common pastures, but no other general comments on the nature of land-use in the vicinity of such sites can be made with any certainty.

Only thirteen metal objects datable to the Late Saxon period have been recorded, all found during metal-detecting, and all, bar three, in areas not defined as coeval occupation sites but in which there were thin scatters of contemporary sherds. A tenth-century buckle decorated with animal heads in the Scandinavian Borre style was found at TF 8943 1305 (HER 4192, Fig. 5.4 1). Two eleventh-century pieces, a stirrup terminal (Fig. 5.4 3) and a zoomorphic strap-end, were recovered from a field on the west side of Great Fransham parish churchyard (HER 20508), along with a penny of Aethelred II (dated 997–1003) in the adjoining field to the north (HER 20542). Four objects were located in the field on the southern and eastern sides of the churchyard (HER 4193): another penny of Aethelred II on LS 8, a ninth- or tenth-century finger-ring in the eastern part of the field, a tenth- or eleventh-century buckle fragment near the southern boundary and part of a late ninth- or tenth-century gold finger-ring close to the eastern edge of the churchyard at TF 8994 1310. The site of a medieval manor house (HER 24783, Med 5) yielded an eleventh-century stirrup terminal. In Little Fransham, apart from a pair of tweezers from LS 17, another tenth-century Borre style buckle frame was found in an area of medieval settlements (Med 9–12, HER 20818, Fig. 5.4 2). Two eleventh-century stirrup-strap mounts were recovered, one from close to another medieval site (Med 85, HER 24771), the other from the same field as LS 19 (HER 24767).

The Domesday evidence
(Table 5.1)

The Little Domesday Book is the only documentary source for Fransham during this period. There are three entries: 8.66, a holding of William de Warenne; 8.68, another of de Warenne with properties in both Rougham and Fransham; 22.11, the holding of Ralph de Tosny. The translated texts will be presented in full (numeration after Brown 1984; TRE = in 1066).

8.66
In Fraudesham 2 free men held TRE of whom Frederic's predecessor held the commendation only, later Frederic. Now W. has it, and Gilbert from him. 1½ carucates of land. Always 4 villeins and 8 bordars[i]. Then 2 slaves. 4 acres of meadow. Always 3 plough-teams. Woodland for 60 pigs. Then 1 mill, now 1 and a half. Value always 40s.

Frederic, William de Warenne's brother-in-law, was killed in 1070. Gilbert also possessed a de Warenne holding in Scarning (8.67).

8.68
In Ruhham and in Fraudesham Toki, a free man, held 2 carucates of land TRE. Always 1 villein. Then 12 bordars, now 10. Then 3 slaves, now 1. 1 acre of meadow. Always 3 demesne plough-teams. 1½ men's plough-teams. Woodland for 10 pigs. Now half a mill. 16 free men. Half a carucate of land. 8 acres of land. Always 1.5 plough-teams. Value then 50s, now 60s. This is by exchange of Lewes. All Fraudesham has 9 furlongs in length and 8 in width. 10d of geld whoever holds there. W. holds.

The reference to Lewes shows that this holding was not one that de Warenne had inherited from Frederic but was one granted to him in exchange for lands in Sussex. Toki, one of several people of this name who occur in Domesday, had been a major landholder in his own right, with manors in Norfolk, Suffolk and Cambridgeshire (Sawyer 1985, 75). His Norfolk *caput* (chief manor) at Castle Acre was to maintain its status under de Warenne (Liddiard 2000, 28–31). 'W.' might be read as William de Warenne or Wimer or Wymer, de Warenne's '*dapifer*' (steward), who held lands of de Warenne in Gressenhall, Lexham, Weasenham, Tittleshall and Castle Acre. The subsequent tenurial descent in these places shows that Wimer is the correct identification.

22.11
In Frouuesham 16 sokemen of Harold TRE. 3 carucates of land. Always 12 bordars. 6 acres of meadow. Then 3 plough-teams, now 4. Woodland for 60 pigs. Always 1 mill. In the valuation of Necton. Eudo son of Clamahoc had 1 carucate of those 3 freely while he lived. Ralph de Beaufour held the same. Now Ralph de Tosny has it in Necton where it lay TRE.

Eudo was a follower of Earl Ralph Guader who was exiled in 1075 (Carthew 1877, 65). In 1086 Ralph de Beaufour still held manors in Launditch Hundred, Swanton Morley, East Dereham and Lexham.

From these three entries it can be seen that the calculation of basic Domesday figures for the vill of Fransham is beset with problems. There is one outstanding difficulty, namely that the second de Warenne holding makes no distinction between vills under the single entry for Fransham and Rougham. *For all subsequent calculations this entry will be halved*, with the awareness that such a division is the result of pure guesswork (it should be noted that at their nearest points the two parishes now bearing the names Fransham and Rougham are 6.2km apart). This problem is further discussed below.

The holding of Ralph de Tosny, like almost all his others which had formerly been King Harold's and spread over seven Hundreds, was considered a satellite or berewick of Necton, but we can be sure that the Fransham entry is complete, with the exception of the valuation, which cannot be guessed (for an outline of de Tosny's Domesday estate centred on Necton see Davison and Cushion 2004, 456–7).

Land
There were 10½ acres of meadow, and woodland for 125 pigs. The total number of carucates, *i.e.* arable land, in the three holdings combined was 5¾ and four acres. This gives a total of 694 acres if the 120-acre carucate is used. What can be said about the linear measurements given for Fransham, 9 furlongs in length and 8 in breadth? The significance of such measurements has been said to defy analysis (Darby 1987, 114), but Mary Hesse's statistical assessment of fifteen Suffolk Hundreds has shown that they relate to the arable land of a vill, and not to its total area. (Hesse 2000). Seventy-two square furlongs are indicated by the linear measurements, and with 10 acres to 1 square furlong, the total of 720 acres exceeds only slightly the 694 acres noted above. If approximations between the Domesday acre and the statute acre, and between the sizes of the Domesday vill and the modern parish are assumed, then approximately 23% of the land area may have been arable in the eleventh century.

If the Domesday linear measurements were taken to refer to a compact, rectangular block of land, and if the modern perch of 16½ feet is assumed to be the basic unit (Hart 1992, 97–100), then the whole of Fransham (9 x 8 furlongs = 1 mile 220 yards x 1mile or 1810m x 1609m) would be too small to fit the known extent of eleventh-century settlement. However, if *c.*160 acres of meadow and pasture, known from medieval sources to have been within and on the edges of the eleventh-century area, are added, then the resultant block of just under 88 square furlongs (9.95 x 8.84 furlongs = 2189 x 1945 yards = 1945m x 1778m) encompasses a more satisfactory proportion of the settlement zone. It would be reasonable to assume that a greater proportion of the land block was not exploited as arable in the eleventh century. An area which included all the settlement zone would amount to more than 162 square furlongs (14.42 x 10.44 furlongs = 3173 x 2297 yards = 2900m x 2100m). This is almost twice the size of the above-adjusted figure and seems too large to be explained by a greater proportion of non-arable. Some of the discrepancy may be due to the post-Domesday foundation dates of some of the outlying settlements, but with so many uncertainties it would be unwise to pursue this matter further.

Plough-teams
A total of 9 demesne plough-teams had risen to 10 in 1086. Men's plough-teams (¾), as opposed to those of free men or sokemen, are recorded only under the Rougham/Fransham holding. These figures are perhaps incomplete, for it is difficult to believe, for example, that the four villeins and eight bordars on de Warenne's Fransham holding had no teams of their own. However, such an omission seems unlikely in view of the obvious value to the Domesday compilers of arable farming not only as a source of taxation, but more importantly as a means of food production (Higham 1990, 43). As an average of 2 plough-teams per carucate has been estimated for East Anglia (Darby 1987, 115), 11½ might have been expected here. Thus, an omission of 1 or 1½ men's plough-teams remains a possibility.

Population
There were 4½ villeins although none was listed under the de Tosny holding. Bordars appear in all three holdings, 26 TRE and 25 in 1086. The slave or serf population, again absent from de Tosny's lands, fell from 3½ TRE to ½ in 1086. Free men, calculated at 8, are confined to the de Warenne Rougham/Fransham entry, while the 16 sokemen were recorded only under de Tosny. It is assumed that this entry 'XVI.soc.heroldi.t.r.e.' is not implying that these men had been removed by 1086. The total recorded population amounted to 60 TRE and 56 in 1086. The latter figure would be adjusted down to 40 if Harold's 16 sokemen were excluded.

Mills
Two mills TRE had increased to 2¾ by 1086.

The Rougham/Fransham problem
The total recorded population for Fransham of 60 TRE and 56 in 1086 falls to 44 and 42 when the Rougham/Fransham totals are deducted. For Rougham

	Holder		Holding		Value		V.	B.	S.	Tenants V.
	TRE	1086	Carucates	Acres	TRE	1086		TRE		
Fransham 8.66	2 freemen	Gilbert of William de Warenne	1.5		40s	40s	4	8	2	4
Rougham & Fransham 8.68	Toki	William de Warenne	2		50	60s	1	12	3	1
	16 freemen	16 freemen	.5	8						
Fransham 22.11	16 sokemen of Harold	Ralph de Tosny	3		Valued in Necton			12		
Wendling 14.12		Richard of the Abbot of St.Edmunds	1		20s	30s				2
		1 sokeman		12				1		
Necton 22.1	Harold	Ralph de Tosny 1 church 5 sokemen		36		3s	32	11	6	32
Necton 22.18		3 sokemen		60						
Dunham 1.212	Stigand	King William 8 sokemen	4	34	Valued in Mileham	19	8 1	2	10	8 1
Dunham 22.12	1 sokeman of Harold	Ralph de Tosnt		30.5	Valued in Necton		4			4
Dunham 46.1	Payne	Reynold the priest and the daughter of Payne, of Edmund son of Payne 3 sokemen	4	43	100s	£8	12	4	4	12
Kempstone 8.65	4 sokemen of Stigand	William de Warenne	1		20s	20s	4		1	4
Longham 66.25		1 freeman of Hermer de Ferres (annexation)	.5			5s	1	1		1
Kirtling 1.214	Stigand	2 sokemen of the King		17	Valued in Mileham					
Gressenhall 8.62	Toki	Wymer of William de Warenne	2.5		40s	£4	10	18	4	10
		18 sokemen 18 sokemen of William de Warenne	1					3		
Scarning 8.62		(a berewick of Gressenhall)	.5 1		Valued in Gressenhall					
Scarning 8.67	Fredregis	William de Warenne	1.5		20s	30s	4	6		4
Scarning 31.40		Ralph Baynard		80 in Bradenham	Valued in Bradenham					
		2 sokemen		12						
Scarning 66.38		1 freeman of Ralph Baynard (annexation)		24		5s				2
Bradenham 8.93	Osmund	1 freeman of William de Warenne		30	5s	5s	3			3
Bradenham 22.2		1 sokeman of Ralph de Tosny	.5							
		8 sokemen under the above sokeman	.5							
Bradenham 31.34	Aethelgyth	Ralph Baynard 8 sokemen 1 church		15	£6	£12 15d	12	6	4	15
Bradenham 66.64		William de Warenne (annexation) 2 freemen	1.5 land for 2 oxen		10s	10s	5	2	1	5

Table 5.1 Domesday statistics: Fransham and surrounding vills

B. 1086	S.	Demesne TRE	Demesne 1086	Villein TRE	Villein 1086	Mills TRE	Mills 1086	Meadow Acres	Swine Wood	Swine TRE	Swine 1086	Sheep TRE	Sheep 1086	Cattle TRE	Cattle 1086	Cobs TRE	Cobs 1086	Goats TRE	Goats 1086	Misc.
8						1	1.5	4	60											
10	1	3	3	1.5	1.5		.5	1	10											
		1.5	1.5																	
12		3	4			1	1	6	60											
6			1		1.5	1	1	6	100		19									
1		1	.5																	
11	6	4	4	10	10	1	1	20	1000		100		105		19		4		80	1 salting
			5																	
1			1					3												
		1	1	1.5	.5			1	20	8	8	6	6	2	2					0.5 market
		1.5	1					1												
		1	1																	
13	2	1	1	5	4	1	1	14	100	4	17		100	4	9	1	2			3 beehives
		1	1																	
	1	3	2.5					1	10											
	1		.5					2	10											
		1						1												
18	1	2	2	2	2	1	2	4	100	30	30		30	10	11	1	1		30	
3		3	2			2	2	4												
5		1	1	1	1			1			20				4					
6		1	1	1	1	1	1	3	30											
			.5					2												
								2	10											
						2	10													
	1	1				4	20													
			1	1																
6		2	2	3	3			8	250	18	18	75	75	9	9	2	1	80	26	
		1.5	1.5																	
2	1		1		1			4	20											

itself, the population in the two other holdings, of the King (1.78) and Hermer de Ferrers (13.17), amounted to 31 TRE and 26 in 1086. This rises to 47 and 40 with the addition of the other half of the Rougham/Fransham total. Rougham had suffered since TRE to judge from the decline in plough-teams on the other two holdings from 7½ TRE to 2½ in 1086. Given that the Rougham/Fransham plough-team figure had increased by 1086 and with the assumption that population and agricultural setbacks are more likely to befall a complete vill than two out of three manors within a vill, then the transference of a 50% portion of the Rougham/Fransham entry to Fransham may be conservative. Indeed, it might be argued that the location of the entry, immediately preceding the measurements and geld liability of Fransham, suggests that Fransham element of this holding was the more important. On the other hand, the order at the start of the entry, 'In Ruhham and in Fraudesham', might suggest the contrary. Davison (1988, 48) saw it as 'mainly in Fransham'.

Fransham compared with surrounding vills
We have seen above that for want of consistent evidence useful comparisons cannot be made between the archaeology of Fransham and that of nearby parishes in this period. Fortunately, the Domesday compilers were thorough and have left a more workable set of data. Rather than setting Fransham against the remainder of Launditch Hundred, it seems more useful to compare it with surrounding vills, two of which, Bradenham and Necton, were in South Greenhoe. The selected vills are those surrounding Fransham and Wendling: Dunham (Great and Little, not differentiated in Domesday), Kempstone, Beeston (not listed in Domesday, presumably subsumed under Mileham), Longham, Kirtling (in Gressenhall)[ii], Gressenhall, Scarning, Bradenham (East and West, not differentiated in Domesday) and Necton.

Geld payments were closely linked to the measurements of vills in ways which are now insoluble (Darby 1987, 113–4; Hesse 2000, 21). Assessments for geld should of course be studied from a hundredal standpoint (Johnson 1906a, 5–9). Fransham appears to have been joined with Wendling and Gressenhall in a leet for the apportionment of geld payments (Johnson 1906b, 210). The subject of leets will be touched upon in Chapter 6 in a discussion of Fransham's late medieval courts leet.

With valuations 'there are all kinds of anomalies and no equation is possible.' (Darby 1971, 118), while Welldon Finn (1967, 176) considered it 'frankly impossible' to assess the accuracy of a valuation. Fransham was worth 65s (70s in 1086), although no value for the de Tosny holding was given, because it was included with that for Necton and its other dependencies. The figure for Bradenham was £6 rising to £12 in 1086 while Gressenhall was worth 40s (£4 in 1086), Dunham £5 (£8 in 1086), Wendling and Kempstone 20s, Longham 5s. The value of the Necton holding on its own was not given. However, it is clear that accurate comparisons between vills are impossible because valuations relate to holdings. As such estates cross over from vill to vill, valid ranking of vills by wealth cannot be achieved.

In terms of total population, including slaves, Fransham compares closely with Dunham (66), Necton (58), Bradenham and Gressenhall (both 53). The total in Scarning (in four entries) reaches only 20 and is surely incomplete. At the other extreme, Wendling totals 10, Kempstone 9, Longham 3 and Kirtling 2. The vills under consideration fall within an area of very low Domesday population according to an assessment by Williamson and Skipper (2005). This is a refinement on the ranking given to Launditch Hundred by Darby (1971, fig. 28), where the large vills of Mileham and North Elmham had boosted the estimate. Free men were scarce in these surrounding vills, with 3 in Bradenham, and 1 each in Scarning and Longham, while 16 are listed under the Rougham/Fransham holding. Sokemen were most numerous in Gressenhall (18), followed by Bradenham (17, including one who had two others under him). Fransham's 16 comprised the third largest group, and Dunham's the fourth with 12. Scarning's low figure of 2 sokemen (the same as that for Kirtling and half that of Kempstone) matches its overall low population figure and further suggests incompleteness. The area in question was in fact in the middle range in terms of sokemen density, and in the lowest category for free men (Skipper and Williamson 2005).

Using TRE figures, a comparison of the unfree population totals will now be made. Fransham's total of villeins, 4½, was very low in comparison with other large vills such as Bradenham (17), Dunham (31) and Necton (32). Gressenhall, on the other hand, had only 10. The latter also had a higher number of bordars (21) than Bradenham (11), Dunham (17) and Necton (12). Fransham, however, contained the most bordars (26). Scarning also had a low villein quota (4) and a relatively high number of bordars (13). Slaves were present in all the large vills, Necton and Dunham having the greatest number (6). Bradenham mustered 5, Gressenhall 4 and Fransham 3½.

Figures for carucates are particularly difficult to interpret because of incompleteness. For example, Bradenham (in three entries) is listed as containing 30 acres, 15 acres (with a church) and 2 half-carucates, but in another entry, the largest, no carucatage is cited. Necton had 36 acres associated with a church and 60 acres held by 3 sokemen, but again there is no reference to carucates. Gressenhall, broadly similar to Fransham in size of population, had 3½ carucates. Dunham, the most populous vill, had 8, along with 3 lots of acres (34, 30½ and 43). These figures should be compared with Fransham's 5¾ carucates and 4 acres.

Necton's 19 plough-teams were by far the most numerous, with 4 in demesne, 10 of the 'men' and 5 belonging to 5 sokemen. Dunham's 12 teams comprised 2 on the demesnes of 2 holdings, 6½ for 2 groups of men and 3½ belonging to 12 sokemen in 3 groups. Bradenham had 10½ teams, 3 on the demesnes and 4 of the men of 2 manors, and 3½ belonging to 17 sokemen in 3 groups. Gressenhall's total of 7 comprised 2 for the demesne, 2 men's and 3 belonging to 18 sokemen. Fransham's total amounts to 9. This included 4½ on the demesne of two holdings, ¾ men's, 3 pertaining to sokemen and ¾ to free men (as mentioned above, the Fransham total of men's teams might be incomplete). There is then only a rather loose correlation between numbers of carucates and of plough-teams.

At the time of Domesday Fransham lay towards the southern end and western edge of the band of heavily wooded country that ran along Norfolk's central watershed (Williamson 1993, 113–4, fig. 3.3). Woodland in the area under consideration is dominated by Necton, which could provide sustenance for 1000 pigs. Fransham's 125 pigs compare with 120 in Dunham and 100 in Gressenhall. Bradenham's 260 may reflect large wooded areas in West Bradenham which may have linked with those of Necton. The woodland of Wendling (for 100 pigs) seems rather large for a vill of this size. It can be accounted for by the northern extension of the parish that contained wooded areas as evidenced by the place names, *Herningshawe* and *Dykewood*. It should of course be remembered that these figures can give only the most general impression of the amounts of woodland that existed in the eleventh century, for, as Rackham (1986b, 75–6) has pointed out, a wood's swine-feeding potential cannot have been reliably related to its size. Warner (1987, 20–1) has suggested that the Domesday swine figures refer to the yields or renders of swine due from private manorially owned woods, and that woods not so owned and/or not suitable for fattening pigs would therefore not have been recorded.

Necton also heads the list of meadow totals, with 20 acres. Bradenham had 18 acres, Dunham 16, Fransham 10½ and Gressenhall 8. Although it is obvious that the Wissey valley would have provided abundant meadowland for Necton and Bradenham, the high position of Dunham is more difficult to explain. Here in the modern parishes of Great and Little Dunham the major meadow resource is the valley of a small stream draining north-west into the Nar. Gressenhall might have had a higher acreage for it is situated on the lower reaches of the Scarning River. Wendling, further up the same stream, has a surprisingly high total of 6 acres.

Apart from those relating to swine and woodland, the Fransham entries make no references to livestock.

Water-mills are the most archaeologically recognisable site-type frequently to appear in Domesday, apart from churches and castles. It is unfortunate, therefore, that the locations of Fransham's 2 TRE mills and the 2¾ (?perhaps more realistically 3) of 1086 were not defined in the archaeological record. They are most likely to have been situated in the eastern part of the study area, near or downstream from the confluence of the major watercourses at TF 916 133. This failure to locate any of these mills may perhaps be explained by the removal of all the earthworks associated with them and the absence or sparsity of any associated pottery. Furthermore, they may even have been situated outside the present bounds of Fransham parish, in Wendling or beyond.

Finally mention must be made of an unusual Domesday entry in the vicinity of Fransham, the half-market in Dunham, which must go some way towards dispelling notions of economic backwardness for this area. A quarter-market is entered under nearby Litcham. If these three quarters, which comprise two out of three references to markets in the Norfolk section of Domesday, were held at the same place, along with the missing quarter, might not the most likely location have been at or near the Roman road crossing in Kempstone? This lies on the south side of the Nar valley close to the junction of the parishes of Kempstone, Great Dunham, East Lexham and Litcham. Perhaps, then, it would not be too fanciful to suggest that the missing quarter, which surely must have existed, should have been entered under Kempstone or Lexham, or both.

Discussion

The first question to be considered is whether the opportunity afforded by the identification of Domesday period settlement sites in this archaeological survey has produced results which are compatible with the Domesday evidence. Two major nucleated settlement sites were identified, while there were three Domesday holdings. It seems rather unlikely that any other major sites remain to be found in non-surveyed areas. If site LS 2 in Little Fransham is to be associated with the de Tosny manor, then the two de Warenne holdings should be related to the probably much larger site in Great Fransham, LS 1. Without overall surface coverage and certainly without excavation, it is impossible even to guess at the number of dwelling houses contained within these two sites. Put differently, it would be rash to estimate, from incomplete surface evidence alone, the quantity of individuals listed in Domesday which might be allotted to each site. In addition, the legal status of occupants, whether slaves or free men, villeins or bordars, cannot be assessed from pottery scatters. Indeed, it is doubtful whether even the most meticulous excavation would be more successful in this. Of the remaining sites, all single settlements or very small groups of settlements, most, given the uncertainties of pottery dating, could have been occupied by 1066, and all by 1086. Here the very small (6%) drop in the recorded population between TRE and 1086 should be noted. This reduction would be compatible with the archaeological evidence were it to be assumed that some of these small sites may have been founded by tenants who had moved out from the two large ones, LS 1 and 2, leaving gaps within the settled areas of both, gaps which would not be identifiable without excavation.

These small sites are almost all situated on common edges or on roads with medieval origins. The exceptions are of some interest. One site, LS 8, lay hard by the edge of Great Fransham churchyard. Might it have been the Rectory until a move to the common edge in the late thirteenth century? Sites LS 9 and 10 both sit back from a common edge. The explanation for this may be no more than that the edge has since moved eastwards. In the case of site LS 9 it is curious that its medieval successor was actually further from the common. Similar movements might also apply in the cases of sites LS 16 and 19, both of which appear to have been replaced by medieval sites situated on common edges.

Domesday is of course silent on common pastures. Williamson (1993, 170) suggested that such sites, lying set back from the common edge, might 'occupy, not so much the edges of residual areas of waste, but sites on the periphery of the established arable land *between* the commons'. It is particularly unfortunate that the Fransham evidence is not sufficient to support or refute this ingenious explanation.

Late Saxon pottery scatters indicative of arable land are disappointingly few and small in the study area (Fig. 5.1), so much so that areas of arable cannot be mapped with any confidence. Those that are visible hardly do justice to the Domesday plough-teams. It must be assumed that either there was little or no need to fertilise arable land at this period (Jones 2004), or that domestic non-organic refuse was not admixed with organic material to any great extent, or that other methods of soil fertilisation, in particular direct dunging, were employed. Many of those sherd-free areas near and between Late Saxon settlement sites and with suitable soils must surely have been cultivated. All the common edges in the outer parts of the parish, except in the northern part of the eastern area adjacent to Wendling, are devoid of both Late Saxon sherd scatters and of contemporary settlement sites. In these parts non-arable land-use must have been the widespread. With such uncertain archaeological evidence to define areas of Late Saxon arable farming this survey makes little contribution to the great question of the origin of open fields. The nature of land-use in the spaces between common pastures remains unclear, and we are no nearer knowing at what dates those areas identified as irregular open fields in the medieval period first became so.

It was suggested in Chapter 4 that outlying areas might have been exploited for a variety of purposes in the Middle Saxon period, as woodland, waste, wood pasture, open grass pasture, and perhaps sporadically as arable. Late medieval sources show that many of these areas, all around the periphery of the parish, carried place names of fields, commons and closes, which indicate former woodland and woodland clearance, names often containing the elements *wudu* (Smith 1956b, 279–80; Williamson 2013, 219–21), and *rod* (Smith 1956b, 86–7). In most of these areas archaeological evidence for both settlement sites and arable farming begins to be widespread in the twelfth century. This of course does not imply that woodland or wood pasture was converted to arable in one operation, and it may well be that in the Late Saxon and early Norman periods the use of such outer areas was beginning a long process of change. It should be stressed, however, that some of these names might denote woodland that had disappeared at a much earlier date. David Hall has suggested that some such names given to furlongs in champion areas of Northamptonshire commemorate woodland converted to arable in the Late Saxon period (Hall 1985, 63; 1988, 101).

In Fransham this process may have involved the establishment of managed demesne woodlands and of defined areas of common pasture. Perhaps as the lords created managed woods out of former wood pasture (Rackham 1976, 135–6; 1986b, 121) the tenants were excluded, and thus some of the remaining areas were fixed for common use. During the eleventh century some tenants, especially those without access to enclosed pasture, may then have found it expeditious to settle on the edges of the inner commons in order to secure their pasture rights. If so, then towards the end of the century the situation would have become more insecure, probably less because of a rising population, and more through seigniorial pressure on outlying areas of wood pasture. A natural result of this uncertainty would have been the rapid abandonment of the two central nucleated settlements, and the start of a rush, rather than drift, to common edges both in the inner and outer areas of the vill in *c*.1100. This large-scale movement may not have been ordered by lords so much as caused by them, as they formalised the layout and fixed the extent of demesne pastures and woodland at the expense of tenants. This explanation has more force than one involving population pressure on its own (*e.g.* Bigmore 1982, 164).

Reference should be made here to *Pillwood*, the south-western extension of Fransham parish. First mentioned in 1273/4 when it was arable (Illingworth and Caley 1812, 434), it must have been part of the royal demesne, presumably attached to Harold's manor of Necton. Its shape and location indicate that it would once have formed part of Necton township. The first element of the place name, *Pil*, shows a place 'where shafts or stakes could be obtained' (Smith 1956b, 64), a wood of which a part at least was managed as coppice.

One place name which may possibly be indicative of former woodland is far from peripheral and is indeed quite central. *Barnards Moor*, a common pasture shared between the two Franshams, was recorded as *Barnardismor* in 1323 (MC 360/54 713x6) and *Bernarsmor* in 1346 (MC 360/70 713x6). This name may possibly contain the Old English past participle *baerned*, meaning burnt (Smith 1956a, 32), and may suggest woodland clearance by burning (Hunn 1994, 193). An alternative explanation involving 'pot-boiler' sites seems less convincing, for more of these are found in other low-lying areas. It is far more likely, however, that the first element in the place name is the personal name Bernard.

If the size, shape and extent of the common pastures were the result of seigniorial rationalisation of much larger areas of wood pasture in the tenth and eleventh centuries, then it would not be necessary to seek much more ancient, indeed Roman, origins for them, as Warner has attempted in north-east Suffolk (Warner 1987, 11). Early or Middle Saxon origins have been claimed for commons in a sample of Cambridgeshire villages, and the same writer has argued for the very much more ancient origin of commons in other parts of England (Oosthuizen 1993; 2013, 19–43). The commons of Fransham, where the evidence has survived, show no signs of having been demarcated by substantial earthwork features. It is therefore difficult to envisage how their edges can have remained recognisable at the end of the long span between the end of the Roman period and the eleventh century, whatever may have been the land-use around them. It is clear, however, that the two debates, on the antiquity of commons themselves, and on the chronology of settlement on their margins, must follow two distinct though obviously interrelated lines. In the absence of hard evidence, the former debate, 'a most obscure problem in English history' (Hoskins and Stamp 1963, 5), will be pursued no more here, while the latter needs further consideration. The Fransham archaeological evidence shows, with unusual clarity, that the process of denucleation and of the colonisation of common edges had begun by the Conquest and was completed with great rapidity at the turn of the eleventh century. Peter Warner argued that 'green-side settlement was well established on some Suffolk clayland commons by the ninth or tenth century'. His failure to locate any firm archaeological evidence to support this was put down to inconclusive pottery evidence, to the 'difficulties in accurately dating early medieval pottery types'. To this he added that Ipswich and Thetford-type wares were 'largely confined to high status sites in East Anglia' (Warner 1987, 17–8). Indeed, he had earlier suggested that 'much of our unidentifiable 'early medieval' pottery.... may ultimately turn out to be late Saxon' (Warner 1983). However, there is to date no hint from the large amount of recent fieldwork in Norfolk either that Thetford-type ware was of high status or that the starting date of early medieval wares can be pushed back into the tenth century. The evidence recovered in this survey does not point to such early origins for common-edge settlement, rather it has shown that along all the edges that were available for examination there was little or no occupation before the eleventh century.

Although it lies entirely on the Boulder Clay, the whole of the study area, with its roughly central Early and Middle Saxon settlement sites, is best seen as comprising what Warner would regard as a primary zone of settlement (Warner 1987, 15–7). The areas of wood pasture that fell to the lord and became managed woodland, and those that emerged as common pasture, lay predominantly on the outer fringes of this primary zone, rather than outside it. It cannot be demonstrated that most common-edge sites were of free status, in contrast to what Warner has shown often to have been the case in marginal areas of secondary settlement (1987, 25–8, 45). Unfortunately, in Fransham the imperfections of the documentary evidence do not allow the identification of the tenure, in the late medieval period, of some of the eleventh-century foundations. Those identified include a roughly equal mix of both freehold and customary tenures and demesne. Such a situation is to be expected of an area of primary settlement in a landscape that was already old by the Norman Conquest.

Endnotes

i   Bordar, a lesser peasant or cottager ranked below a villain.

ii A map of *c.*1595 depicts Kirtling Common in the south-east corner of Longham parish on its border with Gressenhall and archaeological evidence has shown that the bulk of settlement around the edges of the common was not established until the late fifteenth or early sixteenth centuries (Wade-Martins 1980b, 33–9). Two charters of the early to mid-thirteenth century in the Castle Acre cartulary may point to Kirtling having been within Gressenhall (BL Harley MS 2110). William son of Walter of Gressenhall granted 6 acres in the fields of Kirtling and a rent of 8d to Castle Acre priory. William son of Hubert Hunter (*venatoris*) of Gressenhall granted to the priory 8d rent paid to him by William son of Walter, his kinsman, for 5 acres in Kirtling. Of these, one acre of arable land butted on a meadow of Longham, and a part of a meadow called Northmedow lay between the croft of John son of William and the park gate (*portam parci*). The park was surely that of Gressenhall (HER 50576) which was considerably larger than its surviving post-medieval successor (HER 51031) and extended much closer to Longham.

Chapter 6. Medieval Population and Wealth, Manorial and Tenurial Structure

Introduction

Surface traces of the medieval period, overwhelmingly in the form of sherd concentrations and scatters, form the majority of the available evidence. Over a limited period at the turn of the eleventh century the settlement pattern of Fransham had been transformed. The two nucleated settlements (LS 1 and 2) were deserted, and small groups and rows of houses, and single houses, were established on the edges of common pastures, or adjacent to roads, in a process that had begun somewhat tentatively earlier in the eleventh century. By 1200 this pattern had spread over most parts of both Great and Little Fransham, leaving only some outlying areas to be colonised during the course of the thirteenth century. The later fourteenth century saw a widespread contraction of settlement in both outlying and central areas. This archaeological evidence is complemented by an abundance of written sources, almost all of which post-date the period of expansion. Indeed, many were written in periods of severe decline and subsequent recovery, the fifteenth and sixteenth centuries.

All original documents cited in this and succeeding chapters are identified by an abbreviation signifying the repository (*e.g.* PRO, **see p. ix**) and their piece numbers. For the sake of brevity an exception has been made for documents housed in the Norfolk Record Office. The standard prefix NRO has been omitted, as well as box code suffixes, so that, for example, NRO MS 11352 T134D appears as MS 11352 and NRO MS 13084 40A3 as MS 13084. Summaries and piece numbers of all manuscript sources are contained in the Bibliography under *Primary Sources*.

In this and succeeding chapters much use is made of various technical terms relating to manors, courts and tenures. The most accessible source of explanation is Bailey 2002, which includes a glossary.

Population and wealth

National taxation records offer some information on relative wealth, but as has been pointed out, the numbers of tax payers are of 'absolutely no use' in the estimation of true populations because of the small proportions of people who were assessed for tax (Glasscock 1975, xxiv–xxv). Some notion of the relative sizes of population can be gained from the records of the Lay Subsidies of 1327 and 1332 (Willard 1934, 11; Jurkowski *et al.* 1998, 36–8). In 1327, when personal movable wealth was assessed at one twentieth of its estimated value, 45 people in Great Fransham paid a total of £3 2s 2d and 35 in Little Fransham paid £2 15s 5d (TNA E 179/149/7). When personal movable wealth was assessesd at one fifteenth in 1332, 46 people in Great Fransham paid £4 18s 4d and 38 in Little Fransham £3 3s 4d (TNA E 179/149/9).

The sizes of the taxed populations of the Franshams in 1327 and 1332 were not exceptional, with that of Great Fransham being greater than 41.3, the average for Launditch Hundred in 1327, while Little Fransham was smaller (Table 6.1). Both, however, fell below the mean of 58.5. The population of the former declined between the two dates and that of the latter rose. The taxed population totals of 21 Launditch townships were smaller in 1332, while those of 9 had increased. Two places (Gateley and East Lexham) were stable. The number of taxpayers in the whole Hundred declined by *c*.9% between the two taxes.

For the tax of 1334 a fifteenth of the value of Great Fransham was assessed at £5 10s 0d and that of Little Fransham at £3 8s 0d (Hudson 1895, 276–7; Glasscock 1975, 207–8). These figures fall above and below the average for the thirty-two assessed townships in Launditch Hundred of £4 11s 3d. The assessment of Great Fransham lies very close to £5 12s 1d, the average figure for the two Franshams, Wendling and the nine radiating townships (Fig. 1.3). Using parish acreages given by White (1845, 326 and 372), it is possible to arrive at an average value per acre as assessed in 1334. For the above thirteen parishes this was 0.65d (the lowest being Wendling at 0.35d, the highest Beeston with Little Bittering at 0.9d). The acreage values for both Great and Little Fransham were above this average, at 0.7d and 0.84d, while Necton and Scarning fell very close to it, at 0.64d and 0.66d respectively.

On 28 June 1336 a violent rain and hail storm hit Gressenhall [with Great Bittering], Great Fransham, Wendling, Scarning, Swanton Morley, East Dereham and Hoe[i]. All the corn crop was destroyed apart from that growing on limited acreages in certain named fields. In the case of Great Fransham only 20 acres of wheat worth 100s at 5s a quarter and 20 acres of oats worth 40s at 2s a quarter in the west field were spared. In Wendling all the crops were lost (Cal. Inq. Misc. 1916, 389–90, no.1581). In 1337 a commission was set up to assess a reduction of liability to the Lay Subsidy of a fifteenth which had been granted in 1336 (Cal. Fine Rol. 1921, 43). As a result, much reduced sums were levied from the afflicted places, and as part of the reassessment the individual contributions of named people were listed. Thirty-one names paying a total of 40s are listed under Great Fransham. Fourteen people paying 13s 8d are listed under Wendling for the same reassessment. The adjusted sums for each of the seven places were set at between 34.5% and 36.4% of the 1334 levels (TNA E 179/238/111). By 1347 the tax collectors demanded that the assessments be restored to pre-storm levels (Cal. Close Rol. 1905, 255). An inquisition held at East Dereham on 1 July judged that the fifteenths of all seven were at levels below half the 1334 assessments, Great Fransham's being £2 11s 4d, and that the total contribution of all seven (£25 14s 4d) was an increase of £5 14s 4d on the total when they had

	1327		1332	
Beeston & Little Bittering	61	£5 10s 6d	58	£8 12 9d
Beetley	46	£3 17s 3d	37	£3 8s 9d
East Bilney	32	£2 0s 6d	26	£2 9s 0d
Brisley	52	£4 1s 2d	51	£5 3s 9d
Colkirk	34	£1 19s 11d	20+	incomplete
Great Dunham	49	£4 4s 9d	40	£6 17s 8d
Little Dunham	34	£3 13s 8d	19	£3 8s 11d
North Elmham	88	£7 7s 2d	72	£7 4s 0d
Great Fransham	55	£3 2s 2d	46	£4 18s 4d
Little Fransham	35	£2 15s 5d	38	£3 3s 4d
Gateley	34	£1 18 1d	34	£2 7s 4d
Godwick	13	£1 2s 3d	14	£1 0s 8d
Gressenhall & Great Bittering	50	£4 3s 5d	51	£5 0s 3d
Hoe	62	£4 2s 10d	72	£5 12s 1d
Horningtoft	23	£2 4s 6d	21	£2 8s 8d
Kempstone	22	£1 14s 6d	21	£2 5s 10d
West Lexham	19	£1 17s 6d	15	£1 10s 0d
East Lexham	15	£1 15s 6d	15	£1 15s 11d
Litcham	26	£2 7s 9d	25	£3 2s 4d
Longham	24	£3 4s 3d	23	£3 9s 0d
Mileham	37	£3 3s 4d	31	£3 8s 4d
Oxwick	21	£1 13s 4d	23	£2 2s 6d
Pattesley	14	£0 18s 2d	15	£1 7s 0d
Rougham	56	£4 15s 5d	58	£7 8s 0d
Scarning	85	£8 5s 8d	112	£9 13s 10d
Stanfield	30	£2 17s 10d	35	£3 2s 6d
Swanton Morley	103	£6 0s 4d	66	£10 3s 11d
Tittleshall	39	£3 5s ?d	35	£4 13s 3d
Weasenham	88	£7 10s 9d	62	£7 7s 0d
Wellingham	21	£1 8s 6d	18	£1 14s 7d
Wendling	27	£? 10s 4d	24	£1 13s 8d
Whissonsett	28	£2 5s 10d	26	£2 17s 2d
Total	**1323**		**1203+**	

Table 6.1 The Lay Subsidies of 1327 and 1332: numbers of taxpayers and total assessments per vill in Launditch Hundred (after Hawes 2001)

previously been taxed (Cal. Inq. Misc. 1916, 512, no. 2040). Clearly recovery was very slow in coming.

The true damage wrought by the Black Death on the populations of the Franshams cannot be measured directly from documentary sources, although extracts of the proceedings of a Great Fransham manor court held on 18 July 1349 give a chilling hint of the devastation, a list the names of 33 dead tenants and their holdings, which amounted to 21 messuages, 1 toft and 134.75 acres. Seven tenants died without heirs and another 17 left heirs who were underage. As a result, many holdings were seized into the lord's hands. It is not known to what proportion of the tenantry this death toll amounted. At the first court of Gilbert de Fransham, held on 16 September 1343, 24 tenants had paid fealty to the lord, while 32 others had been distrained to do so, *i.e.* they had not turned up at court (MS 13034). These figures may not be completely reliable, particularly because of the late date (*c.*1600) of the extracts, but a 50% mortality rate seems quite likely.

Norfolk assessment rolls for the 1377 Poll Tax do not survive. This is most unfortunate given the generally accepted demographic reliability of this tax (Campbell 2000, 402), which was levied at a flat rate of 4d on all men and women over the age of fourteen except 'honest beggars'. The 1379 Poll Tax was levied at a complex graduated rate on all males and single females over sixteen (Dowell 1965, 92–6; Jurkowski *et al.* 1998, 56–9). Detailed rolls do survive for Launditch Hundred but are imperfect and in part illegible (TNA E 179/149/53; Fenwick 2001, 150–5). Thirty people were taxed in Little Fransham, and the name of only one of these is entirely illegible. Some evasion must have taken place, to judge from contemporary court rolls. For example, the names of three capital pledges who were tenants in Little Fransham and were sworn in at a leet court held on 30 September 1379, do not appear in the above list (MS 13093). Single females may also have been under-reported for only two women, one of whom was a widow and lady of the principal manor, appear amongst the 28 fully legible names. The single entry in which only the surname is legible was almost certainly a woman (Olive Gotte). Under Great Fransham 21 names can be read and there is space for 5 more at the base of the membrane (TNA E 179/149/53/13d). Ten other names on another membrane under a missing heading are almost certainly of Great Fransham residents (TNA E 179/149/53/5d). This suggests a total of 46 or more. The average number of taxpayers for the 22 townships with complete returns is 31.8, but this figure must be too low because full lists for most of the small places, such as Pattersley and Godwick, are extant, while those for some large townships, such as Swanton Morley and Scarning, are incomplete or missing. A full list is given in Fenwick 2001, 82.

The records of the 1381 Poll Tax survive even more patchily than those of 1379 (TNA E 179/149/53; Fenwick 2001, 188–94). It was levied, at a flat rate of 12d, but with some exceptions both higher and lower, on all males and females over the age of fifteen (Dowell 1965, 98; Jurkowski et al. 1998, 60–2). There were 58 taxpayers in Little Fransham, but complete returns are available for only six other Launditch townships (Fenwick 2001, 85). The Little Fransham figures seem more credible than those of 1379. There were 18 married couples named, 1 son, 1 male servant, 13 males and 7 females.

Reduced assessments of the Lay Subsidy made in 1449 indicate that both the Franshams were in a healthier economic state than many of their neighbours (Hudson 1895). The average reduction for the 32 townships of Launditch Hundred expressed as a percentage of the sum set for each place in 1334 was 15%, and this figure includes three places (Pattersley, Beetley and Hoe) that were given no reduction. Great Fransham's allowance was 10%, Little Fransham's 5.88%. In South Greenhoe Hundred, Necton was allowed a reduction of almost 23% and West Bradenham 15%. Apart from the three townships with unreduced tax burdens, Little Fransham received the second smallest allowance in Launditch after Brisley (5.37%), the third smallest being Gateley (6.25%). Fourteen places including the above three were more lightly burdened than Great Fransham.

The manorial structure

Many of the written sources relate to individual manors and to the holdings of monastic houses, and it has been possible to assign a substantial proportion of settlement sites and pieces of land to particular manors and monasteries, both as demesne and tenanted properties. Therefore, it seems most appropriate firstly to present a summary of Fransham's manorial structure and changes therein, before proceeding to a topographical description of the parish and an analysis of the material evidence which will be outlined in Chapter 7.

The most significant post-Domesday document is a late thirteenth-century feodary (*feodarium*), a list of tenants and their lands in Great Fransham linked up the feudal chain to the King. Its contents are shown diagrammatically on Table 6.2 (see facing page), and in simplified translation in Appendix 1. It survives only as a sixteenth-century copy (MS 11352) and as four less complete copies of approximately the same date (MS 13084). No version is dated, but since internal evidence indicates that it was composed between 1277 and 1289, it is probable that the original was drawn up as part of a return to the Hundred Roll Commissioners in 1279–80, an inquiry that has been described as 'a second and more detailed Domesday Book if it had survived in full' (Cam 1930, 28), and that was conceived by Edward I to be precisely that (Raban 2004, 178).

Despite its probably corrupt condition, and, as is apparent on the evidence of other sources, its incompleteness, the feodary is a key source of information, for it presents the manorial and tenurial structure for the first time since 1086 and, unfortunately, for the last. It is also a rare survival, with Hundred Roll returns of 1279 known to survive for very few other vills in Norfolk, seven in Gallow Hundred, Holkham in North Greenhoe, Hevingham in South Erpingham, Sedgeford in Smithdon and the northern part of King's Lynn borough (Raban 2004, 158–61; Greenway 1982; Campbell 1986, Hassall and Beauroy 1993, 215–30; Rutledge and Rutledge 1978)[ii]. The intricacy of the Fransham feodary is emphasised by comparison with the *Nomina Villarum* of 1316, the most commonly cited source. This names two lords under Great Fransham (Blake 1952, 269), while the feodary lists six people under whom customary tenants (villeins) held land. The lords of the *Nomina Villarum* held by knight's service, and their holdings can be equated with those of two lords in the feodary, William de Fransham and Geoffrey de Marscall, who also so held. The complexity of the tenurial situation here is as great as that of Hevingham, whose 1279 return has been published in diagrammatic form (Campbell 1986).

Sadly, Little Fransham is excluded from the feodary which is headed *Fransham Magna*. The document is primarily concerned with detailing tenants and their lands in this vill, with only one external holding (in Beeston) being mentioned. Five tenants-in-chief are listed, as well as the abbot of Wendling who held lands in pure and perpetual alms. Free tenants held lands directly from manorial lords and as sub-tenancies from other freeholders. The combined total of demesne and freehold properties amounts to 18 messuages, 402½ acres of land, 9 acres of meadow, 11 acres of pasture and 12 of wood. The six entries of villeins' lands comprise 154 acres. The overall numbers of customary tenants and messuages is not given and cannot be calculated, with an obscure formula being used, 'n. acres which his villeins hold in villeinage with their messuages' (*n. acr. ter. quas villan. sui tenent in villenag. cum suis mess.*). This lack of detail concerning unfree tenants is found in other East Anglian Hundred Roll returns (Greenway 1982, 76–7; Raban 2004, 94). The total acreage of all demesne, freehold and customary lands in Great Fransham reaches 588½ (along with 6 acres in Beeston). This figure amounts to less than 30.5% of 1,932 acres, the present area of the former civil parish of Great Fransham. If the surviving version is anywhere near complete, then it is clear that the acre in thirteenth-century Great Fransham was a large one. It should be stressed, however, that some lands were certainly omitted, such as the properties of Castle Acre Priory. Other tenants of Wendling Abbey are also missing. Another part of the shortfall in the acreage can be explained by the exclusion of common pastures and

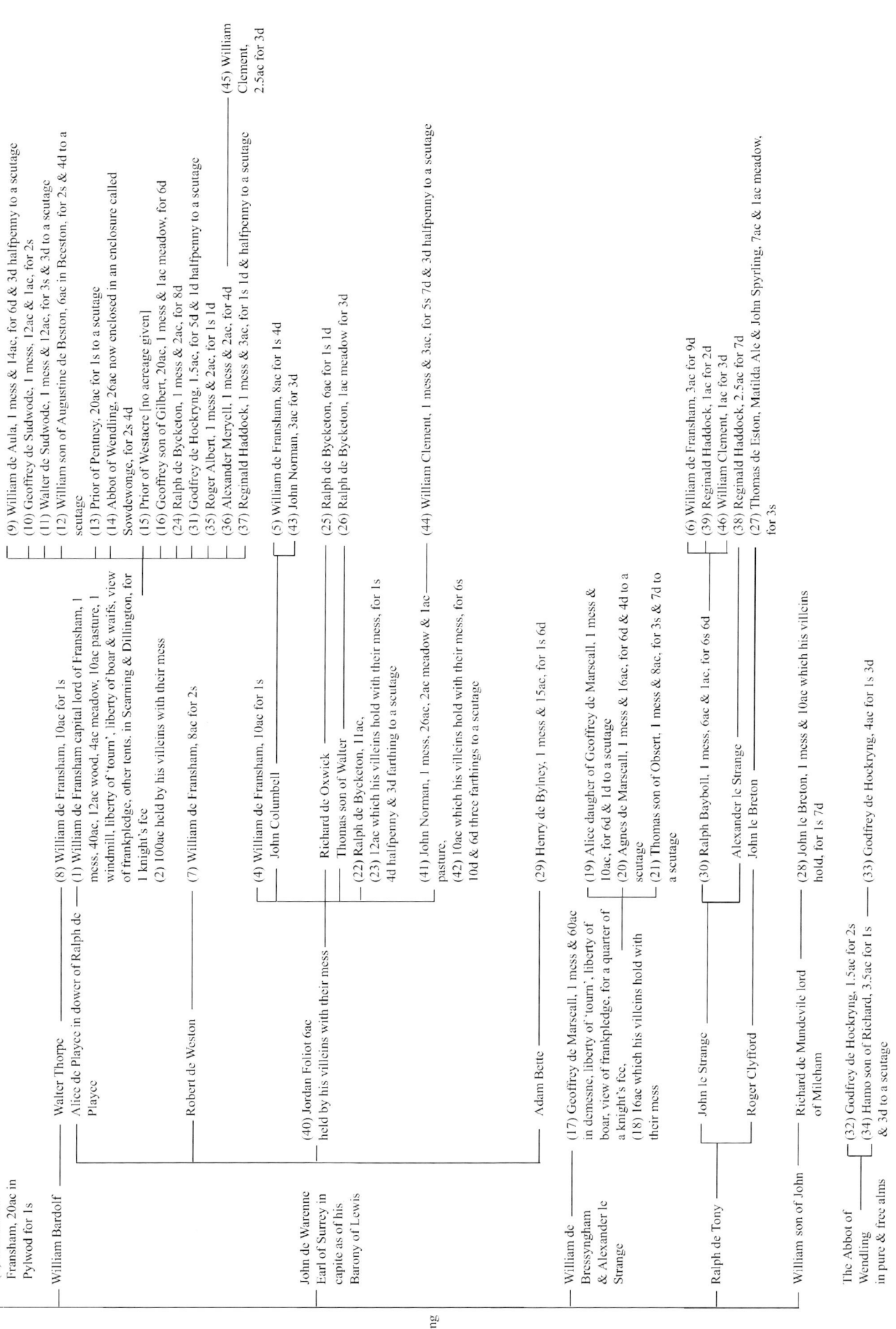

Table 6.2 Diagram showing the Great Fransham feodary of c.1279

wastes, as well as woodland, of which only 12 acres were entered.

As well as the mass of detail contained in the feodary some use has been made of more than 150 medieval deeds, most of which antedate 1350 and include a majority of the later thirteenth century. About half relate to the manors of Wilcoks and Kirkhams in Little Fransham (MC 360/1–78, 713X6; Pl. 6.1 and Pl. 6.2).

Because of subinfeudation[iii] the manorial structure of Fransham in the late thirteenth century and later was much more complicated than it had been in 1086. It will now be explained, with discussion grouped under the three Domesday entries. These discussions will be followed by notes on the lands and rents held by six monastic houses and on the two sets of glebe land.

Great Fransham manor, part of the de Warenne fee

For Fransham the twelfth century is almost an historical blank, with only an episcopal confirmation charter dated 1181 and a group of undated charters in the Castle Acre cartulary making a significant contribution to our knowledge (BL Harley MS 2110). The earliest dated post-Domesday reference to specific lands in Fransham is a final concord of 1198, by which Herveus son of Juliana conveyed 1 carucate of land there to Agnes de Fransham. For this she gave Herveus 1 mark and granted, for 3d annual rent, 20 acres in *Franesham*, comprising 5½ acres *ad longam terram*, 4 acres *ad curtam terram*, 3 acres at the door (*ad portam*) of Fransham church, 3 acres in Ailrich's toft, 3 acres in Juliana's toft, and ½ acre of Brictmar's land (Dodwell 1952, 75, no.174; Rye 1881, 44–5, no.217). None of these parcels has been located or recognised in later sources, and indeed we cannot be certain in which of the two Franshams these lands lay. Agnes de Fransham may have been a member of the family of that name known to have held Great Fransham manor from the late thirteenth to the early fifteenth centuries. For a fine of 1202 concerning 11 acres, again unlocated, see Appendix 3.

In 1274/5 the Launditch hundredal jury stated that William lord of Great Fransham claimed assize of bread and ale and other rights pertaining to the King from the time of the Conquest (Illingworth and Caley eds 1812, 434). In *c*.1279 William de Fransham (Table 6.2, no. 1) was the capital lord of Great Fransham and tenant of Alice de Playce (Plaiz or Playz), mesne tenant of John de Warenne[iv], and there is no doubt that this manor can be equated with the holding of Gilbert at Domesday (Brown 1984, 8.66). Carthew (1877, 34) considered William de Fransham a descendant of Gilbert who in 1086 had also held a de Warenne manor in Scarning (Brown 1984, 8.67). The continuity of the de Fransham line up to *Nomina Villarum* (Blake 1952, 250) and beyond to the death of Geoffrey de Fransham in 1414 remains a distinct possibility. Gilbert was frequently the name of lords of Great Fransham in the thirteenth and fourteenth centuries (*e.g.* Feudal Aids 1904, 539). Some support for continuity may be found in the parallel lordship of the manors of Great Fransham and Scarning Hall in Scarning. Both were held by Gilbert in 1086 and continued to share a common lord until 1414 (Blomefield 1809, 38–9; Carthew 1877, 228–38).

William de Fransham was also a tenant-in-chief (Table 6.2, no. 3), holding 20 acres in *Pylwod* of the King. This had been confirmed by an entry in the Hundred Rolls for 1274/5: William de Fransham was said to hold of the King, as from the time of the Conquest, a *cultur'* (arable land) called *Pilewude*, paying 1s annual blanch farm rent (*ad albam firmam*, *i.e.* payment in cash) to the sheriff of Norfolk (Illingworth and Caley eds 1812, 434). The land was later to be regarded as part of the demesne of this manor. It may possibly be equated with 20 acres in Great Fransham that Geoffrey de Fransham held of Robert son of Robert de Scales, a ward of the King in 1332 (Cal. Inq. Post Mort. 1909, 339, no. 476).

The complexity of the tenurial tree is illustrated by William de Fransham's other holdings, five parcels totalling 39 acres held of five men (Table 6.2, nos 4–8). Eight acres were held of Robert de Weston, another mesne tenant of de Warenne. Nothing else is known of de Weston and it is assumed that this land subsequently became part of the Great Fransham demesne. William was thus also a tenant and sub-tenant. As well as his unknown number of customary tenants, which to judge from the acreage was the highest in the township (Table 6.2, no. 2), William had thirteen free tenants, again the largest number, who held, along with one sub-tenant, eight messuages and at least 125 acres (Table 6.2, nos 9–16, 24, 31, 35–7 and 45). Henry de Bylney held a messuage and 15 acres of Adam Bette, another mesne tenant of John de Warenne (Table 6.2, no. 29). No more is known of Bette, but the de Bylney holding was almost certainly to become regarded as a freehold of Great Fransham manor, for a free messuage and 14 acres, once of William de Bilney, were listed in a Great Fransham rental of *c*.1400.

Very brief extracts from manor and/or leet court rolls from seventeen years between 1272/3 and 1338/9 were made in the sixteenth century. Almost all the entries concern small-scale purprestures (encroachments) upon common pastures (MS 11352).

Much longer extracts of manor court and leet rolls, again sixteenth-century copies, begin in 1330 (MS 13034). However, it is not until a detailed rental of *c*.1400 and an extent of *c*.1430 become available that topography, settlement location and land-use can be considered in any detail. A summary of many of the surviving manorial documents is given in HMC 1914, 318–20 and 324–7.

The detailed rental, dated on internal grounds to *c*.1400, survives in 9 sixteenth-century copies, differing mainly in the glosses, which almost invariably refer to later tenants (MS 13071, MS 13072, 6 versions in MS 13084, and MS 11352). The tenanted lands of this manor were overwhelmingly held by free tenure, there being more than four times as many freehold acres as customary, and almost five times as many free tenants.

The total of annual rents due from 34 freeholders amounted to £1 10s 10d, a hen and a pound of pepper. One tenant owed one boon-work (*precaria*). There were 22 messuages and a portion of a messuage, of which 2 were described as void (*vacat.*), as well as 1 cottage. The total acreage was 247½. This included 13¾ acres of meadow and 8+ acres of pasture. Also listed were 1 headland, 1 yard or garden (*ortum*), 2 closes and 2 lots of 'divers lands'. The monastic tenants were the prior of Castle Acre (a messuage and 6 acres), the abbot of Wendling (38 acres), the prior of West Acre (divers lands, known from sixteenth-century court rolls of Cannons manor to comprise 10 acres), and the prior of Pentney (20½ acres and 1 acre of meadow). The largest lay tenant was Roger de Toftes who held 4 messuages (including 1 void) and 46

74

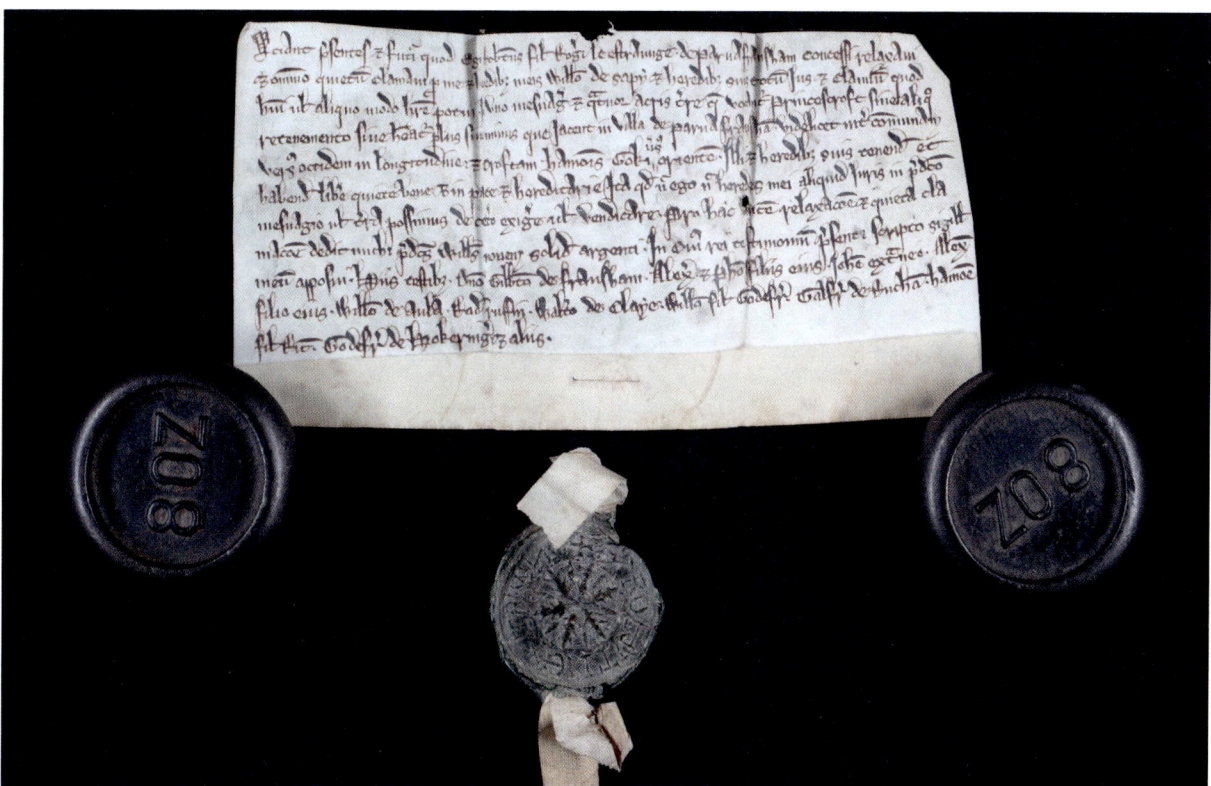

Plate 6.1 Undated quitclaim by Robert son of Roger le Strange of Little Fransham to William de Sapy of a messuage and four acres called *Princescroft*, before 1273 (NRO MC 360/5, 713X6)

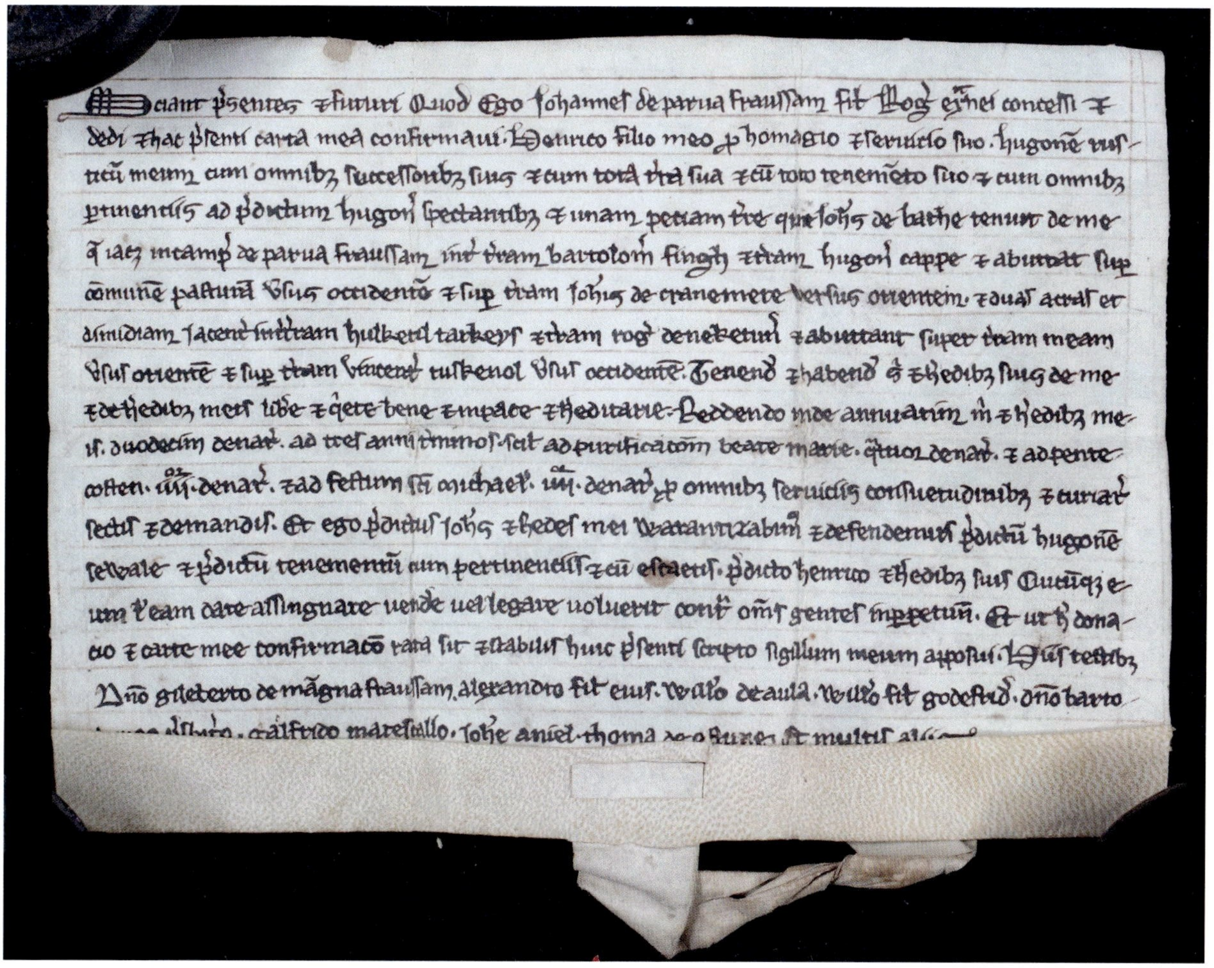

Plate 6.2 Undated grant by John of Little Fransham, son of Roger le Strange, to his son Henry of Hugh his villein (*rusticus*) with all his tenement and land, along with one piece and 2½ acres of land, before 1273
(NRO MC 360/6, 713X6)

acres. Seventeen tenants held lands but no messuage of this manor, and of these three had a single acre each. With the exception of 6 acres in Beeston, and of 1 messuage and most of its associated 16 acres (including 1 yard) in Scarning and Wendling, all lands of this manor lay in the Franshams, and almost all in Great Fransham. Edmund Oldhall (lord of Kirkhams manor in Little Fransham) held a messuage, ¾ acre of meadow, 3 acres of pasture and 7½ acres of land (including 2½ acres in Little Fransham Millfield), for rents totalling 12¾d. Payments of 12½d to Agnes and later Geoffrey de Fransham were recorded in Kirkhams messor's account rolls for 1398–9 and 1405–7 (MS 13125, MS 13130 and MS 13131). However, a rent of 2s for 6 acres in Beeston (Table 6.2, no. 12), which was also held by Edmund Oldhall, was not entered in these rolls.

Of 7 customary tenants, 4 were also freeholders. A total of 6 messuages, 1 close and 59 acres, including 3 acres of meadow and some pasture within a 5-acre piece of land, were listed. Money rents totalled £1 12s 4d. Four hens, 5 eggs and 2 bushels of barley were also due. Three autumn boon-works were owed by one tenant. Another (also a freeholder) who held a messuage, 21½ acres and 3 acres of meadow, paid a rent of 2s, 1s to a scutage, 1 hen and 5 eggs, and in addition owed a relatively heavy burden of labour services: 16 days in autumn, unspecified mowing, hay-making and carrying duties, 4 days of carrying services with his own horse, 1 winter and 1 spring ploughing boon-work, 2 days of winter harrowing and 1 day after the sowing of oats, 2 days of threshing in winter and 1 in Lent. These lands were known as the tenement Wymer, one Thomas Wymer having died seized of a messuage and 20 acres in 1349 (MS 13034). By c.1400 labour services had become unnecessary and had largely given way to money rents. Three ancient customary tenements (*tenementa*, see Douglas 1927, 20–3), which had been let out at fee farm in the 1390s, accounted for £1 9s, almost 90% of the total. One of the three lay in Kempstone and at £1 its rent accounted for 62% of the total. It comprised a messuage and 14¼ acres.[v]

An extent, undated but of *c.*1430 on internal evidence, treats the manor as an entity, despite post-dating a tripartite division in 1414 following the death of the lord, Geoffrey de Fransham (Blomefield 1808, 496; Carthew 1877, 235–8; Carthew 1878, 478–9). It survives in 8 sixteenth-century copies (6 versions in MS 13084 and 2 in MS 11352), derived from 2 different earlier versions, in one of which land parcels are arranged by fields and parts of fields. There are only a few insignificant differences, in terms of acreage and descriptions, between the copies. A total of 632¼ acres of demesne included 31 acres of meadow, 21½ acres of pasture and 1 acre enclosure with underwood, as well as 27¼ acres comprising the 3 customary tenements held at fee farm and mentioned above. Many other parcels of demesne had once been held by customary tenure and others were probably escheated freeholds.

The site of the manor house was identified in the field survey (Med 5, Appendix 2).

The Rougham / Fransham part of the de Warenne fee: East Lexham, Ellinghams, Mascales, Blyfords and Rougholme manors
The Domesday estates of Wimer the Dapifer, which extended into Gressenhall, Kempstone, [East] Lexham, Tittleshall and Weasenham, as well as Rougham and Fransham (Brown 1984, 8.68) passed to the de Stutevilles around the turn of the twelfth century, to the Foliots in 1272/3[vi] and to the Hastings in 1330 (Carthew 1877, 189–96). By the middle of the fourteenth century, and probably earlier, the Fransham fraction of this fee was regarded as part of East Lexham manor. Much confusion remains around the tenurial history of this fraction, and the five at least in part distinguishable elements have been identified. They are discussed below. Documents with links between Rougham and Fransham are summarised in Appendix 3.

Ellinghams manor
In *c.*1279 both Jordan Foliot and 2 of his 6 tenants had customary tenants (Table 6.2, nos 22–3, 40–2). The sub-manor held by John Norman (Table 6.2, nos 41–2) was known as the manor of Ellinghams by 1404. The sole sub-tenant was William Clement (Table 6.2, no. 44), also a sub-tenant of William de Fransham (no. 45). Clement's pair of holdings comprised a messuage and 5½ acres. A charter of 1316 records the granting, by Roger son of William son of Henry Clement of Great Fransham chaplain, of a messuage, 4 acres of arable and 1½ acres of wood in Great Fransham to two other men (TNA E 40/10496). A later endorsement on a release of the same year by William son of Henry Clement of the same property states that the lands are called Elynghams (TNA E 40/10516).

The name derives from Thomas de Elyngham who took out a 10-year lease of 4½ acres of Great Fransham manor land in 1389 (MS 13043) and a 4-year lease of 3 acres of Kirkhams manor land in 1392 (MS 13093). In his will, proved in 1404, John Croupus rector of Little Fransham instructed his cofeoffees to sell his lands, tenements, rents and services in Great Fransham and elsewhere called Elynghammes (NCC 312 Harsyk MF/RO137). One of his executors was Edmund Reve rector of Great Fransham, on whom, with others, lands in Beeston, Great Fransham and Great Dunham lands and rents were settled by fine in 1405 by Thomas de Elyngham and his wife (TNA CP 25/1/168/183.54). Reve had died by 1445 and left no real estate in his will (NCC 32–3 Wylbey MF26). In 1440 Ellinghams manor had been recently acquired (*nuper perquis.*), presumably from Edmund Reve, by William Oldhall, lord of Kirkhams and Wilcoks manors in Little Fransham. Account rolls for 1440–1 and 1442–3 give details of income from and expenditure on the manor of Ellinghams (MS 13039 and MS 13140). In 1440–1 farm rents totalling £1 10s 5d were received from 4 people for 15¼ acres of land, 8 acres of meadow and the pasturing of 2 crofts, and fixed rents (*i.e.* for customary or freehold lands) totalling 1s 11d were paid by 2 tenants. Rents were paid to Beeston, East Lexham and Great Fransham manors. The amount paid to the latter, 1s 2d, matches exactly the rents due from John Croupius to Great Fransham manor in *c.*1400 for a messuage, a void messuage with 2 acres and divers pieces of land. The rent paid to Beeston manor probably relates to John le Breton's possessions held of Mileham in *c.*1279 (Table 6.2, no. 28). In 1442–3 the expenditure was unchanged but income had increased, probably because lordship was by then more firmly established. Thirty-two acres of land, 4¼ acres of meadow and 2 crofts were let at farm for £1 11s 10d, although not all the money was collected. A rent of 4s 4d was not received for 26 acres that were in poor state and needed to be folded with sheep, and 1½ acres were in the lord's hands. Nine tenants (including 2 joint) paid fixed rents amounting to 3s 2d. In an undated, slightly later rental 5 tenants were recorded paying 2s 11½d fixed rent (MS 13175).

All subsequent information on this manor's tenanted lands is derived from a court book which begins in 1576 (MC 1847/1, 741X2). From this source a rough estimate can be made of the amount of tenanted properties. Freehold consisted of a tenement built, 29½ acres of land in 7 holdings, 7½ acres of meadow in 3 parcels, 'divers lands and tenements' and a close. There were only 3 customary holdings, a cottage and 1½ roods, a messuage built with 1½ acres, and 6¼ acres.

East Lexham manor
The second sub-manor, that of Ralph de Byketon (Table 6.2, nos 22–3), his two sub-tenancies (nos 25–6), and three other holdings (nos 4, 5 and 43) must make up the remainder of the manor of East Lexham, details of which are known mostly from much later sources.

Carthew (1878, 662–4) had access to a series of manor and leet court rolls of East Lexham manor running from 1347 to 1377, and his extracts contain several references to Great Fransham. He, irritatingly, gave no indication of the owner of the documents and their present whereabouts are unknown. An East Lexham extent of 1496–7 does not mention any demesne in Great Fransham, though it does refer to the leet court which has jurisdiction over tenants there (KIM 1/8/14). The two main surviving sources for East Lexham manor which do touch on Fransham are both late: two early seventeenth-century copies of an early sixteenth-century rental (KIM 1/8/15 and KIM 1/8/16) and a descriptive list of similar date with tenurial histories and rents arranged by tenants, which is based on 'old' rentals and court rolls dated between 1333/4 and 1609/10 (MC 1812/49, 838X5).

The following statistics can be extracted from these two rather unsatisfactory sources. Freeholds comprised 7 messuages, 2 parcels of messuages (probably the equivalent of 1), 101¾ acres of land, 4 acres of meadow, 1 meadow (no acreage given), 4 tenements (no acreage) and a parcel of a wood (no acreage). In contrast there were only 6 acres of customary land. Three of these included a void messuage and the other 3 certainly contained a standing messuage in 1642.

One part of the above group of freeholds in effect made up the demesne of Ellinghams manor. It consisted of a messuage with 20 acres, 3 tenements and a parcel of a wood. Recorded tenants of these lands were lords of Ellinghams in the sixteenth and seventeenth centuries. Annual rent paid by lords of Ellinghams to East Lexham manor right up the nineteenth century equals the combined rents of these freeholds minus that for the wood.

Mascales manor
One further property element might also have been expected to feature in the feodary, although it cannot be specifically identified therein. This was the manor of Mascales or the lands and rents recently purchased by William Oldhall from Thomas Mascalle in 1442–3 (farmer's and bailiff's account roll, MS 13140). This holding must have been recently acquired as it does not feature in the roll for 1440–1 (MS 13039). As two fixed rents were paid by men of Kempstone and one by a Norwich man, their lands may not have been in Great Fransham. Another fixed rent was paid by the prior of Castle Acre for a meadow in Wendling. The only fixed rent that can be confidently associated with Fransham was one of 3s 4d paid by John Coke for a 20-acre close called *Brakes*. Farm rents were paid by Thomas Mascalle (presumably the same man who had sold the land) for 16 acres, a close called *le Parke* and 4½ acres of meadow. Eight acres were held at farm by 2 men, while other farmed lands were in Beeston and Kempstone. A large enclosure in Great Fransham called *Kynwelshaweclose* with the *laund* there, which should have raised 8s, was not leased out because it was being grazed by the lord's animals. Outgoings for the manor of Mascales included 2s rent to the manor of [East] Lexham, 1d rent to the same for *Kynwelshaweclos*, 7d to the same for suit of court, and 2½d annual *blauncheferme* (a rent required to be paid in coin) to the Hundred bailiff (MS 13140).

Blyfords manor
Part of Wimer the Dapifer's Domesday fee (Brown 1984, 8.68), which caused so much uncertainty in the Domesday entry, can probably be identified with the manor of Geoffrey de Marscall in the feodary (Table 6.2, nos 17 and 18). It is not known when or how this part was alienated from the rest. It was held, for a ¼ knight's fee of William de Bressyngham and Alexander le Strange, mesne tenants of de Warenne (see Davison 1988, 48–9 for a discussion of Rougham). As well as a messuage and 60 acres in demesne and 16 acres of customary land, there were 3 messuages and 34 acres held by 3 free tenants, of whom 2 were named de Marscall (Table 6.2, nos 19–21).

The exceptionally confused evidence for this manor is presented in Appendix 3. Two points should be noted here. Firstly, holders of a ¼ knight's fee of de Warenne in Rougham and Fransham in 1302, 1401–2 and 1428 were all named le Mareschal or variations thereof (Feudal Aids 1904, 416, 454, 539, 595 and 634). Secondly, some freehold rents in Great and Little Fransham were granted to Wendling Abbey both before and after the composition of the feodary. However, neither grantor was a de Marschall, which suggests that the actual ladder of tenure was more complicated.

The chief part (Table 6.2, nos 17 and 18) became the manor known as the manor of *Blyfords* in the mid-fifteenth century, the core of which was an estate consisting of a messuage, 57¾ acres of land, 5 acres of pasture and 4½ acres of meadow, held by William Mascale in 1434/5 of lord Edward Hastings for an annual rent of 10¼d (PD 143/76). The 3 messuages and 34 acres held by 3 tenants (Table 6.2, nos 19–21) are next recognisable as 3 messuages and slightly more than 36 acres in Great Fransham owing annual rents totalling 5s 2¼d to Blyfords manor about 270 years later (MS 424). Most of William Mascale's Great Fransham properties were bequeathed to John Blyford and his wife in his will, which was proved in 1439 (NCC 76 Doke MF26). In 1509 the former Blyford estate was to become a main possession of a charitable trust, the Necton Town Estate (p.190).

Rougholme Manor
Holdings of the free chapel of St Nicholas at Rougholme in Gressenhall, which had been founded by William de

Stuteville in 1249/50 and endowed with lands in Great Fransham and elsewhere in Launditch Hundred and in Bradenham (Blomefield 1808, 515–6; Carthew 1878, 460), do not appear in the feodary. Little information is available on Rougholme manor until a bailiff's account roll of 1441–2 (LEST/GA7) and a rather corrupt rental of the late fifteenth century (TNA SC 11/476). According to the account roll fixed rents in Great and Little [sic] Fransham amounted to 16s 8½d. The parson of Great Fransham paid 1s rent for land late of Ralph de Beeston, and there were 2 farm rents of 3s 6d and 3s. Court roll extracts are available for 1504–34 (MR 28 240X6 and TNA SC 2/192/95). After the Dissolution the manor was split, with part going to Richard Hoo of Scarning (MR 255A), and becoming amalgamated with two former Wendling Abbey manors, Northendhall and Guntons. From post-medieval sources for each part it has been possible to arrive at a list of tenanted lands in Great Fransham, there being no evidence for any demesne there. There was a very minor freehold component: 1 messuage, 1 void messuage with ½ acre, a ½-acre pightle and ½ acre. Evidence for free rents is incomplete, but the total was low, little more than 2d and 2 hens. Customary holdings comprised 2 void messuages, 1 cottage, 57½ acres of land and 2 acres of meadow. The rents amounted to £1 6s 11d, 7 hens and 1 capon. This is a small proportion of £13 12s 3½d, the total annual revenue in rents and farms of St Nicholas' chapel assessed in 1535 (Caley and Hunter 1817, 329).

De Tosny manors in Little Fransham:
Kirkhams, Wilcoks, Sparhams, Cannons and West Bradenham

The single fee of Ralph de Tosny in Fransham (Brown 1984, 22.11), which formed part of the large estate or soke of Necton, had probably been divided into 5 parts by the middle of the thirteenth century. They were to become known as Kirkhams, Wilcoks, Sparhams, Cannons and West Bradenham manors. Two of these (Kirkhams and Sparhams) appear in the Great Fransham feodary of c.1279. There is no surviving return for Little Fransham, and because all 5 manors were dependencies of the manor of Necton, they do not appear in Feudal Aids (1904) except under the year 1316 when the lords of Kirkhams, Wilcoks and Sparhams were listed (Blake 1952, 269).

Kirkhams manor

The largest manor was known as Little Fransham and/or Kirkhams (after a lord who held it in the 1330s). In 1264 the lord was probably Osbert de Caylii, listed as a tenant of Roger de Tosny in his *Inquisition Post Mortem* (TNA C 132/31/3/588). In 1277/8 Ralph de Tosny and John le Logan were judged at the king's court to have dispossessed Adam de Cailly of a messuage and 25 acres in Little Fransham (Rose and Illingworth eds 1811, 195). Some lands held by free tenancy lay in Great Fransham and in the feodary of c.1279 John le Strange, who held of Ralph de Tony, had 1 tenant and 4 sub-tenants there (Table 6.2, nos 6, 30, 38–9 and 46). Two undated releases antedating c.1310 show that the manor had descended from Roger le Strange through his son John and to his son Henry (BL Add Ch 6192; MC 360/35, 713X6)[vii]. Henry le Strange was a lord in Little Fransham in 1316 (Blake 1952).

This manor is more than normally well documented (HMC 1914, 320–7). The earliest court roll is of January 1327, and the fragmentary record of a leet court or view of frankpledge held in 1328 also survives (MS 13090; Pl. 6.3). The latter consists of a list of thirty-one jurors (capital pledges) of the tenantry of Lady le Strange (*de homage. dne. Lastraunge*). Several messors' accounts are entered amongst subsequent court rolls, the earliest for 1329–30 (MS 13091). A short rental of freehold tenants, of those holding lands at farm and of a few customary tenants, dates to c.1375 (MS 13175). A wealth of detail on both free and customary tenants and lands is contained in a rental and custumal of Emma le Strange, dated 6 October 1384, with additions of c.1391 (MS 13176). The evidence provided by this document is supplemented by that from a much more detailed rental made at Michaelmas 1443, with a few later additions (MS 13145, with a faithful sixteenth-century copy, MS 13146). The earliest extant bailiff's accounts are for 1373–4 (MS 13121) and the earliest messor's account roll is for 1383–4 (MS 13122). It is surprising that neither Blomefield (1808, 501–2) nor Carthew (1877, 93) was aware that this manor was the most substantial of the five. The demesne of Kirkhams is inextricably bound up with that of Wilcoks manor because the first surviving extent was compiled more than a century after they were combined. The two sets of demesne will therefore be treated together after descriptions of the tenanted lands of each. Most of the available Kirkhams and Wilcoks manorial sources are summarised in HMC 1914, 320–7.

The following figures can be extracted from the 1384 rental. Freehold lands, under 25 entries and held by 18 tenants, amounted to 4 messuages, 52 acres of land (including a grove) and 4½ acres of meadow, of which 1 messuage, 18¾ acres of land and all the meadows were in Great Fransham. Of these 17 acres and 3½ acres of meadow were of the Baysbolle fee (or in one entry of the tenement Bayesbolle) and were held by 10 tenants for a combined rent of 8s 7¾d. Both acreage and rent totals exceed the overall figures for the holdings of Ralph Baysboll and his three tenants in c.1279 (Table 6.2, nos 6, 30, 39 and 46)[viii]. Other sources, both earlier and later than 1384, provide evidence of additional freehold lands. These were all in Great Fransham and comprised 2 messuages and a portion of a messuage, 11¼ acres of land and ¾ acre of meadow (MS 13091–2, MS 13122–3, MS 13125, MS 13128, MS 13145 and MS 13175). Additional sources, predominantly later than 1384, provide evidence of other freeholds that cannot be ascribed firmly to either Kirkhams or Wilcoks manors, but merely to both. These comprised 2 messuages, a ¼-acre tenement and 48¼ acres, all in Little Fransham, and held in 14 parcels.

In 1384 customary holdings comprised 19½ messuages and a parcel of another, 1 cottage, 126 acres and ¼ rood of land, and 1½ acres of meadow. There were 70 entries for which individual rents and services were given, and 17 tenants. The total of annual rents was £1 13s 8¾d, 20½ hens, 12 pullets and 1 clove of garlic. Services amounted to 44½ autumn boon-works. Parts of 2 tenements were in Necton and 4 entries totalling 2½ acres were in Great Fransham. Additional entries, comprising 7 messuages, 2 parcels of messuages and a ¼ messuage, a parcel of a toft, 40 acres and 4 perches, ¾ acre of pasture, 1¾ acres of meadow and ½ a meadow, appear on the reverse of the role, having been added in or soon after

Plate 6.3 The earliest extant court roll of Little Fransham (Kirkhams) manor, held on the Saturday after the feast of St Agnes, 20 Edward II (24 January 1327) (NRO MS 13090 40A4)

1391. Six tenants paid rents totalling £1 4s 9d and 22 hens, and they owed 21 autumn boon-works and winter works. Seven entries made in 1384 were described as *solidlond.* Soiled land (*solid.* or *soliat.*) was freehold which had fallen into the hands of an unfree, *i.e.* customary, tenant (Davenport 1906, 70). One of these entries carried an increased (*de increment.*) rent, and the rest were *sine servic.* (*i.e.* not owing rent). Four other entries that were not described as soiled also had *de increment.* rents. Some of these holdings were freeholds of other manors, Sparhams and Wilcoks, but there seems to have been little logic in the choice of increased rents or no rent at all. Before the Black Death customary lands were subject to partible inheritance, and afterwards by primogeniture.

In October 1377 Peter le Strange (lord of Kirkhams) was granted the right to hold a weekly market on Thursdays and an annual fair of 16–18 June at his manor in Little Fransham (TNA C 143/390/2; Letters *et al.* 2003, 249). This grant was one of a small group issued in Norfolk between the Black Death and the Peasants' Revolt. Of the other places, Felbrigg (in 1353), Harleston (in 1371), Fring (in 1372), Gissing (in 1378) and Elsing (in 1380), only Harleston was to be a success, and had anyway been holding a market since the early thirteenth century (Dymond 1985, 153–5, fig.14). Little Fransham's failure to achieve urban status can be put down to the large number of rivals in this part of the county, in particular East Dereham and Swaffham. No reference to either market or fair has been found in Kirkhams manorial documents. Perhaps Peter le Strange never had the opportunity to take advantage of the grant, for he died in France within a year of receiving the grant. His will was written at Saint-Malo in August 1378 and was proved in January 1379 (NCC 159 Heydon MF 22).

The moated manor house, which was not occupied after the 1460s, survives as an earthwork (Med 74, Appendix 2).

Wilcoks manor
In 1264 the lord of what was to become known as Wilcoks manor was William de Sapy who held a tenement in Fransham of Roger de Tosny lord of Necton, for an annual rent of 2s 9d (TNA C 132/31/3/588). Sometime between *c.*1273 and 1290 de Sapy granted a messuage and 28 acres with a windmill (pp134–5), homages and villein rents *etc.*, *i.e.* a manor, to Thomas de Cali, rector of [West] Bradenham and others (MC 360/28, 713X6). Both de Cali and de Sapy, along with Johanna widow of Alexander de Welnetham, one of de Cali's cofeoffees, were involved in litigation with de Sapy's son Thomas in 1284 and 1285. Properties involved comprised a messuage and 5 acres, 10 acres and a mill in Little Fransham (TNA JUST 1/1258A f23 and JUST 1/1258B f1d), but it is unclear whether or not these were part of the manor. William Fitz Alexander can be identified as the lord of Wilcoks in 1316 (Blake 1952).

A list of ten capital pledges of the tenantry of Henry le Strange appears above a similar list of Little Fransham men in a view of frankpledge (leet court) of 1328 (MS 13090). Perhaps these ten were tenants of Wilcoks manor, but this is by no means certain.

The earliest rental, titled 'of William Straunge', dates to *c.*1395. It is brief and includes only tenants' names and their rents. There were 27 freeholders who paid annual rents totalling 10s 5½d, 2 hens and 2 capons, as well as 5 customary tenants paying 4s 3d and 3 hens, labour services not being listed (MS 13219). The first surviving court roll of the manor late of (*nuper*) William le Straunge is of 1399. A court held in 1404 was titled *Wilcokys in Parva Fr* (MS 13094). The name Wilcoks, a diminutive, may refer to this William. He may be identified with William le Strange of Little Fransham and William son of Henry le Strange of the same who featured as sole grantee in nineteen Little Fransham deeds, the earliest of 1318 and the latest of 1346 (HRO 8184; PHI/126 577X1; MC 360/37, 39, 54, 56, 59, 60, 62–70 and 77–8 713X6).[ix] The court of William le Strange was named in presentments at a Kirkhams manor court of 1336 and he was named as a free tenant of Kirkhams in October 1348 (MS 13091). He was not mentioned as a living person in post-Black Death courts of that manor.

From 1404 Wilcoks and Kirkhams manors shared a common lord, firstly Emma, widow of Peter le Strange and lord of Kirkhams, and later in that year Edmund Oldhall. The two manors were gradually amalgamated during the fifteenth century. A full rental of Wilcoks tenants and their holdings with abuttals and acreages has been dated to *c.*1420 (MS 13154). By this time a few lands had fallen into the hands of the lord and one free rent had ceased to be paid because it was of an unknown fee, so that 2s 6d, a hen and a capon were no longer included. Freeholds amounted to 13 messuages (including 1 built, 1 void and 1 lately built), a parcel of a messuage, a toft, a barn, 83 acres of land and ½ acre of meadow (in Great Fransham), and free rents totalling 9s 10¾d, 1 capon, 1 pair of gloves and 1 clove of garlic were paid by 22 tenants. Of the above freeholds some parcels were said to be soiled: 2 messuages with 9½ acres soiled of Kirkhams, 1 acre of Sparhams and 7½ acres simply soiled. The properties soiled of Kirkhams and Sparhams are to be found in rentals of those manors. Four tenants held 3 customary messuages (including 2 built) with 10¼ acres for rents totalling 2s, 2 hens, and 12 autumn boon-works. Wilcoks messors' accounts between 1404 and 1421 show that each boon-work was commuted for a payment of 3d (MS 13129, MS 13132, MS 13134 and MS 13136).

The site of the manor house was identified in the field survey (Med 85).

The demesne of Kirkhams and Wilcoks manors
Many parcels of demesne of the combined manor of Kirkhams and Wilcoks cannot be allocated with any certainty to one manor or the other. The earliest surviving extent, prepared in 1502, will be discussed in Chapter 9.

Demesne farming of Kirkhams and Wilcoks manor was practised until at least 1417–8, when the bailiff's account roll listed in detail the produce of the grange (MS 13135). A similar account for 1413–4 had been the last to distinguish between the granges of Kirkhams and Wilcoks (MS 13133). By 1427–8 the demesne was let out in various parcels with the bailiff, William Wyskard, leasing the most land. He held, on a 5-year lease, several buildings with a dovecot, 4 closes next to the site of the manor and 44 acres in several pieces between the manor and the church, along with the crops thereon, at an annual rent of £4 5s 7d (MS 13137). By 1431–2 Wyskard, by now described as farmer and bailiff, was in the first year of another 5-year lease. He held all the buildings outside the moat, a dovecot, and all lands, meadows and pastures pertaining to Kirkhams manor, as well as all pertaining to

Wilcoks, for an annual rent of £15 6s 8d (HRO 8185). Wyskard held the same for the same length of lease, for £16 rent in 1442–3, with 3 tenements which remained in the lord's hands. He also held the rights to all rents, proceeds of courts, wood, underwood, wards, reliefs *etc.* (MS 13140). By 1446–7 much of the demesne was held at farm, either by year or for terms of years, by about eighteen people, Wyskard having reduced his farmed lands to 81½ acres centred on the Kirkhams manor house, his lease being due for termination or renewal at Michaelmas 1447. He must have died soon afterwards, for by *c.*1449 lands formerly held by him had been split between 10 tenants (MS 13142).

During the mid and late fifteenth century many parcels of Kirkhams and Wilcoks demesne were leased out to tenants. Ten of these parcels came to be held by hereditary fee farm, a form of tenure that quite soon became hereditary copyhold. By the sixteenth century this resulted in the distinction between ancient customary land and copyhold becoming first blurred and then extinguished. The situation is complicated by the fact that some of this land at an earlier time had not been demesne but held by tenants, either freely or by customary tenure. The 10 parcels comprised 49¾ acres and included a 7-acre meadow.

In 1485 Sir Edmund Gorges, lord of the manors of Kirkhams and Wilcoks, leased them out to Nicholas Myn (Mynne') and John Stalworthy of Little Fransham, along with the liberty of a foldcourse in Little Fransham and the leet of Milles atte Mor in Great Fransham for a term of 10 years (MS 13234).

Sparhams manor
The third manor in Little Fransham forming part of the de Tosny fee was titled *Sparhams* or Sparham Hall. The medieval manor house stood on or near Sparham Hall, a seventeenth-century house lying in Necton parish at TF 8764 1121 (HER 4209). In 1264 Roger de Clifford held a carucate and the rents and services of 30 villeins in Sparham [in Necton parish] of Roger de Tosny, lord of Necton. De Clifford also held villeins in several nearby places including Fransham, where there were 14 (TNA C 132/31/3/588). By 1272 Sparham manor had been subinfeudated to John le Breton (Blomefield 1807, 47). According to the Great Fransham feodary of *c.*1279 le Breton had 3 sub-tenants and he held of Roger Clyfford of Ralph de Tony (Table 6.2, no. 27). In 1316 Edmund le Bretoun was a lord in Little Fransham and also in Necton with Sparham (Blake 1952). In 1382 possessions in the places that had been listed in 1264 were conveyed by Elizabeth Breton to Ralph, Margaret and John Churcheman (TNA CP 25/1/168/177.73). The Fransham element did not become a distinct entity with its own lord until 1587. However, a late sixteenth-century copy of a rental dated 1385/6 and titled *Sparham hall*, lists tenants and lands in Little Fransham and 4 tenements in Great and Little Dunham and Holme Hale (two of the places listed in 1264), although it contains no information on Sparham or Necton (MS 13162). Separate courts for *Sparham hall et Fransham Parva* were held from 1485 at the latest (Hansell Stevenson 13/07/1972 36). There is no evidence that Sparhams possessed any demesne in Little Fransham.

The 1385/6 rental listed freehold tenants and their lands, as well as tenements, under the heading of customary, which were not held of the manor but which owed rents for the exercise of common rights. Customary entries in many cases did not include the names of tenants, but only the names of tenements. Abuttals or minor details of location were given in only 5 out of 40 entries (nothing will be said here of the final 4 entries concerning properties in the Dunhams and Holme Hale). Freeholds, described in 11 entries, amounted to 1 messuage, 1 cottage, 1 tenement and 24¾ acres. There were 9 tenants whose combined rents totalled 4s 10d and 3 hens, as well as 3 autumn boon-works. One of the latter and 1 of the hens were due from a tenant of a tenement for common rights only. The other two works and another of the hens were the rent for a cottage with 2 acres that were also entered in the 1384 Kirkhams rental as a customary messuage with 2 acres owing an increased rent of ¼d (MS 13176). Three free acres were held by the abbot of Wendling and were in Wendling, although this was not stated. Emma Straunge, lady of Kirkhams, held 5 acres and 1½ roods, and paid 2d rent for rights of common on another 4 acres. Three entries comprising 5 acres, 4 acres and 1½ roods were in Great Fransham, to judge from the tenants' names and sparse details of location.

The picture of customary holdings, with 25 entries, is complex. Tenants' names are given in only 11. Common rights (*communia*) rather than land are the subject of 7 entries, and in 4 of these the rent was payable only when the rights were exercised, 'if the tenant opened the gate onto the common' (*si porta erga communiam habeat apert.*). Some of these 7 must have concerned lands in Great Fransham near the common pasture called *Eastendmoor* in Little Fransham. Three of the named tenants who owed rent only for common rights appeared in the Wilcoks rental of *c.*1395. Fourteen entries, including the 7 above, do not appear in later Sparhams documents. Two of the 14 were for lands outside Fransham, although this was not stated (8 acres at *Bondeswood* and 1 messuage were probably in Necton). One messuage with 2½ acres can probably be identified with a Wilcoks freehold, and 4 other entries concern a total of 4½ acres. The 11 entries that can be followed in court proceedings from 1485 onwards formed the large majority of customary land, and concerned 3 messuages, 2 cottages and 74¼ acres. Two holdings, which paid house-bote (the right to timber and wood for maintenance and building) but for which no messuage was entered, produced archaeological evidence for settlement, and another, without a cited messuage and not owing house-bote, also yielded settlement evidence. The total of customary rents and services amounted to 12s 6¼d, 7s shillings for house-bote, 28 hens, 2 capons, 1 clove, 57½ autumn boon-works, 9 spring ploughing works and 1½d for *flesshese* which might be *flesgabulum*, a due paid by butchers (Latham 1965, 194). Following the start of surviving court proceedings in 1485 a few parcels of land occur, which cannot be identified with any entry in the 1385/6 rental: four pieces of customary land comprising 2½ acres and 1½ roods (including 1 acre in Necton) and 4½ acres of soiled land in five pieces.

Cannons (West Acre Priory) manor
Cannons was not considered as a discrete manor or so named until after the Dissolution. It formed part of the estate of the Augustinian priory of West Acre, which was founded in the reign of Henry I within the de Tosny fee (Vincent 1993; Caley *et al.* eds 1830, 575–6). No

information has been found to bear on the initial granting of lands to West Acre but, given the proximity of the de Tosny caput manor of Necton, it seems probable that the holding was created in Little Fransham early in the history of the priory. It was probably in existence by *c*.1200 (Jurkowski *et al*. 2007, 349). An unstated quantity of land in Great Fransham was held by the priory of William de Fransham in *c*.1279 (Table 6.2, no. 15). The Taxation of Pope Nicholas in 1291 valued the temporalities of West Acre in Little Fransham at 60s 7d, those in Great Fransham at 7s and those in Great Dunham at 1s (Ayscough and Caley eds 1802, 98 and 105). Some land was granted to the priory in 1313 when Constantine son of Geoffrey de Sutton obtained a licence for alienation in mortmain of properties in six places in West Norfolk including West Acre, as well as in Rougham and Fransham. As acreages and details of tenure of all lands *etc*. in all the named places apart from Fransham were given, it is possible that the latter was included in error (TNA C 143/94/18). The 1291 figures were repeated in a list of 1342 (TNA C 260/53/5). One 10¼-acre piece called *Lollemanescroft* was held freely of Kirkhams manor in 1384 (MS 13176) for 8s, an annual rent specified in a charter of 1321 (MC 360/52, 713X6).

A brief rental, titled 'Westakr.' and dated on internal evidence to *c*.1370, survives amongst legal papers assembled in *c*.1600 and relating to Great Fransham manor (MS 13089A). Under the heading 'pasture' (*Herbag*) 10 men were listed with payments totalling 16s, for pasturing on demesne lands. Under 'crops' (*Blad*.) 8½ bushels of barley and 1 hen are written against the names of 3 men and empty spaces are left against 6 others. These payments were probably farm rents for pieces of the demesne, because at the base an addition states that one Thomas Howes had taken out a 7-year lease on 3 acres for an annual rent of 6 bushels of barley. Under 'rents' (*redd*.) 3 men paid a total of 4s 5d, one paying 2 separate rents. These were probably payments for customary holdings.

Some Cannons land, and perhaps the entire manor, was farmed by the lord of Kirkhams in the late fourteenth century (MS 13093), and bailiffs' account rolls show that the lord of Kirkhams and Wilcoks held the whole manor at farm from at least 1412 until 1428, and that large parts of the demesne were sublet (MS 13133, MS 13135 and MS 13137). By 1429 all was back in the prior's hands (MS 13138). In the roll for 1427–8 details of fixed rents are missing, but the total was 2s 6d, judging from a deletion in the roll for 1429–30. Eighteen boon-works were due from 4 tenants (MS 13137 and MS 13138). An account roll of West Acre properties taken in 1435 recorded receipts of 40s from William Pulter for the farm of the manor of Little Fransham, and of 10s 5½d from [blank] Wyscard[vi] of Little Fransham for lands held at farm, with the lease then in its sixth year. In an account roll of 1457 William Deye alias Pulter, farmer of Fransham, recorded a payment of 32s to the cellarer of West Acre inclusive of all arrears, fixed rents and court proceeds, with Deye being responsible for 8s fixed rent to the lord of Kirkhams. The 1505 account roll of Thomas Clarke, bailiff of the priory, cites the total of fixed rents due from Fransham as 44s 9d with 4d for 2 hens (Holkham Hall, Tittleshall Register Rolls 39, 43 and 78). This figure, much larger than that of *c*.1370, must have included payments in lieu of labour services and new copyhold rents for former demesne. A rental book of *c*.1507–10 contains 3 lists on 3 pages under the heading of Fransham, two incomplete, and one with twenty people paying 43s 5½d (CUL Dd VIII 42). No information regarding the acreage and location of demesne and tenanted constituents is available until the start of surviving court proceedings in 1541 (Hansell Stevenson 13/07/1972 36). In 1535 the *Valor Ecclesiasticus*, without employing the word manor, assessed the total of fixed rents due from Little Fransham as 42s 10d, with outgoings of 8s to Giles Capell knight, lord of Kirkhams manor. Rents from land in Great Fransham were not specified (Caley and Hunter eds 1817, 392–3). The payment to Capell was rent for 'divers' lands, *i.e.* the 10¼-acre piece known as *Lollemanescroft* in 1384. The same rent total and outgoings were recorded in an undated, pre-Dissolution West Acre Priory rental (Holkham Hall, Tittleshall Register Rolls 147).

The following figures have been calculated from court records. The demesne, all of which was copyhold by 1541, consisted of 3½ and 10 acres in Great Fransham, and 52½ acres in 11 parcels in Little Fransham. There were only 3 pieces of freehold, 3 acres in Little Fransham, a pightle and 2 acres in Great Fransham. Customary holdings comprised a messuage with 2½ acres, 1 acre that may have once contained a dwelling and which did so by 1623, a messuage with 1½ acres, a messuage with 2 acres, a messuage with 2½ acres, and 4 parcels of land comprising 5¾ acres. A small amount of land in Great Dunham was also subject to Cannons manor, 7½ acres of freehold and 1¾ acres of copyhold.

Although Cannons manor was comparatively small, both in the size of the demesne and in the number of tenants, Carthew considered that the 'greater part' of Little Fransham had been granted by the de Tosnys to West Acre (Carthew 1877, 93).

There was no permanently occupied manorial site in Little Fransham, but an enclosure that may have contained a grange lay in *Quarent*. 16 (Fig. 7.3) where a large proportion of this manor's lands lay (p.150).

West Bradenham manor
A clutch of tenanted lands of this manor lay in Little Fransham very close to the north-east corner of West Bradenham parish. It consisted of 1 free messuage with 3½ acres and 2 customary messuages with 6¼ acres, the direct evidence for which is entirely post-medieval. It is more likely that these lands had been part of the de Tosny Domesday holding in [West] Bradenham (Brown 1984, 22.2) rather than part of either of the de Warenne possessions (Brown 1984, 8.93 and 66.64). The de Warenne and de Tosny manors were united under the lordship of Sir John Knyvet in 1478 (Blomefield 1807, 142–5; Carthew 1883, 7). Surviving manor court proceedings begin in 1496 (NRS 12346, 27C5) and run with gaps from 1499 to 1506 (NRS 11288, 26B2). Single court records are extant for 1609 (Holkham Hall, Davidson, Holkham 953) and 1619 (TNA SC 2/193/4), followed by a continuous series from 1625 to 1797 (PD 299/47–54). The de Tosny identification receives some circumstantial support from two amercements (fines), in 1460 and 1461 at the Little Fransham leet court, for offences in the vicinity of the tenanted lands, the culprit of both occasions being Sir Thomas Tuddenham, lord of the de Tosny manor (MS 13097).

The Barony of Rye

The Domesday possessions of Ralph de Beaufour (Bellafago) within Launditch Hundred lay in Swanton Morley, East Dereham and Lexham. These passed to Hubert de Rye under William II, to the le Mareschalls in the thirteenth century and the Morleys in the fourteenth (Martin and Satchell 2008, 87–8). Two *Inquisitions Post Mortem*, held in 1282 and 1317 found that Godfrey de Beumond, and then Joan Bemond and Walter de Langeton held four knight's fees in Drayton, Scarning, Barford, Fransham and Dunham of John le Mareschale, pertaining to Hockering, the head manor of the barony of Rye (Cal. Inq. Post Mort. 1906, 283, no. 471, and 1910, 51, no. 61). According to an inquisition held in 1360, Walter de Langton, who had died in 1321, and Joan Beumond still held the same, but by then of Robert de Morlee (Cal. Inq. Post Mort. 1921, 502, no. 634). In the *Nomina Villarum* of 1316 Eleanor de Beaumont was a lord in Scarning, and the Bishop of Chester [*i.e.* Walter de Langeton, Bishop of Coventry and Lichfield] was a lord in Drayton, but there is no relevant entry in Barford or either of the Dunhams or Franshams (Blake 1952, 268–9, 280 and 286). A Morley *Inquisition Post Mortem* of 1379 lists knight's fees in Barford, Drayton and Scarning, but not in Dunham or Fransham (Cal. Inq. Post Mort. 1970, 48–9, no. 129).

The Scarning manor became known as Drayton Hall. Two rentals, one early fifteenth-century and the other of 1470/1, contain no reference to Fransham (MS 1890 and MS 2691). Sir William Oldhall, who died in 1460, held a number of Norfolk manors including Kirkhams and Wilcoks, part of Great Fransham and Drayton Hall (TNA PROB 11/4/362). However, no Fransham document contains any reference to Drayton Hall, Hockering manor or any of the lords thereof. Carthew was perplexed by the knight's fees in Fransham and Dunham, and his only explanation was that the one carucate in the de Tosny Fransham manor at Domesday which had previously been held by Ralph de Beaufour (Brown 1984, 22.11) 'must however have been subsequently restored to Beaufoe or to Hubert de Rye' (Carthew 1877, 323–4). This problem remains quite unresolved.

Mileham manor

The feodary of *c*.1279 states that a messuage and 10 acres of villein land in Great Fransham were held by John le Breton of Richard de Mundevile, lord of Mileham (Table 6.2, no. 28). This holding possibly became a constituent of the manor of Ellinghams (p.86). No other evidence has been found of either customary, freehold or demesne lands lying within Fransham and belonging to the Fitz Alan manor of Mileham, which included the greater part of Beeston (Blomefield 1808, 463). John le Breton was presumably he of the same name who was lord of Sparham in Necton (p.81). He held from Richard de Mundevile / Amoundevill / Amundeville, who was married to Maud, grandmother of Richard Fitz Alan, a minor and a King's ward in 1276–7 (Blomefield 1809, 17–8). William son of John, the tenant-in-chief according to the feodary, has not been identified.

Bromehill Priory

A mid-thirteenth century charter confirms the grant of a rent of 1s 1d by Roger son of Gilbert de Fransham to Bromehill Priory (MC 2234/14, 943X1). This Augustinian house near Weeting in south-west Norfolk had been founded, probably in the reign of John, by Sir Hugh de Plaiz, overlord of the lords of Great Fransham manor (Cox 1906, 374–5). The rent was paid by Fucher Galt for 4 acres in *Sûwode* (Southwood in Great Fransham, area O in Chapter 7). The land can be equated with 4 acres of his demesne that had been granted by Roger son of Gilbert de Fransham to Fulcher son of Alfar of Wendling for the same rent. It was at *Sudvude* in his 'external' cultivated land (*in cultura mea forensica*), to the west, apart from ½ acre. This probably means that the other 3½ acres lay in Wendling. The undated charter is endorsed 'Bromhill' (TNA E 40/10539). No further evidence of this rent being paid to, or collected by, Bromehill Priory has been noted. The house was suppressed in 1528 (Knowles and Hadcock 1971, 138).

Castle Acre Priory

The Cluniac priory of Castle Acre was founded in *c*.1087–9 by the second William de Warenne (Pestell 2004, 176) and not by the first as has often been claimed (Caley *et al.* eds 1825 and Carthew 1877). Grants recorded in the priory's cartulary (BL Harley MS 2110) include the tithe of the demesne of Gilbert de Froesham / Fravesham (listed in Warenne's confirmation charters), 2 messuages, 29 acres, 3 perches, a marsh (*marescam*) and a green way (*viridiam viam*) in Great Fransham, as well as a messuage and 8½ acres in Little Fransham. Within the cartulary there are also charters dated 1181[xii], 1249 and 1265 by which the Bishop of Norwich confirmed the monks' possessions. These included two parts of the tithe of Gilbert's demesne in Fransham and the tithes of the assarts (*sartis*) of *Haringeshag*' (Harper-Bill 1990, 147, no. 184).

The manors of Herringshall and Dikewood had been granted to the priory by 1200 (Jurkowski *et al.* 2007, 324). Dikewood comprised a panhandle extension to the north at the western end of Wendling and contained *c*.115 hectares. Its northern half now lies within the civil parish of Beeston with Bittering. Perhaps there was some confusion between lands in Wendling and in Fransham. This may have arisen from ill-defined township boundaries at an early date, when Herringshall and its northerly neighbour Dikewood were not firmly placed within Wendling. Indeed, Dikewood is entered after an entry concerning Scarning and not under Wendling in two of the Bishop of Norwich's confirmation charters (Harper-Bill 1990, 147, no. 184 and 2007, 162, no. 143). It is unlikely that further confusion resulted from the presence amongst grantors to the priory of people surnamed de Francheville and of others called de Fransham. There were two distinct families (Carthew 1877, 231–3). In 1274/5 the Launditch hundredal jury declared that the prior of Castle Acre had recently appropriated free warren in Fransham and Wendling (Illingworth and Caley eds 1812, 435). The priory does not feature in the feodary of *c*.1279. Unaccountably, Blomefield's account of Herringshall and Dikewood occurs under the heading of Dillington, a township lying some distance away and to the north-west of Dereham (Blomefield 1809, 47–9).

Shortly after the Dissolution of 1537 possessions of Castle Acre Priory were granted to Thomas, Duke of Norfolk (Gairdner 1891, 471). Those in Wendling and surrounding townships were named as *Heryngsawe* and *Dykewood*[xiii], and thereafter the two holdings were regarded as one manor. The site of Herringshall manor lies adjacent to the present Manor House[xiv], *c.*600m east of the Fransham parish boundary and retains a curving length of moat, which may once have been fully circular (HER 7291). The probable '*caput*' of Dikewood, now known as *Dykewood House*[xv] and partly surrounded by a rectangular moat, lies 370m west of the Launditch and just over 1km north of the north-west corner of Fransham parish (HER 7273).

Consulted manorial records are post-medieval, the earliest of 1557 (Holkham Hall, Tittleshall Register Books 29). After court proceedings of 1608 and 1620, in the latter of which twenty-one tenants are listed (TNA SC 2/193/3–4), the series runs almost unbroken from 1623 to 1923 (MC 2104, 920X9).

Creake Abbey
The value of rent due to Creake Abbey in Great Fransham was stated to be 10d in 1291 (Ayscough and Caley eds 1802, 98 and 104). This house was first founded as a hospital in the reign of Henry II by Sir Robert and Alice de Nerford, becoming an Augustinian priory in 1206 and an abbey in 1231 (Caley *et al.* eds 1830, 486–90; Cox 1906, 370–1). There is no reference to this rent in the Creake cartulary (BL Add MS 61900; Bedingfield ed. 1966), and no other evidence has been noted. Gilbert de Fransham was a witness to an undated, thirteenth-century, grant of land to the Abbey by Ralph de Gateley (Caley *et al.* eds 1830, 490). The house closed following an epidemic in 1506.

Hempton Priory
Fakenham (*i.e.* Hempton) Priory, an Augustinian house, was founded as a hospital in the reign of Henry I (Caley *et al.* eds 1830, 571–2; Cox 1906, 381; Pestell 2004, 154). The value of its rents in Little Fransham was put at 13s 10d in 1291 (Ayscough and Caley eds 1802, 98 and 110). No details of the names and dates of grantors are known. This value seems very high, given that a farm rent of only 4s was recorded in a receipt book of 1501/2 (BL Add MS 10621). The *Valor Ecclesiasticus* in silent on Hempton lands or rents in the parish (Caley and Hunter eds 1817, 383). The rent for 6 acres remained at 4s in 1544 (TNA E 318/3/84). The acreage was again given as 6 in 1572 (TNA C 66/1091/22). Post-medieval sources suggest there were three parcels of land in three areas, 4½ acres in *Quarent.* 17, a small piece in *Quarent.* 28 and perhaps 2 acres in *Quarent.* 29. The priory was dissolved in 1537.

Pentney Priory
Robert de Vaux had founded this Augustinian house by 1135 (Caley *et al.* eds 1830, 68–70; Cox 1906, 388; Pestell 2004, 208). An undated mid thirteenth-century charter records the gift by Matilda of Fransham, daughter of Bonde, to Pentney Priory of herself and all her land in Fransham, 20 acres of arable and 2 acres 3 roods of meadow. Roger de Fransham was to be paid 1s for every 20s of scutage, and 1d was to be paid annually to All Saints' church (TNA LR 14/571). The grant was confirmed by her son, Ralph son of Roger (TNA LR 14/570). According to the feodary of *c.*1279 the prior of Pentney held 20 acres in Great Fransham of William de Fransham (Table 6.2, no. 1) and William de Fransham held 10 acres of Walter Thorpe who held of William Bardolf who held of the King (Table 6.2, no. 8). In 1291 temporalities in Great Fransham of Pentney Priory were valued at 8s in land (Ayscough and Caley eds 1802, 98 and 102). In 1306 Walter de Thorp held, of Isabel widow of Hugh Bardolf, a knight's fee in *Haleyweythorp* (Gayton Thorpe), Bexwell, Fransham and Gayton, valued at £10 (Cal. Close Rol. 1908, 440). In 1330 the prior of Pentney held a fee in Bexwell and Fransham of Agnes widow of Thomas Bardolf, with an annual value of 100s (Cal. Close Rol. 1898, 8–9; Cal. Inq. Post Mort. 1909, 178, no. 243). There appears to have been a muddle in the feodary, and it has not been possible to determine whether there were two holdings of 10 and 20 acres, or only one, of 20 acres. In *c.*1400 the prior of Pentney held freely of Great Fransham manor, for an annual rent of 1s and 1s 4d to a scutage, 20½ acres with 1 acre of meadow. No suggestion of any other land in Great Fransham has been encountered in later sources. The *Valor Ecclesiasticus* failed to record Pentney's interests here (Caley and Hunter eds 1817, 393–5). This house was dissolved in 1537.

Thetford Priory of the Holy Sepulchre
In 1291 the value of rent in Little Fransham held by the priory of the Canons of the Holy Sepulchre was 6d (Ayscough and Caley eds 1802, 98 and 112). William de Warenne III had founded this house soon after 1139 (Caley *et al.* eds 1830, 728–30; Cox 1906, 391; Davison 1992, 216; Pestell 2004, 155 and 177 f.n. 80). The main source for the priory is silent on this rent (TBA T/C1/10), and nothing further has been found.

Wendling Abbey
This Premonstratensian house was founded in *c.*1265 by William de Wendling, who endowed it with lands in Wendling, Scarning, Little and Great Fransham, Dunham and Kempstone and many other places (Caley *et al.* eds 1830, 889–91; Cox 1906, 421; Pestell 2004, 227). It was the last house of this order to have been founded in England, and amongst the poorest (Colvin 1951, 191–3, 203, and 253; Gribbin 2001, 3–5). The manor of Wendling had been held by the abbot of Bury St Edmunds at Domesday (Brown 1984, 14.12), and Robert de Stuteville held it of Bury. The intriguing story of Wendling Abbey's foundation and its founder, who died in 1270, has been told by Vincent (2001). Amongst substantial groups of deeds recording grants of property to the abbey many concern William de Wendling[xvi]. In 1273 Robert son of William de Stuteville confirmed his grant to the abbey of possessions in Wendling, Scarning, Gressenhall, Little Fransham and Great Fransham (Loyd and Stenton 1950, 25). William de Wendling's gifts to Wendling Abbey are listed in a fine of 1268: they included a messuage, 50 acres of land, 1 acre of meadow and 10s rent in Great Fransham, a messuage, 9 acres of land and 3s rent in Little Fransham (TNA CP 25/1/283/16.446). A revenue roll of 1269 lists the abbey's demesne lands, those in Great and Little Fransham amounting to 54¼ and 4 acres respectively. This figure may be an overestimate, as it includes ¾ acre said to lie at the gate (*ad portam*) of Wendling church. (MS 3813 8A3). The feodary of *c.*1279 must therefore give an incomplete account of the abbey's possessions in Great Fransham, a close of 26 acres and 9 acres held by two tenants and one sub-tenant (Table 6.2, nos 14 and 32–4).

In 1291 lands and rents of Wendling Abbey in Great Fransham were valued at £1 2s and in Little Fransham at 5s 7½d, while the value of its possessions in Wendling itself amounted to £8 16s 7d (Ayscough and Caley eds 1802, 98 and 111–2). Numerous charters record lands and rents in Fransham acquired by William de Wendling before his foundation as well as grants made by other people to the abbey during its early years. The latter included a manor in Scarning and Wendling, later called Northendhall, which had been acquired by William from Roger son of Thomas de Scarning (TNA E 40/10712) and was released to Wendling Abbey by Richard son of Roger Baldwin of Scarning in 1292 (TNA E 40/10919). Both charters carry erroneous later endorsements to the effect that the manor in question was Guntons. However, Guntons manor, which consisted of lands and rents in Scarning, Wendling and West Bradenham, was granted by Matthew de Gunton to Sir Walter de Walcot and four cofeoffees who conveyed it to Geoffrey Malaysel and three others to the use of the abbot and convent of Wendling in 1351. This indenture to the uses makes no mention of Fransham (MS 3808). Wendling Abbey also held another manor called Guntons, in Longham, which had been acquired by c.1448 (Jurkowski et al. 2007, 346).

Guntons and Northendhall manors, which according to late and post-medieval sources also included lands and rents in Fransham, were considered by Blomefield to be of the Warenne fee (1809, 39–40). In several post-Dissolution rentals there are many cases of muddling and confusion between these two manors. The core of Wendling Abbey lands, apart from Northendhall and Guntons, was to become known as the manor of Wendling Nuper Abbis. The amount of land in Great Fransham held of this manor was minimal, consisting of 2½ acres in two parcels and 1 acre of meadow. In 1535 the *Valor Ecclesiasticus* assessed annual rents and farms in the two Franshams at £1 11¼d, with a rent of 1s 6½d due to the lord of Great Fransham (Caley and Hunter eds 1817, 328).[xvii] The house had been dissolved by a papal bull in 1528 and granted to Cardinal Wolsey who fell into disgrace before taking possession. It was granted to Christ Church, Oxford in 1546 (Cox 1906, 423).

Great Fransham Rectory glebe and manor

Great Fransham church was valued at £7 10s 4d in 1254 and at £10 13s 4d in 1291 (Hudson 1910, 102–3). The 1254 value was 74% of the average for parishes in Brisley Deanery, £9 11s 8d, and the 1291 value was 87%. The *Valor Ecclesiasticus* of 1535 assessed the Rector's annual income from tithes and offerings at £6 3s 9½d and from farm rent of the glebe at £2 1s 3d (Caley and Hunter eds 1817, 330).

In 1225 William de Stuteville, lord of the 'Rougham/Fransham' manor, brought an action against Gilbert son of Roger (de Fransham) over the right of presentment to a third part of Great Fransham church (Pat. Rol. 1901, 578 and 596). In 1227 the case was deferred because Gilbert was poised to go on Crusade (Fowler 1959, 69). The outcome of this case is not known but by the fourteeenth century the advowson was held by the lords of Great Fransham (Blomefield 1808, 498–9).

The first reference to a specific part of the glebe occurs in a judgement at Westminster in 1275. William de la Sale of Great Fransham and Hugh parson of the same were in dispute over land (Cal. Close Rol. 1900, 231). Two acres of meadow in Great Fransham were said to be belong in free alms to the church of Fransham and not to the lay fee of de la Sale (Rose and Illingworth eds 1811, 188; Carthew 1877, 344).

The earliest glebe terrier was written in 1613 (ANW/15/2.61). Thirty-one parcels of land amounted to 87¾ acres[xviii]. This figure can have been no less in the fourteenth century and was perhaps larger (Dymond 2002, 91).

There are extant court rolls of the Great Fransham Rectory manor for the years 1324, 1335, 1339, 1344, 1377 (two courts) and 1381/2 (MS 13042) and a late fifteenth-century copy of a rental dated 1343 (Holkham Hall, Longham Bundle 3, 34). Two charter grants made by Alexander, rector of Great Fransham, to Wendling Abbey shortly after its foundation may have involved free lands held of the rectory or of Alexander as an individual. They conveyed, in free alms, the homage and service of one man with 7d rent that he paid for 3½ acres of arable land, and two pieces (*pecie*) of land with rents of 3d and 1d (MS 3802; TNA E 40/11038). After 1381/2 here follows a considerable gap in surviving documentary evidence, during which a Little Fransham document of 1566 (MS 13158) stated of Great Fransham 'The parson thereof keepeth a corte within himself'. A court book commences in 1671 (Priv. Pos. 1). In the first half of the fourteenth century there were about 10 free tenants with 13½+ acres, and 5 customary tenants with 3 messuages and at least 8¼ acres. Free tenants included Gilbert de Fransham and Pentney Priory.

Little Fransham glebe

Little Fransham church was valued at £7 6s 8d in 1254 and at £9 13 4d in 1291 (Hudson 1910, 102–3). The 1254 value was 77% of the average for parishes in Brisley Deanery, and the 1291 value 78%. According to the *Valor Ecclesiasticus* of 1535 the Rector's annual income from tithes and offerings amounted to £5 7s 10½d and farm rent of the glebe to £1 8s 0d (Caley and Hunter eds 1817, 330).

There are indications that the origins of Little Fransham church and rectory may have involved some degree of dependency on Great Fransham, although greed rather than true historical precedence may have been behind the following litigation. In 1223 a case between Ralph de Tosny lord of Necton and Simon de Scarning, rector of Great Fransham over the status of Little Fransham church was heard in the royal court. The rector claimed it was a chapel dependent on his church, while de Tosny said it was a mother church (*matrix ecclesia*) with a cemetery and baptismal rights, and that he held the advowson, as his father had. The court found in favour of the latter, but with de Scarning permitted to hold the church for life, paying an annual allowance of 8 marks to a clerk presented by de Tosny (Fowler 1955, 249, 340 and 482). This dispute resumed in 1242. Laurence de Myllers, the priest who had been presented by Ralph de Tosny to Little Fransham, had died, as had Ralph de Tosny whose heir, Robert, was a ward of the King. Gilbert de Fransham claimed that Simon de Scarning had been presented by his father Roger de Fransham, and that Laurence had never been parson. Gilbert lost the case (Nicol 1991, 234–5). In the same year the King presented Guichard de Charwin[xix] to the church as incumbent (Cal. Pat. Rol. 1906, 303). Robert de Tosny was still underage in 1252 when the King presented Aymo de Grandimonte (Cal. Pat. Rol. 1908, 131). He remained rector in 1288 when he went abroad, having nominated an attorney (Cal. Pat. Rol. 1893, 289).

For the remainder of the Middle Ages the advowson was in the hands of the lords of Necton (Blomefield 1808, 502).

The first glebe terrier, of 1613, lists 24 parcels of land comprising 42¾ acres. Three parcels lay in Great Fransham (ANW 15/2.135).[xx]

The leet of Milles atte Mor
The right to hold leet courts in Great Fransham was held by the lords of Great Fransham and East Lexham, while in Little Fransham leet jurisdiction was exercised by the lord of Kirkhams. A third leet court operated in Great Fransham, that styled *Milles atte Mor* (later *Mills-on-the-Moor*), the earliest surviving record of which is an extract of 1400 (MS 13066, not of 44 Edward III as stated in HMC 1914, 322, the document cited therein (MS 13092) recording a Little Fransham leet court). There is good evidence to show that the court assembled on or near a windmill mound and medieval settlement site (Med 14) near the parish boundary with Great Dunham, Kempstone and Beeston, in Area B (see Chapter 7). The leet jurisdiction had belonged to Geoffrey de Fransham who, by an indenture of 1409, enfeoffed six men in the manor of Great Fransham, the leet known as *Myllys on ye Moor* and other properties, all to be sold after the death of his wife Joan (BL Add Ch 71046). Geoffrey died in 1414 and Joan lived until 1420/1 (NRO Norwich City Court Roll 17m 2/d, MF/RO136/1). By 1427–8 the leet was held by Sir William Oldhall, lord of Kirkhams and Wilcoks, with a rent of 6d being paid to the bailiff of Launditch Hundred for a certain leet held in Great Fransham (MS 13137). In 1429–30 proceeds of 7s 2d from a leet held on the moor at a mill-mound (*tent. super mora. ad mont. mol.*) in Great Fransham were recorded by William Wiscard, Oldhall's bailiff (MS 13138). In 1449 the prior of Castle Acre was amerced (fined) for illegally commoning his flock of *Kempstonhall* next to the leet bush (*versus le lete buske*). Thereafter this feature, which lay in *le Conynger*, was often named in presentments at the leet, but the mill-mound was not mentioned. In 1566 the leet was said 'to be kepte at Mylles on the more at a bushe their called the Leete bushe' (MS 13158).

As well as twelve capital pledges from Great Fransham, four jurors each from Great Dunham, Little Dunham and Kempstone were expected to attend the leet, which was held annually. The lord of Little Dunham paid (or was supposed to pay) a rent of one quarter of wheat each year to the lord of Mills-on-the-Moor, for the right to hold his own leet, a rent finally discharged for a once-off payment of £50 in 1872 (MC 969/2, 858X7). Despite this involvement of men from contiguous parishes, the court dealt exclusively with offences committed in Great Fransham. The location of the court, on the edge of a swathe of common pasture which passed into all 4 parishes, as well as into Beeston, and beyond into East Lexham, Litcham and Mileham, strongly suggests an ancient origin. The extent of this common can be appreciated against a map of heaths and commons in the county as a whole (Barringer 2005a; Macnair and Williamson 2010, fig.35), though it becomes somewhat lost when viewed on a map of East Anglia and Essex (Williamson 2003, fig.30). The men of adjacent Beeston might have been expected to attend the leet. Perhaps they had long been excused for Beeston was subsumed under Mileham, a royal vill at the time of Domesday. It seems likely that the leet had once been concerned with the management of the intercommoning of this huge area of land[xvi]. However, by the fifteenth century it dealt with the normal run of petty transgressions and was not overly concerned with commons-related offences. Where commons were involved, there was no bias towards those nearer the court venue.

At times the villagers of Great Fransham may have felt overburdened with court duties. Many men held land of several manors and attendance at three leet courts may have been tiresome. One example will suffice. A Great Fransham leet was held on Wednesday 11 June 1455 (MS 13049) and another at Mills-on-the-Moor on the following Monday (MS 13048). Five of the 11 jurors at the former were amongst the 12 who attended the latter. One offender and offence were common to both courts, John Mechill and the non-scouring of a ditch at *Emmysfaldgate* [in *Southwoodfield*, see Area O, Chapter 7].

Endnotes

i   An undated petition in French, incomplete and partly illegible, was sent by the people of Gressenhall and Great Fransham (and probably of other vills) to the King and Council asking in desperation for fiscal relief (TNA SC 8/343/16168).

ii   If the Great Fransham feodary does in fact derive from a 1279 Hundred Roll then its discovery need cause no surprise: 'It is possible that what have been assumed to be rentals or surveys elsewhere may equally be transcripts of hundred roll returns.' (Raban 2004, 55).

iii   Subinfeudation: the granting out of a part or parts of a holding by a feudal tenant to a sub-tenant.

iv   The seat of the de Plaiz family had been at Weeting since Domesday, but how and when they acquired the mesne lordship of Great Fransham is unknown.

v   The tenement consisted of a messuage and 15.5 acres in 14 parcels in 12 out of the 32 furlongs listed in a Kempstone field book of 1495–6 (MC 125/10, 600X1). Some versions of the Great Fransham rental of *c*.1400 give an acreage of 16 acres, with the tenement lying in Kempstone and Beeston. A Beeston field book of 1550–1 lists two pieces, both of 0.75 acre, in two furlongs in the western part of that township (Holkham Hall, Davidson, Tittleshall 68).

vi   In 1274/5 the Launditch hundredal jury declared that Robert de Stuteville had recently appropriated free warren in Brisley and Fransham (Illingworth and Caley eds 1812, 435).

vii   In 1243 John [le Strange] son of Roger and Beatrice his wife took legal action against Roger le Strange over a messuage and 1 carucate in Little Fransham which they claimed he held of them by agreement (Brand ed. 1999, 59, no. 304).). The dispute was settled in 1244 when a fine was levied, whereby two parts of the carucate with divers homages and services of freemen, villeinages, woods, meadows, pastures and a mill were to be held by Roger for life with reversion to John and Beatrice and their heirs (TNA CP 25/1/157/69.882; noted in Le Strange 1916, 95).

viii   The earliest reference to the name Baysbolle dates to 1242, when Alice widow of Aylnoth of Wendling took out actions for her right in dower to moieties of lands in Wendling against various people, against Peter Baysbowe for the moiety of an acre in Fransham and against Roger son of the parson for the moiety of an acre of meadow there (Hector 1979, 431).

ix   The many people named le Strange in Fransham is confusing. A fine levied in 1347 may serve as an example, and the William that it includes may possibly be the one in question: John, son and heir of William le Strange of Bayfield, conveyed to John, son of Roger le Strange of Little Fransham, 2 messuages, 60 acres of land, 6 of meadow, 6 of pasture and 2 of wood in Fransham (TNA CP 25/1/165/159.760 and MS 13223).

Endnotes (cont'd/ ...)

x   The Mynne family was to play a major role in both Franshams until the early seventeenth century. The first to appear was Nicholas who must have been 12 years old or more when sworn in as a tithing man at a Little Fransham leet court in 1471 (MS 13099). The rapid rise to gentry status and eventual obscurity of this family would repay an in-depth study.

xi   Almost certainly William Wyscard, bailiff and farmer of Kirkhams and Wilcoks in 1429–34 and 1442–3.

xii   *i.e.* 25 December 1180–24 March 1182.

xiii   The *Valor Ecclesiasticus* valued the manor of *Heryngsall* [and Dikewood] at £15 7s 6d, comprising £2 10s 10d from rents, £8 from demesne lands in the prior's hands, 6s 8d from court receipts and £5 from wood. A rent of 2s was payable to the manor of Middleton for lands in *Heryngsall* (Caley and Hunter eds 1817, 391). Twenty-one tenants were listed in 1620 (TNA SC 2/193/4).

xiv   Named *Heddens Hall* by Faden (1797).

xv   Named *Wendling Farm* by Faden (1797).

xvi   Amongst these are three undated charters showing William de Wendling had held some lands of the Cluniac house of Mendham in Suffolk, a cell of Castle Acre Priory. Eda daughter of Thurstan of Fransham widow and Roger son of Simon of Scarning quitclaimed to Mendham half of the land which Leftein son of Lewin de Wendling had held of Thurstan in Fransham and Wendling (TNA E 40/8979). Eda and Roger released half of the same lands to William son of Leftein, which William then held of Mendham (TNA E 40/12124). Prior Simon of Mendham quitclaimed to the abbot and monks of Wendling 6d rent that William de Wendling had paid for lands and tenements that he had held in Wendling and Fransham (TNA E 42/216). William son of Leftein was probably not the same person as William de Wendling (Vincent 2001).

xvii   Immediately local Wendling Abbey manors valued by the *Valor* comprised Wendling, i.e. Nuper Abbis, @ £23 10 10d; Parva Scarning, @ £2 2s 11d, Poyntons and Northendhall in Scarning, @ £6 1s 11d; Longham Priors with Guntons in Scarning, @ £3 17s 4½d. The situation was complicated by other lands and rents in Beeston, Kempstone, Gressenhall and the Franshams. Post-Dissolution confusion was to be expected (Caley and Hunter eds 1817, 328).

xviii   Dymond arrived at a 'crude estimate' of annual value per acre of 6½d for glebe lands in the *Valor Ecclesiasticus* of 1535 based on evidence from Heacham Deanery (Dymond 2002, 77, f.n. 21). This would give Great Fransham glebe an acreage of 76.15, a 13% shortfall on that given in the terrier of 1613.

xix   It was claimed by one historian (Craster 1909, 249–51) that this man, Guiscard de Charron, was one and the same as Wicard de Sabaudia (*i.e.* Savoy), steward of the Honour of Richmond in 1243 (Cal. Pat. Rol. 1906, 391) and a kinsman of Peter de Savoy, an uncle of Henry III, who arrived in England in 1241. Wicard / Guiscard was present when his brother Stephen, prior of Thetford, was murdered there in 1248. In his narrative of this event Matthew Paris described Guiscard as a 'beastly clerk', *clericum monstruosum*, 'whose belly was like a bladder in frosty weather, and whose body would load a waggon', *cujus venter quasi uter in pruina, cujus quoque cadaver plaustrum oneraret* (Giles 1853, 274–6; Luard ed. 1880, 31–3).

xx   An annual value of 6½d per acre indicates a Little Fransham glebe acreage of 51.69 in 1535, more than 99% of the 1613 figure.

xxi   For courts leet and their origins in pre-Conquest local government see Bailey 2002, 178–89, and for the great antiquity of intercommoning see Oosthuizen 2013, 154–60.

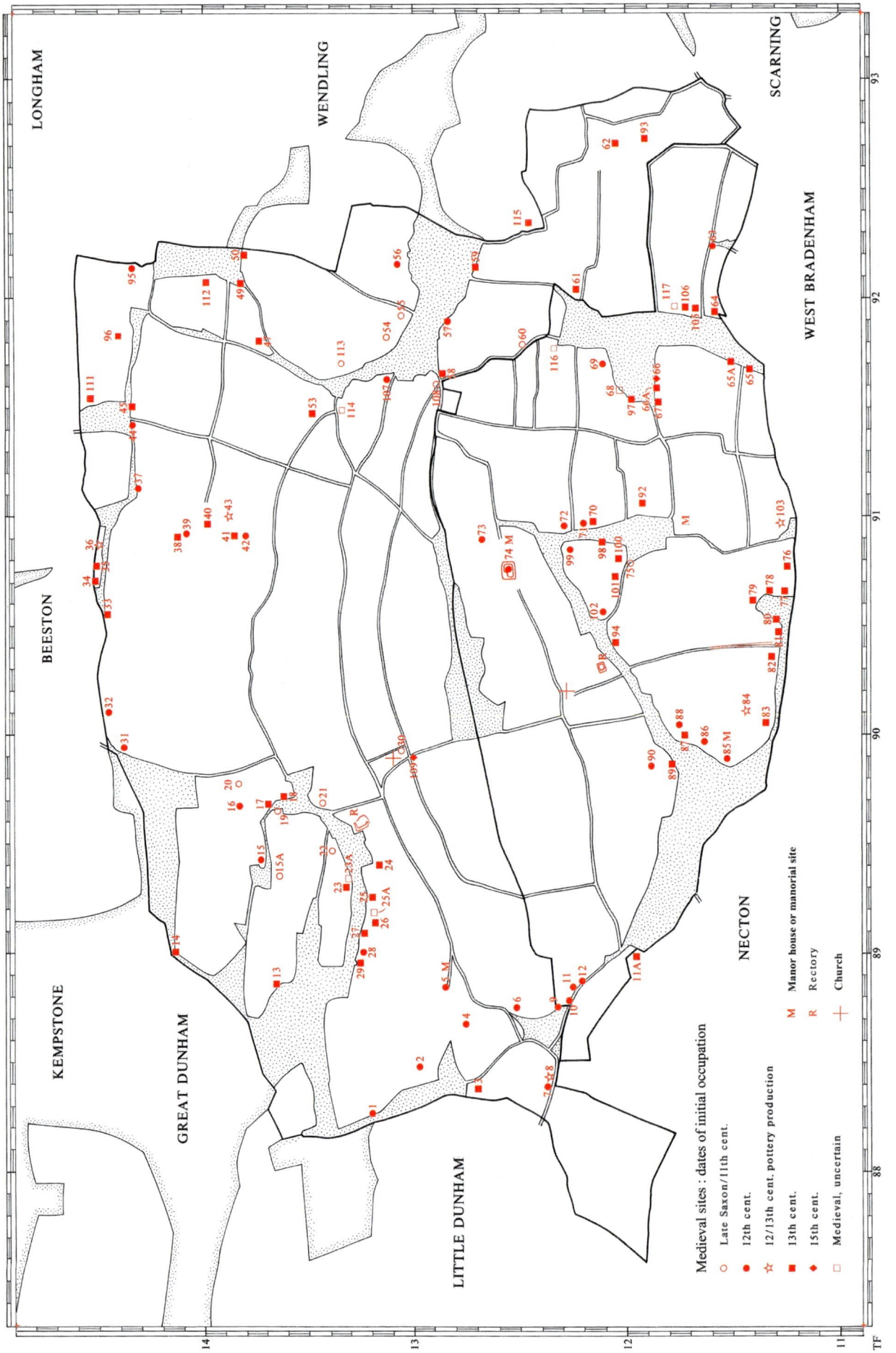

Figure 7.1 Medieval settlement sites known from archaeological evidence, areas of medieval common pastures shown stippled, scale 1:25,000

Chapter 7. The Medieval Landscape

Introduction

Two sources of evidence, archaeological and documentary, are used throughout the following description of the topography of Fransham and its pattern of medieval settlement and land-use. However, it needs to be stressed that though both sources have their own contribution to make, it is not always possible to bring them into line with each other. In those areas where fieldwalking was not possible, such as *Cruddesgrene*, *Hey Green* and *Eastendmoor* in Great Fransham and the present-day elongated village nucleus of Little Fransham, archaeological evidence is either absent or very slight. In such places documents, almost all late medieval or later, are the sole or principal means of reconstructing the earlier medieval pattern of landholding and settlement. Conversely, in those areas where the documentary evidence is vague and of limited detail, reliance is put on evidence collected in the field, and, to restate the obvious, potsherds alone give no clue as to tenurial status or manorial allegiance. The best example of such an area is the great open zone in the northern central part of Great Fransham, where there are numerous medieval settlement sites, about which the documentary evidence is so late in date, vague and incomplete that the topography can be reconstructed only in the barest outline.

Common pastures, route ways and medieval settlements located by field survey are shown on Fig. 7.1. The positions of a small number of other settlements known from documentary sources but with weak archaeological evidence are also indicated.

The locating and dating of settlement sites, and the importance of pottery

As with settlements of earlier periods the surface archaeological evidence for those of the Middle Ages is overwhelmingly in the form of pottery. All peasant houses were constructed of timber and unfired clay and were roofed with thatch. In medieval Fransham ceramic building material, bricks, floor tiles and roof tiles were used only in buildings of importance. Floor tiles were employed only in the two parish churches. Fourteenth- and fifteenth-century plain floor tiles, both English and Flemish of Drury 1993 Groups FT3 and FT6–10, have been recovered from the two churchyards. The distributions of medieval brick and roof tile are remarkably similar: only the two principal manor houses and some of their associated buildings (Med 5 and 74) were roofed with plain flat peg tiles. Dating to the thirteenth and fourteenth centuries these were all of a similar fabric, approximating to Drury 1993 Group RT1. The distribution of these fragments can be seen on Fig. 7.2.

Potsherds provide the fieldwalker with the only means by which the date-range of occupation on medieval sites may be calculated. Indeed, the pottery evidence is crucial in this chapter. It is essential, therefore, to provide a summary of the criteria that have been used to arrive at the many date-ranges given below to sherd concentrations found in the survey. Firstly, however, a number of general points must be made. Medieval pottery traditions were conservative and vessel forms remained unchanged over long periods. Decorative methods were normally simple, and in medieval ceramics there is none of the almost numismatic precision which can be applied to more sophisticated traditions such as Attic figure vases or Roman samian ware. The close dating of any type, form or fabric should always be viewed with moderate scepticism. Dating is normally achieved through the establishment of sequences within which are one or more fixed dates. These dates can be historically based, such as with monastic or castle foundations (even here caution is needed, see Hurst 1962–3) or with dated catastrophes such as fires (such as that in Norwich in 1507, see Evans and Carter 1985). Dating can also be scientifically based, with the use of such techniques as dendrochronology (MacCarthy and Brooks 1988, 4). Without fixed chronological points sequences are merely relative. Where fixed dates are present it is possible to judge certain pottery types to be in use by a certain point, and others to have either ceased circulation or have yet to begin. However, most excavations, especially those in towns, throw up large quantities of potsherds which are residual in the contexts in which they are found, *i.e.* they derive, through the digging of pits and ditches and through levelling, from earlier underlying contexts. Ceramic specialists are still struggling with the problem of residuality which, before it was recognised to be a problem, led to the incorrect dating of many pottery types.

East Anglia does not have the benefit of good published earlier medieval pottery sequences, whether firm or relative. The work of the King's Lynn Survey in the 1960s has provided a sequence from the late eleventh century to the post-medieval period, but this is useful only in the most general terms, with phasing being divided into broad slices such as *c*.1050–1250 (Clarke and Carter 1977, 183–232). Norwich, the scene of pioneering post-war campaigns of urban archaeology by Jope (1952) and Hurst (1963) has failed to provide anything more than a general picture of ceramic developments before the great milestone of the 1507 fire. The city is, however, privileged to have had this picture, from the Roman period to the eighteenth century, admirably portrayed in lucid catalogue form by Sarah Jennings (1981). If it can be argued that Norwich, at a distance of 30km, is too far from Fransham, then the well-defined sequence for Great Yarmouth covering *c*.1000–1250 (Mellor 1976) is of little or no value here. For the purposes of this survey, by far and away the most useful work is that of Bill Milligan on the material from excavations at Castle Acre Castle, 7km west-north-west of Fransham (Milligan 1982 and 1987). Beginning with some pottery antedating the foundation of the castle in the 1070s, the sequence reaches into the late twelfth century. Excavations at Castle Rising Castle have extended this into late medieval times, although there are few useful pottery groups (Milligan 1997).

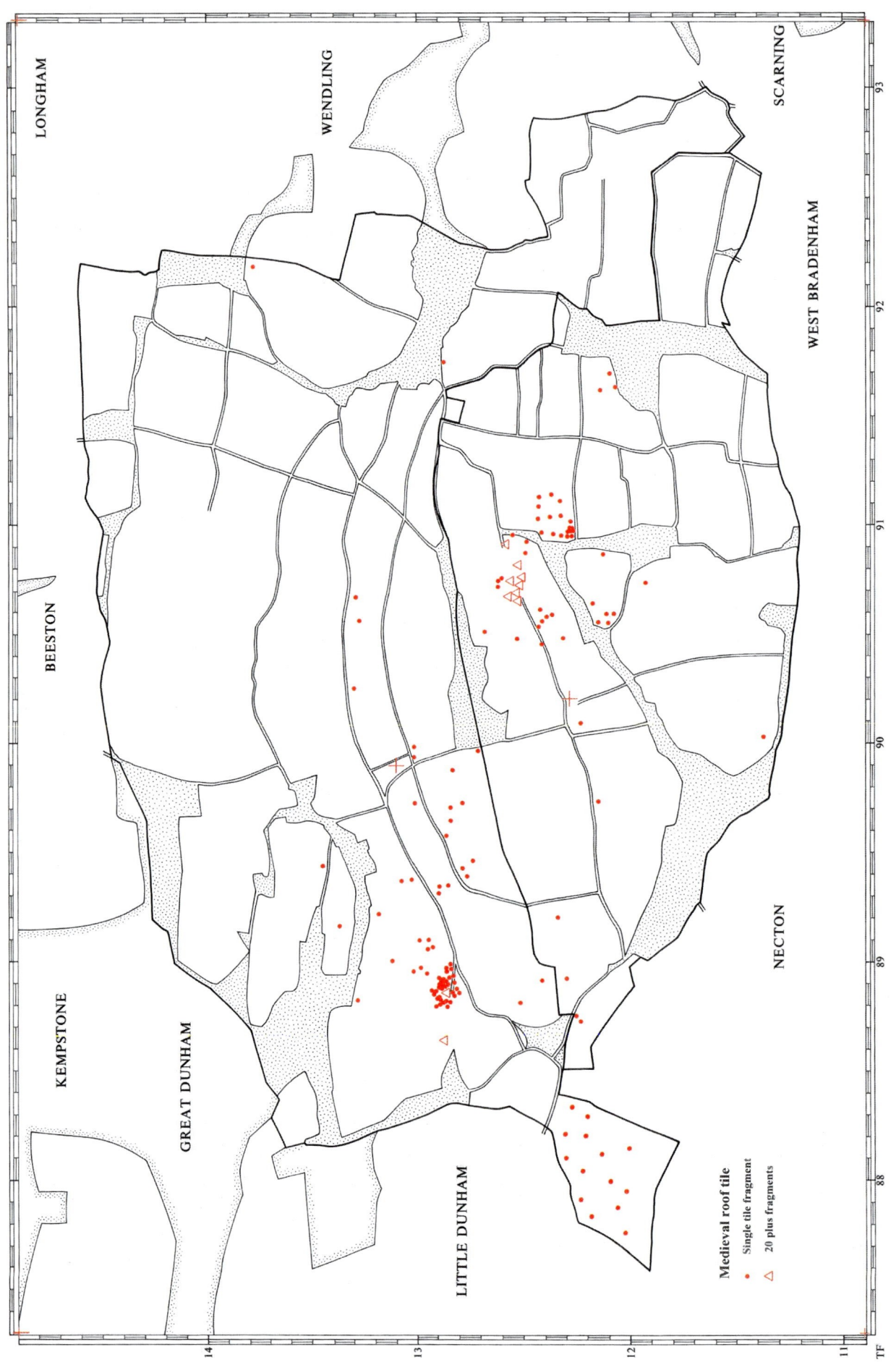

Figure 7.2 Distribution of medieval ceramic roof tile, areas of medieval common pastures shown stippled, scale 1:25,000

There is at present no really reliable typology for the products of the medieval pottery production centre at Pott Row, Grimston near King's Lynn. After a first phase as a rural Thetford-type ware industry (Clarke 1970), Grimston became the dominant producer of glazed wares in Norfolk, particularly in the west and south-west of the county, and its wares reached as far as Iceland in the late thirteenth and early fourteenth centuries (Jennings and Rogerson 1994). Grimston ware amounts to more than 99% of the late twelfth to fourteenth-century glazed pottery found in Fransham. A large quantity of material recovered from excavations at Pott Row, Grimston has been divided into four phases, which fit with reasonable consistency into the broad dating established for Fransham (Little 1994).

In contrast to many of those found in archaeological excavations, potsherds recovered in field surveys are almost invariably small fragments, often so tiny that the forms of the vessels from which they derive must remain unknown. Unglazed cooking wares, the most common medieval pottery group before the fifteenth century, were usually very thin-walled and easily broken. A thirteenth-century cooking pot might shatter into hundreds of sherds, many no bigger than a thumbnail. In addition, the identification of many potsherds found in walking over fields that have been arable for centuries is made more difficult, because they are usually abraded, both on surfaces and in fracture.

For the purposes of this survey what might be described as a relative chronology has been produced. It is based on published material, liaison with colleagues, experience and a degree of intuition. This approach was moderately reliable in the examination of over 33,000 post-Roman sherds found by Bob Silvester during his field survey of Norfolk Marshland for the Fenland project in the 1980s (Rogerson 1988). Date-ranges for more than 280 medieval pottery concentrations were given 'blind', *i.e.* without prior knowledge of the location or potential significance of any of the sites. The resultant pattern fitted most convincingly into Silvester's exposition of the complex development of post-Roman settlement (Silvester 1988, 162–3). Lastly, with regard to the Fransham survey, it should be noted that over 90% of the medieval sites were allotted date-ranges before an examination of the documentary evidence was begun.

The assumption is made throughout this work that there is little or no stratigraphy surviving on any of the archaeological sites identified from sherd scatters in arable fields, and that as a result, for all periods of occupation during which pottery would have been in use, there has been evidence available on the surface of the ploughsoil. In other words, it is not thought likely that, for example, intense fourteenth and fifteenth-century occupation on a particular site can have obscured evidence for a more minor eleventh and twelfth-century phase. Conversely, it is true that a rapid field collection, or one in poor conditions, might miss such an earlier phase of activity, and that up to a point, the more material that is picked up from a site, the more reliable the given date-range will be. Knowledge of this last point provoked additional visits to a number of sites, although as a result there were no alterations to previously estimated date-ranges. In this context it must also be noted that the surfaces of gardens on medieval sites continuously occupied until the present day may give a false and incomplete picture. In such places the normally dark grey soil with its ubiquitous coal and coke fragments militates against the visibility of ancient pottery, in particular unglazed sherds.

The distribution of pottery between settlements

Although the location and identification of medieval settlements is of importance, something must be said of the archaeological evidence recovered from the large tracts of land in between them, tracts that comprised common open fields, enclosures or closes, woodland, meadows and of course common pastures.

All surveyed areas known from documentary sources to have been common open field arable yielded at least a thin scatter of medieval potsherds, as did some areas which had been enclosed from an early date. Because of the somewhat variable conditions in which the survey was conducted, it is not deemed appropriate to estimate an expected mean sherd count per hectare for such areas. Indeed, such a calculation would involve a strong element of spurious accuracy. There is no doubt, however, that sherd scatters were thicker in fields and parts of fields lying close to numerous settlement sites, than they were in more outlying areas. For example, *Woodrowfield* in Little Fransham, which was flanked to north and south by many houses, produced a greater density than *Southwoodfield*, Great Fransham, near which were comparatively few settlements. Sherd numbers in the latter were akin to those in the north-west part of *Millfield*, Little Fransham, or in most of the eastern parts of the central common open field of Great Fransham.

Common pastures were in general devoid of medieval sherds, and normally the transition from open field or arable close to common was as noticeable in the fall-off of pottery finds as they were by soil changes and the presence of headland banks. Meadows were likewise almost sherd free, as were the scarce areas of woodland. Closes and enclosures, many of which may have been pastures for long periods, were rarely free of sherds, but in general the larger ones produced very few. For example, the substantial pieces of demesne surrounding the Kirkhams manor house in Little Fransham, and the similarly large blocks south of the Great Fransham manor house, yielded only a sparse sprinkling of finds. Equally unproductive were two demesne enclosures, known as *Shepehousefield* and *Conyngerlond* in the early fifteenth century, which lay in the northern part of Great Fransham. A foldcourse operated on these two by that date according to the extent of *c.*1430, and the scarcity of potsherds (derived from farmyard middens) can be attributed to direct manuring by sheep. Fieldwork in north-west Norfolk at Ringstead has revealed a similar pattern, with very low levels of medieval sherds on former open field which had formed part of a foldcourse (Leah and Flitcroft 1993, 477–81). There is no evidence for the existence of a rigid manorially controlled foldcourse system during the late medieval period in either of the Franshams, which lay just outside the southern boundary of the Sheep-Corn region and distribution of foldcourses according to Allison (1957, figs I and II), and beyond the limits of the North-West Norfolk farming region in the post-medieval period (Wade-Martins *et al.* 2005). Foldcourses, at any rate, only became widespread in lighter soil regions in the sixteenth century (Whyte 2009, 96–9).

Plate 7.1 Copy of Enclosure Award map, drawn in 1833 (NRO Ca 1/22)

The common pastures

It will become clear in the following pages that common pastures were the most important element to influence the location of settlement sites. Their known extents are shown on Fig. 7.1 and on numerous other maps in this work. The main source for these reconstructions is a map drawn up in 1833 (C/Ca 1/22) a copy of that surveyed in 1805 for the Enclosure Award of 1807 (C/Sca 2/122; Pl. 7.1). On the 1833 copy, the circumstances of whose production are unknown, the edges of former common pastures, with exception of *Barnards Moor*, are carefully delineated in green. These match in fine detail those places on the 1805 map where roads and ways edging or crossing commons are shown with an edge or edges of dashed lines, to signify non-enclosure. In broad and unspecific detail, the conformation of the commons shown on the 1833 map also match those indicated in somewhat distorted scale on Faden's county map (Faden 1797; www.fadensmapofnorfolk.co.uk). There is no suggestion, however, that the common edges shown on Fig. 7.1, and on the many other detailed 1:5000 scale maps of individual sites and groups of sites, lie on precisely the same lines as they did in the medieval period. There are indications of some unrecorded encroachments, big and small, and these are presented below. Two small common pastures, *Southwoodmoor* and *Cruddesgrene*, both in Great Fransham, vanished in the course of the fifteenth and sixteenth centuries. In general, though, the boundaries of commons appear to have hardly shifted between the Middle Ages and the Enclosure Award. Names given to commons on Faden's county map of 1797 are cited in end notes. These bear little or no relation to medieval names.

The allocation of site numbers

Individual medieval settlement sites for which firm archaeological evidence was recovered, have been allotted numbers, Med 1 *etc.* (some numbers not being used because entirely Late Saxon and post-medieval sites were originally included in the sequence). Most medieval sites known only from documentary sources have not been numbered. A few sites or groups of sites, with little or no archaeological evidence but with a lengthy and complex documentary background, have been allotted numbers. Very brief summaries of date-range, as well as tenurial status and manorial allegiance where known, are given in this topographical review. Greater detail for each site is given in Appendix 2, and indications of location, manorial allegiance, tenure and dating are given in Table 7.1.

Documentary references

In the interests of brevity, documentary references to individual sites are not cited in this chapter but will be found in Appendix 2, but those relating to other landscape features, such as roads, closes, fields and commons, are included.

Again, for brevity and clarity some very frequently used documents are not referenced in the following topographical descriptions. Unless otherwise indicated all statements about manors, land, people and places are taken from the following sources:

Great Fransham manor between 1330 and 1413: extracts of court rolls (MS 13034, MS 13043, MS 13044, MS 13045 and MS 13046).

Great Fransham manor in *c*.1400: various versions and copies of a rental (MS 11352, MS 13071, MS 13072 and MS 13084), and in *c*.1430 various copies of an extent (MS 11352 and MS 13084).

Lands formerly of William Mascale in 1434/5: (PD 143/76).

Great and Little Fransham glebe lands: terriers of 1613 (ANW/15/2.61 and 135) terriers of 1635 (ANW/15/1.18 and 46) and terriers of 1677 and 1633 onwards (DN/TER/68/4 and DN/TER/68/5).

Kirkhams and Wilcoks manors between 1327 and 1508, Kirkhams from 1327 and Wilcoks from 1399: manor and leet court rolls (MS 13047, MS 13090–MS 13095 and MS 13097–MS 13100.

Kirkhams manor: rentals of *c*.1375 and *c*.1487 (MS 13175), a rental and custumal of 1384 (MS 13176) and a rental of 1443 (MS 13145 and MS 13146).

Wilcoks manor: rentals of *c*.1395 and *c*.1420 (MS 13219 and MS 13154).

Kirkhams and Wilcoks manor: rentals and extents of 1502 (MS 13053, MS 13155 and MS 13167), 1566 (MS 13158), 1577 (MS 13156 and MS 13157) and 1605 (MS 13159).

Sparhams manor: copy of a rental of 1385/6 (MS 13162) and court books beginning in 1485 (Hansell Stevenson 13/07/1972 36–39 and 42).

Cannons manor: court books beginning in 1541 (Hansell Stevenson 13/07/1972 36–39 and 41).

Names of people listed in fourteenth-century tax assessments: Lay Subsidies of 1327 and 1332 (TNA E 179/149/7 and E 179/149/9), Lay Subsidy of 1337 (TNA E 179/238/111), Poll Taxes of 1379 and 1381 (TNA E 179/149/53).

The piece number for the Great and Little Fransham Enclosure Award map surveyed in 1805 is not cited (C/Sca 2/122).

The locations of some place names found in medieval deeds have not been identified and so the names are not to be found in this chapter. They are listed in Appendix 4.

The spelling of le Strange

To reduce confusion, all references to the many members of the le Strange family are so spelt. The surname is reproduced in a profusion of other ways in various sources: Lestrange, Straunge, le Straunge, Strange, l'Estrange and, in Latin, *Extraneus*.

Land divisions
(Fig. 7.3)

In order to make the complicated picture of the development of the settlement pattern and land-use as clear as possible, the study area will be examined in a succession of fields, furlongs and zones of settlement. Each settlement zone is relatively discrete, and either next to a road or centred (or more accurately spread) around the edges of a common pasture. It should be remembered that a very large proportion of the study area is 'archaeologically visible', *i.e.* arable land. Where normal

	Location	Manor	Tenure	Pottery Dating	Notes
Med 1	Area A	GFr	?	12th–13th century	Within demesne by early 15th century
Med 2	Area A	GFr	?C	12th–13th century	Demesne from 1349
Med 3	Area A	GFr	?	13th–mid 14th century	Within demesne by early 15th century
Med 4	Area A	GFr	F	mid 12th–mid 14th century	Demesne by 1340
Med 5	Area A	GFr	Manor House	12th–14th century	*Hallecroft* in 1330
Med 6	Area A	GFr	C	mid 12th–late 14th century	Demesne by 1374
Med 7	Area A	GFr	F	late 12th–mid 13th century	-
Med 8	Area A	?GFr	?	12th–early 13th century	Pottery production
Med 9	Area A & Quarent. 2	K	F	late 12th–13th century	Customary by 1374
Med 10	Quarent. 2	K	F	late 12th–13th century	Customary by 1374
Med 11	Quarent. 2	K	?F	mid 12th–early 15th century	Customary by 1374
Med 11A	Necton	K	C	13th–14th century	Occupation probably ceased after 1361
Med 12	Quarent. 2	K	F	?12th, 13th–14th century	Customary by 1374
Med 13	Area B	E Lex	F	13th–14th century	-
Med 14	Area B	GFr	?	13th–late 14th / early 15th century	Probably miller's house until mid 14th century
Med 15	Area B	E Lex	F	12th–late 14th century	-
Med 15A	Area B	?GFr	?	mid 11th–13th century	Probably within demesne by *c.*1430. See LS 5
Med 16	Area B	?Blyf	?F	12th century	Perhaps predecessor of Med 17
Med 17	Area B	Blyf	F	13th–17th century	-
Med 18	Area B	GFr	?	13th–14th and ?early 15th century	Within demesne by early 15th century
Med 19	Area B	GFr	C	11th century and later	Site still occupied. See LS 4
Med 20	Area B	GFr	?	late 10th–?early 12th century	Within demesne by early 15th century
Med 21	Area A	Blyf	F	10th century and later	Site still occupied. See LS 7
Med 22	Area A	GF Rect	F	11th–14th century	See LS 6. Perhaps not an ancient freehold
Med 23	Area A	GFr	F	13th–early 16th century	-
Med 23A	Area A	GFr	F	?13th century and later	Site still occupied
Med 24	Area A	Rough GFr	C ?	13th–14th century	Includes two discrete holdings
Med 25	Area A	GFr	F	13th–15th century	A garden by 1553
Med 25A	Area A	GF Rect	F	?13th century and later	Site still occupied
Med 26	Area A	GFr	?	13th–late 14th/ early 15th century	Demesne by early 15th century
Med 27	Area A	GFr	F	13th–16th century	-
Med 28	Area A	GFr	?	12th–14th century	Demesne by 1553 and probably by early 15th century
Med 29	Area A	GFr	?F	13th–14th century	-
Med 30	Area K	GF Rect	? site of Rectory	11th–13th century	Meadow in glebe terrier of 1613
Med 31	Area C	E Lex	F	?mid 12th–14th century	-
Med 32	Area C	E Lex	F	12th–13th century	-
Med 33	Area C	E Lex	F	13th–14th century	-
Med 34	Area C	?E Lex	?F	13th–14th century	-
Med 35	Area C	?E Lex	?F	13th–14th century	-
Med 36	Area C	?	?	12th–early 13th century	Pottery production
Med 37	Area C	?Elling	?	12th–13th century	Probably a 'croft' in 1442–3
Med 38	Area C	E Lex or GFr	F	13th–14th century	-
Med 39	Area C	E Lex or GFr	F	13th–14th century	-
Med 40	Area C	E Lex	F	13th century and later	Site of the post-medieval manor house of Ellinghams
Med 41	Area C	E Lex or GFr	F	13th–14th century	-

	Location	Manor	Tenure	Pottery Dating	Notes
Med 42	Area C	E Lex or GFr	F	12th–13th century	-
Med 43	Area C	?	?	12th–early 13th century	Pottery production
Med 44	Area C	?GFr	?	?12th and 13th–14th century	-
Med 45	Area C	GFr	F	13th–14th century	-
Med 47	Area E	Rough	C	13th–14th century	-
Med 49	Area E	Rough	C	13th–14th century	-
Med 50	Area D	GFr	F	13th–late 15th/ early 16th century	-
Med 53	Area C	GFr	F	13th–14th century	-
Med 54	Area E	GFr	F	11th–14th century	Demesne from 1349, copyhold by 1454. See LS 12
Med 55	Area E	GFr	F	11th–13th century	Demesne by 1386, copyhold by 1537. See LS 13
Med 56	Area E	?Spar	F	12th–14th century	-
Med 57	Area H	GF Rect	C	12th century and later	-
Med 58	Area H	GFr	F	13th–14th century	-
Med 59	Area H	Rough	C	13th–14th and ?early 15th century	-
Med 60	Area H & quarent. 21	?	?F	11th–12th century	See LS 16
Med 61	Area O	GFr K	F C	13th–14th century	Lord of K held freely of GFr. Leasehold of K. Copyhold of K from 1476
Med 62	Area O	GFr	F	13th–14th century	-
Med 63	Quarent. 21	K&W	F	12th century	-
Med 64	Quarent. 29	Spar	?C	13th–14th century	-
Med 65	Quarent. 17	K	C	13th–14th century	-
Med 65A	Quarent. 17	W Brad	C	13th–15th century	Includes two messuages
Med 66	Quarent. 17	K&W	F	15th–17th century	-
Med 66A	Quarent. 17	W	F	13th–14th century	-
Med 67	Quarents. 16 & 17	Spar Cann	C C	13th–19th century	Includes two holdings
Med 68	Quarent. 18	W	F	?13th century and later	Not available for fieldwalking
Med 69	Quarent. 18	K	C	12th–19th century	Includes as many as five messuages
Med 70	Quarent. 27	Spar	C	13th–19th century	-
Med 71	Quarent. 27	K	C	?11th, 12th century and later	Site still occupied
Med 72	Quarent. 25	K&W	?	12th–13th century	On demesne called *Nethiroxmer* in 1502
Med 73	Quarent. 9	K	?	12th century	In a 20-acre demesne close in 1447
Med 74	Quarent. 9	K	Manor House	12th–15th century	-
Med 75	Quarent. 11	Cann	C	11th century and later	Site still occupied. See LS 18
Med 76	Quarent. 15	K ?W	C ?F	13th–19th century	-
Med 77	Quarent. 15	Spar	C	13th–19th century	-
Med 78	Quarent. 15	Spar	C	13th–18th century	-
Med 79	Quarent. 15	Spar	C	13th–18th century	-
Med 80	Quarent. 15	K	C	13th–16th century	-
Med 81	Quarent. 15	Spar	C	13th–16th century	-
Med 82	Quarent. 15	W	F	13th–14th century	-
Med 83	Quarent. 15	W	F	13th–15th century	-
Med 84	Quarent. 15	K	C	12th–early 13th century	Pottery production
Med 85	Quarent. 14	W	?manor house	12th–?14th century	-
Med 86	Quarent. 14	W	F	12th–?14th century	One of three arable closes called *Wilcokks crofts* in 1577
Med 87	Quarent. 14	W	?F	13th–14th century	As Med 86
Med 88	Quarent. 14	W	?F	12th–13th century	As Med 86
Med 89	Quarent. 5	K	?	13th–14th century	*Shephousyerd* in 1392–3

	Location	Manor	Tenure	Pottery Dating	Notes
Med 90	Quarent. 5	K	?	?11th, 12th–13th century	As Med 89
Med 92	Quarent. 28	K	?	13th–14th century	On demesne called *Jekkes* in 1402–3
Med 93	Area O	GFr	F	13th–15th century	-
Med 94	Quarent. 11	K	F	13th–late 16th or early 17th century	-
Med 95	Area D	GFr	C, ?F until 1349	12th–13th century	-
Med 96	Area D	GFr	C	13th–14th century	Site under permanent grass inferred from sherds found in ditch upcast
Med 97	Quarent. 18	Spar	C	13th–19th century	Includes two distinct holdings
Med 98	Quarent. 10	K&W	?	13th–14th century	Probably a pightle of demesne in 1476 and certainly so by 1577
Med 99	Quarent. 10	K	?	Late 11th–14th century	Demesne called *Dufhouscroft* in 1393
Med 100	Quarent. 10	?W	?F	13th–14th century	Possibly called *Prestiscroft* in 1316 or later. Probably a pightle of K&W demesne in 1476
Med 101	Quarent. 10	?K	?C	13th–14th century	-
Med 102	Quarent. 10	K	?	11th and 12th century	Demesne called *Narowsmythclos* in 1429–30. See LS 17
Med 103	Quarent. 16	Cann	?	12th–early 13th century and 14th century	Pottery production, probably with later, 14th-century, occupation
Med 105	Quarent. 29	W K	F Soiled	13th–14th century	Single holding
Med 106	Quarent. 29	W	F	13th–14th century	-
Med 107	Area G	GFr K	FC	12th–13th century, 17th century and later	Single holding
Med 108	Area G	GFr	C	11th century and later	Site still occupied. See LS 15
Med 109	Area M	GFr	F	late 15th–16th century, late 17th century and later	-
Med 111	Area D	?Elling	?	13th–14th century	-
Med 112	Area D	GFr GFr	Soiled F	13th–16th century	Site still occupied or under grass. Includes two distinct holdings
Med 113	Area E	GFr* K K Rough** Elling Cann	C F F C F F	11th century and later	Sites still occupied. See LS 11 *With a bake house in 1537 **With a bake house in 1559–60
Med 114	Area G	GFr GFr GFr* GFr	C F F* F	13th century and later	Sites still occupied * Held of the Prior of Castle Acre who held of GFr in pure and perpetual alms
Med 115	Wendling, next to Area O	?	?	13th century	-
Med 116	Quarent. 19	?Rough Elling	F C	two 13th–14th century sherds only	Sites still occupied
Med 117	Quarent. 29	W K	F Soiled	seven 13th–14th century sherds only	Site not available for fieldwalking

Abbreviations of manor names: Blyf Blyfords, Cann Cannons, E Lex East Lexham, Elling Ellinghams, GFr Great Fransham, GF Rect Great Fransham Rectory, K Kirkhams, K&W Kirkhams and Wilcoks, Rough Rougholme, Spar Sparhams, W Wilcoks, W Brad West Bradenham
Abbreviations of tenures: C Customary, F Freehold

Table 7.1 Medieval settlement sites

fieldwalking and artefact collection was not possible this is made clear in the following description.

Great Fransham parish is described below in land blocks of unequal sizes and shapes, *Areas A–O,* ordered and arranged both for convenience of description and to make highly complex matters as simple as possible. They are the author's invention. Little Fransham is presented by *Quarentinae,* land blocks coined by William Hayward for his survey of 1605 (MS 13159). Numbered 1 to 29, they are abbreviated to *Quarent.* in the following description. The survey is discussed in Chapter 9. It should be noted that Hayward excluded common pastures from his *Quarentinae.*

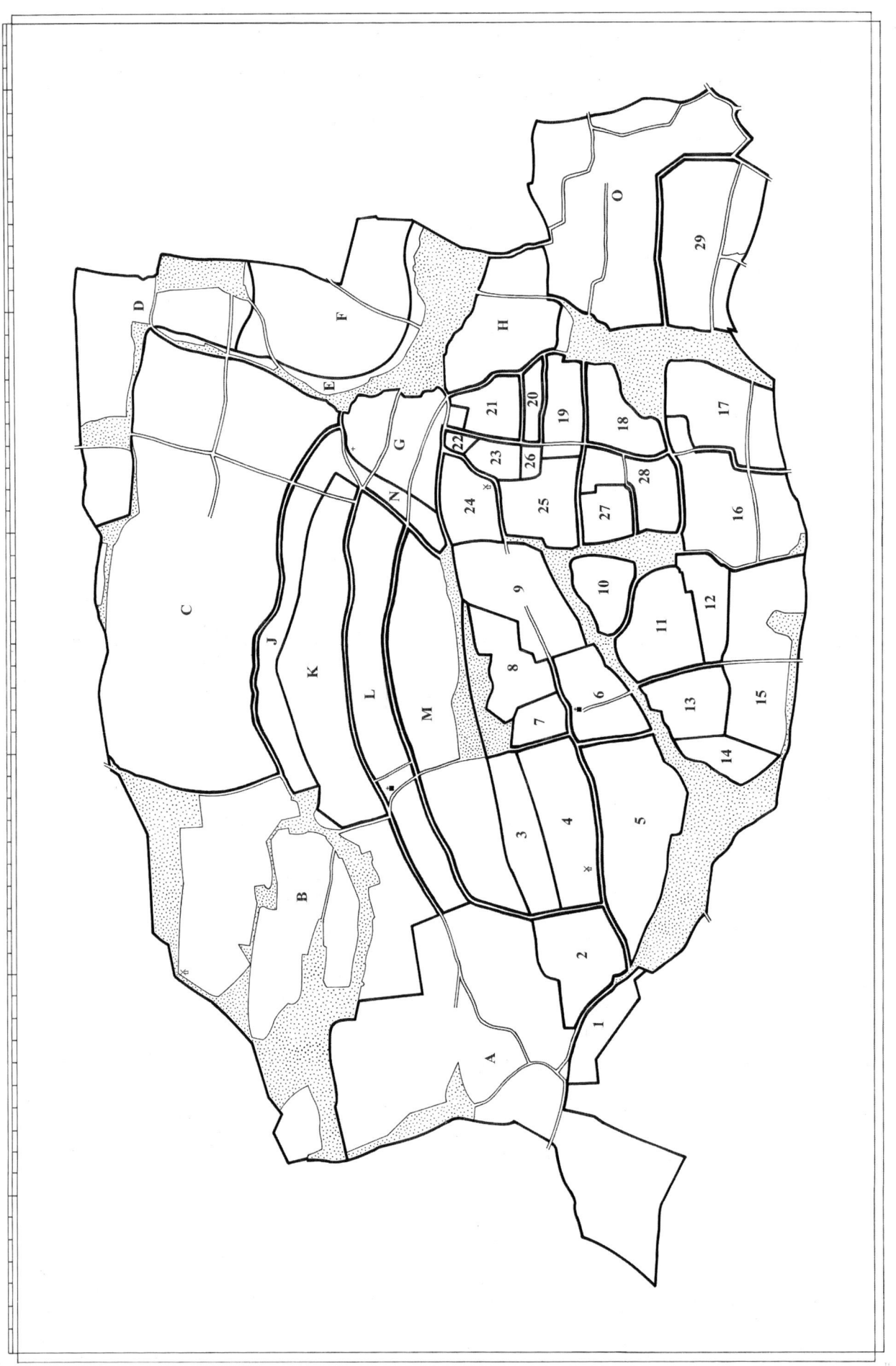

Figure 7.3 Subdivisions of Great Fransham into Areas A–O and Little Fransham in *Quarentinae* 1–29, areas of medieval common pastures shown stippled, scale 1:25,000

Land types

The description of each Area and *Quarent.* begins with a very brief summary of land-use, employing a simplified version of the terminology used by Martin and Satchell (2008, 39–76). The term 'several' means 'held by individual tenants for their own exclusive use'. In Fransham there were many enclosed parcels of land or 'closes' held by tenants and set well away from their dwelling houses. As defined by Martin and Satchell (2008, 45) 'tenement blocks…abutted or encompassed the house and yards of tenements'. For such closes in Fransham the term 'detached tenement block' has been used. Some categories of land type did not occur within the study area, common meadow, common woodland, parkland and several heath. Common heath, *i.e.* dry pasture, has not been recognised here, despite the word 'heath' in several common pasture names. Interchangeable with 'ling' and 'moor' it cannot have implied any great degree of dryness, given the nature of the soil. Many commons were in valleys containing streams. Though these streams were minor the term 'riverside common' is used. As land-use was not static in the Middle Ages, every effort has been made to indicate succinctly where changes are known to have taken place. Finally, in the initial summaries the term 'settlement' means messuage, house, cottage or tenement.

Great Fransham Areas A–O

Area A, the western parts of Great Fransham (Fig 7.4)
Two common pastures, one a medium green with surrounding settlements and tenement blocks, and one linear on the parish boundary, a manor house within a core block demesne, which included wood pasture and an alder carr, and parts of which had been woodland and had incorporated two isolated former common edge settlement sites, and a piece of detached block demesne projecting into Necton parish

A narrow strip of common followed the parish boundary with Little Dunham. It may have been that called *Brancaster more* in 1573 (MS 13079)[i]. The boundary is today marked by a ditch running through woodland, which does not form part of the modern drainage system, has the appearance of considerable antiquity and merges at the north end into an elongated pond at TF 8818 1333. To the east of this common lay two isolated twelfth to thirteenth-century settlement sites (Med 1 and 2) within an area which in *c.*1430 was described as an 80-acre close, part of the demesne of Great Fransham manor and 'where once there was a wood' (*ubi olim silva fuit*). This area, predominantly grassland with poor drainage before later twentieth-century agricultural changes, was known as *Halrode* in 1437 (MS 13048) and *Hallewood* in the sixteenth century (MS 13085). -*rode* is from the Old English **rod*, a clearing (Smith 1956b, 86–7; Ekwall 1960, 390). In a rental of demesne lands of *c.*1430 100 (rather than 80) acres of pasture at (*super*) the manor, with a close and wood belonging, were held at farm. Adam Colyn, the tenant, paid an extremely low annual rent (2d) because he carted away wood for the lord and had made his own fence (MS 13073). *Halrode* was being managed as wood pasture and this may have been the case for a long time (Stamper 1988, 132). The 20 acres in excess were probably in *Dunham Croft*, which lay to the south-west and was apparently held of Little Dunham manor. The lord's crops in *Dunham Croft* were damaged in 1355, as was his barley in *Dunhamlond* in 1366. In the extent of *c.*1430 *Dunham lond* was said to have been sold by the executors of Thomas Isaak of Little Dunham and occupied by them. The meaning of this uncertain. In 1573 a piece of *Isakes* next to *Brancaster more* was let at farm, as was a pightle in *Isakes* in 1582 (MS 13079). In 1621 a parcel of meadow in Little Dunham belonging to Nicholas Mynne [lord of Great Fransham] was called *Isack* (C/Sca 1/5 R117–8) and in 1636 a close in Great Fransham and Little Dunham 'or in one of them' called *Oateclose* and *Isaacs close* contained 39 acres and 25 perches (C/Sca 1/5 R138).

No evidence of the tenurial status of Med 1 has been recovered. It lies immediately south of a point at which a now canalised stream enters the parish. Med 2 may be identified with a probably customary messuage (and 12 acres) which fell into the hands of the lord of Great Fransham in 1349. The pottery, however, suggests abandonment by *c.*1300. An alder carr belonging to the same manor and containing 2½ acres of enclosed land was situated immediately north of this site. The lord's underwood in *le Ker* was damaged in 1369 and in *le Alderker* in 1382. There is no further reference to underwood there, but in 1404 cows damaged the lord's grass in *Halleker*. A road, perhaps along the eastern edge of the common, passed nearby in the later fifteenth century, a ditch being unscoured at *Hallekarre faldgate*[ii] in 1454 (MS 13049), and *Kerlane*, *Halleker lane* and *Kerlanesende* being mentioned in 1473–4 (MS 13048). Another isolated and undocumented thirteenth to fourteenth-century settlement (Med 3) lay next to the common at the northern end of *Dunham Croft*.

South of this common, and set back from its broad southern edge, was another single medieval site, occupied from the mid-twelfth to the mid-fourteenth century and a freehold of Great Fransham manor (Med 4, Fig. 7.5). The area to south of this was demesne of the same manor and known as *Haroldscroft* in 1340, the lord's rye being damaged at *Haroldiscroftsend* in 1334. These seven acres in two pieces lay between the common way on the east and west, butting south on the common way at *Cruddesgrene* and on the common pasture at *Crudds*. In the extent of *c.*1430 their agricultural potential was appreciated, '*et est bona terra*'. They are probably the same as 7 acres at *Colynespytt* held at farm by John Crudde at about the same date (MS 13073). A tree-surrounded pond that survived into the 1990s can be identified with *Colynespytt*. One acre called *Haraldisaker* was let at farm for five years in 1371.

Med 5 lay to the east of *Haroldscroft* and south-east of *Halrode* (Fig. 7.6). As well as unremarkable twelfth to fourteenth-century pottery it produced abundant medieval ceramic building material and mortared rubble, invariably absent from peasant homestead sites in Fransham. These indicate that it was of high status and it can with confidence be identified as the site of Great Fransham manor house. An impressive array of metal finds lends credence to this identification (Fig. 7.7). Occupation may have ceased on the death of Geoffrey de Fransham, the last lord of an undivided manor, in 1414. In *c.*1430 an unnamed 6-acre enclosure lay between the King's highway known as the *Whiteway* on the south and the

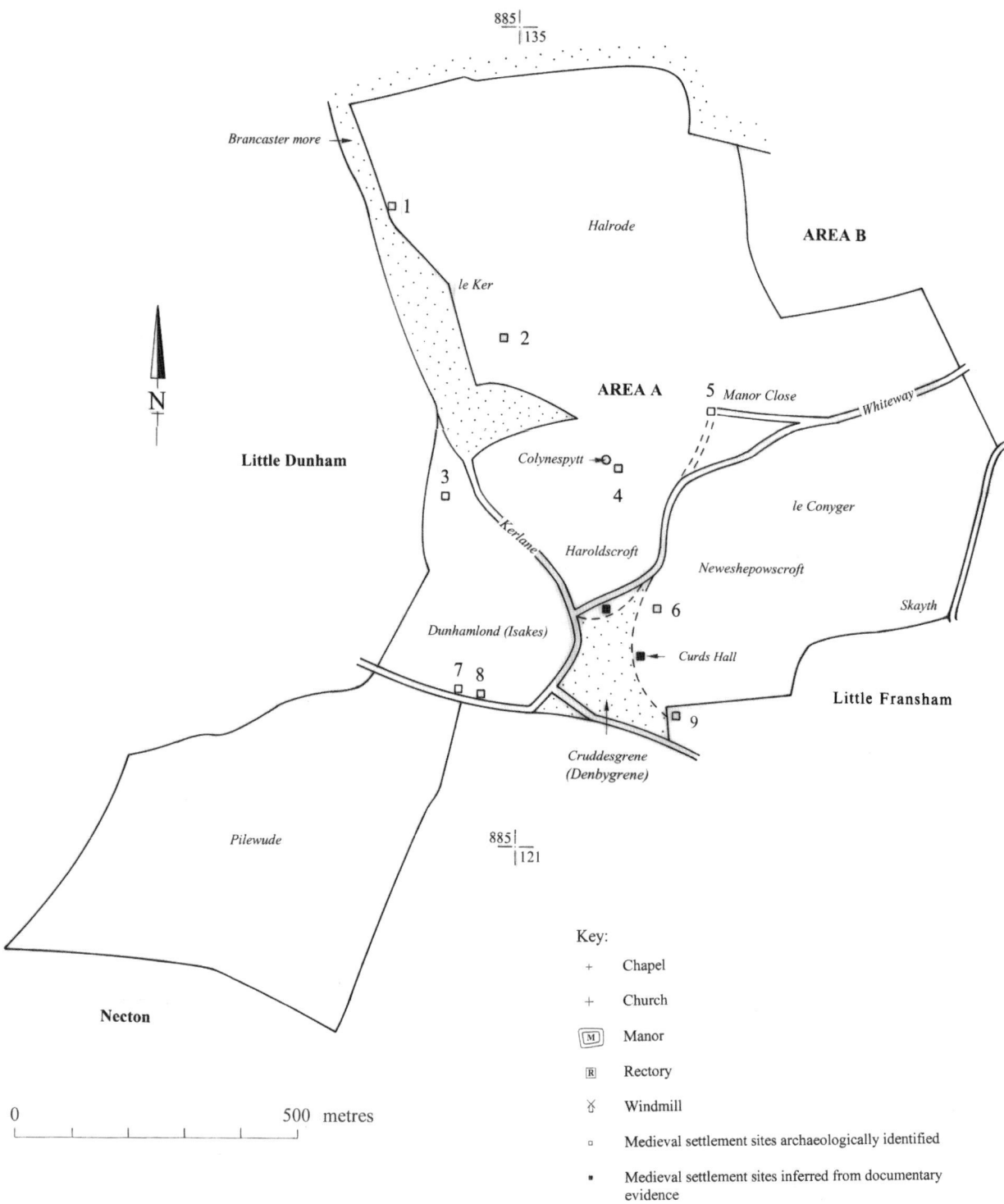

Figure 7.4 Area A, Great Fransham, scale 1:10,560

common way leading from Great Fransham church to the manor on the north. This was known as *Manor Close* in 1511 and as *Halleclos* in 1525 (MS 13056). The 'white' of *Whiteway* is probably from Old English **wiht*, a bend rather than *hwît*, white (Smith 1956a, 273–4; 1956b, 265).

The manor house was surrounded by large closes of Great Fransham demesne in *c.*1430, but it is uncertain whether this was the case in earlier times. A nameless 20-acre lay to the east on the north of the *Whiteway*, and south of the *Whiteway* were three closes, *Neweshepowscroft* (13 acres), *le Conyger* (20 acres) and *Snapespiece* (13 acres). *Le Conyger* must have been a rabbit warren, though no references to rabbits have been found and no traces of earthworks have survived centuries of arable faming. It is no surprise that warrening was carried out during late medieval times in this area of clay soils. Rabbits 'can at a pinch make their burrows in the heaviest clays' (Williamson 2007b, 12; n.b. another close called

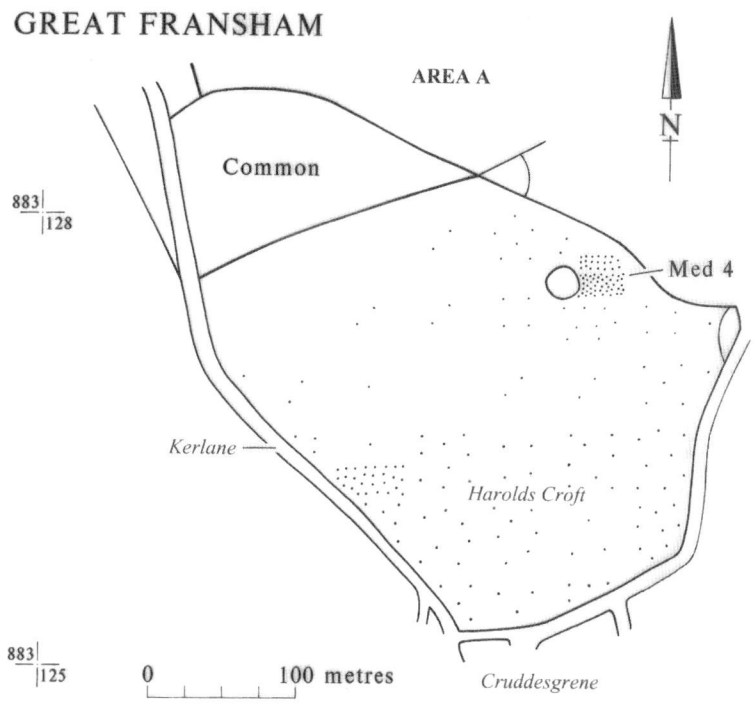

Figure 7.5 Med 4 in Area A, distribution of sherds
(boundaries taken from Ordnance Survey County Series 1928 edition), scale 1:5,000

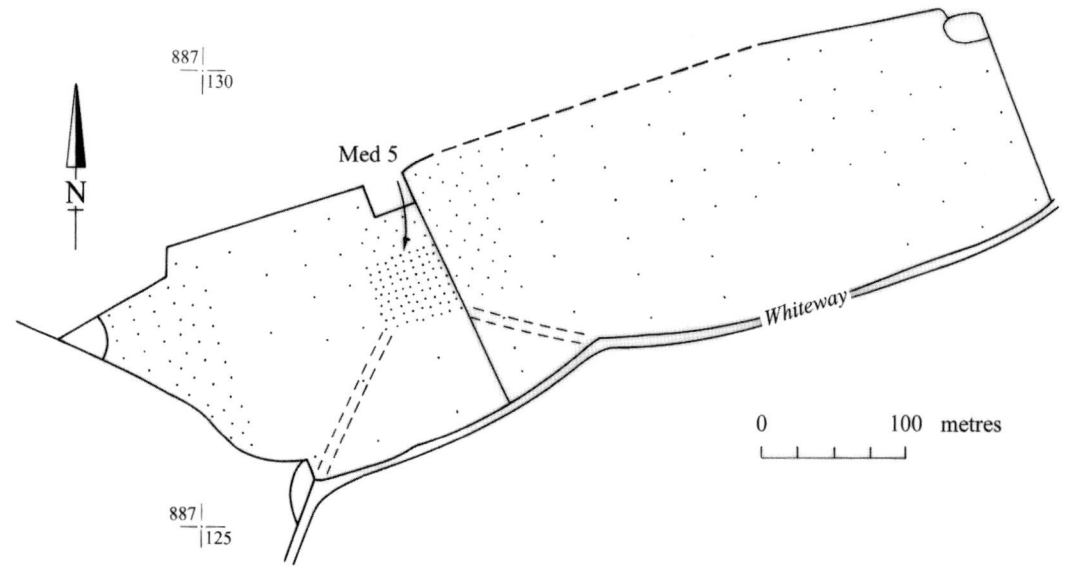

Figure 7.6 Med 5 in Area A, distribution of sherds
(boundaries taken from Ordnance Survey County Series 1928 edition), scale 1:5,000

Conyngerlond or *le Conynger* lay in Area B). In 1355 the lord's crops in *Snape* were damaged by William le Strange and Godfrey Fender. *Snape* may derive from *snap* with the meaning of 'poor pasture' in Middle English or possibly from **snæp* 'a boggy piece of land' (Smith 1956b, 132; Cavill 2018, 390–1). South of these three closes, on the boundary with Little Fransham, lay a 14-acre several pasture called *Skathemedowe*, which, along with *Snapespiece*, extended into area M. The element *Skathe* probably derives from Old English *scçað* or Old Norse *skeið*, a boundary, (Smith 1956b, 103 and 124), but it should be noted that the Old Norse word also has the meaning of race or race-course (Atkin 1978). Though much of this area is low-lying and near a stream, all or parts had previously been arable. Trespass was done by Aveline Harold in *Skayth* in 1330. The lord's peas in *Skathell / Skathil* were damaged in 1348 and 1366. His wheat there was damaged in 1368, his barley in 1369 and his oats in 1371 and 1375. In 1404 John Crudde's servants harvested grass and branches in *Scathilcroft* without licence. By 1443

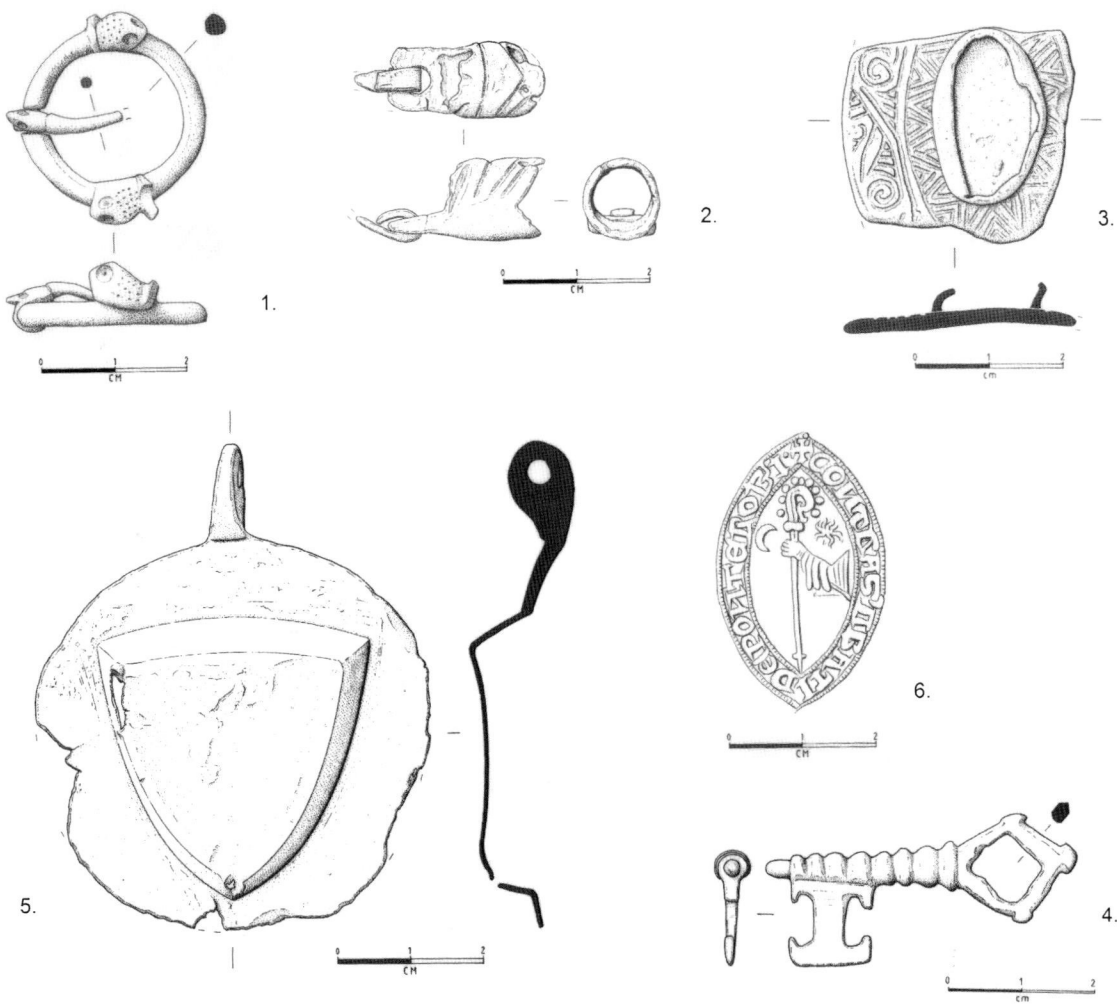

Figure 7.7 Medieval copper alloy objects from Med 5, no.1 annular brooch, no. 2 buckle, nos 3 gilt mount, no. 4 key, no. 5 harness pendant, with no. 6, an impression taken from a seal matrix, scale 1:1

the name had changed to *Skalemedowe*. In 1456 John Maunde was amerced for breaking down John Crudde's *porta caduta* at *le Scalemedowys* (MS 13051).

Cruddes Green sat at the end of the *Whiteway*, at 85m OD, almost the highest point in Fransham. The earliest references to it are to be found in descriptions of the bounds of Necton parish, made in *c*.1427. One witness spoke of a certain green (*viretrum*) next to the house of John Curde and once called *Denbysgrene*, while another mentioned a place called *Curddesgrene alias Cruddesgrene* or *Denbies* (MS 13177). Thomas de Denby occurs in court rolls between 1372 and 1394. None of the area of this small common, which was the focus of several medieval settlements, is available for fieldwalking, being covered with grass, trees and farm buildings, as are areas along its north, south and east sides. Med 6, sitting on the north-east corner of *Cruddesgrene*, is the site of two customary messuages held of Great Fransham manor. Pottery indicates a start of domestic activity in the twelfth century and an end by *c*.1400. This accords well with the documentary evidence.

South-west of these two messuages and lying under grass on the edge of *Cruddesgrene* is the site of Curds Hall, which came to be regarded as the manor house in the fifteenth century and was demolished in the 1930s[iii]. A freehold messuage, once of Thomas Halle, with 24¼ acres (in 12 parcels) was held in *c*.1400 of Great Fransham manor by Roger de Toftes, who must have succeeded Thomas de Denby. There were 2½ acres in the croft which butted north on the common pasture, and on the east of the house lay a 1-acre close, east of which was *Ernyesyard* (Med 6). The site of Curds Hall can be identified with a messuage and 14 acres held by William de Aula [*i.e.* Hall] in *c*.1279 (Table 6.2, no. 9). John de Halle was a taxpayer in 1327 and 1332. By *c*.1427 John Curde or Crudde was tenant (MS 13177). In 1567 and 1569 a tenement called Cruddes with 40 acres in Great Fransham and Little Dunham was held for ½ a knight's fee of the Earl of Oxford as of his honour of Heddingham (TNA E 150/659/7; Traf 710, 92X5).

Another Great Fransham manor freehold was close-by, on the north edge of the green. A messuage with 4 acres, and 10 acres apparently in one piece and lying to the east of the common, were held by Roger de Toftes in *c*.1400. The property was once of William de Bilney. In *c*.1279 Henry de Bylney had a messuage and 15 acres (Table 6.2, no. 29)[iv]. William de Bilney swore fealty to the lord of Great Fransham in 1343. Agnes and John de Bilneie were taxed in 1327 but were not listed under Great Fransham in 1332. In 1349 John de Bylney, tenant of a messuage, had died without heir, and Clement, brother of William, was distrained to swear fealty.

From the south-west corner of *Cruddesgrene* a road ran along the south side of *Dunham croft* west towards Little Dunham. Part of this survives as a sunken way within a belt of trees on the parish boundary with Necton. Med 7 may be another freehold messuage held by Roger de Toftes in *c*.1400, while Med 8, a small pottery production site, may possibly be equated with one of de Toftes' parcels of land which was called *Pottercrofte*. Pottery on both Med 7 and 8 was of the twelfth and thirteenth centuries. Med 9 on the south-east corner of *Cruddesgrene* and lying partly in Little Fransham is noted below under *Quarent*. 2.

The extreme south-west part of Great Fransham forms a 65½-acre projection, reaching far from Med 7 into Necton parish and down into the valley of a tributary of the Wissey. This breaks the cohesion of Fransham's part-ovoid shape and belongs in simplistic geographical terms to Necton. A present-day piece of woodland in Necton parish at its south-east corner is called Pilewood Covert, a name suggesting that wood for stakes, shafts or piles was once grown there, from the Old English *pîl* (Smith 1956b, 64). All the depositions in a dispute of *c*.1427 over tithes there between the vicar of Necton and the rector of Great Fransham included the projection, called *Pylwode*, within Necton. As all the surviving statements on the perambulation of Necton were made by men of that parish this is hardly surprising (MS 13177). The earliest reference to this holding is of 1273/4 when William de Fransham held a *cultura* (cultivated land) called *Pilewude* of the King (Illingworth and Caley eds 1812, 434). The 20 acres in *Pylwod* of *c*.1279 (Table 6.2, no. 3) had increased to 80 by *c*.1430, although an approximately contemporary rental of demesne lands gave the acreage as 66¾ (MS 13073). Many amercements for trespass doled out in Great Fransham manor courts between 1334 and 1413 show that the demesne in *Pilwood* was being used for arable cropping as well as for pasture.

Area B, the north-west of Great Fransham (Fig. 7.8)
Extensive common pastures, small, medium and large greens and a riverside common, detached block demesne and settlements (including the rectory) with tenement blocks, and a demesne windmill

Much of this area is poorly documented and its lay-out is not well understood. A huge swathe of the parish boundary ran across commons, which stretched for various distances into the parishes of Little Dunham, Great Dunham, Kempstone and Beeston. One exception to this was an area of *c*.10 acres of non-common centred at approximately TF 883 136, which appears to have been an intake from the direction of Great Dunham. No documentary evidence has been found to show when this may have happened, although three medieval sherds might perhaps indicate some arable exploitation in the thirteenth or fourteenth centuries.

South-east of this curving sweep of boundary common, tongues of common land and roads ran roughly eastwards dividing the areas between them into three blocks of non-common land. Some inroads into all three had been made by colonisation towards the end of the Late Saxon period (see LS 3–6, Chapter 5). It is quite likely that in each block there were various parcels of land of poorly documented manors, for which there is no reliable evidence and which are not noted in the following descriptions.

The northern block was demarcated on three sides by common pasture, *Wylmondheithe*, *Brounesgrene* and the eastern end of *West End Moor* to the south, a narrow strip on the north-west formed by the end of a common in Great Dunham overlapping the parish boundary, and to the north *Meschalismore*, so called in 1369 and thereafter most frequently known as *Mascallyng*. In the north-west part of the block lay 12 acres in one piece with an enclosure and a foldcourse, part of Great Fransham demesne and known as *Conyngerlond* in *c*.1430. The same enclosure had been called *Quinmillrod* and *Millrod* in 1330, *Mills* in 1334 and *Windmillrode* in 1337. In 1387 *le Conynger* was named in the manor court for the first time, and thereafter both names are used. Frequent amercements for damage to the lord's crops refer to both in the fourteenth century. A single document makes reference to the rearing of rabbits in Fransham, a bill of agreement made in 1461 between two lords of parts of Great Fransham manor, William Vergons and Thomas Sheryngton. This allowed the farmer, Walter Gorges, to continue after the termination of his lease in possession of any lands which he had stocked with rabbits (MS 13413). Another close called *le Conyger* lay in Area A.

The windmill was the mill held by William de Fransham in *c*.1279 (Table 6.2, no. 1) and the old (*vet'*) mill of Gilbert de Fransham in 1356–7 (WIS 11, 163X1). It was the site of a leet court known as *Milles atte Mor* in 1400 (MS 13066) and probably much earlier. It has been suggested that the mill mound, of which there is now no trace, may possibly have been a Bronze Age barrow (Whyte 2009, 148). Med 14, which had thirteenth-century origins and was occupied until *c*.1400, may have begun life as a miller's residence.ᵛ In 1404 damage had been done to the lord's maslin (wheat and rye) at *Millesattemor* by one Richard Duke.

Very few medieval pot sherds were recovered in the area to the south and south-west of Med 14, but at TF 8893 1400, close to the common edge and *c*.170m from the site, metal-detecting produced a thirteenth-century circular silver seal matrix depicting a cinquefoil within the inscription S' WALTER (the seal of Walter).

Med 15 began in the twelfth century and was a freehold of East Lexham manor (Fig. 7.9). On its north side lay 3 acres of William Mascale called *Avelynnescroft*. The predecessor of Med 15 may have been Med 16, an exclusively twelfth-century site set well back from the common edge. Med 17, now within a private garden, was occupied from the thirteenth century and was a freehold messuage of Blyfords manor (MS 424). A large late fourteenth- or fifteenth-century buckle frame was located by metal detector on the former common immediately in front of the site (Fig. 7.10)

The concave eastern boundary of this block was marked by a road, the common way leading from Great Fransham to *Mascallyng*. On its west side in *c*.1430 a 20-acre close called *Halcroft*, demesne of Great Fransham manor, butted north on *Mascallyng* and had an enclosure containing a building (*domus*) at its southern end (MS 13073). It is possible that this building, presumably a barn or similar, occupied the site of a former homestead, Med 18, which was occupied from the thirteenth century to *c*.1400. The first element of this name may be Old English *hall*, a hall or large residence (Smith 1956a, 225–6).

Figure 7.8 Area B, Great Fransham, scale 1:10,560

Field-names containing *hall* can indicate demesne land (Cavill 2018, 189). Alternatively, Old English *haga*, a hedge or enclosure, should also be considered (Smith 1956a, 221). *Halcroft*, which contained the site of an isolated ?late tenth to early twelfth-century settlement (LS 3 / Med 20), was cropped by the lord of Great Fransham between 1330 and 1403. West of this close 4¼ acres of Blyfords manor freehold also butted north on *Mascallyng* (MS 424) as did a 3-acre piece of Great Fransham demesne. A ½-acre parcel of Rougholme manor freehold, lying in this area and held by the tenants of these 4¼ acres and of Med 17, is known only from late fifteenth and early sixteenth-century sources (MR 28, 240X6 and TNA SC 11/476). One customary acre of Rougholme manor lay in a close called *Cuninver* (i.e. *Conyngerlond*) in 1548 (TNA SC 12/3/22), but its history cannot be taken back beyond 1523 (MR 28, 240X6). This acre butted south on a 1¼-acre piece of Great Fransham glebe, a grove in 1548 and partly surviving as a copse at TF 8943 1389. Other land belonging to Rougholme manor must have been nearby, because in 1434/5 William Mascale had held 5 acres lying between Rougholme lands to the east and west and butting north on the heath (*bruarium*).

The central block contained three settlement sites. Towards the west, Med 13, with thirteenth and fourteenth-century occupation, may have been a freehold messuage of East Lexham manor. Med 15A, on the edge of *Brounesgrene* in c.1430, later *Brownsmore*[vi], was of Late Saxon origins and was abandoned in the thirteenth century. On the other hand, Med 19, a pair of Great Fransham customary tenements, was also first occupied in the eleventh century and is still inhabited today. It sat on the edge of another common which by the sixteenth century was known as *West End Moor* (Fig. 7.9). A 10-acre close forming part of this tenement in c.1400 lay immediately west of it. This close, named *Sewlesclose* in

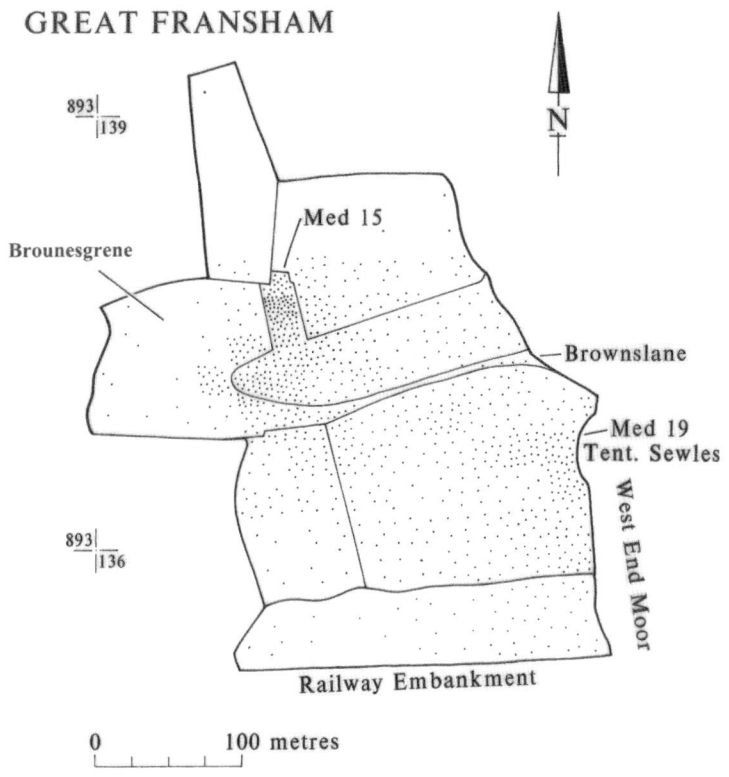

Figure 7.9 Med 15 and 19 within Area B, distribution of sherds
(boundaries taken from Ordnance Survey County Series 1928 edition), scale 1:5,000

1475, butted south on another one, 7 free acres with a pightle of underwood called *Colbiclos* in 1435/6, formerly held by William Mascale, and later to be part of Blyfords manor. Much of this block was taken up with a 30-acre piece of Great Fransham demesne called *le Shepehousefeild* in c.1430 when it lay between the common path leading from *Brounesgrene* towards *Wylmondheithe* on the north and the common pasture of Great Fransham on the south. Between 1330 and 1403 it was known as *Shepehowscroft* and was regularly sown with the lord's crops. By 1404 *Shepehousefield* contained underwood, although in the following year there was damage done to the lord's beans there by Margaret Broun. By c.1430 a foldcourse was associated with this piece and *Conynglond* to the north (MS 13073). A ¼-acre of Great Fransham demesne called *Coddelingescroft* lay somewhere in *Shepehowsefeild* in c.1430.

The rounded western end of this block close to Med 13 consisted of 'divers lands' in a field called *Hallesrod* held by the prior of West Acre of Great Fransham manor in c.1430. They lay next to the common pasture of Fransham called *Fransham Lyng* on the west and butted south on *Hawebushes*. The prior held by military service, and no rent was cited, only scutage, homage and fealty. These are one and the same as the holding of the prior in c.1279 when no acreage or rent was cited (Table 6.2, no. 15), and as *Abbys rode*, a place named in a description of the bounds of the foldcourse of Kempstone in 1356–7 (WIS 11, 163X1). In 1427–8, when West Acre's lands were leased to the lord of Kirkhams and Wilcoks, the rent for 10 acres in Great Fransham late in the tenure of John Maddy was given as 3s 4d (MS 13137). At a leet court held in 1432 this was called *Pryowrsys rod de Westacre* (MS

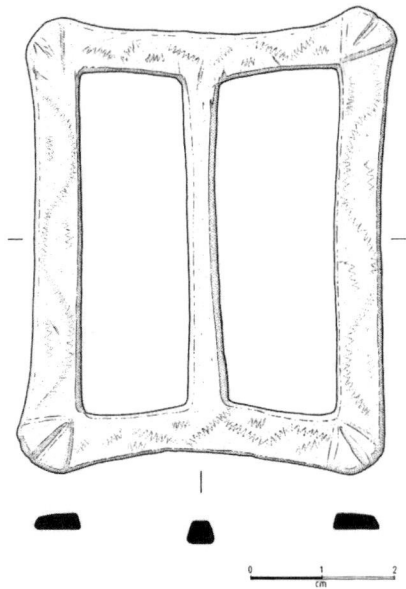

Figure 7.10 Late medieval buckle frame found on former common, close to Med 17 (HER 52913), scale 1:1

13048). By the 1540s the land was copyhold of Cannons manor, 10 acres known as *Abrode*.

The southern block, parts of which were unavailable for fieldwalking, contained four irregularly spaced settlement sites set on the north side of a stream which followed the north edge of the common[vii]. Towards the west end and now under farm buildings lay a customary tenement of East Lexham manor, 6 acres of the tenement Cooks. The earliest sources for this holding are post-medieval but the rent and services due for it, 12d, 7 hens, 35 eggs and 3 work-days (*precariae*), suggest that it was of ancient tenure (KIM 1/8/16 and MC 1812/49, 838X5). It lay between commons on the north and south in *Cockertons* according to a court of 1646 (MS 12832). There was a void messuage in the northern part in *c.*1610. A messuage was standing in the southern part by 1642, and perhaps much earlier. This location is relatively secure as the tenure can be followed with few gaps down to 1807. Med 23 and 23A were both freehold messuages held of Great Fransham manor, the former with thirteenth-century and later pottery and the latter surviving as a sixteenth or seventeenth-century timber-framed house. To the east Med 22, which began life as LS 6 and was not occupied after the fourteenth century, lay on land of unidentified tenure. A 5-acre piece of Great Fransham demesne called *Whippescrofte* lay somewhere to the north of Med 23 and was bounded on the north and east by *Cortelylane* in *c.*1430. It was frequently under the lord's crops between 1353 and 1413.

To the east of *Hallesrod* the outer edge of the common, to the south of the previously described block of land, was for the most part convex and curving, its northern edge following the stream which entered the parish from Little Dunham. A string of settlements along this edge, Med 21, the Rectory and Med 24–9, will be described from east to west.

Permanent grassland and farm buildings prevented fieldwalking at the extreme eastern end of *West End Moor*, but examination of extensive ground disturbance in and around a post-medieval timber-framed building at TF 8981 1346 (PM 5) produced no convincing evidence for a medieval predecessor. Both this site and Med 21 might more properly have been described under Area K.

Med 21, which began life as LS 7, is evidenced by small quantities of medieval pottery recovered from extremely limited patches of bare soil. In 1434/5 it was a freehold messuage with a 2-acre croft called *Normannscroft* held by William Mascale. It was later to become the capital messuage of Blyfords manor. Beyond a north-south road the rectory stood inside a moat within a right-angled turn of the common edge. The north and west arms of the moat, and a stub of the west end of the southern arm, are shown on the Enclosure Award map (Pl. 7.2). Abuttals show the rectory to have been in this position by *c.*1430, but it is possible that an earlier site may have been on the south side of the churchyard (LS 8 / Med 30). In 1613 the rectory was set within 3 acres.

Between the rectory and the Whiteway to the south a 9-acre close of Great Fransham demesne was said to be formerly of Robert de Acre in *c.*1430. He had been taxed in 1332 and the homage and service of someone of that name was listed in a fine levied in 1346 (TNA CP 25/1/164/158.737). This piece is probably the same as *Parsonscroft*, cropped by the lord between 1330 and 1389, and as *Nyneacres* and *le Nineacres* between 1391 and 1404. In a rental of *c.*1430 it was listed as 8 acres with a close lying together below the rectory, held at farm by the rector (MS 13073). The close was separately noted as *Robynscroft acre* in 1366 and as 1 acre with underwood at *Robynsyard* in 1374. In *c.*1430 land of William Mascale bordered the above 9 acres on the west. This cannot be

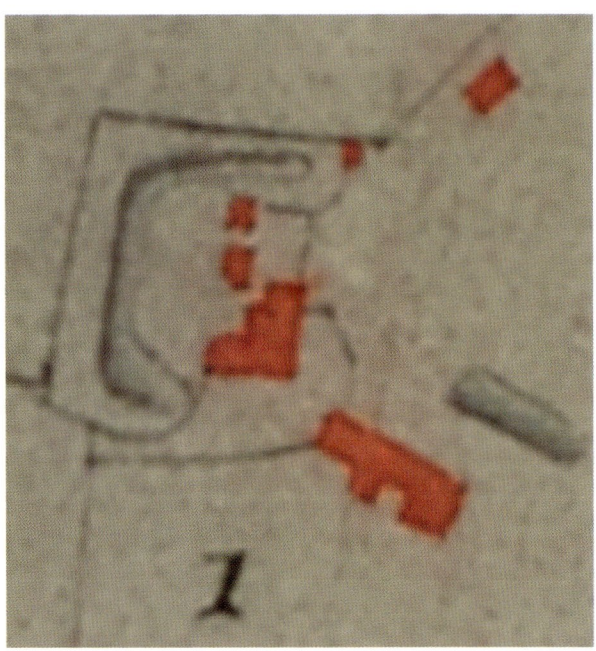

Plate 7.2 Detail from Enclosure Award map, Great Fransham rectory in Area B (NRO C/Sca 2/122)

certainly identified with any piece in a rental of Mascale's former lands of 1434/5.

Beyond this lay a loose row of seven settlement sites (Fig. 7.11; Pl. 7.3)[viii]. Med 24, occupied in the thirteenth and fourteenth-centuries, was of two distinct tenures, a Rougholme manor customary tenement, and a formerly built close and croft, demesne of Great Fransham in *c.*1430. Both properties extended south to the *Whiteway*. Half an acre of Rougholme customary land probably lay near here. It butted south on the common way called *Whyghtlye* in 1523 (MR 28, 240X6) and on the *Whiteway* in 1548 (TNA SC 12/3/22). Med 25, a Great Fransham freehold messuage occupied between the thirteenth and fifteenth centuries, did not reach south to the road. However, 1 acre of Great Fransham demesne, normally held by the tenants of the messuage and in the croft of the same, butted south on the *Whiteway*. To the west of this a post-medieval house masks another site, Med 25A, which was probably a freehold of Great Fransham rectory. The date of initial occupation here is uncertain. In *c.*1400 ¾ acre of Great Fransham freehold lay in the croft of this messuage and butted south on the common way. Med 26 was demesne of Great Fransham in *c.*1430 but its former tenure is unknown. Occupation began in the thirteenth century and may have extended slightly into the fifteenth. The curtilages of this and the following three sites did not extend south to the Whiteway. Most of the land to the south seems to have been Great Fransham demesne, almost certainly the north-east limits of *Halrode* (in Area A). Med 27 was another Great Fransham freehold consisting of a messuage and ½ acre, and settlement thereon began in the thirteenth century. Med 28, a twelfth to fourteenth-century site, lay within Great Fransham demesne by the mid-sixteenth century, but its earlier tenurial history is obscure. The final site in this row is Med 29, with thirteenth and fourteenth-century pottery and tentatively identified as a freehold of Great Fransham manor.

Plate 7.3 Detail from 1946 RAF vertical aerial photograph, part of Area B with West End Moor and Med 22–9 (http://www.historic-maps.norfolk.gov.uk/)

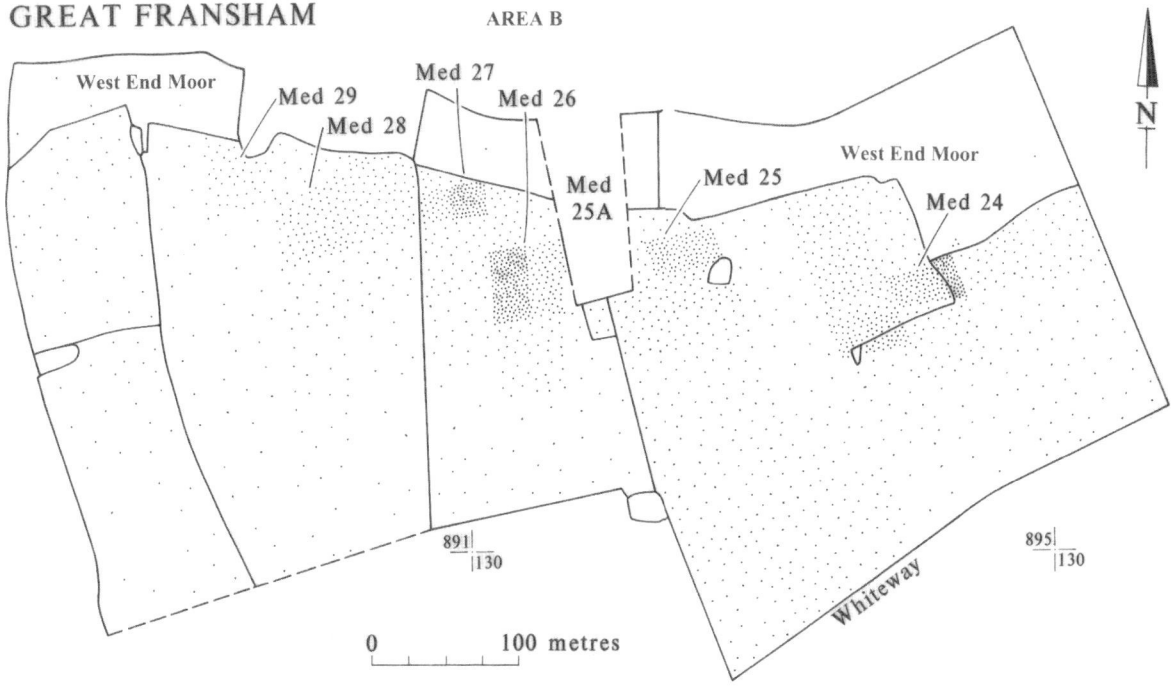

Figure 7.11 Med 24–9 within Area B, distribution of sherds (boundaries taken from Ordnance Survey County Series 1928 edition), scale 1:5,000

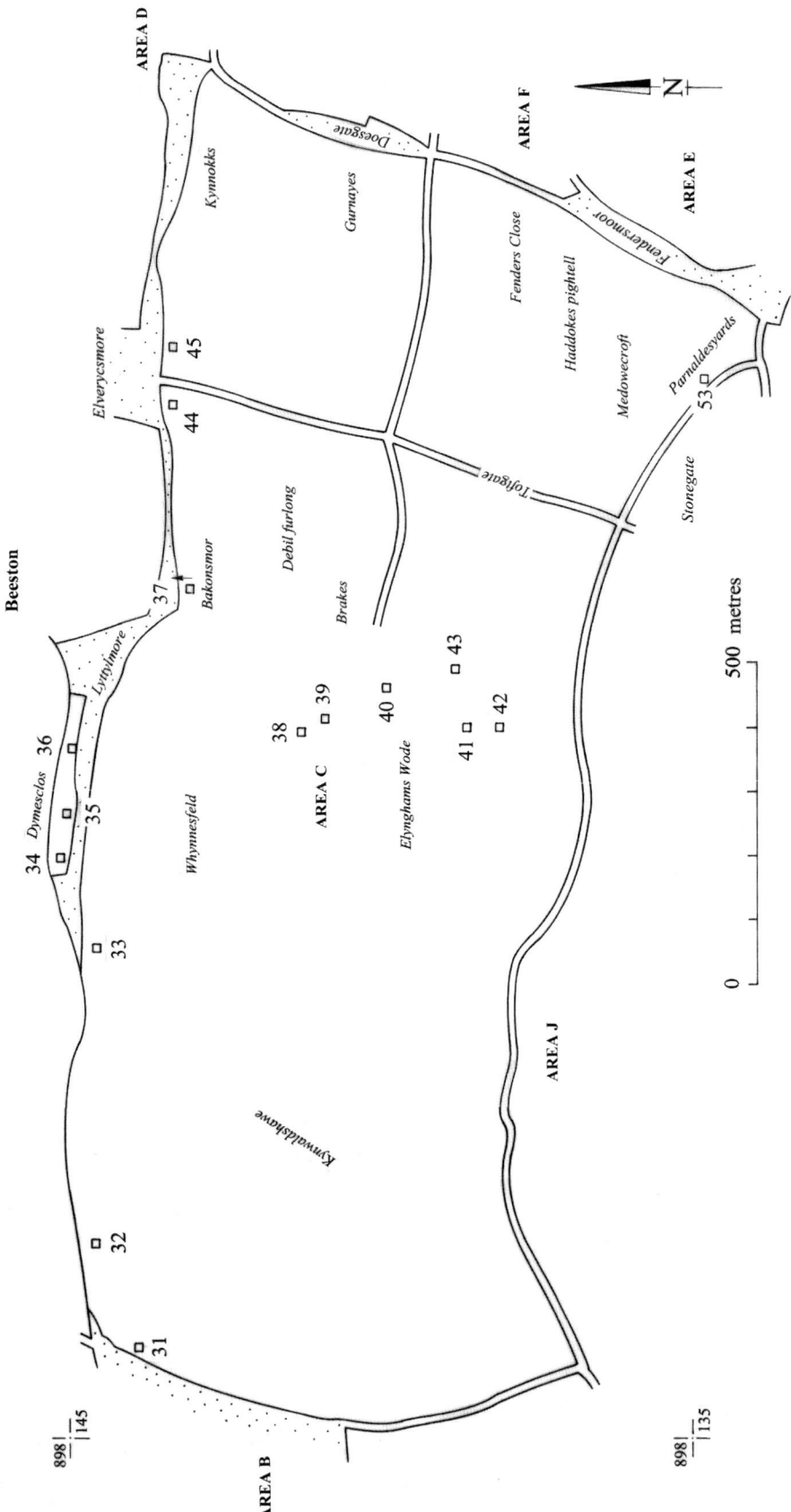

Figure 7.12 Area C, Great Fransham, scale 1:10,560

Area C, north central Great Fransham (Fig. 7.12)
A medium green with settlements and tenement blocks along edges, other settlement sites, detached tenement blocks, open field, (probably demesne) woodland, various small pieces of detached demesne, some perhaps formerly detached tenement blocks

This area comprises a very large south-facing stretch of land, 2km east-west and 700m north-south. It was bordered on the south by a road running along the northern edge of a string of meadows, on the north by the parish boundary with Beeston, on the west by a road and by *Meschalismore*, and on the east by a common and road called *Fendersmoor* and *Doesgate*. The finer points of lay-out and many details of tenure and land-use have been lost, on account of poor or incomplete documentation.

To judge from a sprinkling of medieval sherds the western end, a strip with an east-west width of some 230m, was arable but no field name is known. Two settlement sites at the northern end of this strip, Med 31 and 32, were East Lexham manor freeholds with twelfth-century beginnings, Med 31 continuing into the fourteenth century and Med 32 into the thirteenth. The latter was a messuage called *Kinwalds*. East of this area a rectangular area of *c*.70 acres, 400m wide and extending south from the Beeston boundary as far as Area J, was entirely devoid of medieval sherds. This has been identified as *Kynwaldshawe* in 1371, *Kenwaldeshalle* and *Kyneswaldeshaugh* in *c*.1400. The first part of the name is an Old English personal name, *Cynewald*, and the second is *haga* (or Old Norse *hagi*) meaning a hedge or enclosure, although the Old Norse *haugr*, a hill or mound, is possible and cannot be dismissed on topographical grounds (Smith 1956a, 221–2 and 235–6; Williamson 2013, 213). The word *haga* was often applied in East Anglia to woodland (Martin and Satchell 2008, 100, 188 note 25, and 205). In the words of Della Hooke, places with names containing *haga* 'were most commonly found in little-developed, often densely wooded regions later known to have been used for hunting or as game reserves. They may indeed have already demarcated parts of the woodland set aside for such purposes.' (Hooke 1988, 148; 2012, 41–2). In 1442–3 a rent of 1d was paid for a large close called *Kynwelshaweclos* to East Lexham manor. The close contained timber and underwood as well as pasture (MS 13140). Underwood was illegally cut on the east side of *Kynwelsawe* in 1471 (MS 13048). In 1473 John Yevan was amerced for keeping two fald gates (*portae cadutae*) below *Kewaldeshaugh* (MS 13048), presumably impeding traffic on the common way.

Ellinghams field was the somewhat generalised name given to all the area between *Kynewaldeshaugh* and *Fendersmoor/Doesgate*. A substantial area projecting eastward for up to 300m from the southern half of *Kynewaldeshaugh* was almost devoid of medieval sherds. This may have been *Elynghams Wode*, which was so named in 1442–3 (MS 13140) and was demesne of Ellinghams, the sub-manor of East Lexham. Some of it, near Med 38–42 (Fig. 7.13), may have been common pasture, although no documentary evidence for this has been found. North of this area a thirteenth to fourteenth-century site (Med 33), another East Lexham freehold, lay in the angle between the north-east corner of *Kynewaldeshaugh* and a small common next to the Beeston boundary called *Lyttylmore* in *c*.1430, later *Whynnes moore* (Fig. 7.13). Three sites are set on the north side of this common within a rectangular cut-out, which looks much like an encroachment from Beeston. Either Med 34 or Med 35 Fig. 7.13), both of which were occupied in the thirteenth and fourteenth-centuries, may have been an East Lexham freehold that was to become demesne of Ellinghams. Med 36 (Fig. 7.13) was a pottery production site in the twelfth and early thirteenth centuries. A selection of discoloured pot sherds from this site is shown on Pl. 7.4 along with some 'normal' sherds from Med 35.

The area to the south-east of *Lyttylmore* was open field. In 1442–3 26 acres of Ellinghams demesne lay in parcels (*parcellet.*) in *Whynnesfeld* (MS 13140). In *c*.1430 3 acres of Great Fransham demesne lay in *Debil furlong* south of *Lyttylmore* and north of *Brakes*, as well as three other pieces, two of 1 acre and a ½ acre, close-by. Seven acres of the same demesne in one piece lay someway further south, between the lands of *Brakkes* to the east and west and butting south on *Oxmedow*. *Brakes / Brakkes* is identified with Med 40. Six acres of Rougholme customary land in four parcels, of ½, 1, 1½ and 3 acres, were listed in 1530 (MR 28, 240X6), and 6½ acres in several pieces of the same tenure, not given any details of location in a rental of 1552, probably lay in this field (TNA SC 12/3/23). Two pieces of Great Fransham glebe land also lay here. In 1510 they were to become copyhold of the Rectory manor and held by the Necton Town trust, *i.e.* Blyfords manor (PD 143/79). Eight pieces listed amongst lands formerly of William Mascale in 1434/5 (Blyfords manor) may all have been in this area, although possibly some lay to the west of *Kynewaldeshaugh*. There were 5 acres of pasture, 6 acres of ?underwood (*subbura*), and six parcels amounting to 9¾ acres, the smallest ¾ acre and the largest 2½. Two pieces of Great Fransham freehold, both of 1 acre and held by two tenants in *c*.1400, were in Ellinghams field according to sixteenth-century rentals (MS 13074–6). One of these, called *Selysaker* in 1369, was described as 1 acre formerly of Isabelle Sel in 1370.

A 'cloose of pasture grownde' containing 10 acres in Great Fransham and held by John Tompson of Mileham, yeoman, was the subject of a case in Chancery in 1558–79 (TNA C 3/177/25). Ellinghams manor court proceedings between 1582 and 1600 refer to what must have been the same property, a 10-acre close lying next to *Ellinghams close* for the length of two furlongs was held freely by Tompson (MC 1847/1, 741X2). This may have been fairly recently enclosed from common open field.

Seven further settlement sites (Med 37–42, Fig. 7.13 and Med 44) present great problems of identification. Med 38 and 39 were probably freeholds of East Lexham/Ellinghams manor, and one of them, it is uncertain which, may also have been a freehold of Great Fransham, a void messuage in *c*.1400 lying next to a common pasture on the west. If this was the case then an otherwise unrecorded common pasture may have existed on the west side of Med 38–42, a string of settlements next to which a common might have been expected. Med 40, which had a 20-acre croft, was *Brakes* and in the post-medieval period, if not before, was the site of the manor house of Ellinghams. In *c*.1400 the prior of Pentney held freely of Great Fransham manor 12 acres in the croft of John Brakke. In the mid-sixteenth century this land, which had not been recorded in the *Valor Ecclesiasticus*, was held by the lord of Ellinghams, John Calibutt (TNA C 66/999). Med 40

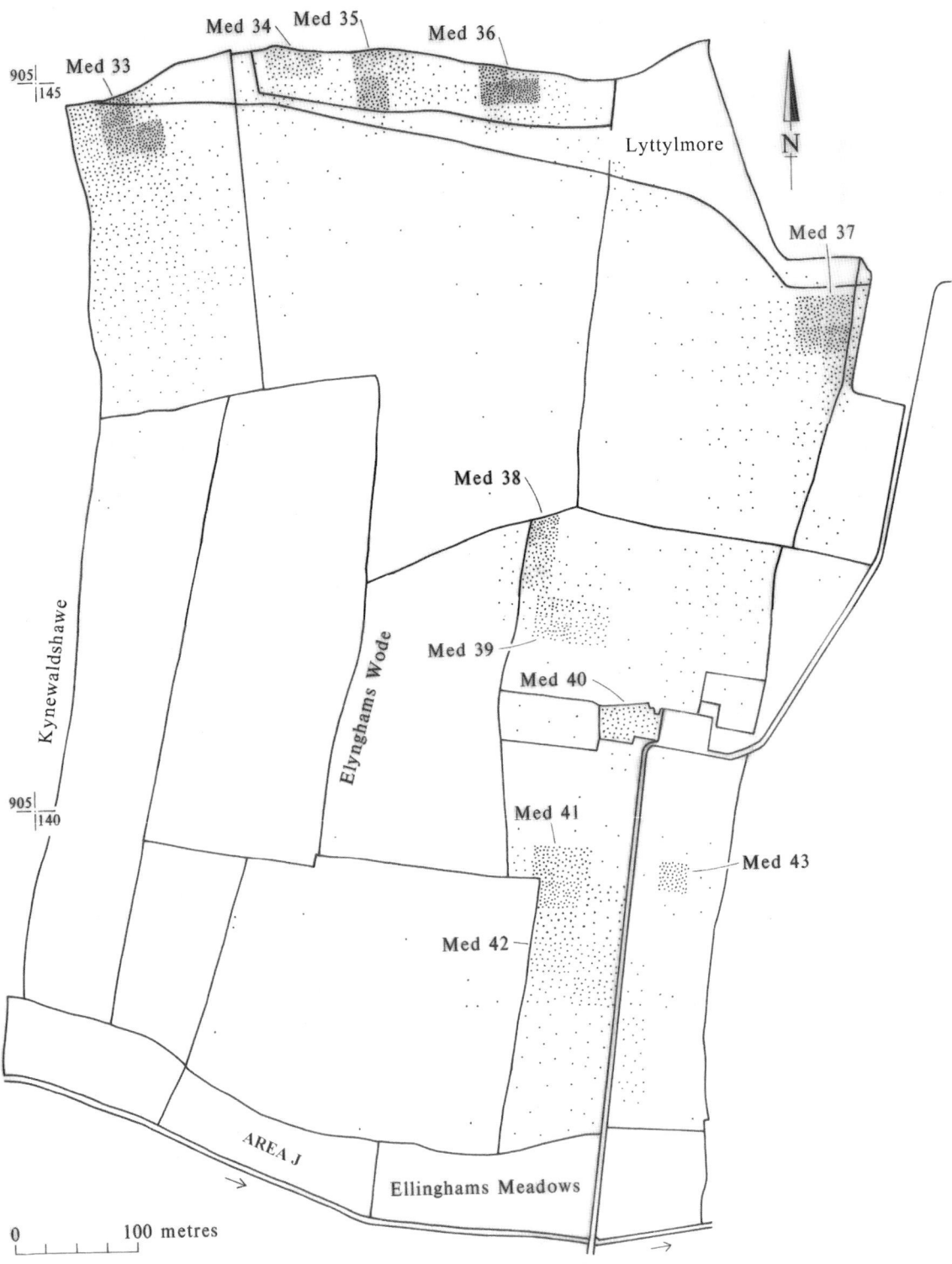

Figure 7.13 Med 33–43 in the central sector of Area C, distribution of sherds
(boundaries taken from Ordnance Survey County Series 1928 edition), scale 1:5,000

was the only one of these five settlements to continue in occupation during the post-medieval period. The tenures and manorial allegiances of the other four sites are unknown. Med 43 was another twelfth and early thirteenth-century pottery production site (Fig. 7.13).

A parcel of a wood, freehold of East Lexham manor was probably situated somewhere in the northern part of this area. It was given no acreage in the two sources that include it (KIM 1/8/16 and MC 1812/49, 838X5) and is almost certainly the same as woodland mentioned in notes re sales of oaks and elms in groves and closes by George

Plate 7.4 A selection of pottery sherds from Med 36 (left) and Med 35 (right)

and Edmund Clement, dated 1564 (Holkham Hall, Longham Bundle 8, 401). The woodland lay next to *Elynghams more* and *Elyngham grene*, which were probably the eastward continuation of *Lyttylmore* and may be equated with *Bakonsmor* mentioned at a leet court in 1450 (MS 13048) and *Baconesgrene* in 1455 (MS 13049). A list, probably beginning in the fourteenth century, of past tenants of the wood was given in *c*.1610, when it was held by Richard Beckham esq.: William Leche, Stephen Bacon, John Canon, John Crudde, John Calybutt, George Clement and Richard Futter (MC 1812/49, 838X5). Calybutt, Clement, Futter and Beckham were all lords of Ellinghams manor.

The eastern side of this ill-understood area was marked by a road called *Toftgate*. This name occurs in 1296/7 when William *ad Pratum* had made an encroachment there (see Med 53 in Appendix 2 for this William). Five acres lying on either side of this way and butting south on meadow were held by Agnes, widow of Gilbert de Fransham, in 1384. Later sources indicate this land was in one piece and lay west of *Toftgate*. It formed part of the *Baysbolle* fee, a group of free lands held of the manor of Kirkhams (see Table 6.2, nos. 6, 30, 39 and 46).

The lay-out within the approximately rectangular area between *Toftgate* and *Fendersmoor / Doesgate* is a little better understood than the above. There is no evidence that any houses lined the eastern edge of this block. In the north-west corner a thirteenth to fourteenth-century site (Med 45) can quite confidently be identified as a freehold of Great Fransham manor. In 1384 a 14-acre piece of the tenement *Kynnokks* lying in the north-east corner were granted at farm by the lord of Great Fransham, along with a messuage and a pightle. The messuage and pightle lay on the east side of the *Fendersmoor / Doesgate*. This tenement had been customary land held by villeins, such as Richard Kynnott, *nativus*, in 1365. The 14-acre close was to remain demesne after 1384. In *c*.1430 there were several other parcels of Great Fransham demesne, apparently lying towards the northern end of this block, one piece of ¼ acre, two of 1½ acres and one of 3 acres at *Gurnayes*. One acre of Great Fransham freehold was called *Gurnaysacre*. Abuttals show that some lands of Pentney Priory and Wendling Abbey were also in this area. Pentney lands held freely of Great Fransham manor comprised 3 acres at *Kynnocks*, 1¾ acres to the east of Med 53 (see below) and 2 acres nearby. Four acres of Kirkhams manor freehold, part of the tenement Baysbolle, lay west of land once of Richard Kynnokes in 1384. These had been held by Geoffrey Leche of Beeston between 1336 and 1348, and then by Cecilia La Leche. By 1443 they were in the hands of the lord of Kirkhams yet failed to appear in any subsequent documents of that manor.

In the central and southern parts were 3 acres at *Meadowcroftsend* and ¾ acre at *Meadowhouse*, both Great Fransham demesne. *Haddokes pightell*, which also lay at *Medowecroft*, contained ¼ acre, butted east on the common pasture and was demesne by 1401. Post-medieval sources enable it to be firmly located at TF 9165 1360. For John Haddok see Med 55 (Appendix 2). Three acres lay near the south-west corner, and there was a ¼ acre at *Cheslond*, both also Great Fransham demesne (MS 13073). Lands of other manors also lay in the central sector, but details of location all come from late sources: 1¾ Rougholme customary acres, 5 acres of Ellinghams customary land at *Medowe Close ende* in *Fenders Close* with 1¼ acres nearby (MC 1847/1, 741X2), and 1 acre of Northendhall demesne (TNA SC 12/3/23). Three acres of Kirkhams demesne lying next to *Toftgate* on the west was

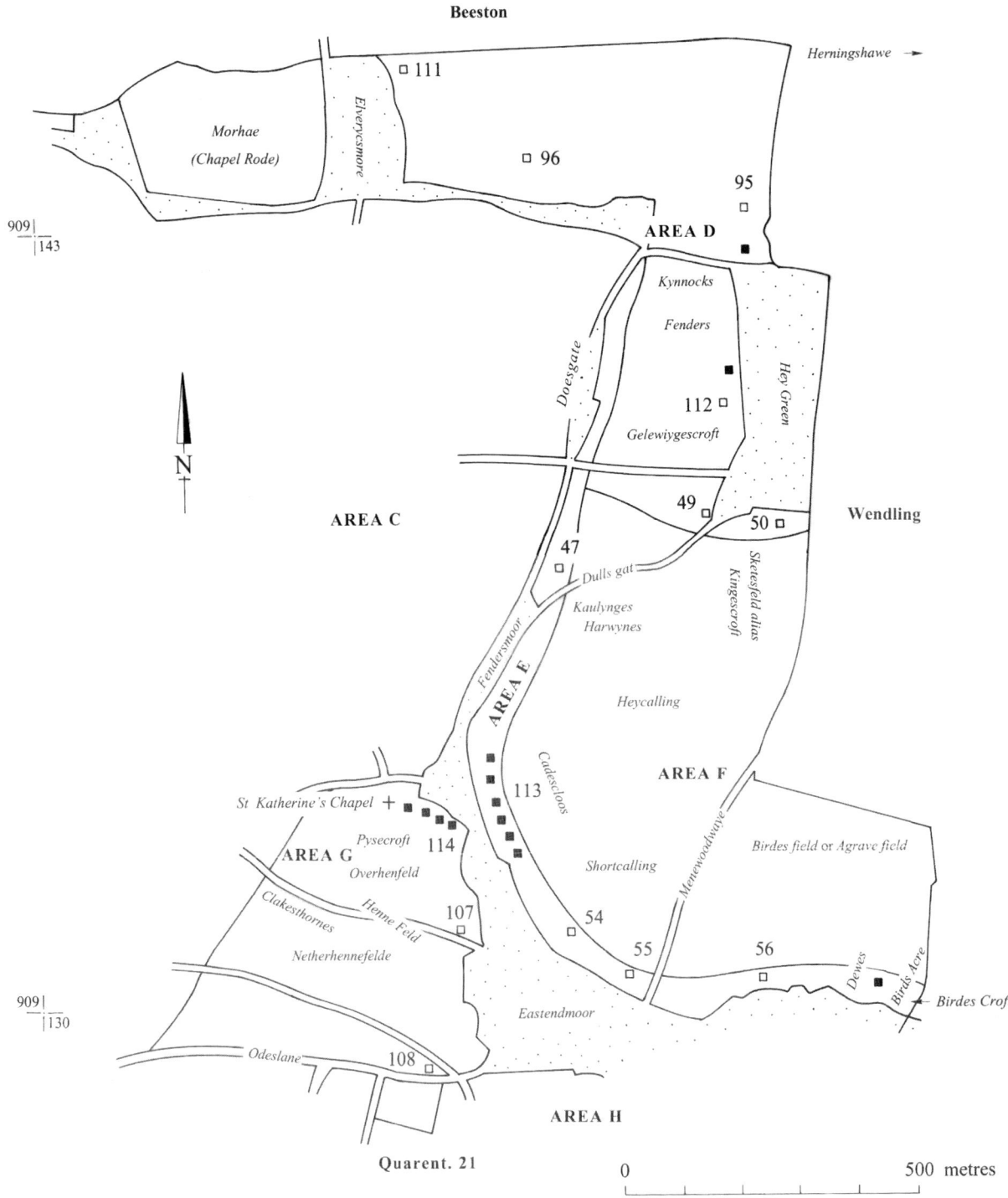

Figure 7.14 Areas D–G, Great Fransham, scale 1:10,560

let at farm in 1378 and 1392. This land had previously been Kirkhams freehold and in several, probably three parcels of the tenement Baysbolle, amounting to 3½ acres. Five other parcels of this tenement, amounting to 5¼ acres and all probably in Ellinghams field, were listed in 1384. The tenurial history of each ends in silence at various times between c.1460 and 1502. To judge from the names of tenants in abuttals, there was also, somewhere in this area, 1 acre of Kirkhams customary land, the tenure of which can be traced from 1384 to 1476.

The only settlement site at the southern end was Med 53, a freehold of Great Fransham manor, a messuage with 8 acres on the croft and 4 acres of meadow. In c.1400 this holding was said to have been once of William in the Medowe, the origin of the meadow house, croft and close names mentioned above. Two Great Fransham freehold pieces were held by the same tenant in c.1400: an enclosure of unstated acreage called *Parnaldesyards* near the south-east corner, and 1 acre nearby butting south on meadow. Two pieces of pasture of Great Fransham demesne lay in the southern part of this area: one acre butted north on *Medowscrofte* and 1¼ acres in or near the south-east corner were said to lie in a close at *Meadowfalgate* in 1540 (MS 13056). The south-west

FRANSHAM
HER 33587 33588 33589 & 34247

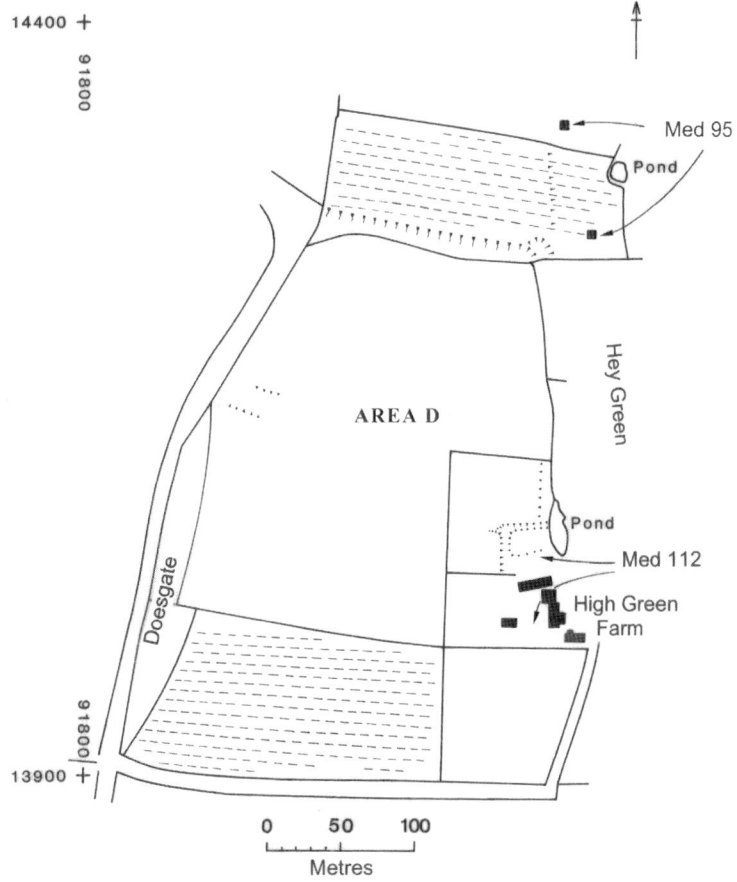

Figure 7.15 Med 112 and surrounding earthworks within Area D, scale 1:5,000

corner was occupied by 3 acres of Great Fransham demesne, lying next to *Toftgate* on the west and butting south on a meadow of William Mascale.

Area D, the north-east corner of Great Fransham, Elverycsmore and Hey Green (Fig. 7.14)
Medium greens edged with dispersed settlements, and tenement blocks

East of *Lyttylmore* along the Beeston parish boundary, the shape of the northern edge of the common pasture strongly suggests a substantial piece of encroachment from Beeston parish southwards, leaving only a thin band of common, little wider than a road, connecting *Lyttylmore* with another common, called *Elverycsmore* in 1548 (MS 13056)[ix]. A slight spread of medieval sherds across these 18 acres shows their use as arable. They can be identified with 15½ acres in Great Fransham, named *Morhae*, which were released by Thomas de Aleby of *Wichereslond* to William de Stuteville sometime before 1259. The land lay between the road leading from *Herningshawe* (*i.e.* Herringshall) towards Acre on the south and the fields of Beeston on the north (LEST/NK 1). The field-name *Morhae* is probably derived from Old English *môr* / Old Norse *mór* 'a high tract of barren uncultivated land' (Smith 1956b, 42–3) and Old English *(ge)hæg*, Middle English *hay* meaning an enclosure (Smith 1956a, 214–5). As mentioned above, the setting of this piece strongly suggests an intake from the waste. It can also be equated with 18 acres called *Chapelrode*, first demesne and later copyhold of Rougholme manor, the tenurial descent of which can be traced from 1441/2 (LEST/GA 7).

A majority of the land lying between the two arms of *Elverycsmore* and extending to the Wendling boundary was arable in medieval times. Most of the eastern and all of the northern edge of the common is now under grass and has not been subjected to fieldwalking. Three isolated settlements are known (Med 95, 96 and 111). It is probable that Med 95, a twelfth and thirteenth-century site, was a customary holding of Great Fransham manor which migrated southwards in the fourteenth century to the edge of *Hey Green* after a major encroachment on the common. This encroachment would have effectively separated *Elverycsmore* from *Hey Green*. Most of its area (almost 3 acres), apart from the site of the re-established house, became arable, as evidenced by the slight surviving traces of ridge-and-furrow (Fig. 7.15; frontispiece, aerial

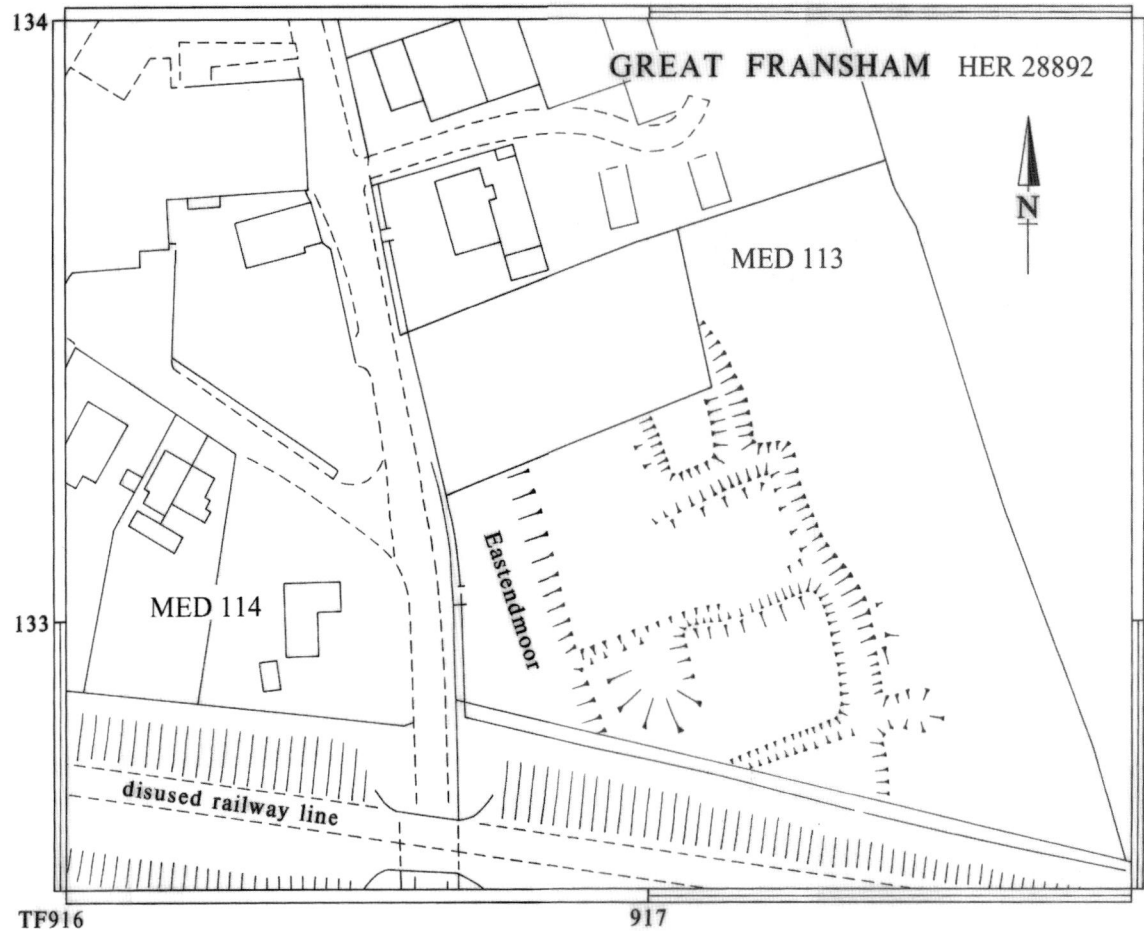

Figure 7.16 Med 113, earthwork site within Area E, scale 1:1,250

photograph). In c.1400 Castle Acre Priory held 6 acres in one piece, freehold of Great Fransham and butting south on the common pasture. This common was named as *Hey Green* in 1553 (MS 13077) when the 6-acre piece was said to lie in *Herningshaw*, i.e. in Wendling and to the east of Med 95^x. In c.1430 *Hey Green* had 7 acres in one piece lying on its north side. To the west, Med 96, inferred from finds found in soil upcast from a ditch next to non-surveyed land, was also probably a Great Fransham customary holding butting south on *Elverycsmore*. This included 8 acres in one piece butting north on Beeston field. West of this lay land of Ellinghams manor. Med 111, a thirteenth and fourteenth-century site in the north-west corner hard by the Beeston boundary, was a freehold of Ellinghams manor, and lay within *Dymesclos* in 1480–3 (MS 13048).

Hey Green now lies under grass. It was butted midway along its western edge by two inhabited holdings. Both were held of Great Fransham manor and have been grouped together as Med 112 (Fig. 7.15). To the north a messuage with 1 acre was described as soiled in 1397. On the south side of this lay a freehold messuage with 1 acre and a 'portion' of another messuage. Several people with the surname le Heigh, Heigh and Hey were tenants in the fourteenth century. The common may have taken its name from this family. It should be noted that along the opposite, eastern edge of the common, on arable land in Wendling parish, there is no surface indication of medieval settlement. Other lands lying between *Hey Green* and *Doesgate* included a 3-acre enclosure called *Fenders*, which was Great Fransham demesne in c.1430, and a customary messuage lay at its western end (see Area E). A 9-acre close called *Kynnocks*, demesne of Northendhall manor in the sixteenth century (TNA SC 12/3/23 and 24), lay at the northern end. It can be identified with a croft, once of Osmund the merchant (*mercatoris*) granted by Roger son of Thomas of Fransham to William son of William de Wendling, the founder of Wendling Abbey. The charter is endorsed '*Kinnokes croft*' (TNA E 40/12003). Two other charters, of 1265–74, also relate to this land (see Med 112, Appendix 2). An 8-acre piece, butting east on *Hey Grene* and held by Wendling Abbey as freehold of Great Fransham in c.1400, was probably the same land, as were the abbey's 8 acres called *Gelewiygescroft* in Great Fransham in 1269 (MS 3813). Both pasture and meadow of Castle Acre Priory occur in several abuttals. Neither can be identified with any certainty amongst the properties listed in the priory's cartulary (BL Harley MS 2110). Probably also in this area were 8¾ acres of East Lexham freehold, apparently lying in one piece and butting west on the common pasture called *Kynnockersmore* and east on *Collysyarde* and *Moltysyarde*, which were perhaps related to one or more of the messuages on the western edge of *Hey Green*. Ridge-and-furrow survives as low earthworks over an area of 1.86 hectares to the south-west of Med 112 (Fig. 7.15).

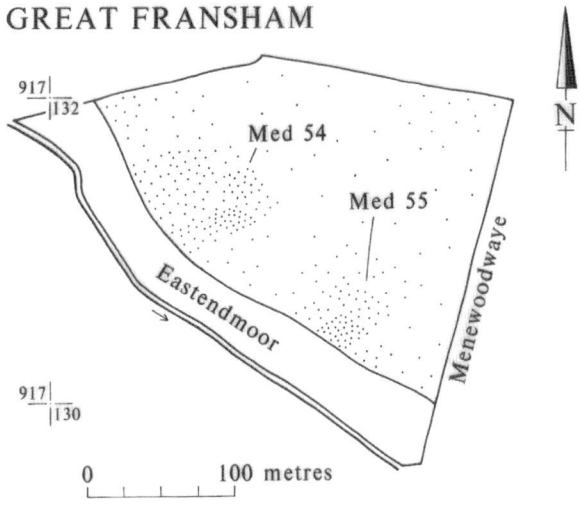

Figure 7.17 Med 54 and 55 within Area E, distribution of sherds (boundaries taken from Ordnance Survey County Series 1928 edition), scale 1:5,000

Med 49 was the third settlement on the western edge of *Hey Green*. Lying at the south-west corner of the common and occupied in the thirteenth and fourteenth centuries, it was a Rougholme manor customary messuage with 8 acres, through which ran the king's highway, according to seventeenth-century abuttals. Land of this tenement extended from *Hey Green* to *Kenoxe Layn, i.e. Doesgate*. The southern end of *Hey Green* was edged by a Great Fransham freehold messuage occupied from the thirteenth century to *c.*1500, Med 50. This was edged on its east side by a free ½ acre of the same fee.

A point of egress from Fransham into Wendling in this area is suggested by an amercement of 1465, when Ralph Lawdy, an inhabitant of *Hey Green* or thereabouts, was found to have re-hung inadequately a *porta caduta* towards (*versus*) *Heryngshawewong*[xi] (MS 13048).

Area E, the eastern and northern edges of Doesgate, Fendersmoor and Eastendmoor, Great Fransham (Fig. 7.14)

Riverside common pasture edged with settlements and tenement blocks, some dispersed, some closely spaced

Doesgate, a road running south from the east end of *Elverycsmore* and set in a shallow valley was also called *Kynnoks Lane*. At TF 9155 1337 the stream met two others flowing from the west. South of the confluence *Eastendmoor* broadened out on either side of the enhanced stream and curled to the east, nowhere achieving a width of more than 350m before crossing the Wendling parish boundary. The topography of the confluence and its surroundings was drastically altered by the construction of a railway embankment in the mid-nineteenth century and subsequently by the erection of industrial, now agricultural buildings. The following description begins at the northern end.

The first 400m are under grass and fall within Area D. A customary messuage of Great Fransham manor lay opposite an associated 14-acre piece of the tenement Kynnokks in the north-east corner of *Ellinghams field*. It is assumed that this holding had been of customary tenure before it was granted at farm in 1384. The house lay within a ¼-acre pightle at the west end of *Fenders*, a close of Great Fransham demesne. As this was described as formerly built in *c.*1430 while the tenement Kynnokks was said to be built, (*i.e.* standing) at the same time, there had probably been two houses here. South of land associated with Med 49 lay Med 47, a thirteenth and fourteenth-century site on customary land of Rougholme manor. South from a point at TF 9165 1342 a length of 250m, covered by buildings and grass and therefore unavailable for fieldwalking, contained a row of properties containing at least six house sites and held of various manors, grouped together as Med 113: a messuage with 1 acre in the croft and 1 acre enclosed, both customary holdings of Great Fransham; a messuage with 1¼ acres in the croft, freehold of Kirkhams; a messuage and 1 acre, freehold of Kirkhams; a Rougholme customary cottage; 2 Rougholme customary acres; a messuage with 1½ acres in the croft, a free and later customary tenement of Ellinghams; a messuage and croft, freehold of Cannons. Such a densely packed group of documented messuages is illustrated by the fortunate survival of the earthworks of parts of three or more tofts in a pasture field to the north and scrubland to the south of the railway embankment (Fig. 7.16).

To the south-west of this group two sites, Med 54 and 55, both with eleventh-century origins (LS 12 and 13) and both freeholds of Great Fransham manor, were more widely spaced (Fig. 7.17). Med 54 was occupied into the fourteenth century and Med 55 into the thirteenth. East of a farm track, a path known as *Menewoodwaye* in *c.*1430 (Old English adjective *m?ne*, common, Smith 1956b, 33), the northern edge of *Eastendmoor* no longer survives as far as the Wendling boundary, having been destroyed without archaeological record by road construction in the mid-1970s. Henry Wrendham had placed a boundary on the common at *Menewood* in 1305/6 without the assent of the community. *Menewoodwaye* survives only at its southern end. It probably ran north along the eastern boundary of Fransham up to and perhaps beyond the north-east corner of *Hey Green*. The common wood may have been what was to be known as Dikewood and Herringshall, areas of Wendling in which there is good documentary evidence for woodland, assarting and wood pasture in the twelfth century[xii].

Med 56, the extant northern part of a twelfth to fourteenth-century site, might possibly have been a freehold of Sparhams manor (Fig. 7.18). A messuage and 3 acres in the croft, held freely of Blyfords manor and void in 1550 lay on the east side of Med 56 and west of land once *Dewes* (MS 424).

The lay-out of properties in this area is ill-understood and confused. The earliest record of an Ellinghams customary holding of a cottage called *Wyndhams* with 1½ roods was in 1576, when it was held by John Wyskard gent. and lay next to a vacant tenement of unstated tenure also held by Wyskard. This may be one and the same as a messuage held in two halves which appears only in a corrupt late 15th-century Rougholme rental. There are two entries, the second of which is very muddled, incomplete and partly duplicated. No indication of status of tenure is given. William Pratt jun. held half a mess once of Henry de Wendham [and] of Richard [—], for the rent of one hen. William Schort & Simon Heyghe held the other half, once of Richard le Heye and afterwards John le

GREAT FRANSHAM

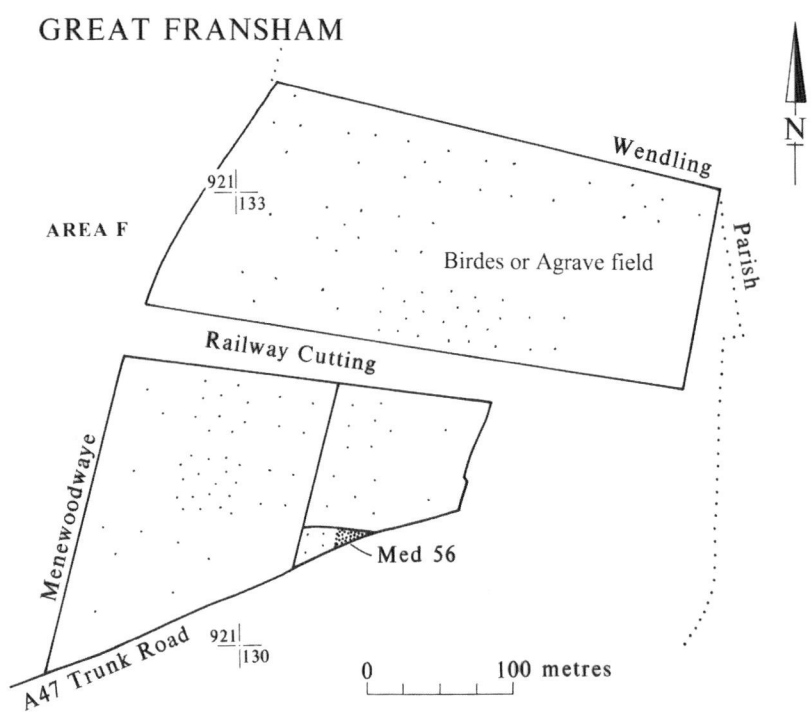

Figure 7.18 Med 56 within Area E, distribution of sherds
(boundaries taken from Ordnance Survey County Series 1928 edition), scale 1:5,000

Heye, rent [—]. The same document lists John Fynch and 'now' Nicholas Petyfere as tenant of a pightle called *Chyleyspyghtell*, once of Henry de Wendling and afterwards Richard le Hey, with a rent of 2 hens (TNA SC 11/476). It seems likely that de *Wendling* was a mistranscription of de *Wendham*. Henry de Wendham was witness to a deed of *c*.1274–90 (MC 360/21, 713X6). John Fynche was a juror at leet courts between 1425 and 1451 (MS 13048) as was Nicholas Petyfere between 1480 and 1504 (MS 13035, 13048, 13052, 13054, and 13166–7). In 1473 Robert and Thomas, sons of Henry Mayken [of Wendling] had stolen apples from William Cades's garden at *Petyfers* (MS 13048). In 1508 Thomas Wyskard gent. was distrained to do fealty and for suite of court for land late Petyfers, at a Rougholme court. In 1528 he was distrained for 12 years arrears of rent of 2 hens per annum owed for *Childes Pictell* which lay in Great Fransham next to the messuage once of Henry de Wendling and afterwards of Richard de le Hay (MR 28, 240X6). In *c*.1555 amongst his lands listed by John Wyskard gent., son of Thomas, was a pightle called [a] hempland once William Cade's called *Fynches modo Petyfers*, along with an unlocated messuage with a croft adjoining containing 2 acres. In the same document the farm rent paid by Thomas Nekyr[xiii] for a messuage with a close called *Petyfers* was given as 13s 4d. Another holding in the same list, a messuage with a 2-acre croft once Shortes and owing rent to Blyfords manor, may be related to the messuage in two halves mentioned above.[xiv]

The next property to the east was probably a messuage and 4 acres of the customary tenement Cristmasse, held of Sparhams manor and documented from 1385/6. *Birds acre*, a freehold of Northendhall or Guntons manor in 1552, lay to the east of this and to the west of 1 acre of the tenement Cristmasse. The final piece was ¾ acre in *Birdes croft*, held probably freely of Northendhall or Guntons manor, and located next to *le Procession way*, i.e. the parish boundary, in 1552 (TNA SC 12/3/23). It is very likely that the Wendling Abbey manor customary tenement Byrddes lay at least in part within Fransham. In 1446/7 it comprised a messuage, 3 acres, ½ rood and 6 perches (Holkham Hall, Longham Bundle 3, 34). In 1482 Henry Mayken, tenant of Byrddes, was amerced at a Mills-on-the-Moor leet court for ploughing over the processional way between Great Fransham and Wendling (MS 13048), and in 1518 Simon Bronde was amerced at a Wendling Abbey manor court for damaging the processional way in *Byrds Feald* with his cart (Raynham Hall, RAW Norfolk manorial, T–W).

Area F, north and east of Doesgate, Fendersmoor and Eastendmoor, Great Fransham (Fig. 7.14)
Predominantly common field

The western part of this area, lying south of *Hey Green* and *Dulls gat*, comprised a common open field known as *Kaulynges* or *Harwynes* field, along with six acres in one piece containing land and pasture in Fransham called *Kingescroft*. This piece was granted by William son of Walter Faber of Wendling to Castle Acre Priory, probably in the twelfth or early thirteenth century. It butted north on the common pasture (BL Harley MS 2110). Probably the same six acres in Fransham were quitclaimed by Philip son of Odo of Fransham to the priory in a fine of 1234 (TNA CP 25/1/156/57.595)[xv]. In 1550 1½ acres of demesne of Northendhall manor lay in *Sketesfeld alias Kingescroft*. Small pieces of Great Fransham demesne, totalling 7 acres and listed in *c*.1430, were all later to be copyhold, and it is likely that some or all had formerly been held by customary tenure: 1 acre in two pieces at *Kynggescroft*, lying to the west of Castle Acre Priory land and butting north on *Hey Green*, ½ acre butting west on

Doesgate, 1 acre at *Doesgate* butting west on *Fendersmoor*, 1 acre at *Fendors* butting west on *Fendersmoor*, ½ acre in the furlong (*stadium*) called *Shortcalling* butting east on *Kynggescroft*, ¾ acre in *Shortcalling*, 1½ acres in the same furlong butting east on *Menewoodwaye*, and ¾ acre lying east to west in *Heycalling* furlong. In *c*.1400 five of the above pieces (1 acre butting north on the common; 1 acre, two ¾ acres and ½ acre, all aligned east-west) had been part of a 12-acre customary holding associated with Med 96 in Area D. There were 3 acres of Great Fransham freehold here, in three pieces, two of which butted west on *Doesgate*. In 1505 6 acres of freehold, whose manorial allegiance is uncertain, lay between lands of Great Fransham manor on both sides and butted west on *Fendoures mor* (MC 2755/4/1, 1004X2). In the mid-sixteenth century 3½ acres of former demesne of Cannons manor in 'divers' pieces in Great Fransham had become copyhold. These are probably the same as 3 acres of West Acre land held at farm in 1427–8 (MS 13137). The names and associations of various tenants in the post-medieval period suggest that these pieces lay in this field, as do abuttals on lands of West Acre Priory for several pieces of Great Fransham demesne listed above. Three pieces of Blyfords manor freehold lay in *Short callinge* in 1550: 1¾ acres and 2 acres, both butting east on *Manhoode stye* (an eighteenth-century mistranscription of *Menewood stye*) and a further 2½-acre piece (MS 424). The first and second parcels, butting east on the path called *Menewoodstye*, had been conveyed by charter in 1505 (MC 2755/4/1, 1004X2). The element *stye* derives from the Old English *stîg* or Old Norse *stigr*, a path or narrow road (Smith 1956b, 152). To the east of Med 113, 2 acres of Rougholme customary land lay enclosed in *Cadescloos* (TNA SC 12/3/23).

The area between *Menewoodwaye* and the Wendling boundary was known as *Birdes field* or *Agrave field*. North of the above-mentioned parcels flanking *Eastendmoor*, it contained the following in 1549: 1 acre in *Birdes felde* and ¾ acre in the same called *Mugelles thre rodes*, freehold of Guntons manor, 1¼ acres with ½ acre to the north, both in *Birdes croft*, held by uncertain tenure of Rougholme manor (TNA SC 12/3/23). To the north of the latter lay customary land of Great Fransham rectory, an acre of copyhold mentioned in the will of Christopher Crowe of Wendling, proved in 1560 (NCC 110 Bircham), and called a 'large acre' in 1729 (DN/TER/68/4/7). Two pieces of 5 acres each, freehold of Blyfords manor, butted west on *Manhood stye* (see above) and 1¾ acres of the same holding were to the north of the close late *Dewes* which lay on the common edge (MS 424). Two parcels of customary land held of the manor of Wendling Nuper Abbis are known from predominantly post-medieval sources. The first parcel lay in two pieces comprising 1¾ acres in *Birdsfild* in Great Fransham and butted east on the common path in 1588 (BL/MA 42). The same two pieces were said to lie in Wendling in 1556, when they had been sold by John Wenne to John Barton gent. (Christ Church Oxford 3d.2.1). One piece can probably be equated with ½ acre of the tenement Charlepoynts held by John Kenting in 1446/7 (Holkham Hall, Longham Bundle 3, 34). Kenting surrendered ½ acre of the tenement Richard Charlepoynts at *Agrave* in Great Fransham in 1465 (TNA SC 2/194/21). In 1636 the second parcel of Wendling Nuper Abbis customary land, ¾ acre, lay at *Bird stile* in Great Fransham or Wendling (MS 4129). *Byrds style* had been damaged in 1518 (Raynham Hall, RAW Norfolk manorial, T–W). In 1558 the same parcel had been said to lie in Wendling next to a pightle called *Pomfrettes* (Christ Church Oxford 3d.2.1). The same description was given in a rental of the same year or slightly earlier (Christ Church Oxford MS Estates 53). This piece may be among 16½ acres in Wendling and Fransham held by Leffei son of Lewin de Wendling and granted to Castle Acre Priory by Laurence son of Elfer of Wendling in the thirteenth century. Philip, prior of Castle Acre, confirmed his grant of the same to Leiffein son of William de Wendling, to be held for a rent of 2s. Prior Philip's charter, using the perch as a quarter of an acre, lists eight pieces in Wendling and one of three perches in Fransham. A note in a sixteenth-century hand adds that these lands were held by the abbot of Wendling (BL Harley MS 2110).

Area G, west and south of Eastendmoor, and Henfield, Great Fransham (Fig. 7.14)
Settlements and tenement blocks, a chapel, common field, detached block demesne, small amounts of demesne pasture

The area, to the south and west of the former confluence of the three streams at TF 9155 1337, is poorly understood, not only because of changes in the courses of these streams, the construction of the railway embankment and of buildings, but also because of some uncertainties in the documentary record. The roughly triangular area north of the embankment was not available for fieldwalking, because of the presence of buildings and a plantation. However, an area measuring 40m by 26m and centred at TF 9157 1332 was examined under very poor soil conditions. Twenty-five medieval sherds were recovered from the southern half, a high total in such circumstances and suggestive of medieval settlement. This has been designated as Med 114, to represent a number of houses known from documentary sources to have run in a row west from *Eastendmoor* along the south side of a road, which was apparently flanked by a tongue of common pasture.

At the western end stood the chapel of St Katherine, first recorded in the will, proved in 1388, of Simon Fyncham, rector of Great Fransham who left 2 quarters of barley for its repair and 1 quarter to the guild of St Katherine (NCC 103 Harsyk). Other wills, including some of Little Fransham and Wendling inhabitants, bequeathed gifts to the chapel and/or guild between 1444 and 1530. The dedication indicates a post-Conquest foundation (Farmer 1987, 77). The chapel had ¼ acre on the north side called *Chapilyards* and another ¼ acre lay to the north of that. The latter was granted out as customary land of Great Fransham manor in 1395. Near the chapel a ¾-acre piece of East Lexham manor freehold butted north on a meadow of Great Fransham manor, and 3 more acres were probably close by (KIM 1/8/16). To the east of the chapel, ¾ acre once built upon lay in *Henfield* at *le Chapell*. It was demesne of Great Fransham in *c*.1430 and subsequently held by customary tenure. Next to this was a messuage, freehold of Great Fransham in *c*.1400. Another free messuage, held in *c*.1400 of the prior of Castle Acre who held of Great Fransham in pure alms, may have been the adjoining property, to judge from the distribution of lands held by subsequent tenants, but no abuttals were given in any document. At the same date the easternmost property was another Great Fransham freehold, which butted east and north on the common. More tenurial details are given under Med 114.

South of the railway embankment there is only a slight medieval sherd scatter along the eastern edge of the medieval *Henfield* and the western edge of *Eastendmoor* until Med 107 is reached. This was described as a messuage with a ½-acre croft in 1372, although only twelfth and thirteenth-century sherds were recovered. It was both a freehold of Great Fransham and a customary holding of Kirkhams manor. No further medieval sites were apparent in the next 100m stretch to the south, beyond which the common edge is covered by farm buildings.

At TF 9160 1287, a road called *Odeslane* entered the common from the west with another road joining from the north-west, after which the common edge swung through a right angle to head to the east. The common way was obstructed by overhanging branches at *Odesfalgate* in 1449 (MS 13048). On the corner of the common, now beneath standing buildings, and butting south and east on the common was a customary holding of Great Fransham manor (Med 108), which on the evidence of a few Late Saxon sherds found in the arable field to the west, had begun in the eleventh century (LS 15).

The earliest reference to *Henfield* is in a late thirteenth-century charter recording the grant by Geoffrey de Hockering to Wendling Abbey of a rent payable for two pieces of land in *Henne Feld* (MS 3809). The name derives from Old English *henn*, wild fowl (Ekwall 1960, 235). At the northern end of the field, south of Med 114 and west of *Eastendmoor* were 5 acres of Great Fransham demesne called *Pysecroft* in which an illegal path had been made in 1362, and which was let at farm in 1366. By c.1400, *Pysecroft* was held by customary tenure and included pasture at one end. Another 5-acre piece lay in the croft of one of the Great Fransham freehold properties at the northern edge of the field. It was held freely of Sparhams manor, and 1½ roods of the same tenure probably lay close by. On the south side ran a common path described in c.1400 both as leading from Great Fransham towards Dereham and as leading towards Great Fransham church. At the same date five pieces of Great Fransham freehold land lay in *Henfeld*: three held by William Grenehode, 1½ acres and ¾ acres, both in the western part, and 2½ acres in *Overhenfeld*, a close of unstated acreage, once of John Haddock (and butting east on the common, and further west, 2 acres at *Clakthornes*.

Clackthornes appears to have been situated just to the south of the crossing of the *Whiteway* over *Fenbridge*. As well as these 2 acres there were two pieces of Great Fransham demesne pasture close by, to the north and west, each of 1¼ acres, one called *Clackthorndes* in c.1400 and the other called *Clackthorns* in 1603 (MS 13080). The Great Fransham freehold piece disappears from the record after 1547/8 (MS 13076), and it is unclear whether it was one and the same as 2 acres of Cannons manor freehold called *Clawthorns* in Great Fransham which were first mentioned in 1642. They were known as *Cleath hornes* and adjoined *Chappel Close* in the will of John Spencer proved in 1658 (TNA PROB 11/274/546), as *Clack* at a manor court held in 1676, and as *Cloathhans* in the will of Daniel Spencer proved in 1690 (ANW W30.43 1690). The place name occurs in two undated charters of the middle of the thirteenth century. In one deed Henry son of William of Fransham granted to William son of Leftheyn of Wendling, for a payment of ½ a mark and an annual rent of 2d, a meadow in Fransham at *Clakesthornes* butting on *Fenbrige* between the meadows of Richard son of Hamon and Roger son of Fuka, as well as a ½d rent formerly paid by Robert Mendham to Henry for a pit (*fovea*) belonging to the meadow. An endorsement states that the meadow was of 1 acre (TNA E 40/10540). The second charter lists both the meadow at *Clakethornes* (with the same abuttals) and the pit amongst holdings granted by Ralph son of Henry son of William of Little Fransham to William son of Leftheine of Wendling (TNA WARD 2/53/179/10). The first element is either Old English *clæcc* 'hillock', the Old Norse equivalent *klakkr* (Smith 1956a, 96 and 1956b, 5), both indistinguishable in place-names as the Middle English form *clakke*), or the Old Norse personal name *Klakkr*. The second element, the same form in Old English and Old Norse, is *þorn*, a thorn-tree or hawthorn (Smith 1956b, 204).

In 1343 one freehold acre of Great Fransham Rectory manor lay in a furlong (*quarentina*) called *Netherhennefelde* (Holkham Hall, Longham Bundle 3, 34). Land of uncertain acreage and tenure, and held of Blyfords manor, lay in *Netherhenfeld* in 1550 (MS 424). This was probably the same land as that of William Mascall, which was to the north of 5 acres of Great Fransham demesne in *Henfeld* in c.1430. These 5 acres butted west on meadow and lay on the north side of the king's highway leading from Wendling towards Great Fransham church.

Below the southern edge of *Henfield* and to the south of *Odeslane* a rectangular piece of Great Fransham parish, containing just over 2 acres, projects south into Little Fransham *Quarent*. 21. This rather anomalous salient is also depicted on the Enclosure Award map. This has been tentatively identified with 2½ acres butting north on *Odeslane* and held freely of Great Fransham manor by Edmund Oldhall in c.1400, when they were said to have been once of Peter le Strange knt. and once of Thomas de Beston. By 1547/8 this land was held by one John Harydance, all of whose freeholds lay in Great Fransham (MS 13076).

One piece of land in *Henne Feld* butted east on a meadow of Sir William de Fransham called *Presmedwe* according to a late thirteenth-century charter (MS 3809). It is hard to judge where this meadow was located. Later evidence indicates that where *Henfield* did not butt east on crofts or messuages it ran up to the common pasture of *Eastendmoor*. It is possible that the piece (*pecia*) of land lay in the extreme north-west corner of the field near St Katherine's chapel, if the *pres* element meant 'priest'.

Area H, the southern edge of Eastendmoor, Great Fransham, and land to the south (Fig. 7.19)
Settlements with tenement blocks flanking a common pasture in Area E, one isolated settlement, some detached tenement blocks, common field, land-use of parts of the area not known

At the west end of the common edge and next to the Little Fransham parish boundary, facing Med 108 across the funnel-shaped entrance to *Eastendmoor*, was Med 58, a thirteenth- and fourteenth-century freehold of Great Fransham manor. A row of four documented messuages lay close together within a short distance to the east, but

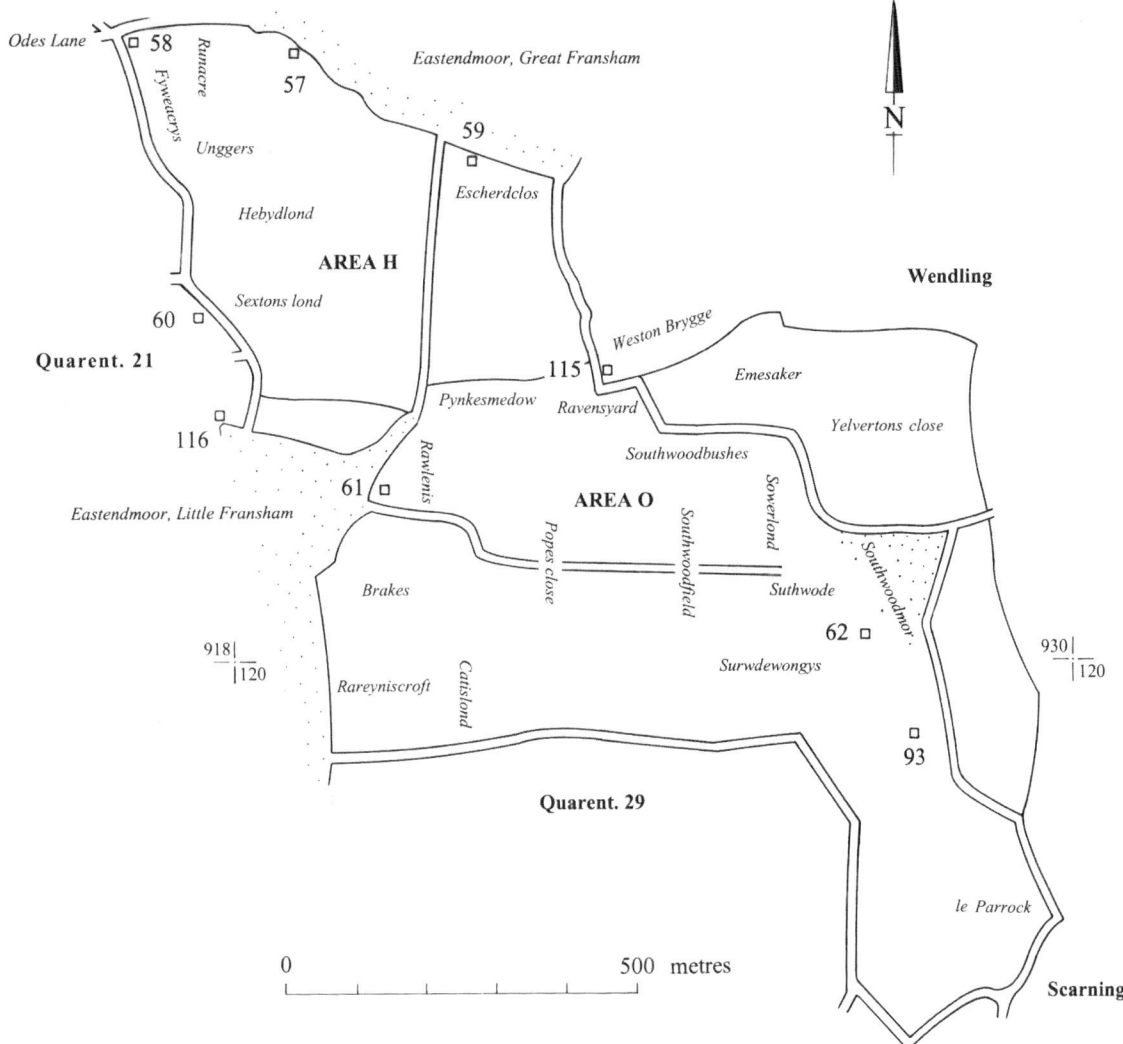

Figure 7.19 Areas H and O, Great Fransham, scale 1:10,560

the sites of probably three of these are now beneath a trunk road. All these three were freeholds, and from west to east, they were held of Guntons, Blyfords, and Ellinghams manors. The fourth messuage was a customary tenement of Great Fransham Rectory manor and may have comprised two distinct messuages before the late fourteenth century. Further details of all four will be found under Med 57. A spread of pottery from the destroyed sites is visible to the west of Med 57 on Fig. 7.20. Beyond a considerable gap and next to a way leading to the south was Med 59, an isolated site occupied from the thirteenth to c.1400 and a Rougholme customary holding. Entrance into land south of Med 57 is indicated by *Pratts Faldgate* cited in 1477 when Thomas Harlewyn was amerced for leaving a watercourse there unscoured (MS 13048). In 1523 Edmund Pratt had inadequately repaired a *porta caduta* at the end of the lane next to his messuage.

Various pieces of land were associated with the above properties, both in their crofts and to the south in a field that does not appear to have been named. Med 58 had ¾ acre in its croft. The composite site Med 57 was accompanied by 2 acres in the croft of the Blyfords freehold messuage and lands amounting to 8 acres were associated with the Ellinghams freehold messuage in 1642, before which their acreage was unspecified. They lay to the south of *Eastendmoor* against the Wendling boundary (Mills and Reeve 12/03/70 Mason Necton deeds). There were two acres in the croft of the Guntons freehold with 1 customary acre called *Runacre / Ronacre* butting north on *Odes lane*, formerly demesne of Northendhall manor in 1549 (TNA SC 2/192/96, SC 11/473 and SC 12/3/24). Two acres of Great Fransham freehold, which in c.1400 lay in the croft of Adam Ringolles with lands of the abbot of Wendling to the west and north, were later held by tenants of the Blyfords and Ellinghams freeholds. In c.1400 this land was once of Hamon de Hokeringe. An earlier tenant, John Jenior, had died seized of 2 acres of the tenement Hokerynge in 1366. In 1385/6 a rent of one hen was due from Adam Ringolde, tenant of the tenement once of Adam Hokering, to Sparhams manor for rights of common. By the seventeenth century rent was paid to Sparhams for 1 freehold acre, as well as for common rights. A Godfrey de Hockryng held land of William de Fransham in c.1279 (Table 6.2, nos 31–3. Adam Ringolde also had property in Little Fransham (*Quarent.* 29). Approximately 8 acres were associated with the two customary messuages of Great Fransham Rectory manor. Med 59 lay within four acres of Rougholme customary land called *Escherdclos*. A road ran south from the eastern end of *Eastendmoor*

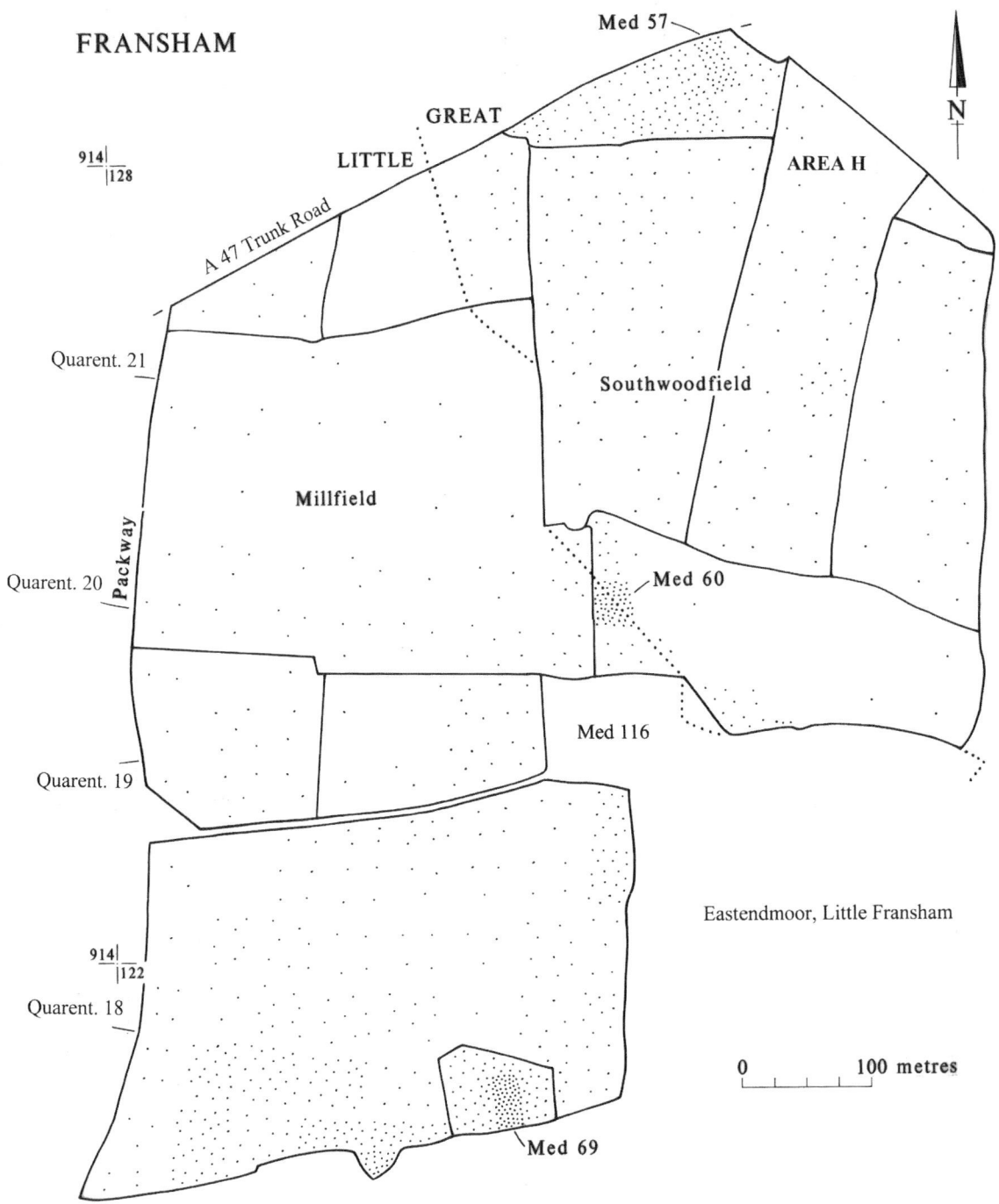

Figure 7.20 Med 57, 60 and 69 in *Quarentinae* 18–21 and Area H, distribution of sherds (boundaries taken from Ordnance Survey County Series 1928 edition), scale 1:5,000

along the Wendling parish boundary. This survives in part as a sunken way flanked by ditches.

The parish boundary between Great and Little Fransham followed a way running south-west to the north-west corner of *Eastendmoor*, Little Fransham. In the north-west of this area 5 acres of Kirkhams and Wilcoks land, aligned north-south, can probably be identified with land of Henry le Strange called *Fyweacrys* and abutted in an early fourteenth-century charter (MC 360/39, 713X6). Part of the Wilcoks demesne and called *le fyveacres* in c.1420, it had become copyhold by 1502. Although most often said to be in Great Fransham, it was included within Little Fransham Millfield *Quarent*. 21 in the 1605 survey. To the south, ¼ acre, the eastern end of *le Lund*, a 7-acre Wilcoks freehold, lay within Great Fransham, the rest being in Little Fransham *Quarent*. 21. One Kirkhams and Wilcoks customary acre said to be in the same *Quarent*. and east of the above freehold must also have been in Great Fransham. By 1392 these 1¾ acres were said to be soiled. Elsewhere nearby lay two pieces of Kirkhams customary land, ½ acre at *Unggers* in 1384 and 1 acre called *Hebydlond* at the same date. The latter was of the tenement Osyers (see Med 69 in *Quarent*. 18). Two acres of Great Fransham freehold lay in this area. One called *Sextons lond* was held by the abbot of Wendling and apparently butted west on Little Fransham. The other acre was said to be once of John Parson in c.1400. He had sworn fealty for 1 acre in 1353 and may have been the

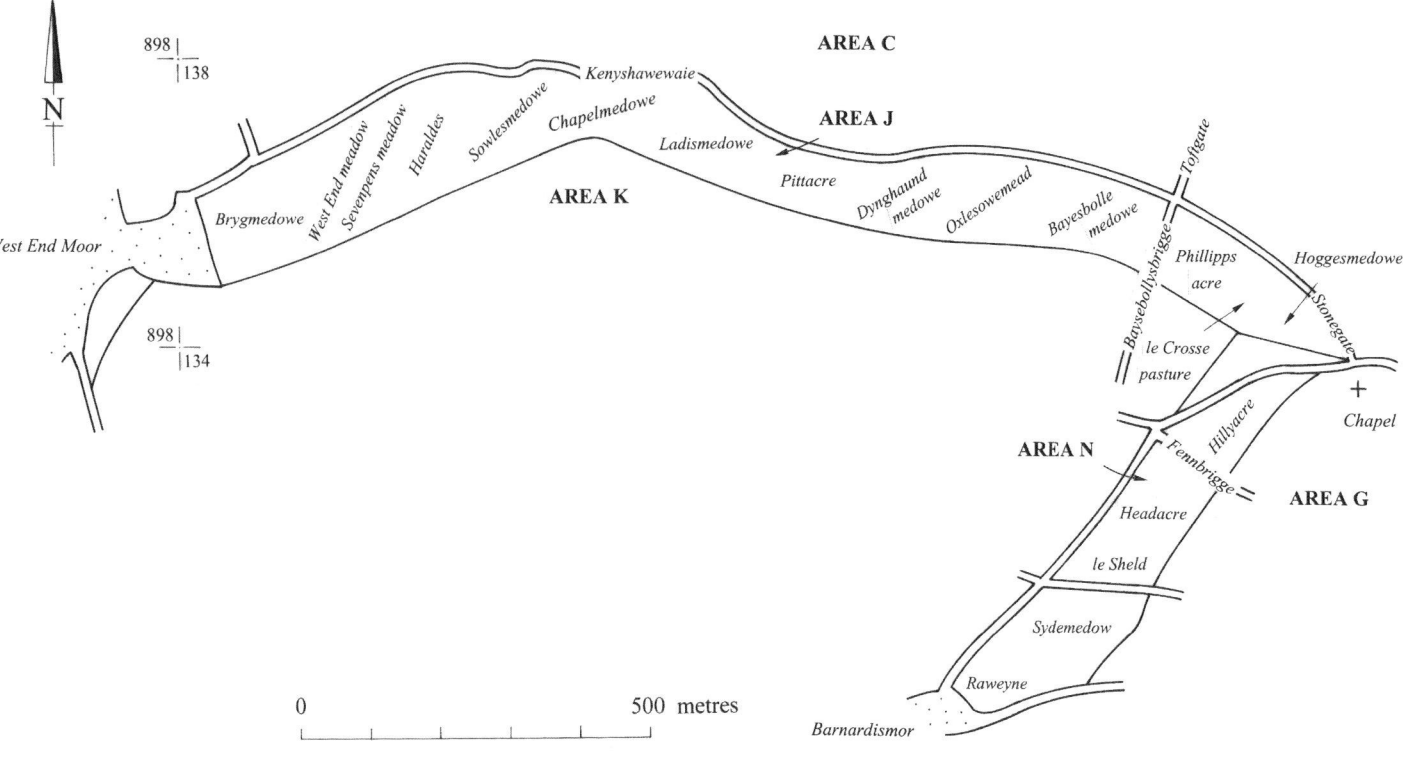

Figure 7.21 Areas J and N, Great Fransham, scale 1:10,560

tenant of Med 56 (in Area F). A 4½-acre piece of Blyfords manor freehold probably lay to the north-east of *Eastendmoor*, Little Fransham. Only one piece of Great Fransham demesne lay in this field, ¼ acre that in *c*.1430 was held at farm in his close by John de Southwood, tenant of Med 58. Pentney Priory may have held 1 acre here in *c*.1400. It lay to the west of land of John de Southwood and butted south on an unlocated common way called *Heygate*. 1¾ freehold acres of uncertain manorial allegiance, which were conveyed in 1505, lay west of Pentney Priory land and butted north on *le Sextensacre, cf. Sextons lond* above (MC 2755/4/1, 1004X2).

A single eleventh and twelfth-century settlement site (LS 16 / Med 60) sits on the Great and Little Fransham parish boundary (Fig. 7.20). The tenure of the land containing this site is not certain, but it was almost certainly a freehold (see Little Fransham *Quarent.* 20. The sum of all the parcels listed above does not account for the whole of the area under discussion. It is clear that a considerable amount of land remains untraced in the available documentary record.

Area J, North Meadows or Ellinghams Meadows, Great Fransham (Fig. 7.21)
Apart from demesne pasture at the eastern end, all meadow, both demesne and several

An arc of valley meadows, by the sixteenth century known as *North or Ellinghams Meadows*, flanked the stream running east from *West End Moor* as far as *Fendersmoor/ Eastendmoor*. This was the main meadow resource for the whole of Fransham. It has proved extremely difficult to make sense of the distribution of individual parcels of meadow along this stretch, so that there is a consequent lack of precision in the following description, which will run from west to east. The difficulty arises from the multiplicity of intermingled, often small parcels, the chronological range of the sources, and the confusion of abuttals. Many meadows, it seems, were on one side of the stream only, while others were on both. A road known as *Kenyshawewaie* and variously described as a common way, pack way or market path, followed the northern edge of meadowland for the full length.

Three acres called *Brygmedowe* in 1434/5 had been held by William Mascale, whose lands later formed the core of Blyfords manor, and John Blyford held *Brigmedow / Briggemeadow* in 1447 and 1461 (MS 13048). In 1560 *Brigges medowe* was next to (*i.e.* to the east of) *West Common* (MS 13059). In 1434/5 a meadow late Thomas Maskell's lay to the east. In later sources Thomas Mascale's meadow is given varying acreages, 4½ acres in 1442–3 (MS 13140), 6 acres in 1543 and 1547 (TNA C 142/70/6 and TNA C 142/85/18), and 8 acres in 1553 and 1557/8, when it was known as *West End meadow* (MS 13077 and 13078). It is very likely that the increase was the result of the incorporation of 3 acres of Great Fransham demesne called *Sevenpens meadow / Sepensmedowe* in *c*.1430, a name which was not recorded after this time. Thomas Mascalle's lands formed part of East Lexham manor. East of this was a Great Fransham glebe meadow, probably one of ¾ acre, but perhaps another of 4 acres, and east of this lay ¾ acre of Kirkhams and Wilcoks demesne meadow followed by one of Rougholme manor (see below). Beyond here the situation becomes more confused.

Amongst Great Fransham demesne meadows listed in *c*.1430 were two formerly associated with dependent

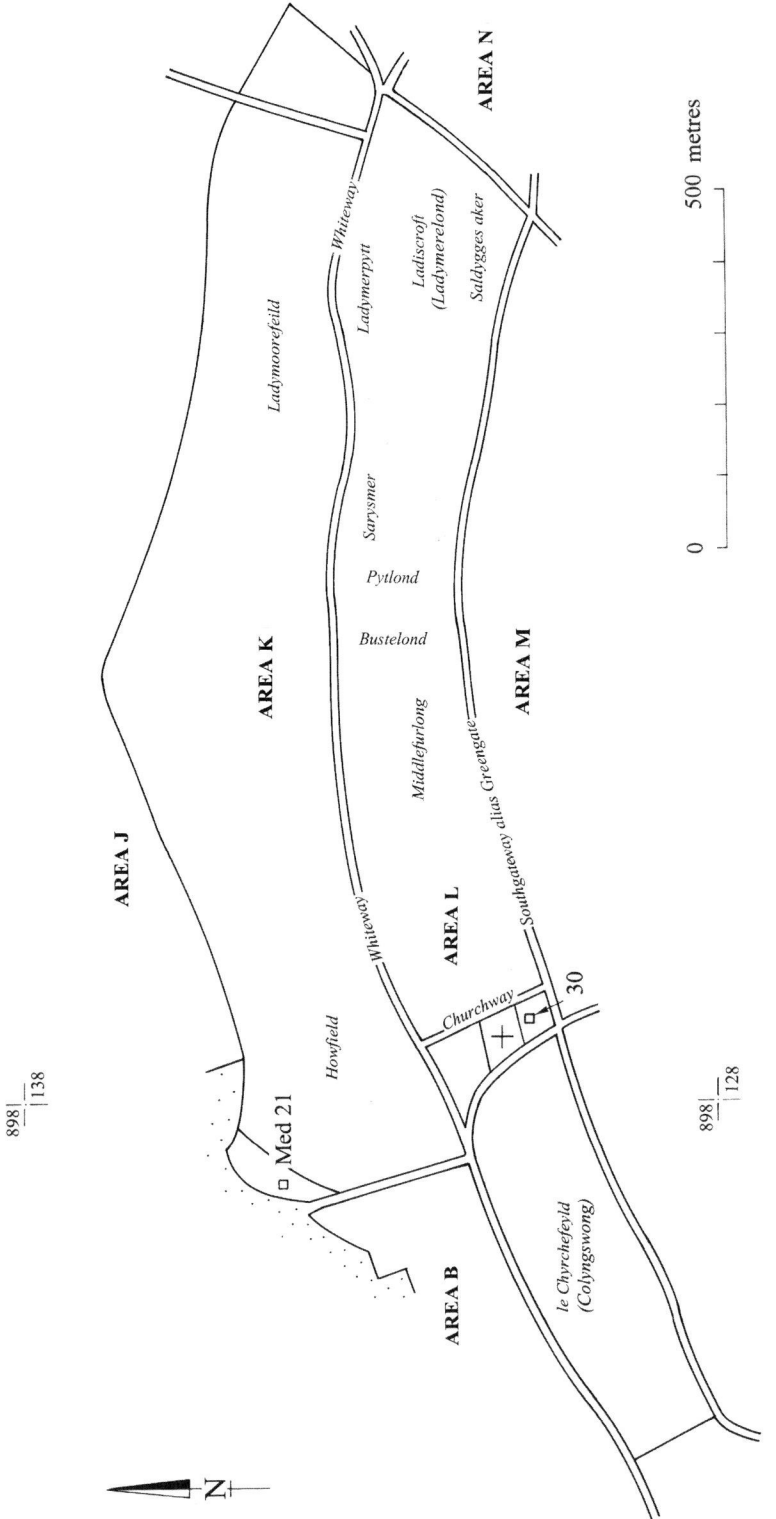

Figure 7.22 Areas K and L, Great Fransham, scale 1:10,560

tenements, 3 acres of meadow called *Haraldes* (see Med 4) and to its east another 3 acres called *Sowlesmedowe*, once part of the customary tenement Wymer (see Med 19). The other demesne meadows, apparently listed from west to east, were *Ladismedowe* (4 acres), *Dynnshtund/ Dynghaund medowe* (¾ acre), *Oxmedowe* (3 acres, *Oxlesowemead* in 1413), unnamed 2 acres, *Bayesbolle medowe* (1¾ acres), and *Phillipps acre* (1 acre). To the west of the latter, a ¼ acre was the only meadow of the Little Fransham glebe. At the eastern end, within the angle of two joining streams, at *c*.TF 9140 1337, lay 3 acres called *le Crosse pasture*, which butted north and south on Great Fransham demesne meadows, that to the south almost certainly being *Phillipps acre*.

Various demesne meadows of Kirkhams and Wilcoks (Little Fransham) manor also lay here. Four and a half acres in four pieces were listed as freehold in 1384. Three had fallen into the lord's hands before 1400 (MS 13125) and the fourth by 1443. None can be unequivocally related to later documents which are all sixteenth-century. The most reliable of these is an extent of 1577, copied verbatim in a survey of 1605. The most westerly meadow contained ¾ acre. For a short time, it formed part of a customary holding, between *c*.1390 and 1392/3 when it lay to the south of *Kynwaldeshaghe* and west of a meadow of Rougholme manor (MS 13123). It was also a freehold of Great Fransham, held in *c*.1400 by Edmund Oldhall lord of Kirkhams. Between 1444 and *c*.1566 it was again held by customary tenure. A 2-acre meadow lay further east, with another containing 1 acre called *Pittacre* on its south side. On the east side of *Baiebollesbridge* lay ¾ acre with a further ½ acre immediately to the east. Nearby was a ¼-acre meadow, and finally, on the west side of the above-mentioned piece of Little Fransham glebe meadow was a 1½-acre piece. The earliest reference to *Baysebollysbrigge*, by which *Toftgate* passed over the stream, was in 1417–8 when John Glas was paid 20d by the bailiff of Kirkhams and Wilcoks for raising the causeway for a length of 20 roods (MS 13135). On the west side of the bridge lay 4¾ acres of meadow in two pieces, once of Ralph de Beeston. In 1429 they were conveyed, along with other possessions, by two trustees of the late Geoffrey de Fransham to William de Oldhall, lord of Kirkhams and Wilcoks, and others (MS 13227), but their previous history and manorial allegiance is unknown. Let at farm as fee simple lands in 1476 (MS 13141), they were to become copyhold of Kirkhams and Wilcoks by 1521 (MS 13103). To judge from an abuttal concerning 3 acres of Great Fransham demesne lying north of the stream and east of *Toftgate*, there must have been a meadow of William Mascale on the east side of the bridge. This was probably the 1½-acre meadow listed in 1434/5.

Two acres of customary meadow belonging to Rougholme manor lay towards the western end (MR 28, 240X6). The Master of the Chapel of St Nicholas at Rougholme was ordered at a leet court to repair a causeway at *Kynwellsawe* in 1455. When the order was repeated in the following years up to 1460 the causeway was at *le Chapelmedowe* or *Chaplemedowys* (MS 13048 and MS 13051). Of East Lexham manor there were an unlocated 4 acres and a meadow (no acreage given) at *Baybolsbrigg* (KIM 1/8/16). Both these were freeholds and were to pass into the Blyfords manor in the seventeenth century. That element of East Lexham that became Ellinghams manor also had meadows here, as evidenced by abuttals referring to sixteenth-century lords. Two acres of meadow with 2 acres of land and meadow on the south side, butting north on *Kenyshawewaie*, and ½ acre of meadow at the south end of *Ellingham way*, all freeholds of Ellinghams, are known from records of late sixteenth-century manor courts (MC 1847/1, 741X2). The latter is very likely to be the same as ½ acre which had been held freely of Kirkhams manor in *c*.1375 and was located at *Toftgatyshende* in *c*.1395. Soon after then, this and other possessions of John Philip clerk passed to John Croupius, rector of Little Fransham and lord of Ellinghams (MS 13125 and MS 13128). Three meadows containing in all 1 acre, held by Pentney Priory freely of Great Fransham manor, were to be subsumed into Ellinghams manor in the sixteenth century. One other Great Fransham freehold meadow, 1 acre, also became part of Ellinghams manor. Five further Great Fransham freehold meadows totalling 7 acres were held by five tenants. One acre at the far, eastern end was called *Hoggesmedowe*. It was associated with most easterly messuage grouped under Med 114 (in Area G). Nearby was a 4-acre piece with 1 acre on its side, but the other three pieces have not been securely located. One freehold 1-acre meadow, held of Guntons manor, lay on the north side near the east end, at *Medowfalgate* (TNA SC 2/192/96 and TNA SC 12/3/23). In 1450 a ditch on the south side of *Medowys Faldgate* in a meadow of Great Fransham manor was unscoured and William Cade was amerced (MS 13048).

The road that followed the northern edge of *Ellinghams Meadows* crossed low-lying ground at its eastern end to join *Fendersmoor / Eastendmoor*. Here, in the vicinity of Med 53 (in Area C), it appears to have been called *Stonegate*. In 1369 John Boure leased two parcels of Great Fransham demesne meadow on either side of *Stonegate* next to a place called *Cornebelys*. The names *Stongate* and *Stonweye* occur in several amercements at Mills-on-the-Moor leet courts between 1483 and 1496. *Stonegate* passed through the close firstly of Thomas Cade, then of William Large senior and finally of Thomas Drowry. It was always associated with a common stream (MS 13048 and MS 13052), and the 'stone' element suggests it was a causeway. The king's highway called *Stone Lane* was last recorded at a leet court held in 1573 when it was blocked by overhanging trees and an unscoured common drain (MS 13062).

Area K, north of the Whiteway, Great Fransham (Fig. 7.22)
Common field and one 10-acre block of glebe land

The lay-out north of the *Whiteway* and west of Med 21 and the rectory has already been described under Area B. The remaining part was open field. It has proved impossible to arrive at precise information on the disposition of lands because of the vagueness of abuttals, with the *Whiteway* not being named in abuttals of *c*.1430. This may have led to confusion with lands lying north of *Southgateway* which ran parallel to the south (Area L). Fortunately, sixteenth-century sub-headings and glosses in several versions of the extent do give road names. The following list of lands must be incomplete.

The western part of this area was known as *Howfield* (perhaps Old English *hôh*, a spur of land, or Old Norse *haugr*, a hill or mound (Smith 1956a, 235–6 and 256–7)). Here there was just one piece of Great Fransham demesne, *Kynnokkshalfacre*, and only two pieces of freehold of the same manor, both held by John Crudde, 1¾ acres at *le Howe* and 2½ acres, called *Howlond* in one version of the rental of *c.*1400 (MS 13071). In 1434/5 lands late of William Mascale included 1 acre in *Hewefeld* and ½ acre in the same furlong. One piece of freehold of Great Fransham Rectory manor, 2 acres held in 1335 by Walter Corbel lay at *le Howe*, and three pieces (¾, 2 and 3 acres) were said to lie in the same furlong (Holkham Hall, Longham Bundle 3, 34).

Some land listed below may also have been in what was known as *Howefield* but may well have lain further east. Thirteen pieces of Great Fransham demesne, amounting to 13¼ acres, lay north of the *Whiteway*. The smallest parcel contained ½ acre and the largest 2 acres, and all bar two were aligned north to south. Of the thirteen pieces three were of customary tenure, 1 acre of the tenement Sewles in *Churchfield* but certainly north of the *Whiteway* and next to 1 acre of the tenement Flyntes, and ¾ acre of the tenement Sewles. Two acres in two pieces lay at the eastern end and butted east on the demesne meadow called *Phillipps acre*. Only two pieces of Great Fransham freehold land in this area have been identified. Both were of 1 acre and both butted north on meadows. Of the lands late of William Mascale listed in 1434/5 only two pieces, of 1 acre and ½ acre, are likely to have been north of the *Whiteway*, although abuttals on his lands in the Great Fransham manor extent suggest that there were more pieces. Twelve parcels of Great Fransham glebe, amounting to 27¼ acres and a pightle, appear to have been in this area. The largest contained 10 acres and the smallest ¼ acre. Three pieces were said to lie in *Ladymoorefeild*. Two acres of freehold of Great Fransham Rectory probably lay north of the *Whiteway*. They were of the lands '*terr.*' *Willori* and were held by Gilbert de Fransham in 1335 and 1343 (MS 13042 and Holkham Hall, Longham Bundle 3, 34). However, a charter of 1323 records the conveyance of various lands in Great Fransham including this piece, or one with identical abuttals, by Gilbert to William le Strange (MC 360/54, 713X6). This land is likely to be the same as 2 acres butting south on the common way called *Whiteway als. Ladymerwaye* recorded in a will of 1568 (NCC 88 Ponder). A ¾-acre piece of Rougholme customary land lay in *Estfeld* in 1548, next to glebe land on the east and butting south on *Whytt way* (TNA SC 12/3/22). It was associated with land containing Med 47 in Area E.

Area L, the parish churchyard, Middlefurlong, between the Whiteway and Southgateway alias Greengate, Great Fransham (Fig. 7.22)
Churchyard with church, common field intermingled with detached block demesne and detached tenement blocks

To the east of *Snapespiece* (in Area A) lay land of John Maynard in *c.*1430. He held ¾ acre of Great Fransham freehold in *c.*1400, which lay to the west of demesne land. In *c.*1430 the latter was described as one piece of 15 acres in *le Chyrchefeyld*, and was said, at the end of the sixteenth century, to have been called *Colyngswong* (MS 13089). There were two other pieces of demesne, ¾ and 5 acres, in the same area. Three pieces of Great Fransham freehold, held by John Crudde in *c.*1400 and amounting to 6 acres, lay in Middlefurlong and probably in this vicinity, as did 2½ acres of Great Fransham glebe, and 2 freehold acres at *Southgate* butting south on the king's highway and formerly held by William Mascale in 1434/5. Immediately west of the church 8 acres of glebe were in one piece between the king's highways to the north, south and east.

All Saints' churchyard contains slightly more than one acre, with the church placed centrally (Pl. 7.5). The extent of the yard to the north and perhaps the east is quite generous, and it may have been enlarged in those directions at some time, although no written evidence for this has been found. The parish church (Cautley 1949, 199; Messent 1936, 87; Mortlock and Roberts 1985, 56; Pevsner and Wilson 1999, 366–7) consists of a thirteenth-century square west tower, north porch, nave measuring 11.6 by 6.2m internally and chancel measuring 10.2 by 6.2m internally. The chancel arch is of the mid-fourteenth century. The south aisle, 11m long, survives only as a four-bay arcade consisting of thirteenth-century circular piers reset on Perpendicular bases and carrying Perpendicular arches. The aisle itself was pulled down in 1801 and had been roofed with lead[xvi]. This accords with instructions made by Geoffrey de Fransham, lord of Great Fransham manor, in an indenture of 1409. Those in whom he had enfeoffed this manor and others were to pay for the roofing with lead of St Mary's chapel in the church, to be carried out in the same manner as that of the south aisle (BL Add Ch 71046). Blomefield's description of the location of the memorial brass of Geoffrey de Fransham (ob. 1414), at the entrance of 'an ancient chapel' at the east end of the south aisle, strongly suggests an almost separate building (Blomefield 1808, 499)[xvii]. The site of the former aisle is visible as a slight hollow outside the Victorian south wall of the nave, but there is no clear indication of an extension beyond the junction of nave and chancel as might have been expected of a chapel added to the east end of the aisle. However, in 2002 drainage trenches on the south side of the chancel disclosed the lower parts of two east-west flint and mortar walls with internal faces 3.8m apart. The outer face of the northern wall was 4.1m south of the chancel south wall. Subsequently resistance survey by John Simmons recorded not only an extension of the south aisle east of the junction of nave and chancel but also a detached square structure whose north-west corner lay close to an angle buttress at the south-east corner of this longer aisle. It was the north and south walls of the building that had been revealed in the drainage trenches. The west wall was recorded during archaeological excavation conducted in 2007 during further drainage work (Crawley and Sillwood 2010). Geoffrey de Fransham had probably built St Mary's as his own mortuary chapel. His very fine brass is now in the chancel.

Two acres of Great Fransham demesne lay on the east side of the churchyard. To the north 2 acres of glebe were bordered on the east by the *Churchway*, on the east side of which were another 4 acres of glebe. South of the churchyard 1 acre of glebe meadow lay next to the *Churchway* on the east. This acre contained LS 8 / Med 30, a settlement of the eleventh to thirteenth centuries. Nine acres formerly of William Mascale also lay east of the church and butted south on the king's highway. Two other pieces of former Mascale land, containing 1 and 6 acres, also lay somewhere in *Middlefurlong*. A fine but

Plate 7.5 All Saints' church Great Fransham in Area L, from the south-east, July 2018

incomplete twelfth-century sword scabbard chape was found to the north-west of the churchyard at TF 8973 1313 (Fig. 7.23). Eight further pieces of Great Fransham demesne totalling 20¾ acres and aligned north-south can be located in *Middlefurlong*: 2½ acres called *Bustelond* or *Buskelond* and 1½ acres called *Pytlond* and a 1-acre parcel, all of the customary tenement Sewles, three 1-acre parcels, ¾ acre butting north on a pit called *Sarysmer,* and 12 acres called both *Ladymerelond* and *Ladismerwong* (MS 13073) in *c*.1430, and *Ladiscroft* in 1335. A pit named *Ladymerpytt* was listed in a rental of *c*.1500–20 (MS 13048). Land called *Ladysmeer* is shown on the Tithe map of 1838 at centre TF 910 132 (DN/TA 189), and a large pit, filled in during the 1980s, appears on the Enclosure Award map at TF 9090 1332. This was probably *Ladysmere* (Old English *mere*, a pool, Smith 1956b, 38–9). The lady in question remains unidentified. She may have been a lady of the manor. The *Whiteway* curls a little to the north around the side of the pit.

East of *Ladyesmerelond* all known parcels of land were aligned east-to-west, reflecting the gentle downward slope towards a stream. In the south-east corner of this area 5 acres of Great Fransham demesne lay next to Southgateway on the south and butted west on *Ladyesmerelond*. This piece must be the same as 4½ acres that were let at farm for four years in 1367, with an additional abuttal stating that *le Rawynmede* lay to the east. Nearby were another ½-acre piece of demesne, and 2 acres of Great Fransham glebe with 1 acre of Little Fransham glebe at their west end. Both pieces of glebe were said to lie in *Ladymoorclose / Ladimer close* in 1613. In *c*.1400 4 acres of Great Fransham freehold lay at *Ladismer* and butted west on demesne land. In 1335 an acre of Great Fransham Rectory freehold butted west on the furlong called *Ladismer* and to the east of it was 1 acre of the same tenure. The latter was called *Saldygges aker* in 1324 and *Saldyngesakre* in 1343 (MS 13042 and Holkham Hall, Longham Bundle 3, 34). The former acre can be identified with a piece butting west on *Ladyemere* and east on *Forthemedowe*, which was conveyed in 1578, 1589 and 1590 (MS 13260–1).

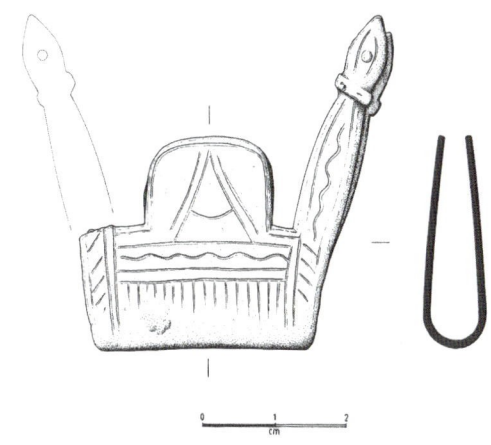

Figure 7.23 Twelfth-century copper alloy sword scabbard chape (HER 20542), scale 1:1

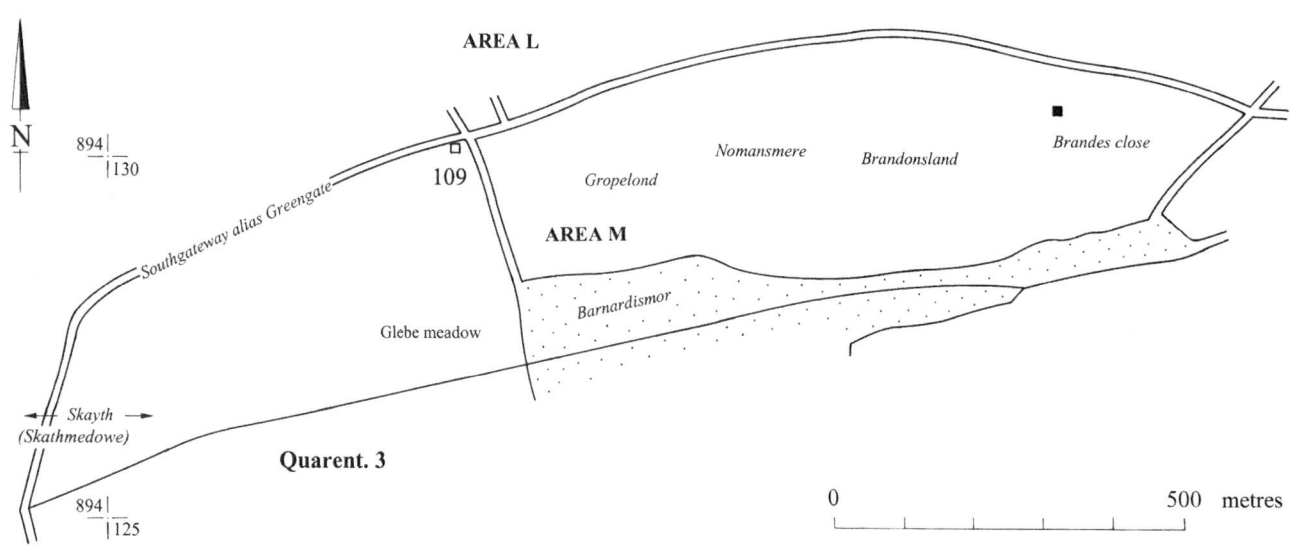

Figure 7.24 Area M, Great Fransham, scale 1:10,560

Area M, South of Southgateway alias Greengate, Great Fransham (Fig. 7.24)
Detached block demesne, glebe meadow, riverside common, common field intermingled with blocks of glebe, and one solitary settlement

At its west end *Southgateway* curved southwards to the Little Fransham boundary cutting through *Skayth* or *Skathemedowe* and *Snapespiece*, closes of Great Fransham demesne partly within area A. Metal-detecting located a copper alloy rotating banner, which would have surmounted a thirteenth- or fourteenth-century horse harness, somewhere in the area of *Skayth* (Fig. 7.25.1). East of *Skayth* lay 3 acres of pasture formerly of Peter le Strange knt. and held freely of Great Fransham manor in c.1430 by Edmund Oldhall, lord of Kirkhams and Wilcoks. These 3 acres lay south of *Snape* or *Snapespiece* and west of 7 acres of Great Fransham glebe meadow, which in turn lay west of *Barnards Moor* common. North of the glebe meadow and west of the church there is a serious shortfall of identified parcels of land. There was certainly 1 acre of Great Fransham glebe and 1½ acres of demesne as well as two 2-acre pieces of the Great Fransham customary tenement Sewles. In the north-west part of this sub-area was a 2½-acre piece of freehold, the earliest record of which occurs as late as 1596. It lay on the east side of *le Snape* in *le Chirchfeild*, butting north on *Southgateway* and south on *Scalemedowe* (MS 13268). In the north-east corner a house 'att the chyrch gate' was said to be new in 1499 (Med 109).

East of the road crossing the stream from Little Fransham the parish boundary passed through *Barnards Moor* common, of which approximately 13 acres lay in Great Fransham. *Barnardismor* was first recorded in 1323, the first element surely being the name *Bernard*. No documentary or field evidence for any medieval settlement sites along the northern edge of this common has been found. The area between the common and *Southgateway* contained many parcels of land, all aligned north-to-south and many butting south on the named common. As usual, the sequence in which they lay is not clear. The west end was taken up with 10 acres of glebe within which a medieval copper alloy book clasp was recovered during metal-detecting (Fig. 7.25.2). The north-to-south *Churchway,* which occurs in abuttals for glebe lands to the north of *Southgateway,* is not mentioned and may therefore have terminated on the north side of this piece. Four other parcels of glebe, of ½, 1, 1 and 6 acres all butted south on the common, one of which, probably the 6-acre piece, was known as *Nomansmere* (no man's (Cavill 2018, 300) and Old English *m?re*, a boundary, or possibly *mere*, a pool (Smith 1956b 33–4 and 38–9)). One of the 1-acre pieces lay on the east side of 1 acre of Little Fransham glebe. There were six pieces of Great Fransham demesne, comprising four of 1 acre (one called *Grope Acre*), 1½ acres, and 5 acres called *Gropelond* which lay west of *Nomansmere* (Old English *grôp*, a ditch or drain, Smith 1956a, 210). Two pieces of the Great Fransham customary tenement Sewles, of ¾ and 2 acres, butted north on *Southgateway*. Two Great Fransham freeholds butted south on the common, 1¾ acres first recorded in 1372 and 3 acres called *Brandonsland* at *Nomansmere*. William le Strange was granted 1¼ acres butting south on *Barnardismor* in 1323 (MC 360/54, 713X6), which he held freely of Great Fransham Rectory manor in 1324 and 1335 (MS 13042). Other parcels in this area comprised the *Lamp land*, a 4-acre piece of Great Fransham (former) glebe first named in 1575 (MS 13079), two freehold pieces, of 1 and 1¼ acres, butting south on *Barnaldesmore,* which had been held by William Mascale in 1434/5, and 7 acres in five pieces forming part of the Necton Town estate in 1598 and almost certainly including some lands once of William Mascale (PD 143/82). The eastern end of this block of land consisted of a close of 9 acres held freely of Kirkhams manor in c.1375 by John Philip clerk, but in the hands of the lord of Kirkhams by 1383–4 (MS 13122). It was not named until 1605, when it was called *Brandes close*.

Rather surprisingly this 9-acre piece was recorded in a rental of c.1395 as butting north on a messuage once of William Tomeys. In 1342 William Thomas had died seized of a Kirkhams customary messuage and 1 acre in the croft, and his son William was admitted. In 1351 a messuage and ½ acre formerly held by the late William

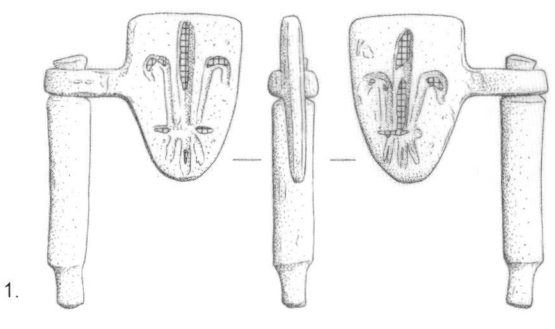

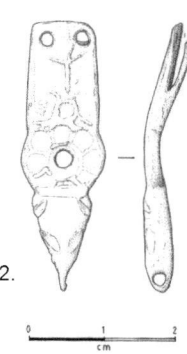

Figure 7.25 Two medieval copper alloy objects (HER 23075 and 20587), scale 1:1

Thomas were retained in the lord's hands, and in 1372 a messuage in Great Fransham formerly of William Tomeys was leased to John Philip clerk, for a rent of 1s per annum for four years. Philip was listed in a rental of freeholds of c.1375 as paying a rent of 4d three times a year for a messuage. In 1391–3 the messuage was said to be formerly of John Philip (MS 13123). This property was to be subsumed under Ellinghams manor through a grant to its lord, John Croupius, in c.1398 (MS 13125). There is no archaeological evidence for a settlement site that might match this messuage, in its rather anomalous position near the edge of a common open field. It probably lay south of *Southgateway* within the curtilage of Crowe's Hall, a standing house and farm buildings, at TF 9076 1309. It may be more than a coincidence that this location was a short distance to the southwest of *Ladyesmerelond* and of MS 1 / LS 1, the core settlement of Middle and Late Saxon Fransham. Perhaps it perpetuated some memory of former habitation.

Area N, Saint Katherine's Meadow, Great Fransham (Fig. 7.21; Pl. 7.6 and Pl. 7.7)
All demesne and several meadow

This group of meadows, which took its name from the chapel that stood in area G, close to the south of the junction with *Ellinghams meadow,* was also known as *Southmeadow* and *Forthmeadow* (Old English *ford*, a ford or crossing place, Smith 1956a, 180–4). Through the meadow flowed the stream that to the west formed the boundary between the Franshams. It was crossed by two roads, the eastern continuations of *Whiteway* and *Southgateway*, the former being called *Fennbrigge* or *Forthbridge*, the latter still marked by a spread of flint rubble on both sides of the stream. A meadow called *Forthemedwe* lay west of a piece of land in *Henfield*, the rent due for which was granted to Wendling Abbey in the late thirteenth century (MS 3809). Not surprisingly the majority of the area was demesne of Great Fransham manor. In c.1430 *Saint Katherine's meadow* contained eight parcels of that demesne totalling 11¾ acres. In the north-east lay *Hillyacre*, also called *Bilacre* (MS 13073), and this was probably next to ½ acre at *Headacre*, the pair being identified with 1½ acres lying at *St Katherine's well* in 1553 (MS 13077). Another 1-acre piece nearby was also called *Headacre* and lay at *Sheldesendes*. One and half acres at *le Fenbrigg* appear to have been called *Halftheshed* in 1553 (MS 13077) and a meadow at *le Sheld* contained ¾ acre. An illegal way was made over the lord's meadow called *Sheldmedowe* in 1370 (possibly Old English *sceldu, shallow water or stream, rather than *scçla a hut, Smith 1956b, 103–4). *Sydemedow* containing 1½ acres lay to the east and another piece with the same name and acreage lay to the south. South of this a 4-acre meadow called *le Rawyn*[xviii] butted the parish boundary and another meadow also called *Rawyn* in Little Fransham (*Quarent*. 24). The lord of Great Fransham's meadow called *Raweyne* was damaged by William Short's cattle in 1364. West of the junction of these two meadows the valley bottom was occupied by the common pasture, *Barnards Moor*.

There were only three parcels of Kirkhams and Wilcoks demesne in *Saint Katherine's meadow*. *Wellacre* was named *Wellemedow* in 1477. Half an acre and 5 perches of meadow were said in an extent of c.1510 to lie at the pit (*puteum*) called *Saint Katherine Welle* (MS 13162). This pit has not been identified in the field. 'Well' means a stream or spring, from Old English *wella* (Smith 1956b, 250–3). Half of *le Scheld medowe* was granted out as part of a customary tenement in c.1390, and its size was given as ¾ acre in 1502. One other piece, of ½ acre, lay somewhere to the north-east, next to a ¼-acre meadow held by Pentney Priory. Both the latter and 1 acre held by John de Poketon were freeholds of Great Fransham manor in c.1400. One other freehold parcel of meadow, a ¼ acre of uncertain manorial allegiance, lay in *Forthmedowe*. It was named as *Thyrlyngges Dokeland* in a charter grant of 1505 (MC 2755/4/1, 1004X2).

In 1410 Geoffrey de Fransham, lord of Great Fransham manor, was granted licence to divert a twenty-five perches long and fifteen feet wide road crossing his meadow, so as to improve and enlarge the meadow and keep it enclosed. The road was in Great Fransham and led from Wendling to Little Dunham (TNA C 143/442/2). It must have been the *Whiteway* and the meadow *St Katherine's*. The length, 137½ yards at a 5½ yard perch, is only slightly greater than the width of the former meadow where it was crossed by *Fenbrigge*, from TF 9120 1326 to 9131 1322. This attempt to push traffic north to cross over the streams at their junction, an area still subject to frequent flooding, was not successful. The road continued in use but had been stopped up by 1805, leaving only the wet route available for the modern traveller.

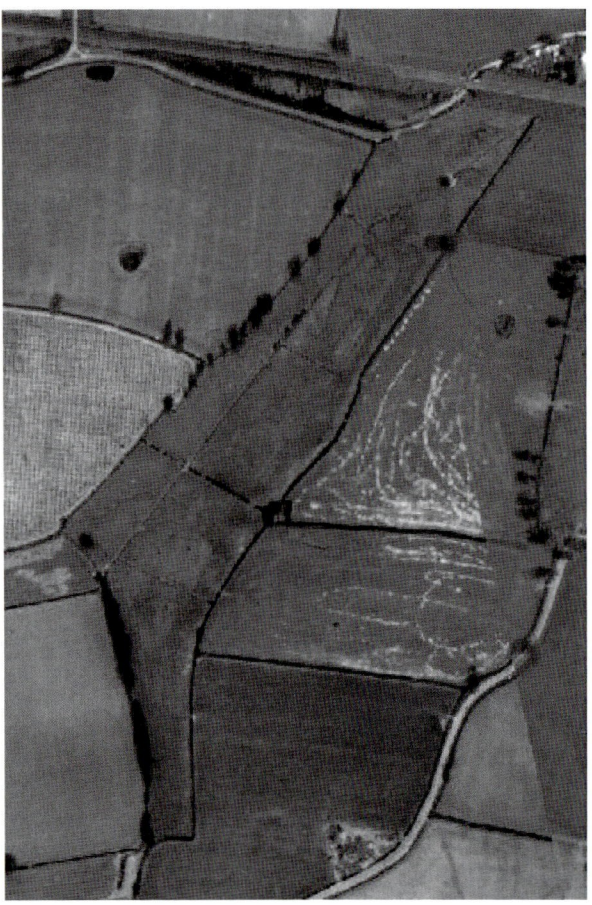

Plate 7.6 Detail from 1946 RAF vertical aerial photograph, centred on St Katherine's meadow in Area N (http://www.historic-maps.norfolk.gov.uk/)

Plate 7.7 Detail from 1988 vertical aerial photograph, centred on St Katherine's meadow in Area N (http://www.historic-maps.norfolk.gov.uk/)

Area O, Southwoodfield, Great Fransham (Fig. 7.19)
Predominantly detached tenement blocks, with a detached Wendling Abbey demesne block, a small green edged by one settlement with another nearby, two other settlements, one on a common pasture edge, one next to a meadow, a small piece of demesne woodland, and a restricted area of common field

In Great Fransham and at the northern end of the eastern edge of *Eastendmoor*, Little Fransham, lay a 5-acre piece of Kirkhams demesne, named as the tenement *Rawlenis* and in use as pasture in 1383–4 (MS 13122). It was to become customary or copyhold in 1476. Med 61 (Fig. 7.26), a thirteenth and fourteenth-century site on the eastern edge of the common of Little Fransham called *Eastendmoor*, lay just outside the south-west corner of *Rawlins*, a piece well located in later sources. South of Med 61 a 350m length of ground bordering the common edge and forming the boundary between the Franshams was not available for fieldwalking. Within this area lay the greater part of an enclosure of 20 acres called *Brakes*, listed amongst lands that had paid rent to Thomas Mascall in 1442–3 (MS 13140). An abuttal in a grant of 1303 suggests that Gilbert le Marescal was then the holder of this land (TNA E 40/10610). In 1442–3 the 'manor' of Mascalls, that had been recently purchased by Sir William Oldhall, was a dependency of East Lexham manor. (MS 13140). *Brakes* was held at the time by John Coke who died in 1442 and who as John Cook or Kooc held extensive Kirkhams customary lands close by in Little Fransham. Thomas Marschale / Mascale had been amerced several times in Little Fransham leet courts for offences at *Brakkys* and *Brakksdyke* between 1370 and 1406. A messuage called *Brakkes* in 1446–7 can probably be identified with Med 61 (MS 13142). In 1385/6 the tenement and lands once of Bracks owed the lord of Sparhams manor a rent of one hen for common rights. The acreage was given as 18 in c.1555.

The western side of *Brakkys* bordered the eastern edge of *Eastendmoor*, Little Fransham, but its south end was separated from the Little Fransham boundary by several small pieces of land. A Kirkhams customary ½ acre called *Catislond* lay at *Brackiscroftesende* in 1384 and lay north to south at the north end of ½ acre of Kirkhams soiled land. The two together were later to be regarded as 1 acre of soiled land, named *long acre* in 1605. To the west of *long acre* 2 acres of Northendhall or Guntons demesne butted west on the common of Little Fransham (*Eastendmoor*) and were copyhold by 1549 (TNA SC 2/192/96). This can be confidently equated with a messuage and 2½ acres in the croft in Great Fransham, once of Robert Rasthyens, which were let at farm by Wendling Abbey to Richard Angeville and his wife in 1303. The property butted west on the common of Little Fransham (TNA E 40/10610). There may also be a connection with *Rareyniscroft* containing 2 acres in Great Fransham which was held by

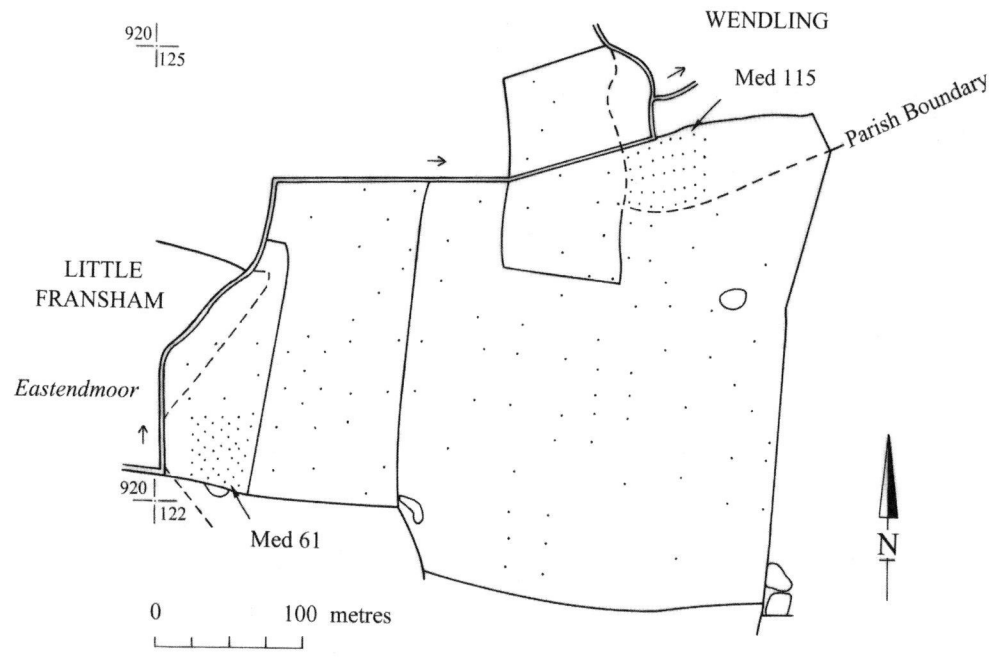

Figure 7.26 Med 61 and 115 within Area O and Wendling, distribution of sherds (boundaries taken from Ordnance Survey County Series 1928 edition), scale 1:5,000

Wendling Abbey in 1269 (MS 3813). To the east of *long acre* was ½ acre of Great Fransham freehold also running north-south, which according to a charter of 1507, lay at the east end of a close called *Brakkys* (Gardner H). This ½ acre lay next to land of Wendling Abbey and at the south end of 5½ acres of Great Fransham freehold. These two pieces were later combined with two other pieces containing 1 acre and 2 acres of land and meadow and were known as *Popes close* or *Popys clos* by the 1540s (MS 13076 and MS 13167). These last four parcels, along with 2 acres in two parcels in *Southwoodfield* were held by Thomas Junyor in *c*.1400 and were once of John Rodeland. In 1366 John Jenior had died seized of 10 acres of land and meadow of the tenement Hosyer, held by military service for 3s rent.

The largest individual parcel of land in *Southwoodfield* lay to the east of *Popes close* along the boundary with Little Fransham. In *c*.1400 the abbot of Wendling held 28 acres butting south on the field of Little Fransham. Twenty acres of arable in two pieces in Fransham, said to be 'by the perch of Fransham' (*per perticam de.*) were granted by Adam son of John de Hecham and his wife to William de Wendling in 1253. The deed is endorsed '... Sowdoles' (TNA E 40/8769). The grant was confirmed by the levying of a fine in 1254 (TNA CP 25/1/157/82.1212). In 1269 Wendling Abbey had 28 acres in two pieces called *Surwdewongys* (MS 3813) Twenty-six enclosed acres called *Sowdewonge* were held by the abbot of William de Fransham in *c*.1279 (Table 6.2, no. 14). Later variations of the name included *Southwong*, *Sowdewonge* and *Sowdsclose* (MS 13048, MS 13067 and MS 13074–5). The king's highway ran along the south side (MS 13067). No medieval potsherds were found in the area of this close (west of Med 62, Fig. 7.27).

In *c*.1400 a grove of the lord of Great Fransham lay on the east side of the above 28 acres. It was described as a 1-acre close with underwood in *c*.1430. In 1331 Geoffrey de Suthwood was amerced in the manor court for lopping ash, oak, maple and apple trees in the wood at *Suthwode* and Alexander Fynch was said to have made a path through the lord's wood there. To the north lay 1 acre of demesne at *Emmestile*, to be equated with *Emesaker* which was granted at farm in 1374. *Emmesfaldgate* was first mentioned in 1450 when Henry Ramme was amerced for flooding the common way by failing to scour a ditch there. A ditch and a watercourse, both unscoured, and an un-repaired *porta caduta* at *Emmies Faldgate* were cited when John Colyn and John Mechil were amerced in 1455 (MS 13048).

A common called *Southwoodmore* or *Southwode greene* lay to the east of the lord's grove and *Emesaker*. It had disappeared by the mid-sixteenth century (a tentative indication of its size and shape is shown on Fig. 7.19). Enclosure came about through the co-operation of the three landowners in the immediate vicinity who made the common into a quasi-private pasture. In 1391 Nicholas Southwood, Thomas Fuche and John Suthwode, freeholders, came to the Great Fransham manor court to announce a mutual agreement. This was to the effect if any of their heirs or assigns were to common on *Southwode greene* with their sheep (*bidentibus, ovibus, matris, multonibus, agnis*) by day or night, between 2 February and 1 August, then they were to obtain a licence from the lord at the manor court. The green was said to have been enclosed by the same free tenants. This appears to have been some form of enclosure by agreement (Kerridge 1969, 99; Williamson and Bellamy 1987, 105) and to have marked the beginning of the end of *Southwode greene* as a common, although an amercement for overcommoning was recorded as late as 1434 (MS 13048). By 1451 the name had changed to *Wardesgrene*, probably after a tenant of nearby lands in the earlier fifteenth century, Nicholas

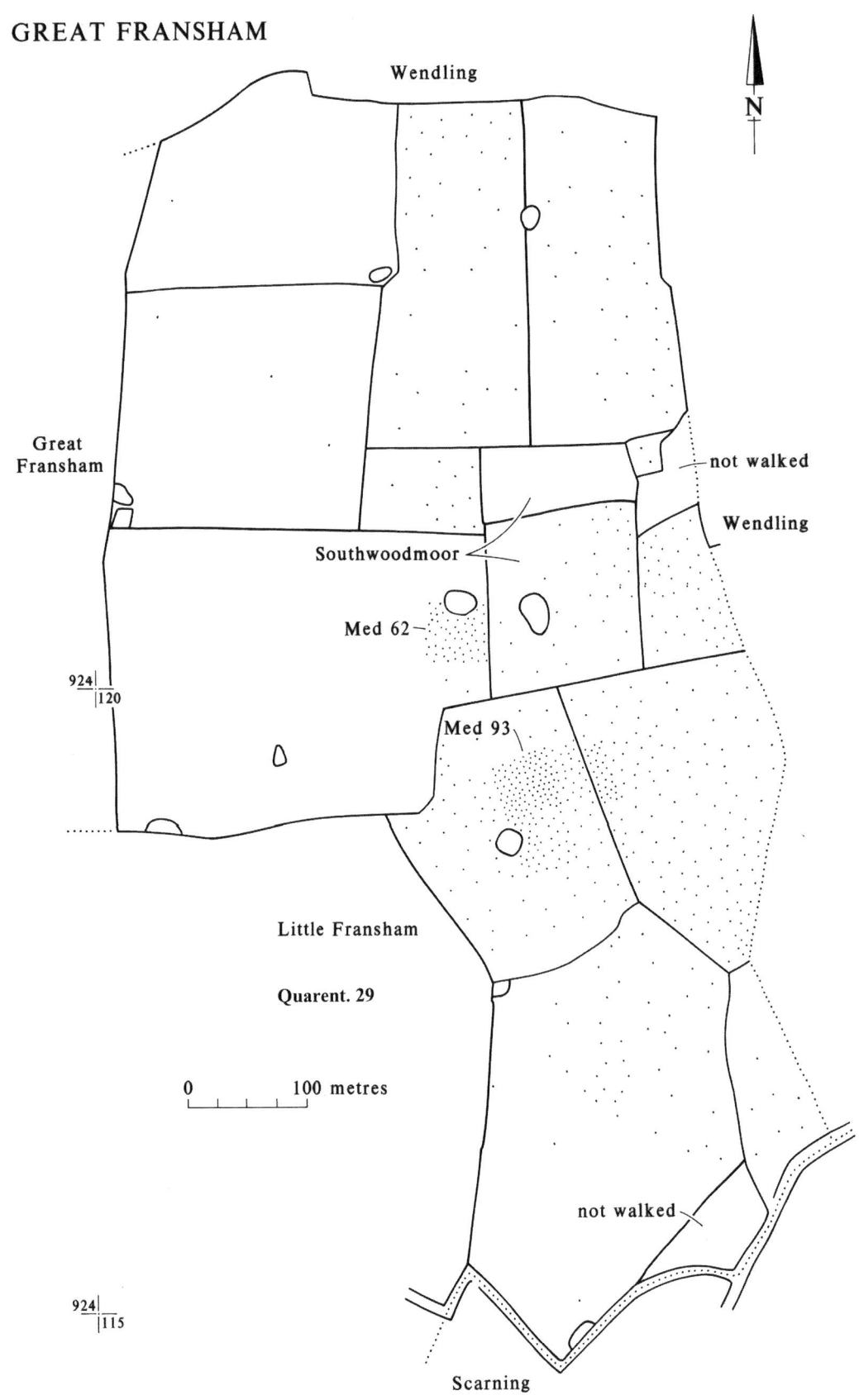

Figure 7.27 Med 62 and 93 within Area O, distribution of sherds
(boundaries taken from Ordnance Survey County Series 1928 edition), scale 1:5,000

Warde. In 1473 another local landholder, John Colyn, was amerced for keeping part of the common called *Wardysmor* closed all year with a *porta caduta* (MS 13048). Whether *Sowdes Falgate*, cited in an amercement of 1490, was the same as this remains uncertain (MS 13052), but *Wardes Faldgate* named in 1508 must have been (MS 13067). By 1545 there was no longer a common pasture here: a close called *Sowdismore* in Great Fransham was itemised in the will of Robert Hogan, which was proved in 1547 (TNA PROB 11/21/569). An indenture dated 1548, lists various lands owned by Thomas Hogan esq., one of Robert's sons, including a close called *Sowds more* in Great Fransham (Mills and Reeve 12/03/70 Mason Necton deeds).

To the north of the common were several pieces of Great Fransham freehold. Two parcels were each of 2 acres and, to the north, one contained 5 acres. The latter was to be known as *Yelvertons close*, after Nicholas Yelverton gent., a tenant in the early sixteenth century (MS 13056). All three lay west of a close called *Southwoodbushes* and the 5-acre piece butted north on a meadow of Wendling Abbey. One acre, held by Thomas Junyor in *c*.1400 (see *Popes close* above), was on the east side of *Southwoodbushes* and butted north on a meadow of Castle Acre Priory. One acre of Great Fransham demesne called *Sowerlond* lay next to land of John Pope on the west in *c.* 1430. *Sowerlond* also butted north on a Wendling Abbey meadow and south on *Southwong* and was near *Sowdes more* (MS 13056 and 13079). One acre of Guntons demesne lay between two pieces of Great Fransham manor land in 1552, that to the east probably being *Yelvertons close*, and butted south on *Sowdwong* and north on a close late of Wendling Abbey called *Medowclos* (TNA SC 12/3/23).

The course of the parish boundary is such that it includes within Wendling all of the low-lying parts of the valley carrying a stream which emerges from the north-east corner of Little Fransham *Eastendmoor* and runs along the north side of *Rawlins*. As the valley base is the most suitable place for meadowland, it must be assumed that most if not all of the following meadows were in Wendling parish, although in no case was this stated. As well as meadows of the monastic houses of Wendling and Castle Acre mentioned in several abuttals, there was 1 acre of Great Fransham freehold immediately east of the north end of *Popes close*. This was held by Paul Harlewyn in *c*.1400 and was once of John de Weston and Alexander Fynch. The latter had made an illegal path at *Suthwode* in 1331. He was listed amongst Scarning taxpayers in 1327 and 1332 and amongst tenants of lands in Wendling, Great Fransham and Little Dunham in a fine of 1346 (TNA CP 25/1/164/158.737). He died in 1349. In 1370 Simon Fincham, rector of Great Fransham, and William Shorte had bought 1 acre of meadow lying at *Weston Brygge* from John de Weston. This bridge was probably at TF 9233 1243 and carried a road, which further north followed the Wendling/Great Fransham boundary, over the stream. On the south-east side of the bridge in what is now Wendling parish lay Med 115, an isolated thirteenth-century settlement site, part of Great Fransham demesne called *Ravensyard* in 1369 (Fig. 7.26). Somewhere nearby, a 1-acre piece of Wendling Abbey meadow in *Harwynsmedowe*, was copyhold of the manor of Wendling Nuper Abbis by 1558 or slightly earlier, and a marginal note states that it lay in Fransham (Christ Church Oxford MS Estates 53). In 1639 it was specified as being in Great Fransham (NCC 190 Green). Five acres of meadow associated with an Ellinghams freehold messuage that lay on the south side of *Eastendmoor* in Great Fransham (Med 57) were probably in this area, but the acreage was not specified until 1642 (Mills and Reeve 12/03/70 Mason Necton deeds). *Pynkesmedow*, of unknown tenure, lay near *Weston Bryyge*, probably to the west.

To the south of the lord's wood and west of *Southwode greene* was Med 62, occupied in the thirteenth and fourteenth centuries, and a Great Fransham freehold messuage with 1½ acres (Fig. 7.27). South of this, Med 93, a thirteenth to fifteenth-century site, another Great Fransham freehold consisting of a messuage and 9 acres with pasture, butted east on a common way (Fig. 7.27). In *c*.1400 these two tenements shared a common tenant. One acre held freely by Wendling Abbey of Great Fransham manor probably lay in this area. In *c*.1400 it and another acre far to the north (in Area H) were both known as *Sextons lond*. To east, west and south of Med 93 were three parcels of Great Fransham freehold land comprising 9 acres, along with 1 acre of pasture, held by William Prior and his wife in *c*.1400, and formerly by John Shortwood. In 1396 John de Shortwode had died seized of 10 acres of free land. One of these three parcels lay to the west. It contained 2 acres, was on the north side of *Southwoodlane* and had a ditch (*fossat.*). This might possibly be equated with 2 acres of arable in Fransham conveyed sometime before 1265 by Geoffrey son of William de Sudwode to William de Wendling, which lay next to William's new ditch at *Sudewodewong* (TNA E 40/8506). The fact that most, if not all of William's lands were given to Wendling Abbey suggests that this equation is not correct. In the south-east part of *Southwoodfield*, 1 acre of Great Fransham demesne lay in *le Parrock* and south of a common way (Old English *pearroc*, a small enclosure or paddock, (Smith 1956b, 60–1) or a small grass enclosure (Cavill 2018, 315)). In 1552 1 acre of Northendhall or Guntons demesne lay in *le Parok* on the east side of the Great Fransham piece, and both were pasture (TNA SC 12/3/23). At a leet court held in 1548 this was called *Padlocks close* (MS 13056). Both these pieces were probably within an area almost devoid of medieval pot sherds centred at TF 9285 1160 (Fig. 7.27).

A large proportion of one free tenement held of Great Fransham manor and listed in the rental of *c*.1400 may have been in Wendling and Scarning. It is probably the same as that held by Walter de Sudwode in *c*.1279 (Table 6.2, no. 11). In *c*.1400 the tenement consisted of a messuage, a garden and 16 acres, including 4 acres of pasture, and was held by Nicholas Bettes alias Sowde, and formerly by William son of Walter de Southwood. Walter, probably the grandson of the Walter of *c*.1279, was listed under Great Fransham as a taxpayer in 1332. He had died in 1349 seized of a messuage and 16 acres, leaving his underaged daughter Isabelle as heir. In 1368 Nicholas Bettys and Isabelle his wife were parties to a fine conveying various properties in West Bradenham, Scarning, Great and Little Fransham (TNA CP 25/1/167/ 170.1331). The messuage butted east on an unnamed common and may have been in Wendling, somewhere east of *Southwode greene*. Ten acres including 3 of pasture lay on the eastern side of a common in Wendling. It is likely that this common was *Hulverstreet* and if so then the land lay in Scarning. One acre of Bettys'

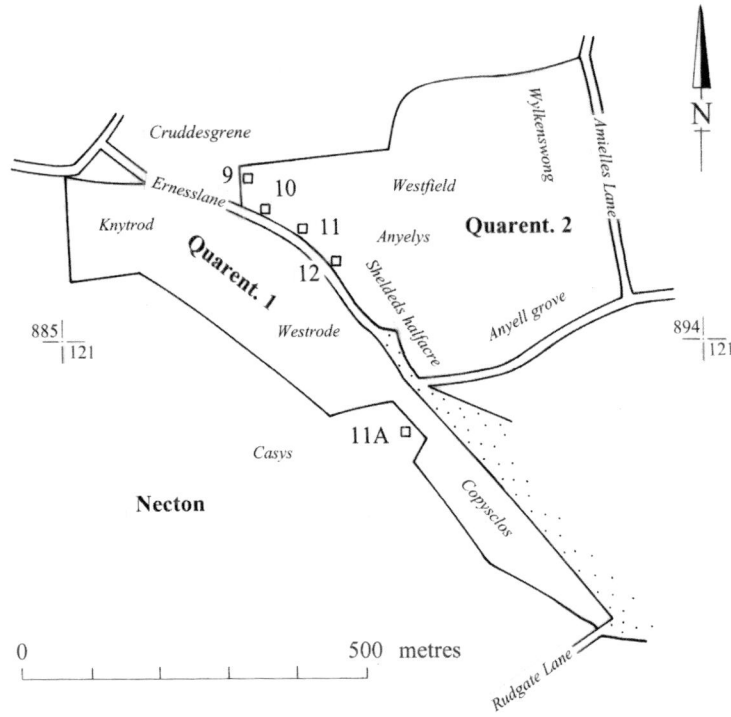

Figure 7.28 *Quarentinae* 1 and 2, Little Fransham, scale 1:10,560

pasture lay east of the tenement of Roger Hanke. This surname has not been encountered in Fransham documents. A Roger Haut was a Wendling Poll Tax payer in 1379. Two acres were at *Hulverhegge* and in 1557 they were said to lie in *Hulverstrete* in Great Fransham (MS 13058). This indicates that they were in the far south-east corner of the parish at TF 9295 1160. One acre lay next to the land of Wendling Abbey on the west and butted north on *Greengate*. In 1537 it was said to be in Great Fransham (MS 13074–5). One acre lay in the field of Scarning and another lay in the same place. A garden (*ortum*) called *Musterdyard*, acreage unstated, was also in Scarning. In 1369 Nicholas Bettys was amerced at the manor court for blocking a watercourse at *Kattesfaldegate*. This is the earliest reference to a *faldgate* in Fransham documents (Appendix 5).

Lands of one tenement, all said to be in *Southwoodfield*, Great Fransham in c.1430 when they were part of the demesne of Great Fransham manor, have presented the greatest problems of location, and no archaeological evidence of a settlement site was found. A ½-acre close and 6 acres in the croft, where once there was the messuage of Gilbert Echerard, lay between land of the tenement Ravenes west (Med 115) and land of Alexander Anger east, and butted north on the tenement of Henry Ram. A William Echard had been a taxpayer in Great Fransham in 1327 and 1332 (see also Med 59 in Area H, which lay in *Escherdclos*). Someone called Henry Ram held land in Little Fransham in c.1420 (*Quarent*. 13), but a Henry Ram alias Grene held parcels of five named customary tenements of Wendling Abbey manor in 1446/7 (Holkham Hall, Longham Bundle 3, 34). Alexander Anger held at farm a Great Fransham demesne meadow (*Oxmedow*) in c.1430, but in 1402/3 Geoffrey Anger and Alexander his son of Wendling held at farm *Swankescroft* in Wendling. The conclusion must be that the lands once of Gilbert Echerard lay in what is now Wendling, and that the parish boundary was less precisely defined in the Middle Ages. That the conformation of some medieval parishes could be far more complex before rationalisations were brought about to simplify the levying of tithes has been amply demonstrated by Warner (1986).

Little Fransham *Quarentinae* 1–29

Quarent. 1, the western edges of Little Fransham (Fig. 7.28)
Detached block demesne

On the south-west side of *Ernesslane* and to the south of *Cruddesgrene* lay three pieces of demesne land which flanked the parish boundary with Necton. *Knightsrod*, a 9-acre piece, lay to the north-west and belonged to Great Fransham manor, although in Little Fransham. Amercements in the manor court show that it was regularly cropped between 1330 and 1390. In c.1427 the men of Necton considered *Knytrod* to lie within their parish (MS 13177). The central piece, *Westrode*, contained 6 acres and was recorded as demesne of Kirkhams manor in 1409. In the mid-thirteenth century, one piece of 2½ acres in *Westrade* was granted by Roger le Strange of Little Fransham to his son John and Beatrice daughter of Agnes de Sparle. The deed is endorsed *West rode* (MC 360/4, 713X6). The third piece, *Copysclos*, was granted out as 4 acres of customary land in 1409. It was made up of a pair of 2-acre former freeholds, both of Wilcoks manor. Both are observable, as allowances for rents unpaid, in the earliest surviving Wilcoks messor's account roll, for 1404–5 (MS 13129). The eastern part was in the hands of the lord and the western was cultivated by the lord (*in cultura dom.*). The latter had previously been held by the abbot of Wendling and can be identified with a

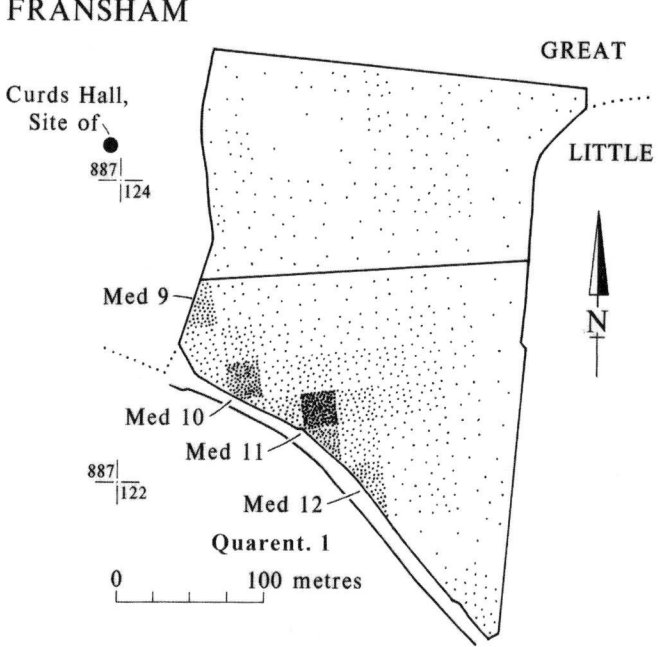

Figure 7.29 Med 9–12 within *Quarentina* 2, and field adjacent in Area A, Great Fransham, distribution of sherds (boundaries taken from Ordnance Survey County Series 1928 edition), scale 1:5,000

tenement in Little Fransham, the rent of 6d for which Robert son of Roger ad Scalam granted to Wendling Abbey between *c.*1265 and 1273 (TNA E 40/10573). The wording of this charter was closely followed in a rental of 1386/7 (NNAS G1/7). Although these 2 acres were certainly in *Copysclos*, they were said to lie in *le Westrode* in a detailed Wilcoks rental of *c.*1420.

An adjunct in Necton
A single settlement and detached block demesne

A single thirteenth to fourteenth-century settlement site (Med 11A) sits in Necton within a re-entrant of the Necton/Little Fransham parish boundary, close to the north-east end of the Lyng, a common pasture and at the meeting point of *Westrode* and *Copysclos*. This was the messuage of a 10-acre customary tenement of Kirkhams manor first recorded in 1343, which was in the lord's hands by 1422.

To the south-west of Med 11A lay a close of Kirkhams demesne called *Casys* where the lord's crops were damaged in 1374. Two pieces of 20 and 11 acres were cropped at *Casies* in 1402–3 (MS 13127). In 1605 *Cases* consisted of 29 acres and 10 perches of pasture in Necton. Abuttals placed it between Necton grounds to the west and south, *Rudgate Lane* to the east, *Lingsendcloses* (*i.e. Copysclos* and *Westrode* in *Quarent.* 1) and the common *lynge* to the north.

Quarent. 2, *Westfield*, Little Fransham (Fig. 7.28)
Four common pasture edge and roadside settlements, a small piece of demesne woodland, tenement blocks, and common field

A road, known as *Ernesslane* by 1395, ran towards the south-east corner of *Cruddesgrene*, and just before its entry into the common it was edged on the north-east by a row of four medieval sites, Med 9–12, along the margin of *Westfield* (Fig. 7.29). Med 9 straddled the parish boundary. All four had twelfth-century origins. Two sites, Med 9 and 10, did not survive beyond *c.*1200. Med 12 lasted into the fourteenth, and Med 11 continued to be occupied into the fifteenth century. Their tenurial origins are uncertain, although one or more may have been freeholds of Kirkhams manor. By 1384 they had been granted out, with 18 acres and meadow, by the lord of Kirkhams as a single customary tenement. Much of this had become demesne by 1391.

Westfield, containing 31½ acres, was bordered on its east and south sides by *Amielles Lane*, and on the north by the parish boundary with Great Fransham. A 3 or 4-acre piece aligned north-south lay in the north-east part to the west of a lane. Butting north on *Skalemedows* in Great Fransham, it was a Kirkhams freehold, first documented in *c.*1375 when the tenant was John Wylkynesson. It became demesne at some time after 1384 and was known as *Wylkenswong* in 1392. To the south were 3 acres of Kirkhams demesne which were at least in part sown with peas in 1372. This piece had probably formed part of the customary tenement associated with Med 9–12 in the 1380s before reverting to demesne in 1391. It butted south on *Amielles Lane*, and lay east of *Anyell grove*, first named in *c.*1427 (MS 13177) and containing 3 acres. To the north-west of the grove lay another piece of Kirkhams demesne containing about 4 acres, which was named *Anyelys* in 1372, and a close called *Anyel* in 1379. It was also an element of the above-mentioned customary tenement. It was probably here, *Danyell cloos*, that a crop of *bulmong* was sown in 1402–3 (MS 13127). This was grown for fodder and consisted of a mixture of oats and legumes (Campbell 2000, 227–8).

The remainder of *Westfield* contained two pieces of Wilcoks freehold, of 6 and 5 acres, entered but not given abuttals in a rental of *c.*1420, to be equated with lands once of Thomas Denby in a rental of *c.*1395, and associated with a messuage in *Quarent.* 13 by *c.*1420. Both pieces were aligned east-west. According to a charter of 1480 the holding was divided into three pieces comprising 10½ acres: 4 acres at the northern end of the field, 5 acres further south and a 1½ acre north-south headland (MS 13409). In both *c.*1420 and 1480 the 5-acre piece was said to lie next to land of Great Fransham Rectory on the south. This was 1 acre of customary land known only from a mid-16th-century list of lands held by John Wyskard.

Three pieces of Kirkhams customary land are known from a rental of 1443 to have once formed part of the tenement belonging to Med 11A. Half an acre aligned east-west was south of the Great Fransham Rectory piece. Two acres were also aligned east-west, and 5 acres lay north-south, butting south on demesne called *Anyellysclos*. Finally, there were two pieces of Great Fransham demesne, ¾ acre aligned east-west and ½ acre running north-south, known as *Sheldeds halfacre* in *c.*1430.

The location and alignment of 1 acre of Wilcoks free land in *le Westfeld* once of Isabelle Fastolf, which in *c.*1420 was held by John Couper parson of Scarning (rector 1412–23), cannot be determined. One later gloss in the rental suggests this was held by John Croupius, rector of Little Fransham, who died in 1404, and another gloss casts doubt on this (*dubit.*). Elizabeth Fastolf had paid the same rent (1d) in *c.*1395. In any event there is no mention of this freehold acre in later rentals.

Quarent. 3, *Longmeadow*, Little Fransham (Fig. 7.30)
Demesne meadow only

One piece of Kirkhams and Wilcoks demesne lay on the west side of the common way at *Barnards Moor* along the boundary with Great Fransham. The first record of its name was in 1471 when Edmund Tenmarke was amerced at the manor court for cutting and stealing underwood and thorns (*spin.*) growing in *Longmedowe*. Thereafter it was invariably described as pasture. By 1566 it was estimated to contain 24 acres, which accords well with an area within four fields shown by the survey to be devoid of medieval sherds.

Quarent. 4, the northern part of *Bullesfield* (Fig. 7.30)
Common field and detached block demesne, some of which were probably engrossed common field strips, and a windmill

The name of this field is derived from a free tenement called *Bules* or *Bolys* (see *Quarent.* 5). By the fifteenth century most of this area consisted of large blocks of Kirkhams and Wilcoks demesne, but the evidence is not there to tell whether any of these were the result of the engrossing and enclosure of smaller parcels of tenanted lands. In the later fifteenth and sixteenth century these demesne lands went through various confusing and poorly understood rearrangements in which consistently large acreages were involved. The 1605 survey has been used to elucidate the lay-out of lands, which will be described from east to west.

The whole of the eastern side along the edge of *le Greenway* leading to Great Fransham consisted of a 5-acre piece known as *Longclos* by 1476 (MS 13141), which in 1502 was said to lie in *Chirchfeld* with *le Salowdyke* along its western side. West of this were two pieces of demesne, of 3½ and 3 acres, which covered the full length of the field from *Longmeadow* to an east-west *packway* on the south. The two were sown with rye in 1401 when they were described as 7 acres in one piece at *Huberdeslaneshende* (MS 13126). Variations in cropping area and the resultant confusion in an understanding of field lay-out can be seen from the following year when barley was grown on 14 acres at *Hoberdslanesende* (MS 13127). A 4-acre piece of Kirkhams customary land lay on the west side of the two pieces of demesne. From 1444 it was part of a tenement, the messuage of which lay on the west side of *Huberdslane* in *Quarent.* 5. One acre, later to be incorporated into the 4 acres, lay at the northern end next to *Longmeadow*, at *Kerbusk* in 1384. At the southern end ¾ acre of Cannons manor customary land butted south on the *packway*. Its tenurial history is known only from 1531. Next came 5 acres of Little Fransham glebe stretching the full length of the field. At the south-west corner of this lay ¾ acre of Wilcoks freehold, which in *c.*1420 lay at *Barghmyllehill* and butted south on the

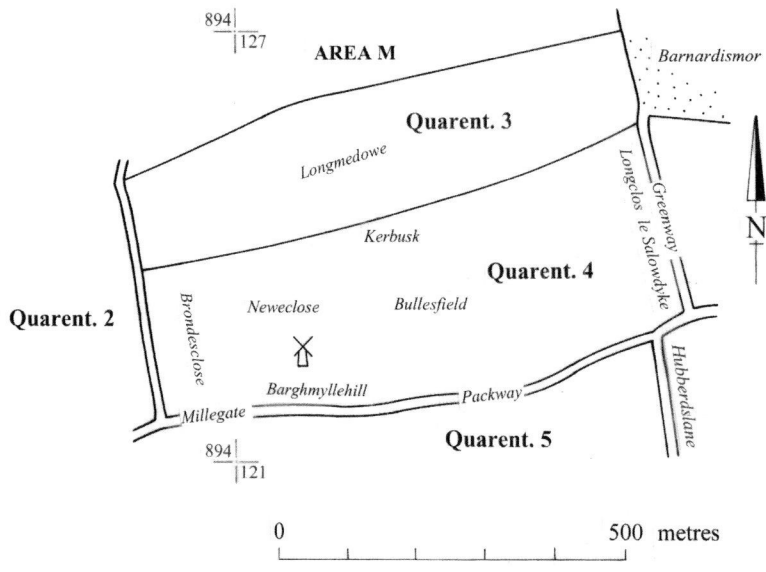

Figure 7.30 *Quarentinae* 3 and 4, Little Fransham, scale 1:10,560

king's highway. This piece occurs in several fourteenth-century charters. In 1331/2 Margaret widow of William at Rode of Little Fransham granted ¾ acre to William son of Henry le Strange, which butted north on William le Strange's mill (MC 360/60, 713X6). John son of William Atterode quitclaimed all rights in the same piece and other lands, including 3½ acres called *Millereslond*, to William in 1338 (MC 360/68, 713X6). The same ¾ acre was the subject of another, undated, quitclaim between the same parties, in which it was said to butt south on the way leading to Little Fransham church. (PHI/126, 577X1). Interestingly according to two of the deeds the land to the east was not glebe, but of William le Strange. The third was silent on this. Another ¾-acre Wilcoks freehold, held by Alexander Broun in the 1330s, lay on the west side, also at *Barghmyllehill* in *c*.1420. John Syger, the tenant in *c*.1395 was amerced at a leet court in 1377 for ploughing over the common way at *Millegate*. Another piece of glebe, 2½ acres, butted south on the way and, wrapping around the last piece, extended north to *Longmeadow*. West of here two large Kirkhams and Wilcoks demesne closes were separated by 1 acre of glebe, all three lying the full length of the field. First came *Neweclose*, first named in 1433 and containing 15 acres, and to the west beyond the acre of glebe a close of 11 acres. This was named *Brondesclose* in 1526 (MS 13251). In 1492 one piece containing 14 acres in *Bolesfeld* was granted in hereditary fee farm (a form of copyhold) to Simon Bronde, his wife and Robert Bronde clerk. Fourteen acres in *Bullysfeld* were described as newly enclosed in 1511. One small piece of Northendhall or Guntons demesne cannot be located. In 1552 ¾ acre lay in *Boolesfeld* between lands of the lord [of Little Fransham, *i.e.* Kirkhams and Wilcoks] and butted south on a common path (TNA SC 12/3/23). The latest record of this piece is in 1559, when the rent was paid by Master [Edward] Mynne (TNA SC 11/486). It was probably incorporated into one of large blocks of Kirkhams and Wilcoks demesne.

Quarent. 5, the southern part of *Bullesfield* and the north-west part of the main village, Little Fransham (Fig. 7.31; Pl. 7.8 and Pl. 7.9)

Detached demesne blocks, some probably enclosed from common field, a small piece of demesne woodland, and settlements with tenement blocks edging a riverside common

This area will be described from east to west, beginning with *Bullesfield* and ending with properties fronting the common pasture in the main village. *Huberdslane* marked the eastern edge. The messuage of William Huberd was abutted in a charter of 1318 (HRO 8184). It lay at the south-east corner of this *Quarent* and more detail is given below. William Huberd was a witness to several charters between 1323 and 1361, and William Hubert was a taxpayer in 1332. In the corner between *Huberdslane* and the *packway* forming the northern boundary of the area was a 4-acre piece of Kirkhams and Wilcoks demesne which, with another 1½ acres to the west, must equate to 6 acres lying on the west side of *Huberdislane* in 1502. South along *Huberslane* another 3 acres of demesne were unnamed until called *Allens close* in 1605. The origins of this name are unknown. West of the above 1½ acres of demesne lay *Hamondescroft*, which was first recorded by name as 7 acres of arable in 1482,

when it was granted out as customary land. It had been Kirkhams and Wilcoks demesne called *Shephouscroft* in 1402–3 when 7½ acres were sown with the lord's oats (MS 13127), but again the Hamond element of the name cannot be explained. The next piece to the west consisted of 5½ acres of demesne pasture 'now' called *Townesend-close* in 1605. This must be the same as 6 acres near *Shepehouscroft* which butted on *Bolesyerd* and had been sown with the lord's crops in 1402–3 (MS 13127). In 1605 a pightle of pasture called *Bullesgrove* lay on the west side of the last piece and north of the *common lyng*. A grove called *Bolys* was first recorded in 1485 (MS 13234).

The names *Bolys* and *Bullesfield* derive from a free tenement which fell into the hands of the lord sometime between 1384 and 1398–9. In 1335 Thomas de Stowe was distrained to swear fealty to the lord of Kirkhams for a tenement once of William Godefrey. Someone of this name and of Fransham was a juror of Launditch Hundred in 1274/5 (Illingworth and Caley eds 1812, 434). William Godfrey of Little Fransham and William son of the same appeared in several charters between *c*.1273 and 1321. Thomas de Stowe was a taxpayer in 1327 and held a free rent on land in *Quarent*. 16. In 1340 William le Strange was said to have acquired a messuage and 14 acres from de Stowe and he was distrained in 1345. In *c*.1375 John Crupes (Crupius or Croupius, rector of Little Fransham 1362–1404) held 14 acres and a messuage, formerly of William Godfrey, called *Bules*. Between 1398 and 1407 allowances were made in Kirkhams messor's accounts for rents unpaid for the lands lately held by John Croupius that were in the lord's hands (MS 13125, MS 13128, MS 13130 and MS 13131). In the last two accounts the lands were said to pertain to the manor of Wilcoks. In the Wilcoks messor's accounts for 1404–5 the sum of 11d was entered as a claim, for a payment (*shot*) collected by the bailiff of Launditch Hundred and by the bailiff of the green wax of the same hundred for the tenement Bolys, which was in the lord's hands (MS 13129). Kirkhams and Wilcoks bailiff's accounts for 1427–8, and later, record payments of 1s 4d in sheriff's aid and a 2s fine for suit to the hundred court for lands and tenements once of Henry Benedick and William son of Godfrey (MS 13137). In 1384 John Croupius' messuage of the tenement once of William Godesfreston lay between land of the lady of the manor east and of David Anyell west, and butted south on the common called *le Lyng*. The site of the messuage, for which there is no archaeological evidence, and perhaps of *Bolys* grove, may be Ling's End Farm (at TF 8960 1187).

In 1605 nine acres called *Lingeclose* lay to the west of *Hamondescroft*, between *Shepehousecroft* / *Townesend-close* on the south and the *packway* on the north. To the west lay 16 acres also called *Lingeclose*, bordered by the *packway* on the north and by *Bullesgrove* and the *common lynge* on the south. The name *Linge close* does not appear until 1566. Hedges or fences around the lord's close called *Boles* were broken down and stolen in 1443. An enclosure at *le Ling* and 18 acres in *Bullfield* were held at farm in 1484 (MS 13162). It is likely that *Wylkynsclos*, which contained 8 acres and was leased out several times between 1427 and 1485, was in this area and not in *Quarent*. 1 where there had been a close of the same name (MS 13137 and MS 13141). The changeable situation in south-east *Bullesfield* is exemplified by the 1502 extent in which an 8-acre close and three pieces with a combined acreage of 36 all lay between the common way on the

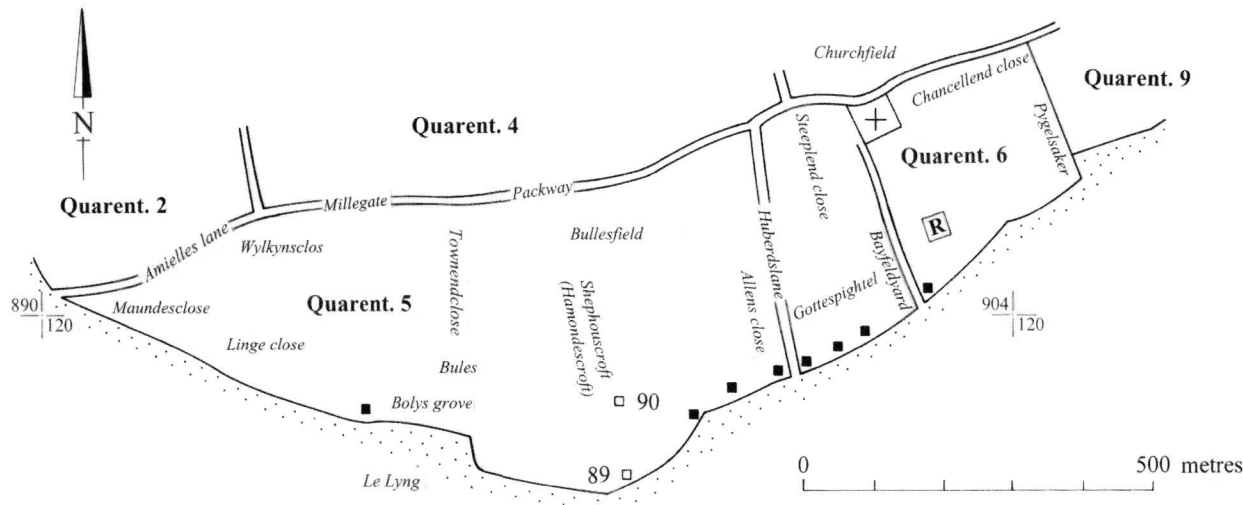

Figure 7.31 *Quarentinae* 5 and 6, Little Fransham, scale 1:10,560

north and the common pasture on the south. West of the 16 acres in *Lingeclose* lay 5 acres called *Maundesclose*, lying between *Aniels lane* on the north-west and the *common lynge* on the south. This was named after John Maunde senior who held at farm 18 acres to the east of *Bolesgrove* on a 5-year lease from 1476 (MS 13141) and was holding 18 acres in *Bullefeild* in 1484 (MS 13162). His widow Joanna took out a 20-year lease on this and other lands in 1485.

The most easterly property fronting on the common pasture was a Kirkhams customary tenement in the later fourteenth century, but previously had been a freehold, the messuage of William Huberd abutted in a charter of 1318 (HRO 8184)[xix]. One acre with a messuage called *Tuskenolnysines* was granted to Roger Tuskenol a villein (*nativus*) in 1365. In 1384 it was held by John de Wilton and was once of Richard de Wesenham. The messuage lay next to *Hoberdslane* on the east, and two pieces of land were included in the tenure, 1 acre at *Kerbusk* in *Quarent.* 4, and 1½ roods in *Quarent.* 8. The rent was 6s and no work services were required, suggesting that this was not of ancient tenure but a regrant under new terms. This is supported by the messor's accounts for 1383–4 in which the rent is entered with receipts for farmed lands and not included in the total of customary rents (MS 13122). In 1451 Edmund Tenmark, the tenant, was granted at farm the 3 acres of demesne that lay immediately north, to enlarge his messuage and to enclose and build it with timber and wood. A watercourse, flowing from the west and now largely culverted, ran along the front of the property and followed the common edge.

The next property to the west was entered in the Wilcoks rental of *c.*1420 as 2¼ acres of freehold in *Barghmyllefeld*. It butted south on the common pasture and watercourse and was held by William Chapman. The eastern of a pair of ¾-acre pieces at the south end of *Quarent.* 4, was part of the same tenement. The rent for these 3 acres was 2½d, but there was no mention of a messuage. The same rent had been paid by Katherine Hobbes in *c.*1395. However, in the Wilcoks messor's accounts for 1420–1 an allowance was made for the rent which was unpaid because the land was in the lord's hands after the death of Margaret Hobbes, daughter of Richard Hobbes and wife of William Chapman. Richard Hobbes / Hobbys had been a taxpayer in 1379 and 1381. The land in question was described in the account as 3 acres with a messuage, along with 2 customary acres in *Quarent.*12. Three shillings were collected as farm rent for the same lands (MS 13136). The freehold parts may have remained in the lord's hands until *c.*1450. In 1502 when it was next described, the land in the croft of this messuage had been reduced to 2 acres.

On the west side of the above, and to the south of the watercourse, lay a Kirkhams customary messuage. In 1384 a tenement, once of Roger Casy, contained 10 acres with a messuage in Necton (Med 11A). Casy, tenant of a messuage and 10 acres in Necton and 1 acre in Fransham, had died in 1361. The tenement was granted to Geoffrey son of Roger Tussenol in 1374. He was a taxpayer in 1379 and 1381 and died in 1405. His underaged son William died in 1410 when the holding was said to be in Little Fransham. Half was retained by his mother and the rest seized by the lord. By 1422 it was all in the hands of the lord. It was probably in 1423, when it was granted out anew to John Ward and Isabelle his wife, that the messuage was 'relocated' to this position. The tenant of the messuage in Little Fransham was one John Carter, to judge from an abuttal for the adjoining freehold in *c.*1420. In 1443 the 10-acre tenement once of Roger Casy, held by John Gleymesford, included a messuage with 2 acres in the croft, 7½ acres in three pieces of land in *Quarent.* 2 and ½ acre in *Quarent.* 20. In 1447 the tenement, including a messuage built, was granted to Henry Hokeryng and his wife.

Next to the west lay a 1¾ acre pightle of glebe land. Nothing is known of this piece, but it is tempting to suggest that a house might once have stood in it. The final property fronting the common was demesne of Kirkhams called *Shephousyerd* in 1392–3 (MS 13123). This contained two settlement sites, Med 89 and 90, the former lying on the south side of the watercourse, and the latter to the north (Fig. 7.32).

Plate 7.8 Detail from 1946 RAF vertical aerial photograph, area including the main village of Little Fransham, *Quarents*. 5, 6, 11 and 12 (http://www.historic-maps.norfolk.gov.uk/)

Plate 7.9 Detail from the Enclosure Award map, area including the main village of Little Fransham (NRO C/Sca 2/122)

LITTLE FRANSHAM

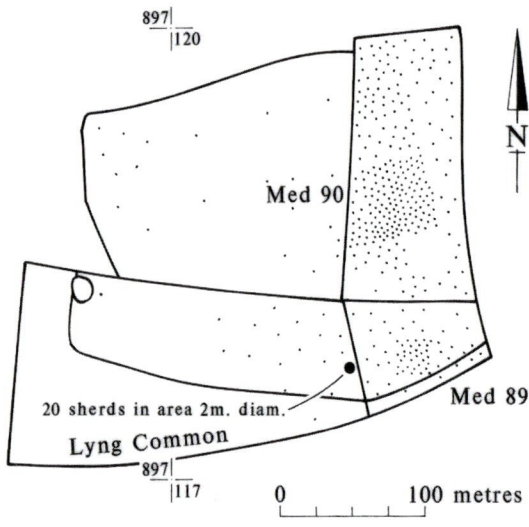

Figure 7.32 Med 89 and 90 within *Quarentinae* 5, distribution of sherds (boundaries taken from Ordnance Survey County Series 1928 edition), scale 1:5,000

Quarent. 6, the parish churchyard, the rectory and the north-east part of the main village, Little Fransham (Fig. 7.31; Pl. 7.8 and Pl. 7.9; Pl. 7.10 and Pl. 7.11)
Churchyard with church, rectory within block of glebe, settlements, some with tenement blocks, edging a riverside common

In 1613 almost the whole of the eastern part consisted of 12 acres of glebe, with house, yards and 'homeclose' which butted south on the common. None of this land is now arable so that no fieldwalking was possible. The medieval rectory lay within a square moated enclosure (HER 7289, Pl. 7.10), *c*.30m by 30m internally and with rounded corners. A house, which may or may not have been medieval[xx], stood within the moat in 1804, when a faculty was granted for its demolition and for the building of a new and much larger dwelling some distance to the north (DN/FCB 5/1). The petition (DN/FCP 8/1) includes a plan of the old house, moat and outbuildings (Fig. 7.33)[xxi] and one of the proposed new house. The moat, with its island empty of buildings, is shown on the Enclosure Award map, lying at TF 9029 1213, *c*.40m north of the common edge. In 1566 the rectory was 'mooted round aboute with [missing]'. Until 1988 the north and east arms of the moat survived as slight linear depressions. The west arm, hard up against the edge of the neighbouring property, remains as a deep V-shaped and largely dry ditch. The south arm was a water-filled moat-like feature more than 10m wide, which extended south-east beyond the junction with the eastern arm, to end in a pond that is depicted as a separate feature on the Enclosure Award map. In 1988 the southern arm was massively deepened and partly widened by a tracked excavator. The resultant spoil, from which only late post-medieval building material was recovered, was spread to the south and over the island, thereby obscuring the northern and eastern arms. The south end of the latter, mechanically sectioned in the process, was seen to be 12.5m wide, 2m deep and flat-based. A tip-line down the west side and across the base contained a mass of post-medieval pan-tiles and bricks.

Chancellend close contained 3 acres. It lay south of a way leading east to the Kirkhams manor house in *Quarent*. 9, and north of the above 12 acres, and butted west on the churchyard. This may have been 3 acres lying at Little Fransham church (*ad ecclesiam*) granted by William le Strange to John [Croupius] the rector in 1359 (BL Add Ch 71040). This piece was sometimes sown with crops by the lord of Kirkhams. Barley was growing on 3 acres and ½ a rood butting west on the cemetery in 1402–3, barley on 3 acres *ad ecclesiam* in 1412–3 and oats on 3 acres at *Chyrchgate* in 1413–4 (MS 13127 and MS 13133). A ¾-acre pightle east of the 12 acres butted north on *Chancellend close*. In 1613 an 8 feet wide strip in *Hallcroft* east of a ditch running down the east side of *Chancellend close* and the pightle was thought to be glebe. This does not appear in any later glebe terrier, apart from one version of 1635.

The parish church of St Mary the Virgin lies 260m north of the common edge and stands centrally within an almost square churchyard containing 0.632 acre / 0.255 hectare (Pl. 7.11). In the same way as All Saints' church, 870m to the north, it sits on the crest of a very slight rise. The present church lacks a tower which is said to have fallen in *c*.1700 (Bryant 1903; Cautley 1949, 199; Messent 1936, 88; Mortlock and Roberts 1985; Pevsner and Wilson 1999, 521–2)[xxii]. The late twelfth-century font is the earliest part of the fabric although several reused pieces of ashlar in the north wall appear to be Norman, to judge from their tooling. The nave, measuring 16 by 7m internally, has a medieval hammerbeam roof and is flanked by a south porch. William Martenet, once Vicar of Sporle, left 20s in his will, proved in 1438, for the making of a porch on the south side of the nave (NCC 66/7 Doke). The chancel measures 11 by 5.7m internally. It has been suggested that in the 1340s or 1350s the nave and chancel were designed by an architect who was responsible for work at eight other Norfolk churches, all but one of which lie in centre of the county. The distinctive treatment of

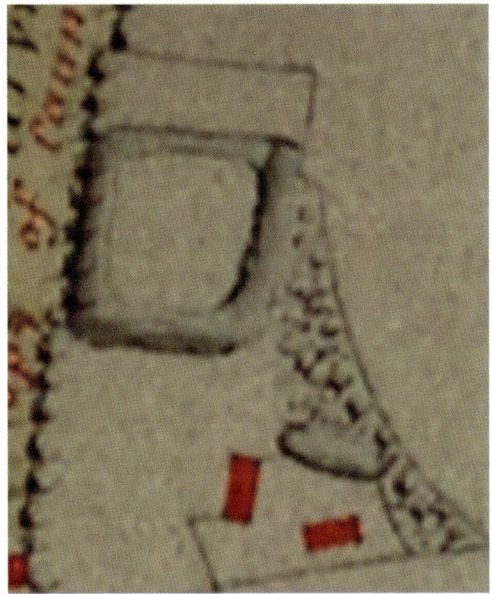

Plate 7.10 Detail from the Enclosure Award map, Little Fransham rectory in *Quarent*. 6 (NRO C/Sca 2/122)

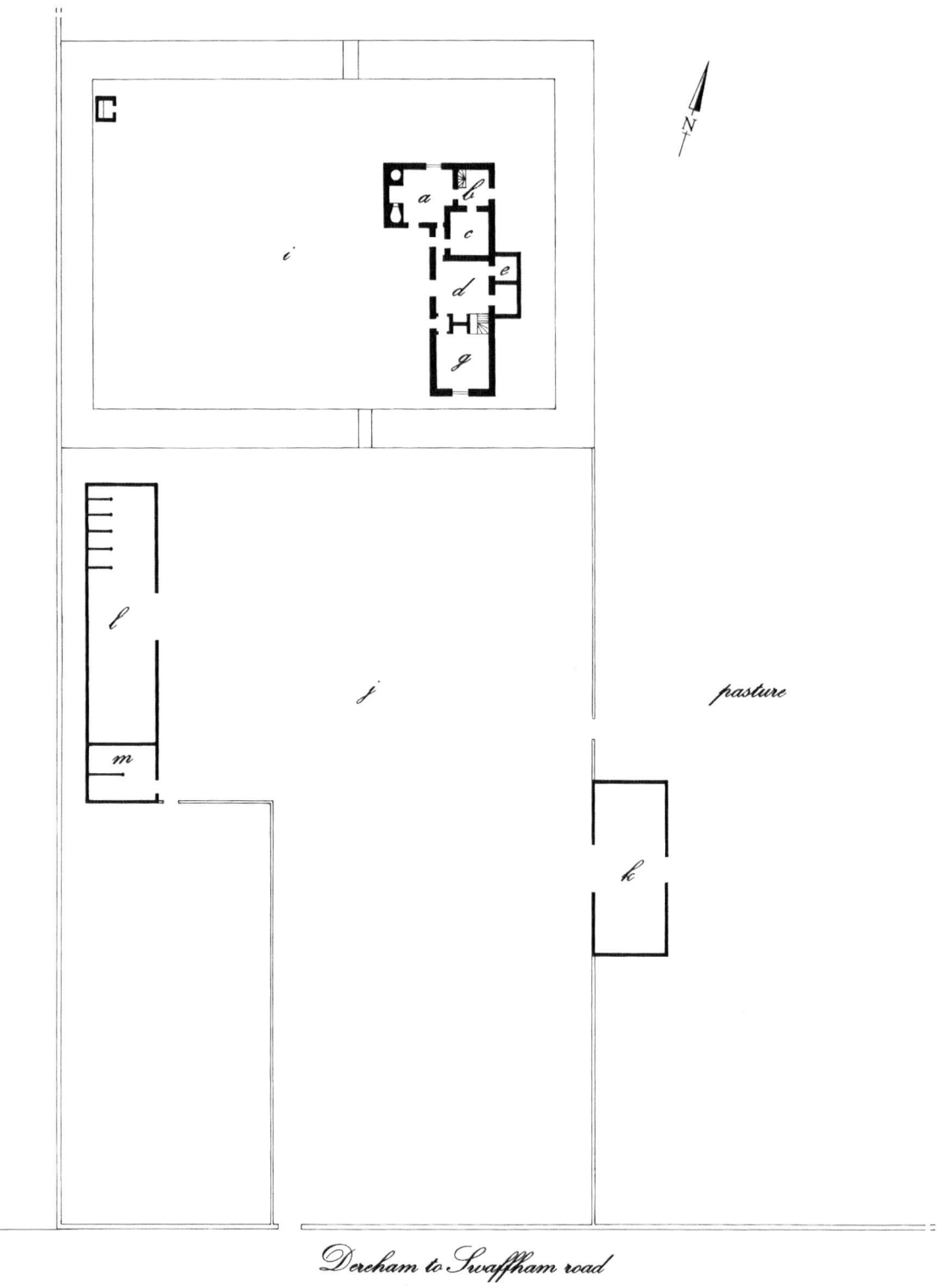

Figure 7.33 Plan of Little Fransham rectory in 1804, scale not given

window tracery in these churches is claimed to be stylistically similar (Fawcett 1980). It is uncertain how a mid-fourteenth-century date can be squared with a clause in the will of John Croupius, Rector of Little Fransham, which was written and proved in 1404. He requested his executors to arrange for the making of two windows on the north side of the chancel *in petr. in glasyng*, i.e. both tracery and glass (NCC 312 Harsyk). Either the work was not carried out or new windows in an old and matching style were made.

Steeplend close, which contained 4 acres and had been a settlement site in the Late Saxon period (LS 2), filled the angle between the *packway* on the north and *Huberdslane* on the west.

Properties fronting the watercourse that ran eastwards along the north side of the common will now be described from west to east. On the corner of *Huberslane* and the common a Kirkhams and Wilcoks freehold ¼-acre tenement with yard was recently built in 1583 (MS 13064), but an abuttal in the Kirkhams rental of 1384

Plate 7.11 St Mary's church Little Fransham in *Quarent.* 6, from the south-east, July 2018

shows that this was then the messuage of John Wilkenessson. John son of William / John Williamson was a taxpayer in 1379 and 1381. The property itself was not listed in the 1384 rental. In 1423 and 1425 John Wylkenson (probably son of the former) was amerced at the leet court for not scouring a watercourse on the east side of *Hoberds* / *Hooberdislane*. He held free land in *Quarent.* 1 and customary land in *Quarents.* 11, 12 and 15, and died in 1429. It is hard to understand why this property escaped inclusion in any fifteenth-century rental. On its east side lay a Kirkhams freehold messuage held by William Gaude for an annual rent of 1d in 1384. He had paid the same rent in *c.*1375 but was not taxed in 1379 or 1381. He died in 1406 seized of a messuage and ½ acre formerly of Geoffrey Gaude. The property fell into the lord's hands because William Gaude had been a bastard. Three years later it became customary land, a messuage with a newly-made ¾-acre close, thereafter to be known as *Guadesyard* or *Gaudes*. Rent was received for a cottage here in 1427–8 (MS 13137) and for the herbage of a cottage here in 1429–30 (MS 13138). Thereafter this piece was described as a close, a pightle or as land, but was reoccupied by a house in the 1580s.

Lying north of *Gaudes* and of the property to the west, and butting west on *Hoberdslane,* was a ½-acre pightle known as *Gottespightel* or *Magotesclos*. It was in the hands of the lord of Wilcoks manor between 1399 and 1421, and probably for some time after that (MS 13129, MS 13132, MS 13134 and MS 13136). By 1502 it had become a Kirkhams and Wilcoks freehold. Did the name *Magotesclos* refer to Olive Gotte, tenant of the next property to the east? A pightle once of Humphrey Gotte was abutted in two charters of 1316 and one of 1323/7 (MC 360/46, 47 and 78, 713X6). East of *Gaudes*, 5 acres with a messuage were held freely of Wilcoks by Richard Maunde in *c.*1420. They were late of Olive Gotte his mother, who had paid the same rent (2½d) in *c.*1395 and had been a taxpayer in 1379 (partly illegible, …Gotte) and 1381 (Cotte). The charters cited above show that a 3-acre piece, which must have part of these 5 acres, was conveyed in June 1316 by John the Carpenter and Joanna le Caly his wife, to Henry son of Peter de Scarning, by Henry to William de la Rode in October that year, and by Edward de Stowe rector of Runcton Holme [in west Norfolk] to William son of Henry le Strange between 1323 and 1327. Next to this freehold lay a ¾-acre piece which, according to both the glebe terriers and a court roll of 1677, butted north on *Steplendclose* (MC 1850/1, 858X9). This was Kirkhams demesne called *Bayfeldyard* in 1372 and *Bayfeldcroft* in 1373 when the lord's corn crop was growing there. In *c.*1375 John Stalonn paid 2s 6d farm rent for a close called *Bayfeldeyard*. John Stalonde and his wife were taxpayers in 1381, but not in 1379. In 1383–4 no rent was received for a messuage called *Bayfeld* because it was being grazed by the lord's animals (MS 13122). In the fifteenth century it was normally let at farm along with *Gaudes* to tenants of the freehold lying between the two, and by 1502 it was copyhold.

The church path ran along the east side of *Bayfeld* and beyond it was a customary tenement of Cannons manor, a

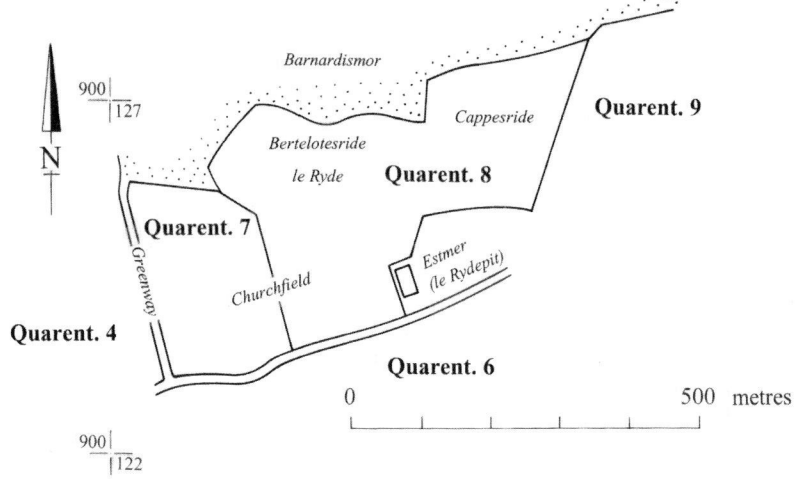

Figure 7.34 *Quarentinae* 7 and 8, Little Fransham, scale 1:10,560

messuage and 2½ acres in the croft, which was never given any abuttals but probably extended north to the churchyard. The earliest direct reference to this property is in court proceedings of 1591, when the croft size was given as 1½ acres, but on all subsequent occasions it was said to comprise 2½ acres. On its east side ½ acre of Cannons demesne, copyhold after 1555, lay between glebe land to the north and east, and the croft to the south and west. To the east of the croft and the ½ acre a 180m length of common edge was butted by a 12-acre block of glebe land. Beyond this lay 1 acre of Cannons copyhold which butted north on the large piece of glebe and Kirkhams demesne land in *Quarent.* 9. In 1541 this piece was called *Pytylacre* and contained 1 acre of meadow. Numerous amercements, often involving the rector and/or the prior of West Acre, in earlier Little Fransham courts leet had referred to this place and a related stream/ditch and bridge, for example *Pykelesdyke* in 1377, a watercourse at *Pygelsaker* in 1392 and 1393, and *Pykelsbrygge* in 1406. The pightle contained a dwelling house by 1623, but whether it did so in the Middle Ages is unknown.

Quarent. 7, the western part of *Churchfield*, Little Fransham (Fig. 7.34)
Common field

This area was bounded by the *Greenway* on the west, *Barnards Moor* on the north, and the *packway* or way leading to Kirkhams manor house on the south. All nine land parcels were aligned north-south. From west to east they were: 1 acre of Kirkhams and Wilcoks demesne, 1 acre of the Sparhams customary tenement Cappes (Med 70 in *Quarent.* 27), 3 acres of glebe, 1 acre of the same Sparhams tenement, 2 acres of glebe, 2½ acres of Kirkhams and Wilcoks demesne, ¾ acre of glebe, ¾ acre of Northendhall or Guntons demesne, ½ acre of glebe. The last two pieces of glebe butted north on *Reed Close* (see *Quarent.* 8). The piece between them was incorrectly said to butt north on *Capride* (TNA SC 12/3/23). The first piece in the above list must be the same as 1¼ acres conveyed by Geoffrey Gotte of Little Fransham to William le Strange [probably the lord of Wilcoks] in 1346. The piece lay between the green way (*viridiam viam*) west and the land of Hawys Tarkeys east, and it butted south on the way leading to the church and north on *Barnardismor* (MC 360/70, 713X6).

Quarent. 8, the eastern part of *Churchfield* and area to the north and north-east, Little Fransham (Fig. 7.34)
Detached block demesne, core block demesne, and common field

Caprede, in the north-east part, contained 10 acres of Cannons demesne, and was copyhold in the sixteenth century. When held at farm by the lord of Kirkhams it was normally cropped, *e.g.* with rye in 1378 when Ralph Kyng's cows did damage, and with barley in 1412–3 when 20 acres at *Caprede* and *le Rede* were sown (MS 13133). The earliest reference to this piece is in a mid-thirteenth-century charter. Godfrey son of John of Little Fransham granted a rent and various lands to Robert de Sancto Thoma, including a piece (*pecia*) called *Bertelotesride* lying between *Cappesride* and the moor, *i.e.* *Barnardismor* (MC 360/13, 713X6). The second element in these names is Old English *r?d, a clearing (Smith 1956b, 89–90). *Bertelot*, a personal name, is a double-diminutive of Bartholomew (Reaney and Wilson 1991, 30 under the name Bartlet). *Cappes* is a surname (*cf.* the tenement Cappes in Little Fransham, Med 70 in Appendix 2). On the west side of *Caprede* lay *le Ryde*, first recorded in 1360. It was Kirkhams demesne containing 8 acres, or 10 acres according to several fifteenth-century sources in which it is called *Redeclos* (MS 13097 and MS 13142). The northern parts of this close, which must have contained *Bertelotesride*, and of *Cappesride* both appear to have been cut out of the southern side of *Barnardismor*. Despite their use as arable land in the late fourteenth and early fifteenth centuries neither close has produced a scatter of medieval sherds. The southern end of *Redeclos* wrapped around the north-east corner of *Churchfield* to end at *le Rydepit* or *Estmer* (see *Quarent.* 9).

South of *Redeclos* in *Churchfield* proper, 5 acres of Kirkhams demesne were aligned east-west. Barley grew on 5 acres below *le Ryde* in 1402–3 (MS 13127). South of here were five smaller pieces all aligned east-west and listed from north to south: ¾ acre of the Sparhams customary tenement Benedict Heved (Med 77 and 78 in

Quarent. 15); ¾ acre of Kirkhams customary land associated with Med 71 in *Quarent.* 27; 1½ roods of Kirkhams customary land (all of these butting east on *le Rydepit*); ½ acre of glebe; ½ acre of Kirkhams demesne. The southern edge of the latter was followed by the way leading from the church to the Kirkhams manor house (Med 74).

Quarent. 9, the manor house of Kirkhams and land surrounding, Little Fransham (Fig. 7.35, Pl. 7.12 and Pl. 7.13)
Manor house and core block demesne

All of this area was demesne of Kirkhams manor. The western part was known as *Halcrofte* and contained about 14 acres. In 1446–7 23½ acres in the croft of the manor must have included land in *Hall close* to the east (MS 13142). In 1484 two pieces in *Hall crofte*, 7 and 6¼ acres, were held at farm by two tenants (MS 13162) and in 1502 *Halcroft* contained 18 acres. This land ran from *Caprede* and *Redeclos* in the north to the common and a Cannons customary acre in the south, with *Churchfield* and 12 acres of glebe on the west.

Le Rydepit still exists, up against the eastern edge of *Churchfield* at TF 9043 1245, as an unusually flat-based and rectangular pit, approximately 1m deep, but appearing deeper from *Churchfield* because of a substantial rise at the headland. In the late fourteenth century the pit was called *Estmer*. Old English *mere* meaning a pool (Smith 1956b, 38–9) is the second element, but the descriptive *east* cannot indicate its position in relation to the Kirkhams manor house. Illegal pasturing took place at *Estmer* in 1372 and in the same year the lord's barley at *Estmerewong* was damaged by cows. In 1373 the lord's rye at *Estmer* was damaged by Christina le Dey to the value of 1 peck. In *c.*1375 Vincent and Petronilla Fysher paid rent for pasturage (*herbagium*) at *Estmere*. In 1428 Richard Maunde had damaged the lord's barley growing on 5 acres at *Rudpytte*. *Le Rydepit* was named in an abuttal of 1443 and in the following year William Wyskard was amerced for fishing in the lord's private water (*seperali aqua*) at *Redepyt*.

In 1995 a small pond was mechanically excavated in the base of the pit and the following stratification was recorded for a depth of 1.1m down to water level: 0–15cm topsoil, 15–45cm redeposited boulder clay, 45–70cm peat with much wood and one cut animal bone, 70–90cm dark grey peaty silt with one sherd of Romano-British pottery, dipping downwards to the south and perhaps the filling of a recut, 90–110cm pale grey organic silt with twigs and wood fragments. The impression gained from this rapid and informal observation was that the lower deposits were of great antiquity.

Halclose contained 30 acres and lay to the east of *Halcrofte*. It extended from *Barnards Moor* in the north to the common in the south, and to *Drovelane* in the east. This way (*Drovieslanesende* in 1429, *Drouteslane* in 1431) ran along the edge of a demesne meadow called *Raweyn* in *Quarent.* 24. One twelfth-century settlement site (Med 73) sat in an isolated position towards the north-east corner of *Halclose*. The manor house (Med 74) stood slightly to the west of centre on a site first occupied in the twelfth century and was surrounded by a moat. The earliest documentary reference to the house is of 1373–4. The archaeology of the site and what is known of the maintenance and demise of the manor house complex, as well as details of subdivisions within *Halclose* are given under Med 74 in Appendix 2.

Quarent. 10, north and west of Cannons Green, Little Fransham (Fig. 7.36)
Core block demesne (with a dovecot) containing five former settlements

Common pastures surrounded all of this area except on the south-west where it was edged by a road, called *Chouneslane* in 1379. By the fifteenth century, all was demesne of Kirkhams and Wilcoks. Of five settlement sites (Med 98–102) all had been abandoned by the end, and probably by the middle, of the fourteenth century (Fig. 7.37). Two of these (Med 99 and 102) began in the twelfth century, and the others in the thirteenth, with

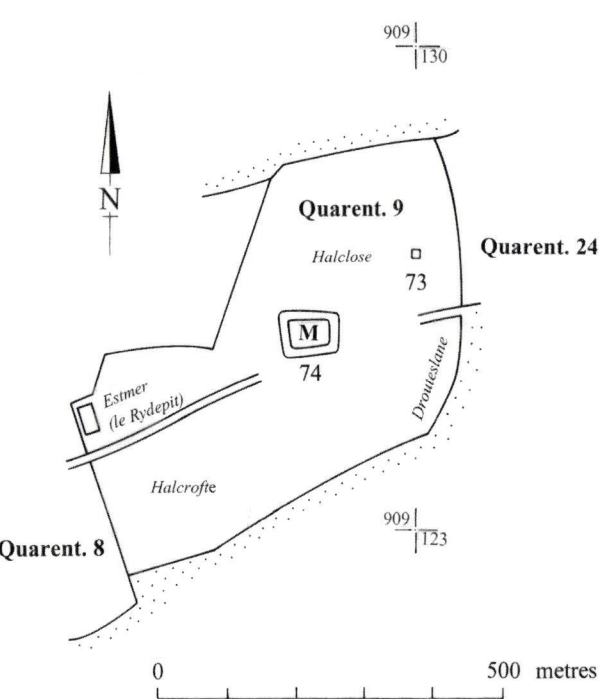

Figure 7.35 *Quarentina* 9, Little Fransham, scale 1:10,560

Plate 7.12 Detail from the Enclosure Award map, Kirkhams manor house site (Med 74) in *Quarent.* 9 (NRO C/Sca 2/122)

occupation on Med 99 possibly starting before 1100. Documentary evidence touching on the history of these settlements is extremely sparse.

Arrowsmithsclose took up the north-west part. Amounting to 12 acres, it was first named, as *Narowsmythclos*, in 1429–30 (MS 13138) and contained Med 102, a settlement that failed to survive into the thirteenth century. *Dovehouseyard* in the north-east corner contained 2 acres and the dovecot of Kirkhams manor, as well as Med 99. It was named *Dufhouscroft* in 1393. The 1605 survey listed a row of three pightles (½, 2 and 1 acre) down the east side and at the south end of the field. Med 98 and Med 100–1 lay within them. There are few earlier references to these pightles. Med 100 may have been a freehold of Wilcoks manor and Med 101 a customary tenement held of Kirkhams. Soilmarks of the recently levelled earthworks of Med 100 and 101 were recorded by Ordnance Survey aerial photography in 1971 (Fig. 7.38).

Quarent. 11, the south-east part of the main village, *Chewnesfurlong* and the north-west part of *Woodrowfield*, Little Fransham (Fig. 7.39; Pl. 7.8 and Pl. 7.9)
Settlements with tenement blocks flanking a riverside common, common field, and a small piece of demesne woodland

The common formed the northern edge of this *Quarent.* and *Middlefurlong* the southern. A church path marked the west side, *Chouneslane* and *Cannons Green* the east. The description begins at the west end of four

Plate 7.13 Detail from 1946 RAF vertical aerial photograph, Kirkhams manor house site (Med 74) in *Quarent.* 9 (http://www.historic-maps.norfolk.gov.uk/)

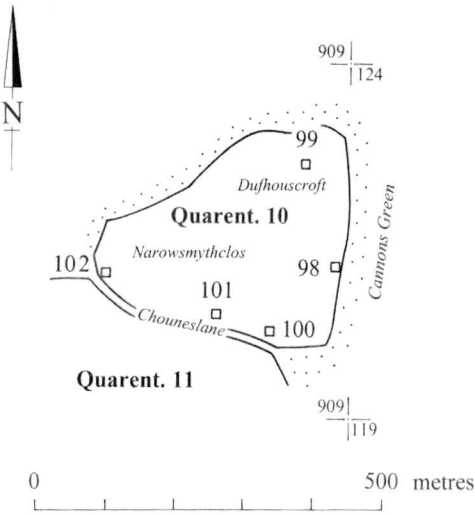

Figure 7.36 *Quarentinae* 10, Little Fransham, scale 1:10,560

properties edging the common before moving on to the open field to the south. On the east side of the church path but included by William Hayward in *Quarent.* 13, was a Kirkhams freehold messuage at *Fisherbrigg*, once of John Fisher in 1384, when it was held by Alice daughter of Vincent Fisher and her sister Margery. John Fysher had been a juror at the manor court between 1336 and 1340. Eustace Fysher, a taxpayer in 1327 and 1332 (Fissor / Fisor), had died seized of a freehold cottage in 1361, with Vincent Fysher as his heir. He appeared as [illeg.] Fyssor and Vincent Fyshor in the 1379 and 1381 Poll Tax lists. In 1443 this piece contained ½ acre and was held by Joanna Base along with another freehold, a parcel of a messuage and parcel of a croft, also containing ½ acre, which had not been included in the 1384 rental. By 1502 the two had been combined as a messuage with 1 acre. In *c.*1375 the former piece lay next to a messuage once of Juetta Gardener. In 1385/6 this Sparhams customary holding was described as 1½ acres with a cottage, once of Inotte [sic] Gardener, but no abuttal was given. Thereafter the cottage was not mentioned in any record, and the area had shrunk to ¼ acre by 1493. Between then and 1597 this ¼ acre shared the same tenant as the Kirkhams freehold, but it was engrossed by the lord of Sparhams in 1598. *Jowettesbrygge*, where the tenant of the Kirkhams piece blocked the church path in 1422, must be the same as *Fisherbrigg*. The adjoining property on the east consisted of 2½ acres of Cannons customary land. Its tenurial history does not begin until 1521, but it may be significant that one Cannons rent payer in *c.*1370 was Vincent Fisor (MS 13089A). In the sixteenth century the piece was held by the tenants of the property to the west. A bake house in need of repair was mentioned in 1578 and a messuage built was conveyed in 1599. It seems very probable that the plot had been the site of a separate dwelling before the late fourteenth century. A house now standing on the site contains fragments of probably seventeenth-century timber framing (HER 51406).

On the east lay Med 94, a Kirkhams free, and sometimes customary, holding called *Segars* that was occupied from the thirteenth century until *c.*1600. Two acres lay with the messuage in 1502, but there were 3 acres

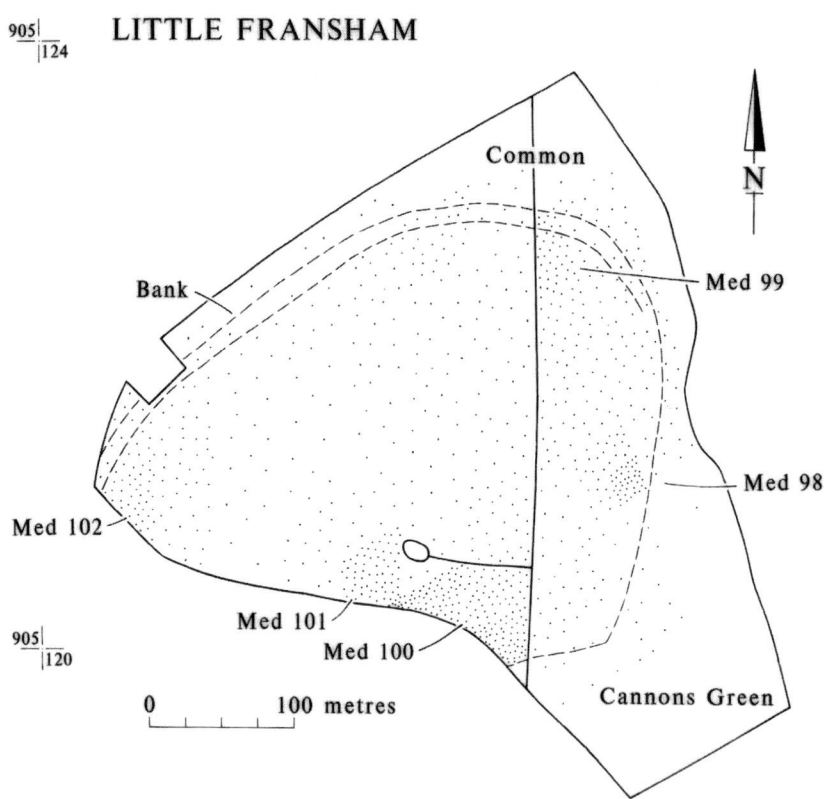

Figure 7.37 Med 98–102 in *Quarentina* 10, distribution of sherds (boundaries taken from Ordnance Survey County Series 1928 edition), scale 1:5,000

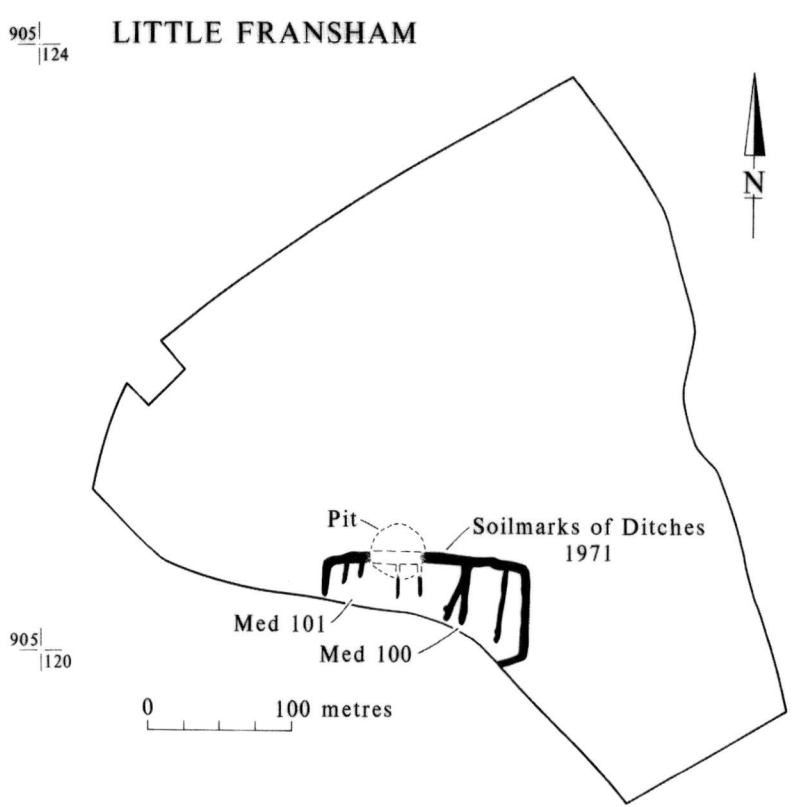

Figure 7.38 Med 100 and 101 in *Quarentina* 10, with soil marks plotted from an Ordnance Survey vertical aerial photograph (sortie no. OS/71046 Frame no. 036), scale 1:5,000

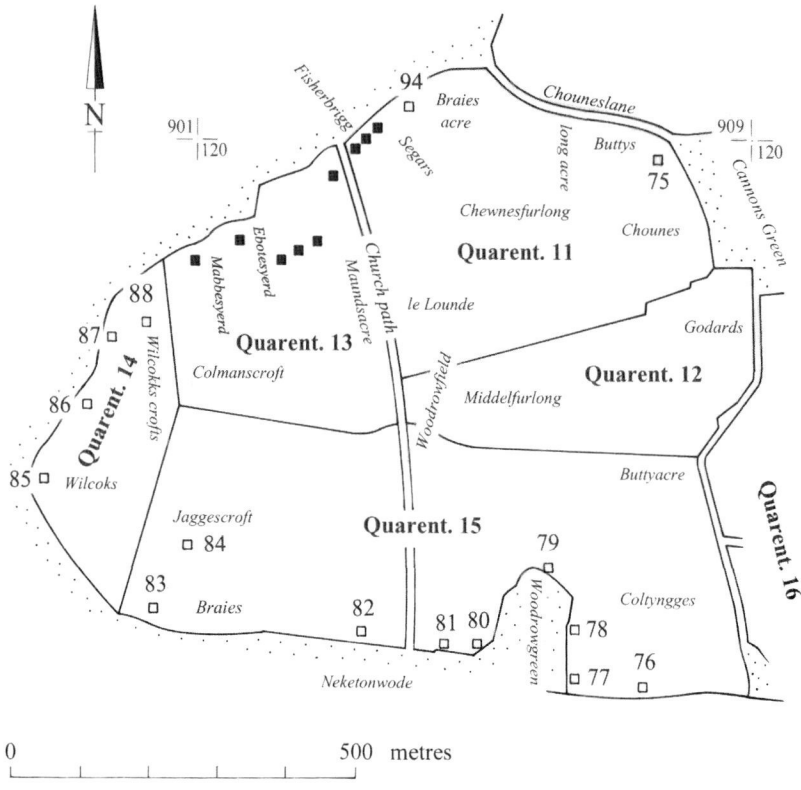

Figure 7.39 *Quarentinae* 11–15, Little Fransham, scale 1:10,560

in the croft in 1596 (MS 13268). Beyond *Segars* were 1¾ acres of Kirkhams freehold known from 1442 and held for an annual rent of a red rose. Beyond this to the east and south-east along the common edge and then along the side of *Chouneslane*, there was no further settlement site until Med 75 is reached. This was a Cannons customary tenement fronting north-east onto the entrance of *Chouneslane* into *Cannons Green*. First documented in 1546, it is still occupied by a house and farm buildings, and to judge from sherds found immediately to the south, settlement was established there in the eleventh century (LS 18).

The remainder of this area was occupied by *Chewnesfurlong*. This contained a large number of land parcels that in the southern part were aligned north-south. At the east end were 4 acres of Kirkhams demesne in a close called *Chounes* in 1378. Barley was growing on 11½ acres at *Chounescroft* in 1402–3 (MS 13127). West of this lay 4½ acres of Kirkhams and Wilcoks demesne, first recognisable as 4½ acres at *Chounes* in 1446–7 (MS 13142). In the 1490s both these pieces became copyhold. On the west side of the latter lay ¼ acre of the Kirkhams customary tenement held in 1384 by John Wilkensson. This was part of what became known as the tenement Wylkenson and lay in *Jownesfurlong*. West of here the sequence of strips becomes impossible to unravel. It included ½ acre of the same tenement, 1 acre of Wilcoks soiled land (by 1502 said to be ¾ acre), ½ acre of Wilcoks soiled land, ½, ¾ (in the furlong called *le Lounde* in 1502), 1, 1 and 2 acres of Kirkhams and Wilcoks freehold, ¼ and ¾ acre of the Sparhams customary tenement Benedict Heved (Med 77 and 78 in *Quarent.* 15). A further 3 acres of this tenement may also have been in this *Quarent.*, but after one mention, at a court held in 1531 when they were passed by Nicholas to Edward Mynne, sources are silent on their fate. *Lounde* is derived from Old Norse *lúndr*, a small wood or grove (Smith 1956b, 27–8).

To the west of Med 75 and north of *Chounescroft* a 1-acre grove of Kirkhams and Wilcoks demesne called *Chounes* was first recorded in 1432. It butted north on *Chewneslane*, and on its west side was ¼ acre of glebe described as a pightle in 1502 and 'sometime a hempland' in 1613. West of this was another ¼-acre piece of glebe, which extended west along the headland between furlongs of north-south strips on each side, with several of the strips listed in the previous paragraph butting onto it from the south. *Buttys*, lying north of this ¼ acre, comprised 1 acre of Kirkhams demesne. It carried the lord's oat crop in 1371, was called *Bottylond* in 1450 and *Buttyacre* in 1476 (MS 13141). *Buttys* lay next to Chowneslane on the north but was presumably aligned east-west. At its west end a Kirkhams and Wilcoks freehold, the *long acre*, butted north on the common. The north-east corner of this *Quarent.* contained three pieces of Kirkhams and Wilcoks freehold running north-south, ¼, ½ and 1 acre. Further to the west *Braies acre*, named after an early fifteenth-century Wilcoks free tenant, was associated with a messuage in *Quarent.* 15 (Med 83) and butted north on *Segars* (Med 94). In the same area were two ½ acres and ¼ acre of Sparhams soiled land. One ½-acre piece of the Sparhams customary tenement Godfrey butted north on the common, somewhere to the east of *Segars*. The messuage of this tenement was in *Quarent.* 15. Three acres of the Sparhams customary tenement Benedict Heved (Med 77 and 78 in *Quarent.* 15) lay to the south-west of *Segars*. There were 6½ acres associated with the *Segars* messuage in addition to the croft. These were listed in 1502 but somehow missed by William Hayward in 1605. As *Segars* was one point of contention in a legal dispute between the lord of Kirkhams and Wilcoks and Richard Beckham, the lord of Cannons and Sparhams, in the 1590s (MS 13162), it is not surprising that the latter managed somehow to conceal these lands from the surveyor of the former. Of these, ¼ acre, two ½ acres and 2½ acres were probably in this part of the field. The final piece, 2¾ acres, was specified as running the length of two furlongs in 1596 (MS 13268). It probably ran along the church path at the west end of *Quarent.* 11 and 12. One Kirkhams customary ½-acre, that in 1384 had been associated with a messuage in *Quarent.* 27 (Med 71), almost certainly lay in this *Quarent*. Although its tenurial history can be followed up to 1588, when it fell into the hands of Richard Beckham, by 1605 William Hayward was unable to find it (*non invent.*).

Quarent. 12, *Middlefurlong*, *Woodrowfield*, Little Fransham (Fig. 7.39)
Common field with a piece of block demesne, perhaps a former tenement block

All parcels were aligned north-south. At the eastern end lay *Godards*, 5 acres of Kirkhams demesne, the north-east part of which butted on *Cannons Green*. To the east ran a road called *Cannons, Coltings or Goddards Lane* (the present day *Goggles Lane*). The lord's barley growing in *Godards* was damaged in 1365, as were his peas in 1371 and his oats in 1372. In 1374 a close of unstated acreage and a certain pasture (*herbagium*) at *Godards* were surrendered and regranted as customary land. A former customary tenement in this area, perhaps the above close, and perhaps in a non-surveyed location on the south-west edge of *Cannons Green*, is suggested by the decision of the manor court jury in 1393 to elect the tenement *Godardes* to the office of messor. It was in the lord's hands. *Godards* became copyhold in 1483. Next to the west was a 6-acre piece of demesne, first distinguished in 1476 when 6 acres at *Goodards* were held at farm on a 5-year lease (MS 13141). This piece, *Godards* and the two pieces, of 4 and 4½ acres, in *Chewnesfurlong*, made up a sizeable block of demesne. In 1412–3 11 acres at *Godardys* were sown with wheat and in the next year 21 acres at *Godardes* and *Chounes* were sown with barley (MS 13133). Next came 1½ acres of soiled land, listed under both Kirkhams in 1384 and Wilcoks in *c*.1420, which butted north on *Chounescroft* (in *Quarent*. 11). On the west were three parcels of the Kirkhams tenement Wylkenson which were separately listed in 1384, as ¾ acre, ½ acre and 1½ roods, the first two said to be above (*super*) *Middelfurlong*. Abuttals written some time after 1443 state that all three butted north on *Bochelylond*, a name not encountered in other sources. By 1463 all three were considered as one piece. To the west of here the order of individual parcels becomes uncertain. Half an acre and ½ rood next to *Middelfurlong* was said to be once of Sara Bray in 1384 and can probably be equated with a Kirkhams freehold piece of the same size of which Hugh Bray had died seized in 1327. In 1605 it was reduced to ½ acre and was considered soiled. Three pieces, two ½ acres and ¾ acre of Kirkhams customary land, were granted as 1¾ acres in *Waderowfeld* to John Sygger in 1391. This was called *Hobbyscroft* some time after 1443. The tenement *Hobbyslond* had been elected to the office of messor in 1374. One ¾-acre parcel of the Kirkhams customary tenement of Roger Knot (Med 80) lay in this area, as did several pieces of Sparhams customary land, two ¾ acres and ½ acre of the tenement of Benedict Heved (Med 77 and 78). Sparhams soiled land, 1¼ acres first mentioned in 1531, also probably lay in this furlong as may some or all of 3 acres of the Sparham customary tenement once of William Coo. This land was never given abuttals. Along the western part of the headland between this *Quarent.* and *Quarent.* 11 lay ¾ acre of glebe. In the 1605 survey it was described as 'the short 3r of the Rectorie' when abutted by two of the above small parcels of Kirkhams and Wilcoks land.

Quarent. 13, the south-west part of the main village and *Colmanscroft*, Little Fransham (Fig. 7.39; Pl. 7.8 and Pl. 7.9)
Settlements with tenement blocks, edging riverside pastures, and two very small detached demesne closes (perhaps once containing houses), detached block demesne in an ancient enclosure, and one freehold acre

West of the church path lay a Kirkhams customary tenement, described in 1384 as a messuage and 1½ acres held by John Bernham and once of Henry Knyght. In 1330 a messuage was seized by the lord because Christina daughter of Hugh Bate had married without licence. In 1331 she paid a fine and Henry Knyt, a villein (*nativus*), swore fealty. Christina died in 1335 seized of a messuage and 2 acres which she and her husband had jointly acquired, her nearest heir being her son David aged two. In 1337 Alan de Barsham paid a fine for permission to lease 2 acres with a messuage from Henry Knyt for a 13-year term, de Barsham to render services to the lord for the duration. David Knyt, villein, was reported to have left the lord's demesne in 1348. John de Bernham held a messuage and croft containing 2 acres of the tenement Knyghts on a 5-year lease from 1363. In 1372 he was granted a customary messuage built and 1½ acres of the tenement Knights, to hold for a new annual rent of 3s and a hen, one work day of autumn reaping and suit of court every three weeks. In 1393 de Bernham surrendered this holding, on his deathbed, to John de Pykenham and his wife. It was to be divided into two distinct holdings in 1490, and one part was still called *Peckingham* in 1768 (MC 1850/4, 858X8).

To the south-west of *Pykenhams* lay a tenement with a complex tenurial background, which in the later sixteenth century was to become the *de facto* manor house of Sparhams and Cannons. It is now known as Little Fransham Old Hall. One element was described as a free messuage with 2 acres in the croft in 1552, held of Wendling Abbey by Matilda Mynne (TNA SC 12/3/23). A charter of 1265–74 records the grant by Thomas Spurnn of Fransham to Wendling of a rent for 2 acres there for the maintenance of a light in the abbey church. A sixteenth-century endorsement states that the land was held by Matilda Mynne and was at that time built up (*edificatur*; TNA E 40/10463). Matilda was the widow of Edward Mynne, lord of part of Great Fransham manor and a major landholder in Little Fransham, who died in 1543 and whose descendants were to acquire both Sparhams and Cannons manors. Another element was a Sparhams free messuage held by John Sefepens in 1385/6. Richard

Sevepens was a taxpayer in 1379, as were he, his wife and his son Richard in 1381. Both these properties are listed in the Inquisition Post Mortem of Edward Mynne. They were said, erroneously, to have been held of Sir Giles Capell, as of his manor of Little Fransham, *i.e.* Kirkhams and Wilcoks (TNA C 142/70/6). The error was repeated in the Inquisition Post Mortem of Nicholas Mynne, son of Edward, who died in 1546 (TNA C 142/85/18). A third part of this holding was a freehold Wilcoks messuage held by Walter Lexham in *c*.1420 for the annual rent of a capon, the previous tenant having been William Foun or Fowne since *c*.1395 (MS 13129, MS 13132, MS 13134, and MS 13136). By 1480 this was described as ¾ acre, with no reference to a messuage. In 1605 it was held by Richard Beckham, who had married into the Mynnes and had become lord of Cannons manor in 1577 and of Sparhams in 1587. The land was stated as 'being the weste parte of his messe'. Beckham also paid 6d rent for two purprestures 'before his howse'.[xxiii]

On the west of the above lay a small enclosure of Kirkhams and Wilcoks demesne called *Ebotesyerd* in 1434. In 1446–7 it was a pightle called *Mounte Joyes* (MS 13142). Between 1404 and 1416 a rent of 1 capon paid by John Monioye was recorded in Wilcoks messor's account rolls (MS 13129, MS 13132 and MS 13134). By 1420–1 the rent was unpaid because the land (unspecified) was in the lord's hands. In 1605 this was a hempland or parcel of arable containing ½ acre. Next to the west was a Wilcoks freehold messuage held by John Smyth in *c*.1420. The rent of a farthing suggests that the tenant in *c*.1395 may have been John Crudde, although a John Smyth had been a taxpayer in 1379 and 1381. No acreage was given for this property until 1676 when ½ acre was cited (MC 1850/1, 858X9). Eleven freehold acres in *Westfield* (*Quarent.* 2) were associated with this house from *c*.1395 when the tenant of lands once of Thomas Denby, *i.e.* John Crudde, was liable for the rent. Next came another small piece of Kirkhams and Wilcoks demesne, a close called *Mabbesyerd* in 1434. In 1502 it contained ½ rood and was called *le hemplond*. By 1577 it was a garden of ½ acre and in 1605 an enclosed hempland of the same size. Beyond this was a Cannons customary messuage which was first recorded in 1541 as built, with a stable adjoining and 2½ acres. Tenants' names can be taken back to 1507 through various abuttals and a rental (CUL Dd VIII 42). The most westerly house to front on the common in this *Quarent.* was a Wilcoks freehold messuage with 2 acres in the croft in *c*.1420, when it was held by Henry Ram. There is no entry in the rental of *c*.1395 to match this property. In 1427–8 and 1429–30 no rent was received for 1¾ acres on the west side of Henry Ram's messuage because they had been exchanged with the lord for the same amount of land elsewhere (MS 13137 and MS 13138). Presumably land to the side of the property was swapped with land behind it. It may well be the same as the messuage of Alice Suengeden / Swengeden abutted in two charters of *c*.1273–90 (MC 360/29, 713X6 and NRS 12710, 37F4) and with *Swengendenscroft* abutted in a charter of 1333 (MC 360/63,713X6). However, the Sparhams rental of 1385/6 lists a customary holding consisting of 2½ acres with a messuage of the tenement Swingden and lying in a croft called *Swingdons*. Nothing more is known of this Sparhams holding, but the Wilcoks freehold continued as an entity until 1677, after which it was 'lost' amongst the documentation of the Cannons land adjoining on the east.

Colmanscroft butted on the south side of many of the common edge properties listed above. In 1359 William le Strange granted John [Croupius] rector of Little Fransham various lands including 3 acres in *Colmanscroft*. (BL Add Ch 71040). By 1402–3 it was demesne when maslin (wheat and rye) was sown on 5 acres in one piece in *Colmanscroft* (MS 13127). From 1475 the area of this piece remained fairly consistent at 7 acres (MS 13141). One acre of Kirkhams and Wilcoks freehold lay in *Colmanscroft* along the eastern edge. In the late fifteenth century it was held by members of the Maunde family who resided just to the north in the Wilcoks freehold between *Mabbesyerd* and *Ibotesyerd*. Consequently, it was known as *Maundsacre* in the sixteenth century and later. It was specified, though not named, as 1 acre of pasture held of Henry Capel as of his manor of Little Fransham, in the Inquisition Post Mortem of Edward Mynne who died in 1572 (TNA C 142/165/147).

Quarent. 14, Wilcoks in south-west Little Fransham (Fig. 7.39)
Manor house, barn, dovecot and core block demesne, some incorporating former settlements, all edging a large green

All of this *Quarent.* consisted of Wilcoks demesne by the early fourteenth century. A string of three loosely spaced settlement sites (Med 86–8) followed the common edge as it curved round to the south-west (Fig. 7.40). Med 86 and 88 had twelfth-century origins and Med 87 began in the thirteenth. Two were abandoned in the fourteenth century and one (Med 88) in the thirteenth. These sites coincide with three arable closes called *Wilcokks crofts* containing 5½ acres, which were first listed in 1577 (and amounted to 6 acres in 1605). To the south a 24-acre close called *Wilcoks* was edged on the west and south by a common extending to the Necton parish boundary. Med 85, a twelfth to fourteenth-century settlement, sat close to the western edge of *Wilcoks*. Although there were no archaeological indications that this was a site of high status, it is likely to have been the manor house of Wilcoks. A barn, a dovecot and other buildings stood within the close in the first half of the fifteenth century.

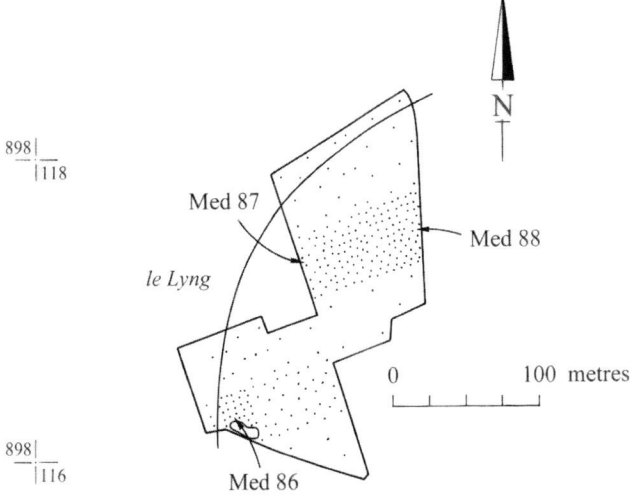

Figure 7.40 Med 86–8 within *Quarentina* 14, distribution of sherds (boundaries taken from Ordnance Survey County Series 1928 edition), scale 1:5,000

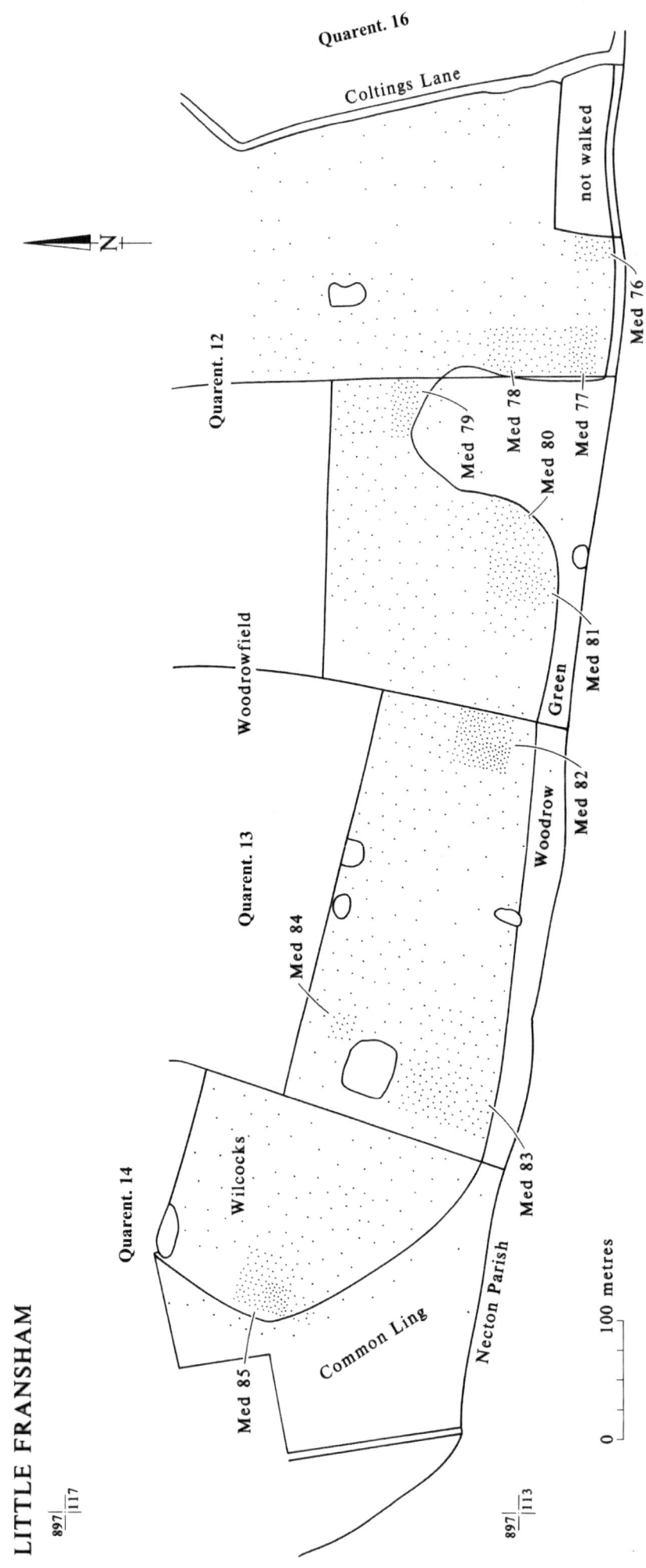

Figure 7.41 Med 76–85 within *Quarentinae* 14 and 15, distribution of sherds (boundaries taken from Ordnance Survey County Series 1928 edition), scale 1:5,000

Quarent. **15,** *Woodrow* **and south of** *Woodrowfield,* **Little Fransham (Fig. 7.39)**
Settlements and tenement blocks flanking a medium green, and one piece of detached block demesne

Almost the whole of this area was taken up with settlement sites (Med 76–84) and their adjoining lands, the sites butting south on a long narrow common following the parish boundary with Necton (Fig. 7.41). South of the common lay Necton Wood.[xxiv] The area will be described from west to east.

Med 83 occupied between the thirteenth and fifteenth centuries, was a 3½-acre Wilcoks freehold tenement called *Braies*, first detectable in *c*.1395. A messuage was mentioned in 1429, but the property was said to be void in 1455. Med 84, a concentration of twelfth and early thirteenth-century sherds representing pottery production, appears to have been a Kirkhams customary holding of a messuage and 3 acres for which there is evidence from 1339. One acre, probably of the same tenement, lay to the south-west. Abuttals of 1443 to the north and west of these two were onto land of the prior of West Acre that was customary land called *Jagges* in 1566 and 1575 (MS 13104). Two acres named *Jaggescroft* were listed amongst lands of the priory in 1427–8 (MS 13137). Possibly there may have been a muddle in 1537 between this piece and 2 acres given the same name in *Quarent.* 16. It seems as though the former West Acre land was no longer recognised by 1605, for both the Kirkhams pieces were said to lie next to Wilcoks on the west and at the north end of a close called *Braies* (i.e. Med 83). To the east another Wilcoks free tenement consisted of 5 acres with a messuage in *c*.1420. Within it lay Med 82, a thirteenth and fourteenth-century site. Near the common edge at a point where it bulged sharply northwards to form *Woodrowgreen*, were two closely spaced sites (Med 80 and 81), both occupied from the thirteenth to the sixteenth century. Med 81 to the west was a Sparhams customary holding, the tenement Godfry in 1385/6, the messuage of which was associated with 6 customary and 2 soiled acres in this *Quarent.*, as well as 5½ acres in *Quarents.* 11, 18 and 27. Med 80 was a Kirkhams customary holding, the tenement of Roger Knot, who was tenant in 1384. There were 2 acres in the croft, and 2¾ acres in two pieces (3 acres by 1605) were associated, lying to the north of Med 81, with the church path running down the west side. Another ½ acre was in *Quarent.* 12. Med 79, a thirteenth to eighteenth-century site, was a Sparhams customary tenement, called Hotche *quondam* [once of] Dagnet in 1385/6 and *quondam* Dagonetts in 1485. There were 1¾ acres in the croft. Half a rood, probably in *Quarent.* 12, lay at *Daginotis croftisend* in 1335. To the north-west lay 4¼ acres of the Kirkhams customary tenement Wylkenson, first recorded in 1384. It butted north on *Woodrowfield*, i.e. *Quarent.* 12. To the south-west were two sites (Med 77 and 78), both of which began in the thirteenth century and continued in occupation throughout the post-medieval period and beyond. Both have been identified as the messuage containing 1¼ acres and the 2-acre croft of the 11-acre Sparhams customary tenement Benedict Heved listed in a rental of 1385/6. South of Med 76 and 77 the common narrowed to a track, described as the common way below *Neketonwode* in 1443. Med 76, which lies immediately adjacent to a small (1.6 acre) piece of non-surveyed non-arable land on the east, had been a freehold in the early fourteenth century, but by 1384 was a Kirkhams customary tenement, held by William Coltyns as a messuage and 1 acre in the croft, and ½ acre with a messuage in the same croft. This double dwelling and its land were surrounded on the east and north by a large block of Kirkhams and Wilcoks demesne called *Coltyngges* in 1418, when it contained 9 acres of oats (MS 13135). In 1482, when *Coltyngs* became copyhold, it was divided into 9 acres in one piece and 1 acre at the north end. In 1502 the latter, called *Buttyacre*, lay north of a common way. *Coltinges* butted north on *Godards* and on 6 acres of demesne in *Quarent.* 12.

Quarent. **16** *The Rode* **(Fig. 7.42)**
Core block demesne including some woodland and an uninhabited manorial centre

This subdivision was used by Hayward in his 1605 survey by default, *i.e.* he employed numbers 15 and 17 but was silent on 16. This omission was the result of the complete absence of Kirkhams and Wilcoks demesne and (by 1605) of tenanted land here, the entire area appertaining to the manor of Cannons. Med 103, isolated in the south-west corner near the north edge of *Coltinges* green, was a twelfth- and early thirteenth-century pottery production site. It may have been occupied by people other than potters further into the thirteenth century. Medieval pot sherds were scattered very thinly over this *Quarent.*

In 1321 William Godefrey son of William Godefrey granted to Thomas de Stowe, rector of Wetheringsett [Suffolk] 8s free rent due out of lands and tenements held by the prior and convent of West Acre in a field called *le Rode* and elsewhere in Little Fransham (MC 360/52, 713X6). The prior of West Acre was distrained to swear fealty to the lord of Kirkhams in 1336. In *c*.1375 the same rent, for *le Rode* and *Lylmannescroft* was due to Kirkhams, as it was in 1384 when the prior's holding was described as 10 acres with a grove, called *Lollemanescroft* and lying in *le Rode*. The piece lay next to Stephen Coltyng's land on the west and butted south on a common way. It almost certainly lay in the south-west corner of the *Quarent.* The same free rent of 8s appears as expenditure for 'divers' lands in Little Fransham paid to Giles Capell knt., lord of Kirkhams, in an early sixteenth-century account roll of the priory (Holkham Hall, Tittleshall Register Rolls 147) and as income in a Kirkhams and Wilcoks rental of 1532/3 (HRO 8186).

In the early fifteenth century up to 1428 Cannons manor was held at farm by the lords of Kirkhams and Wilcoks. In 1412–3 barley grew on 53 acres in *Canonsclos* and in the following year 50 acres in *Canonysrode* were sown with oats (MS 13133). After surviving Cannons manor court records begin in 1541 ten parcels of land totalling 52 acres in *le Rudde* are discernible, all copyhold except 3 free acres called *Fynchesclos*, and a pightle and 4 acres called *Cannons Pightle* which had been demesne and became copyhold in 1542 (and freehold by 1680). One of these ten, the largest at 11 acres, in the centre of the *Quarent.* was called, rather than lay in, *le Rudde*.

Cannons Pightle occupied the north-west corner of the *Quarent.* at the south end of *Cannons Green*. The Enclosure Award map depicts a substantial water-filled ditch on the north and part of the east sides of a rectangular

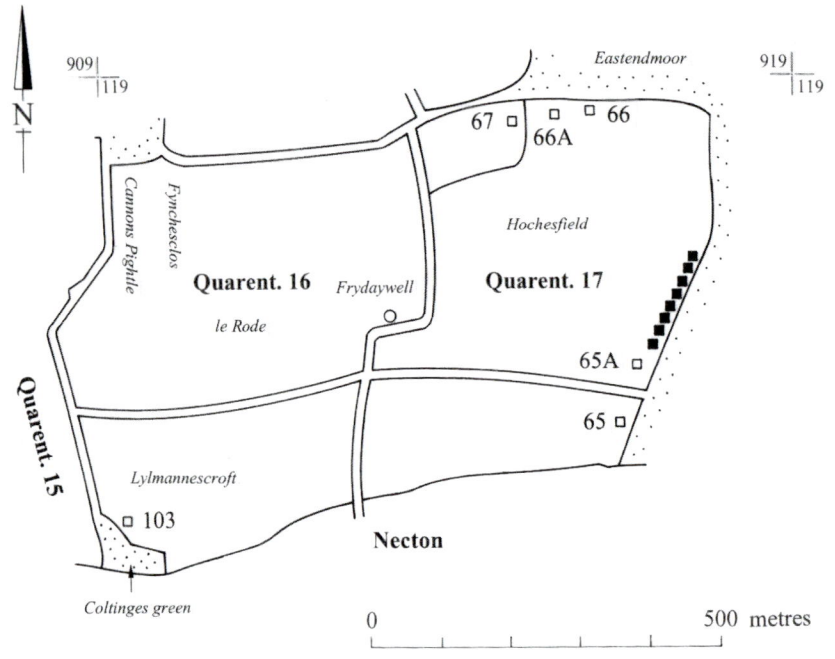

Figure 7.42 *Quarentinae* 16 and 17, Little Fransham, scale 1:10,560

enclosure (Pl. 7.14). At the Tithe Award this was called *Manor Pightle* (DN/TA 168). Traces of wide ditches are still visible in the field on the north, east and south sides. The west side is marked by a kink and a realignment in *Goddards Lane*. The site, measuring *c.*100m north-to-south by *c.*60m east-to-west, has the appearance of a manorial enclosure surrounded by a narrow moat. However, neither medieval building material nor a large number of sherds was recovered during field survey. This suggests that Cannons lands were farmed out to tenants who had no need to reside on the site of the manor farm, although the initial intention of the priory may have been the establishment of a grange, farmed in hand with its buildings protected by a moat.

Plate 7.14 Detail from copy of Enclosure Award map (NRO Ca 1/22), Cannons grange in *Quarent.* 16. The same area on the original map is largely obscured by a crease

Quarent. 17, the southern and western margins of *Eastendmoor*, and *Hochesfield*, Little Fransham (Fig. 7.42)
Settlements and tenement blocks edging a riverside common, and common field

There is now no visible division between this area and *Quarent.* 16. A field called *Hoches* was bordered on the east and north by a common pasture, *Eastendmoor*[xxv]. Most of this field was taken up with land in the crofts of the messuages lining its east and north sides. In the centre, however, there were some small parcels that lay in an open field. From its southern end at the meeting point of West Bradenham, Necton and Little Fransham parishes *Eastendmoor* follows the valley of a northward flowing stream which eventually joins the main stream issuing out of Great Fransham at TF 9263 1256 into Wendling parish. Minor watercourses join *Eastendmoor* from each side, but only that from the west has dictated the shape of the common by producing a pronounced projection. Settlement sites will be described northwards from the Necton boundary and then westwards, after which arrangements within *Hochesfield* will be outlined.

Med 65 (Fig. 7.43), a thirteenth and fourteenth-century site, can be identified as the house of the Kirkhams customary tenement Hoches, first recorded in 1348. The messuage had two acres in the croft. A John Hoche appeared in a court roll of 1347 and survived the Black Death. His ancestors must have given their name to the adjoining field. The tenement Hoche was probably quite old by John's time for it had become very dislocated by 1348, when four tenants held parcels of 1¼, 1 and ¼ acres and 1½ roods. In 1353 John surrendered a messuage and 2 acres and at the same time five other people holding parcels of the tenement were listed, the smallest piece of land being ¼ rood. In 1384 the tenement was held by three people, and divided into a messuage with 3¼ acres, 1¾ acres and ¼ rood. The abuttals of 1443 show that 2 acres

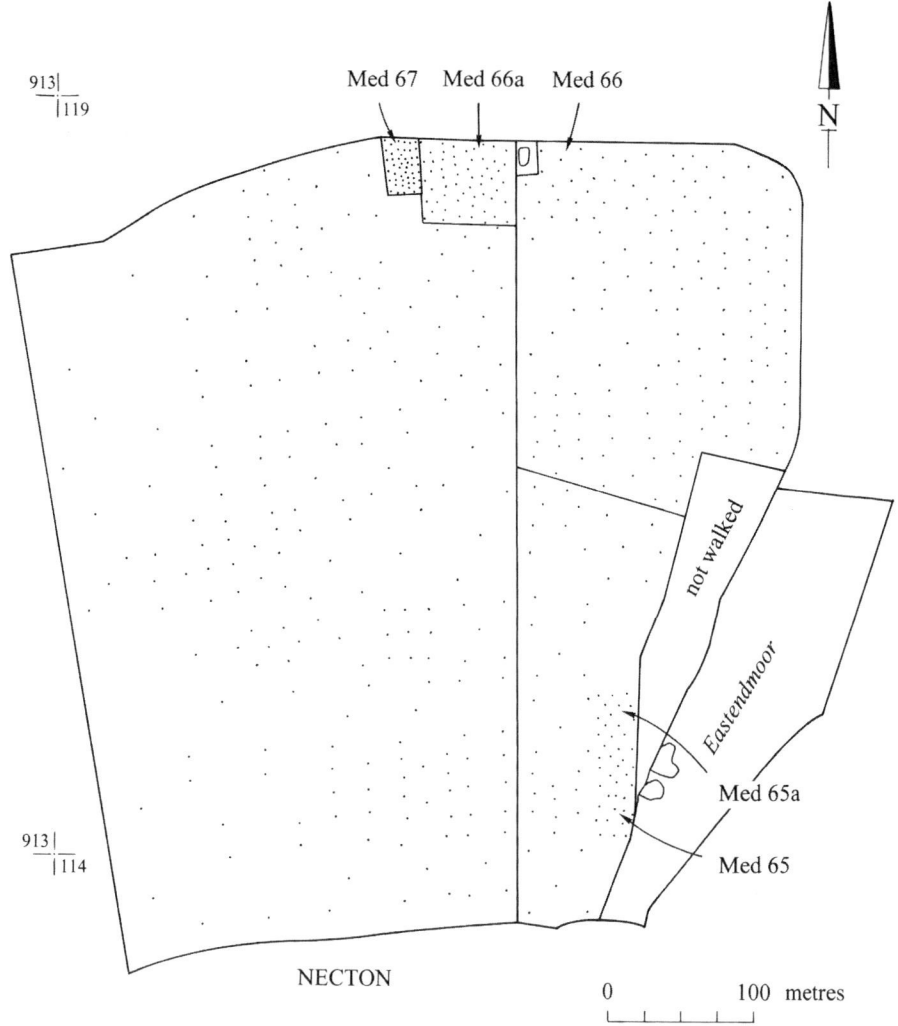

Figure 7.43 Med 65–7 in *Quarentina* 17, distribution of sherds
(boundaries taken from Ordnance Survey County Series 1928 edition), scale 1:5,000

were in the croft, and that other parcels, 1¼, 1 and ¾ acres lay in the field, the ¼ rood having been 'lost'. Med 65A (Fig. 7.43), occupied from the thirteenth to the sixteenth century, was a customary holding of West Bradenham manor, a messuage with a croft containing ½ acre called Bloggs.

To the north of Med 65A a stretch of 140m along the edge of the common was inaccessible, beneath two houses and gardens, and at the north end a large concrete hard-standing. The following eight house sites (numbered **1** to **8** below) are known, therefore, only from the documentary evidence. An average of only 57 feet (3.5 perches, 17.5m) of frontage per messuage is very narrow, compared, for example, with a 75-feet average for tenth to fourteenth-century properties at Caldecote in Hertfordshire (Beresford 2009, 58 and 81). It is not excessively narrow when compared with other sites on the mid-Norfolk clays, for example Thuxton (Butler and Wade-Martins 1989, fig 5). There is also good documentary evidence for very narrow properties on the eastern edge of this common (see *Quarent.* 29).

1. A West Bradenham manor customary holding and a messuage containing ¼ acre with 5½ acres in the croft. Of the 5½ acres in the croft 2 were once of Alexander Nowlys and the rest once of Roger Richers. In 1553 this and Med 65A were said to contain 6 acres when sold by John Nicholls to William Stalworthie of Beeston (Hood, Vores and Allwood, 14/03/1980 Box 56). Abuttals in Kirkhams and Wilcoks documents of 1566 and 1575 show that this was held by John Stalworthy jun., late of John Nicoll (MS 13158 and MS 13104). It was the holding of William Allison in 1605. He, 'dwelling on the Fee of Bradenham at the south end of the comon called Eastendmore', paid 1d for his 'libertie of commonage' to the lord of Kirkhams and Wilcoks according to the 1605 rental, which includes an abuttal describing this holding as a messuage. From 1625 this was held jointly with Med 65A (PD 299/47–54).

2. A freehold of Wilcoks and soiled of Kirkhams manor, this property was listed in the Kirkhams 1384 rental as a messuage and 4 acres in *Estende* and in the Wilcoks rental of *c.*1420 as 3 acres with a messuage. The tenant in 1384, John Whitlok, had been a taxpayer in 1381 (Quytlok). In 1411 it was granted to John Blog (see Med 65A). He was not a Fransham man but a 'blood' villein from another of the lord's manors (*nativus de sang. ut de maner. de Oldhalle in Estderham*). The Kirkhams messuage was associated with 1 acre called *Hevedlond* (*i.e.* headland, Cavill 2018, 186–7), ¾ acre in *Hochisfeld* butting on the king's highway next to *Neketonwode* and another ¾ acre. The Wilcoks messuage had 2½ acres adjoining the croft on the west, 1½ acres and ¼ acre at *Wodebarres*. By 1575 these parcels had been rationalised, by rearrangement and reallocation, into 6 acres of soiled land on the site of the messuage, croft and land to the west, and 1½ acres in two adjoining pieces in *Hochesfield* with a common path on the south (MS 13104).

3. A messuage with 3½ acres in the croft held freely of West Bradenham manor, though mentioned in abuttals of *c*.1420 and later, is absent from the manor court books which begin in 1625 (PD 299/47–54), although it appears as a free rent of 3d in the 1750s (PD 299/59). Tenants' names gleaned from abuttals were Alexander Sewale in *c*.1420, Richard Necoll in 1443, John Nycoll senior in 1502, Thomas Alanson in 1566, Thomas Allison in 1605 and John Allison in 1632. An Alexander Sewale was a taxpayer in the 1379 and 1381. The property was cited as a messuage built with a 3½-acre croft called Nycolls held of the manor of West Bradenham, in the Inquisition Post Mortem of Edward Mynne, who died in 1543 (TNA C 142/70/6). In his will Mynne wrote of his 'mease' purchased from John Nycolles (NCC 188–93 Cooke).

4. A messuage built and 1¼ acres was a Wilcoks customary holding in *c*.1420, associated with ¾ acre in *Quarent*. 26. In *c*.1395 it was held by John Serviant. He had appeared as John Seriaunt in the 1379 Poll Tax and as John Turkeys (an alias) in 1381. In 1400 John Tarkeys died seized of 2 acres with a messuage of the tenement Tarkeys. His sons John (aged 2) and Thomas (aged 3 weeks) were admitted, John paying a heriot of one cow. In 1404–5 an allowance was made in the messor's accounts for a rent of 3d and half a hen due from the tenement late of John Serviant because it had been freed (*manumiss.*) for six years, this year being the last. John Tarkeys was tenant in *c*.1420.

5. This was also a Wilcoks customary tenement consisting of 1¼ acres with a built messuage in *c*.1420. Almost certainly this holding and its neighbour to the south were the result of the subdivision of one property. Their rent was the same, although here three rather than two work days in autumn were required, and the two tenants shared responsibility for discharging the office of messor. Edmund Sawler (alias Edyman), who had been a taxpayer in 1381, was tenant in *c*.1395. He also held Med 106 in *Quarent*. 29. The two adjoining tenements were held as one by 1426 and had a variety of names attached to them in fifteenth-century court rolls, Rudlondes, Bucles and Fylippes.

6. Another Wilcoks customary tenement, 2 acres with a messuage called Brydes and 2 acres in *Quarent*. 29, were held by William Smyth in *c*.1395 and by John Fendours alias Maunfras by *c*.1420. Evidence for partible inheritance comes from the tenement Brydes or Byrdys. In 1400 William Smyth had died and his two sons aged 3 were admitted and then died. Four aunts were heirs, and they were admitted in the following year. Three immediately remitted all rights to one, Christina, who was admitted.

7. Two acres of Wilcoks customary land in one piece called *Peryscroft* were held by the same tenants as no. 3 in 1400 and *c*.1420. There was no reference to a messuage until 1455 when a void messuage was alienated by the tenant, John Maunfras. It may have contained a residence at some earlier stage because the tenant was liable for election as messor and it had a tenement name, Piers in 1400. In the fifteenth century the name was spelt in a great variety of ways: Pers, Petrus, Perters, Persses, Persys, Perys and even Parsones. From 1430 this was held jointly with no.5. In 1550 they were described as a messuage built with 4 acres (MS 13169).

8. The most northerly site consisted of 1.5 acres surrendered by William Blak to the use of Walter Martynet at a Kirkhams court in 1373. He does not appear in the 1379 Poll Tax list, but an Alice Martynet does in the 1381 list. The property was described as 1½ soiled acres with a messuage at *Gernyshil* held by Walter Martinet of Kirkhams manor in 1384, and as 1½ soiled acres held of Wilcoks by John Sevepens in *c*.1420. William Martinet was cited as rent payer in the Wilcoks rental of *c*.1395. A very low annual rent, 1½d, was due to Wilcoks, but none (*sine servic.*) was due to Kirkhams, an arrangement that often occurred in such cases. The land was said to be with a pightle in 1430 and with a messuage in 1431. Interestingly, as late as 1682 this land was described as a pightle or close of soiled land (*pightell vel clausum terra soliat.*) called Blacks (MC 1850/1, 858X9).

The remaining stretch of the western edge of *Eastendmoor* to the north of this compact group of settlements was not built up. It consisted of land of Hempton Priory. This piece occurs in abuttals from *c*.1420 but its size was not stated until 1632 when the will of John Allison, a weaver, gave it as 4½ acres (ANW 346 Sharpe). After a right-angled turn to the west the common edge was similarly devoid of settlement until after *c*.170m where lay Med 66, a Kirkhams and Wilcoks freehold messuage with 2 acres which was not occupied until the fifteenth century (Fig. 7.43). The croft was aligned lengthways along the common edge and reached east to the right-angled corner. The earliest reference was in *c*.1420 when it was named as the messuage of John Tarkeys, presumably the same person who held unfree land to the south. Close to this on the west lay Med 66A, a Wilcoks freehold messuage called *Boteres* in *c*.1420 (Fig. 7.43). By 1430 this was associated with 2½ acres of Kirkhams soiled land lying to the south in *Boterscroft*. Med 67 was the most westerly dwelling of this group and sat at the south side of an entrance into *Eastendmoor* from the west (Fig. 7.43). Occupation began in the thirteenth century on this 3-acre Sparhams customary holding, part of the tenement Jocks, once of Hamond Jocke, which in 1385/6 consisted of 12 acres with a messuage and a cottage. The western part of this site fell within *Quarent*. 16, and was copyhold of Cannons manor.

The tenement Tukele containing 4½ acres was held by John Rodland of Norwich in 1353, and the tenement Tokelys amounted to 5 acres in 1384. There was never any reference to a messuage associated with this Kirkhams customary holding, the tenant of which was nevertheless liable for messor duties. In 1443 the tenement consisted of two pieces, of 2 and 3 acres, and both were well abutted. Two acres lay between land of the tenement Hotches on the east and a common way on the west and butted north on a common path and *Frydaywell*. A good candidate for this pit or pond is a large depression, now ploughed over, at TF 9133 1156. Three acres lay on the south side of the above with the common way on the west and another common way below *Neketone wode* on the south. One other piece of Kirkhams land also butted south on the way by Necton Wood. This was 1 acre of soiled land which had been surrendered by Margaret de Cawston in 1370, and which by 1384 had become part of a customary tenement centred on a messuage in *Quarent*. 27 (Med 71).

Quarent. 18, the south-east part of *Millfield*, Little Fransham (Fig. 7.44)
Settlements, with tenement blocks, edging a riverside common, three several meadows, and common field

North of Med 67 the edge of *Eastendmoor* turned north as a road approached from the west into a typically funnel-shaped common entrance (Rackham 1986b, 141–2). Med 97, lying on the north side of the funnel, consisted of two parts, distinct in tenurial terms but both Sparhams customary holdings (Fig. 7.45). Occupation commenced in the thirteenth century and continued to the nineteenth. The south part comprised a tenement with 2 acres in the croft, parcel of the tenement once of Hamond Jocke (see Med 67). The house was probably the cottage listed in 1385/6. The north part was parcel of 5 acres once of Edmund Jocke in 1385/6. A messuage was first mentioned in 1507. It had 2½ acres in the croft. Land of Edmund Jok in Little Fransham was abutted in a deed of 1361 (MC 360/75, 713X6). Both elements of Med 97 butted west on a north-south road, normally called *le pack way*. Half an acre of meadow was associated with the northern element and lay to the south-west of the croft. One acre of land was also associated and lay somewhere to the north in this *Quarent*.

Med 68 sat close to the north of Med 97 at a point where the edge of *Eastendmoor* curved to the east (Fig. 7.45). It was a Wilcoks freehold messuage with 3 acres in one piece, first definitely recorded in *c*.1420. It probably began life in the thirteenth century, although the actual frontage was not available for fieldwalking and it may therefore have earlier origins. This property also butted west on *le pack way*. The above-mentioned ½ acre of Sparhams customary meadow lay on the west of ¼ acre of the tenement Cristmasse, another Sparhams customary tenement, the messuage of which was in Great Fransham (Area E). The meadow also adjoined two other pieces of meadow. All three were between the ends of the crofts of the two elements of Med 97 and butted on *le pack way*. To the south, 1 acre described in an abuttal of 1443 as the meadow of the prior of West Acre had become copyhold of Cannons manor by the mid-sixteenth century. To the north was 1 acre of Kirkhams demesne land called *le Redmedwe* in an abuttal of 1315 (MC 360/44, 713X6). The prior of West Acre was ordered to repair a ditch there in 1373 and 1374, and pasturage there was let at farm in 1383–4 (MS 13122). By 1384 this had become part of a Kirkhams customary tenement, the messuage of which lay in *Quarent*. 27 (Med 71). The ground here is quite poorly drained to this day and is visible on Fig. 7.45 as a potsherd-free zone.

To the north-east beyond Med 68 lay Med 69 (Fig.7.20), a site where the archaeological and documentary evidence have been the most difficult to reconcile. What appears as one quite convincing pottery concentration (twelfth- to nineteenth-century) has had to be matched with four Kirkhams customary messuages and a Wilcoks freehold messuage, which were listed in the rentals of 1384, *c*.1420 and 1443 and which cannot be

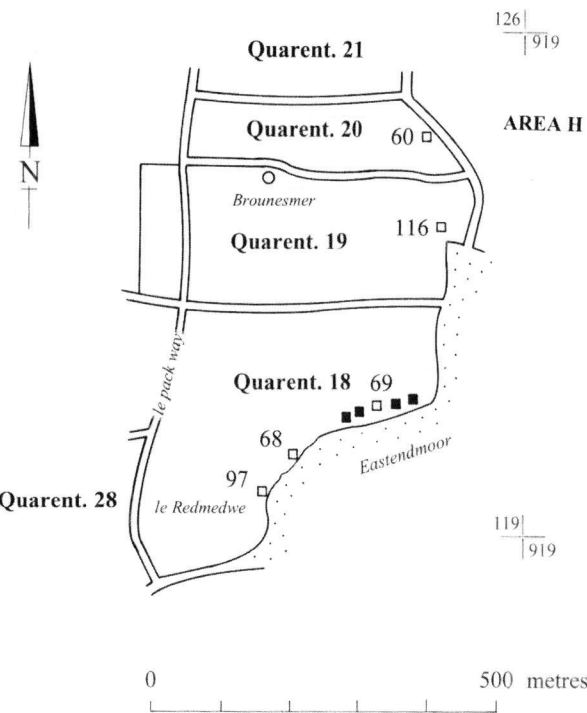

Figure 7.44 *Quarentinae* 18–20, Little Fransham, scale 1:10,560

placed elsewhere with any conviction. A total of 10¼ acres in the crofts of these messuages, appearing under eight separate entries in the 1443 rental, along with several parcels of ¼ and 1 acre, make up much of the remainder of this *Quarent*. By 1605 the situation had been rationalised and the following were listed: two messuages and 1½ acres, an 8-acre close called *the Crofts*, 4 acres enclosed called *Old Close* and a 1½-acre parcel. Six acres of Sparhams customary land, in 'divers' pieces, were probably in this *Quarent*. They were part of a tenement centred on a messuage in *Quarent*. 27 (Med 70). Two

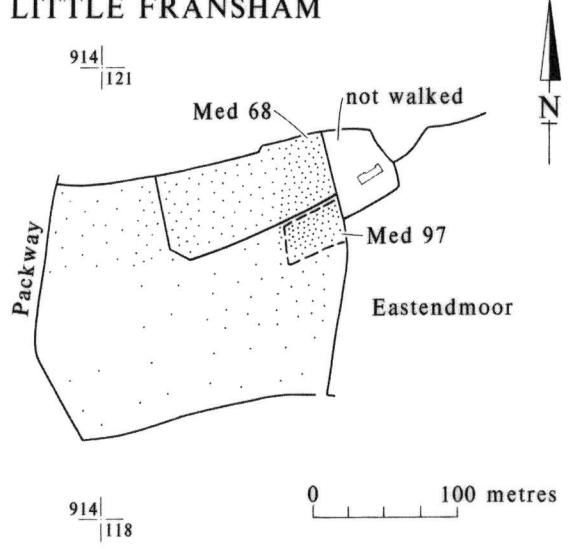

Figure 7.45 Med 68 and 97 within *Quarentina* 18, distribution of sherds (boundaries taken from Ordnance Survey County Series 1928 edition), scale 1:5,000

153

acres of the Sparhams customary tenement Godfry, centred on Med 81 in *Quarent.* 15, lay in the same area. Finally, a 1½-acre piece of Kirkhams and Wilcoks freehold was said in a charter of 1478 to have been conveyed in 1465. It lay in the *Northfeld* between lands of John Maunde and butted west on Kirkhams and Wilcox demesne (MC 3115/1/1, 1037X4). In 1502, it was between the same lands on the west side of *the Crofts* and butted west on the *le pack way.*

Quarent. 19, south central part of eastern *Millfield*, Little Fransham (Fig. 7.44)
Common field, one piece of detached block demesne, one settlement edging a riverside common

This area was separated from *Quarent.* 18 to the south by an east-west church path. The west end lay on the west side of *le pack way* which divided 5 acres of Kirkhams and Wilcoks demesne into two equal parts. These are probably the same as 6 acres in *le Myllefurlond* held at farm in 1451. To the east of the *pack way* four pieces were aligned north-south: 1½ acres freehold of Ellinghams manor; 1¼-acre freehold of uncertain manorial allegiance identified in a document of *c.*1555 and described in a release of 1678 as containing a pit called *Brenchmere pitt* and butting south on the church path (MC 3115/1/6, 1037X4); ¾ acre of Sparhams customary land, part of the tenement Cristmasse, the messuage of which lay in Great Fransham (Area E); a 1¼ acre Kirkhams customary land lying next to *Brounesmer* and part of a tenement associated with Med 71 in *Quarent.* 27. *Brounesmer* in 1384, *Brownesmerpytt* in 1502 is probably a ploughed over depression at TF 9155 1242. An otherwise unidentified freehold acre was said to lie on the north side of *Brounismere Pytt* in *c.*1555. East again were two pieces of Kirkhams customary land (¾ and ½ acre) running east-west and below them two more (½ and 2 acres) aligned north-south. In 1605 two Kirkhams customary pieces, both associated with Med 69, lay to the south-east, *Hirnclose* containing 7½ acres and 1½ acres of woodland called *the Grove.*

The east end of this *Quarent.* contained a messuage which, although of considerable size by the late sixteenth century, has proved very difficult to identify in terms of tenure and manorial allegiance. It may possibly have been a freehold of Great Fransham manor. Only two medieval sherds have been found on the premises, now known as Willow Farm, all of which is built up or grassland, but in view of the lengthy and obscure documentary evidence that has led to the identification, the site has been designated as Med 116 (Pl. 7.15).

Quarent. 20, north central part of eastern *Millfield*, Little Fransham (Fig.7.44)
Common field and one isolated settlement

A way ran east to west across the north side of this area. The most northerly piece was an east-west piece ¾ acre of Kirkhams customary land described as in the *Lound* in 1443 and on the south side of it in *c.*1555. Three pieces butted west on *le pack way*. On the north lay ¾ acre of Little Fransham glebe, then Kirkhams customary ½ acre associated with a messuage in *Quarent.* 5 and located in *Estmyllefeld* in 1443, and on the south a ½-acre parcel of 5 acres of Sparhams customary land once of Edmund Jocke (see Med 97 in *Quarent.* 18). To the east of these were another ½ acre of Sparhams customary land and possibly 1 acre of Great Fransham freehold held by John Ede and his wife in *c.*1400. Various abuttals indicate that some parcels of unidentified land, probably all freehold and most, if not all, held by tenants of Med 116 in the post-medieval period, lay in the eastern part of this *Quarent.* They must have amounted to *c.*5½ acres. Two such pieces are listed in a release of 1678, 1½ acres butting north on the *Lound* (in *Quarent.* 21) and, immediately to the west, 1 acre aligned east-west (MC 3115/1/6, 1037X4). Within this poorly documented area, LS 16 / Med 60, an eleventh- and twelfth-century site, sits astride the parish boundary and partly in Area H (Fig. 7.20).

Quarent. 21, the northern part of eastern *Millfield* (Fig. 7.46)
Detached tenement blocks

The southern part was occupied by a 7-acre close of Wilcoks freehold, the most fully documented piece of uninhabited free land in Little Fransham. A charter of *c.*1273–90 recorded the grant by Robert son of John the reeve of Little Fransham to William de Sappe of three rents: 1d, one autumn work day and one hen owed by Robert's sister for a part of the land known as *le Lund*, 1d paid by Robert Nel for a part of *le Lund* and ½d paid by Ralph Hoyp for 1 rood in the field of Little Fransham (MC 360/27, 713X6). *Lund* is indicative of a small wood or grove (Smith 1956b, 27–8). William Greenhood of Great Fransham, who held Med 53, was tenant in *c.*1395 and *c.*1420. In 1490 *Lound* in *Millefeld* contained 7¼ acres of which 1 rood lay in Great Fransham. In 1502 3 acres lay in *le Short Lownd* to the west of 4 acres in *le Long Lownd*, and ¼ acre [at the east end] butted east on land of the abbot of Wendling. The annual rent remained consistently at 1d between *c.*1395 and 1600 (MS 13148). By 1605 it had increased to 1½d and the area had decreased to 7 acres. The most elaborate abuttals occur in a release of 1678 (University of Chicago Library, Norfolk Collection of Misc. English Deeds Box III Folder 20). On the north side of the *Lound* a 4-acre piece of Kirkhams customary land was aligned east-to-west. Its tenurial history begins somewhat tenuously in 1347, and it was said to be both in *le Lounde* and called *le Lounde*. It was usually held jointly with a 5-acre piece of Kirkhams customary land to the north, most of which lay within Great Fransham. This was aligned north-to-south and Med 58 sat at its north end. It was called *Fyweacrys* in the early fourteenth century (see Area H). Some unidentified land lay to the west of this piece, and to the west of that a rectangular piece of Great Fransham parish (in Area G) projected south from *Odeslane*. One element in this unidentified land may have been 1¾ Kirkhams customary acres said in 1384 to lie in *Northfeld* and to be of the tenement of Godfrey de Hokerynge. The piece was termed soiled in 1392 and detailed abuttals of 1443 show that it was aligned north-to-south. Its tenurial history ends in *c.*1487.

Quarent. 22, the northern end of western *Millfield*, Little Fransham (Fig. 7.46)
Common field

In the north-east corner 1½ acres of Great Fransham demesne butted north on the king's highway leading from

Plate 7.15 Looking north-east from the Pack Way across *Quarent.* 19 towards Med 116

Wendling to Great Fransham church. Next to the west ½ acre butted north on *Odeslane*. In the Kirkhams rental of 1384 this was described as soiled, and in *c*.1420 it was said to be free of Wilcoks and soiled of Kirkhams. To the south lay ½ acre of the Sparhams customary tenement Cristmasse and to the west ½ acre of Great Fransham demesne that also butted north on *Odeslane.* The north-west corner was taken up with ½ acre of Kirkhams and Wilcoks demesne. In 1409 when granted out as part of a customary tenement, it was described as lying below *Mylclose* and butting north on the common way leading from Dereham to Swaffham. It lay next to *le Wyndemyllecote* in 1447 when it was leased at farm, and at *le Mill close corner* in 1484 (MS 13162). One Wilcoks customary acre about which there is no tenurial information later than *c*.1420 may also have been in this *Quarent.* A fragment of a thirteenth-century seal matrix was found in the south-east corner of this area.[xxvi]

Quarent. 23, north-west part of western *Millfield*, Little Fransham (Fig. 7.46)
Common field

All parcels were aligned north-to-south. Two acres of Kirkhams and Wilcoks demesne in the south-west corner butted north on ½ acre of the same demesne. The latter lay at *Myllehill* when granted at farm in 1476 (MS 13141) and was 'grassgrounde lyinge at waste' in 1605 when 'the way lieth upon it'. To the east ¼ acre of the Sparhams customary tenement Cristmasse butted north with a pit (*cum uno le pytte*) on the king's highway, and it lay next to another Sparhams piece, ½ acre once of Edmund Jocke (Med 97). East of the 2 acres of demesne, ½ acre of the tenement Cristmasse may or may not have extended north to the road. The next piece certainly did, 1½ acres of Kirkhams and Wilcoks freehold that was not recorded until 1502. It was listed in a release of 1678 and lay on the east side of a 2-acre piece of freehold that remains unidentified (MC 3115/1/6, 1037X4). Abuttals suggest that in the central part of this *Quarent.*, apart from 1 acre of Sparhams customary land once of Edmund Jocke (Med 97), there were one or two other small, probably freehold parcels. One such ½-acre piece was associated with Med 116 and in *c*.1555 it was said to butt north on *St Katerines Gappe*, a toponym not noted in other sources. To the east lay 1 acre of Kirkhams customary land associated with Med 71 (*Quarent.* 27). It was in two parts but held by the same tenant in 1384. By 1502 it was temporarily in the lord's hands and was called *Sokelyngacr.* Next to this, 1 acre of Cannons customary land marked the eastern edge of this *Quarent.*

Quarent. 24, *Great Millclose* and *Rawen* meadow, Little Fransham (Fig. 7.46)
Core block demesne with a windmill and a demesne meadow

This area consisted entirely of Kirkhams demesne, an 18-acre enclosure called *Great Milclose* and to the west a 7-acre meadow called *Rawen*.

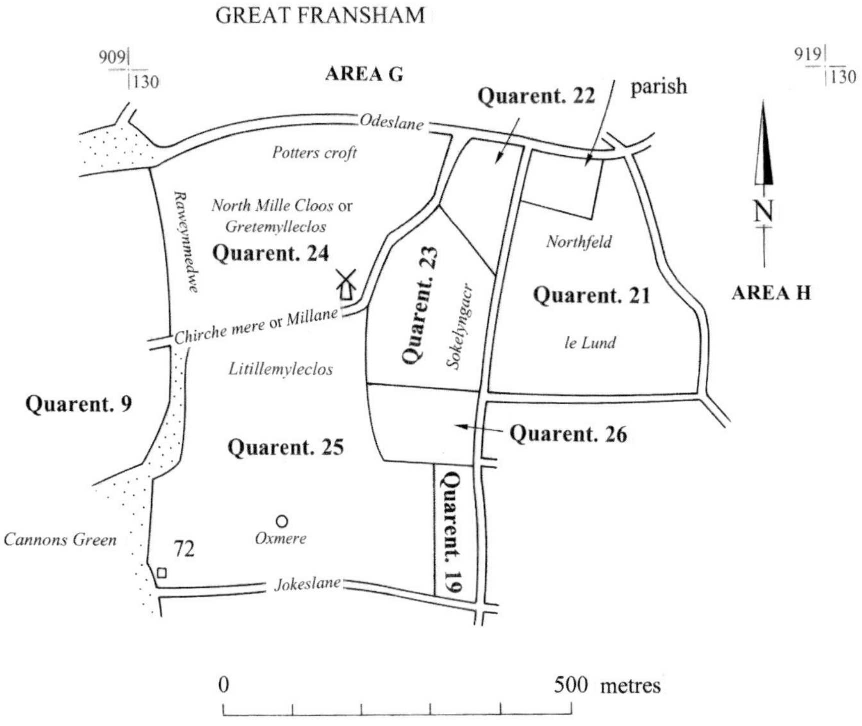

Figure 7.46 *Quarentinae* 21–26 and the west end of 19, Little Fransham, scale 1:10,560

According to the 1605 survey a mill hill stood at the south-east corner of *Great Milclose*. No trace of this survives. The northern edge was followed by *Odeslane* and the southern and eastern by *Chirche mere* or *Millane*. No evidence of medieval domestic occupation was recovered in the survey, but LS 20, a Late Saxon pottery production site, covered much of the close. It is possible that 5 acres in one piece in the croft called *Potters croft* on the north next to *Kyngesway*, for which Emma le Strange lady of Kirkhams manor paid a free rent to Sparhams manor in 1385/6, lay in *Great Milclose*. If this is the case then *Kyngesway* can be equated with *Odeslane*, often called the king's highway.

Bailiff's account rolls show that a windmill functioned between 1373 and 1430. In 1373–4 sixteen quarters of wheat were received from the Kirkhams mill, and 8s 11½d were spent on various repairs to the mill-house: *le Garyte* was made, an iron key bought, the tower (*bert[achia]*) roofed, a sail-yard made, and twenty-four hurdles (*clat.*) were bought for the fold (*fald.*) (MS 13121). Six quarters and four bushels of grain were received as farm rent for the mill in 1394–5 (MS 13124). John Maunfras jun. and Adam Webster were amerced at a Kirkhams manor court in 1394 because their cows had damaged wheat at the lord's mill.

In 1400–1 one quarter and four bushels of oats were handed to John Base for sowing on a piece of land next to the lord's mill. In the same year three quarters and five bushels of oats, and one bushel of wheat, were received by the bailiff from the miller (MS 13126). Twenty-five shillings and 9d were paid by the miller, Thomas Yool, directly to the lord in 1402–3. In the same year 17¼ acres were sown (crop type unknown, margin missing) at *Milleclos*, and ploughing took place in *le Milneclos* (MS 13127). In 1413–4 twenty acres in *le Mylleclos* were sown with oats (MS 13133). In 1417–8 and 1427–8 a farm rent of 26s 8d for the windmill was received from Roger Grene (MS 13135 and 13137), and 23s 4d were received in 1429–30, when 16d were expended on mending the sails and 5d on buying a lock and key for the store-house (MS 13138). John, servant of William Crudde, stole *chyppes* (?beams) from the building (*domus*) called *Mille Cote* in 1429.

No rent was received in 1431–2 and 1432–3 because one millstone was broken and other repairs were needed (HRO 8185 and MS 13096). The situation had not improved by 1436–7 (MS 13139) and in the next year the mill was totally in decay (MS 13037). The mill's life was certainly at an end by 1438–9, when 3s was expended on the carting of a millstone from Little Fransham to Hempstead (HRO 8179). The latest surviving bailiff's account roll, for 1442–3, recorded that the recent rent of 23s 4d was not received because the mill was totally in decay and devastated (MS 13140).

In 1450 the close north of *Chirche mere* or *Millane*, differentiated for the first time from that to the south, was called *North Mille Cloos*, and in 1454 it became *Gretemylleclos*.

The *Rawen* meadow occupied a valley on the west side of *Great Milclose* and ran north from the point at which *Millane* entered a tongue of common, down to the Great Fransham parish boundary where it butted a meadow with the same name. The earliest record is of 1417–8 when six men were paid 1s for half-a-day's mowing of 4 acres in *Raweynmedwe* (MS 13135). It was said to contain 8 acres in 1446–7 (MS 13142) and 7 acres in 1502. Probably in the 1480s, and certainly by 1502, the *Rawen* had become copyhold and remained so thereafter.

***Quarent*. 25, *Little Millclose* and the northern part of western *Millfield*, Little Fransham (Fig. 7.46)**
Core block demesne, common field and one piece of detached block demesne containing a settlement

The western edges of this area and of *Quarents*. 27 and 28 consisted of *Cannons Grene* and were followed by a minor north-flowing watercourse and *Jokeslane*, a roadway first named in 1392.

Little Milclose lay to the south of *Millane*[xxvii], and stretched eastwards from *Cannons Green* in the west to a furlong in *Millfield* (*Quarent*. 26). In 1402–3 barley was grown on 6 acres of Kirkhams and Wilcoks demesne in *le Milleclos* (MS 13127). These must have been in *Little Milclose* because 17¼ acres, almost the full area of its larger neighbour to the north, were also cropped that year (see *Quarent*. 24). This piece contained 10 acres and was named *Litillemylleclos* in 1447 when granted out at farm. It was called *Parva Millecloos* in 1476 (MS 13141). In 1502 when its size was still given as 10 acres it was the 'other field' (*alium campum*), as opposed to its larger neighbour, and was named *Litilmelfeld*. In 1605 it had reduced to 8 acres, with William Hayward's measured survey arriving at a figure of 9 acres and 30 perches.

Flanking the south side of *Little Milclose* were 3 acres of Cannons copyhold at *Oxmere*, whose tenurial history can be traced from 1535. Half of this land, 1½ acres at *Oxmere*, was entered in bailiff's accounts in 1427–30 when Cannons manor was held at farm by the lord of Kirkhams and Wilcoks (MS 13137 and MS 13138). In 1552 on the south side of the above (which was said to be enclosed) ¾ acre of Northendhall or Guntons demesne lay in *Oxmerecloos* on the north side of glebe land in the same close (TNA SC 12/3/23). The glebe consisted of ¼ acre in a close called *Oxmere* butting west on the common pasture, and butting on it from the west was a ¾-acre piece in the same close. To the south lay 8 acres of Kirkhams and Wilcoks demesne called *Oxmeare* in 1605. Lying east-west, they butted west on the common, *Cannons Green*, and were divided into two parcels, 4¼ acres on the west which were called *Nethiroxmer* in 1502, and 3¾ acres on the east called *Overoxmer*. Med 72, a twelfth and thirteenth-century site, lay at the west end of the former where there was a parcel of meadow in 1605. On the east side of *Overoxmer* 1½ acres of Kirkhams and Wilcoks demesne were aligned north-south. When all three pieces were held at farm in 1476 they were said to be at *Oxmer*. They were newly enclosed in 1577. To the east of the 1½ acres of demesne lay ¾ acre of glebe, also aligned north-south, beyond which were the 2½ acres of demesne lying west of *le pack way* but in *Quarent*. 19. A *church path* ran along the southern boundary of this *Quarent*.

A late thirteenth-century charter records the grant of ¼ acre aligned east-west next to glebe land in the field of Little Fransham at *Oxmere*, by William the chaplain, son of Ralph son of Henry, of Little Fransham, to Hubert son of Hugh of Castle Acre (MC 360/37, 713X6). In 1325 Alice daughter of John Norman quitclaimed all rights in one piece of land in Little Fransham called *Oxmerewonges* to William son of Henry le Strange of Little Fransham (MC 360/56, 713X6). Geoffrey Sewale granted various lands in Little Fransham to Walter de Schortwode chaplain in 1351. These included 1½ acres in *Estfeld* at *Oxemere* (MC 360/73, 713X6). In May 1373 the lord of Kirkhams granted to Simon Elyot for life rights of pasture of a pit at *Oxmere* with *le Groop* (ditch) there for an annual rent of six pullets. Elyot was amerced, in August of the same year, for damaging the lord's peas and beans at *Oxmerewong*. In October John Wilps had made an illegal way over the demesne at the same place. In 1378 the lord's rye growing in *Oxmere* had been damaged. The pit which gave its name to this area can with reasonable confidence be located at TF 9113 1235. Here a large (50m diameter) depression, now ploughed over apart from a small central pit, is crossed by an east-west hedge. The boundary, but not the pit, is depicted on the Enclosure map.

***Quarent*. 26, within the northern part of western *Millfield*, Little Fransham (Fig. 7.46)**
Common field

This small furlong, aligned east-west, lay between *le pack way* and the eastern ends of *Little Milclose* and the Cannons customary 3 acres in *Quarent*. 25. Seven parcels of land are listed from north to south: two pieces of Kirkhams and Wilcoks demesne, 1½ acres on the north, 'being a headland' in 1605, and ½ acre; a piece of unidentified size and tenure held in 1605 by the tenant of Med 116; ¾ acre of Wilcoks customary land associated with property no.3 on the western edge of *Eastendmoor* in *Quarent*. 17; ½ acre of Sparhams customary land parcel of 5 acres once of Edmund Jocke (Med 97); another piece of unidentified size and tenure held by tenants of Med 116 in the sixteenth and seventeenth centuries; ¾ acre associated with Med 69 until 1599 (SRO E3/10/9.16). This last parcel was butted on the south by demesne land at the west end of *Quarent*. 19 and by a 1½-acre piece in the south-east of *Quarent*. 25.

***Quarent*. 27, central part of western *Millfield*, Little Fransham (Fig. 7.47)**
Two settlements, with tenement blocks, edging a riverside common, and one piece of detached block demesne

This *Quarent*. did not extend east as far as *le pack way*. A pair of medieval sites sat next to the eastern edge of *Cannons Green*. On the south side of the *church path* was Med 71, a Kirkhams customary holding on a site first occupied in the twelfth century. There were 4 acres in the croft. The property is still occupied. On the south side of this property lay Med 70, a Sparhams customary tenement, once of Hugh Cappe in 1385/6. This was first occupied in the thirteenth century and abandoned in the nineteenth. There were 4 acres in the croft.

Next came a 4-acre piece of Wilcoks demesne called *Balepeece* in 1605 when it was divided into two pieces, enclosed pasture to the west and 'feilde grounde' in the east. William Hayward's survey measured these at almost 5 acres (1¾ acres and 3 acres 35 perches). Until the 1480s this land was called *Bathescroft* or *Bathe*. In 1402–3 peas were sown at *Bathescroft* (MS 13127) and in 1404 the lord of Wilcoks' barley growing in *Bathe* was damaged by animals. In 1476 John Maunde junior (also known as de la Chekir) held at farm 7 acres at *Bathe* and two other pieces for an annual rent of 4s 1d (MS 13141). In 1484 John att Checker held at farm 7 acres at *Bale* with the same other lands for the same rent (MS 13162). Thereafter *Bale* or variants thereof was the name. Sometime before 1273 John of Little Fransham, son of Roger le Strange, granted to his son Henry a villein named Hugh with all his possessions, 2½ acres and a piece (*peciam*) of land held by John de Bathe. This lay between lands of Bartholomew Fingh and Hugh Cappe (*cf.* Med 70) and butted west on the common pasture (MC 360/6, 713X6). In 1326 Henry le Strange of Little Fransham instructed Bartholomew Anyel of the same place, by letter of attorney, to deliver possession of a piece called *Bathelond* and of another piece (in *Quarent.* 29) to his, Henry's, son Geoffrey (MC 360/57, 713X6). In 1385/6 John Croupius, rector of Little Fransham, held freely of Sparhams manor, 1 acre once of William le Strange lying in the croft of *Baths*.

The south edge of this *Quarent* was followed by a path known as *Jekkespath* in 1502 and *Jecks mere* in 1577. It was also often called a *church path*. Between it and *Baths*, a 3-acre piece of Sparhams customary land ran east from the common edge as far as *le pack way*, i.e. it passed through into *Quarent.* 28. This was a constituent of the tenement Godfry, the messuage of which was in *Quarent.* 15 (Med 81). Abuttals from 1599 onwards stated that this piece ran for the length of two furlongs (*quarentinae*).

Quarent. 28, the southern end of western *Millfield*, Little Fransham (Fig. 7.47)

Detached block demesne in two pieces, one containing a riverside common edge settlement, a small piece of demesne woodland, and common field

This *Quarent.* was L-shaped, crossing north over *Jekkespath* and wrapping around the eastern end of *Quarent.* 27. In the north-east corner within the junction of the *church path* and *le pack way* lay 3 acres of Kirkhams and Wilcoks demesne. Aligned east-west this piece was first recorded in 1446–7 when it was held by Henry Warde, the tenant of Med 71, and it lay at the end of his croft (MS 13142). South of this were 2 acres of the Sparhams customary tenement once of Hamond Jocke (Med 67 and 97), and south again were 2½ acres of Wilcoks freehold which were not entered in the rental of *c.*1420 and were first recorded in a Kirkhams rental of *c.*1487. This piece butted west on *Balepiece* and east on *le pack way*. On the south side of this lay a piece of Hempton Priory land known only from abuttals. Its acreage is unrecorded, but it was probably very small. Next came the eastern part of the long Sparhams 3-acre piece, already noted under *Quarent.* 27.

Seven acres of Kirkhams and Wilcoks demesne, called *Jeckespeece* in 1605, ran the full length of this *Quarent.* along the south side of *Jekkespath* from *Cannons Green* to *le pack way*. In 1402–3 peas were grown in *Jekkes* (MS 13127). In the north-west corner was *Jeckesgrove* which contained ¾ acre and was first named in 1429, and to the south of it lay a 'small parcel' of 20 perches recorded only in 1605. Med 92, which was occupied in the thirteenth and fourteenth centuries, probably lay within *Jeckesgrove* while a small Late Saxon site (LS 19) a little further to the east was within *Jeckespeece*. South of the demesne all four parcels of land stretched the full length of the *Quarent.* They are listed from north to south.: a Sparhams customary ½ acre of the tenement Benedict Heved (Med 77 and 78); a Kirkhams customary ½ acre associated with Med 71 and called *Wrenglond* in 1384; a 3-acre Sparhams customary piece, once of Hamond Jocke (Med 67 and 97), known as *le Long closse* by 1577; 1¼ acres of Sparhams customary land, possibly of the tenement Hastings. This last piece lay next to the common path and the common

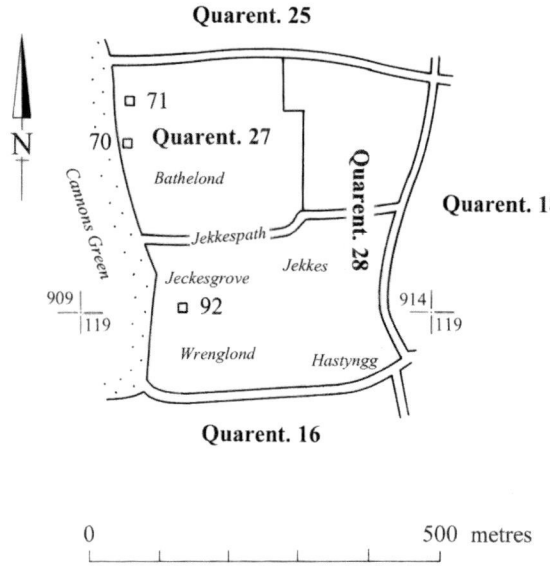

Figure 7.47 *Quarentinae* 27 and 28, Little Fransham, scale 1:10560

pasture on the south, the common pasture presumably being a narrow tongue emanating from the western extension of *Eastendmoor*. In 1385/6 the tenement Hastings had contained 4 acres. Its name is found in amercements at several courts leet: a watercourse at *Hastyngg* in 1394–5 and at *Hastyngesdych* in 1407, a close called *Hastynges* in 1440, a watercourse at *Hastyngeslane* in 1445 and an illegal clay pit on the common at *Hastynggsclosse* in 1492. The 1¼-acre piece in this *Quarent.* was never ascribed to the tenement Hastings and is not noted in manor court proceedings until 1598. Land of the tenement, variously estimated at 2½, 2 and 3 acres, was conveyed on three occasions in 1507, 1520 and 1527. So, this identification remains dubious and the fate of the remaining 2¾ acres is unknown.

Quarent. 29, *Eastfield* and the eastern edge of *Eastendmoor*, Little Fransham (Fig. 7.48)

Numerous settlements, some closely packed, with tenement blocks, all edging a riverside common, common field, and detached tenement blocks

Firstly, settlements along the eastern side of *Eastendmoor* will be described from south to north, and this will be followed by a description of *Eastfield*. Med 64 was occupied in the thirteenth and fourteenth centuries (Fig. 7.49). It sat almost on the West Bradenham parish boundary within a 3-acre piece of the Sparhams customary tenement once of Hamond Jocke (see Med 67 and 97)[xxviii]. North of Med 64 a sunken way and modern road, called *Maryoneselane* in 1392, runs west onto *Eastendmoor*. On the north side of the road two thirteenth and fourteenth-century sites partly survive as slight earthworks (Fig. 7.50). Med 105 was a Kirkhams customary tenement of a cottage with 1 acre in 1384 when it was held by Marion Soutere, whose name may have been given to the adjacent lane. In *c.*1420 it was listed as freehold of Wilcoks and soiled of Kirkhams. In 1439 the tenant, Walter at Brook, was amerced for blocking the common watercourse at *Maryonesfaldgate* with an ash

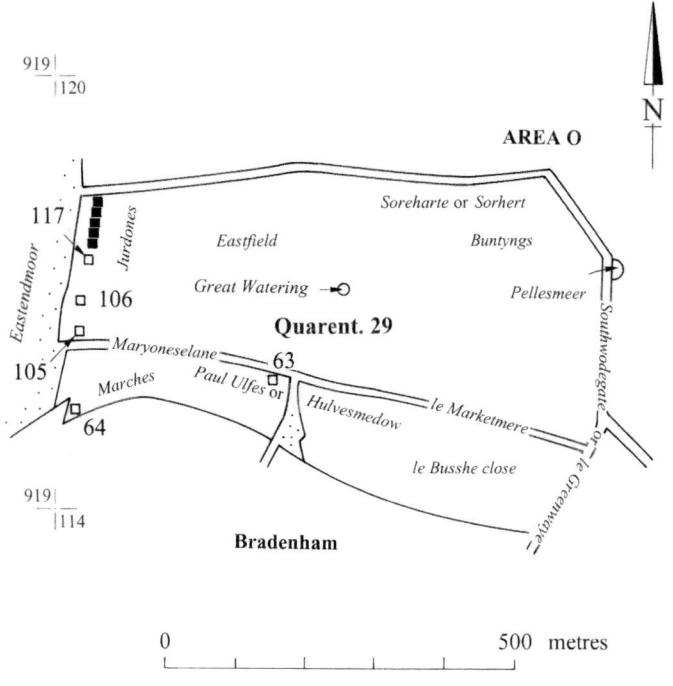

Figure 7.48 *Quarentina* 29, Little Fransham, scale 1:10,560

tree. Med 106, a Wilcoks freehold messuage with 1½ acres, was said to be no longer standing in *c*.1420. North of this a ditched and wooded enclosure marks the site of Med 117, another messuage held freely of Wilcoks and soiled of Kirkhams, which was said to be void in *c*.1420. The remaining 80m length of the common edge within Little Fransham is covered with grass and buildings. The following properties appear to have been contained therein, the first five being Kirkhams customary holdings.

1. A messuage and 2 acres of the tenement Kirkham, lying at *Jurdones* and held by Margaret Smyth in 1384. This land was held by Walter Pouly in 1443. After *c*.1460 (MS 13144) it was not distinguished as an individual property.

2. A messuage and 2 acres of the tenement Sparhamhalle, held by Margaret Smyth in 1384 for a *de increment*. rent of one farthing. It was called *Smythyecroft* and lay next to *Chirchemer*, presumably a path, on the north. This is the same as 2 acres with a cottage, freehold of Sparhams manor, held by John Powly in 1385/6 for two autumn work days and a hen. It was of the tenement Dunninge once of William Jordan and was called *Smythiecroft*. Walter Powley held it of Kirkhams as soiled land in 1443, but it is not discernible in rentals after *c*.1460 (MS 13144). The property was mentioned only once in Sparhams court proceedings: in 1487, after the death of the tenant, an inquiry was ordered into whether the tenure was customary or soiled. The matter was not reported back to the court.

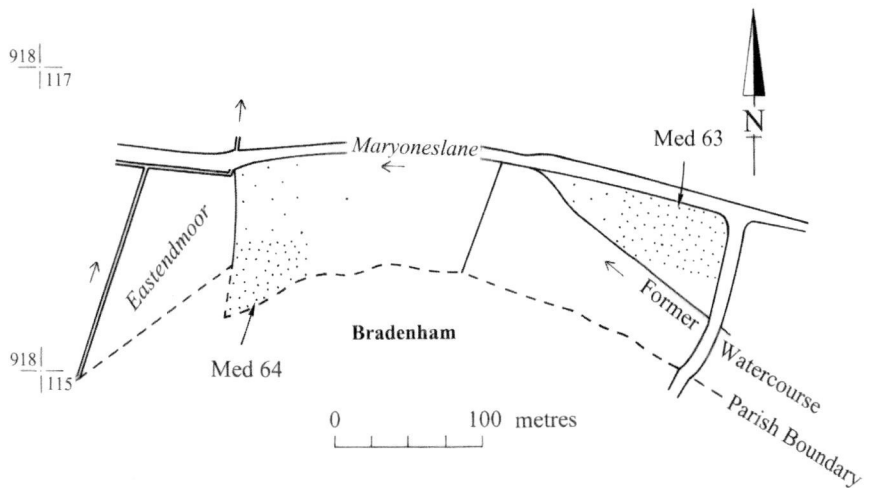

Figure 7.49 Med 63 and 64 within *Quarentina* 29, distribution of sherds (boundaries taken from Ordnance Survey County Series 1928 edition), scale 1:5,000

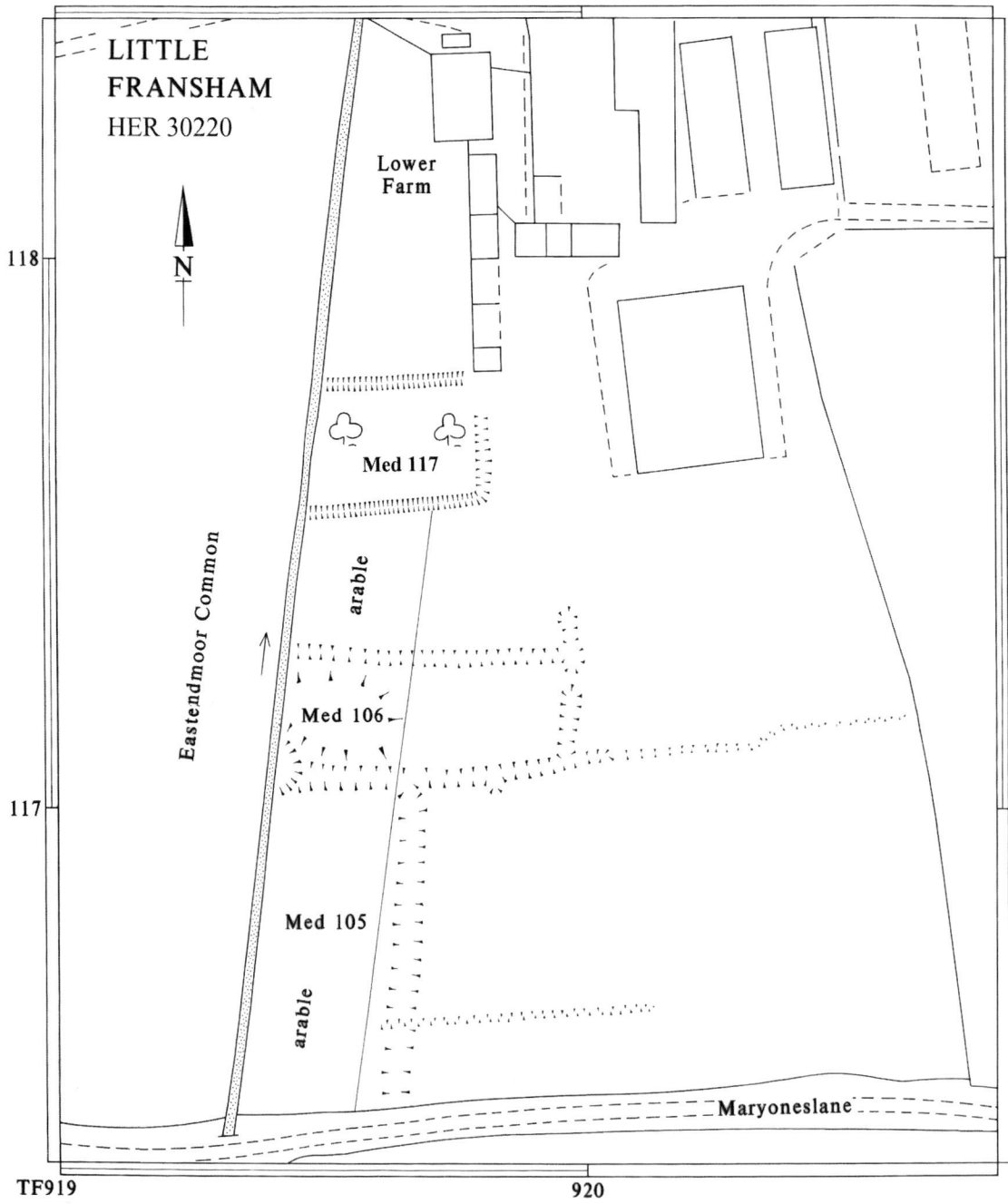

Figure 7.50 Med 105–6 and 117 earthworks, within *Quarentina* 29, scale 1:1,250

3. A messuage and ¼ acre of the tenement Renggis held by Adam Ryngolfs was entered in 1391, or slightly later, as an addition to the 1384 rental. The tenement Renggis consisted of six elements in 1384, comprising a messuage, a parcel of a messuage and 10½ acres. Henry Renge, the first of that name, appeared in a court roll of 1351. His lands were seized by the lord in 1355, and thereafter neither he nor any other Renge was mentioned. The tenement name was last used, in the context of a messor election, in 1493.

In 1395 this property was described as a cottage of the tenement Renges but was not individually distinguished thereafter. Adam Ryngolde held land in Great Fransham (Area H). He (Ryngolf) was a Little Fransham taxpayer in 1379 and 1381.

4. A parcel of a messuage of the tenement Renggis once of Nicholas Jurdan and held by Adam Ryngolfs was entered as an addition to the 1384 rental. A parcel of a messuage at *Jordonys*, measuring 10 perches in length and 1 perch 8 feet in width, had been conveyed by Thomas Pouly to Adam Ryngolfs in 1364.

5. A parcel of a messuage of the tenement Robert Edildes held by Adam Ryngolfs was also entered as an addition to the 1384 rental. It was 5½ perches long and 2 perches 1 foot wide. In 1365 Robert Edild and his wife had conveyed a parcel of a messuage once of Nicholas Jordan and of exactly the same size to William Large. Ryngolfs was admitted in 1391 to what must have been the same property, measuring 5 by 2 perches, and he conveyed it to Beatrice Tullboye in 1394. When she died in 1409 it was

Plate 7.16 Lower Farm on the western edge of Eastendmoor, Little Fransham, in *Quarent*. 29, July 2018

described as a cottage called *Renges* and ¼ rood. In 1443, when held by Thomas Stalworthy, it lay between his messuage on the north and Walter Pouly's messuage called *Rengys* on the south. After *c*.1487 the property was no longer individually itemised.

6. A messuage and 4 acres in the croft, freehold of Guntons manor, lay at the northern end of this stretch next to the boundary with Great Fransham. This messuage with 7¼ acres of arable in Little Fransham features in two fifteenth-century charters, of 1472 and 1495 (Gardner F and G). According to the earlier one the grantors had been enfeoffed in the lands by the late Thomas Stalworthy. In 1513 John Stalworthy acknowledged in the manor court that he held freely a messuage built in which he lived with 4 acres in the croft called *Jurdons croft* once of William Shortewode (TNA SC 2/194/22). For the tenement Jordans see Med 105. A seventeenth-century house, Lower Farm (HER 29820), stands on this site, at TF 9196 1183 (Pl. 7.16).

Eastfield stretched to the east from these common-edge properties as far as the Great Fransham and Scarning boundaries. Medieval potsherds were quite sparsely distributed particularly towards the eastern end. John Stalworthy's free lands associated with the Guntons freehold were listed in 1552 (TNA SC 12/3/23) and in an undated rental in English (TNA SC 12/3/24): 2 acres at the east end of the croft, 1 acre on the north of it, 1 acre in two pieces next the last, 1½ acres in a new close once of William Soutwode, 2 acres in two pieces between his lands on all sides and lying next to a large pond ('*magnum adaquarium voc. a great Watering*'), 1½ acres soiled of Little Fransham manor next to *le Marketmere* on the south. The latter piece may be the same as 1 soiled Kirkhams and Wilcoks acre butting south on *Market meare* held by George Stalworthy in 1605. *Market meare* was the easterly continuation of *Maryoneslane*. The best modern candidate for the 'great Watering' is a water-filled pond at TF 9233 1172. From 1549 John Stalworthy also had 8 acres of Northendhall or Guntons demesne in Little Fransham as copyhold, along with 2 acres in Great Fransham immediately north of his house (TNA SC 2/192/96 and TNA E 40/14712). He had previously held them at farm for a term of years, beginning in 1525 (TNA SC 11/473 and TNA SC 12/3/24). An earlier conveyance of these lands is recorded in two near-identical charters dated 10 and 31 May 1299. In the first Robert de Sancto Omero of Necton, and in the second Robert de Sancto Thoma of the same, granted, for 20s, to Thomas son of Alexander de Scarning, Agnes his wife, Agnes daughter of Alexander de Ringstead and Thomas' heirs a rent of 1s 9d due from Thomas and his wife for a tenement in Little Fransham. Abuttals were given: between the boundary (*divisam*) of Nicholas Jordan and land of the abbot of Wendling, butting west on the common pasture of Little Fransham and east on the messuage of Geoffrey de Suthwode. That this tenement was John Stalworthy's farmed lands is confirmed by an endorsement on one document, '*Johannes Staworthi modo tenent ad firmam*'

(TNA E 40/10574–5). Two acres lay at the east end of a close called *Soreharte* or *Sorhert* and was a headland, '*terra curta voc. a Shortlond*'. This butted both north and east on Great Fransham, the Wendling Abbey close called *Soudes* (*i.e.* the 28-acre *Sowdsclose*) to the north. In Stalworthy's new close 1½ acres lay on the south side of a piece of Sparhams customary land that he had acquired in 1532, ½ acre of the tenement Benedict Heved (Med 77 and 78 in *Quarent*. 15). Four acres, also in his new close, butted both south and east on the *Market mere*, and must therefore have been next to a kink in this road at TF 9269 1146. Half an acre was in the same close on the north side of the *Great Watering*. This suggests that this close was large, the pond and the kink in the road are 400m apart.

Kirkhams and Wilcoks customary lands in *Eastfield* were listed in 1384 but abutted in far more detail in the 1443 rental. The tenurial history of a pair of Kirkhams customary tenements, Edildes and Renggis, along with parts of other tenements and various soiled lands in *Millfield* and *Eastfield* (see Med 69), is exceptionally complicated and confusing. By 1457 all had fallen into the hands of one tenant, John Wyot, and in 1520 were split into two holdings, one on each side of *Eastendmoor* (MS 13103). The holding in this *Quarent*. was thereafter often cited as the tenement Wyates, lands and/or messuages called Wyotts *etc*. Various pieces of land, apart from the messuages on the common edge already described, can be listed but rarely located. All were probably to the north of the *Market mere* and most, if not all, were aligned east-west. The following were freehold of Wilcoks in *c*.1420 but listed amongst Kirkhams customary holdings in 1384: 1 acre called *Boketonlond*, ½ acre of meadow called *Dowesmedow,* ¼ acre called *Pellisrode*, 1¼ acres and ¾ acre called *Pellislond* and a pit called *Pellesmeer* in a charter of 1472 (Gardner F), ½ acre called *Pellis* next to the common way called *Southwodegate* on the east[xxix]. *Pellesmeer* can probably be identified with a water-filled pit on the boundary between the two Franshams at TF 9273 1175. Of the tenement Edildes there were three pieces each of 1½ acres and ½ rood, including one in *Mydylfurlong* and one in *Rengyscroft*. Of the tenement Renggis there were 5 acres, two pieces of 1¾ acres including one butting east on *le Greenwaye* (probably one and the same as *Southwodegate*), ½ acre in *Mydyfurlong*, ¼ acre above *Sawlepit*, ½ acre nearby and butting east on *le Greneway,* and ½ acre. Two and a half acres were soiled of Kirkhams and of the tenement Gunton, *i.e.* of Guntons manor, and butted east on *Southwodedyke*. Half an acre of Kirkhams customary land was called *Flatlond*. Held jointly with Med 105 (the messuage of Marion Soutere at the west end of this *Quarent.*) was a piece of 1 or 1¼ acres, freehold of Wilcoks and soiled of Kirkhams, which butted east on *Pellismere*. There were two other pieces of similar tenure, ½ acre butting east on *le Greenway* and ¼ acre.

Four pieces of Wilcoks freehold also lay north of the *Market mere* and were described in *c*.1420. Three of them were arranged in a line west to east: ½ acre, 2 acres and 1 acre that butted east on the green way (*viam virid.*). One acre at *Southwodedike* was held by John the bastard of Petronilla Ryngolf in *c*.1420, for the rent of a pair of gloves. In 1605 these were entered as 5 acres in four pieces without any further detail.

Two other properties, both held of Guntons manor, probably lay somewhere in *Eastfield*, perhaps in or near the north-east corner. In a Guntons rental of 1481/2 the rent of one John Betys was given as 1½d and the entry is glossed 'Nich Mynnes' (Holkham Hall, Longham Bundle 3, 34). In 1513 a Guntons court heard that Nicholas Mynne had purchased 3 acres of customary land and a soiled close at *Buntyngs* that lay next to his land on the north and east, for which a rent of 1½d was liable (TNA SC 2/194/22). In 1516 Mynne accepted that he had purchased them (TNA SC 2/194/23). His daughter-in-law Matilda was listed in two undated rentals as holding the same lands, in Little Fransham, for the same rent (TNA SC 11/478 and TNA SC 12/3/24). The same rent for 3 acres called *Buntynges* due from John Fisher [of Scarning] was listed in another undated rental (TNA SC 11/473). This place name occurs only three times in Little Fransham records: in 1517–19 John Boor was amerced for failing to scour his ditch at *Buntyngesfaldgate* (MS 13103).

The area of *Eastfield* south of the *Market mere* and east of the land containing Med 64 was almost all held by free tenure. Eighteen enclosed acres called *Ulnesmedowe*, freehold of Kirkhams and Wilcoks in 1605, lay along the south side of the *pack way*. This was a pasture called *Paul Ulfes* itemised in a letter of attorney of 1326 (MC 360/57, 713X6). Its name was *Hulvesmedow* in 1425 and *Ulvesmedowe* in 1426. Richard Necoll was amerced, in 1440, for keeping closed a close called *Ulfes* when it should have been open. In 1444 Necoll and his heirs were granted licence to keep enclosed throughout the year 3 acres of meadow called *Ulvesmeadowe* lying in *le Estfeld* on either side of the common way, a capon to be paid for the licence at Easter. In 1443 Necoll's rent of a capon was for two parcels of virtually private (*quasi seperales*) meadow, but no name, acreage or abuttals were given. In 1450 he was amerced for allowing branches to overhang *le Market mere* at *Marionesfaldgate* next to *Ulvesmeadowe*. In 1502 John Nicoll held an 18-acre piece of land called *Olvis* for an annual rent of a capon, valued at 3d. Both Richard and John Nicoll were tenants of the West Bradenham freehold messuage on the west side of *Eastendmoor* in *Quarent*. 17 (property no.3). In the early sixteenth century John Nicoll and his successors were frequently amerced at courts leet for offences concerning flooding, blocking and encroaching on the common way, at *Hullsmedowe*, *Hulbys* and *Ulvesmedowe* (MS 13100 and MS 13102). In 1526 the unnamed tenant of lands late of John Nichols senior [Edward Mynne], who had blocked both ends of the king's highway at *Ulvesmedowe* with hedges, was ordered to erect a fald gate at each end of this way which separated his own land on each side. At the same court he was amerced for flooding *Maryones lane* at *Ulvesmeadowe* (MS 13103). The sum of these court proceedings shows that there were two roads, one the east-west *Market mere* or *Maryones lane*, the other a north-south route running out of West Bradenham and through *Ulvesmeadowe* from a tiny area of common depicted on the Enclosure map but not named in any document. The cause of the flooding was a small stream, now piped underground, which crossed the north-south road and flowed in a north-westerly direction across the western part of *Ulvesmedowe* to meet *Maryones lane* at *Maryonesfaldgate* and then to join the stream which marks the east side of *Eastendmoor*. One property listed in the Inquisition Post Mortem of Edward Mynne (ob. 1543) was a piece of land and meadow in *Estfeld* in Little Fransham called *Elvys*, containing 18 acres and held [*sic*] of the manor of West Bradenham (TNA C 142/70/6). In

1679, 18 enclosed acres were called *Hulls* and in 1682 *Bullsmead*, with the rent due to Kirkhams and Wilcoks manor remaining one capon (MC 1850/1, 858X9).

Within these 18 acres was a pasture close, named *Podyngwong* in 1570 (Gardner L). The lord of West Bradenham was amerced at a Little Fransham leet court in 1451 for not scouring a watercourse at *Podyng wonggesend*. Richard Nycoll blocked a common watercourse at *Puddyngys wrongesende* in 1467. That year and the next he had diverted a watercourse at *Puddyngs wong*. These names may indicate wetness, and are perhaps derived from Old English **puddel*, a pond, water-filled pit, puddle *etc.* (Smith 1956b, 74)[xxx]. *Podyngwong* lay at the west end of *Ulvesmeadowe* and south of 1½ acres of meadow which butted west on the pasture close containing Med 64. North of the minor watercourse, within the angle between the two roads, and almost certainly in these 1½ acres was a lone twelfth-century settlement (Med 63, Fig. 7.49). Might this have been the dwelling place of Paul Ulfe?

In 1605 the next property to the east was a 4-acre piece of Kirkhams and Wilcoks freehold called *Bushshie close*. It lay next to the *pack way* on the north and butted east on Scarning 'groundes'. Two acres of these four are known from *c.*1395 when John Pomfrey paid 4d free rent to Wilcoks manor. In *c.*1420 his widow Margaret held 2 acres lying together in *Estfeld* next to *le Marketmere* on the north and butting east on a green way (*virid. viam*). The tenure of these 2 acres and the 4d rent can be followed to 1488 when it was held by Henry Shokete. The other two acres, which lay on the south side, first appear in a charter dated 1478 in which there is reference to a conveyance of 1465 (see Med 66 in Appendix 2). The piece bordered land of Henry Chokett of Scarning on the north and of Hempton Priory on the south. It was in *Estfeld* and butted on *le Greneway* east and on land of John Nycolles west (MC 3115/1/1, 1037X4). In 1502 land to the north was of Thomas Hey.

By 1539 the two 2-acre pieces had been combined. John Wyskard of Little Fransham conveyed by charter to Thomas Hogan 4 acres once of Thomas Hey *notarius*. The land lay next to the common way on the north and butted east on *le Greneway* and west on land of Edward Mynne, *i.e. Ulvesmedowe* (MC 1122/5, 805X8). The close can probably be identified with one in Little Fransham mentioned in the will of Robert Hogan of East Bradenham gent., proved in 1547 (TNA PROB 11/21/569), and in an indenture of 1548 (Mills and Reeve 12/03/70 Mason Necton deeds). In 1566 the rent for 4 acres in *Eastfield* was 6d as it was for *le Busshe close* in 1577 (MS 13104). In the extreme south-east corner of the parish lay 2 acres of Wilcoks customary land associated with a tenement called *Brydes* on the west edge of *Eastendmoor* in *Quarent.* 17 (property no.5). In *c.*1420 this piece was in *le Estfeld* next to land of Hempton Priory on the north and butted east on *le Grengate*. In 1502 it bordered land late Michills on the south (this was a 24-acre freehold close in Scarning held of the manor of Guntons). In 1605 the 2 acres lay 'in the eastfield by Skarninge ground on the south and butting east upon Skarninge'. The size of the above piece of Hempton Priory land is not known.

Endnotes

i   *Branchester Lane*, marked on the Ordnance Survey First edition map in Little Dunham parish at TF 8750 1338, was perhaps the westward continuation of a lane through the common, which may once have exited Great Fransham at TF 8815 1340. Faden (1797) labelled this *More Common*.
ii   There are many references to *faldgates* or *portae cadutae* (literally 'fallen gate') in Fransham sources. In some cases, they appear to have been either simple gates at entrances to commons or fields, or erected (usually illegally) across roads or paths. Very often they are associated with ditches and watercourses and so may well have been falling gates, *i.e.* drawbridges. A clear explanation of meanings has been given by David Yaxley (2003, 76). A list of references to faldgates in court proceedings is given in Appendix 5.
iii   A Ground Penetrating Radar survey of the site of the house and its immediate surrounds was carried out in 2012 by Michael de Bootman. Abundant buried remains of masonry wall foundations were recorded, but no attempt has been made here to interpret the results (HER 4203). The house was named *Cads Hall* on Faden's map of 1797.
iv   A circular lead seal matrix inscribed + S' HENRICI : DE BILNEIE was found during metal-detecting in Area M at TF 8973 1291 (HER 20508), 1.1km east of the messuage (HER 20508).
v   Another mill lay to the north-west of Med 14 in Beeston. This was the mill of Ralph de Beeston. In 1356–7 Giles Gwene, a 92-year-old villein of Castle Acre Priory, described in a sworn statement the boundaries of the Kempstone foldcourse: one length ran from the old mill of Gilbert de Fransham along a path called *Market Stye* to Ralph de Beeston's mill (WIS 11, 163X11). In *c.*1400 Edmund Oldhall held, of Great Fransham manor, a freehold close once of Ralph de Beeston at *Shepehousecroft*. Butting south on the common pasture of Great Fransham it must therefore have been in Beeston and can be identified with 6 acres held by William son of Augustine de Beeston in *c.*1279 (Table 6.2, no. 12). A sixteenth-century tenant of this land, Sir Roger Townshend, also held freely of East Lexham manor a piece of land in a close called *le Roode* / *le Rodes* in Fransham [sic] with the liberty of a windmill, once of Ralph de Beeston and Edmund Oldhall (KIM 1/8/16 and MC 1812/49, 838X5). In 1553 Henry Skott held of Great Fransham manor 'certayne land late Sir Roger Townsend in Rawlinges Close in Beston' (MS 13077). A slight mound is still visible at TF 8925 1430 and medieval pottery was found on one brief visit (HER 18227). The Fransham Enclosure map names this area 'Rowlands', while 'Mill Hill' is written here on the Beeston Enclosure map of 1814 (C/Sca 2/187).
vi   Named *Brownsmore Common* by Faden (1797).
vii   The eastern part of this common was named *High Green* by Faden (1797).
viii   The area containing Med 24–7 (HER 4192), now one field incorporating the adjacent part of the former common to the north, has been subjected to intense metal detecting. Medieval metal objects were almost entirely absent from the former common but were prolific on the settlement sites and to south of them. Outstanding items include three seal matrices, two thirteenth-century lead circular personal examples, of Thomas son of H...., probably Henry (at TF 8925 1311) and of John son of William (at TF 8931 1313), and a fourteenth-century copper alloy piece inscribed, in Norman French, * IE SV SEL BON LEL AM (I am the seal of a good and loyal friend), found at TF 8922 1310.
ix   Named *Mole Hill Common* by Faden (1797).
x   Hey Green was named *Frans High Green* by Faden (1797).

Endnotes (cont'd/ ...)

xi The element *wong*, which occurs in a number of Fransham field-names, seems almost always to indicate a piece of cultivated land enclosed (either temporarily or permanently) from an open field. (Rebecca Gregory pers. comm.)

xii Within the Castle Acre cartulary there is a charter of 1180/2, by which the Bishop of Norwich confirmed the monks' possessions (BL Harley MS 2110). These included the tithes of the assarts (*sartis*) of *Haringeshag*' (Harper-Bill 1990, 147, no. 184). Another confirmation charter, of 1265, gives more detail: the tithes of the *sartis* of *Heringeshae*, in Wendling all the tithes of Great and Little *Dichwud* of the demesne once of Reginald son of Elwold, both of Giffard's fee and of that of William de Francheville (Harper-Bill 2007, 162, no. 143). Amongst several charters in the cartulary a number mention wood pasture (*nemus*). Roger de Tosny granted Castle Acre Priory his *nemus de Haringeshae* with all land and assarts belonging. This was confirmed in further charters by his son Ralph and by William de Warenne, 3rd Earl of Surrey (1138–48). Confirmation charters of Henry II (1154–89) cited the de Tosny gift as the *boscum* (wood) *de Heringeshage*. Both wood and wood pasture in Dikewood (*Dichewde*) are included in grants by William and Peter de Pelleville and Richard de Cambeis. These woodland-related references in Dikewood and Herringshall deeds, however, are far outnumbered by those to land (*terra*), on some occasions described as arable. Honeypot Wood, a medieval wood (Barnes and Williamson 2015, 206–7), lies a short distance to the north-east of the site of Heringshall manor.

xiii Thomas Nekyr of Great Fransham was a carpenter of 'regional significance' who worked in the 1530s at Thetford Priory and Hengrave Hall, Suffolk (Dymond 1995, 27; Dymond 1996, 574–5 and 774).

xiv In 1600 John Wyskard's son-in-law Robert Davy gent. gained a licence to demolish the cottage called Wyndhams. In his will, proved in 1639, he left one tenement called *Pettifers* to his wife and executrix Dorothy, to sell within two years, with 'the land thereto adjoining or belonging both free and copie as they lye nowe enclosed And of long time have so done' (NCC 190 Green, MF 412).

xv On the Enclosure Award map '*Kings Close*' is written along the parish boundary at TF 9230 1330 and '*Six Acres*' slightly further to the west, both in the area known as *Birdes field* or *Agrave field.*

xvi A faculty for the demolition of the south aisle and for the building of a wall on the south side of the nave was granted in 1801. The aisle had been much decayed' and 'supported by two very ugly Buttresses which make a very awkward and unseemly appearance'. Lead from the aisle roof, weighing 4½ tons, was to be sold for £81 (petition DN/FCP 7/7; faculty DN/FCB 4/2). The new wall was erected immediately south of the aisle arcade. A faculty for various works, including the demolition and rebuilding of this wall, was granted in 1878 (DN/FCB 8). This part of the building was in a parlous state until repair works were completed in 2010.

xvii St Mary's was not a guild Chapel. The four Great Fransham guilds were of All Saints, St Anne, the Holy Trinity and St Katherine (Blomefield 1808, 499, Taylor 1821, 72; Farnhill 2001, 185).

xviii The etymology of *Raweyne* is obscure. The *eyn* or *weyn* might be Middle English *leyne* 'tract of land' or perhaps Old Norse *eng* 'meadow' having lost its final g. *Ra(w)* may be Old English *râ* / Old Norse *rá* 'roe, roe-buck' (Smith 1956b, 78), or possibly Old Norse *vrá* 'nook or corner of land' (Smith 1956b, 232–3). So 'meadow where roe deer are found' is a possible meaning. (Rebecca Gregory pers. comm.)

xix Ralph Nel of Little Fransham granted 2 acres to William son of Henry le Strange. The land lay between land of the said William on the west and the green way (*viridiam viam*) of Henry le Strange on the east and butted south on William Huberd's messuage.

xx The parsonage was 'a very ancient Building, much out of repair and very unfit for the Residence of a Clergyman'. Much earlier, in 1535–8, the rector's 'mansion' was said by the incumbent Ralph Orrell to be ruinous and decayed, as were his other buildings and the chancel of the church, through the neglect of his predecessor, Thomas Chester. Attempts were made to extract £30 for repairs from Chester's executor (TNA C 1/864/44–6).

xxi The key to the letters on the plan with dimensions, where given, in feet and inches: a, kitchen 13' x 15'; b, backhouse [*i.e.* bakehouse] 10' 6" x 7'9"; c, dairy 14' x 12'; d, hall, 15' x 13' 6"; e, pantry 6' 9" x 5' 9"; f, cellar 7' 6" x 5' 9"; g, parlour 15' x 15' (5 bedrooms on the Chamber Floor [*i.e.* first floor]; h, mote; i, garden; j, yard; k, barn, 45' x 20'; l, cow and straw house, 69' x 18'; m, stable, 13' x 18'.

xxii The source for a date of *c.*1700 is unknown. Bryant (1903) was the first to cite such a date. Bill Wilson noted the date stone of 1583, set near the apex of the gable of the nave west wall high above a 'domestic, transomed four-light window' (Pevsner and Wilson 1999, 521). There is no visible material in this wall that need be later than the sixteenth century. An upper story on the south porch is of brick and is dated 1743 in large iron letters. A dry area trench, dug probably in the 1970s along the nave west wall, cut through the bases of the north and south tower walls. In 1742 a faculty was granted for the sale of two bells. Three had been 'hanging in a thatched shed in the churchyard which is now so much decayed that the bells are in danger of falling which said bells by reason of their hanging so low are and for many years have been of no real use but that one of these bells when hung in a proper place to be erected and that you request to be over the church porch will be sufficient and very usefull' (DN/FCB 2/1). It seems much more likely that the thatched shed had become much decayed after the *c.*160 years that had elapsed since the 1580s than after a mere four decades. In 1552/3 there were three bells. (L'Estrange 1874, 134).

xxiii The area of the two purprestures amounts to *c.*1½ acres. The next reference after 1605 is in a short rental of 1780–92. Hamond Alpe esq. paid an annual rent of 2s for 'two pieces of waste with a pond enclosed' (MC 969/8, 858X7). The ovoid pond, centred at TF 9026 1193, is extant.

xxiv Arable land in Necton immediately south of the Fransham boundary, measuring 740m east to west was examined over a width of *c.*50m, under good soil conditions. The area stretched from TF 8989 1132 to 9062 1120. No medieval pottery was recovered, suggesting that this land may have not been arable, and was probably woodland, throughout the Middle Ages.

xxv The southern part of *Eastendmoor* was named *Spencers Green* by Faden (1797) and the remainder *Eastend Common*.

xxvi Found by metal-detector at TF 9140 1265 (L157, HER 21629), about one quarter of a circular lead seal matrix is inscribed …]ONILL[…

xxvii On the Enclosure Award map of 1805, the Turnpike Road ran along what had been the northern and western edges of *Little Millclose*, along the lines of *Millane* and *Drovelane*. At some time before the Tithe map of 1839 the Turnpike was realigned to run directly from the north-east to the south west corner of the close, a route still taken by the A47 trunk road.

xxviii Close to the south of here and in West Bradenham parish, may have been the tenement and lands once of Adam Marche, the tenant of which, in 1385/6, owed the lord of Sparhams a rent of two capons for common rights, if and when such rights were exercised. Various amercements of Little Fransham and West Bradenham people in courts leet between 1394 and 1469 for offences concerning unscoured ditches and watercourses at *Marches*, *Marchesdyk* and *Marcheswell*e, and the common at *Marches*, suggest that Adam Marche's property was in this area. His dwelling may have been at TF 9176 1136, where an isolated concentration of medieval and post-medieval sherds was located close to the south-east edge of *Eastendmoor* (HER 28350).

xxix The ¾ acre piece is quite likely that which was conveyed in 1492 and 1498 according to a charter grant transcribed by Carthew (1879, 184–5) and owned by him. Its present whereabouts is unknown.

xxx If Old English **puddle* is the origin of this name then the *yng* is difficult to explain. 'pudding' field-names are not unusual for land with soft, sticky soil (Cavill 2018, 343), but no medieval examples are known. The Oxford English Dictionary gives the sense of 'stuffed entrail or sausage' from the thirteenth century but the sweet pudding sense only comes about in the sixteenth. Such an origin is not impossible but unlikely given the date. The final *s* in *Puddyngys* and *Puddyngs* might indicate some personal name but no suitable candidate has come to light. The place-name Pudding Norton (near Fakenham, Norfolk) should be also noted. The prefix *Pudding*, first recorded in 1302, remains unexplained. (Rebecca Gregory pers. comm.)

Chapter 8. The Middle Ages, an Overview

In this chapter frequently cited documents are not individually referenced. They are listed in Chapter 7, *Documentary references*.

Settlement numbers and population
(Fig. 8.1)

While only six settlement sites were occupied in the tenth and twenty in the eleventh century, thirty-eight located in the survey had origins in the twelfth century, although four of these (Med 16, 63, 73 and 102) did not continue to be occupied into the thirteenth century. In addition, eleven sites which had begun in the eleventh century were still occupied in the twelfth, though one of these (LS 3 / Med 20) did not survive long after *c*.1100. Settlement was initiated on fifty-four sites in the thirteenth century. A total of nineteen sites (with the addition of one in Wendling, Med 115) had failed by the end of the thirteenth century. This total is distorted by five small pottery production sites but does not include any sites that had begun after 1200. Forty-five sites were deserted in the fourteenth century. Of these two had begun in the eleventh, thirteen in the twelfth and twenty-nine in the thirteenth century. No site with a fourteenth-century starting date was located. Of eight for which there is only limited ceramic evidence, six (Med 23A, 25A, 112–4 and 116) are still occupied to one degree or another by buildings, one (Med 117) is obscured by trees and shrubs, and another (Med 74) is the surviving earthwork of the Kirkhams manor house. They were all occupied by the thirteenth century, with Med 113 commencing in the eleventh if not the tenth century. The origins of Med 116, an inaccessible site, remain obscure.

A total of one hundred and five sites (or one hundred if the pottery making sites are excluded), for which there is archaeological evidence, were in existence in the thirteenth century. Even allowing for the fact that many of these were single settlements, and complete coexistence at any moment is not claimed for them all, the total makes a considerable contrast with the figure of eighteen occupation sites, including two nucleated settlements, for the eleventh century. The large population increase implied by these figures accords with the upward trend recorded in documents elsewhere in Norfolk (Hallam 1988, 515–6 and 541–2). Almost one half (44%) of sites ceased to be occupied in the fourteenth century[i]. This is a startling figure, which amounted to 'a *shocking decay*; a great dilapidation and constant pulling down or falling down of houses' (Cobbett 2001, 36), but it should be moderated by the likelihood that a higher percentage of inaccessible sites, those known only from documents, would have either survived the troubles of the fourteenth century or have been resettled soon afterwards. These statistics, rough as they are, nevertheless seem remarkable as a physical manifestation in one locality of two major trends of medieval demography, the population optimum of the thirteenth century and the disastrous decline in the fourteenth. In the world of archaeology both trends are far better known from the study, through their surviving earthworks, of shrunken and deserted nucleated settlements. A combination of a relatively dispersed settlement tradition and the twentieth-century mechanised agricultural 'improvement' of Norfolk has prevented the county from entering the top league of medieval settlement studies.

In a review of another piece of Norfolk fieldwork (Davison 1988) the writer ended by stating that 'the real puzzle for Norfolk is to explain how and why this county ever came to support such a high density of people and settlements' (Dyer 1990). The 'why' in the above cannot be answered by the study of one parish, but perhaps the 'how' is not so far outside the remit of this survey.

Given the remarkable total of deserted settlement sites located in the field survey and the many sites which remain inaccessible beneath existing houses, is there any way of arriving at an estimate of the size of Fransham's population at the apogee of the later thirteenth century? Only one method, fraught with considerable difficulties of interpretation and chronology, has been considered. This involves the counting of all references to dwellings or former dwellings, *i.e.* messuages and cottages, to be found in documents of the late fourteenth to sixteenth centuries, and the multiplication of the total by 4.5, the size of an average household. Numbers of messuages and cottages under each manor are given in Chapter 6. The total of houses in Great Fransham is sixty-two, and the total for Little Fransham, for which much fuller documentary coverage survives, is sixty-five. These figures suggest a population of 572, a figure remarkably close to 592, the total for the two parishes in the mid-nineteenth century (White 1845, 333).

Direct documentary assistance is not forthcoming for the period of high expansion in the twelfth and thirteenth centuries. Thirteenth and early fourteenth-century deeds illustrate the frantic conveying of mostly small pieces of land by freeholders, but they are silent on the processes involved in the multiplying of settlements. The manor court records of Great Fransham manor and of Kirkhams in Little Fransham show that the land market was buoyant in the two decades or so before the Black Death, but there are few references to the establishment of new settlements. A high population and partible inheritance triggered some such new building in Little Fransham. For example, in 1327 Bartholomew son of John Jordan surrendered a 40-feet square building plot (*placea mess.*) to the use of his son Adam. In 1328 Bartholomew Jordan the white died seized of a sixth part of a customary messuage, a rood with a large cottage and a freehold messuage and 5¾ acres, as well as other lands. His wife was still living, and he left three sons as heirs. His widow, Cecilia, quitclaimed all rights etc. in the above plot, which was her father's, to one of her sons, Adam. At one court in 1339 Thomas Clerk (*clericus*) surrendered a 40-feet square plot on the west side of his messuage to the use of his son Adam, and he also surrendered a rood in his messuage to the use of another son, Roger, who immediately surrendered the same back to his father for life to build a cottage on it. Three years later both Adam

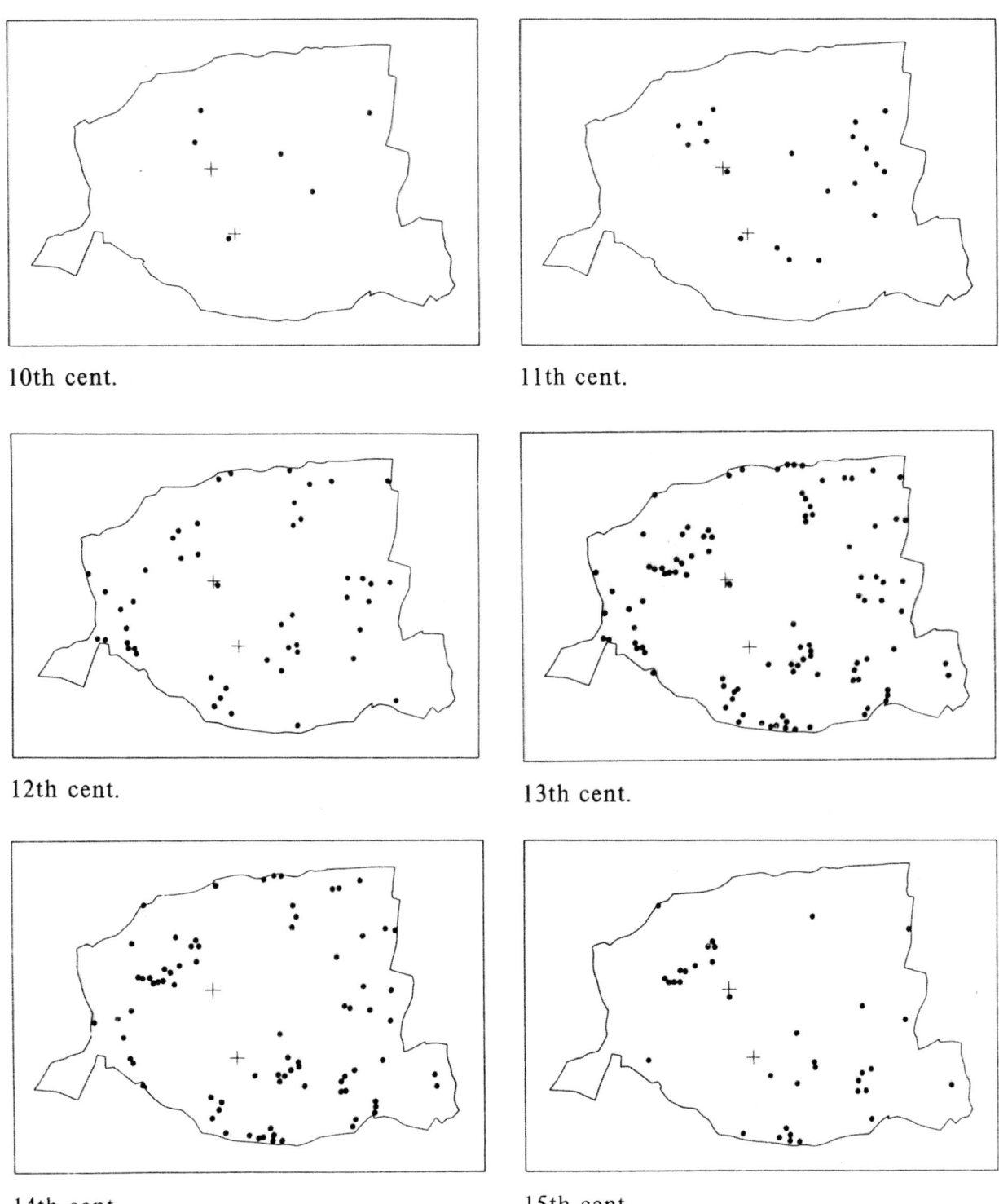

Figure 8.1 Schematic plans showing archaeological sites in occupation by century, Late Saxon and medieval

and Roger, who were in Necton, were described as *anelpimen* (landless villeins). In 1343 their father had died having surrendered 1 acre to Roger, and Adam and Roger were heirs to 1½ acres. Thomas' widow Matilda was left with ½ acre in *Woodrowfield*. For the tenement Thomas Clerkes in 1384, see Med 84.

Settlement distribution

Early references to messuages and cottages such as the above cannot often be located on a map, for the earliest surviving rolls are very sparing in their use of place names, and what were probably crucial courts for the linking of pre- and post-Black Death tenures in Little Fransham Kirkhams manor, those in 1349 and 1350, do not survive, there being a gap between 23 October 1348 and 22 June 1351. A list of thirty-two dead tenants and their lands in the Great Fransham manor court roll extract for 18 July 1349 has few definite links with entries in the preceding nineteen years of extracts, although the tenurial succession of the majority of these lands can be followed from that time onwards. We are forced, then, to use archaeological evidence for occupation sites and the documentary evidence of later dates for the locations of commons and fields known to suggest ways in which the study area was settled and exploited in the boom years between 1100 and the Black Death.

In western Great Fransham a great cluster of twelfth-century sites is to be found around *Curds Green* and roads leading to it. This was an area devoid of Late Saxon activity. Colonisation was dominated by Great Fransham tenants, both free and customary, with a few of Kirkhams manor also making an impression. The common, which must have been very small, was to fall within Great Fransham when the two vills became distinct, probably in the years around 1200. Two sites to the north (Med 1 and 2) were swallowed up into demesne in the thirteenth century. Place names in this area show that much of this colonisation must have been at the expense of woodland or wood pasture. North-east of here the common later known as *West End Moor* had been well settled in the Late Saxon period, and further expansion was to take place in the thirteenth century. The long valley-bottom common east of this was colonised in the thirteenth century by free and customary tenants of several manors, and a Late Saxon site (LS 5/ Med 15A) on the south side of the tiny *Brounesgrene* common to the north-east was joined by a new settlement nearby in the twelfth century (Med 15). The edges of *Wylmondheithe*, the curiously shaped common in the north-west part of Great Fransham, were settled sparsely and only after *c*.1200. Here East Lexham manor was dominant.

East Lexham manor and its dependency Ellinghams were also behind the exploitation of the north-central part of the parish, between *Ellinghams field* and what had been a substantial area of woodland, *Kynwaldeshawe* and *Elynghams Wode*. Here there was an overwhelming preponderance of freeholds, and it is particularly disappointing that because of the paucity of the documents, the lay-out of so much of this area is so dimly perceived. The east end of Great Fransham had seen some settlement around *Fendersmoor* and *Eastendmoor* common in the eleventh century. The relatively small number of new twelfth-century sites can be put down to the large inaccessible lengths of common edge, but infilling did occur in the thirteenth. Here, the documentary evidence shows that several manors were involved in the establishment of new settlements (see particularly the composite 'site' Med 113). This process must have involved a strong degree of co-operation between lords, and, most probably, between tenants.

Hey Green in the far north-east was settled in the thirteenth century. It lies at the southern end of what had probably been a large tract of woodland and wood pasture until the twelfth century, *Herningshawe* and *Dikewood* (now in Wendling and Beeston parishes), most of which was granted to Castle Acre Priory (see Chapter 7, f.n. xii).

Southwoodfield, the large area of Great Fransham which hooks around the east side of Little Fransham, does not appear to have been opened up until the thirteenth century, apart from one odd site with eleventh century origins, which sits on the boundary between the two Franshams (LS 16 / Med 60). The margin of a lost common, *Southwoodmore*, appears to have attracted only one settlement site within Fransham in the thirteenth century (Med 62), although another of the same date (Med 93) lay a little to the south (Fig. 7.19). Others, however, may lie nearby, in Wendling. Once again, freeholds seem to have been dominant in this area, whose name, along with many tenants who were members of the Southwood family, suggests an area of woodland surviving into twelfth century or beyond.

West of *Southwoodfield* into Little Fransham, the edges of the valley-bottom common, *Eastendmoor*, have not produced any evidence of settlement before 1200, although some such might lie on the largely obscured eastern side. One isolated site (Med 63), not fronting onto this common, was occupied only in the twelfth century. Documents, and to a lesser extent the archaeology, show that in some places there was dense settlement around *Eastendmoor*, although nearby there were considerable lengths which remained unsettled. Tenements in these dense clusters were shared amongst several manors, with once again a mix of free and customary tenures. Here, as with *Eastendmoor* in Great Fransham, the mechanisms whereby the initial settlements were carried out under the control of distinct manors must have involved no small degree of co-operation.

West of *Hochesfield* in Little Fransham, a large area of heavy soil called the *Rode* and part of Cannons manor, was almost free of medieval sites. One, devoted to pottery production at the south-west corner (Med 103), probably took advantage of the underwood resources available here, or across the parish boundary in *Necton Wood*. *Cannons Green*, another low-lying common pasture, had seen settlement on both sides in the eleventh century, and was to witness some infilling in the thirteenth. Where known, all settlement sites were of customary tenure.

Woodrowgreen, a narrow common between houses and open field arable to the north and woodland to the south certainly has 'the appearance of the last wave of an advancing tide of clearance' (Dyer 1991, 40). It was lined with many settlement sites, particularly densely at its eastern end (Med 77–83). None of these was in place until the thirteenth century. To the north-west Med 85 sat on the edge of the *Lyng*, a continuation of *Woodrowgreen*. Here there was evidence for twelfth-century occupation, as there was at two more sites along this edge, Med 86 and 88.

The present 'main village' of Little Fransham, a linear common edge settlement strung out along a slight valley, masks any archaeological evidence. It is unfortunate that here, so close to the second nucleated Late Saxon site and to the parish church, where the documentary evidence for the late medieval pattern of tenures and manorial allegiances is so good, no opportunity was taken archaeologically to date the origins of the tenements. There surely must be a late eleventh- or twelfth-century component somewhere in this built-up area. A few sherds of Late Saxon pottery on Med 90 at the western end of the northern side give a hint that this may be so.

The manor house of Kirkhams (Med 74) sat *c.*150m from the nearest common pasture in the midst of a large tract of demesne containing only one other settlement site, Med 73, where occupation was restricted to the twelfth century. This block of demesne bordered a substantial area of glebe land surrounding the rectory, and beyond which lay the parish church at a distance of 0.6km from the manor house.

The relationship of principal manor house and church was rather different in Great Fransham. Here the manor (Med 5), again with substantial demesne closes to the north and south, was, at over 1km, much further from the church and the nearest common lay more than 300m distant. It is worth noting that there is no evidence of settlement at this site before the twelfth century.[ii]

Unlike the two principal manors, Great Fransham and Kirkhams, the manor house of Wilcoks (Med 85), that had split off from Kirkhams, the main de Tosny manor, probably in the twelfth or early thirteenth century, was situated on a common edge. Both rectories were in similar locations. Likewise, the apparently uninhabited manorial enclosure of Cannons manor, presumably established in the twelfth century, was also sited on a common edge. Thus, it appears that most secondary manorial sites were positioned similarly to the majority of tenants' houses.

The overall picture of settlement distribution at the thirteenth-century high point is one of a mixture of small nucleations or hamlets, some tightly packed rows, others loosely strung out, within a sprinkling of dispersed sites, a pattern that conforms to what would be expected in an East Anglian 'ancient' or 'woodland' landscape (Williamson 2003; 2007a, 89–91). Only in Little Fransham is anything akin to a sizeable village in a physical sense of the word discernible, in this case an irregular double row strung along both sides of a common pasture, the only nucleation to survive into the modern period, albeit in a much thinned-out state. However, no one locality in either Great or Little Fransham can have been regarded as *the* village or centre of the community, holding economic, administrative or political sway over dependent hamlets (Jones 2010).

It is significant that Fransham sits directly on the western boundary of Mid-Norfolk, local region 2 in the Anglia sub-province of the South-Eastern province of Roberts and Wrathmell's (2000) map of English rural settlement. This local region is marked by high densities of dispersion, while to the west the Goodsands, local region 1 of the Wash (east) sub-province, is characterised by low densities. This boundary may have been much sharper in the thirteenth century.

The dynamics of settlement: chronology, manorial allegiance and tenure

We have, in both Little and Great Fransham, a pattern in which during the twelfth century, following tentative moves made in the eleventh, certain common pastures attracted both freehold and customary settlements held of various manors, while others, in particular *Eastendmoor* and *Woodrowgreen* in Little Fransham, and possibly *Hey*

Green in Great Fransham, had to wait until the thirteenth. There are few obvious clues, in either soil type or topography, to indicate why certain common edges and certain parts thereof were settled earlier than others. The great central area of Fransham was for the most part empty of settlement in the medieval period, with Little Fransham church and Kirkhams manor house near the southern edge, Great Fransham manor house to the west, and Great Fransham church, (with possibly for a brief period its rectory, LS 8/Med 30), being prominently alone just north of the middle. This area of predominantly medium soils, with good drainage on south and north-facing slopes, contained the prime agricultural land, three furlongs of Great Fransham (*Middlefurlong* and two nameless) with their two dividing roads, the *Whiteway* and *Southgateway* alias *Greenway*, the smaller *Henfield* to the east, Little Fransham *Westfield*, *Bullesfield* and *Churchfield* to the west and south, as well as the two principal valleys and one tributary with their meadows. In the centre, *Barnards Moor*, in a valley bottom, was the only common pasture to be shared between the two parts of Fransham, and the only one that was not edged with settlements. Another peculiarity of this common lies in the way in which at both its east and west ends, *i.e.* downstream and upstream, it gave way to demesne meadows. This is particularly noteworthy at the west end where the abrupt change from common pasture to meadow is marked by a road. The name of this common suggests woodland clearance.

In close proximity to the more peripheral commons there is a fairly consistent pattern of place names indicating the former presence of woodland, *e.g. Curds Green* with *Knightrode*, *Hey Green* with *Herningshawe*, *Woodrowgreen* with *Necton Wood*, and *Southwoodmore*. With the scarcity of early documents, there is no direct evidence for the large amount of assarting that took place in these areas during the twelfth and thirteenth centuries (*cf.* Hallam 1988, 154–6), although it should be remembered that *Pilewude* was called a *cultura* (arable) in 1273/4. There is a tendency for this former woodland pattern to be strongest where the earliest evidence for common-edge colonisation is in the twelfth and thirteenth centuries. *West End moor* and *Eastendmoor* in Great Fransham, and probably the common in the present-day village nucleus of Little Fransham with its south-eastern continuation, *Cannons Green*, are less closely associated with wood names, and these were the common pastures which attracted settlements along their edges in the eleventh century. Two of these commons were placed more centrally within the vill, although this cannot be said of *Eastendmoor*, Great Fransham, unless Wendling is considered to form part of the same land-unit, surely a tendentious and anachronistic suggestion for the eleventh century. All these commons were in valleys while most of the peripheral commons were situated on watersheds or high ground. One exception is *Eastendmoor*, Little Fransham, which was set in a valley. It lies, however, between areas with wood names, the *Rode* to the west and *Southwood* (field) to the east.

In almost every part of the vill, the lordship of free and customary messuages and lands was mixed. It should be remembered, however, that the situation in Little Fransham was not so complex as it at first may appear, for three manors, Kirkhams, Wilcoks and Sparhams were all off-shoots from one Domesday holding, and may not have split until well into the period under review. Cannons manor had also come from the de Tosny holding, but earlier, presumably during or soon after the reign of Henry I. It is interesting that West Acre Priory was not given the best land, but a block of rather heavy soil adjoining *Necton Wood*, as well as only two tenements in the 'main village'. East Lexham manor does seem to have had a considerable dominance in northern Great Fransham, while the holdings of the chapel of Rougholme were almost all in the eastern part of the parish.

Who then was behind the widespread migration of settlement to the common edges? It was clearly not the work of energetic and independent freemen on their own (*cf.* Roberts 1977, 169), if the tenurial status of sites as described in later medieval documents are to be believed. It has already been argued that the eleventh-century beginnings of the movement may have been the result of seigniorial activity in the defining and restricting of areas of common pasture, rather than of direct lordly dictate. There may have been a higher degree of seigniorial control in the twelfth and thirteenth centuries than there had been before or was to be after. However, it is most likely that pressure on remaining pasture resources and the need to cultivate more land towards the extremities of the vill made the rush desirable for tenants both free and unfree. It might be thought that the former would have found it easier to initiate the migration to the commons, and that they were soon emulated by the latter. Such an assumption, however, is not supported by the few instances where both documentary and archaeological evidence are available. A certain weakness in lordship would have allowed some movement by villeins, who, we know from later court rolls, were frequently committing acts contrary to custom before being allowed to continue after the payment of a fine. Perhaps soon after a few initial movements to the commons during the eleventh century, the practice became accepted and even encouraged by the authorities. This led to the rapid desertion of the two main settlements (LS 1 and 2), and thereafter new common edge settlements emerged as the normal response during the twelfth century, on the part of lords and tenants, to each pang of land or pasture hunger caused by a rising population. The establishment of new settlements was to continue into the thirteenth century. In assessing the differing initiatives played by lords and tenants in this process of settlement relocation, it is well to remember that much took place at a time before the regular meeting of the manor court became the norm in the early thirteenth century (Harvey 1989, 41).

It now remains to examine whether the disposition of free and customary settlements around the common edges and their manorial allegiances possess any degree of patterning which might illuminate the seigniorial and non-seigniorial forces at work behind the processes of colonisation. It must be remembered, however, that the picture is far from complete, both because of the number of settlements evidenced only from documents and whose foundation dates are thus unknown, and because there is a significant proportion of archaeologically observed sites of uncertain manorial allegiance and tenurial status. Emphasis should also be placed on the uncertainties surrounding the relationship between the later medieval manorial structure of Fransham and the much simpler structure recorded in Domesday. The events that must have taken place in the intervening centuries, perhaps particularly during the Anarchy of the mid-twelfth century, cannot be assessed.

Some customary tenements known from documents of the late fourteenth century and later might have once been freeholds that had escheated to the lord at an earlier date. In addition, the relationships between free tenants and lords were much more fluid before the passing of the Statute of *Quia Emptores* in 1290, as can be seen in the conveyance of rents and services in many early charters. Even customary tenements and tenants may have passed from one manor to another. Some thirteenth-century charters record the transfer of villeins and their land between lords, although in two of the following three examples the grantor and grantee were father and son. Roger le Strange of Little Fransham quitclaimed to his son John all rights etc. in Roger son of William son of Baldwin with all his brood or family (*secutella*), his tenement and his rents (MC 360/38, 713X6). John of Little Fransham, son of Roger le Strange, granted to his son Henry the homage, service, tenement and lands of Hugh his villein (*rusticus*) and those of Hugh's successors (MC 360/6, 713X6; Pl. 6.2). John, son of Simon formerly parson of Fransham, granted to Alexander, son of Adam de Gressenhall, two acres of arable in Great Fransham along with Matilda daughter of Laurence, her two sons and all their brood (*sequela*), customs and services (Nottingham University Library Mi D 3617/1). Such grants of serfs along with their families and their lands were very rare after the twelfth century (Bailey 2002, 33).

In Great Fransham, where the documentary evidence is less complete, there were certainly major variations in tenure around the edges of different commons. For example, around *Curds Green* and along adjacent roadways, freeholds, all of Great Fransham manor, predominated. This area lies quite close to the site of the Great Fransham manor house. Four Kirkhams customary holdings were strung out to the south–east in Little Fransham and one in Necton. Some, at least, of these had been freeholds at some date before the late fourteenth century. This whole area seems to have been colonised in the twelfth century and later.

To the north-east of *Curds Green* around *Brounsgrene* and *West End moor* the manorial situation is more complex. Great Fransham freeholds are again most common, but East Lexham, Rougholme and Blyfords manor holdings are also present. Some settlements began in the eleventh century, and at least one of these (LS 3 / Med 20) was a customary tenement. The poorly documented north central area of Great Fransham was, as has been said, dominated by East Lexham manor freeholds, and here once more there was no settlement before the twelfth century.

Hey Green in the extreme north-east, an area mostly unavailable for field survey, seems to have been settled exclusively by free and customary holdings of Great Fransham manor. Here again the situation may have been more complex, but for want of further documentary evidence we cannot be sure.

Houses were rather densely packed around parts of the edges of *Fendersmoor / Doesgate / Eastendmoor*, the common that crossed the parish boundary into Wendling (Fig. 7.14). Settlement was at its tightest on either side of the confluence of three streams in the area of the hamlet now known as Crane's Corner[iii]. Most of this locality could not be surveyed, but the ceramic evidence was sufficient to show the presence of eleventh-century settlements. Here there were freeholds of Great Fransham, Kirkhams and Cannons manors, and customary messuages of Great Fransham and Rougholme. Close to the south on the west edge of this common, one twelfth-century site with relatively sound documentary evidence (Med 107), both a freehold of Great Fransham and a customary messuage of Kirkhams, indicates that much caution should be used both in the mapping of tenures and in the making of inferences from their distribution. Further to the south and west there were also freeholds of Blyfords and Guntons, and customary holdings of Great Fransham, Great Fransham rectory, Rougholme, and Sparhams manors, but it was only from two freeholds and one customary holding of Great Fransham manor that any evidence for eleventh-century origins was forthcoming. In this area also, however, the sites of many houses have been destroyed or were not available for survey.

Southwoodfield in Great Fransham, which took up all the south-eastern part of the parish, was bordered on its eastern edge by another common, *Southwoodmore* or *Southwode greene* This was edged by a single house, a freehold of Great Fransham manor (Med 62), with another somewhere to the east in Wendling, while a third (Med 93) lay a little to the south. The archaeological evidence, which is available for two of these three, points to the start of occupation in the thirteenth century.

The edges of *Eastendmoor* in Little Fransham were colonised by over thirty house-sites, many of which were located by fieldwalking. Where the archaeological evidence was available, it pointed overwhelmingly to a thirteenth-century phase of initial settlement. Only one site (Med 69) produced twelfth-century material. Holdings of Wilcoks manor, mostly freehold but with one group of four customary tenements along with customary tenements of Kirkhams, were distributed in tight clusters along certain stretches of the common edge. Holdings of only three other manors were present there: a solitary freehold, probably of Rougholme manor, at the north end, a pair of West Bradenham customary messuages and a freehold of the same manor near the south-west corner, and three Sparhams customary tenements close together on either side of the entry of a road near the mid-point of the western side.

Cannons Green was far more sparingly edged by houses than *Eastendmoor*. Kirkhams and Wilcoks manors were pre-eminent, with only single customary tenements of Sparhams and one of Cannons. No freeholds were identified, but it is possible that one site (Med 100) located on what was demesne of the combined manor of Kirkhams and Wilcoks in the later fifteenth century may have formerly been held freely of Wilcoks.

Apart from a twelfth or thirteenth-century pottery production site at its eastern end, *Woodrowgreen*, most of the edge of which was open to fieldwalking, was lined with sites that began in the thirteenth century. A Wilcoks freehold lay at the west end, and beyond this was a tight cluster of seven customary messuages held of Kirkhams and Sparhams manors. Further west again two Wilcoks freeholds were more widely spaced. At the rear, northern end of the more westerly of the pair was a probable Kirkhams manor customary tenement, a probable pottery production site with twelfth-century origins (Med 84).

The unusual location of this site might conceivably reflect an earlier line of the common edge.

Beyond an arc of four sites which included the Wilcoks manorial centre (Med 85) and two others where occupation began in the twelfth century, the present-day village of Little Fransham overlies rows of medieval settlements on the north and south sides of a common pasture. These included freeholds of Wilcoks and Kirkhams manors (the latter only occurring on the edge of this common), a single freehold of Guntons, and customary messuages of Cannons, Sparhams and Kirkhams manors.

All the above evidence, for free and customary tenures, manorial allegiances and archaeological dating, suggests a limited degree of patterning. Firstly, wherever there is close spacing of houses on a common edge, both tenures are always present. There is no place where more than four customary messuages occur without an accompanying freehold, except along the eastern part of *Woodrowgreen*, Little Fransham, where there is a run of seven with a solitary freehold at its eastern end. Secondly, in such cases there is always some admixture of manorial allegiance. At places where the variety of manors is greatest, there is the strongest likelihood of an eleventh-century element. There is no evidence that freeholds have any tendency to begin at an earlier date than customary holdings, and at least two of the latter (LS 4 / Med 19 and LS 15 / Med 108) were first founded in the eleventh century. Where settlements were widely spaced, and particularly in some of the more outlying areas, such as *Curds Green* and *Southwoodmore*, Great Fransham, or the western end of *Woodrowgreen*, Little Fransham, there is a predominance of freeholds, and a marked tendency for occupation to begin in the thirteenth century.

Adjacent to these outlying areas there was a preponderance of large parcels of land and closes that went with nearby freeholds, and a scarcity of normal open field strips. This implies that in the thirteenth century there was a large-scale process of the enclosure by free individuals of former waste, woodland or pasture. However, it is also possible that the enclosures took place at an earlier date and were carried out by men who lived nearer the centre of the vill, and whose descendants only moved their dwellings to the periphery in the thirteenth century. In contrast to the outer areas, a more normal open field arrangement predominated nearer the centre. However, it should be stressed that the evidence for the field systems of both the inner and outer zones is almost entirely late medieval.

It is a moot point whether a more complete archaeological coverage in which all parts of the study area were subjected to field survey, along with a more even amount of late medieval documentary evidence for all the manors involved, would have contributed more coherent explanations of the processes involved in common edge settlement. It is tempting to suggest, however, that if court rolls and other manorial documents of the thirteenth century were available, then the picture would be very much clearer, for it was in that century that settlements were still being made in earnest. The assumed degree of inter-manorial co-operation touched upon earlier would perhaps then be discernible.

The tenemental system

Throughout Chapter 7 frequent mention was made of named tenements or *tenementa*, particularly those forming part of the manors of Kirkhams, Wilcoks and Sparhams in Little Fransham, and to a lesser degree in Great Fransham manor. These holdings, a peculiarity of medieval East Anglia, were considered by Douglas (1927, 17–66) to be 'derived from a single primitive holding', the Danish bovate of 12½ acres, while Gray (1915, 351–2) saw them as the result of the adaptation by Danish invaders of a pre-existing system of landholding akin to the *iuga* of Kent (Witney 1982, 231–3). Campbell (1980, 179) suggested that at Martham in east Norfolk *tenementa* were created as fiscal units by seigniorial authority in the early twelfth century but may not have become finally fixed until the early thirteenth. Whatever its origin, the tenemental system, whereby a group of customary lands distributed quite compactly and close to a peasant's house, carried a single name and the liability for its tenant or tenants to perform the duties of messor when elected at the manor court, was still of some significance in Little Fransham in the middle of the fourteenth century. Lucid summaries of the system have been given by Bailey (1989, 48–52) and Williamson 2003, 80 and 127–30). That the system was far from uniform can be seen in Burghall manor, Holkham, where each *tenementum* also contained a portion of the demesne (Hassall and Beauroy 1993, 48).

The term *messor* is often translated as hayward (see Thornton 2012, especially 213–14, for a succinct overview of the office). In Little Fransham the messor's duties seem to have been restricted to the collection of both free and customary rents in money and kind, of monies owed in lieu of labour services, and of farm rents, the presentation to the lord or his bailiff of annual accounts, and the payment of any shortfall. There is no evidence that he was expected to perform the tasks expected of a messor in a Midland manor, such as the impounding of stray animals, the guarding of the crops in the fields, the maintenance of the 'hays' (hedges) that surrounded the fields, and the presenting of offences to the manor court (Homans 1941, 293–7; Bennett 1937, 178–81). Multiple lordship and weak seigniorial authority in places such as Fransham would have made the execution of such duties by an official of a single manor almost impossible. The messors of Forncett, Norfolk, seem to have been burdened a little more than their Fransham counterparts. Their role was mainly financial, as in Fransham, but they were also responsible for overseeing conveyances of customary land and for other court duties (Davenport 1906, 25). In Forncett, unlike Fransham, the messor was appointed by the lord until the 1370s. Thereafter *tenementa* were elected, not so that a tenant thereof could be sworn in as messor, but so that a money charge per acre could be raised for use as the messor's stipend (Davenport 1906, 50–1).

Kirkhams manor court records give a very full picture of messor elections, and they show that the close connection between *tenementa* and messor duties was not necessarily ancient. Details of seventeen elections between January 1327 and February 1346 are known. In all cases the elected tenant's name, and nothing else, was given, without reference to a named tenement. In 1335 the jury stated that 6 acres and no less should *fac. offic. messor*, i.e. that a tenant must hold 6 acres or more before he might be elected. At the same time the burden of office was valued at 40d. Roger Cacy (see Med 11A) was elected, but Adam Jordan was willing to do the job and was sworn in. In 1337 Nicholas Edild was elected 'for the tenement that he held'. In 1342 three men, who held 3 acres, 1 acre and 1 acre were elected, but Adam Jordan was charged with carrying out the duties and was sworn in. Roger Cacy, who was said to hold 10 acres, was elected in 1343. A change of emphasis took place in August 1346 when the *land* of Roger Knyght was elected. In March the following year it was ordered that 40d and 4 bushels of wheat be levied from Knyght, presumably as payment for a licence not to act as messor (Knyght's lands were all or partly in Necton). In December 1347 the unnamed tenants of the lands (*terrarium*) Edyld were elected. The next surviving election record shows the situation had changed: in October 1353 the tenement Edild was elected, the constituent parts of the tenement were listed with acreages, the five tenants were named, and Robert Edild, who held the largest portion, was sworn in. From this point on, it was almost invariably the tenement that was elected and the main tenant who was sworn in.

Frequently the acreage of the holding was given, and when there were several tenants a list of the various parts was supplied. During the course of the fifteenth century the system of electing messors on the basis of named tenements began to break down. There is no doubt that the office of messor was not a popular one, for very often the post was left unfilled after the jury had chosen a tenement which was in the hands of the lord. The manor court jury sometimes took advantage of the lord's, or at least his bailiff's, ignorance by electing a fictitious or half-forgotten tenement. Some examples taken from the manor of Wilcoks will illustrate this habit.

In 1438 the tenement Boles (in fact a former Kirkhams freehold in *Quarent.* 5) was elected, but its contents were unknown, and it was in the lord's hands. The tenement Wilcokks, containing 1¾ acres in *Bolesfeld* (*Bullesfield*, in *Quarent.* 5), was elected in 1487 but was in the lord's hands. At other times no tenement name was given, as in 1473 when 3 acres in the lord's hands (*III acr. in man. dom.*) were elected. On some occasions the description of the tenement was very minimal, as for example in 1496 when the court roll entry reads *Wilcocks Offic. messoris Elig. Tent.* [blank] *cont.* [blank] *Et est in man. dom.*

Kirkhams manor tenants much more rarely made such evasive choices, probably because they were more numerous than those of Wilcoks, so that any one individual would not be elected for several years. Even at this late date, at the same court held in 1496, a real Kirkhams tenement was elected and its constituent parts and tenants were listed. The tenement of John Wilkinson contained 7½ acres and ½ rood held by five people. The largest landholder, John Wiskard, who held 4¼ acres, was elected. On some occasions the tenant of a *tenementum* which had been granted out for a money rent was shown not to be liable for messor duties. For example, in 1483 the 10-acre tenement late of John Gleymesford (in *Quarents.* 2, 5 and 20) and held by John Maunde, was elected, but the jury found that Maunde held it on the grant of the lord without the burden of messor duties (*ex concessione domini sine onere officii messor.*), and that therefore the lord was liable to carry out the task.

Customary lands which had been in the lord's hands for a prolonged period, or which were let out in different combinations and for 'new' rents, were not burdened with messor duties. A useful example of this is a widely scattered post-Black Death Kirkhams holding of between 7 and 9¼ acres which first appeared in 1351 and was associated with a messuage in *Quarent.* 27 (Med 71). Although the holding remained intact until some time after 1527, and although it was sometimes called a tenement and given names such as Jurdons (the earliest recorded tenant) or Hoberds (William Huberd, a tenant, died in 1427), a tenant was never elected as messor. Other holdings were known as *tenementa* but were not apparently liable for messor duties. A messuage and 1½ acres (in *Quarent.* 13) called the tenement once of Henry Knyght in 1384, later the tenement Pekehams, was unburdened (Knyt was tenant in 1330, John de Pykenham in 1393). Part of this holding was called the tenement Brandes in 1616 (MS 13415), after a family called Bronde or Brande, several members of which were tenants between 1524 and the 1580s.

The tenement of John Wilkinson also serves as a good illustration of these two interrelated aspects of the tenemental system, the frequently non-ancient names which the holdings carried and the tendency for these names to change from time to time. John Wilkennson held this unnamed tenement in 1384 and was liable for messor duties. In 1429 a certain tenement, which the late John son of John Wilkyn had held for the term of his life, was seized into the lord's hands. The name of the tenement Wilkinson thereafter remained unchanged, except in 1463 when it was named the tenement William Blak and Wylkynson, and in 1487 when its constituent parts and their tenants were listed, and it was called the tenement Tussenoll. An unusual aspect of this tenement was that at no time was a messuage said to form part of it. John Wilkensson also held a freehold messuage and 4 freehold acres in 1384.

The geographical compactness of East Anglian *tenementa* marks them off from the normally scattered holdings of the Midland peasant, and in general the admittedly late evidence of Fransham suggests that the pattern here was no different. Drawing once again on the tenement of John Wilkinson, it can be seen that, apart from one acre which lay far away in Great Fransham, probably in *Ellinghams field*, all the lands were in *Woodrowfield* (*Quarents.* 11, 12 and 15). There were, however, some *tenementa* whose lands were more widely flung. For example, in 1385/6 the tenement Benedict Heveds, held of Sparhams manor, was said to comprise 11 acres with a messuage containing 1¼ acres (Med 77). Evidence from court proceedings beginning in 1485 shows that pieces were to be found in no less than 7 *quarentinae*.

Evidence concerning messor elections derives almost exclusively from the manors of Kirkhams and Wilcoks. Interestingly, although much emphasis was placed on tenement names in Sparhams manor, the very full manorial court records, beginning 1485, contain no reference to the elections of messors, presumably because the practice had been abandoned earlier in the fifteenth century. The evidence for Great Fransham manor, in which *tenementa* were generally compact and did not have apparently ancient names, is so limited that it can be given in full. In 1396 the tenement of Thomas Lalle (with lands entirely in Kempstone and widely distributed) was elected to the office of messor, and the tenant, of the same name, was exempt because he held it for a money rent of 20s in place of all services. In 1397 the tenement of William Gybbes was chosen but was in the lord's hands. This situation was repeated in the following year with the tenement Kynnockys. In 1399 the tenement Wymers was elected, but the court roll extract does not indicate whether the post was filled by the tenant, Nicholas Sewles, who was dead by 1400.

In the early sixteenth century there were fewer references to the election of messors. The last-named tenant to be elected was Nicholas Mynne, who held 5½ acres of the tenement of Roger Knott in 1515. This was a Kirkhams holding, and there was no mention of a Wilcoks messor. The final recorded election was in 1516 when the Kirkhams tenement of John Wyton, containing a vacant messuage and 10 acres called Cassys (Med 11A), was chosen. No messor was named, for this tenement was completely (*totaliter*) in the lord's hands (MS 13167). The death of the role of the messor, after the confidently provocative way in which manor court juries had dealt with the problem for many decades, neatly symbolises the new relationship between lord and tenants which emerged in the early modern period.

The pottery industry

One comment must be made on a curious result of this survey, one perhaps of more interest to the archaeologist than the historian: the five small and discrete sites which were producing pottery of early medieval type in the twelfth and probably early thirteenth century. This is an almost unparalleled type of site in Norfolk. One place, at Blackborough End, Middleton, in West Norfolk has been claimed as a production centre of broadly similar pottery (Rogerson and Ashley 1985). Only one comparable site has been recorded close to Fransham, a small concentration of misfired sherds in Gressenhall parish (HER 29236). The five sites in Fransham should be set against the background of the two Late Saxon pottery production sites identified in the survey, which form an equally unusual pair. There is, moreover, no reason to believe that the quality of the Fransham clays had any special appeal to potters.

Whatever the significance of these discoveries to medieval ceramic studies, they are not without some faint echoes in field names found amongst the documentary records of the parish. The homage and rent paid by Matilda daughter of Odo of Great Fransham for a piece of land called *Potterescrof'* in Little Fransham, which Matilda held of Roger Christemesse, was conveyed by the latter to Thomas de Estune, clerk, in one undated thirteenth-century deed (MC 360/34, 713X6). In another 1 acre in *Pottescroft* lying between the lands of Roger Nephew and Walter Cristemesse was granted by Ralph son of Henry son of William of Little Fransham to William son of Leftheine of Wendling (TNA WARD 2/53/179/10). In a third deed Ralph Parle of Great Fransham granted 1 acre at *Poteriscroft* in Little Fransham to Katherine daughter of Roger, clerk, of Colton (TNA WARD 2/53/179/15). A rent of 3d for *Potters lund* with an adjacent croft was cited in an indentured memorandum of agreement, dated 1297, between William son of Ralph of Oxborough and Thomas of Scarning and his wife Agnes atte Halle. This land was probably in Little Fransham (TNA E 40/10519). In another undated, thirteenth-century, charter grant an acre of meadow in Fransham lay next to *Potekinesaker* (TNA E 40/8885). In 1385/6 Lady

Emma le Strange, lady of the manor of Kirkhams, held freely of Sparhams manor five acres in one piece called *Potters croft*. Roger de Toftes held 4½ free acres called *Potterscrofte* of Great Fransham manor in *c*.1400. None of these names can be equated with any of the five above-mentioned archaeological sites, although Lady Emma's *Potters croft* may echo a large Thetford-type ware production site (LS 20).

Taken together, the above place names are strongly suggestive of a potting tradition in Fransham, and this is reinforced by the field evidence. It has been claimed that such names coupled with occupational personal names (of which no examples earlier that the fifteenth century have been noted) are a 'reasonable guide to the existence of an industry' (le Patourel 1968, 121). One authority has suggested that minor medieval place names have been undervalued as evidence for medieval pottery making (Moorhouse 1983, 105). Of the Fransham potters themselves, whose skills stood at the base of medieval crafts, we have no information, but we can be sure that they were of low status (Steane 1985, 242–3). Cherry has suggested that medieval rural potting was often a part-time trade carried out by peasants (Cherry 1991, 204). The small size and scattered distribution of these sites indicates that itinerant potters made occasional visits to Fransham. Further examples of such transient activity would be expected were detailed field surveys to be conducted elsewhere in the area.

Late Medieval decline

The loss of forty-five archaeologically identified settlement sites and the failure to found any new settlements in the fourteeenth century, along with the establishment of only two new ones (Med 66 and 109) in the fifteenth, provide unequivocal evidence of decline. Manorial sources are in the main too late to reveal in detail how the Black Death and subsequent plagues hit the population. The gap in surviving Kirkhams manor court rolls between 23 October 1348 and 22 June 1351 denies us a list of those who had died, and it is only in the case of Great Fransham manor that some idea of the scale of mortality can be gained. A court roll extract for 4 July 1349 records the deaths of thirty-two tenants, of whom seventeen left heirs who were underage and seven had no heir. There is no roll of tenants from the immediately preceding years with which to compare these figures, but it is certain that the effect of the Black Death was devastating, with 'profound consequences in many ways' (Hoskins 1955, 92). In *c*.1400 this manor had forty-one tenants.

To judge from deductions made in the Lay Subsidy of 1449 the wealth of the Franshams seems to have been reduced by less than that of their neighbours. Great Fransham's contribution was a deduction of 10% of the 1334 assessment, Little Fransham's 5.8% (Hudson 1895, 276–7 and 286–7). These percentages were low in comparison with an average deduction for places in Launditch Hundred of 15.1%, and lower than that for Wendling (17.1%). They were also lower than those for all places surrounding the Franshams and Wendling: Little Dunham 26%, Great Dunham 12.7%, Kempstone 32%, Beeston and Little Bittering 16.7%, Longham 24.2%, Gressenhall and Great Bittering 25%, Scarning 12.5%, East Bradenham 19%, West Bradenham 15.2%, Necton and Sparham 22.5%. The total due from Great Fransham had climbed from eleventh to tenth largest in Launditch Hundred and that due from Little Fransham from seventeenth to fourteenth.

Manorial records are of limited value in assessing wealth or population. Lists of tenants in rentals and in first courts of new lords are not very useful indicators of population because they frequently included people resident outside the vill, because they are concerned only with one manor, and most importantly because they take no account of sub-tenants and of those who held no land (Hatcher 1977, 14). Juries at courts leet were staffed by freeholders only, so that lists of jurors and of those who were essoined, are also of no real use in assessing population size. A list, renewed on 7 October 1423, of those liable to attend the leet court of Little Fransham contains 60 names. These were of all those males aged 12 and over residing within the precinct of the leet, which was presumably coterminous with the parish. Multiplication by a factor of 2.5 might give a rough figure for the complete population. The resultant figure is 150, considerably below 325, the figure for Little Fransham's population in the late thirteenth century, which was derived from the possible number (65) of houses then existing. Unfortunately, no other comparable list has been found for either Great or Little Fransham.

Agrarian organisation, land-use and landscape change

There is no evidence that in the late medieval period a highly regulated system of open field or common field arable farming on the Midland pattern was practised in the Franshams. Rather the prevailing system was an irregular one in which 'there was not any discernible method of communal crop rotation' (Hall 1982, 20), and in which common grazing rights on the fields were restricted to the harvest shack. This system conforms with Campbell's sub-type B(i) (1981a, 114). A very useful typology of common field systems has recently been proposed (Martin and Satchell 2008, 22). Both Franshams belong to Type 2B, in which the common fields are variable in number and dominate farming practices, where there is some confusion between fields and their subdivisions and where 'the strips belonging to each holding tend to be clustered in the vicinity of the holder's house and there is less evidence [than in Type 2A] for communal cropping and folding arrangements.' Specific evidence for communal cropping has not been noted but cooperative procedures for the regulation of pasturing stock on harvested fields and on commons are often featured in manor court records.

In some parts of Great Fransham, such as Areas B and O, evidence for common fields was very slight or non-existent, and enclosures predominated. These consisted of land held in severalty (in individual ownership): tenement blocks, *i.e.* closes, crofts and yards attached to settlements (Martin and Satchell 2008, 45); closes held by free or customary tenants and detached from dwellings; and demesne closes. A distinction has been made between Type A 'block holdings', closes that had never been in multiple holdings and Type B 'consolidated holdings' created through the engrossing of strips (Martin and Satchell 2008, 22–3). It is reasonable to assume that many blocks were of great antiquity and of

Type A, for example *Kynewaldshawe* (in Area C) and *le Lund* (in *Quarent.* 21). We cannot date the formation of common fields. It may have been a protracted process in any one community, over several centuries on either side of the Norman Conquest. In any event it happened at a time in which detailed records were not made. So, some apparently Type A holdings might in truth be Type B, having been formed at an undocumented date from consolidated strips. Such a process might have resulted in a demesne close or one held by a tenant.

Certainly, both parishes contained common fields that had 'field' names and in which there were generally a large number of parcels, of widely divergent sizes. On the other hand, some fields, such as *Shepehousefield* (Area B) and the western end of *Middlefurlong* (in Area L), and large parts of *Bullesfield* (in *Quarents.* 4 and 5), consisted of sizeable pieces of demesne when first documented. The multiplicity of manors and the absence of any field book or 'dragge' make the reconstruction of the disposition of holdings in any one field extremely problematic, although the superior documentation available for Little Fransham reveals the landscape in slightly more detail. By the late sixteenth century, if not earlier, the enumeration of separate strips in rentals and in conveyances at manor courts may often have perpetuated ancient tenurial and legal distinctions between parcels of land which, because of engrossment, may not have existed on the ground. It is quite likely, however, that until the middle of the fifteenth century these distinctions were for the most part real. For it is otherwise not easy to explain why the Kirkhams manor rental of 1443 was far more detailed in its enumeration of many small parcels of land than that of 1384 had been. However, almost a century after the Black Death, with a smaller population laying claims to the land, it is clear that the coalescence of strips into Type B closes was underway.

It is difficult to form a clear picture of how groups of once distinct tenements, messuages and crofts appeared as they came under single ownership in the late medieval period. Equally, it is hard to understand the physical realities that prevailed in open fields after formerly discrete parcels of land fell into the hands of fewer tenants. The impression gained from the Kirkhams rental of 1443, in which abuttals were refined and updated from those of 1384, is that open-field strips were still definable realities. It is unlikely that such an effort would have been made to perpetuate so thoroughly in writing a lay-out that had changed on the ground. In Little Fransham, at least, the situation was soon to change.

A rash of agreements concerning the placing of boundaries (*bunda*) between pieces of land, recorded in Kirkhams and Wilcoks manor and leet courts during the 1460s shows that Type B closes were being created (such actions are absent from earlier court rolls). For example, in 1462 Richard Wiskard paid a fine for placing a boundary between his lands and those of Thomas Rous [in *Hochesfield*]. At the same court John Wyot and Thomas Stalworthy paid for erecting three boundaries between their lands at *Jurdons* in *Eastfield*. In 1464 the suitors at the leet court were ordered to place bounds between the lord's and Richard Wiskard's lands in *Hochesfield*, the lord's and Geoffrey Maunde's in *Churchfield*, and John Maunde senior's and John Wyot's in *Millfield*. John Wyot was amerced for placing, without licence, a boundary between his and Thomas Stalworthy's lands in *Eastfield* in 1465. Further examples followed in 1467, involving lands in *Hochesfield*, *Eastfield*, *Westfield* and at *Pekylbrygge* (south of the rectory). This process of piecemeal enclosure was to continue apace into the sixteenth century.

Amercements for pasturing before or after shack time, which were imposed in leet and manor courts, are indicative of communal arrangements, along with numerous references to the maintenance of fald gates (*falgatae*), many of which allowed access into the fields and commons for pasturing animals, while others were raised or lowered over streams and ditches (see Appendix 5 for a list of references to fald gates in court proceedings). This situation is markedly similar to that in eastern Norfolk where Campbell (1980, 174) found that the 'only clearly documented common right applied to subdivided fields.....was the right of common grazing on the aftermath of the harvest known as harvest shack'. The number of animals that any tenant was entitled to pasture on common fields and pastures, commonly known as a 'stint', was also subject to communal control. Many amercements for overcommoning were qualified with statements to the effect that the offender had exceeded his quota by reason of his tenure. However, actual figures of total permitted numbers were never given, although in some cases the number and breed of animals that the offender had pastured were stated.

Endnotes

i   A large fall in population as a result of the Black Death did not always result in a concomitant desertion of dwellings in all communities, e.g. Great Horwood, Buckinghamshire (Tompkins 2012).

ii The whereabouts of a predecessor is uncertain. One possibility, for which there is no evidence, is the rectory site. It is conceivable that the lord moved his house from there to Med 5 and the rector's residence was relocated from next to the churchyard at Med 30. Occupation, however, persisted here until *c.*1300. If the above tentative suggestion was correct then a tenant would have taken over from the rector.

iii The name commemorates William Crane, blacksmith and wheelwright, who set up a wagon-making plant here in the late nineteenth century.

Chapter 9. The Post-Medieval Period

The archaeological evidence

The settlement pattern within the study area has altered little since relative stability set in during the fifteenth century. As a result, with the overwhelming majority of post-medieval settlement sites still occupied, the contribution of archaeological field survey here is slight in comparison with that made in earlier chapters.

Just as in the case of preceding periods, the most important means of dating the few post-medieval sites located during field survey has been through an analysis of the pottery. The largest ceramic group, which can be dated to the later fourteenth, fifteenth and early sixteenth centuries, comprises late Grimston glazed ware. This consists predominantly of jugs, for the most part undecorated, and normally thickly lead-glazed on the exterior, in rather shapeless globular and baggy forms, often with wide strap handles (Jennings 1981, 50). Other distinctively late forms are bowls, often glazed internally, and bung-hole cisterns (Little 1994, fig.63). The date of the demise of the Grimston pottery industry is uncertain, but it had probably occurred by the mid-sixteenth century.

Fransham lies outside the western boundary of the main distribution area of Late Medieval and Transitional Ware (LMT), a major group of lead and copper glazed wares which was identified and described by Jennings (1981, 61–71). LMT dominated the markets of Norwich and eastern Norfolk from the middle of the fifteenth until the third quarter of the sixteenth century, and it is now known through the work of Mike Hardy and the Suffolk Archaeological Unit to have been produced on a large scale along the Waveney valley in north-east Suffolk (Anderson *et al.* 1996). So useful in dating late medieval and early post-medieval sites in eastern Norfolk, its scarcity in Fransham makes its value in this survey somewhat limited. Nevertheless, it occurs in small quantities on all settlement sites of this date-range.

Glazed Red Earthenware (GRE), a major class of oxidised lead-glazed pottery manufactured in several places in the county, was considered by Sarah Jennings (1981, 157–8) to have come into production at some time in the first half of the sixteenth century. Further work on Norwich ceramics suggested to her (pers. comm.) that the changeover from LMT to GRE took place in the 1560s to 1580s. GRE continued as the dominant pottery type well into the eighteenth century. It is extremely common in Fransham, although because there is no established local sequence for its development throughout its long currency, its dating remains rather speculative.

Late medieval German stoneware is very rarely found in Fransham, while the frequency of stoneware increases markedly from the sixteenth century. It was never common, however, and remains of only minor importance in the dating of settlement sites.

In general, late medieval and early post-medieval potsherds are scarce over the areas of the open fields and closes, and they never achieve the densities of earlier medieval material. In fact, fifteenth and sixteenth-century sherds are so sparsely distributed that it might be argued, from almost negative archaeological evidence, that there was a large-scale reduction in arable farming at this time. This scarcity of sherds, however, has been noted in the course of other Norfolk field surveys (Davison 1990, 22, 41 and 71; 1994a, 18). It was not merely the result of the decline in crop production and the rise of pastoral farming which undoubtedly took place in the centuries after the Black Death. Although changes in the pattern of manuring and in rubbish disposal practices may also partly explain the sparse distribution of sherds, it is far more likely to have been the result of a reduction in the use of large and easily breakable ceramic vessels for cooking purposes, and of rises in the use of smaller, more durable ceramic pots and, more importantly, of metal vessels (McCarthy and Brooks 1988, 107).

The documentary evidence

Around the middle of the sixteenth century most manors in both the Franshams are reasonably well covered by documentary sources, both rentals and court records, but after the beginning of the seventeenth the picture becomes much patchier in Great Fransham. Although Geoffrey de Fransham's death in 1414 had resulted in the division of Great Fransham manor amongst three of his five sisters, the holding appears to have been regarded as a single entity, in terms of the demesne and tenanted lands, throughout the fifteenth and sixteenth centuries, despite extremely complex divisions of tenure and inheritance, and enormous confusion resulting from leasehold tenancies of the manor, none of which will be explained here. In 1602, following a dispute in Chancery, the manor was permanently split between two lords, Sir Arthur Capell (who was also lord of Kirkhams and Wilcoks in Little Fransham[i]) and Nicholas Mynne esq. (MS 13391–13393, TNA C 78/128/4). Capell, the plaintiff, retained two-ninths, the demesne of which comprised 110 acres. His portion, styled 'Mills-on-the-Moor *una cum* Great Fransham', is relatively well documented. Court records begin in 1606 and continue into the nineteenth century, but with major gaps between 1616 and 1670 and between 1726 and 1787 (MS 13170, MS 13415, MC 969/1, MC 969/2 and MC 969/8, 858X7). The history of the other seven-ninths retained by Mynne the defendant, and styled 'Great Fransham', is very obscure, the only surviving manorial documents being court proceedings for 1668–71 and 1674–6 (MC 1847/1, 741X2; Priv. Pos. 1). The tenurial histories of the many freehold properties dependent on Mynne's part of the manor slip almost entirely from view after the beginning of the seventeenth century.[ii]

East Lexham manor, the second largest holding in Great Fransham, is also represented only sketchily in the documentary record, although extant court records of a sub-manor, Ellinghams, begin in 1576 and continue intermittently into the nineteenth century. This manor was styled *Ellinghams cum Rustins* in 1576 and *Ellinghams,*

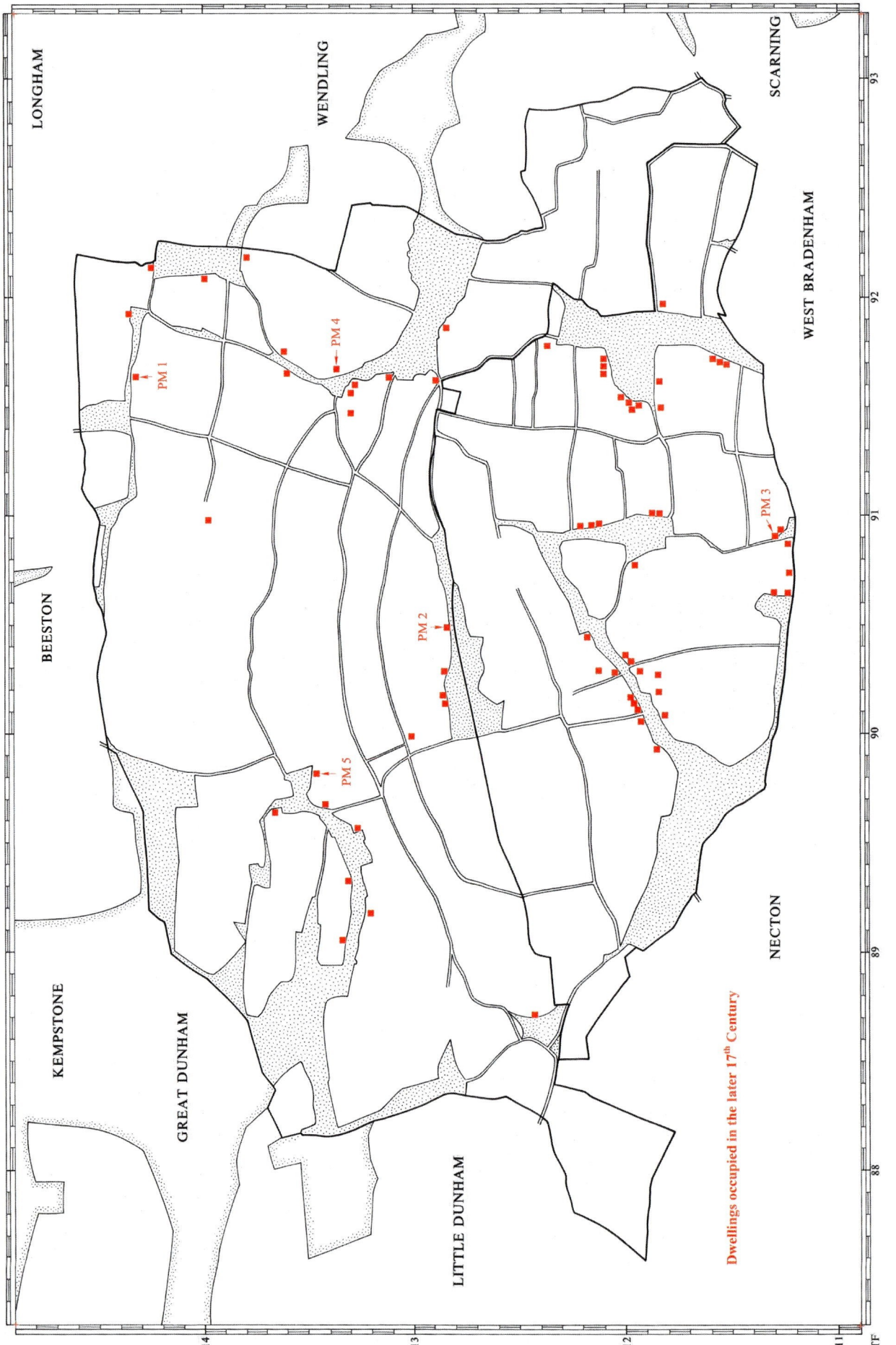

Figure 9.1 Post-medieval houses occupied in the later seventeenth century, areas of medieval common pastures shown stippled, scale 1:25,000

Rustins cum Curtlings in 1587 (MC 1847/1, 741X2). It was to become joined with part of the manor of Rougholme in the seventeenth century. The *Curtlings* element probably derives from *Curtlys*, a freehold of East Lexham manor, and the *Rustins* from *Rusteyns*, a freehold of Great Fransham manor and/or from *Rusteyn*, a freehold of East Lexham manor. These holdings, and others, were effectively demesne of this East Lexham sub-manor. No court rolls of the main part of East Lexham manor are known, and the only major sources are two early seventeenth-century documents already described (p.77). Bailiff's accounts for 1556–61 touch on one freehold tenement, Med 15 in Area B (KIM 1/8/12). Court roll extracts with some lists of jurors for 1625–70 contain some relevant material (MS 12832). Additional scant information can be found in short rentals for 1727 (KIM 1/8/18) and for 1790–1810 (MS 12835–12837).

There are court roll extracts of Rougholme manor for 1504–9, 1516–21, 1527–8, 1530 and 1534–5 (MR 28, 240X6 and TNA SC 2/192/95). Courts held in 1638 and 1640, and courts held jointly with Ellinghams cum Rustens in 1668 and thereafter, are recorded in a court book (MC 1847/1, 741X2). In 1550 Nicholas le Strange of Hunstanton knight acquired the late free chapel of St Nicholas called Rougholme and all its lands including those in Great Fransham by royal grant (Cal. Pat. Rol. 1925, 334–5). In 1552 le Strange sold part of Rougholme manor to Richard Hoo, lord of the manors of Northendhall, Scarning Parva and Guntons, all formerly amongst the possessions of Wendling Abbey (MR 255A).

In 1543/4 these three manors had been granted by the king to Robert Hogan or Hoogan who in 1548 had conveyed them to Richard Hoo (Carthew 1878, 683 and 697). Hoo's holdings are enumerated in a detailed rental of 1549 with additions of 1552 listing his Rougholme acquisitions (TNA SC 12/3/23), and they are also covered by other rentals of the 1550s (TNA E 36/98, TNA SC 11/478, SC 11/483, SC 11/485, SC 11/486, and TNA SC 12/3/24) and a court book for the years 1548–68 (TNA SC 2/192/96). After a gap of almost half a century two court books for the combined manors continue their history from 1615 until Enclosure and beyond (EVL 595 and 596). Further information can be culled from short rentals covering the period between 1710 and 1776 (EVL 599 and 601–4).

Wendling Abbey had been granted to Cardinal Wolsey in 1528 but he fell from royal favour in the following year. In 1546 the Abbey was granted to Wolsey's foundation Christ Church, Oxford. That part of the Abbey's holdings known as the manor of Wendling Nuper Abbis was thereafter held by lords who held of Christ Church (Carthew 1878, 683–5). Only three parcels of copyhold land comprising 3½ acres lay in Great Fransham. Their tenurial histories can be followed in a series of court books beginning in 1588 and continuing into the nineteenth century, with only one gap, between 1608 and 1645 (BL/MA 42; MS 4129–30 4E; NRS 24133–4 119X). There is also a rental of demesne and tenanted lands dated 1777 (NRS 24136 119X).

The sixteenth-century history of Castle Acre priory holdings in Fransham, which formed part of the manor of Herringshall and Dikewood in Wendling, is extremely uncertain. Very few court rolls survive, with records of single courts in 1557 (Holkham Hall, Tittleshall Register Book 29 and 1559 (TNA SC 2/192/102). After records of individual court sessions in 1608 and 1620 (TNA SC 2/193/3–4), four court books give almost uninterrupted coverage from 1623 to 1840 (MC 2104/1–2104/4, 920X9), and there is a rental book for 1750–1851 (MC 2104/6, 920X9). The tenure of only one piece, 6 copyhold acres of pasture called *Kingscroft* in Great Fransham (Area F), can be followed with confidence. Some of the other Castle Acre lands known from medieval sources are described as 'certain free lands and tenements' without any details of acreage or location and remain utterly obscure.

Great Fransham Rectory manor emerges from obscurity in 1671 with the start of a court book that continues into the nineteenth century (Priv. Pos. 1). A glebe terrier of 1729 is the first to list free and copyhold tenants, their lands and rents (DN/TER/68/4). Both documents tally well with each other, but it has proved impossible to establish many convincing links between their contents, in terms of the identification of tenanted lands, and what is known from fourteenth-century sources.

In consequence of these great shortfalls in available records much of the post-medieval history of settlement and land-use in Great Fransham remains uncertain. Little Fransham, on the other hand, is much better known, with manor court records for Kirkhams and Wilcoks and for Sparhams surviving with some gaps from the sixteenth to nineteenth centuries, and those for Cannons being equally continuous from 1541. Consequently, the sequence of tenure of almost all occupied properties and of the majority of tenanted lands can be followed from the sixteenth century to the Enclosure of 1807.

Margaret Spufford (1974, 56) found that a will 'gave much more comprehensive information than, say, a court roll entry', but this has not been found to be the case in this study, which is aimed at the history of land and property rather than of tenants and families. Of 311 Great and Little Fransham wills dating between 1377 and 1807, only 25 (8%) named the manor of which property was held, all such land being copyhold. Of 49 other wills made by residents of 27 other places, which yielded information relevant to Fransham, only 4 (8%) gave details of the parent manor. Obviously in the study of a one-manor community wills are a much more useful tool[iii]. Even here, however, wills have been valuable in one respect: they are normally quite unequivocal on the question of whether a house was standing or not, for the 'howse in which I dwell' cannot have been a decayed or empty messuage, or a mere site, at the time when a will was composed. Court rolls and rentals on the other hand were often infuriatingly out of date, giving no indication of whether the messuage or tenement comprised a house that was standing and occupied, or long since vanished.

Inquisitions Post Mortem have proved to be of limited help. Eight sixteenth-century inquisitions and one of the early seventeenth century have been examined. Most contain inaccuracies and obscurities with regard to manorial allegiance, and in some cases the evidence they provide clashes with that available in manorial sources and in wills.

Use has been made of twenty probate inventories of Fransham residents, the earliest of 1584 and the last of 1667. The social historical value of such documents is not the remit of this work, but some inventories have yielded good evidence for the comparative size of dwellings as perceived through the enumeration of rooms and outbuildings, particularly in the case of two larger houses (Med 40 and Med 116).

Population

The parish registers of Great Fransham begin in 1558 (PD 683/1) and those of Little Fransham in 1538 (PD 682/1). No attempt has been made here to use these sources for demographic analyses, although they have been of value in both filling gaps in tenurial histories of individual properties and in explaining, on occasions, the circumstances behind changes in ownership.

Some indications of population can be gained from national taxation records, especially the Lay Subsidies of 1524 and 1525. This tax was levied on people aged 16 or more whose movables were assessed at an annual value of £2 upwards or whose annual wages exceeded £1 (Sheail 1968, 31; Spufford 1974, 13–14). Records for Launditch Hundred are imperfect, with the numbers of taxpayers not surviving for 1524 and missing for many places in 1525. Twenty-seven people were assessed in Little Fransham and 18 in Great Fransham (TNA E 179/150/213). With the use of Patten's (1979, 79) formula, the total population of the Little Fransham can be estimated at 102 and that of Great Fransham at 68. Of surrounding parishes, Necton had 67 taxpayers in 1525, West Bradenham 29, Kempstone 6 and Beeston 32 (Sheail 1968). Fuller figures relating to Launditch Hundred are available for the Lay Subsidy of 1543. Thirty named places were assessed, and the average number of assessed people per place was 26.6. Little Fransham had 37 taxpayers and Great Fransham 24. Totals of taxpayers in surrounding Launditch parishes were 14 in Little Dunham, 35 in Great Dunham, 5 in Kempstone, 42 in Beeston, 30 in Wendling and 48 in Scarning. The most populous places were Swanton Morley, Gressenhall and North Elmham (77, 54 and 51), while Little Bittering and Godwick both produced only 2 taxpayers (TNA E 179/150/310).

Several late sixteenth-century court records yield some demographic information, giving lists of jurors and of others attending courts leet. For example, in 1577 as well as 20 jurors, 21 other people were present at a Little Fransham leet court, and at a Kirkhams and Wilcoks manor court held immediately afterwards, a further 11 people, all copyholders, were listed. Of these 4 are known from various sources to have been residents of Great Fransham or elsewhere (MS 13104). Sparhams and Cannons manor courts for the same year add only one other name of someone living in the parish. Thus, it can be shown that at least 49 males aged 12 or more were resident in Little Fransham in 1577. A similar exercise for 1599 results in a figure of 45 (SRO E3/10/9.16).

Returns made by the clergy of Norwich diocese to the Bishop in 1603 gave numbers of communicants, non-communicants and recusants for each parish (Jessop 1888). The assembled figures, representing adults of more than 13 to 15 years, seem to have been far from exact. There were 120 communicants and no others in Little Fransham, and the number for Great Fransham was 100, again with no others. Of 43 totals given for parishes in the Deanery of Brisley and Toftrees, 33 were expressed as multiples of 10, and 5 as multiples of 100. Little Fransham appears in joint seventeenth place within the Deanery, and Great Fransham in joint eighteenth. These figures cannot be very reliable, despite Jessop's claim (1888, 2) that the information furnished 'would give as near an approximation to a census of the population as in those days had ever been aimed at.' (Jessop 1888, 2). David Yaxley (2005 has suggested that the 1603 figures may represent c.60% of the total population. This calculation would give rather high figures of 200 for Little Fransham and 167 for Great Fransham. Following Patten's (1979, 82) method of adding 40% of the figure given to account for underage members, we arrive at totals of 168 for Little and 140 for Great Fransham.

The Hearth Taxes of 1664 and 1666 provide some indication of population, although it must be remembered that paupers and persons living in houses with an annual value of less than £1 were exempted (Frankel and Seaman 1983, 61; Seaman 1991, 25 and 28). In 1664, 27 Great Fransham householders shared 69 hearths, and 29 Little Fransham householders 67 hearths. In 1666, 29 people in Great Fransham paid £3 3s for 63 hearths, and 31 people in Little Fransham paid £3 9s for 69 hearths. Using a household multiplier of 4.75 (Patten 1979, 85), total taxed populations can be estimated as: Great Fransham 128 in 1664 and 137 in 1666; Little Fransham 137 and 147. Lists of exempted households in 1664 survive for only 37 Norfolk parishes, three of which, East and West Bradenham and Necton, are adjacent to Fransham. In them 18%, 39% and 23% of households were exempted (Longcroft 2006, 62–3, Table 8.1). These figures, averaging at 27%, would produce populations of 163 for Great Fransham and 174 for Little Fransham.

Although it has been possible to identify the manorial allegiance, tenure and geographical location of all houses in the Little Fransham hearth tax lists of 1664 and 1666, there was no such success for Great Fransham. The results for the former are shown in Table 9.1 and Figs 9.2 and 9.3.

When the 1670–3 Hearth Tax exemption lists for Little Fransham are considered the situation becomes complex and bewildering. The lists contain between 13 and 15 names (TNA E 179/338/422, E 179/335/890, E 179/336/535 and E 179/337/344). For example, fourteen people were exempted in 1670. Two had been taxed in 1666 (nos. 25 and 28). One had been taxed in 1664, but another person was listed as occupier of his dwelling in 1666 (no.13). One was a sub-tenant replacing the tenant's son who was listed in 1666 (no.26). Seven were widows, including one who had been taxed in 1665 but not in 1666. One man may have lived in part of a property listed in 1666 (no.28) or may not. The locations of the dwellings of two men, known otherwise only from the parish register are unknown[iv].

In 1676 the Church of England conducted a survey of all conformists, recusants and dissenters, known as the Compton Census. The returns for the diocese of Norwich appear to have listed all men and women of 16 years or more (Whiteman 1986, 189–90). There were 110 conformists and no others in Little Fransham, and 106 conformists and 1 dissenter in Great Fransham (Whiteman 1986, 224–5). Patten's (1979) method for adding an estimate of underage people gives figures of 154 for Little and 150 for Great Fransham. The total populations of 3,569 and 3,696 recorded for Brisley deanery in 1603 and 1676 (excepting Hoe which was assessed with East Dereham in 1603), show an increase of only 3.56%. This is higher than the figure of 1.12% given

178

1664				1666		
Order	Tenant	Number of hearths		Order	Tenant	Tenure
1.	Peter Large	2	2	2.	Peter Large	Wf Cc
2.	Widow Blunkall	2	2	1.	William Munsell	Kc
3.	Widow Fox	1	1	4.	Robert [Roberts]	KWf
4.	John Chapman	1	2	3.	John Chapman	Kc
5.	William Ashley	2	2	5.	William Ashley	Wf
6.	John Woodrow	7	7	6.	John Woodrow	WEf Sf
7.	Randolph Mynns	2	2	7.	John Mynn	Wf
8.	Widow Wright	2	-	-	-	Kc
9.	Mary Bastard	2	2	8.	William Powley	Cc
10.	Thomas Ashley	3	3	9.	Thomas Ashley	Kf
11.	William Sheene clk	3	3	10.	William Shene clk	Rectory
12.	William Large	2	2	11.	Henry Large	Cc
13.	Widow Powley	2	2	12.	Widow Pawley	Cc
14.	William Plowright	2	2	13.	John Goodson	Kc
15.	John Large	2	2	14.	John Large	Sc
16.	Anthony Bunting	1	1	16.	Anthony Bunting	Sc
17.	John Powly	2	2	15.	John Pawley	Sc
18.	William Powly	2	2	17.	William Pawley	Sc
19.	George Large jun.	2	2	19.	Thomas Allison	Wf
20.	Edward Shene	2	2	20.	Edward Shene	Kc
21.	William Minn	2	2	21.	William Mynn	Kc
22.	Mrs Davy widow	7	7	22.	Mrs Davy widow	f
23.	John Stalworthy	5	5	23.	John Stalworthy	WEf
24.	George Large sen.	1	1	24.	George Large sen.	Kc
25.	William Claxton	2	2	25.	William Claxton	Wc
26.	Robert Allison	2	2	26.	Robert Allison	Bf
27.	Edward Buddle	1	1	28.	Edward Buddle	Cc
28.	Widow Goodson	1	1	29.	Widow Goodson	Sc
29.	Richard Goodson	2	2	30.	Richard Goodson	Sc
			1	18.	Robert Danger	KWf
			1	27.	Widow Allison	Bc
			1	31.	James Dey	Sc

Key to tenures: c = customary, f = freehold
B = Bradenham, C = Cannons, E = Ellinghams, K = Kirkhams, R = Rougholme, S = Sparhams, W = Wilcoks, WE = Wendling

Table 9.1 Hearth taxes in 1664 and 1666, Little Fransham

by Whiteman (1986, 194–5, table 8.1) who did not include recusants and non-conformists in the 1676 total.

Clearly the estimation of total populations from the above religious and fiscal sources is far more approximate than accurate, although one trend is quite clear. Whereas the population of Great Fransham had been only about two-thirds of that of Little Fransham in the first half of the sixteenth century, it was catching up fast by 1603, the size of both communities increasing between 1525 and 1603, Little Fransham by 65% and Great Fransham by 106%. In contrast, the first three quarters of the seventeenth century saw little change with neither place achieving the 26% overall increase for Norfolk between 1603 and 1676 (Patten 1979, 85). Little Fransham's population fell by almost 1% and Great Fransham's rose by about the same amount.

If the 1676 figures are to be trusted, then the populations of both parishes must have grown during the eighteenth century. According to the census of 1801 the population of Great Fransham was 207, consisting of 38 families dwelling in 35 houses, and that of Little Fransham 214, with 46 families in 42 houses (Census Office 1831; www.origins.org.uk/genuki/NFK).

Settlement

For those medieval settlement sites still occupied at the present day written evidence has proved to be much more informative than archaeological, given all the problems of non-availability for field survey. Many such sites, particularly in the main village of Little Fransham, have well documented tenurial histories that have been

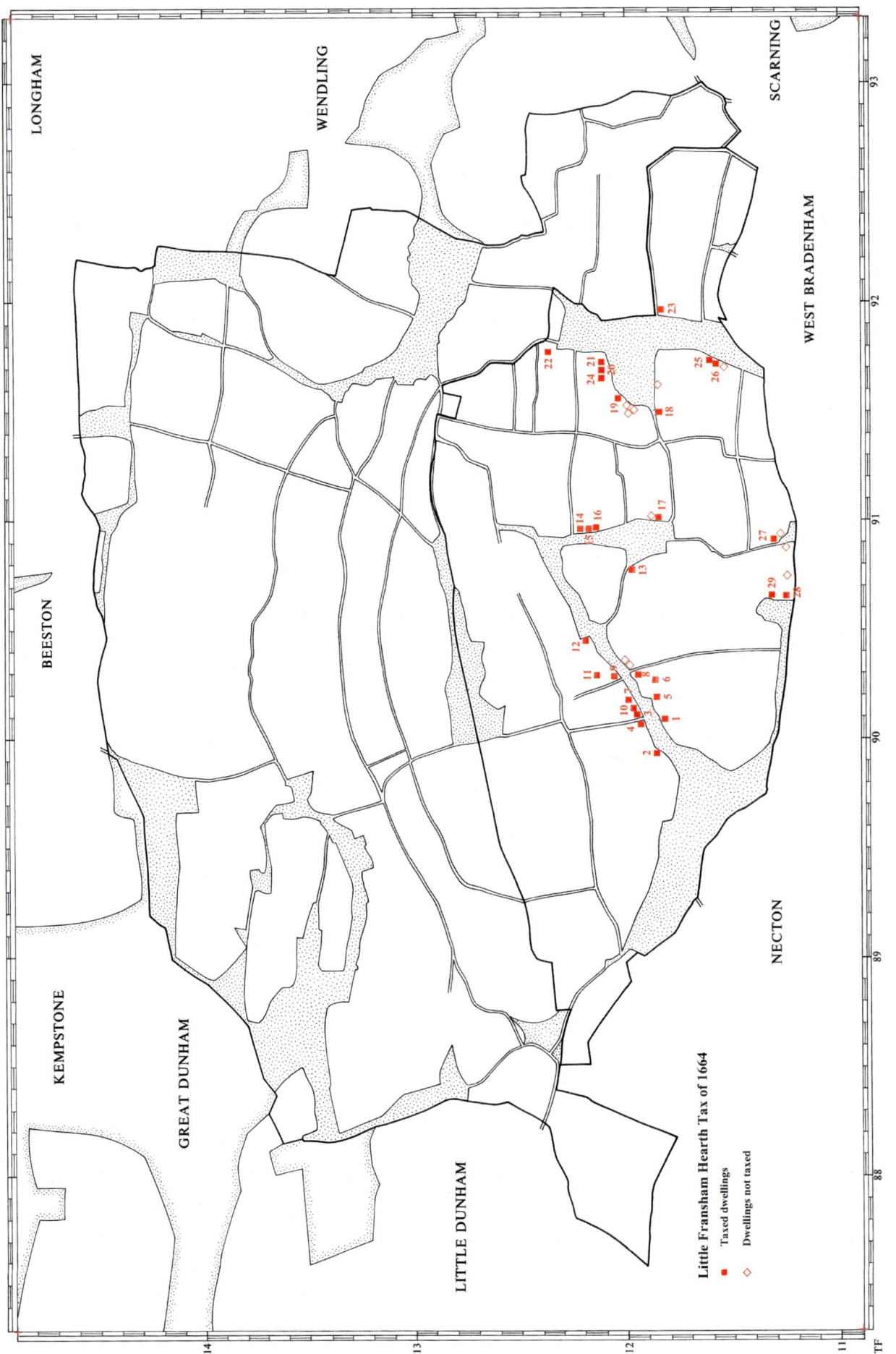

Figure 9.2 Little Fransham, houses listed in the 1664 hearth tax, areas of medieval common pastures shown stippled, scale 1:25,000

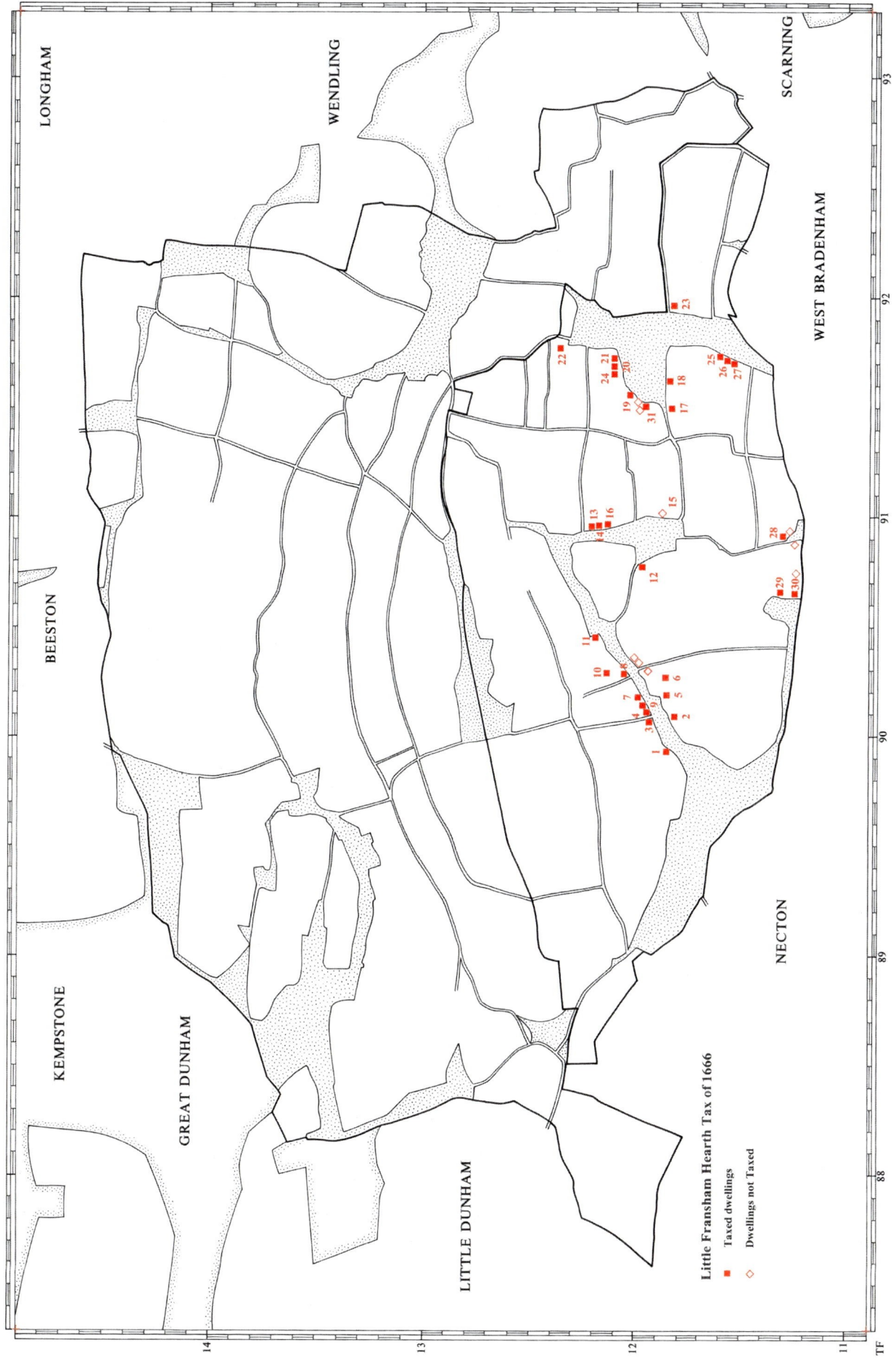

Figure 9.3 Little Fransham, houses listed in the 1666 hearth tax, areas of medieval common pastures shown stippled, scale 1:25,000

followed down to the Enclosure. Some other settlements were new foundations of the post-medieval period (Appendix 6). Three in Great Fransham (PM 1, 2 and 4) are known primarily or entirely from archaeological evidence. Details of PM 3, in Little Fransham, have been extracted from both field and written evidence, while PM 5 is an extant post-medieval house in Great Fransham without documentary evidence. The origins of a number of other properties, new foundations of the post-medieval period, can be established from documents although the sites are not accessible for field survey. The locations of PM 1–5 are shown on Fig. 9.1, along with all houses known from documentary evidence to have been occupied in the later seventeenth century.

On the basis of the archaeological evidence, seven medieval settlement sites are known to have been deserted at various dates between the late fifteenth/early sixteenth and the seventeenth centuries (Med 17, 23, 27, 50, 66, 80 and 94). Two were abandoned in the eighteenth (Med 78 and 79), six in nineteenth (Med 67, 69, 70, 76, 77 and 97), and two in the twentieth century (Med 40 and 68). One other (Med 50) was re-occupied in the eighteenth and abandoned once again in the twentieth century. Eleven sites with varying degrees of archaeological evidence for medieval and early post-medieval occupation, and including some with good documentary evidence, are still occupied today (Med 19, 21, 23A, 25A, 71, 75, 108, 112, 113, 114 and 116). It should be remembered that one of these (Med 112) represents two medieval holdings and that two others (Med 113 and 114) were in reality multiple medieval holdings, six and four respectively. Three sites, now deserted, were first occupied in the sixteenth and seventeenth centuries (PM 1–3). Another (Med 109) had been established at the end of the fifteenth century but was soon abandoned. It was reoccupied in the seventeenth and abandoned once more in the twentieth. In addition three high status sites should be added to the list of those inaccessible for fieldwalking: Little Fransham rectory which remained within its moat until a new rectory was built to the north-east in 1804, Great Fransham rectory, formerly moated and still occupied; Curds Hall, a manor house in the fifteenth century, and the largest dwelling in the Franshams in 1664 and 1666, with eleven hearths (Frankel and Seaman 1983, 61; Seaman 1991, 25). It was demolished in the 1930s and its site is now under permanent grass.

Signs of any reverse in population stagnation before 1500 are few. Hints of recovery during the fifteenth century can be seen in the establishment of houses on new sites, Med 66 (Little Fransham *Quarent*. 17) and Med 109 (Great Fransham Area M), and another in the division into two parts of the Kirkhams customary tenement Pykenhams in the north-east corner of *Quarent*. 13 in Little Fransham. In 1490 the tenant John Dabbe conveyed 1¼ acres including part of the house, hempland and arable in the croft to John Hawke, his wife and his son, and retained a cottage and a ¼ acre garden for himself. The latter parcel survived as an inhabited holding in the early nineteenth century. The building on the former was partly demolished in 1616 (MS 13415) and the property was said to be void in 1677 (MC 1850/1, 858X9). In 1590 the tenant, Richard Beckham, paid 6d for a licence to move a small building (*parvam domum*) standing on the former and to re-erect it on a 30 x 30 feet plot in the south-east corner of a Kirkhams copyhold pightle called *Bayfeild* on the north side of the common in *Quarent*. 6 (MS 13206). The building was 'now made a Smithsforge' in 1605 and was described as a smith's shop in 1775 (MC 1850/4, 858X9)

Manorial sources reveal that the later sixteenth century saw a minor surge in the establishment of new settlement sites in Little Fransham. One example is PM 3, a Cannons copyhold in *Quarent*. 16 which was built by 1589. In the late 1590s Med 76 in *Quarent*. 15, which had been deserted since the late fifteenth century, was occupied by a newly built cottage. Other new dwellings appeared in places unavailable for field survey. In 1580 ½ rood of Sparhams customary and formerly arable land in *Quarent*. 28, part of ½ acre which was a constituent of a tenement whose house lay in *Woodrowfield*, *Quarent*. 15 (Med 77), was conveyed by John Harwyn to Robert Wyskard. Part of a tenement built stood on the land (*desuper edificat.*). In the same year Harwyn conveyed to Wyskard another ½ rood, part of a ½-acre arable strip and an element of a Kirkhams customary tenement whose house lay in *Quarent*. 27 (Med 71). These two tiny pieces of land lay together and butted west on *Cannons Green*, the Sparhams one to the north. Their sequence of tenure as a single dwelling place can be traced to Enclosure[v]. The house of John Powly/Pawley contained two hearths in 1664 and 1666 (Frankel and Seaman 1983, 61; Seaman 1991, 28). A nineteenth-century house still stands at TF 9102 1185.

At some time before 1670, during a gap in surviving records of Kirkhams and Wilcoks court proceedings, another copyhold cottage was to be built, immediately to the north of John Powly's house, on 3 perches of land that had been part of the demesne called *Jeckespeece*. The cottage was first mentioned at a court held in 1679, although its tenant, Prudence Large widow, had been exempted from payment of the Hearth Tax in 1671–3 (TNA E 179/338/422, E 179/335/890, E 179/336/535 and E 179/337/344)[vi]. Again, this minute property's history can be followed to Enclosure. Between 1568 and 1572 another cottage was built by Robert Wyskard further north in *Quarent*. 27 on a ½-rood piece of land of the ancient Sparhams customary tenement Cappes (Med 70). After six years Wyskard sold the cottage to one Gilbert Ranson.

Another example of expansion in the housing stock is a ¼-acre free tenement and yard described as newly built in 1583 and lying on the east side of *Huberdslane* in the main village of Little Fransham at TF 9011 1193 (*Quarent*. 6). This was erected on the site of an ancient Wilcoks free tenement probably last occupied in 1429. The list of its tenants is continuous from the late sixteenth century, and a row of nineteenth-century cottages stands there today. Immediately east of this property a Kirkhams free tenement, that had become a customary holding in 1409 and no longer contained a dwelling house after the 1430s, was again built up in the late 1570s or early 1580s. Robert Robynson (*recte* Roberts) and Paul Turner, tenants of these two properties, along with Gilbert Ranson and Robert Wyskard, tenants of the two new dwellings in *quarents*. 27 and 28 (see above), were all amerced at a Mills-on-the-Moor leet court for illegally commoning on *Barnards Moor* where, as tenants of newly built cottages, they had no rights to do so (MS 13064).

By 1611 another new settlement had been established at the southern end of a 10-acre piece of Kirkhams and Wilcoks copyhold called *Coltings* in *Quarent*. 15, on or close to the site of a long-deserted Wilcoks free messuage. Katherine Rayner and her daughter Dorothy, wife of Richard Wadelow alias Cooke, were admitted to a copyhold tenement and 1 rood now surrounded by a hedge and ditch, on the surrender of John Mynne, tenant of the 10 acres. He received £15 from the women who also paid an entry fine of £1 (MS 13415). The low annual rent of 3d remained unchanged in 1795 (MC 1850/5, 858X8). The house, termed a cottage from 1614, lay at TF 9087 1124 where a row of nineteenth-century cottages stands today, although by Enclosure its tenure had been swapped with that of Med 77. A further example of a reoccupied site in this area is to be found at Med 78, part of a Sparhams customary holding that was described as newly built in 1613.

Details of the establishment of new houses in Great Fransham are much more sketchily documented. As outlined above, the population of Great Fransham almost caught up with that of Little Fransham during the late sixteenth and seventeenth centuries, and some examples of the creation of new dwellings are known. At a Mills-on-the-Moor leet court held in 1582 three people, Simon Allen, John Dennis and John Tompson, who had newly built tenements, were amerced for commoning illegally on the common of Great Fransham (MS 13063 and MS 13065). The same three, with the addition of John Cornewell, all with newly built cottages, were amerced again in 1583 at the same court sitting at which the above-mentioned men of Little Fransham had been penalised for the same offence (MS 13064)[vii]. Simon Allen and John Tompson have been associated with known sites (PM 1 and PM 2), and John Cornewell probably occupied a house on the (now inaccessible) site of St Katherine's chapel in Area G. It is possible that John Dennis' house was the westernmost in a row of dwelling sites of post-medieval origin in Area M, mentioned in the will of Thomas Bailey in 1670 (see below).

In 1530 Nicholas Myn of Little Fransham had bequeathed in his will a chalice 'that I bought of Mayster Crudde' to St Katherine's Chapel (in Great Fransham Area G) along with 2s to the Guild of St Katherine, which might be used for repair of the chapel (NCC 3–5 Alpe). By 1547/8 Thomas Cornell, who lived further south (see Med 57), was freehold tenant of the chapel, paying Great Fransham manor an annual rent of a halfpenny (MS 13076) and in 1553 the chapel was said to have one rood belonging on its north side (MS 13077). It can probably be identified with the only property described in the will, proved in 1558, of Thomas Cornell alias Wryght: 'one parcell of lande inclosed with an ould dyke and with a certen howse bilded therupponn' and a rood of land belonging, which he had purchased from Nicholas Mynne gent. (ANW 253 Teylor and ANW 553 Hychekoke)[viii]. John Cornell, a son of Thomas, was listed as the rent payer in one rental of 1570 (MS 13077), but his brother Edward appeared in another of the same date. Mother Wright or Cornell paid the rent between 1573 and 1582 (MS 13079). There is no further record of the ex-chapel until 1674 when John Brocke, following the death of Thomas his father, swore fealty at a Great Fransham manor court for a freehold messuage called *Chappell House* (Priv. Pos. 1). In 1699 John Brock, blacksmith of Great Fransham, bequeathed his house called *Chappell hurn* with a hempland and rood belonging to his son Thomas (ANW 23 1699–1700).

In the Middle Ages there was no settlement site in Great Fransham along the northern edge of *Barnards Moor* (Area M). However, there is post-medieval documentary support for three properties there, although no evidence indicates when they were first established, and there is archaeological evidence for a fourth (PM 2). The westernmost lay at TF 9014 1284 where a north-south row of nineteenth-century cottages now stands. In his will of 1670 Thomas Baly or Bayly, butcher of Great Fransham, left to his nephew Thomas a messuage or tenement with grounds at *Barnards Moore*, along with 1¾ acres of arable land butting north on the green way leading towards the windmill (*i.e. Southgateway*) and south on the said grounds. A copyhold ½ acre lying within the 'homestall' of the messuage was to be surrendered by John, a brother of the elder Thomas (TNA PROB 11/333/157). In 1676 John Baley, carpenter of Great Fransham, bequeathed his messuage or tenement with 3 acres to his wife for life with reversion to his son George (ANW 1676–7.108). A series of deeds show the descent of the property between 1682 and 1820 (NRS 3828–3838, 13E4; BRA 925/3/1–3, 109X6). Abuttals concerning a confidently located piece of glebe land in glebe terriers between 1677 and 1740 serve to confirm the location of the property, which in 1779 butted south on Berners Moor. At Enclosure it contained 2 acres 3 roods and 19 perches and was the freehold of John Bunn. The present property comprises 2.92 acres and incorporates the line of *Southgateway* at its northern end.

In 1657 Edmund Allenson, yeoman of Great Fransham, bequeathed to his grand-daughter Agnes, wife of William Phillips, a house and ½ rood butting south on *Barnewells* [sic] *Moore* (TNA PROB 11/266/496). This must have lain to the east of the above house, probably at TF 9018 1287, where a nineteenth-century house stands and where at Enclosure a copyhold messuage and 1½ roods of the Capell portion of Great Fransham manor was deemed to lie (for this bizarre transference of tenure see Med 108).

The third dwelling lay further to the east. In his will, proved in 1670, Samuel Harsnett of Great Fransham esq. [lord of the main portion of Great Fransham manor] gave the churchwardens and overseers of the poor in the parish, for the sole use of the poor, his tenement or cottage lately purchased from Mr Denry, together with lands belonging (TNA PROB 11/334/163). The 1735 glebe terrier listed a small cottage with an adjoining parcel of about ½ acre which was for the use of the poor of the parish. In the 1740 terrier this was described as a messuage or tenement with a ¾-acre piece belonging. The latter butted south on the said house and lay between land of the Earl of Essex on the west and of Necton Town on the east. On an undated, eighteenth-century, framed linen list of parochial charities, which is preserved in the parish church, the property is given abuttals and described as 'One piece of Land on which a House formerly stood containing by Estimation three Roods'. Abuttals are the same as those of 1740, with the addition of land of the Earl of Essex north and *Barnards Moore* south. The site can be identified with a ½-acre plot of town land depicted, without a building, on the Enclosure map at TF 9027 1285.

There is further documentary evidence for post-medieval activity in this part of Great Fransham. In April 1592 Adam Hicke, miller of Great Fransham, conveyed a parcel of land to Ralph Powley of Little Fransham. In

September 1598 the latter conveyed by charter to his eldest son, William Powley of Little Fransham, a 60-feet square parcel with a newly built windmill on it (*nunc de novo superstruct. et edificat.*). It lay between land of Nicholas Mynne gent. lord of Great Fransham manor on the east and Ralph's land on the west, and it butted north on *le Greenewaie* and south on Ralph's land (HRO 8182). The will of Richard Skynner, miller of Great Fransham was proved in December 1601. He left no real estate. The places of residence of people named in the will suggest he was of Beeston origin (ANW 214 Bastard).

In his will, proved in September 1603, Ralph Powlye of Little Fransham left to his eldest son William his windmill in Great Fransham and all his other lands there including a tenement with 5 acres, which had been purchased from Nicholas Powlye (ANW 207 Wigget). Ralph's dwelling house was in Little Fransham (Med 67 in *Quarent.* 17). In 1613 1 acre of Little Fransham glebe lay near the windmill and butted north on the common way and south on *Barnards more*. An indenture of 1655 referred to a 1-acre parcel of arable in *Church Field*, butting north on the *Greenwaie* and on land 'whereon ye Mill standeth' (Mills and Reeve 12/03/70: Mason Necton deeds). The eventual fate of the mill is not recorded. A close called Mill Field is shown on the Tithe map, centred at TF 903 131. The mill probably stood in the north-east corner, but it has left no surface trace.

The western edge of *Eastendmoor* in Great Fransham had not been settled in medieval times. A ¼-acre plot of Great Fransham demesne land called *Haddokes pightell*, first recorded in 1401 lay at the east end of Area C. There is no evidence that it contained a house before the late seventeenth century. In 1666 John Shinquin's dwelling contained two hearths, although two years earlier it had been recorded, presumably in error, as having five (Frankel and Seaman 1983, 61; Seaman 1991, 25). In his will, proved in 1681, John Shinkin of Great Fransham, husbandman, bequeathed his dwelling house and land belonging called *Haddocks Pightle*, which he had purchased from John Hamond, to his son John (ANW 452 1680). He had acknowledged at a Great Fransham manor court in 1674 that he held by copy of court roll a tenement and ¼ acre of free land acquired from Hamond (MC 1847/1, 741X2). Thereafter the descent of the property can be followed through several wills. By 1794 it contained a blacksmith's shop and was known as *the Checker* (ANW 167 1783). This was presumably a public house, as it was to be in 1845 (White 1845, 333). A nineteenth-century house called *Chequers* now stands slightly to the south of a house depicted on the Enclosure map, at TF 9166 1358.

Only one house in Little Fransham stood on common pasture in 1807 (at TF 9052 1214, *Quarent.* 10), and in view of the great stability and integrity of commons there right up to Enclosure it is appropriate that its origins are well documented. In 1793 William Askew of Little Fransham requested the lord of Kirkhams and Wilcoks to grant him a piece of ground, part of the 'waste and soil' and now 'staked out' on which to build a cottage. He was admitted as a copyholder paying an annual rent of 6d. In 1813 the messuage was described as being 'in two dwellings'. A nineteenth-century house still stands.

The common pastures and the common fields

As the greater part of the commons of both Franshams remained intact until 1807, the integrity of these tracts of land must have remained important to the inhabitants during the post-medieval period. In the sixteenth century amercements for minor encroachments were as frequent as they had been earlier. Subpoenas for large sums seem to have forced most offenders to release their illegally acquired land, and there are only two recorded cases of licensed encroachments or purprestures, both in Little Fransham: 1 acre of the northern edge of *Eastendmoor* in 1598 (Med 116 in *Quarent.* 19) and an area of slightly more than 1½ acres on the north side of Little Fransham Old Hall (*Quarent.* 13), first recorded in 1604 (MS 13150).

Court rolls, particularly those of better documented Little Fransham, show that communal management of shared pasture resources was continued into the late sixteenth century with almost the same thoroughness as in the Middle Ages. It should be noted, however, that amercements concerning fald gates (*portae cadutae*) in leet courts had ceased before the middle of the century (Appendix 5). Apart from many amercements of people from neighbouring communities for illegal commoning, in both Franshams there were frequent indictments of local tenants for over-commoning, usually using the same formulae as in earlier times, that a tenant had pastured more animals than he was permitted by reason of his tenure. However, in no case was the permitted number of beasts ever stated. There were also frequent proclamations and amercements concerning the pasturing of animals on the common pastures and fields at non-permitted times of the year. All this is at variance with a statement near the end of a Kirkhams and Wilcoks extent and rental of 1566 that the common of Little Fransham contained 140 acres 'whereupon all th'inhabytants there maye keep their cattell [animals] without stinted' (MS 13158). On 1 April 1594 it was determined at a Little Fransham leet court that 'the orders heretofore made concerninge sheepe putt upon the Common by the inhabitants shall be dissolved henceforth', but no replacement order was made (MS 13210). Subsequent Little Fransham court records up to 1616 and after 1670 when surviving records resume, contain no presentments for offences concerning over-commoning by local people, apart from one case involving Richard Beckham in 1597[ix] and another concerning horses in 1670. Animals are mentioned only in affirmations of, or minor changes in, byelaws, relating to the impounding of un-rung pigs and stray cattle, horses and sheep by the pinders (officers annually elected at the leet court). Between 1710 and 1724 there were regular statements regulating the cutting of 'firrs and whinns' (furze and gorse) on the commons and their sale, and thereafter non-specified byelaws were reconfirmed annually (MC 1850/1–3, 858X9; MC 1850/4–5, 858/X8). Such actions by the court suggest that, in Little Fransham at least, the conservation of firewood resources had become more significant than that of communal pasture. This can probably be explained by the greater availability, from the late sixteenth century onwards, of enclosed grassland, as well as by the concentration amongst a smaller part of the general population of the need for pasture, with fewer inhabitants directly dependent on animal husbandry.

The inhabitants' high regard for their commons is exemplified in an agreement over their ancient customs made between the rector of Little Fransham and the township in 1648, as a confirmation of what had been confirmed as customary in a previous agreement of 1584 (FX 110/1; Carthew 1879, 190–1). As well as several clauses on tithes of firewood, fruit, livestock, hay and grain it was agreed that Samuel Cushinge [rector] 'shall not keep or feed any cattell or any other thinge upon the common paster of the town nor fell nor carry away any fuell out of the said common paster aforesaid in the right or title of the parsonage of littell Fransham aforesaid without the consent of the whole Townshipp'. The tone suggests that as far as commons were concerned the community saw itself as proprietor, or at least as the chief holder of rights. The same self-confidence was in evidence almost one hundred and forty years later when, in 1787, the jury of the Little Fransham leet gave 'leave to the Earl of Essex or to the Tenant of a certain Piece of Land called Wilcocks to cast down the present Fence or Row thereto belonging next the Common called the Whinn Common in Little Fransham and to raise a new Fence in a direct Line instead thereof; And which Land so to be inclosed shall be enjoyed for ever hereafter by the said Earl of Essex and his Heirs without any Interruption whatever' (MC 1850/4–5, 858X8). A plan of 1804 (DN/FCP 8/1) depicting Little Fransham rectory and its curtilage suggests that the community's control over its commons had diminished immediately before Enclosure: an encroachment including outbuildings extended south to the turnpike road, which ran along the line now taken by the A47 trunk road (Fig. 7.33).

Demesne lands

Far more is known about the demesne of Kirkhams and Wilcoks in the sixteenth century than of any other manor. Two versions of an extent of 1502 survive. One is neatly laid out but contains no acreages (MS 13155). The other does so, but is rough, unfinished and damaged (MS 13167). The minimum total acreage amounted to 300. Pasture is mentioned six times, thrice on its own, twice with land and once with meadow. A number of closes were probably pasture although not specified as such. There were also four groves.

In almost all cases, the parcels enumerated in 1502 can be equated with names occurring in fifteenth-century court rolls and in later and more complete documents. An extent, in English, of 1566 (MS 13158) divided the demesne into pasture, arable, meadow and woodland ('groves'). Acreage totals were, respectively, 164, 138½, 7¾, and 5¼, giving a total of 315½. Two identical versions of an extent of 1577 (MS 13156 and MS 13157) gave measurements in acres, roods and perches. These amounted to a total of 375½ acres and 22½ perches, a figure excluding the lands of one customary tenement temporarily in the lord's hands. Most entries are described as land [*i.e.* arable], closes or meadow, and only four, comprising just over 14½ acres, as pasture. It can be assumed that many of the closes were under grass. There were also four groves together containing a little over 6 acres.

A survey of the manor of Kirkhams and Wilcoks, also in English, and made by William Hayward in 1605, contains an extent of the demesne as well as a detailed rental of freeholds and copyholds, and was accompanied by a map or 'plott', which, most regrettably, does not survive. Notwithstanding its late date this document remains the key to any reconstruction of Fransham's medieval and post-medieval landscape.

Both demesne and tenanted lands were located in 29 *Quarentinae*, and these enable a reliable reconstruction of the distribution of holdings despite the lack of the map. It should be stressed that these *Quarents*. (Fig. 7.3) were not the equivalent of furlongs or of long established subdivisions of the open fields, and they bear little relationship to any arrangements that existed earlier. Rather they were precincts or blocks, often separated by roads, into which Hayward chose to divide the parish for his own convenience. Areas where divisions between holdings were complex he subdivided into a greater number of *Quarents.*, but where ownership was straightforward or of little concern to Kirkhams and Wilcoks, he adopted a simpler approach. For example, *Millfield* was subdivided into nine *Quarents.*, while all of *Eastfield* was treated as one, *Quarent.* 29. In dividing the parish in this somewhat arbitrary way, Hayward was following a practice that had become common in the sixteenth century (Campbell 1981b, 12–3). Demesne lands in Little Fransham, which lay in 23 *quarents*. were given 'the true measure...by Statute measure', *i.e.* in acres, roods and perches, as well as 'the contente by the comon estimacon or by evidences' of twenty named tenants, in acres and roods. There are only minor differences between Hayward's detailed measurements and those entered in the 1577 extent (MS 13156–7). For example, *Wilcocks* contained 20.3.11 in 1577 and 20.2.10 in 1605, and the measurements for *Colemanscroft* were 4.0.17 and 4.1.5. As regards demesne meadows in Great Fransham Hayward's abuttals and measurements were not his own work, but were copied (and translated into English), from the 1577 survey. Total acreages by each method of calculation for lands in Little Fransham given at the end of the 1605 extent are shown in Tables 9.2 and 9.3.

The pasture land in Beeston was a close called *Knightwodd*, centred at TF 9000 1460)ˣ. That in Necton was named *Cases* and centred at TF 8905 1176.

Managed woodland was not a predominant feature of the Fransham landscape in the sixteenth century. The role of woodland within these two parishes has been clearly set within the context of Norfolk by Barnes and Williamson (2015, 76–86). By an indenture of 3 March 1526, all timber, wood and underwood 'growing of in & abought' *Wylcokks Close* in *Quarent.* 14 and in twenty-three other named places in Little Fransham, including *Annyellys*, *Bullys* and *Jecks* groves (in *quarents.* 2, 5 and 28), and *Elys grove* which is probably to be identified with *Chownes* in *Quarent.* 11, were sold by the lord of Kirkhams and Wilcoks, Sir Giles Capell, to Thomas Wyskard, Nicholas Mynne and Edward Mynne. The price was £14, the felling was to be completed by Michaelmas 1528, and a clause aimed at allowing sufficient regrowth was included. Many of these trees must have been growing in hedges and in thin strips along boundaries, to judge from some of the places described, *e.g.* 'the row by hobberds lane', 'the dykerowe on the Westside of the same brondesclose', 'the borders without Redepitt', and simply 'hotches' (MS 13251). When Sir Edmund Gorges leased Kirkhams and Wilcoks manors and other holdings to Nicholas Mynne and John Stalworthy for a term of 10 years in 1485, wood

Acres by estimation	Demesne in Little Fransham	Measured statute acres, roods and perches
176	Pasture *	192.2.15
124	Arable	118.3.20
31.5	Meadow	32.1.25
12.5	Wood	11.3.0
0.5	Parcel of waste	0.1.30
342.5	**Total**	**356.0.10**

* The totals include 24 acres estimated and 29 acres and 10 perches measured for a pasture close called Cases in Necton.

Table 9.2 Acreages of Kirkhams and Wilcoks demesne in Little Fransham given in the 1605 extent (MS 13159)

Acres by estimation	Demesne outside Little Fransham	Measured statute acres, roods and perches
3	Pasture in Great Fransham	2.2.10
9	Arable in Great Fransham	7.2.15
7.75	Meadow in Great Fransham	-
14	Pasture in Beeston	14.0.0
24	Pasture in Necton	29.0.10

Table 9.3 Acreages of Kirkhams and Wilcoks demesne outside Little Fransham based on the 1605 extent (MS 13159)

from four 'grovys clepyd' called *Anyell*, *Bolys*, *Jekks* and *Chounys* had been specifically excepted (MS 13234). When Sir Giles Capell leased the same for a term of 21 years to John and Edward Mynne in 1532, the four groves and all oaks and other timber growing therein and elsewhere on the manor and other lands were excepted (MS 13253). Almost identical exceptions were made when the lease was renewed in 1543 and 1555, with Edward and Nicholas Mynne as lessees. On these occasions ash trees were specified along with oaks (MS 13256–7).

Only one of the four groves, *Amielles* or *Anyells* was still wooded in 1605. The others, *Bulls*, *Chownes* and *Jecks*, were described as 'three several pightles late converted from Woodgrownde to pasture' in a lease of 1603 (MS 13279). *Anyells* did not last much longer, 'being of late woodground and stubbed upp' in 1637 (MS 13326; Barnes and Williamson 2015, 77). The other woodland listed in 1605 comprised 8 acres 1 rood and 10 perches of 'wodde and bushshes' in the close called *Wilcocks* in *Quarent.* 14, which also contained 12¼ acres of pasture. This woodland also had gone by 1607 when *Wilcoks* consisted of 24½ acres of pasture (MS 13301).

The only other reference to woodland in Little Fransham relates to wood pasture. Five copyhold acres of Cannons manor, which had been called *Jaggs* and *Fynches* in 1537 when there had been no mention of woodland, were described as two pieces of pasture and wood called the Grove in 1613. They lay in *Quarent.* 16.

Although there had been some wood pasture in late medieval Great Fransham, there was only a tiny amount of managed woodland. In c.1430, out of a total of 632¼ acres, Great Fransham manor boasted only 1 acre enclosed with underwood, in Area O. In 1613 the rectory glebe included a 1¼-acre grove (in Area B). It was described in an abuttal of 1548 as a *grovetta* (TNA SC 12/3/22). By 1677 it had been converted to pasture. A parcel of a wood, freehold of East Lexham manor, can be equated with groves purchased with other lands for £120 by George and Edmund Clement of Longham in 1563 from John Calybutt esq., lord of Ellinghams manor. These lay in the northern part of Area C. Accounts of 1564 itemised various sales of trees: 4 oaks in the grove at 8s each, 5 elms and 2 oaks in the close in the upper furlong for 20s, 1 oak in *Dymes closse* for 5s 8d, 1 oak 'without ye hold of ye dyke toward Elynghams more' for 5s, 2 oaks in the grove 'being ye Fayrest' for 26s 8d, 1 oak in the grove by *Elyngham grene* for 9s, 23 oaks in the north-east corner of the grove for £6. Sale of underwood is indicated by two entries: all the grove at 8s per acre to be felled in two years, and 4 acres of wood at 15s per acre (Holkham Hall, Longham Bundle 8, 401). Most of the northern part of Area C is depicted as tree covered on Faden's map (surveyed in 1790–4), but a very much smaller wooded area, centred on TF 9082 1430, is shown on the Enclosure map (surveyed in 1805).

One useful source for the land-use over a considerable part of Great Fransham in the late sixteenth century is an undated group of lists of lands with their rents or potential rents, probably the property of Henry Mynne gent. (ob. 1589), lord of Great Fransham manor and holder of many other lands, particularly of East Lexham manor. One summary list comprised 487 acres, none of which was arable, 312 were pasture, 49 meadow and 126 wood (MS 13085). Of 80 acres in *Hallwood* (Area A) 30 were meadow, 10 pasture and the remaining acres were not described. Might they have reverted to woodland? In another list a 6-acre 'boschy grove' lay at *Hallwood Gate* and nearby *Dunham Close* contained 20 acres of 'wood and boschys'. There were 80 acres in *Pilwood* (Area A) 'whereof X is run in boschys'. In the next close, probably in Little Dunham or Necton, 3 out of 12 acres had similarly 'run'. Under the heading 'The scituation about the mansion late Curds' a 1-acre grove lay beside *Ernys* and *Curds croft*, and 2 out of 16 acres in the 'great close afore the gate' had also 'run'. All the above land parcels were in Area A. According to one list, *Kinwalsawe Wood* (in Area C) contained 30 acres of pasture. In another the acreage of *Peretre close* with *Kynnashall Wood* was given as 40 acres.

A survey book of 1595 detailing lands of Nicholas Mynne gent., lord of Great Fransham manor, listed most of the parcels contained in the above-mentioned document as well as many pieces of arable in Great Fransham. It gave very different figures (MS 13084). All the above mentioned lands were described as pasture, and the woodland total amounted to only 64¼ acres and 36½ perches. If these figures are to be believed, then Mynne must have embarked on a policy of rapid and widespread woodland clearance. Perhaps, then, one of the interrogatories prepared in 1598 and to be answered by witnesses in a Chancery suit between Sir Arthur Capell and Nicholas Mynne may not have been wide of the mark, 'Item, whether you do knowe or have hearde what tymber trees and woodes growing upon the demeasnes or landes parcell of the saide manner have been felled by the Defendant or his Anncestors or by his or their procurement And what is the valewe of the woodes so

Date	Length of lease in years	Acreage, land-use and location	Annual rent	Lessee	Notes	MSS reference
1601	7	9ac in GFr	£2-5s-0d	William Poley of LFr yeoman	-	MS 13274 40C2
1603	7	12ac, 5ac, 0.5ac & 5ac arable in GFr	£4-17s-5d	Thomas Baxter of GFr yeoman	surrendered 1607	MS 13276 40C2
1603	7	3ac & 1ac arable in GFr	£0-14s-8d	William Costyne of LFr carpenter	-	MS 13277 40C2
1603	7	5ac arable in GFr	£1-15s-0d	Robert Davye of LFr gent.	-	MS 13278 40C2
1603	at the lord's will	4ac meadow, 1.5ac pasture, 0.75ac arable & 14ac meadow or pasture in GFr, & 3 pightles pasture (1ac 1 rood & 19 perches) in LFr	£5-7s-4d	Robert Clarke of LFr wheelwright	-	MS 13279 40C2
1604	7	5ac & 7ac pasture in GFr	£4-4s-0d	Andrew Sammes of GFr fishmonger	cancelled 1607	MS 13280 40C2
1604	7	3ac arable in GFr	£0-12s-0d	William Myller of GFr husbandman	-	MS 13281 40C2
1604	11	29.75ac pasture in 3 closes in GFr	£6-0s-0d	Richard Beckham sen. of LFr gent.	cancelled 1606	MS 13282 40C2
1604	21	12.5ac arable or pasture in GFr	£2-10s.0d	Cecily Thurrold of GFr widow	-	MS 13283 40C2
1604	11	14ac pasture in Beeston	£4-10s-0d	John Souldan of Beeston fishmonger	land seized for non-payment of rent 1607	MS 13284 & MS 13285 40C2
1606	9	29.75ac pasture in 3 closes in GFr	£6-0s-0d	Richard Owles of GFr yeoman	surrendered 1608	MS 13286 40C2
1607	21	14ac pasture in Beeston	£4-0s-0d	Andrew Sammes of GFr fishmonger	-	MS 13275 40C2
1607	21	9ac 30 perches & 2ac 25 perches pasture, 0.75ac pightle & 9ac arable in LFr	£7-10-0d	Henry Large of LFr butcher	-	MS 13287 40C2
1607	21	9ac 3 roods 30 perches pasture, 5ac, 1ac & 0.5ac arable in LFr	£5-6s-8d	William Costyne of LFr carpenter	-	MS 13288 40C2
1607	21	3ac pasture, 0.75ac, 0.5ac & 0.25ac meadow in GFr	£2-0s-0d	Richard Beckham jun. of LFr gent.	-	MS 13289 40C2
1607	21	3ac arable in LFr	£1-0s-0d	Agnes Powley widow & William Powley her son of LFr	-	MS 13290 40C2
1607	21	3ac 2 roods 25 perches & 4ac 20 perches pasture in LFr	£2-0s-0d	Robert Roberts of LFr carpenter	-	MS 13291 40C2
1607	21	4ac 3 roods 35 perches arable & pasture, 1ac & 1ac 10 perches pasture in LFr	£2-3s-4d	Gilbert Ransun of LFr husbandman	-	MS 13292 40C2
1607	21	18ac pasture in LFr, 1ac & 1.5ac meadow in GFr	£7-3s-4d	Thomas Michel of GFr husbandman	surrendered 1611	MS 13293 & MS 13294 40C2
1607	21	1.5ac & 3.75ac arable, 5ac 2 roods 20 perches & 6.75ac pasture in LFr	£4-13s-4d	John Brooke alias Daye of LFr husbandman	-	MS 13295 40C2
1607	21	5ac 25 perches & 4.25ac pasture in LFr	£2-5s-8d	John Howell of LFr blacksmith	-	MS 13296 40C2
1607	21	5ac, 3ac 2 roods 25 perches & 3ac arable in LFr	£2-5s-8d	Nicholas Turner of LFr taylor	-	MS 13297 40C2
1607	21	9ac 1 rood 15 perches, 2.5ac, 2.5ac, 2.5ac, 1 ac 2 roods 12 perches & 0.5ac arable & 0.5ac pasture in LFr	£3-13s-4d	Robert Davye of LFr gent.	'Licence to sublet & 5ac arable in GFr added in 1608, 3ac arable in LFr added 1609'	MS 13298 40C2
1607	21	7ac arable & 2ac 20 perches pasture in LFr	£2-0s-0d	William Henson of LFr husbandman	-	MS 13299 40C2
1607	21	33ac pasture in LFr	£13-10s-0d	Henry Large of LFr butcher & John Bretton clerk of LFr	'surrendered, no date given, see 1608'	MS 13300 40C2
1607	21	5ac & 7ac pasture, 12ac, 5ac, 0.5ac & 12.5ac arable in GFr	£12-1s-6d	Andrew Sammes of GFr fishmonger	-	MS 13302 40C2

Date	Length of lease in years	Acreage, land-use and location	Annual rent	Lessee	Notes	MSS reference
1607	21	9ac & 0.5ac arable in GFr	£2-5s-0d (for 9ac) & £0-3s-4d (for 0.5ac)	Andrew Sammes of GFr fishmonger	-	MS 13303 40C2
1607	21	8ac 2 roods 15 perches arable in LFr	£2-0s-0d	Thomas Large of LFr butcher	-	MS 13304 40C2
1607	21	16.75ac arable & 9.25ac pasture in LFr	£6-13s-4d	Thomas Large jun. & Henry Baylye, both of LFr butchers	-	MS 13309 40C2
1607	21	11ac & 24.5ac pasture, 15ac arable & 28ac 20 perches meadow in LFr & 29ac 10 perches pasture in Necton	£26-16s-8d	Andrew Sammes of GFr fishmonger & John Mynne of LFr yeoman	cancelled 1607	MS 13301 40C2
1608	21	11ac & 24.5ac pasture, 15ac arable & 28ac 20 perches meadow in LFr & 29ac 10 perches pasture in Necton	£26-16s-8d	Andrew Sammes of GFr fishmonger	-	MS 13305 & MS 13306 40C2
1608	21	3ac & 1ac arable in GFr	£0-14s-8d	William Costyne of LFr carpenter	renewal of 1603 lease	MS 13307 40C2
1608	21	33ac in LFr	£13-10s-0d	William Beckerton of GFr yeoman & Henry Large of LFr butcher	-	MS 13308 40C2
1609	21	29.75ac pasture or arable in 3 closes in GFr	£6-13s-4d	Edmund Ruston of GFr mason	see 1606	BL Add Ch 6193
1611	21	11ac & 24.5ac pasture, 15ac arable & 28ac 20 perches meadow in LFr & 29ac 10 perches pasture in Necton	£26-16s-8d	Simon Woodrowe of GFr yeoman	'see 1607 & 1608, surrendered 1620'	MS 13310 40C2
1612	18	18ac pasture in LFr, 1ac & 1.5ac meadow in GFr	£7-3s-4d	Edmund Chapman of LFr yeoman	see 1607	MS 13311 40C2
1612	18	3ac arable in GFr	£0-15s-0d	William Myller of GFr husbandman	renewal of 1604 lease	MS 13312 40C2
1612	18	5ac arable in GFr	£1-15s-0d	Robert Davye of LFr gent.	This land added in 1608 to lease of 1607	MS 13313 40C2
1613	17	0.5ac, 0.5ac 24 perches, 4ac 2 roods 20 perches & 1ac arable, & 4ac 1 rood 5 perches meadow in LFr	£4-6s-8d	Walter Beckham of Beachamwell son of Richard Beckham of LFr gent.	-	BL Add Ch 71050
1616	14	16.75ac arable & 9.25ac pasture in LFr	£6-13s-4d	Nicholas Thurrolde of GFr yeoman	see 1607	MS 13314 40C2
1621	9	15ac pasture in LFr	£3-0-0d	George Large son of Henry Large of LFr butcher	arable in 1611 in 1611 when leased to Simon Woodrowe	MS 13316 40C2
1621	9	28ac 20 perches meadow in LFr	£6-3s-4d	Simon Woodrowe of GFr yeoman	see 1611	MS 13317 40C2
1621	9	11ac & 24.5ac pasture in LFr	£10-13-4d	John Powley of LFr yeoman son of John Powley late of LFr yeoman	leased to Simon Woodrowe in 1611	MS 13318 40C2
1622	8	29ac 10 perches arable or pasture in Necton	£7-0s-0d	Lettice Cricke widow of Necton & her son Thomas Cricke	pasture in 1611 when leased to Simon Woodrowe	MS 13319 40C2
1630	21	1ac 2 roods 7 perches, 3ac 2 roods 25 perches & 3.75ac arable, 5ac 2 roods 20 perches, 6.75ac & 3ac 2 roods 25 perches pasture in LFr	£7-0s-0d	John Brooke alias Daye of LFr yeoman	-	MS 13321 40C2
1631	20	33ac 3 roods 30 perches pasture with a barn in LFr & 7ac 2 roods 15 perches & 0.5ac arable in GFr	£0-3s-4d for 0.5ac arable & £19-16s-8d for the rest	Margaret Couper of Swaffham widow & Walter Lardge of Swaffham husbandman	surrendered in 1636	MS 13322 & MS 13323 40C2
1636	14	3ac 1 rood 30 perches *late woodground and stubbed upp*	£1-6s-8d	John Brooke alias Day yeoman of LFr	surrendered by widow in 1642	MS 13326 40C2

Table 9.4 Leases of Sir Arthur Capell's demesne lands 1601–37

felled and of the severall spoiles and wastes there done?' (MS 13221).

The Capell/Mynne dispute over Great Fransham manor, or at least over two of the nine parts into which it was divided[xi], opened on 3 July 1598 with a royal writ of *oyer and terminer* (MS 13391). One of the first moves of Sir Arthur Capell of Little Hadham (Hertfordshire) was to lease out the demesne to one Bernard Johnson, a yeoman of the same place. Two indentures, dated 7 and 9 August 1598, itemised all the lands concerned, giving names and acreages. The total was 504½ acres and 2 perches, but land-use details were not included (MS 13270 and MS 13271). Legal notes, which recorded that Nicholas Mynne and one Henry Tharrolde had entered and claimed possession of the lands a few days later, included acreages by land-use: 129 acres of arable, 283 of pasture, 67 of meadow and 24 of woodland, total 503 acres (MS 13390).

From 1601 Sir Arthur Capell's demesne lands, of Kirkhams and Wilcoks and of his portion of Great Fransham, were leased out for terms of years ranging between seven and twenty-one to a variety of local people, as evidenced by fifty surviving indentured leases, the latest of which is of 1637 (Table 9.4). Rentals of 1613 and 1618 reveal the large discrepancy between the income derived from Kirkhams and Wilcoks ancient free and customary rents on the one hand and leased-out demesne on the other (MS 13151–3). In 1613 thirty-one tenants paid £5 13s and 2 capons in free and customary fixed rents, while the revenue from nineteen leases amounted to £112 1s 4d. In 1618 the latter remained the same but fixed rents had been reduced by 1s 4d. Great Fransham figures for 1614 provide the same contrast: the total of free and customary rents was 14s 9d and one hen, while leases brought in £26 18s 2d (MS 13083). Under the Commonwealth all lands of Sir Arthur Capell, son of the above-mentioned Sir Arthur, were sequestrated (TNA SP 23/73)[xii]. One rental lists amounts of rent due for leases running for 21 years from Michaelmas 1655 (MS 13173). Rents from ten Great Fransham leases amounted to £38 16s 2d and those from fifteen Kirkhams and Wilcoks leases to £147 3 4d. Unfortunately, there is no seventeenth-century rental of free and customary lands subsequent to that of 1618.

Only three eighteenth-century leases have been located. Two of these show that large agglomerations of land fell into the hands of members of the Case family, which established itself in Great Fransham from the 1660s. The Cases were farmers in the modern sense of the word[xiii]. In 1739 Thomas Case, a tanner, took out a 21-year lease for an annual rent of £89 15s from William Capell, Earl of Essex, on 211 acres of Kirkhams and Wilcoks and Great Fransham demesne in 22 parcels, all pasture apart from 44¾ acres of arable, 45¼ acres of arable and pasture, and 1 acre of meadow. A barn in *Hall Close* in *Quarent*. 9 was included (MS 13328)[xiv]. In 1761 the 21-year lease of Edward Case tanner from the Countess of Essex was for more than 230 acres in 29 parcels. These included a much higher proportion of arable, 130 acres (MS 13337). Both leases stipulated an additional charge of 20s on every acre ploughed that had been pasture for the previous fifteen years.

Enclosure

The landscape of Fransham had long been a melange of irregular open fields and closes, and as has been explained in Chapter 8, the practice of engrossment by the piecemeal enclosure of strips formerly held by different tenants had accelerated in the late fifteenth century. The process was to continue throughout the sixteenth to eighteenth centuries, though this was rarely stated specifically in court rolls. On the contrary, redundant land descriptions of individual land parcels were often to continue in use, giving the very misleading impression of subdivided open fields, which were in reality made up of enclosures held in severalty[xv]. The situation is much more clearly visible through the documentary sources in Little than in Great Fransham.

Throughout the sixteenth and seventeenth centuries the holdings of the Stalworthy family in *Eastfield* (*Quarent*. 29) were made up of a many individual parcels, held of Kirkhams, Wilcoks, Guntons and Sparhams manors by free, customary/copyhold and soiled tenure. At least 58 acres can be calculated from the evidence of court rolls and rentals. All John Stalworthy's free and customary Guntons lands listed in 1552 lay next to other pieces held by him in one or more directions, and several pieces were said to lie in his close or new close (TNA SC 12/3/23–4). Ten acres in 5 pieces held of Guntons/Northendhall manor by the Stalworthys were granted as customary land in 1549 (TNA SC 2/192/96) but were leased out to the same for 99 years in 1568 (Gardner A). According to a survey of 1605 George Stalworthy's Kirkhams and Wilcoks lands comprised 30½ acres and a parcel and lay 'all in Eastfeilde in the inclosed grounds neare to his free messuage [Lower Farm at TF 9196 1183, Pl. 7.15] excepte the foresaid long acre'. This piece, which lay in Area O in Great Fransham, was clearly unenclosed. In 1611, when John Stalworthy had inherited from his late father, named tenants of the manor were ordered to place metes and bounds between his bond land called *Longeacre* in Great Fransham *Southfield* and the free lands of Robert Davey gent. (MS 13415).

Abuttals in a one-year lease of 1719 for what had been the Stalworthy farm were not concerned with the ancient verbage of manor courts and described a small and compact farm of 63 acres consisting of a messuage and 1 acre, eight closes of 7, 3, 5, 16, 12, 3, 5 and 3 acres, and two pightles containing 6 acres and two containing 2 acres (Gardner BB). Earlier manorial documents show that the farm consisted of at least 46 once individually itemised parcels of land.

Where documentary evidence has survived other examples of small-scale enclosure through the combination of pieces of land have been noted in Little Fransham. Three freehold parcels of unknown manorial allegiance in *Mill Field* (*Quarents*. 19 and 20), comprising 3¾ acres and first recorded in 1678, were within a close with 2 acres of Kirkhams and Wilcoks demesne by 1712. Two contiguous pieces in *Quarent. 23*, 1½ acres of Kirkhams and Wilcoks freehold known from 1502 and 2 free acres held of an unknown manor remained separate in 1678, but they were described as a 3-acre close in 1712 (MC 3115/1/6 and 11). *Bushshie Close*, 4 acres in *East Field* (*Quarent*. 29) first named in 1539, was composed of two 2-acres pieces of Kirkhams and Wilcoks freehold. By

1712 it had grown to 6 acres, the additional 2 acres being a Wilcoks customary piece (MC 3115/1/11, 1037x4).

The story of one 18-acre freehold close in Little Fransham, *Ulvesmeadowe* in *Quarent*. 29, was especially complex. Within it a 7½-acre close of land and pasture was conveyed in 1567 as was a 1½ piece of meadow in 1570. The latter lay next to a pasture close called *Podyngwong*, also within the 18 acres. In 1648 the 7½-acre close contained 'certain divisions or separacions therin lately made', and these still stood in 1712 (MC 3115/1/2, 5 and 11, 1037x4). By 1724 they had been removed and the enclosure was now called *Eastfield Close* (MC 3115/1/12, 1037x4). With its annual rent remaining at one capon for the full 18 acres this property can have attracted little interest from the lord of the manor. The final occasions on which it was named, and its complete acreage given, were in 1679 *Hulls Meadow*, and in 1682 *Bullsmead* (MC 1850/1, 858X9).

Much less material detailing enclosure in Great Fransham has survived. *Crowes Close* in Area M probably emerged in the first half of the sixteenth century and may have been named after Robert Crowe of Wendling who held lands in Great Fransham and died in 1541. There is no documentary evidence to shed light on the processes by which it became enclosed. The close is described as new in one sixteenth-century copy of an earlier rental (MS 13084, version C). It contained a 5-acre piece of Great Fransham demesne called *Gropelond* and 1 other acre of the same. According to later sources it also included 4 acres of glebe called the *Lamp land* in 1575 (MS 13079), 3 acres and 1 acre of Great Fransham customary land leased in 1603 (MS 13277), and 7 acres in five pieces of Necton Town land leased in 1598 (PD 143/82).

The Necton Town or Blyfords estate

In 1509 the core of what was to become a small farm, in the modern sense of the word, with its farmhouse at Med 21, was created when Nicholas Mynne of Little Fransham granted to seventeen men of Necton and Thomas Wyskard of Little Fransham, lands which had been held by William Mascale and then John Blyford in the early fifteenth century (p.202). The descent of the property from Blyford through various people, including John Crudde, to Nicholas Mynne is recorded in eighteenth-century copies of four deeds preserved in the Necton parish papers (MS 424). On the evidence of a rental of 1434/5 (PD 143/76), Mynne's grant of 1509 (PD 143/77), which included additional lands comprising 1 acre in *Howfeld* (Area K) and 1 acre between *Kynoldshaugh Wood* and *Elynghams* (Area C), amounted to a messuage and 69¼ acres as well as income from various freeholds.

The estate was increased in size four times after its foundation. In 1510 three churchwardens (*propositi*) of Necton were admitted to 3 copyhold acres of Great Fransham rectory manor, lying in two pieces in Area C. The land was described as demesne, but it is unclear whether it had up to then been glebe proper or customary land of the manor (PD 143/46). In 1530 three Necton trustees were admitted to 9 acres of land and meadow, copyhold of Rougholme manor, lying in Areas C and J. The property had been alienated to the trustees by the tenant, Henry Toly, in 1517 (MR 28, 240X6). In 1553 Richard Hoo, lord of part of Rougholme manor, leased these 9 acres to the Necton trustees for 99 years at an annual rent of a capon and a down payment of £6 13 4d (MS 424; TNA SC 12/3/23). By 1582 the Necton churchwardens or trustees were tenants of various free lands and tenements held of Ellinghams manor for an annual rent of 5¼d. In the absence of Ellinghams court records antedating 1576 it is not known when this property was acquired, and neither acreage nor details of location were ever given (MC 1847/1, 741X2). Sometime in the early seventeenth century the estate was augmented by 30 freehold acres and 2 messuages that had been held by Nicholas Mynne of East Lexham manor in *c*.1610. The entry in a document of this date is glossed '*Blyfords modo ville de Necton*' (MC 1812/49, 838X5). The property lay in the western part of Area C, including Med 31 and 33, and in Area J. The sum total of all the above holdings amounts to 111¼ acres, 3 messuages and divers lands. This is not far short of the 117 acres 3 roods and 28 perches held by Necton Town before Enclosure. Churchwardens' accounts for 1536–1735 record the receipts of annual rents from farmers of Blyfords (£4 in 1536, £40 in 1701, £65 in 1724) and of monies from the sale of timber, as well as frequent expenditure on construction and repair work of the farm house and buildings (PD 143/46–8). After 1644 there was no further entry of receipts for Blyfords freehold lands. As the total had been only 5s 2¼d, it was no great loss. The final entry, in 1646, reads 'Quit rents not paid this year'.

At Enclosure the Necton Town charity was awarded 127 acres 3 roods 29 perches in five allotments which involved considerable rearrangement and included land in places it had not previously occupied. The reconstituted estate comprised compact blocks in Areas B, C, J. K and L.

The end of the study period and the Parliamentary Enclosure of 1807

This study of one parish seems to end on an anti-climactic note: without doubt the picture of life, land-use and settlement in the eighteenth-century is very much less full than that of the preceding three hundred years. Fransham becomes archaeologically less visible as its settlement pattern stabilised into a state that was scarcely to alter before modern times, and as farming practices, with an increase in pasture (and probably changes in manuring techniques) left much less artefactual debris strewn across the fields[xvi]. Documentary evidence is also sparser and very much less informative.

The map surveyed in 1805 for the Enclosure Award of 1807 (C/Sca 2/122) would, if used on its own, *i.e.* without earlier written sources, give a very misleading picture of the true pattern of land holdings before the Award. Part of its heading, 'as allotted in 1807' makes this clear. Each land block allotted to an individual is bordered by hedge-like lines except where a public road forms a border. Within these bounds simple lines denote boundaries of fields and closes. The majority of these are almost certainly accurate indications of hedge lines, but some around areas of copyhold may be notional. New areas of copyhold were allotted 'for and in lieu of common rights'. These, which were created both from the common pastures and former freehold land, were added to old pieces of copyhold and in some cases moved into compact blocks. The larger allotments, such as that of Hamond Alpe esq. in Little Fransham, were sub-divided into blocks of freehold and of copyhold held of each manor. These bear little relation to the disposition of pre-Enclosure tenures. Similarly, large areas of demesne included elements that had previously been copyhold. The two glebe holdings, previously subdivided into many parcels, were rendered into discrete blocks, that of Little Fransham, formerly in 24 pieces, into one self-contained estate.

Endnotes

i   Sir William Capell, of Rayne in Essex, held his first court as lord of Kirkhams and Wilcoks in 1502 (MS 13053). He had acquired this lordship in 1500 from Sir Edmund Gorges, grandson of Sir William Oldhall, along with part of Great Fransham manor, the Norfolk manors of Dersingham and Oldhall in East Dereham, and the manor of Ditton Valence in Cambridgeshire (Essex Record Office A8173). The Fransham holdings continued in the hands of the Capells (Earls of Essex from 1661), later of Hadham and then of Cassiobury in Hertfordshire, until 1851.

ii   As well as the lordships of seven ninths of Great Fransham manor, Sparhams and Cannons, Nicholas Mynne esq. had acquired large amounts of copyhold and freehold land held of various manors, including Great Fransham, by the time of his death in 1631 (Carthew 1878, 486). There are vivid descriptions of the resultant tenurial confusion and blurring of boundaries in the Decree in Chancery of 1602 concerning his unsuccessful dispute with Sir Arthur Capell (TNA C 78/128/4 and MS 13393). One example will suffice: Capell claimed that Mynne had 'obteyned the possession of dyvers of the auntient copyholde lands and tents. of the said mannor and pulled downe and defaced the auntient dwelling places of the same and also defaced suppressed and concealed the severall meres and boundes of them'. The details of the post-mortem disposition of Mynne's estate are unknown, but it is likely that the tenurial histories of many elements were lost forever. Some clues as to complexities of the break-up can be seen in changes in abuttals in two sequential Great Fransham glebe terriers, of 1613 and 1635 (ANW/15/2.61 and ANW/15/1.18). In the former there were 22 abuttals onto Mynne's properties. Their equivalents in the latter comprised 3 onto lands of his widow and 19 onto lands of 10 different people.

iii   Wills, of course contain much valuable information. For example, they often specify the occupation of the testator. Although not entirely relevant to a landscape history a list of occupations seems worthy of inclusion, if only to give a general impression of the range of activities being undertaken. The job descriptions of clerk, parson and rector have been excluded, along with the following titles: esquire, gentleman, husbandman, knight, singleman, spinster, widow, wife (one example only) and yeoman. The earliest occurrence of the title yeoman was in 1565 (Great Fransham) and the latest in 1758 (two wills, Great Fransham).

Great Fransham
Blacksmith 1699, 1794, Butcher 1602, 1633, 1643, 1670, 1690, Carpenter 1559, 1676, Cooper 1701, Cordwainer (*i.e.* shoemaker) 1744, Farmer 1760, 1766, 1782, 1794, 1801, 1801, Hosier 1690, Labourer 1599, Miller 1601, Shepherd 1602, Shoemaker 1616, Tailor 1634, 1697, Tanner 1761, Thatcher 1726, Weaver 1615, Woolchapman 1642, 1647, Worstead weaver 1684

Little Fransham
Blacksmith 1681, Bricklayer 1685, Butcher 1579, 1600, 1625, 1651, 1656, 1658, 1673, 1681, 1690, Carpenter 1524, 1595, 1620, 1623, 1627, 1682, Cordwainer (*i.e.* shoemaker) 1664, 1669, 1796, Farmer 1771, 1785, 1797, 1799, Knacker 1695, Labourer 1601, 1650, 1661, Linen weaver 1674, 1687, Rope maker 1577, Tailor 1625, 1662, Thatcher 1613, 1696, Weaver 1607, 1632, Wheelwright 1685, Worstead weaver 1679

iv   The two men, Thomas Monk and William Thompson, must have been undertenants. The most likely locations for their dwellings are two neighbouring properties in *Quarent.* 13, a Kirkhams freehold and a Cannons copyhold. The former was described as 'built' in the early seventeenth century and the latter on several occasions both before and after the 1670s. They shared a common absentee tenant at this time.

v   A 20-perch 'small parcel' of Kirkhams demesne itemised in the 1605 extent was leased at farm for a term of eighteen years in 1611 to Margery Goldinge widow, tenant of this property. The parcel, which lay in her farmyard? (*bartona*), lay on the north side of her Sparhams plot and south of *Jecksgrove*. She was to allow sufficient access from time to time to the lord and his assigns from the common called *Cannons Greene* into the field called *Jackes Peece* (MS 13415).

vi   3 perches = 90.75 square yards = 75.9 square metres, *i.e.* only 8.7m^2, a very limited space.

vii A national attempt to curb unregulated cottage building was soon to occur, in 1589 with an *Act against the erection and maintenance of cottages*, 31 Eliz. 1, c.7 (Pickering 1763, 409–11).

viii Amongst a large royal grant in fee simple of many chantries, chapels *etc.* to Cecily Pickerell of Norwich widow in 1563 were St Katherine's chapel in Great Fransham and lands thereof, and 'the guildehall' there (Cal. Pat. Rol. 1948, 566–7).

ix   At Kirkhams and Wilcoks manor courts Richard Beckham, lord of Sparhams, was singled out as an overcommoning offender. In 1592 he was subpoenaed 100 shillings for the offence (MS 13208). In 1593 he was said to have depastured twenty-five sheep contrary to a court order of 1584, though there is no surviving record for a court in that year (MS 13209). Five years later he was accused of depasturing sixty sheep (MS 13214). This dispute seems to have settled down thereafter.

x   In 1429 Sir William Oldhall, lord of Kirkhams and Wilcoks, along with various cofeoffees including Sir John Fastolf, acquired various lands amongst which was a grove called *Knyghtwode* in Beeston formerly of Ralph de Beeston, from cofeoffees of the [late] lord of Great Fransham, Geoffrey de Fransham (MS 13227). The grove was freehold of the manor of Mileham. Several bailiff's account rolls for the period 1427–43 record payments of the rent to Mileham as well as receipts for the sale of underwood and occasionally timber from there (MS 13137–8, HRO 8185, MS 13096, MS 13139, MS 13037, HRO 8179, MS 13038–9, MS 13140). The location of *Knyghtwode* can be established from a Beeston field book of 1550/1 (Holkham Hall, Davidson, Tittleshall 68) and from abuttals given in Hayward's 1605 extent, in which it was described as 14 acres of pasture with 'diverse small timber trees upon it'. However, it was 'newly converted from woodgrounde' according to leases of 1604 (MS 13275, MS 13284–5).

xi   Tenurial complexities arising from the tripartite division of Great Fransham manor in 1414 have not been presented here in any detail. One example will perhaps serve as an example of the confusion. In 1538 Sir Giles Capell conveyed by bargain and sale to Edward Mynne, yeoman one ninth of the manor of *Moche* Fransham 'third parte of the third parte and porcion….commonly called Mawde of Bestons parte….whiche Mawde was sometime wiff of John Markaunt of Beston and afterward called Mawde Smyth (MS 13255).

xii Sir Arthur Capell was executed for treason in 1649.

xiii Useful background information on the Case family can be found in Barney 2000.

xiv The barn is probably a single building shown at TF 9068 1237. Two buildings are depicted in the same position on the Tithe Map, as they are on the Ordnance Survey 1st edition 1:2500 scale map of 1883, by then within an enclosure. There were agricultural buildings here until the 1960s.

xv   The consolidation of ownership of strips in the open fields, and the persistence of tenurial distinctions between strips in documentary sources after the enclosure of such fields, was explained in practical terms by Corbett (1897, 85–7).

xvi One late sixteenth or early seventeenth-century object found by metal detector in a field (HER 20518) a short distance to the north-west of Curds Hall is worthy of mention: a silver hawking vervel inscribed W SPRYNG // OF PAKENHAM. This records the owner of the bird. The Spring family of Suffolk produced several Williams. The most likely candidate is Sir William Spring (1588–1638) (https://en.wikipedia.org/wiki/William_Spring_of_Pakenham, accessed 20/12/17). Perhaps he was one of Nicholas Mynne's hunting party guests at the hall. His son William (1613–1654), should also be considered (https://en.wikipedia.org/wiki/Sir_William_Spring,_1st_Baronet, accessed 20/12/17). The vervel can be viewed on the Portable Antiquities Scheme database (NMS-092867).

Chapter 10. Postscript

The study of the landscape through time is now a well accepted discipline, whether it be called landscape history or landscape archaeology. The expanse to be researched may be wide or small, and there is no need to justify the choice of Fransham parish as the study area. I have attempted in this examination of one place to go a little deeper into the available sources than time normally permits one person, and have become aware, particularly towards the end of the work, of the real inadequacy of a one-person project. Without regularly receiving the opinions and sharing the expertise of others during both the amassing of data and its synthesis, I have trod at times a solitary path, and I look with envy at such places as Whittlewood and Shapwick that were subjected to large-scale collaborative investigations (Jones and Page 2006; Gerrard with Aston 2007). Landscape archaeology has been described as 'the application of archaeological techniques to understanding changing relationships between culture, environment, biology, and structural elements such as geology and topography' (Gerrard with Aston 2007, 7). This only serves to underline the above-mentioned deficiency.

I derive some comfort, however, from the fact that the written and material sources I have drawn upon will survive for others to use. There is little chance that hitherto unrecorded historical documents relating to Fransham will come to light in the future, but at least the large majority in the public domain will remain for future enquiry. The fieldwork so far carried out is a mere sample: most of the archaeology of Fransham has yet to be identified, recorded and interpreted. Many thousands of potsherds as well as hundreds of pieces of metalwork have been removed from the topsoil but a much greater quantity must still remain, and through the almost complete absence of archaeological excavation, the archaeological resource remains largely intact beneath the ploughzone.

The evidence presented has been very variable in quantity and quality, as well as being of the *longue durée*, from the Lower Palaeolithic to the post-medieval period, from the densities of late prehistoric struck flints over the arable surface to trends in the levels of land rents in late and post-medieval times. Huge emphasis has been placed on the twelfth to sixteenth centuries, the Middle Ages and the early stages of the early modern period, and rightly so because it is to this stretch of time that most of both the field and the documentary evidence belongs.

The Roman period and the enormous stretch of time before it have yielded little surprise. The tiny number of Palaeolithic finds plug a slight gap in the record, but significant amounts of activity on clay soils during the Mesolithic are no longer out of the ordinary. Likewise, some low level of exploitation of heavier land from the earlier Neolithic to the Iron Age is also to be expected over much of the British lowlands. However, that exploitation began before the later Neolithic is of some greater interest. Perhaps the absence of truly heavy soil here explains this. It may well be that further intense fieldwork in areas of more intractable clay will firmly demonstrate a lack of activity before the Late Neolithic / Early Bronze Age.

The Middle to Late Bronze Age remains elusive through the frailty of the pottery, though a good proportion of the struck flint must belong here, and the few recent finds of metalwork have shed a little more light.

It is only in the Iron Age that discrete settlement sites become demonstrable from the surface archaeological record in the form of, usually rather feeble, concentrations of potsherds, but work has hinted that the density of occupation may have been underestimated, some sites perhaps being missed because so slight, others masked under Roman sites prolific in ceramics. On the lighter soils there were subtle suggestions, in the form of sprinklings of potsherds, of areas of arable farming.

The Romano-British situation appears also to have been unremarkable, with an average density of easily found rural settlements dispersed across the area, and iron smelting as the only demonstrable industry to supplement agriculture of an ill-defined type. Areas of arable exploitation have been suggested from potsherd scatters, but on a scale far less extensive than in some other places, for example Whittlewood (Jones and Page 2006, 52–3) and Barton Bendish (Rogerson 1997, 14–6). The continuity of some minor Roman routes into the medieval period as furlong boundaries and roads was unexpected, and parallels should be sought elsewhere in this area of Norfolk.

That the results for the post-Roman period are of greater intrinsic interest should probably not be denied. Some contraction of the population and of the area settled, or at least of detectable signs of activity, certainly occurred after the later fourth century, but surface indications of dispersed settlements, albeit slight, were identified, and thanks to recorded metal-detecting an inhumation cemetery was located. The great questions of the fifth century, the Late Roman / Early Saxon transition, political, demographic, cultural and social, are no better understood following this study, though this is hardly a failure: fieldwalking alone is not equipped to answer them. The close proximity of the largest Early Saxon settlement to a contemporary cemetery and to the medieval parish church is especially interesting, an arrangement that cries out for further work beyond the collection and plotting of objects in the ploughsoil.

The shift of settlement to a new location in the seventh century is not without precedent. It was first emphasised forty years ago (Arnold and Wardle 1981) and became known as the 'seventh-century shuffle'. More out of the ordinary is the existence by the end of the seventh century of a single settlement, or possibly two (if the possibility of an undiscovered site somewhere in Little Fransham is accepted), nucleation after a period of dispersal that stretches back into prehistory. However, it remains a moot point as to whether *nucleation* is the right term to use here because of the small size of the one known site.

The location of the eighth to ninth-century settlement (MS 1) close to the centre of the oval formed by the parishes of Wendling and Fransham remains highly intriguing, but any significance should probably be dismissed as mere coincidence. The assemblage of finds is quite unremarkable, and there is no suggestion of 'high' status. Nucleation in the eighth century is the norm in this part of East Anglia (Rippon 2008, 186–9), and despite its small size, MS 1 conforms to this. With the changeover from Ipswich ware to Thetford-type pottery in the second half of the ninth century the settlement remained in the same place but grew larger (LS 1), and was soon joined by a second nucleation in Little Fransham (LS 2)

There was, then, a phase where nucleation may have been the sole form of settlement, from the seventh to the eleventh century in Great Fransham (LS 1), and from the ninth or perhaps tenth to the eleventh in Little Fransham (LS 2). This phase was a short-lived aberration that terminated in a centrifugal scattering back into dispersal and the abandonment of both sites before c.1100. Of some interest is the tentative start of this process involving a phase in which, before the end of LS 1 and 2, a few settlements were established a short distance back from the edges of common pastures. These were subsequently abandoned. Edward Martin has recently proposed some research directions in which East Anglian rural settlement studies should move. With the above observations in mind I hope that this work has made some small contribution, albeit intensely localised, to two of these, the origins of dispersed settlement patterns and the origins and development of common pastures (Martin 2012, 245–6).

As might have been predicted, the survey recovered no good evidence to flesh out details of the practice of agriculture in the Late Saxon period, apart from vague indications of the extent of arable, and the processes by which an irregular pattern of open fields came into being have not been elucidated. Though open fields were widespread by the thirteenth century when documentation becomes profuse, we are no nearer postulating a firm date for their beginning. Indeed, there is nothing in this study which points unequivocally to open field origins before the Norman Conquest. In stark contrast to this shortcoming the identification of two areas of pottery production (LS 14 and 20) came as an enormous surprise.

Throughout the twelfth and thirteenth centuries more and more settlements were established in both Franshams, some isolated and others grouped into rows, some tightly spaced, others well spaced out, but almost all along the edges of common pastures. Definitions of 'dispersal' and 'nucleation' are sorely needed when dealing with compact rows of houses such as those at the south end of Eastendmoor, Little Fransham or at the northern end of Eastendmoor, Great Fransham (Med 113 and 114). The forces behind this great change, from concentrated to spread out settlement, have been discussed, but no sound explanation has been found, beyond a necessity to live close to fast diminishing areas of pasture at a time when an increasing population required more arable land.

Similarly, attempts to find patterns in the distribution of settlements by status of tenure and manorial allegiance have met with limited success, primarily because of incompleteness of the evidence, with the tenure of so many settlements being uncertain and the manorial structure being so fluid, obscure and complex. These attempts were also risky, for they were carried out in full awareness of the dangers inherent in straying too far into others' fields of expertise, 'archaeologists should concentrate on being archaeologists and resist the temptation to draw heavily on other kinds of evidence, historical or linguistic' (Sawyer 1983, 46). Though guilty as charged, in mitigation I wish to stress how much less would have been learnt from a 'stand-alone' archaeological field survey without recourse to historical manuscripts, and it is difficult to imagine such a project gaining approval in these times of inter-disciplinary cooperation. I prefer to hope for a future when the norm will be 'a far more integrated study of medieval archaeology, where scholars are encouraged to engage with source materials beyond their traditional remit' (Reynolds 2009, 429).

Since the late nineteenth century documentary sources have played a major role in the study of the origins and development of field systems, and, of course, written evidence is the sole repository of information on agricultural organisation. What has been learned of Fransham's fields and has the collection of archaeological data made any useful contribution? At a rather basic level late medieval land-use over most of the study area has been plotted, although in most places it has proved impossible to draw firm lines on a map. The bewilderingly intermingled arrangement of irregular common open fields and enclosures, and indeed the process of piecemeal enclosure which probably persisted throughout the medieval period and well beyond, have rendered the task of accurately mapping land-use through time almost impossible.

Both the material and the written evidence suggested a major reduction in population and considerable settlement desertion in the fourteenth and fifteenth centuries, with no appreciable sign of recovery until well into the sixteenth. Along with these trends were those of piecemeal enclosure, the agglomeration of holdings and the gradual emergence of compact farms. There is nothing new here, and indeed it would have been surprising had a different picture emerged. However, there is some satisfaction in the fact that the two forms of evidence, where they were available in detail, have shown themselves to be complementary.

Parliamentary enclosure in 1807, the most recent major landscape change, removed all the common pastures at one stroke, along with the little that was left of the open fields. It had great effect on the pattern of landholding but little on that of settlement. Thereafter a few houses were built on former commons, and several outlying farms and groups of farm buildings were established. Late twentieth-century changes involved the destruction of many miles of hedgerows, some of which were probably of great antiquity, the demolition of several outlying farms of both medieval and nineteenth-century origin, and small-scale housing developments on former commons and fields. Despite all these events, the greater part of the settlement pattern is still recognisably that which came into being at the start of the twelfth century.

The lives of the present population (433 people in 187 households according to the census of 2011) do not, however, display such strong elements of continuity. Drastic reductions in numbers of those employed on the land over the last sixty years have resulted in the disappearance of most of the services that supported farming. The agricultural element within the community is still of great importance but those employed on the land are few. Fransham, like most English villages, now exists largely for the benefit of the commuter by car, the retired person and the 'second homer'. Again, in the same way as in much of England, most people now travel by car, coach,

Plate 10.1 Looking south-west from just north of Med 94 along the A47 trunk road which runs through the former common pasture of Little Fransham's main village, November 2018. The village sign is near bottom right

bus and lorry through, rather than to the study area, most notably along the A47 trunk road (Pl. 10.1 and Pl. 10.2). I hope that, by way of contrast to such precarious modernity, this work has shown something of the ways in which earlier inhabitants shaped their own lives by exploiting and sometimes changing the landscape which surrounded them and on which they depended.

Emphasis has already been laid on the considerable limitations of this archaeological survey carried out by a single person without the back-up of excavation and other specialist services, and insufficiencies resulting from the use of documentary sources by a non-specialist have also been stressed. However, it has been most pleasing to note that a recent work of considerable importance has made great use of the thesis on which this volume is based and on data from more recent fieldwork contained in the Norfolk HER (Fleming 2016, especially 99–106, 113–4). It is to be hoped that once the paper records relating to the survey have been digitised and made freely available online, future scholars will find food for further useful thoughts.

Despite these shortcomings I remain confident that the understanding reader will not consider this work to be entirely without merit or justification. Those who do disapprove should consider that both the landscape of Fransham and the relevant manuscripts can be revisited by future enquirers. Perhaps one such future scholar will bring to bear a theoretical approach of the sort that has not been taken in this study, which is unashamedly of the traditional 'over empirical' variety (Rippon 2009, 243).

Plate 10.2 The village sign erected in 1991 on former common pasture in Little Fransham, a representation of the monumental brass of Geoffrey de Fransham (ob. 1414) in All Saints' church, Great Fransham

Appendix 1.
Translation of the Great Fransham feodary of *c*.1279

(Norfolk Record Office MS 11352 and MS 13084 40A3)

All acreages refer to land (*terra*) unless otherwise stated. It is reasonable to assume that all rents were annual, although this is nowhere specified. All entries, apart from demesne holdings and those relating to villeins, must concern freeholds. They all include the phrases *per lib. service.* or *per service*. As these variations are random and are the copyist's inconsistencies, they have not been included. For the sake of brevity, greater use is made here of the phrase 'as above' than the copyist made of *ut super*. I have numbered the entries.

The dating of the original text from internal evidence is reasonably secure. A *terminus post quem* can be found in the accession of Jordan Foliot to the lordship of Gressenhall on the death of Sir Richard Foliot in 1277/8 (Blomefield 1808, 512). No useful dates in the 1280s have been noted, until the death of William Bardolph junior, lord of Wormegay, in 1289 (Carthew 1877, 51). All the other major figures were living in the 1280s.

Fransham Magna

1. William de Fransham is the capital lord of Fransham and holds in the same vill one messuage and 40 acres, 12 acres of wood, 4 acres of meadow and 10 acres of pasture, one windmill, liberty of bull, boar and waif, and view of frankpledge. He holds these of Alice de Playce for the service of one knight's fee, for this holding and for others in Scarning and Dillington. The said Alice holds the same as her dowry of Ralph de Playce, and Ralph holds of John de Warenne Earl of Surrey, who holds it in chief of the lord King as of his barony of Lewis.

2. The same William holds 100 acres, which his villeins hold from him with their messuages [*quas villain sui tenent de eo in villenagio cum suis mess.*], of the same Alice for the same service, and the said Alice holds as above.

3. The same William holds 20 acres in Pylewod of the lord King in chief, paying 12d as 'blanch-farm' [*ad albam firmam*] to the castellan of Norwich [*ad Castn. Norwici*].

4. The same William holds 10 acres of Jordan Foliot for 12d. The same Jordan holds of Earl Warenne who holds of the King in chief.

5. The same William holds 8 acres of John Columbell for 16d. The same John holds of Jordan Foliot who holds as above.

6. The same William holds 3 acres of Ralph Baysboll for 9d. The same Ralph holds of John Lestraunge, and the same John of Ralph de Tonie, and the same Ralph of the lord King in chief.

7. The same William holds 8 acres of Robert de Weston for 2s. The said Robert holds of the said Earl who holds as above.

8. The same William holds 10 acres of William Bardolf, who holds of the lord King.

[Entries 9–16 concern lands held of William de Fransham who held of Alice de Playce who held as above]

9. William de Aula holds one messuage and 14 acres for 6d, and 3½d to a scutage.

10. Geoffrey de Sudwode holds one messuage and 12 acres and 1 acre [of land, ?recte meadow] for 2s.

11. Walter de Sudwode holds one messuage and 12 acres for 3s, and 3d to a scutage.

12. William son of Augustine de Beston holds 6 acres in Beeston for 2s, and 4d to a scutage.

13. The Prior of Pentney holds 20 acres in the same vill [presumably Fransham rather than Beeston] for 12d to a scutage.

14. The Abbot of Wendling holds 26 acres now enclosed in one close called Sowdewonge for 28d.

15. The Prior of West Acre holds [no acreage given] for 4d to a scutage.

16. Geoffrey son of Gilbert holds 20 acres and one messuage and 1 acre of meadow for 6d.

17. Geoffrey de Marscall holds one messuage and 60 acres in demesne of William de Bressyngham and Alexander Lestraunge for one quarter of a knight's fee, with liberty of bull and boar, and view of frankpledge. The said William and Alexander hold of Earl Warren who holds as above.

18. The same Geoffrey holds, by the same service of the said William and Alexander, 16 acres which his villeins hold in their villeinage with their messuages.

[Entries 19–21 concern lands held of Geoffrey de Marscall who held as above]

19. Alice daughter of Geoffrey de Marscall holds a messuage and 10 acres for 6d, and 1d to a scutage.

20. Agnes de Marscall holds a messuage and 16 acres for 6d, and 4d to a scutage.

21. Thomas son of Osbert holds one messuage and 8 acres for 3s, and 7d to a scutage.

22. Ralph de Bycketon holds 11 acres in demesne of Jordan Foliot for 16¼d, and 3¼d to a scutage. The same Jordan holds of Earl Warenne who holds as above.

23. The same Ralph holds of the said Jordan by the said service 12 acres which his villeins hold in villeinage with their messuages.

24. The same Ralph holds one messuage and 2 acres of William de Fransham for 8d. The said William holds of the said Alice as above.

25. The same Ralph holds 6 acres of Richard de Oxwick for 13d. The said Richard holds of Jordan Foliot who holds as above.

26. The same Ralph holds 1 acre of meadow of Thomas son of Walter for 3d. The said Thomas holds of the said Jordan who holds as above.

27. Thomas de Eston, Matilda Ale and John Spyrling hold 7 acres and 1 acre of meadow of John le Breton for 3s. The said John [le Breton] holds of Roger Clyfford who holds of Ralph de Tonie who holds as above.

28. John le Breton holds in the same vill one messuage and 10 acres which his villeins hold, for 19d, of Richard de Mundevile, lord of Mileham, who holds of William son of John who holds of the lord King in chief as above.

29. Henry de Bylney holds one messuage and 15 acres of Adam Bette for 18d. The same Adam holds of Earl Warenne who holds as above.

30. Ralph Baysboll holds one messuage and 6 acres and 1 acre of land [?recte meadow] of John Lestraunge for 6s 6d. The same John holds as above.

31. Godfrey de Hockryng holds 1½ acres of William de Fransham for 5d, and 1d to a scutage. The same William holds from the said Alice as above.

32. The said Godfrey holds 1½ acres of the Abbot of Wendling for 2s. The said Abbot holds in free and pure alms.

33. The said Godfrey holds 4 acres of Hamo son of Richard for 15d. The same Hamo holds of the said Abbot who holds as above.

34. Hamo son of Richard holds 3½ acres of the Abbot of Wendling for 12d, and 3d to a scutage. The same Abbot holds as above.

[Entries 35–7 concern lands held of William de Fransham who held of Alice de Playce as above]

35. Roger Albert holds one messuage and 2 acres for 13d.

36. Alexander Meryell holds one messuage and 2 acres for 4d.

37. Reginald Haddok holds one messuage and 3 acres for 13d, and ½d to a scutage.

38. Reginald Haddok holds 2½ acres of Alexander Lestraunge for 7d. The said Alexander holds of John Lestraunge who holds as above.

39. The same Reginald holds 1 acre of Ralph Baysboll for 2d. The same Ralph holds of John Lestraunge who holds as above.

40. Jordan Foliot holds in the same vill 6 acres which his villeins hold in villeinage with their messuages, of Earl Warenne who holds as above.

41. John Norman holds one messuage, 26 acres, 2 acres of meadow and 1 acre of pasture of Jordan Foliot for 6s 10d, and 6d to a scutage. The said Jordan holds as above.

42. The same John Norman holds 10 acres which his villeins hold from him in their villeinage with their messuages, by the same service, of Jordan Foliot who holds as above.

43. The same John holds 3 acres of John Columbell for 3d. The said John [Columbell] holds of Jordan Foliot who holds as above.

44. William Clement clerk (*capellanus*) holds one messuage and 3 acres of John Norman for 5s 7d, and 3½d to a scutage. The said John holds of the said Jordan who holds as above.

45. The same William holds 2½ acres of Alexander Meryell for 3d. The said Alexander holds of William de Fransham who holds of the said Alice as above.

46. The same William [Clement] holds 1 acre of Ralph Baysboll for 3d. The said Ralph holds of John Lestraunge as above.

Appendix 2. Gazetteer of Medieval Sites

This gazetteer lists medieval sites for which there is some archaeological evidence. The introduction to each entry begins with the national grid reference. This is followed by the Area letter (for Great Fransham) or *Quarent.* number (for Little Fransham), the Norfolk Historic Environment Record (HER) number, soil type and, finally, height above Ordnance datum. Where possible, a summary of the tenurial history down to the Enclosure Act of 1807 is given. Frequently cited documents are not individually referenced. They are listed Chapter 7 *Documentary References*. Site locations are shown on Fig. 7.1.

The following numbers, Med 46, 48, 51, 52, 91, 104 and 110, have not been used in this gazetteer, because the sites to which they were formerly allotted are Late Saxon or post-medieval.

Med 1 TF 8827 1319 (Area A, HER 20520). Heavy soil, 79m OD (Fig. 7.4). Concentration of 12th and 13th-century sherds, 40m east-west x 30m north-south, on the eastern edge of an elongated common pasture running along the Little Dunham parish boundary, and immediately south of a stream flowing eastward through the boundary. Very few sherds occur as outliers in fields to the north, south and east. No direct documentary evidence has been found, but this site lay on the eastern edge of 80 acres of enclosed demesne of Great Fransham manor, which was former woodland in *c*.1430. In 1595 pasture called *Hallwood* 'in the wholl together with the Spring at the north part thereof' contained 49½ acres and *Hallwood meadowe* contained 23¾ acres and 20 perches. All this land came into Nicholas Mynne's portion of the manor in 1603.

Within a freehold block of more than 123 acres of William Mason esq. following Enclosure.

Med 2 TF 8848 1297 (Area A, HER 20521). Medium-heavy soil, 80m OD (Fig. 7.4). Concentration of 12th and 13th-century sherds, 50m x 50m, set back 80m to the east and 60m to the north from the edge of a common pasture. A scatter of sherds fans out in all directions except to the north, suggesting that the site lay within a compact arable block of 3.9 hectares (9.6 acres) bounded on the south and west by common pasture and on the north and east by enclosed demesne (see Med 1). A large ditch, now ploughed over and visible as a pronounced dip, bounds the concentration on the west. There is no certain documentary evidence, but this site may be identified with a probably customary messuage and 12 acres held by John Hastell who died without heir in 1349, his lands being seized into the hands of the lord of Great Fransham manor. *Le Alderker* above *Hastelisdiche* was mentioned in 1382, and a ditch at *Astelsdyke* on the south side of *Halleker* in 1439 and 1440. A stream next to *Astellsyard* was not cleaned in 1447. The location of this land was not known in the late 1590s (MS 13089).

On free land of John Drosier esq. following Enclosure.

Med 3 TF 8838 1270 (Area A, HER 20519). Medium-heavy soil, 85m OD (Fig. 7.4). Concentration of 13th to mid-14th-century pottery, 40m x 40m, lying close to the boundary with Little Dunham parish and flanked on the east by a probably medieval road, at the north end of Great Fransham demesne known as *Dunham croft*. No documentary evidence has been found.

On free land of John Drosier esq. following Enclosure.

Med 4 TF 8868 1275 (Area A, HER 20518). Medium-heavy soil, 82m OD. (Figs 7.4 and 7.5). Concentration of mid-12th to 14th-century sherds, 30m x 30m, lying immediately east of a circular pit. This site is probably to be identified with a ½-acre close at *Colins pitte ubi fuit messuagium quondam Harald*, part of the demesne of Great Fransham manor in *c*.1430. Aveline Harold was amerced for trespass in 1330. The tenants of the lands of Beatrice Harrold were distrained to do fealty in 1330 as were the tenants of *Harhalds* in 1343. *Haraldscroft* was demesne of Great Fransham manor by 1340. The messuage had been associated with 7 acres in two pieces which lay to the south of it between two roads and to the north of *Cruddesgrene*. A 3-acre meadow called *Haraldes* lay in Area H.

On free land of John Drosier esq. following Enclosure.

Med 5 TF 8885 1285 (Area A, HER 24783, extending east into G69, HER 24784). Medium soil, 80m OD (Figs 7.4 and 7.6). Concentration of 12th to 14th-century sherds, medieval ceramic peg roof tile fragments and flint nodules, with some medieval bricks, 55m east-west x 45m north-south, with a ploughed-over pit immediately to the south-west, lying *c*.100m north of a medieval road, the *Whiteway*. The farm manager reported that flint and mortar footings had been pulled out by an excavating machine, probably in the 1950s. This site is that of the manor house of Great Fransham manor. Six acres in a close were listed but not named in *c*.1430. The close was bordered by a road on its south side, and by another road, leading from Great Fransham church to the manor, on the north.

Finds recovered during metal detecting include a penny of Henry I (*c*.1125–35), fifty-five coins ranging from Stephen to Henry VII[i], eight medieval jettons, three lead papal bull seals, two of Innocent III (1198–1216) and one of Gregory IX (1227–41), five 13th and 14th-century seal matrices, one in copper alloy inscribed + CONTRAS' ABATI DE PONTE ROB'I· (Counterseal of the Abbot of Robertsbridge[ii], Fig. 7.7.6), two lead inscribed + S' ROGERI : KNIT (Seal of Roger Knight), and + S.' ROG [.....]I IOh' (Seal of Roger son of John), and two copper alloy inscribed * SIGILLV·SECRETE (Secret seal) and * TIMETE DEVM (Fear God). Amongst other copper alloy objects are dress accessories including a 12th-century annular brooch with animal-head projections (Fig. 7.7.1; Ashley 2006, fig.1 no.7), a gaping-mouth beast buckle of the mid-12th to early 13th century (Fig. 7.7.2), parts of a 12th-century sword scabbard chape, a fragmentary gilt mount possibly from a book cover (Fig. 7.7.3), an unusually elaborate rotary key (Fig. 7.7.4), twelve pieces of horse furniture including harness pendants (Fig. 7.7.5) and a swivelling heraldic 'banner', spur fragments, and numerous pieces of cast cooking vessels, some of which may perhaps be post-medieval. Amongst comparatively few certainly post-medieval objects were ten coins (Philip and Mary to William III), and a two Nuremberg jettons.

It seems very likely that a standing manor house would have merited a specific entry in the extent of *c*.1430. A rental of demesne lands of about the same date shows that almost all were leased out to numerous tenants (MS 13073). An abandonment date cannot be fixed with any certainty, but the pottery suggests that occupation had ceased probably before *c*.1400, and more certainly by 1414 when the manor was divided on the death of Geoffrey de Fransham. The de Fransham family may have long placed more emphasis on their Scarning residence. It may be significant that when, in 1337, the Lay Subsidy payments of Great Fransham and Scarning were apportioned amongst the inhabitants at a variable rate reflecting their moveable wealth, Geoffrey de Fransham's contributions under the two vills were so different. In Great Fransham he paid 4s out of a total for the township of 40s (10%), while in Scarning his contribution was 13s 4d out of 75s (17.8%).

Manor Close, containing 7 acres, was held at farm in 1511 by Richard Maunde [of Little Fransham]. Henry Skepper of Necton, the tenant, was amerced at a manor court in 1526 for failing to maintain a *porta caduta* next to *Maundesclose* next to *Halwoodlane* (MS 13056). By 1537 this was known as *Skeppers Close* and contained 6 acres (MS 13075). *Skeppers grove* contained 8¼ acres of wood in 1595 and 8 acres in 1598.

One question in an interrogatory of 1598 for the Chancery case between Sir Arthur Capell complainant and Nicholas Mynne gent. defendant asked 'whether you knowe.......that the defendant or his Anncestors......have changed, defaced or concealed the Ancient mannor house and scite of the saide mannor.....?' (MS 13221). The same words were used in the decree of this case issued in 1602, with the addition of 'pulled downe….filled upp….suppressed….. removed' (TNA C 78/128/4; MS 13393). In 1621 a parcel of meadow or pasture in Great and Little [sic] Fransham was known as *Shepperds* or *Skeppards grove* (C/Sca 1/5 R117–8) and in 1636 a close or piece of ground called *Shepperds alias Skeppers grove* contained 7¾ acres and 17 perches and lay next to the *Greate New close* on the east (C/Sca 1/5 R138).

A concentration of 13th or 14th-century ceramic roof tiles *c*.200 west of the site (HER 20521) may perhaps mark the site of a manorial building, perhaps a barn, although there is no supporting documentary evidence.

On free land of William Mason esq. following Enclosure.

Med 6 TF 8875 1251 (Area A, HER 20509). Medium-heavy soil, 84m OD (Fig. 7.4). Concentration of mid-12th to late 14th-century sherds, 40m north-south x 30m east-west, lying on the east edge of a common pasture, *Cruddesgrene*. This was probably a 4-acre close of Great Fransham demesne once *Ernescroft* in *c*.1430, which lay next to a close of John Crudde on the west. In *c*.1400 a 1-acre close of Great Fransham freehold, which was later to be held by John Crudde, butted east on *Ernyesyard* and lay next to a messuage, which Crudde was also later to hold, on the west. Two Great Fransham customary tenants called Erny died in 1349: John had held a messuage and ¾ acre, and Cecilia a messuage and 1¾ acres. In 1374 a messuage and 5 acres called *Ernys* were leased out for a term of 8 years. There are three entries in a series of undated (late 16th-century) documents that consistently group *Ernys croft* and *Curds Croft* together. Each time they are listed after 'the situation of the howse late Courds' (MS 13085).

On free land of John Drosier esq. following Enclosure.

Med 7 TF 8839 1237 (Area A, HER 20446). Heavy soil, 87m OD (Fig. 7.4). Concentration of late 12th to mid-13th-century sherds, 30m x 30m, lying immediately north of a probably medieval road, outside the north-east corner of a large piece of demesne of Great Fransham manor called *Pylwod*. This may be identified as a Great Fransham freehold messuage held by Roger de Toftes in *c*.1400, once of John Leche. A person of this name swore fealty in 1343. The messuage, which was not accorded any acreage, lay next to the lord's land on the east and butted south on the common path leading to Dunham. In 1537 the same messuage was said to be held by John Crudde (MS 13074).

On free land of John Drosier esq. following Enclosure.

Med 8 TF 8843 1236 (Area A, HER 20446). Heavy soil, 87m OD (Fig. 7.4). A pottery production site is evidenced by this concentration of discoloured, predominantly oxidised, and partly under- and overfired 12th to early 13th-century unglazed sherds, 40m x 40m, but without any pronounced soil discoloration. There is no documentary evidence. A 4½ acre piece of Great Fransham freehold called *Potterscrofte* held by Roger de Toftes in *c*.1400 was probably somewhere near this site, but as the former butted west on a common way, they are unlikely to be one and the same. A group of nine similarly discoloured sherds was found amongst a slight concentration of normally fired sherds at TF 8852 1262, some 270m to the north-north-east, with the occasional sherd to the east in the same field (G57, HER 20518). This concentration, shown on Fig. 7.5 and lying on the east side of *Kerlane*, is more likely to have been *Potterscrofte*.

Both Med 8 and the slight concentration were on free lands of John Drosier esq. following Enclosure.

Med 9 TF 8875 1232 (Area A and *Quarent*. 2, HER 20818 and 20448). Medium soil, 85m OD. (Figs 7.4, 7.28 and 7.29). This site straddles the former boundary between Great and Little Fransham and lay at the south-west corner of a common pasture, *Cruddesgrene*, on the north side of the junction between the green and a road approaching from the south-east called *Ernneslane* in 1395. Later 12th and 13th-century sherds cover an uncertain area. The part within Little Fransham is under arable, while that within Great Fransham lies under grass. Part of this was ploughed up and sown for pheasant cover in 1992. A surprisingly large number of sherds was recovered despite poor surface conditions, although the western edge of the concentration was not defined. Its extent from north to south was *c*.40m. This was one of three messuages which were part of a customary holding of Kirkhams manor in the late 14th century (see Med 11).

On free land of John Drosier esq. following Enclosure.

Med 10 TF 8878 1227 (*Quarent*. 2, HER 20818). Medium soil, 85m OD. (Figs 7.28 and 7.29). Concentration of later 12th and 13th-century sherds, 30m x 30m on the north side of *Ernneslane*. It may have been one of three messuages forming part of a Kirkhams customary holding in the late 14th century (see Med 11).

On free land of John Drosier esq. following Enclosure.

Med 11 TF 8884 1225 (*Quarent*. 2, HER 20818). Medium soil, 85m OD. (Figs 7.28 and 7.29). Concentration of mid-12th to early 15th-century sherds, 30m east-west and max. 50m north-south, set within a ditch to the north, east and west, and butting south on *Ernneslane*. This enclosure is clearly visible, as a recently ploughed earthwork, on several 1946 RAF vertical air photographs, and is still partly visible as a soil mark.

William Couper held a customary messuage and 18 acres of Kirkhams manor by 1374. In 1384 Robert Anyell and his wife, who had been taxpayers in 1381, held a customary tenement of the same manor, which included 2 meadows, 18 acres, ½ acre with a messuage and three messuages. The latter were described as once of William Leche, Cecilia Mundham and Nicholas Syger, and formerly Coupers. No abuttals were given. Despite this lack of information, it is likely that this site may be the messuage with ½ acre, and Med 9, 10 and 12 may be the other three messuages. Much of this holding was in the hands of the lord by 1391. Part had been regranted as bond land divided into three parcels in *Westfield* by 1443, and part became demesne, perhaps for the second time, including a close called *Anyelles* by 1446/7 (MS 13142), and a grove called *Anyell / Anyell grove* by 1427–8 (MS 13177 and MS 13097).

On free land of John Drosier esq. following Enclosure.

Med 11A TF 8899 1196, HER 23089). Medium-heavy soil, 82m OD (Fig. 7.28). Concentration of 13th and 14th-century sherds 60m north-south x 30m east-west, in Necton parish immediately adjacent to the boundary with Little Fransham. The site lies in the south-east part of a small bulge of Necton parish into Little Fransham at the north-west end of a common pasture of Little Fransham called the *common lynge* in 1605. A moderate spread of sherds is present over the remainder of the bulge. Slight signs of a bank aligned north-west to south-east form the south-west boundary of the concentration. Unusually clear soil changes occur close to the site: heavy soil to the north and medium, almost light, soil to the south-east. This site can be identified with a Kirkhams customary messuage and 10 acres in Necton. In 1343 Roger Casy, who held 10 acres, was elected at the manor court as messor. In 1361 a messuage and 10 acres in Necton and 1 acre in Little Fransham, of which John Casy died seized without heir, were taken into the lord's hands. In 1374 a tenement once of Roger Cacy containing 10 acres with a messuage was granted to Geoffrey son of Roger Tussenolf. Geoffrey died in 1405, seized of a messuage and 9½ acres, and when his son William, aged 2, did not attend court the property was again taken by the lord. William had died by 1410 when half of the holding, now said to be in Little Fransham, was in the lord's hands and half was held by William's mother Johanna. In 1422 the tenement Casyes was elected to the office of messor but was in the lord's hands. In August 1423 John Ward and his wife were admitted to a tenement containing a messuage and 10 acres once of Geoffrey Tuskenolf in Little Fransham, to hold for ancient rents and services. Apart from an entry in a leet roll in October that year, Ward was never to appear again in court proceedings. In 1429 the tenement Casys was in the lord's hands and held at farm by one Thomas Reve (for Reve see Med 89). In a perambulation of Necton parish in 1427 this site was called a certain close or croft called *Kayscrofte* (MS 13177). In 1441 the tenement Wardes alias Tussenolf was granted to John Gleymesford and his wife and heirs to hold for a money rent. In 1443 and 1444 when the tenement TussenolI was elected to the office of messor it was said to be in the lord's hands and held at farm by Gleymesford.

The detailed rental of 1443 listed a messuage in *Quarent*. 5, three pieces of land in *Quarent*. 2 and one in *Quarent*. 20, totalling 10 acres. The muddle about whether this tenement by then lay in Necton or Little Fransham had at last been put right: the word '*Neketon*' was deleted, underlined by pecking and superscribed '*Fransham parva*'.

In 1449, when the tenement Casyes was elected to the office of messor, it was said to contain 10 acres and a messuage void and unbuilt (*vacuo non edificat.*, an unusually definite description of desertion) and to be in the lord's hands. This messuage was Med 11A, while that in *Quarent*. 5 continued to be occupied. The tenement Casyes, still in the lord's hands, was last elected to the office of messor in 1489.

Med 12 TF 8887 1220 (*Quarent*. 2, HER 20818). Medium soil, 84m OD. (Figs 7.28 and 7.29). Concentration of ?12th and 13th to 14th-century sherds, 30m east-west x max. 40m north-south, lying to the south-west of Med 11 and on the north side of a medieval road. This may be one of three customary messuages held of Kirkhams manor in the late 14th century (see Med 11).

On free land of John Drosier gent. following Enclosure.

Med 13 TF 8885 1364 (Area B, HER 20796). Heavy soil, 77m OD (Fig. 7.8). Concentration of 13th and 14th-century sherds lying on the edge of *Wylmondheithe* (or *Fransham Lyng*), a common pasture. Of uncertain extent because it lies partly outside the area available for examination. This is probably to be identified with a messuage with 8 acres of the tenement Curtlys, freehold of the manor of East Lexham, known from an incomplete rental of *c*. 1550 (KIM 1/8/16). In the early 17th century the tenement Curtelyns was held by Nicholas Mynne, and it had been held by John Crudde and his father before him. In 1451/2 John Crudde and William Cade had sworn fealty for it (MC 1812/49, 838X5).

Running east from the east of *Wylmondheithe* was a road called *Cortelylane* in *c*.1430. Related place names occur in several amercements at courts leet: a watercourse at *Curtely sex acr* in 1434, ditches at *Kyrtely* in 1440, ditches against *Sexacrys* and at *Curtely* in 1443. Each offence involved a member of the Crudde family (MS 13048).

Following Enclosure, a house lying immediately to the south-west of Med 13 on former common and now demolished was freehold, and rentals show that it was held of East Lexham manor in the late 18th and early 19th century (MS 12835–7). On free land of Sarah Beck following Enclosure.

Med 14 TF 8905 1414 (Area B, HER 20797). Medium-heavy soil, 80m OD (Fig. 7.8). Concentration of

13th to late 14th or early 15th-century sherds, 45m east-west x 30m north-south, lying at the west end of a common pasture called *Meschalismor* in 1369 and later *Mascallyng*, and adjacent to the boundaries with Kempstone and Great Dunham parishes, in the nearest parts of both of which were large tracts of common pasture.

This lay within Great Fransham demesne and may have been the house of a miller. The background is fully explained in Chapter 6. By *c.*1430 the area was called *Conyngerlond*, 12 acres in one piece with a close. Perhaps this close contained the miller's house, the windmill and the site at which a leet court styled Milles atte Mor was held.

On free land of Deborah Bunting following Enclosure.

Med 15 TF 8942 1372 (Area B, HER 20264). Heavy soil, 73m OD. (Figs 7.8 and 7.9). Concentration of 12th to late 14th-century sherds, 25m east-west x 40m north-south with a strong spread to the south-west, situated on the east edge of a common pasture called *Brounesgrene* and north of a roadway shown on the Enclosure map of 1805. This site can be identified with a void messuage, freehold of the manor of East Lexham in *c.*1550, when it was held by Thomas Toly, once of Edmund Browne. The messuage had a 2-acre croft to the east, lay next to *Brownsmore* and a garden of Great Fransham manor west, and butted south on a common way called *Brownslane* (KIM 1/8/16). The croft is indicated by a moderate spread of sherds to the east. A piece of Great Fransham demesne called *Jonesyard* lay in *Shepehousefield* next to *Brownsmore* on the west in *c.* 1430. This was almost certainly the garden. Thomas Toly held at farm from Great Fransham manor a little pightle, probably the same piece, in 1547/8 (MS 13076). It is probably evidenced by the area of sherds to the south-west of the messuage.

In the bailiff of East Lexham manor's accounts for 1555–6 an allowance was made for the rent (5½d) due from a messuage built and croft in Great Fransham now in the hands of the lord because the former tenant, Thomas Tolie, had been hanged in Norwich for various offences (*perdicibus*). This allowance was still being made up till the last surviving account, for 1560–1 (KIM 1/8/12). It is judged that the bailiff's use of the word built (*edificat.*) was an error. Tolie lived not far away at Med 17. This property was not entered in an early 17th-century list of East Lexham holdings (MC 1812/49, 838X6).

At the quarter sessions in Norwich held on 27 July 1555 four members of the Toly family were condemned to be hung, drawn and quartered. William of Wicklewood yeoman, Richard of London barber, Thomas of Great Fransham yeoman and John of Norwich tailor were found guilty of counterfeiting nine gold coins of the Kingdom of France called 'French Crownes' at Wicklewood on 25 February 1555. The judges said that the said 'frenchcrownes' were not issued by this realm (*non fuit propria cunia huius Regni*) but were still [valid] currency (*Cunia curreas*) in England (C/S 3 Box 4).

Amongst a royal grant of monastic properties and lands of attainted people made to Thomas Guybon of King's Lynn esq. and William Mynne of London gent. in 1558 were a tenement and 8 acres in Great Fransham in the tenure of Nicholas Golder, late of Thomas Tolye, attainted (Cal. Pat. Rol. 1939, 291).

Within a block of Necton Town lands following Enclosure.

Med 15A TF 8935 1363 (Area B, HER 20623). Medium soil, 72m OD (Fig. 7.8). Occupation began in the middle of the 11th century (LS 5) and continued into the 13th. It probably lay within Great Fransham demesne called *Shepehowscroft*.

On free land of Henry Stanford following Enclosure.

Med 16 TF 8967 1383 (Area B, HER 20802). Medium soil, 70m OD (Fig. 7.8). Concentration of 12th-century sherds, 40m east-west x 60m north-south, set back *c.*120m north of a medieval road. A few sherds of Thetford-type ware may derive from LS 3 to the east. It probably lay west of Great Fransham demesne called *Halcroft* and on Rougholme manor land or on Blyfords freehold associated with Med 17, of which it may have been the predecessor.

On free land of Edward Wellingham following Enclosure.

Med 17 TF 8968 1369 (Area B, HER 20609). Medium soil, 67m OD (Fig. 7.8). Profuse 13th to 17th-century sherds were recovered from flower beds in a garden. A spread of early post-medieval bricks was present. Its extent is uncertain, but it did not reach arable areas available for fieldwalking *c.*30m to the east or *c.*60m to the north. This site lies immediately north of a stream and a medieval road, *Brownslane*, which connected two areas of common pasture, *West End moor* and *Brounesgrene*. It is possible that this site was a successor to Med 16. It is to be identified as a freehold messuage with 1 acre in the croft, a freehold of the manor of Blyfords, which was listed in a rental of 1550 as being held by Margaret Toly widow. It had been held by her husband Henry and in the later 15th century by Alexander, then William then Thomas Pynne (MS 424). The abuttals do not include one to the south. To the north lay land of the said Margaret, and according to the same rental she held 4½ acres in one piece which butted north on *Mascallyng*, the common which lay to the north along the parish boundary. A ½-acre parcel of Rougham freehold probably lay on the west side. It had been held by the same members of the Pynne family and Henry Toly swore fealty for it in 1507 (MR 28, 240X6). See Med 15 for Thomas Toly, probably the son of Margaret. By 1589 the rent 'for Toolys' was paid by Nicholas Mynne gent. and Edward Mynne gent, was named as tenant in 1627. By 1644 Richard Alpe was tenant (PD 143/46).

A large double-looped fifteenth-century buckle frame found during metal-detecting on the former common pasture in front of the property at TF 8967 1366 (HER 52913, Fig. 7.10).

On free land of Edward Wellingham following Enclosure.

Med 18 TF 8971 1361 (Area B, HER 20606). Probably medium-heavy soil, 66m OD (Fig. 7.8). Profuse 13th, 14th and possibly early 15th-century sherds were recovered from a vegetable bed in a garden on the eastern edge of *West End moor*. The extent of the spread cannot be assessed, although it was absent from a formerly arable field 30m to the north-east. It lay near the south-west corner of a 20-acre close called *Halcroft* with a building (*domus*) at its southern end, demesne of Great Fransham manor in c.1430. In a rental of the same date this was described as 21 acres with an enclosure at the southern end containing a building (MS 13073). A gloss in the extent states it was held at farm by Henry Toly, probably early temp. Henry VIII (for other people called Toly see Med 15 and 17). In 1575 and 1581–2 it was called *Tolyes* or *Toolys close* (MS 13079). *Halcroft* contained the site of LS 3 / Med 20, but it should be noted that there is an apparent gap of occupation between Med 19 and 20, covering most of the 12th century.

On free land of Edward Wellingham following Enclosure.

Med 19 TF 8964 1367 (Area B, HER 35264) (Figs 7.8 and 7.9). The Late Saxon origin of this site, (LS 4), as well as its occupation in the medieval period, is inferred from a spread of sherds in adjacent part of the field immediately to the west (HER 20624). It is still occupied by a house and garden. Its documentary history, as two customary holdings of Great Fransham manor, the tenements Wymers and Flyntes, is relatively continuous from the mid-14th century. Because the documentation is so full, more detail of the tenurial descent will be given for this site than for any other.

Thomas Wymer, a taxpayer in 1327, 1332 and 1337, swore fealty to Gilbert de Fransham in 1343 and had died by July 1349, seized of a messuage and 20 acres, leaving Adam Sewles and Nicholas Large as heirs. Adam Sewles was ordered to repair a damaged building (*domo fec. ruinosa*) of the tenement Wymerys in 1371. Adam Sules was a taxpayer in 1379. Nicholas Sewles was admitted to the tenement Wymers on the surrender of Adam in 1385. In 1399 the tenement Wymers, which contained 26 acres of land and meadow, was elected to the office of messor. According to the rental of c.1400 Nicholas Sewles held a messuage, 21½ acres and 3 acres of meadow once of Wymer, for an annual rent of 2s and 16 autumn workdays. Sewles had died by 30 October 1400 when his son John was admitted to the same, of the tenement Wymers, paying a heriot of a mare, valued at 16s. The rental enumerates the tenement as a messuage and 10 acres enclosed, with two pieces of land in Area J, three in Area K and four in Area L. The meadow lay in Area H.

In 1391 John Flynt, a taxpayer in 1379, had died seized of a cottage, and his wife and co-tenant Margaret was admitted. In c.1400 Nicholas Sewles held a customary messuage once of John Flynt and Eustace Fisher for the rent of a halfpenny. It lay next to his tenement and land (i.e. Wymers) on the east. One Eustace Fisher, free tenant of a cottage in the north-west corner of *Quarent*.13 in Little Fransham, had died in 1361.

Sometime after 1400 the tenement Wymers fell into the lord's hands so that by c.1430 its constituents were listed in an extent of the demesne. Unfortunately, there are several discrepancies concerning acreage and abuttals between the rental and the extent. The former is probably more reliable on the pieces in the fields, while the latter describes the messuage and its close or croft as a 12-acre close where once there was the tenement Sewles. In a roughly contemporary rental of lands let at farm John Codling paid 9½d per acre for two closes once of Sewles containing 10 acres (MS 13073).

The cottage or messuage once of John Flynt was not entered in the extent of c.1430, although 1 acre of the tenement Flyntes in Area K was listed. A cottage built called Flyntys was conveyed in 1455 (MS 13049). According to a rental of the 1470s or 1480s William Evan held a close called *Sowles* with 1 acre in the field for 4s (MS 13078). Richard Miller was amerced for not scouring his ditch at *Sewlesclose* in 1475 (MS 13048). In 1496 John Miller failed to come to court for admittance to a customary cottage built, but he was admitted in 1498. By 1502 a cottage built was held by Thomas Futche who conveyed it Thomas Pynne, his wife and his son (MS 13035). *Millers Close* appears in three copies of farm rents dated 1511. It had lately been let as copyhold for a rent of 5s. One list stated that it was in decay and another that William Steade paid the rent. In two lists of customary rents of the same date John Futche's rent for *Sowlisclosse / Solleys close* was given as 3s (MS 13056). In 1521 and 1528 Henry Toly was amerced for not scouring a ditch at *Miller Lane* and *Myllers close* (MS 13068). In 1530 John Flegge was admitted to a cottage built called *Myllers* on the surrender of Henry Toly and his wife. In 1544 Flegge showed his copies for the cottage and for a 5-acre close near *West End moor* next to the common way leading to *Brownesmore* on the north, butting west on *Sewles close* and east on the cottage called *Millers* (MS 13056). Clearly *Millers close* had been created out of the eastern part of *Sewles close*. From this point the history of the two closes will not be considered.

A tenement called Fynts [sic] formerly held by Richard Miller was seized in the lord's hands in 1504 (MS 13166). According to two rentals of 1537 a messuage once of Nicholas Sewles and John Flynt was held by Robert Crowe, with the rent unchanged at a halfpenny (MS 13074–5). There is no later reference to the property which was probably soon subsumed under its neighbour to the east.

In 1553 John Flegge's rent for his house was 1d (MS 13077). In 1557 a cottage called *Millers* passed from John Flegge to John Asshill, and then to John Cannon in 1558. In 1560 it went to William Antingham (MS 13058). He was buried at Great Fransham in 1588. By 1591 Thomas Dymes was tenant (MS 13062) and in 1595 he paid 4d rent of customary rent for cottage once of William Antingham. In 1603 the property was allotted to Sir Arthur Capel's portion of Great Fransham manor (styled as Mills-on-the-Moor with Great Fransham). The fate of Thomas Dymes is unclear, but he must have been followed by an otherwise unrecorded tenant because in 1603 John Johnson paid 4d rent for a cottage late Rustons once Antinghams (MS 13080). In 1605 it passed from Johnson to James Barker. A messuage late in the tenure of Thomas Daynes (i.e. Dymes) was seized by the lord because the tenant James Barker had fled after perpetrating a certain felony. In 1614 the cottage passed through the hands of two people at one manor court sitting in an affair concerning unpaid debts probably from a mortgage, before Richard Sheene was admitted (MS 13415). Sheene's rent was recorded as 4d in the same year (MS 13083). There then follows a gap in the sequence caused by the lack of any manorial documentation until 1670. Sheene's final appearance in the parish register was in 1623, for a birth.

In his will, proved in 1662, Richard Dames yeoman of Great Fransham left his copyhold messuage there to his son Robert and his wife for their lives, with reversion to Robert's son Richard (original will no.95). In 1670 Robert

Danes the guardian of Richard Danes paid a fine of 6d for a licence to pull down an animal? shed (*betem domum*) standing on Richard's customary tenement. In 1671 Robert "had suffered a certain coppiehold Tenent. of Richard Danes to be soe ruinous that the same is become Inhabitable [sic] and fallen downe". It was forfeited and seized by the lord. In 1673 Richard Daines had forfeited a customary rood with a standing building (*domus super inde erect.*) because he had cut down five pollard trees growing there. It was again seized into the lord's hands and Robert Birch was admitted, for a rent of 4d.

By 1678 Birch had died, seized of a parcel of pasture containing ¼ acre at *Westendmoore*, on which a certain building (*domus*) lately stood. No one claimed the property and a first proclamation was read out. A second followed in 1679. After a third in 1680 the property was seized by the lord and Samuel Walker was then admitted, for a rent of 1s 6d.

In 1726 Walker had died, having surrendered all his lands to the use of his will in 1707. His daughter, Elizabeth Howard widow, brought the will to court. In this, Samuel Walker, a thatcher of Great Fransham, had left his messuage or tenement, copyhold of the manor of Mills-on-the-Moor in Great Fransham, to Elizabeth and her daughters Mary, Sarah and Amy Howard (ANW 7.92 1725). These three girls were admitted to a cottage or tenement containing ¼ acre (MC 969/1, 858X7). There then follows a gap in court records until 1787.

In 1778 Dorothy Younge surrendered a cottage or tenement with ¼ acre to the use of James Harrold of Great Fransham yeoman (evidence from a court held in 1793). According to a rental of 1780–92 Harrold paid 1s 6d rent for a cottage late Richard Daines (MC 969/8, 858X7). In 1793 he surrendered a cottage or tenement with ¼ acre adjoining to the use of Cook Leath of Little Ellingham, farmer, who immediately surrendered the same to the use of his will (MC 969/2, 858X7). In his will (proved in 1801) Edward Leath of Great Fransham farmer left all his properties in Great Fransham, Stow Bedon and Rocklands to his son Cook, of Little Ellingham, farmer (NCC 140 Francklin). To judge from Cook's property portfolio at Enclosure, these lands comprised about 150 acres.

Following Enclosure, Cook Leath was allotted 2 acres 1 rood and 18 perches of Mills-on-the-Moor with Great Fransham copyhold, of which 2 roods and 18 poles were allotted for and in lieu of the mess and 1 rood to which he stood admitted, and 1 acre 3 roods were allotted for and in respect of common rights. The rent was increased by 2d.

The present house, a 19th and 20th-century structure stands on low lying ground at TF 8965 1365, in what is probably an encroachment onto the common, and in the same position as a building on the Enclosure map. To the north of the house the grass covered surface rises to what must have been the site of the medieval house. Here four medieval sherds have been recovered from minute patches of bare soil and molehills. One fresh sherd was found during the examination of various builder's trenches around the house.

Med 20 TF 8978 1383 (Area B, HER 20793). Medium soil, 70m OD (Fig. 7.8). This was first occupied in the ?later 10th century (see LS 3, Chapter 5), but was deserted by 1100 or soon after. It may have been succeeded by Med 18 after a gap in occupation covering most of the 12th century, and it lay within the same close of Great Fransham demesne.

On free land of Edward Wellingham following Enclosure.

Med 21 TF 8968 1343 (Area A, HER 25553). Probably heavy soil, 67m OD (Figs 7.8 and 7.22). This site, which borders the southern edge of *West End moor*, might perhaps be more accurately placed in Area K. It is evidenced by a small sample of Late Saxon, medieval and post-medieval sherds recovered in poor soil conditions from the garden of Church Farm (see LS 7). This site is identified with a messuage with 2 acres in the croft, which was held, along with 67¼ acres in twenty-three parcels, by William Mascale of Edward Hastings, lord of Gressenhall and East Lexham. Mascale had died by 1439 (NCC 76 Doke). Only one messuage appears in a rental of his lands dated 1434/5, but the abuttals do not fit very well with the location of this site: in *Normannscroft*, between his land on both sides and butting south on the common way (PD 143/76). This way could be equated with the *Whiteway* and that the common to the north was omitted need not be a difficulty because the document rental does not give more three abuttals for any entry. However, Mascale's lands on both sides remains a problem because a way and beyond that a common lay to the west. Mascale bequeathed this estate to John Blyford and Agnes his wife.

During the life of the Blyfords the estate passed to three men who then granted it to four others, including William Yelverton knight. In 1462 these in turn conveyed it to five others, including Thomas Lardge and two other Larges of Great Fransham, with exceptions being made for certain elements during the lives of the Blyfords and for forty days after their deaths: a room called *le Gosechambyr* (recte guest?) at the west end of the hall in the messuage where John Blyford lived, all rooms adjoining the chamber, a garden next to the chamber, a pond (*stagnum*) in the garden, a parcel of land for firewood (*terrae profocale*, Latham 1965, 195), the pasturage of a close called *le Briggemeadowe*, a stable for the Blyfords' horse and their friends' horses, 1 acre of arable in Great Fransham in two pieces called *Broad half acre* and *Pyt half acre* with 10d rent from land pertaining called *Curtileys* (cf. Med 13). In 1468 three surviving cofeoffees granted the estate to John Crudde and four others, and in 1489 when two of the latter were dead the surviving pair released their interest to Crudde. In 1491 he granted the same to his wife and five others, including Nicholas Mynne, to the uses of his will (MS 424). In 1509 Mynne, of Little Fransham and the sole surviving grantee, conveyed the estate to seventeen men of Necton and Thomas Wyskard of Little Fransham (PD 143/77). Thus, the manor of Blyford became a constituent of what became known as the Necton Town estate.

Necton churchwardens' account books for 1536–1699 and 1657–92 (PD 143/46–7) contain several references to building and repair work at Blyfords. Timber was taken there in 1536–7 and a new pair of gates was made in 1546–7. Bricks and lime were taken there, carpenters, masons and thatchers worked there, and an oven was made there at various times between 1666 and 1688. Of the wills of those who held the lease of Blyfords in the post-medieval period only one, that of William Thorold, husbandman of Great Fransham, which was proved in 1567, makes reference to the house: two beds in the 'fire howse' and 'my casses standinge uppon the chamber over the fier howse wt all the lynin their beinge..' (ANW 259 Mendham).

The farmhouse and farm buildings were the only ones on Necton Town estate lands in Great Fransham following Enclosure. The present Church Farm house is a 19th-century brick-faced clay-lump structure, and the farm buildings are 19th and 20th-century.

Med 22 TF 8946 1338 (Area A, HER 20613). Medium-heavy soil, 69m OD (Fig. 7.8). Concentration of 11th to 14th-century sherds (see LS 6), 70m east-west x 50m north-south on the northern edge of a common pasture, *West End Moor*. There is a roughly circular and particularly dense sherd scatter in the centre, *c*.30m diameter. Pasture fields lie to the east and west.

On free land of Henry Stanford following Enclosure.

Med 23 TF 8929 1332 (Area A, HER 20613). Heavy soil, 69m OD (Fig. 7.8). Concentration, 35m north-south x 20m east-west, of 13th to early 16th-century sherds on the northern edge of a common pasture, *West End Moor*, with a stream running along its southern edge. This may be identified with a messuage and 1½ acres butting south on a common way and held by Thomas Mascall senior in *c*.1400, freehold of Great Fransham manor, once of Katherine de Whistede and Henry Capell. Henry Capellus was a taxpayer in 1332 and 1337. Henry the chaplain (*capellanus*) was amerced at the Great Fransham manor court for trespass in 1337. From *c*.1400 this property and Med 23A (immediately to the west) were held by the same tenants and from *c*.1560 they were amalgamated. The tenurial history of the pair can be followed to 1655.

On free land of Henry Stanford following Enclosure.

Med 23A TF 8933 1331 (Area A, HER 14166). Heavy soil, 69m OD (Fig. 7.8). A timber-framed 16th or 17th-century house now sits within a garden of 0.13 hectare on the northern edge of *West End Moor* and immediately east of Med 23. Ten medieval and three post-medieval sherds have been found on patches of bare soil. It is probably to be identified with a messuage and 2½ acres butting south on a common way and held by Thomas Mascall senior in *c*.1400, freehold of Great Fransham manor. It was once of Katherine de Whistede and John Wyllers. A Katherine de Whistede had held at farm 1¼ acres of Great Fransham demesne for 5 years from 1353. Thomas Mascale was a taxpayer in 1379. He also held Med 23.

There is no 15th-century documentary evidence, but by 1511 the free rent of Edmund Agges shows he held this and Med 23, as did John Futche in 1515/6 (MS 13056). John Colyn senior was tenant in 1537 (MS 13074–5) and in 1544 he had died seized of a free tenement called *Aggs* with 2 acres (MS 13056) and his widow Matilda was tenant in 1547/8 and 1553 (MS 13076 and MS 13077). John Collyn was said to have sold a free messuage to Christopher Dokett who had sold it on to John Hammond of Swaffham. He swore fealty for a free tenement called *Agges* with 6½ acres. This amount of land is too much for this piece and Med 23 alone, but the rent (10d) was the same (MS 13059). In his will (proved in 1565) Robert Collenge, yeoman of Great Fransham, left his lands etc. called *Agses* to his brother Henry, his mother Matilda to have occupancy for life (ANW 2 Mendham). William Colyn's free rent for *Agges* was 10½d in 1573 and 1575 and he paid the same in 1581–2, as did Andrew Sammes in 1595 (MS 13079). The will of William Collen yeoman of Wendling (proved in 1598) made money bequests to Sammes, his wife and Christian Sammes (ANW 355 Lyncolne 1597–8). Andrew Sammes was buried in 1608. The rent for various Great Fransham demesne lands leased out to Andrew Sammes fishmonger in 1607 was paid by Simon Woodrowe in 1609 and he still held these lands in 1614 (MS 13082–3). Similarly, a group of Kirkhams and Wilcoks demesne lands formally held by Sammes were leased out to Woodrowe, a yeoman, in 1611 (MS 13310; see Table 9.4). An abuttal concerning a piece of glebe in 1613 was on land occupied by Simon Woodrowe 'in the right of Andrew Sames and his heirs'. Woodrowe's wife was called Christine and it is very likely that she was the 'Christian' of William Collen's will.

In his will (proved in 1630) Woodrowe left to Christine his mansion house and 8 acres in six pieces in the field of Great Fransham (ANW 125 Sharpe). The total of Great Fransham free land held by the 16th-century tenants of this property had amounted to 3 messuages, a cottage and 5¾ acres. Christine Woodrowe's will (proved in 1655) mentions only one property, her tenement in Great Fransham occupied by Thomas Homes, although she was described as of Great Fransham. It was to be divided between two of her children (TNA PROB 11/251/211).

On free land of Henry Stanford following Enclosure.

Med 24 TF 8940 1316 (Area A, HER 4192). Medium-heavy soil, 70m OD. (Figs 7.8 and 7.11). Three concentrations, merging into each other, of 13th and 14th-century sherds lying next to a right-angled turn in the southern edge of a common pasture, *West End Moor*.

The eastern part may be identified with a cottage and 2 acres once of Roger Parse listed in a corrupt later 15th-century rental of Rougholme manor (TNA SC 11/476). In 1521 Joanna widow of Edmund Agges had sold a void customary messuage with 2 acres in the croft held of Rougholme to William Godfrey alias Smyth. He was admitted in 1523 to the same, which butted south on the *Whygtlye* (MR 28, 240X6). The messuage was still described as empty in 1548, when it butted south on the *Whiteway* and was held by William Sammes (TNA SC 12 3/22). In 1572 he left his lands etc. to his wife for life with reversion to his son Luke (ANW 163 Busbye). By 1633 the messuage was described as built, as it was in 1640, when it butted north and east on the common pasture and south on the common way. Its tenurial history, as copyhold of the manor of Ellinghams, Rougholme etc., can be traced intermittently (MC 1847/1, 741X2) until Enclosure, when it was described as a copyhold messuage and yard containing 2 acres and was held by Henry Stanford. The Enclosure Award map shows two small buildings to the north of the medieval concentrations at TF 8938 1322. Here there are plentiful post-medieval brick fragments, but virtually no pottery. This suggests that the built messuage of 1633 and later was not a dwelling house.

In *c*.1430 the western part of the site can be identified with an enclosure of ½ acres with 2½ acres in the croft once built and called Parles (cf. Roger Parse above), demesne of Great Fransham manor. It lay north of the *Whiteway* and next to land of the Master of the Chapel of Gressenhall on the east. Underwood was destroyed in Parlisyard in 1368 and the lord's wheat was damaged in

1369. In a rental of *c*.1430 a messuage and croft called Parles contained 3 acres and were let to farm (MS 13073). In 1537 this was held by William Godfrey as customary land (MS 13075). He was tenant of the adjoining Rougholme property. In 1547–8 Parles croft was held at farm as 3 acres of pasture by Thomas Asshyll (MS 13076). A Ralph Parle of Great Fransham was the grantor of one 13th-century charter (TNA WARD 2/53/179/15), and the name of Roger Parle occurs in a Little Fransham deed of a similar date (BL Add Ch 71036).

Med 25 TF 8925 1319 (Area A, HER 4192). Heavy soil, 71m OD. (Figs 7.8 and 7.11). Concentration of 13th to 15th-century sherds, 50m x 30m on the southern edge of a common pasture. This can be identified with a messuage, freehold of Great Fransham manor, once of John Sevenpens and held by John Maynard in *c*.1400 for an annual rent of 6d. It butted north on the common pasture and lay next to the messuage of Thomas Mascall on the west. Adam Sevepens, who was distrained to do fealty in 1343, died in 1349 seized of a messuage. He left his underaged son John as heir. People called Sevepens lived in Little Fransham in the 14th and 15th centuries, and Isabelle Sevepenes was a Great Fransham taxpayer in 1379.

In 1537 the rent was paid by John Colyn senior. At a manor court in 1544 it was said that he had died having sold a tenement built once Futches and certain free lands to Robert Colyn (see Med 23A). He in turn had sold all to John Colyn who swore fealty. In 1547 it was said that John had sold the same Robert (MS 13056). Robert Colling paid the rent in 1553 (MS 13077) and in his will, proved in 1565, Robert Collinge yeoman of Great Fransham left his lands etc. called *Futches* to his daughter Grace (ANW 2 Mendham). The rent for this property is not entered in any subsequent rentals, but the tenancy may have fallen into the hands of Andrew Sammes, for a gloss in one version of the rental of *c*.1400 reads "It is thought by Andrew Sammes that all ye land wch Jo. Collyn had is nowe his" (MS 13084 Book B). Sammes died in 1608.

It should be noted that despite the mid-16th-century references to a messuage built there was no archaeological evidence to support occupation here beyond *c*.1500.

A cottage stood on the west side of this messuage in *c*.1400. It was a freehold of Great Fransham manor, once of Osbert de Mundeforde and John Norman and held by David Anyell, the tenant of Med.27. In the 16th century it was held by the tenants of the messuage. Its description in a rental of 1553, when the tenant was Robert Colling, ends 'and it is his garden' (MS 13077).

On free land of Henry Stanford following Enclosure.

Med 25A TF 8918 1318 (Area A, HER 13725). Heavy soil, 71m OD. (Figs 7.8 and 7.11). A late 17th-century timber-framed farmhouse, now known as Cook's Meadows, stands near the southern edge of the former common pasture. Only five medieval sherds were found in that part of the back garden now incorporated into an arable field, and four more were found in bare patches of soil at the rear of the house. It is possible that this stands on an earlier site. Abuttals show that the site contained a messuage held by Thomas Mascall in *c*.1400 (see abuttal for Med 25) and by William Gryffyn in 1553 (MS 13077). Apart from Med 23 and 23A, the only other messuage known to have been held by Mascall (one held of East Lexham manor) was certainly not in this location.

After 1553 there is a gap in information, but from the early 17th century a series of Great Fransham wills, and from the late 17th century several entries in the court book of Great Fransham Rectory manor, provide a reliable tenurial history. In 1605, John Denyes, husbandman, left to his son Edward all his mansion house and grounds, which he had purchased from the late Henry Mynne of Little Fransham (ANW 221 Sawyer). Mynne had died in 1589. In 1657, Edmund Allenson, yeoman, left all his properties to his wife Agnes for life, his son Nicholas thereafter to inherit the house and lands which he had purchased from Edward Dennis (TNA PROB 11/266/496). In 1683 John Mawby acknowledged at the Rector's court that he held freely a messuage and 10 acres, late of Samuel Cushing clerk and *proinde* (i.e. then, but certainly an error) of Edmund Allyson.

In 1690 John Malby, butcher, left all houses and lands, which he had purchased from Samuel Cushinge clerk, to his kinsman John Malby (ANW W39.53 1690). In 1700 John Malby, yeoman, left his houses etc. and 16 acres of arable and pasture, all purchased from Mr Samuel Cushion, to his daughter Elizabeth (ANW 244 1699–1700). She married John Stanford of Great Fransham in 1702. The heirs of John Malby were amerced for default of suit of court in 1703. John Stanford held 10 acres and a messuage, for 2s rent, in 1729, 1735 and 1740. In 1758 John Stanford, yeoman, did not specify any landed property in his will (ANW W60.111 1758). In 1779 Thomas Stanford (one of John's sons) acknowledged that he held freely a house and 10 acres formerly Maltbys.

In 1782 Thomas Stanford, farmer, ordered all his freehold and copyhold properties in Great Fransham, Necton and Holme-next-the-Sea to be sold by his executors, one of whom was his brother Samuel of Little Massingham (ANW W42.51 1782). Samuel Standford acknowledged that he held a messuage and 10 acres formerly Maltby's later in 1782. In his will, proved in 1801, Samuel Stanford gent. left all his property in Great Fransham and Raynham (and in Withersdale and Mindham [sic], Suffolk) to his son Henry Stanford of Little Massingham gent. (ANW W68.72 1801). In 1807 Henry Stanford of Litcham gent. acknowledged that he held a messuage and 10 acres, late Samuel Stanford's.

On freehold land of Henry Stanford following Enclosure. Buildings are depicted on the Enclosure map.

Med 26 TF 8914 1318 (Area A, HER 4192). Heavy soil, 71m OD. (Figs 7.8 and 7.11). Concentration of 13th to late 14th or early 15th-century sherds, particularly dense in its western part, 40m x 40m, near the southern edge of *West End Moor*. This may possibly be identified with ½ acre of demesne of Great Fransham manor in *c*.1430. It was described as a close where once there were two closes, lying on the north side of the *Whiteway* and butting north on the common pasture. During the 16th century its tenants were consistently the men who held Med 27.

On free land of Henry Stanford following Enclosure.

Med 27 TF 8909 1323 (Area A, HER 4192). Heavy soil, 70m OD. (Figs 7.8 and 7.11). Concentration of 13th to 16th-century sherds, 30m east-west x 25m north-south, on southern edge of *West End Moor*. This may be identified with a messuage, freehold of Great Fransham manor, held in *c*.1400 by David Anyell for 3d annual rent (for a Robert Anyell see Med 11). It was once of Robert Hoverd. Robert Hubert, who was a taxpayer in the 1327 Lay Subsidy and swore fealty in 1343, died seized of a messuage and ½ acre in 1349, leaving his son Robert as heir. It had once been held by John Curd, presumably at some time in the 15th century, according to a rental of 1553 (MS 13077). The tenure of this piece can be traced from 1507 to 1595 in continual association with the demesne close that may be identified with Med 26. In his will, proved in 1507, Robert Parker of Great Fransham left to his wife Agnes the tenement and croft in which he lived (ANF 5 & 20 Grantham). Thomas Parker was tenant in 1511–2 (MS 13056), as was John Colyn in 1537 (MS 13074–5). He had sold certain lands to William Sammes in 1539 (HRO 8181). After his death in 1572 (see Med 24) his widow remarried, and her husband William Thorold was the rent payer in 1582 (MS 13079). William lived until 1602 and his wife until 1606, but by 1595 they must have sold this property to Nicholas Mynne, one of the lords of the manor, for according to a rental of that year he paid a free rent of 3d for land, the recent tenure of which was succinctly summarised, *pro terr. quondam Sammes olim Collen & antea Parker & nuper Wm Thurrolde iure uxis*.

On free land of Henry Stanford following Enclosure.

Med 28 TF 8900 1323 (Area A, HER 20523). Heavy soil, 71m OD. (Figs 7.8 and 7.11). Concentration of 12th to 14th-century pottery, 60m east-west x 40m north-south, on the southern edge of *West End Moor*. The documentary evidence is very slight. In 1553 the tenant of Med 27, William Sammys, held at farm 1 acre of Great Fransham demesne that butted north on the common pasture and lay next to his messuage on the east (MS 13077). This acre cannot be identified in the extent of *c*.1430, although it is likely to have been within a 20-acre close of Great Fransham demesne lying on the north side of the *Whiteway* and below the manor (Med 5).

On free land of William Mason esq. following Enclosure.

Med 29 TF 8895 1324 (Area A, HER 20523). Heavy soil, 71m OD. (Figs 7.8 and 7.11). A small concentration of 13th and 14th-century sherds, 25m east-west x 15m north-south, on the southern edge of *West End Moor*. This may not be a sufficiently large area to merit confident designation as a site, although it appeared quite discrete from Med 28. In common with the latter there is no certain documentary evidence, although it might be identified with a messuage once of Agnes Dene, freehold of Great Fransham manor in *c*.1400, which was held by John Crudde. Stephen Dene was a taxpayer in 1327. The messuage was listed in one rental of 1537 (MS 13074) but no reference to it has been found in any other document.

On free land of William Mason esq. following Enclosure.

Med 30 TF 8992 1306 (Area L, HER 4193). Light-medium soil, 73m OD (Fig.7.22). Immediately south of All Saints' churchyard, this site began life in the 11th century (LS 8), and its pottery, which is concentrated in an area of 30m x 30m, runs up to the end of the 13th century. Its position suggests that it may perhaps have been the original site of Great Fransham rectory, though there is no proof of this. The 1613 glebe terrier described this land as 1 acre of meadow, between the king's highway on the west and the church way on the east, butting south on the king's highway and north on the churchyard.

In a close of glebe containing 25 acres and 10 perches following Enclosure.

Med 31 TF 8994 1438 (Area C, HER 20812). Heavy soil, 74m OD (Fig. 7.12). Concentration of ?mid 12th to 14th-century sherds, 60m east-west x 30m north-south, on the eastern edge of a common pasture called *Mascallyng*, along which a north-south road ran in the medieval period. This may be tentatively identified with a messuage and 17 acres of the tenement Cornubells, freehold of East Lexham manor in *c*.1550 (KIM 1/8/16) and held with another messuage that has been equated with Med 33. A Roger son of William Columbel of Fransham was party to a charter of *c*.1265–73 (TNA E 40/10571).Walter Columbel of Great Fransham appeared in several charters between 1304 and 1317. He was a taxpayer in 1332.

In *c*.1610 it was held by Nicholas Mynne. A later gloss added that the land was then part of the Necton Town estate (*Blyfords modo ville de Necton*). No details of location were given (MC 1812/49, 838X5). This property and Med 33 were probably mentioned in the Inquisitions Post Mortem of Edward Mynne (ob. 1543) and Nicholas Mynne (ob. 1546) as a messuage with a close adjoining called *Petrie Clos alias the Grete Clos* and another close called *Netherclose* adjoining *Kenellhawgh Woode* in Great Fransham (TNA C 142/70/6 and C 142/85/18).

On free land of Cook Leath gent. following Enclosure.

Med 32 TF 9010 1445 (Area C, HER 20811). Heavy soil, 74m OD (Fig. 7.12). Concentration of 12th and 13th-century sherds, 70m north-south x 35m east-west butting north on the parish boundary with Beeston, along which ran a road, called *Knightwood Lane*, in 1805 (Enclosure map). Immediately north of the boundary lay *Knyghtwode*, demesne of the manor of Kirkhams held of the manor of Mileham from 1429. This site can be identified with a messuage called *Kinwalds* and 8 acres, freehold of the manor of East Lexham, which is entered in a rental of *c*.1550 (KIM 1/8/16). No contemporary tenant's name was given, but the holding was once of Thomas Mareshall and afterwards held by John Norman Esq. It lay on the west side of *Kinwaldyshaghe*. In *c*.1610 it was said to be held by Nicholas Mynne for an annual rent of 2s, and that it had been held by military service according to court rolls of 1345/6 and 1468/9. It had been amongst lands amounting to 48 acres of which John Norman had died seized in the reign of Edward III (MC 1812/49, 838X5). Roger Norman was a taxpayer in 1327 and Alice Norman in 1332. For John Norman see Med 25.

Med 33 TF 9056 1445 (Area C, HER 20789). Heavy soil, 76m OD. (Figs 7.12 and 7.13). Concentration of 13th and 14th-century sherds, 50m east-west x 35m north-south, close to the parish boundary with Beeston on the southern edge of the west end of a common pasture called *Lyttylmore* in *c*.1430, *Whynnes moore* in 1503 (MS 13035) and *Whinny Green* in 1805. This is perhaps to be identified with a freehold of the manor of East Lexham described in *c*.1550 as 9 acres with a messuage lying on the east of *Kinwald*, i.e. *Kinwaldyshaghe* (KIM 1/8/16). No contemporary tenant's name was given, but the holding was once of William Mareshall and lately held by John Crudde (who died in 1499). In *c.*1610 the property was held by Nicholas Mynne and reference was made to a court of 1361/2 at which Edward Maskall had sworn fealty for 9 acres on the east of *Kinwalds* for which he paid a rent of 2s (MC 1812/49, 838X5). Later in the 17th century this was to become part of the Necton Town estate (see Med 31).

The site sits at the northern end of a former 8½-acre field which is shown on the Enclosure map within a 61-acre block of Necton Town lands. The field carries a medium density of medieval sherds which contrasts with the sherd-free area of *Kinwaldyshaghe* to the west, with a virtually sherd free-area to the south and with an area with sparse sherds to the east. This field must represent a compact 9-acre holding with a messuage at its north end.

Med 34 TF 9070 1451 (Area C, HER 20788). Heavy soil, 76m OD. (Figs 7.12 and 7.13). Concentration of 13th and 14th-century sherds, 30m east-west x 20m north-south. This site along with Med 35 and 36 sits on the northern edge of *Lyttylmore* (see Med 33) and immediately south of the parish boundary with Beeston. The boundaries of this common shown on the Enclosure map indicate that all three sites were set within what appears to be an encroachment, well defined and rectangular, and probably carried out from Beeston parish. In *c.*1550 John Calibutt [lord of Ellinghams manor] was listed as holding, freely of East Lexham manor, the tenement Qwynes, once of Edmund Reeve (rector of Great Fransham 1388–1444) and before him of John Philip. No acreage was given (KIM 1/8/16). In *c.*1610 the tenement Quinnys alias Whynnys was held by Richard Beckham gent., another lord of Ellinghams, for an annual rent of 2s 6d (MC 1812/49, 838X5).

On free land of Rev. Baily Wallis [lord of Ellinghams] following Enclosure.

Med 35 TF 9077 1450 (Area C, HER 20788). Heavy soil, 76m OD. (Figs 7.12 and 7.13). Concentration of 13th and 14th-century sherds, 30m x 30m, lying on the north side of *Lyttylmore* (see Med 34).

Med 36 TF 9087 1449 (Area C, HER 20788). Heavy soil, 76m OD. (Figs 7.12 and 7.13). Concentration of discoloured, predominantly oxidised under- and overfired 12th to early 13th-century sherds lying on the northern edge of *Lyttylmore* (see Med 34). Although no obvious soil discoloration is present, this site must have been dedicated to pottery production.

Med 37 TF 9112 1430 (Area C, HER 20787). Heavy soil, 75m OD. (Figs 7.12 and 7.13. Concentration of 12th and 13th-century sherds, 40m north-south x 25m east-west on the south edge of a common called *Bakonsmor* in 1450 (MS 13048) and *Baconesgrene* in 1455 (MS 13049). It is possible that this site was a croft of Ellinghams manor let at farm for one year in 1442–3 to Henry Deymes for 8s rent. It lay on the north side of the plot or building in the same place, *ex part. borial. plac. ibm.* (MS 13140). The place in question was Ellinghams, probably Med 40.

On free land of Rev. Baily Wallis [lord of Ellinghams] following Enclosure.

Med 38 TF 9090 1412 (Area C, HER 20774). Heavy soil, 72m OD. (Figs 7.12 and 7.13). Concentration of 13th and 14th-century sherds, 40m north-south x 20m east-west, lying immediately south-east of a large pit, now ploughed-over but shown on the Enclosure map. The definition of this concentration is unusually clear in all directions except to the south-east, towards Med 39. It sits on the eastern edge of what may have been common pasture (see Med 40). Perhaps this site and Med 39 might be identified as two holdings, the tenements Totefacs and Rusteyn. Both were freeholds of East Lexham manor in *c.*1550 when they were held by John Calibutt (see Med 40), and both were once of Edmund Reeve and John Philip (see Med 34). Both were listed simply as a tenement, an acreage was not given for either, and there was no reference to a messuage (KIM 1/8/16). Richard Beckham held both in *c.*1610, for annual rents of 4½d and 1s 5d (MC 1812/49, 838X5).

A mid thirteenth-century charter records the sale of two acres of arable of the fee of William Rusteng butting west on a common pasture of Great Fransham, and of Matilda daughter of Laurence [a villein] and her two sons and all their household (*sequela*). The grantor was John son of Simon a former parson of Fransham, the grantee Alexander son of Adam de Gressenhall (Nottingham University Library Mi D 3617/1). In 1250 lands in Fransham held by William Rusteng and John son of the parson were the subject of a successful plea by Avelina once wife of Roger de Skarning (Crook ed. 2002, nos 1415 and 2017). William Rusteng was accorded the title *dominus* (knight) when witnessing an undated thirteenth-century charter concerning Kempstone and Beeston (TNA WARD 2/52/177/91). Two acres with a void messuage called Rusteyns and butting west on a common pasture, were held by John Croupius (rector of Little Fransham, 1362–1404) in *c.*1400, as freehold of Great Fransham manor. Properties in many Norfolk parishes in Norfolk including both the Franshams (including a messuage in Great Fransham) were conveyed by fine from Ralph de Kyrketon and his wife to William Rusteng in 1280 (TNA CP 25/1/159/109.174). The heirs of Henry Rusteyn had been distrained to attend the manor court in 1343. The void messuage was held by Edmund Reeve in the 1430s (MS 13048), John Crudd in 1491/2 (MS 13052), by John Calibutt in 1537 (MS 13074–5), and by John Futter in 1569 and 1574 (MS 13062). The tenement name, Rusteyn, survived as an element in the title of the manor of Ellinghams, Curtlins, Rustins etc. Croupius, Reeve, Calibutt, Futter and Beckham were all lords of Ellinghams manor.

No one of the above three freeholds can be firmly identified with this site or with Med 39, 41 or 42, but it seems likely that all three lay in this area. If the Great Fransham freehold void messuage was one of these then its abuttal is the only evidence for a common on the west side of this group of sites, along with that concerning the two acres of arable in the above-cited mid thirteenth-century charter.

This site or Med 39 may have been a croft of Ellinghams manor, formerly held by John Pumfret, which was not let at farm for 5s rent in 1442–3. It lay on the west side of the plot or building in the same place, the place being Ellinghams, Med 40 (see Med 37).

On free land of Rev. Baily Wallis [lord of Ellinghams] following Enclosure.

Med 39 TF 9092 1408 (Area C, HER 20774). Heavy soil, 72m OD. (Figs 7.12 and 7.13). Concentration of 12th and 13th-century sherds, 25m x 25m. See Med 38.

On free land of Rev. Baily Wallis [lord of Ellinghams] following Enclosure.

Med 40 TF 9097 1398 (Area C, HER 20775). Heavy soil, 70m OD. (Figs 7.12 and 7.13). Concentration of 13th to 20th-century sherds in the area of *Hill Farm*, which was demolished in the 1960s. Sherds of the 16th and 17th centuries were extremely sparse. The site of the farmhouse and outbuildings lies under concrete immediately east of the concentration and is thus not available for fieldwalking. It was called *Ellingham House* on 19th-century editions of one-inch Ordnance Survey maps. Despite the shortage of ceramic evidence for 16th-century occupation, it is tempting to identify this site with a messuage built of the tenement Hoywicks with 20 acres in the croft, which was held by John Calibutt gent. as freehold of the manor of East Lexham in *c*.1550. This, the only piece held of this manor by Calibutt which was said to contain a building, butted north on a common pasture and south on a common way, and lay between land late of John Curde on the west and lands late of the prior of Pentney and of Great Fransham manor on the east (KIM 1/8/16). In *c*.1610 Richard Beckham held a messuage built once of Geoffrey Brake and 20 acres in the croft of the tenement Oxwicks for an annual rent of 2s 6d (MC 1812/49, 838X5).

Evidences from earlier court rolls were cited in *c*.1610. In 1333/4 John Sconings of Pentney clerk came into court and swore fealty for a messuage and 22 acres in Great Fransham that he had purchased from John de Oxwick. He later sold the same to Geoffrey son of John le Leche, who was distrained to swear fealty in 1343/4. In 1350/1 the heirs of Geoffrey le Leche were distrained to pay reliefs for the tents. Oxwicks and Totfayts. In 1338/9 John Philip clerk swore fealty for 1 acre of the Oxwicks fee that he had purchased from Christopher de Cycestre.

Two cases of disputed land in Fransham, both involving a much earlier John de Oxwick, were heard before the king's court in 1199 and 1200. In one 15 acres were claimed by Reginald de Lenne and Matilda his wife in a suit against Turstan Clober and John de Oxwick (Palgrave 1835, 414). In the other case Matilda widow of Roger Passur' had recovered unspecified land from de Oxwick in the king's court but he had prevented access to it. She was successful (Fowler 1922, 235, 251 and 349). There may of course have been no connection or descent between these two men called John de Oxwick, separated by more than a century, nor indeed between the lands in question.

This site was that of the post-medieval manor house of Ellinghams and the dwelling house of Richard Futter of Great Fransham gent. [lord of Ellinghams] who was buried on 18 August 1590. His probate inventory, drawn up on 26 August, listed the following elements of the property: hall, kitchen, kitchen chamber, buttery, buttery chamber, hall chamber, dairy, 'bulting' house [flour store], brew house, chambers over the last three, stable, barn and yards (DN/INV 6/122).

Henry Beckham gent. married Alice Futter at Great Fransham in December 1590. She was buried there in March 1591, and he married Dorothy Bullock in 1594. He was buried on 28 November 1598 and his will, in which he was styled of Great Fransham gent., was proved on 11 December, with Dorothy as executive. The only properties noted were a house and lands in Beeston (NCC 147 Adams). At this time Richard Beckham, whose house was in Little Fransham, was lord of Ellinghams. Henry Beckham's probate inventory was taken on 4 December (he was styled as late of Great Fransham). The following were listed: parlour, hall, kitchen, kitchen chamber, buttery, parlour chamber, dairy, dairy chamber, brew house, brew house chamber, hall chamber, malt chamber, store house, 'Lyllhouse' (containing plough, harrows, querns, stool, hemp), barn, cart house, and garden (DN/INV 15/185).

On free land of Rev. Baily Wallis [lord of Ellinghams] following Enclosure.

Med 41 TF 9091 1385 (Area C, HER 20766). Heavy soil, 68m OD. (Figs 7.12 and 7.13). Concentration of 13th and 14th-century sherds, 35m north-south x 30m east-west. See Med 38.

On free land of Rev. Baily Wallis [lord of Ellinghams] following Enclosure.

Med 42 TF 9091 1380 (Area C, HER 20766). Medium-heavy soil, 65m OD. (Fig. 7.12 and 7.13). Concentration of 12th and 13th-century sherds, 40m north-south x 20 east-west. See Med 38.

On free land of Rev. Baily Wallis [lord of Ellinghams] following Enclosure.

Med 43 TF 9100 1387 (Area C, HER 20766). Heavy soil, 65m OD. (Fig. 7.12 and 7.13). Concentration of discoloured, predominantly oxidised, under- and overfired 12th to early 13th-century sherds in a very restricted area of *c*.12m diameter with a small number of sherds in the surrounding *c*.25m. There was no obvious soil discoloration apart from a few flecks of burnt red soil. This represents a short or very small-scale episode of pottery production.

On free land of Rev. Baily Wallis [lord of Ellinghams] following Enclosure.

Med 44 TF 9141 1433 (Area C, HER 20784). Heavy soil, 72m OD (Fig. 7.12). Concentration of ?12th, 13th and 14th-century sherds, 45m east-west x 20m north-south, lying west of a medieval road called *Toftgate* and immediately south of another road running along the south edge of a common called *Bakonsmor* or *Baconesgrene*. The road is that running from *Herningsaw*e to Acre abutted in a charter dating to before 1259 (LEST/NK I). No documentary evidence for this site has been found, but it is possible that it relates to the place name *Gurnayes* appearing in descriptions of four parcels of Great Fransham demesne in *c*.1430 and of one Great Fransham freehold piece in *c*.1400.

On free land of Rev. Baily Wallis [lord of Ellinghams] following Enclosure.

Med 45 TF 9150 1433 (Area C, HER 20784). Heavy soil, 71m OD (Fig. 7.12). Concentration of 13th and 14th-century sherds, 40m north-south x 30 east-west, on the south side of *Elverycsmore*. This can be identified with a void messuage, once of John Filip clerk and once of William Thomeys, held freely of Great Fransham manor by John Croupius in *c.*1400 for an annual rent of 1d. It lay next to *Toftgate* on the west and butted north on the common pasture. Another messuage of William Thomeys and later of Croupius lay far to the south next to *Southgateway* (Area M).

A linear depression, *c.*10m wide and now ploughed over, ran southwards from the road *c.*30m east of the site for *c.*90m. Part of this feature is shown as an L-shaped pond on the Enclosure map. It may have been dug as a boundary to this site, although it may have been an oddly shaped marl pit.

On free land of Rev. Baily Wallis [lord of Ellinghams] following Enclosure.

Med 47 TF 9180 1373 (Area E, HER 21627). Heavy soil, 61m OD (Fig. 7.14). Concentration of 13th and 14th-century sherds on eastern side of *Doesgate*. In 1548 this was at the west end of 4¼ acres of Rougholme customary land lying next to the king's highway called *Dulls gat* on the south and butting west on *Kenoxe Lane*. The rent owed by the tenant, Thomas Byrston, for this land and ¾ acre in Area K, 2s 8d and 2 hens, suggests that this land may once have contained a messuage (TNA SC 12/3/22). The two pieces together are probably the same as a toft and 5 acres listed in a corrupt later 15th-century rental, without the rent being included. The property was held by William Ryngolf, 'now' Fynch, and was once of Hamon Shengham and then of Edmund Hey (TNA SC 11/476). Hamon de Sengham / Shengham was a taxpayer in 1327 and 1332. In 1552 Thomas Burston paid the same rent for 4 acres once of John Futche (MR 255A). The same piece was described in 1669 as 4½ acres of pasture in a close called *Doesgate*. Its tenure can be followed until 1753 when it was surrendered to the use of one Stephen Allen in trust for John Bayley, lord of Rougholme manor.

On free land of Abel Brereton following Enclosure.

Med 49 TF 9206 1382 (Area D, HER 21627). Medium-heavy soil, 68m OD (Fig. 7.14). Concentration of 13th and 14th-century sherds, 30m x 30m, butting east on the common pasture called *Hey Green*. This was a Rougholme customary messuage with 8 acres, first noted in a corrupt late 15th-century rental as once of Sketes and held by [ ] Large, no rent cited (TNA SC 11/476). Geoffrey Sket was a taxpayer in 1332. William Large was amerced for failing to scour a watercourse at *Skeetes faldgate* in 1480 (MS 13048).

Along with 1¾ acres nearby at the eastern end of Area C, this property appears in the will of Agnes widow of William son of Robert Large, which was written in 1519 and proved in 1541. She asked her executors to sell, with first option of purchase to her eldest son, a void messuage and 10 acres of 'lond closyd lyenge in II closis at [blank] to the seyd mese adioyning' (ANW 219 Athowe). According to two rentals of 1548 and *c.*1550 both pieces were held by William Benett for an annual rent of 5s 3d (or 5s 6d) and 3 (or 2) hens. Eight acres called *Sketts* butted east on *Hye grene* and west on *Kenoxe layn* (TNA SC 12/3/22). At a manor court held in 1548 this land was called *Skythclosse* (TNA SC 2/192/96). The tenurial history can be followed up to Enclosure.

Copyhold of the manor of Ellingham Curtlings etc. held by Abel Brereton following Enclosure.

Med 50 TF 9218 1380 (Area D, HER 21620). Medium-heavy soil, 68m OD (Fig. 7.14). Concentration of 13th to late 15th or early 16th-century sherds, 40m north-south x 30m east-west, within a larger area of 18th to 20th-century pottery and building material, lying at the southern end of *Hey Green*. In *c.*1400 Henry Sewles held freely of Great Fransham manor 2½ acres, a messuage and ¼ acre, once of Hamon Sponer and once of Leffeyn and Dymyng, butting north on the common pasture and lying next to the same on the west. Robert Leffeyn was a taxpayer in 1332. Thomas Leffen and John Dunynge swore fealty for free lands in 1343. Thomas died in 1349, seized of a messuage and 2¼ acres, with an underaged son, Hamon, as heir. In 1366 John Sponer died seized of a messuage and 1½ acres, which he had held for a rent of 5d, the same as that in the rental of *c.*1400. His wife Emma died in 1370, seized of 1 acre of arable, a messuage built and ½ acre. Her son Hamon was distrained to swear fealty. Elot Sponer was a taxpayer in 1379. After a documentary gap in the 15th century, the tenurial history can be traced from 1537 until 1595. In 1553 the common abutted to the north and west was named as *Haygrene* (MS 13077). After 1553 the rent was combined with a ½-acre piece immediately to the east, which had been held by the same tenant in *c.*1400. By 1659 this had become a messuage or tenement with 1 acre belonging, copyhold of Great Fransham manor, one of very few cases in Fransham to involve conversion of free tenure to copyhold in the post-medieval period. The pottery evidence shows that it was not occupied at this date. However, a messuage at the southern end of *High Green* called *Spooners* with outhouses, barn, stables etc. and 2½ acres in the croft was conveyed in 1769 as part of a total of 55 acres of copyhold and freehold in Areas D, E and F (NRS 12175, 27B6).

Copyhold of Great Fransham manor held by Thomas Ralleson following Enclosure

Med 53 TF 9147 1347 (Area C, HER 20752). Medium-heavy soil, 56–7m OD (Fig. 7.12). Concentration of 13th and 14th-century sherds, 40m east-west x 30m north-south, sitting on the north edge of former meadow (see LS 9). This is the only medieval site in Great Fransham that is so situated. This was a messuage with 8 acres and 4 acres of meadow held freely of Great Fransham by William Grenehode in *c.*1400 for an annual rent of 1s 4¾d. The property was once of William Shorte and William in the Medowe. William *ad Pratum* was fined for a purpresture at *Toftgate* in 1297/8. William *in Prato* was a witness to a charter of 1327 (TNA E 40/10111). William atte Medewe was a taxpayer in 1332, as was William Short in 1379. A gloss in one version of the rental (MS 13072) indicates that it had been held by William Cade who appeared in leet court proceedings between 1438 and 1475. In his will, proved in 1488, Thomas Cade of Great Fransham left *Medowclos* to his wife (ANW 195 Fuller alias Roper). Thomas Fueche [Futch] of Great Fransham left 10 acres formerly of Thomas Cade to his son John, in his will that was proved in 1504 (NCC 54/5 Ryxe). Thomas Wyskard was tenant by 1515–16, and paid free rent once *Modowes* (MS 13056). By 1553 John

Wyskard was tenant (MS 13077). His rent was not paid (*nunc detent.*) in 1595, although he had died aged about 100 in 1593.

On free land was held by Lady Essex [lord of Mills-on-the-Moor with Great Fransham manor] following Enclosure.

Med 54 TF 9182 1312 (Area E, HER 20745). Medium soil, 55m OD. (Figs 7.14 and 7.17). Concentration of 11th to 14th-century sherds, 40m x 40m on the north-east edge of the common pasture of Great Fransham called *Eastendmoor* (see LS 12). After Henry Duke had died without heir in 1349, his messuage and 6 acres were seized into the hands of the lord of Great Fransham manor. In 1365 the messuage and 2 acres in the croft along with ¾ acre at the head of the croft at *Kaulynges* were granted at farm to John de Weston for a term of 5 years. This was repeated in 1371 when Aveline de Weston's annual rent for 2¾ acres with a messuage once of Henry Doukys was set at a quarter of barley. Aveline de Westoun was a Little Fransham taxpayer in 1381. A close once built called *Dukes* with a croft containing 2 acres was listed amongst the demesne of Great Fransham manor in *c.*1430. It lay between land of Ellinghams on the south and of Thomas Cade on the north and butted west on the common pasture. The earliest evidence for this land being granted out as copyhold was in 1454 when Ralph Lawdy, his wife and their heirs were admitted to 2 acres of escheated land with a garden or yard (*orto*) called *Dewks* (MS 13049). It was described as 2 acres of demesne with a garden or yard of escheated land called *Dukks* in 1544 (MS 13056) and as 'one close called *Dusks* sometime edified' with a 2-acre croft in 1553 (MS 13077). John Bride, tenant of Med 108, held the property by 1537 (MS 13075) and surrendered it in 1574 when Adam Bosome gent. was admitted (MS 13062). Bosome, a major landholder in Wendling and Great Fransham, died in 1612, having left all his properties to his wife for her life and then to his cousin John Bosome of Horningtoft (ANW 97 Dewpleet). The copyhold rent remained at 1s 2d between 1454 and 1595 (MS 13049 and MS 13084).

On free land of Thomas Ralleson following Enclosure.

Med 55 TF 9192 1305 (Area E, HER 20745). Medium soil, 55m OD. (Figs 7.14 and 7.17). Concentration of 11th to 13th-century sherds, 30m x 30m, on the north-east edge of a common pasture, *Eastendmoor* (see LS 13). This is probably to be identified with an enclosure once Haddokks with 1 acre in the croft, which was demesne of Great Fransham manor in *c.*1430. It lay between land of William Ringolls on the north and John Maceon on the south and butted west on the common pasture. John Haddock swore fealty to the lord of Great Fransham manor in 1343 and died seized of a messuage and 1 acre in 1349, with his underaged son John as heir. In 1353 half a messuage of which John Haddok had died seized was let at farm to John Seel during the period of John Haddok the younger's minority, for an annual rent of a bushel of oats. Edmund Heye took out a 10-year lease on 3 acres called *Haddocks* in 1386, for an annual rent of 6 bushels of barley. By 1537 John Large was the copyhold tenant of the 1-acre close once of Haddock and his rent was 1s (MS 13075). A freehold close once of John Haddock lay in Area G and *Haddokes pightell* in Area C.

On free land of Thomas Ralleson following Enclosure.

Med 56 TF 9215 1306 (Area E, HER 20747). Medium soil, 60m OD. (Figs 7.14 and 7.18). Concentration of 12th to 14th-century sherds, of uncertain extent because its southern part was removed by the construction of a cutting of a new trunk road in the mid-1970s. It was *c.*20m east-west, and a minimum of 10m north-south. The northern edge of *Eastendmoor* common pasture lay slightly to the south. It is possible, but by no means certain, that this might be identified with 4 acres of Sparhams freehold which were held by John Haddock in 1385/6 and were once of John Person. In 1495 Robert Large swore fealty for 4 acres in Great Fransham once of Haddock. There is no mention of a messuage in Sparhams sources. Amongst properties listed in the Inquisition Post Mortem of Edward Mynne (ob. 1543) was a void messuage in Great Fransham with adjoining croft called *Parsones* and containing [illeg.] acres (TNA C 142/85/18). This may have been the void messuage late of Edward Mynne now of John Harydance which lay on the west side of a void freehold messuage of Blyfords manor in 1550.

On free land of Thomas Ralleson following Enclosure.

Med 57 TF 9190 1287 (Area H, HER 20636). Medium soil, 56m OD. (Figs 7.19 and 7.20). Concentration of 12th to 14th-century sherds, 30m x 30m, on the southern and western edge of *Eastendmoor* common pasture. Close to the north of this site the land is obscured by the A47 trunk road which was diverted in the 1950s and widened in the 1970s. A fairly strong spread of medieval and post-medieval sherds along the southern edge of this road to the south-west of this site, and another spread to the west on the north side of the road, suggest that further concentrations once existed on the road line along the common edge. The Enclosure map shows three buildings on this line. A messuage and 3 acres, copyhold of Great Fransham rectory manor, was situated on this site following Enclosure. It is unclear which of the two customary messuages held of this manor in the 14th century this might have been. One was been held by Adam Ryngolf until 1377 when it passed to Nicholas Ryngolf, a taxpayer in 1381. Adam, a Little Fransham taxpayer in 1381, held property in *Quarent.* 29. As both messuages fell into the hands of John Haddock in 1377 and 1381/2 (MS 13042), they may have been close together.

Three holdings now covered by the trunk road probably include, firstly, a messuage built with 2 acres in the croft held freely by Margaret Pratt widow of Blyfords manor in 1550. This messuage butted north on the common pasture and lay next to a common path on the east (MS 424). Secondly, Margaret Pratt also held a free tenement built and certain lands of Ellinghams manor at the same period. The first court at which this property was mentioned was held as late as 1576, but reference was made then to a court of 1492/3. Neither acreage nor abuttals were to be given until 1642 (Mills and Reeve 12/03/70: Mason Necton deeds). The Pratt family had been in Great Fransham since the late 1460s. Beatrice Pratt, a widow, bequeathed her dwelling house and properties to her son Edmund in 1472 (NCC 263 Jekkys). In 1503 Edmund left his house and lands to his wife Margaret with reversion to their son Edmund (NCC 350–1 Popy). In 1532 Edmund passed on his house and lands, both freehold and copyhold to Margaret his wife, with reversion to their son, Thomas (NCC 35 Mingaye). The will of Thomas Pratte husbandman, proved in 1572, specifies copyhold land held of the parsonage of Great Fransham (ANW 268 Busby). This hints at a connection between all the above mentioned holdings. The third and most westerly property was a Guntons freehold messuage with a croft of unstated acreage. A free rent of 3d due from Thomas Cornwell alias Wright was listed in one post-Dissolution rental (TNA SC 11/473). In another the same rent was due for 'one messe wherin he dwelleth with the croft and land adjoining' (TNA SC 12/3/24). The Latin version of this in a rental of 1552 was deleted (TNA SC 12/3/23). Cornwell died in 1558 and his son Edward swore fealty for the same (TNA SC 2/192/96). Edward's rent was entered in a rental of 1559 (TNA SC 11/486).

On free land and Great Fransham rectory copyhold land of Rev. Baily Wallis following Enclosure.

Med 58 TF 9165 1286 (Area H, HER 20638). Medium soil, 59m OD (Fig. 7.19). Concentration of 13th and 14th-century sherds, 25m x 25m, on the south-west edge of *Eastendmoor* common pasture and immediately east of the former boundary with Little Fransham parish. This can be identified with a messuage and ¾ acre in the croft once of John att Bour and Henry de Skarning which John de Southwood held freely of Great Fransham manor in *c*.1400 for an annual rent of 4d. It lay next to land of Edmund Oldhall on the east and butted north on the common pasture. Henry de Skernynge did fealty in 1343. John de Southwood was probably the same as John de Schortwode of Little Fransham. John Wroo, tenant of 5 acres of Kirkhams and Wilcoks copyhold to the south, held this in 1511/12. Thomas Cornell alias Wright (see Med 57) was tenant in 1537 (MS 13074–5) and was so at his death in 1558. The property remained in his family for the rest of the 16th century, and in 1603 it passed into Arthur Capel's portion of Great Fransham manor. Between 1603 and 1614 it was held by George Elmedon [of Weasenham] and was inexplicably described as 'sometime [of] Thomas Anguishe (MS 13080–3). A gloss added to the 1614 rental (MS 13083) indicates that John Mynne and John Burnham were later tenants. The property must have been included in a free and copyhold enclosure in Great Fransham lying next to *Millfield* on the west that was cited in the will of John Mynn yeoman of Little Fransham, proved in 1651 (ANW 381 1648–52).

On free land of Rev. Baily Wallis following Enclosure.

Med 59 TF 9214 1270 (Area H, HER 23886). Medium-heavy soil, 56m OD (Fig. 7.19). Concentration of 13th and 14th and ?early 15th-century pottery, 40m north-west to south-east x 20m, on the southern edge of *Eastendmoor* common pasture. The site lies in the north-west corner of 4 acres of Rougholme customary land called *Escherdclos*, of which Edmund Pratt had died seized in 1504. In 1535 Margaret Pratt held a 3-acre close called *Esshe yard* (MR 28, 240X6). In 1548 it was given abuttals: between the king's highways east and west and butting north on the common. The annual rent due from Margaret Pratt was 2s 2d and 2 hens (TNA SC 12 3/22). In 1660 *Ashwood* contained 4 acres. In 1686 it was called *Ashyard alias Ashwood*, and lay between *Towlins Lane* west, the road leading from *Sowdesfield* east and *Eastend More* north. Its tenurial history has been traced to Enclosure.

Correctly located on the Enclosure map as 3 acres 3 roods and 6 perches, copyhold of the manor of Ellingham Curtlings etc. and held by Ambrose Thompson.

Med 60 TF 9178 1248 (Area H and *Quarent.* 21, HER 20629 and 20822). Medium soil, 62m OD. (Figs 7.19 and 7.20). Concentration of 11th and predominantly 12th-century pottery, 25m north-south x 20m east-west (see LS 16), lying across the boundary between Great and Little Fransham. It lay on free land of uncertain manorial allegiance that was held by tenants of Med 116 in the 16th century and may have been the original site of a tenement that was to move south to Med 116.

In a close called Wilkins, freehold of Anne Overton following Enclosure.

Med 61 TF 9203 1223 (Area O, HER 23890). Heavy soil, 58m OD (Figs 7.19 and 7.26). Concentration of 13th to 14th-century sherds, 30m north-south x 25m east-west, in Great Fransham, on the east edge of *Eastendmoor*, a common pasture of Little Fransham. This may be identified with the tenement Rawlenis which John Pauli was holding at farm for a rent of 7s in 1383–4, the third year of a 7-year lease from the lord of Kirkhams manor (MS 13122) It was almost certainly the same as 5 acres once of Peter le Strange knight held freely of Great Fransham manor by Edmund Oldhall [lord of Kirkhams] in *c*.1400. A gloss in one version of the Great Fransham rental (MS 13084 Book D) cites a charter to support this. This document survives as a quitclaim of 1352 whereby Robert Toly released his rights in 5 acres of meadow in Great and Little Fransham and a rent in Scarning to John le Strange, which had been given to him by Elizabeth widow of Ostelin of Whinburgh (BL Add Ch 71038). At a Little Fransham leet court held in 1366 Peter le Strange [lord of Kirkhams] was said to have blocked a watercourse at *Rawlenysbrygge* and a similar complaint was made in 1374. The bridge lay on the eastern edge of *Eastendmoor* at TF 9200 1221, just to the south-west of this site.

The tenement Rawlyns continued to be held at farm in the late 14th and 15th centuries, until 1476 when it was granted out as copyhold to John Stalworthy and his heirs for a new rent of 3s 4d. It was described as a piece of land and meadow in Great Fransham called *Rawlynnes*, containing 5 acres with a pightle at its west end, and lying next to the common pasture of Little Fransham. The tenure continued until 1806 and the rent remained unchanged, with the name more often being *Rowlands* rather than *Rawlings* from 1675. In 1801 the tenant, Thomas Henry Case of Great Fransham gent., conveyed by lease and release a 1-acre piece at the west end, late part of an enclosure called *Rawlins*, to William Watlin farmer of Little Fransham, along with a nearby messuage (Med 116) and adjoining lands (Salmon C and D). Following Enclosure this was to be regarded as 1 acre 1 rood and 34 perches of freehold. In 1806 Case conveyed the remaining part to Ambrose Thompson of Middleton, who was admitted to 5 acres, rather than 4 acres. After Enclosure in 1807 Thompson was admitted to a piece of Kirkhams and Wilcoks copyhold containing 4 acres 3 roods and 19 perches, which was situated *c*.200m north of *Rawlings / Rowlands* (MC 1850/4–5, 858X8).

The medieval settlement on free land of William Watling, and the rest on free land of Ambrose Thompson following Enclosure.

Med 62 TF 9270 1204 (Area O, HER 25548). Medium soil, 60m OD. (Figs 7.19 and 7.27). Concentration of 13th and 14th-century sherds, 35m north-west to south-east x 20m. A messuage and 1½ acres, freehold of Great Fransham manor, once of Sibil de Southwood, were held by Thomas Futche for an annual rent of 1¾d in *c*.1400. The property was in *Southwoodfield* next to land of the Abbot of Wendling on the east and butted north on the lord's wood. According to the Great Fransham extent of *c*.1430 this wood butted south on an enclosure of Nicholas Warde and lay next to a common pasture called *Southwoodmore* on the east. *Southwoodmore*, may therefore have lain to the north-east of this concentration. Thomas Futche also held another nearby freehold, Med 93. Nicholas Warde was probably tenant in the earlier 15th century, the common being called *Wardesgrene* in 1451 and *Wardysmor* in 1460 (MS 13048). A gloss in one version of the rental of *c*.1400 stated that this was held by Robert Hogan (MS 13084 Book B). He died in 1547.

On free land of Matthew Nelson esq. following Enclosure.

Med 63 TF 9223 1159 (*Quarent*. 29, HER 25560). Heavy soil, 67m OD (Figs 7.48 and 7.49). Concentration of 12th-century pottery, 40m east-west x 30m north-south, set within a triangle made by two medieval roads to the east and north and a stream to the south-west. The site lay at the northern edge of a pasture called *Paul Ulfes* in 1326 (MC 360/57, 713X6) and an 18-acre close called *Hulvesmedow / Ulvesmedowe*, a freehold of Kirkhams and Wilcoks first mentioned in 1425 and 1426. It is tempting to suggest that this was the messuage of Paul Ulfe.

On Cannons manor copyhold of Charles Senkler following Enclosure.

Med 64 TF 9194 1156 (*Quarent*. 29, HER 25561). Heavy soil, 64m OD (Figs 7.48 and 7.49). Concentration of 13th and 14th-century sherds, 30m north-south x 25m east-west, on the east edge of *Eastendmoor* common pasture close to the parish boundary with West Bradenham. The site was within a 3-acre piece of the Sparhams 12-acre customary tenement once of Hamond Jocke, the two messuages of which lay in *quarents*. 17 and 18. In 1570 an abuttal named it l*e Bond Closse* (Gardner L) and in 1581 it was described as an enclosed pasture (MC 3115/1/2, 1037X4). The first reference to this piece as a part of this tenement was in 1572, and in 1578 it was given details of location: lying next to the common on the west, butting north on the common. In 1694 it butted north on the king's highway. There was never any suggestion that it had once contained a settlement. In 1724 a 3-acre close of 'rich' pasture, copyhold of the Sparhams tenement Jocks, was named *Bond Pightle* (MC 3115/1/12, 1037X4).

It is possible that this settlement site had once been within another Sparhams customary holding, the tenement and lands once of Adam Marche, held for an annual rent of two capons, which was listed in the rental of 1385/6 (see Chapter 7, end note xiii). Many amercements in courts leet between 1394 and 1469 refer to a place called *Marches*. This lay next to a watercourse and very close to the West Bradenham boundary, apparently in the south-west corner of *quarent*. 29.

On Cannons copyhold of Charles Senkler following Enclosure.

Med 65 TF 9167 1142 (*Quarent*. 17, HER 24776). Medium soil, 65m OD (Figs 7.42 and 7.43). Concentration of 13th and 14th-century sherds, 20m x 20m, on the west edge of the south end of *Eastendmoor*. This can be identified with a Kirkhams customary messuage and 2 acres surrendered by John Hoche to Thomas Powley in 1353. Hoche had made his first appearance in a court roll of 1347. The tenement Hoches was first mentioned in 1348. In 1353 it consisted of 5 acres and ¾ rood, held by six tenants, in the following parcels: 2 acres (messuage not specified}, 1¼ acres, 1¼ acres, 1½ roods, 1 rood and ¼ rood. The messuage was associated with 3¼ acres both in 1384 and in 1443 when it was given abuttals for the first time. It and 2 acres in its adjoining croft butted south on the common way below *Neketonwode*[iii], and north on the remaining 1¼ acres. The tenement had three tenants in 1384, whose rents and services totalled 2s, 1 hen and 4 autumn boon-works. The ¼ rood of 1353 was still separately itemised, but it was not included in the 1443 rental. The tenant of the messuage in 1384, John Pauly (Poule / Pouly) was a taxpayer in 1379 and 1381. In the 15th century land to the north and west of this site was known as *Hochesfield*. After 1513 the whole of this tenement became part of the demesne of Kirkhams and Wilcoks manor (MS 13102).

On free land of Charles Senkler following Enclosure.

Med 65A TF 9169 1150 (*Quarent*. 17, HER 24776). Medium soil, 65m OD (Figs 7.42 and 7.43). Concentration of 13th to 15th-century sherds on the western edge of *Eastendmoor*, 35m north-south, but of uncertain width east-west because separated from the common edge by an 18–30m wide strip of grass. In the area of Med 65 and this site and to the north metal-detecting has recovered a halfpenny of Edward I–III, two coins of Elizabeth, and one of James I. Copper alloy objects include a medieval dress fitting, ?harness mount and vessel fragments, and 15th or 16th-century thimbles and a purse bar.

In 1553 John Nicholls of LFr husbandman sold his messuages, lands, tenements, cottages, meadows, pastures and feedings in LFr, amounting to 6ac, copyhold of West Bradenham manor, to William Stalworthie of Beeston husbandman for £24. Nicholls and Elizabeth his wife were to have the cottage built where they dwelled reserved to them until 9 days after the surviving one of them had died with all the other premises, which amounted to property no.1 (p.151). Excepted from this arrangement and presumably where it was intended that Stalworthie should live was this site, a house built on the south side of the above with two yards or pightles 'lying bounded owte with old dikes' and containing ½ acre (Hood, Vores & Allwood 14/03/1980 Box 56)[iv]. In the event, William Stallworthie was buried on 24 December 1558, John Nycholls on 4 March 1559 and Elizabeth on 14 March.

After a long gap the tenurial descent, identical to that of property no.1, can be followed from 1625 to 1797 when it was consistently described as a messuage with adjoining croft called *Bloggs* containing ½ acre. No abuttals were given, and there were no references to standing buildings. The name *Bloggs* must be derived from John Blog, a customary tenant of Kirkhams manor (see property no.2, p.151). An orchard and hempland were mentioned. (PD 299/47–54).

Following Enclosure, the tenant, Anne Griggs, who had been admitted in 1797 to both the above properties, was said to hold 8½ acres of West Bradenham copyhold lands with 'the site of two ancient buildings'. Her West Bradenham copyhold allotment of 9 acres 3 roods and 38 perches was in an entirely different location, in *Eastfield* at centre TF 925 117. The correct site fell within free land held by Charles Senkler. The often misleading and fictitious nature of the rearrangements that took place in 1807 are well illustrated by this example.

Med 66 TF 9162 1186 (*Quarent.* 17, HER 24778). Heavy soil, 64m OD (Figs 7.42 and 7.43). Sparse concentration of 15th to 17th-century sherds, 30m east-west x 20m north-south, containing a smaller, 20m x 10m, area of post-medieval brick rubble, on the south edge of *Eastendmoor*. Amongst metal-detector finds from the northern part of the field containing this site were five medieval coins, the earliest of Henry III and the latest of Edward IV, and including a Venetian *soldino* of 1400–13. Medieval objects included several buckles, an annular brooch and a belt fitting. Late 15th and 16th-century pieces were quite numerous, but there were few from the 17th or 18th centuries.

This messuage can first be recognised in an abuttal of c.1420 for Med 66A stating that this was the messuage of John Tarkeys, the tenant of a Wilcoks customary tenement to the south (property no.3, p.152). In 1478, when granted to Henry Jonsone, his wife and others by John Crudde and Silvester Boor, it was described as a messuage built, with 2 acres in the croft, butting *Esteendemour* on the north and east. In 1465 it had been conveyed by William Brook and his eponymous son to the late Geoffrey Powly (MC 3115/1/1, 1037X4). A freehold of Kirkhams and Wilcoks manor, the property was held by John Nicoll junior, late Henry Johnson in 1502. In 1511 John Neve swore fealty for 5½ acres of free land that he had purchased from John Nycoll, and this site appears in Neve's will, proved in 1521, as the place in which he dwelled (ANW 28 Randes).

John Alyson had died seized of free and customary lands in 1555, with his son Thomas as heir (MS 13169). According to his will, proved in the same year, John had already sold Thomas his house and lands. He specified that his widow Alice was to have 'the chamber that she dwell in and the medowe down to the more' (ANW 351 Barnham). In 1566 Thomas Alanson paid a rent of 3d for 2 acres of land called *Neves* and he still held it in 1605 when it lay next to *Eastendmore* on the north and butted east on the same. This shows the croft lay lengthways along the common edge. Thomas Allison was buried in 1607 and in the will of Thomas Alansone, weaver, of Little Fransham, written in 1599, mentioned 'the chamber wherein Joane tayler dwelt being of parte of the premisses & halfe of the Entree of the Mansion house and thereto set up builde & finishe a chimney' (ANW 194 Wells). His son John, also a weaver, died in 1631 and in his will, proved in the following year, he left all his properties to his wife for her life and then to his son Robert (ANW 346 Sharpe). The probate inventory of his widow Martha, dated 1633, lists a kitchen, hall, dairy and chambers (Inv.39 no.360). In 1638, in an indenture leading to the uses of a fine, John Allanson, linen weaver and son of John, was named as owner. Along with the messuage there were outhouses, barns, a stable and homesteads within 2 acres and the whole amounted to 4 acres (MC 3115/1/4, 1037X4).

By 1658 Thomas Powll butcher of Little Fransham was tenant. He died that year leaving all his properties in Little Fransham to his wife and then to Nicholas Gibbs of Swaffham (TNA PROB 11/286/603). In 1664 Gibbs settled this property by fine on Robert Dunger (MC 1683/22b, 821X4). In 1666 the house of Robert Danger contained one hearth (Seaman 1991, 28). In 1695 it was probably amongst properties which were the subject of a fine whereby Robert Allison and his wife and others conveyed possessions in Little Fransham and other places to various people including Thomas Rudd (MC 1683/27, 821X4).

In 1712 the property was the capital messuage of Robert Allison, butcher. By 1724 he had moved to Gressenhall, and his son John was a yeoman of Horningtoft. An undertenant, Robert Roome, lived in the house. In 1761 the farmhouse, described as 'good', was occupied by John Reeve when acquired by Edmund Senkler of Barwick (MC 3115/1/11–18).

In rentals of 1780–92 the rent due from Hamond Alpe gent. for 'late Dingers free' was 3d (MS 13165 and MC 969/8, 858X7).

On Kirkhams and Wilcoks copyhold land of Money Griggs following Enclosure.

Med 66A TF 9158 1185 (*Quarent.* 17, HER 24780). Heavy soil, 65m OD (Fig. 7.42 and 7.43). Concentration of 13th and 14th-century sherds, 40m north-south x 25m east-west on the southern edge of *Eastendmoor*. This was a messuage called *Boteres*, freehold of the Wilcoks manor in c.1420 when it was held by John Sevepens for an annual rent of 6d. Geoffrey Boter was a taxpayer in 1327 and 1332. In 1502 a messuage called *Boters* was held by John Nicoll junior. He almost certainly sold this land to Thomas Wyskard from whom it passed to his son John who held it in 1566. All of the latter's lands in Little Fransham were left in 1593 to his wife Anne with reversion to his son-in-law Robert Davy (NCC 83 Clearke). In 1605 this piece was held by Robert Davy and described as pightles with a void tenement called *Butchers*. Abuttals show that it lay on the south edge of *Eastendmore* between Med 66 to the east and Med 67 to the west. In Robert Davy's will, proved in 1639, this was named as *Butchers Pightill*, near the dwelling house of William Henson, Med 67 (NCC 190 Green). From 1693 to Enclosure and beyond it was held by various members of the Powley family. The rent remained unchanged, 6d being due from Peter Powley for a free pightle between 1780 and 1792 (MS 13165 and MC 969/8, 858X7).

A rectangular enclosure of 0.85 acres was still shown on the 1958 edition of the Ordnance Survey 1:10560 map Sheet 91SW.

The messuage was associated with 2½ acres lying in *Hochesfield* to the south. This land appeared as customary land of Kirkhams manor in a court roll of 1377 and in the rental of 1384. In 1430 it was described in a Wilcoks manor court roll as soiled land in *Boterscroft*. In 1605 it was soiled land called *Butcherscroft* and was still soiled land once of John Neve (a tenant from 1516–21) in 1615 (MS 13415).

Both messuage and 2½ acres were on Sparhams copyhold land of Peter Powley following Enclosure.

Med 67 TF 9152 1184 (*Quarents.*16 and 17, HER 24779 and 24777). Heavy soil, 65m OD (Fig. 7.42). Concentration of 13th to 19th-century sherds with 18th and 19th-century building material, 50m x 50m, on the southern edge of *Eastendmoor* common pasture close to its south-west corner. Metal-detector finds from this site and Med 66A include two medieval buckles and coins of Elizabeth I, Charles I and William III. Four buildings are depicted on the Enclosure map. The Ordnance Survey 1928 edition 1:2500 map shows only a 0.192 acre enclosure with the west and south boundaries marked by dashed lines. This site can be identified with two holdings, a Sparhams customary tenement of medieval origin and a Cannons copyhold which contained a messuage in the 17th century.

The eastern part was customary land of Sparhams manor and parcel of 12 acres with a messuage and a cottage once of Hamond Jocke in 1385/6. In 1514 it was described as 3 acres built of the tenement Jocks, and its tenurial history has been followed until 1807. The house was quite consistently described as a tenement built, with a barn and stable first being noted in 1531 when the roofs, thatch and daub of both were defective.

In 1529 Cristina was left this property in the will of her late husband William Heylott als. Reder (ANW 500 Randes) and immediately after admittance she was amerced for failing to carry out repairs. In 1530 Cristiana Lyle was amerced for not fixing her roof while in 1532 and 1534 Walter Lyle was the offender. In Lay Subsidy lists for 1542–4 Walter Lyle '*alyen borne*' was assessed to pay 8d for goods (TNA E 179/150/310) and Walter Leigh '*Alien*' to pay 5d (TNA E 179/151/317). Walter Lee was buried on 12 February 1555. He was probably a Fleming from Lille.

Abuttals of 1575 stated that the tenement lay south of *Eastendmore* and *Rudde Lane*. The will of Mary Hunson widow, proved in 1648, mentions the shop chamber, parlour, kitchen and chamber above (ANW 5 1648–52). Her daughter Jane, wife of William Powley, was admitted. The house of William Powly / Pawley contained two hearths in 1664 and 1666 (Frankel and Seaman 1983, 61; Seaman 1991, 28). The property remained with the Powley family until after Enclosure.

The western part of this site formed part of a 12-acre piece of customary land held of Cannons manor. This lay in Cannons Rudde and is known from 1558. The first reference to a house or tenement is in the will of John Poulie yeoman of Necton, which was proved in 1604 (ANF 413 Offwood). His Cannons manor lands were left to his son Thomas (in 1603 another Powley, Ralph, had surrendered the eastern Sparham manor part to his son George). The messuage was associated with 2 acres of the 12 from 1624. The messuage had recently fallen down (*nuper delapsum*) in 1680, and in 1695 it was described as void. In 1699 the tenant, Peter Powley, was granted licence to demolish and never to rebuild (*destruere et devastere…inperpet. Custodire in Ruina absque ulla redificaceon.*). The 2 acres containing the site remained with members of the Powley family, in later years all from neighbouring parishes, until 1779, when it was taken up by Peter Powley, the tenant of the eastern part. It should be noted that none of the ceramic building material on either part of the site need be earlier than the 18th century.

On Sparhams copyhold land (eastern part) and Cannons copyhold land (western part) of Peter Powley following Enclosure.

Med 68 TF 9157 1203 (*Quarent.* 18, HER 28877 and 20819). Heavy soil, 62m OD. (Figs 7.44 and 7.45). A ½-acre close (L116) on the north-west corner of *Eastendmoor* contained a house until the 1970s and is now a plantation. Two medieval and two late 15th or 16th-century sherds were recovered from a minute patch of bare soil in the centre. To the west a formerly separate 1½-acre field produced a dense scatter of 13th to 19th-century sherds and a small quantity of 19th-century building material, particularly at its eastern end.

Evidence for the tenurial descent of this property has been particularly discontinuous and unsatisfactory. It may be identified with a messuage and 3 acres in one piece and butting east on the common pasture, freehold of Wilcoks manor, held by Alexander Powly, once of Thomas Powly, in *c*.1420. To judge from the rent (1d), it had been held by Margaret Pauly in *c*.1395. This property may be the same as a tenement with 3½ acres of free land, formerly of Mountjoy held of Wilcoks manor with a rent of 1d by Richard Aggys who had bought it from the executors of Thomas Wright in 1481. It is absent from the exhaustive rental of 1502. Edward Mynne had died in 1543 jointly seized with his wife of a messuage and adjoining 3½-acre croft in Little Fransham (TNA C 142/70/6). In 1557 John Crispe swore fealty for a messuage with 2 acres in the croft held jointly with his wife Faith, daughter of Thomas Wiscard, for an annual rent of ½d (MS 13169). John Cryspe was buried in 1576. Robert Hunt paid a halfpenny rent for a free tenement in 1600, and in 1605 Edward Chapman held for the same rent by the right of his wife, Hunt's widow, a free messuage and a 2-acre croft, butting west on the *pack way* and east on *Eastendmoor*. Chapman's land was abutted on the north of Med 97 in 1621. He was buried in 1635. The order in which householders were listed for the 1664 Hearth Tax suggests that the house, which had two hearths, was then occupied by George Large junior (Frankel and Seaman 1983, 61). In 1666 Large was not listed and his place was taken by Thomas Allison (Seaman 1991, 28). Rentals of 1780–92 suggest the property was held by Edward Sharpin whose free rent was ½d (MS 13165 and MC 969/8, 858X7).

On Sparhams copyhold land of John Baly following Enclosure (see Med 97). A building is shown on the Enclosure map in the same position as the recently demolished house.

Med 69 TF 9170 1210 (*Quarent.* 18, HER 20820). Medium-heavy soil, 60m OD. (Figs 7.20 and 7.44). Concentration of 12th to 19th-century sherds with 18th and 19th-century building material, butting south on *Eastendmoor*. A well-defined area of dark soil, 20m east-west x 40m north-south produced almost all the finds. Very limited metal-detecting produced a 13th or 14th-century buckle plate and parts of two others. A formerly separate 1.2-acre enclosure (L117) is shown with three subdivisions on the Enclosure Award map, the central and western ones with buildings. The pottery concentration lies in the central subdivision, while almost all the western one is now a ploughed-over pit. The documentary evidence for this site is complex.

The following five customary holdings in the Kirkhams rental of 1384 are relevant:

- Half a messuage and 4 acres of the tenement Osyeres held by Agnes Smyth, the lady of the manor's villein (*nativa dominae*). Agnes was a taxpayer in 1381. One Vincent Hosyer died seized of a tenement in 1327. In 1395 William de Clare was admitted to this holding which was called *Dunyngs*. In 1429 this and c) were called the tenement Clares. It butted south on a common pasture in 1443 when it was held by Geoffrey Pouly.

- 2 messuages and 3 acres of the tenement Osyeres held by Agnes Smyth. The rental of 1443, when all were held by Walter Pouly, shows that 1 acre was in Great Fransham, 1 messuage with 1 acre in the croft was surrounded on the east, west and north by other lands and therefore may have butted south on a common, and that another messuage and 1-acre croft butted south on a common.

- Half a messuage of the same tenement held by Margaret Smyth (*nativa dominae*), which was associated with 4 acres. These were in 7 parcels in 1443, and the half messuage butted south on a common. All were held by Walter Pouly in 1443.

- Quarter of a messuage and 2 acres of the tenement Edildes, in *Edildescroft*, held by Agnes Edild. In 1443 this was held by John Pope between land of Walter Pouly on all sides except to the west.

- Parcel of a messuage [probably ¼], 3 acres and half a messuage of the tenement Edildes, held by Robert Edild. In 1443 the parcel and the half messuage were together and butted south on a common. There were 3 acres in the croft which butted west on the common mill path (i.e. the *pack way* to the west). Walter Pouly was the tenant. The name of John Edild occurred in a court roll of 1328. Nicholas Echyld was a taxpayer in 1332, as was Robert Edel / Edyld in 1379 and 1381. Agnes, the last of that name to appear in court rolls, was not mentioned after 1395. In 1347 the tenement Edild was elected to the office of messor, as it was again in 1353 when the tenants and their lands were listed. Agnes held the same as above, her brother Robert three quarters of a messuage and 2½ acres, Geoffrey Sewale 1½ acres, John Sewale 1 acre, William Jurdon 1½ acres, ¼ acre, ½ acre and ½ rood. This gives a total of 1 messuage, 9 acres and 1½ roods. In 1360 there were 4 tenants and 10 acres. The total was increased to 11¼ acres and ½ rood in the 1384 rental with additions of c.1391.

A messuage called Fawkes, held by Margary Smyth, next to the messuage of Robert Edild on the east, and associated with 4½ acres in five parcels and ½ acre of meadow, some of which land was in *Eastfield*, some in *Millfield*. The messuage and lands were also entered in the Wilcoks manor rental of c.1420 as freehold. In 1443 these were all held by Walter Pouly.

All the above and other lands to the east and west of *Eastendmoor* were in the hands of John Bocher who had married the widow of Walter Powley, probably in 1447. In 1457 Bocher conveyed a messuage built and 42 acres to John Wyot. Thereafter sundry tenement names, in particular Clares, Edilles, Rengs and Souters, and variety of acreage totals and numbers of messuages were employed to describe this large holding. In 1520 it was split into two, one part in *Eastfield* and the other in *Millfield* (MS 13103), and members of the Stalworthy family were tenants of both halves until 1626.

In 1566 the western half comprised 24 acres and this site was described as a tenement with 12 acres of pasture, lying next to *Eastendmore* on the south. In 1605 the total was 27 acres and this site was listed as two messuages and 1½ acres, lying next to *Eastendmore* on the south and Edward Chapman's messuage (Med 68) on the west. Part of the estate was separated off following the will of Richard Stalworthy, who died in 1626 (ANW 54 1626–9). By 1664 / 1666 there were two houses here, that of William Mynn with two hearths and that of George Large sen. with one (Frankel and Seaman 1983, 61; Seaman 1991, 28). The tenurial history has been followed into the early 19th century.

In 1807 one messuage and 21 acres, copyhold of Kirkhams and Wilcoks were said at the manor court to have been held by Money Griggs before Enclosure. After the Award, as well as the messuage and its croft, his main allotment, 18 acres and 18 perches, was made up of the northern part of the former common of *Eastendmoor*, with lands to the north of the messuage and formally part of the holding going to Lady Essex as freehold. Griggs also received a block of land in the north-east corner of *Hochesfield*, (*Quarent.* 17) which he had not previously held. Three small enclosures lying together, two with buildings, are shown on the Enclosure map.

Med 70 TF 9098 1215 (*Quarent.* 27, HER 24768). Medium-heavy soil, 66m OD (Fig. 7.47). Concentration of 13th to 19th-century sherds, with some 18th and 19th-century building material, 50m north-south x 30m east-west on the eastern edge of the common pasture known as *Cannons More* in the 16th century. This was recorded as 12 acres of customary land once of Hugh Cappe, without reference to a messuage, in the Sparhams manor rental of 1385/6. Land of Hugh Cappe was abutted in an undated deed of 1273 or earlier (MC 360/6, 713X6). A tenement built with 10 acres had been alienated in 1507 by John Maunde fletcher, and later that year the holding was called a tenement called Cappes with 9 acres of the same tenement, when John surrendered the property to Richard Maunde. This John Maunde seems to have been the same person as John Maunde de Cheker who had appeared in various Kirkhams and Wilcoks manor court and leet court proceedings in the 1480s and 1490s. An amercement at a leet court in 1512 refers to Richard Maunde's messuage at the *Chekyr* (MS 13102). This name suggests that the building may have been an alehouse (Mabey 1996, 204–7). There were 4 acres in the croft, and the remaining lands of the tenement were in *Quarent.* 18 (6 acres) and *Quarent.* 7 (2 acres).

In 1529 a tenement called Cappes with 2 acres of the same were split off from its associated lands. This was described as void in 1541, but by 1556 it was once more built, as evidenced by the will of John Stalworthy senior (NCC 369 Beeles). In 1568 a ½-rood pightle, a parcel of 2 acres adjoining the tenement Cappes, was detached and granted to another tenant. By 1572 this was newly built with what was to be described as a cottage in 1578 (later abuttals show the ½ rood to have been at the south-west corner of the 2 acres). The house of Anthony Bunting, tenant of the cottage, had one hearth in 1664 and 1666 (Frankel and Seaman 1983, 61; Seaman 1991, 28). In 1773 the tenancy of the cottage was reunited with that of the main part of the tenement. In 1779 it was 'now dilapidated' and in 1781 the tenant, Matthew Buscall of Fakenham gent. was said to have 'pulled down and laid waste the cottage lately standing'. Surface archaeological evidence of this site was not distinguishable from that of the main house.

The main house was detailed as a tenement called Cappes containing 1 acre and 1½ roods with gardens adjoining in 1586. In the same year the tenants paid a fine to pull down a bake house on the north side of their tenement. A barn on the same had a damaged roof in 1587, and again in 1592 and 1594. The main parts of this tenement had been in the hands of members of the Stalworthy family from before 1521, and remained so until 1626, when the holding was dispersed following the death of Richard Stalworthy. The lands were reunited in the course of the 17th century, and the evidence of several wills shows that the house continued to stand. In 1664 and 1666 the house of John Large (a butcher) had two hearths (Frankel and Seaman 1983, 61; Seaman 1991, 28). The tenement name was still in use in 1787 when Matthew Buscall, late of Little Fransham and then a schoolmaster of King's Lynn, was admitted.

Following Enclosure Matthew Buscall was declared to have held 1 messuage, 10 acres and 20 perches copyhold of Sparhams manor. The messuage was located on this site, with two buildings being shown on the Enclosure map.

Med 71 TF 9096 1219 (*Quarent.* 27, HER 23905). Medium soil, 65m OD (Fig.7.47). This site is inferred from a spread of sherds in flower-beds and in an arable field to the east of a 19th-century farmhouse on the eastern edge of the former *Cannons Green*. The odd late Thetford-type sherd might suggest the site began in the 11th century, but ceramic evidence becomes prolific in the 12th. The earliest documentary evidence occurred in a Kirkhams manor court roll of 1351 when a customary messuage and 7 acres held of Kirkhams manor by Bartholomew and Margaret Andrews were granted to Roger Attcheys and his wife. In 1362 William Jordan surrendered a messuage and 5 acres in one parcel and 2 acres in another to the use of his wife and daughter. In 1363 the lord of Kirkhams granted to his villein William, son of Nicholas Jordan, a messuage and 7 acres, once of Adam Syger. The latter had been a free tenant before the Black Death and this messuage had probably formed part of his 17-acre freehold (see Med 94).

In 1374 the holding was described as a messuage and 8 acres with 1 acre of meadow. In the rental of 1384 Peter son of William Jordan held a messuage, 9½ acres and 1 acre of meadow. The messuage and 4½ acres lay next to the common pasture on the west. The other parts of the holding comprised *Redemedow* in *Quarent*.18, ¾ acre in *Churchfield* (*Quarent.* 8), ½ acre in *Woodrowfield* (*Quarent.* 11), 1 acre in *Eastmillfield* (*Quarent.* 23), 1 acre of soiled land in *Hochesfield* (*Quarent.* 17), 1¼ acres in *Millfield* near *Brounesmer* (*Quarent.* 19), and ½ acre in *Millfield* (*Quarent.* 28).

The whole tenement was in the lord's hands by 1391–2, probably because of the tenant's death (MS 13123). In 1393 all except the soiled land in *Hochesfield* were granted out to Thomas Pytecok. The tenure of these pieces can be followed throughout the 15th century. William Meryell, whose name was to be attached to the house and croft, had been tenant between 1464 and 1496. In 1502 all parts of the tenement were in the lord's hands and therefore described in the extent rather than the rental of that year. In 1504 a ruined cottage called *Meriell* with 8 acres of land and 1 acre of meadow were granted out to Robert Dabbe and his wife.

The tenement was split up in 1527 when the messuage and 4-acre croft were alienated by Robert Dabbe to Nicholas Wen (MS 13013). In 1566 John Large held these, 'pasture ground Landes sometyme called Meryelles and now called Wendes being a litle cotage upon the same…', and they were listed as a tenement called *Merielles alias Wennes* in 1605. The rent for the cottage and 4 acres was 2s 10d in 1532–3 (HRO 8186). The same rent was paid for a tenement and land called *Merriells* between 1780 and 1792 (MS 13165 and MC 969/8, 858X7). The house was probably occupied by undertenants, William Plowright in 1664 and John Goodson in 1666. It had two hearths (Frankel and Seaman 1983, 61; Seaman 1991, 28). The tenant, Peter Large, lived in *Quarent.* 13. The tenancy of the house and croft can be followed throughout the 17th and 18th centuries to the admittance of George Watson, late of Little Dunham and now of Little Fransham, hosier, in 1794.

A Kirkhams and Wilcoks copyhold messuage and 5 acres of George Watson following Enclosure.

In 2008 four archaeological evaluation trenches were excavated in advance of development in the western part of the croft. A ditch aligned north-north-west/south-south-east and containing 13th to 14th-century sherds was recorded immediately north-east of the farmhouse and a north-east/south-west aligned ditch, without finds but probably ancient was recorded *c.*10m further east. Negative results were achieved in the other two trenches (HER 51769; Boyle 2008). The 19th-century farmhouse has since been demolished and replaced.

Med 72 TF 9096 1229 (*Quarent.* 25, HER 23903). Heavy soil, 65m OD (Fig. 7.46). Concentration of 12th and 13th-century sherds (with a few possibly late Thetford-type), 40m north-south x 30m east-west, lying on the east edge of *Cannons Green* and at the west end of Kirkhams and Wilcoks demesne land called *Nethiroxmer* in 1502 and *Oxmeare* in 1605. The place name *Oxmerewonges* occurs in a charter of 1325 (MC 360/56, 713X6).

On Kirkhams and Wilcoks copyhold land of Thomas Crowe following Enclosure.

Med 73 TF 9090 1268 (*Quarent.* 9, HER 20828). Medium-heavy soil, 63m OD (Fig. 7.35). Concentration of 12th-century sherds, 25m x 25m, lying within a close on the north side of Kirkhams manor house (Med 74), said to contain 20 acres in 1447 (MS 13142). In 1476 this was called *Northclos* (MS 13141) and in *c.*1484 was listed as a close behind the hall (MS 13162). In 1502 a 10-acre close of pasture with a pightle lay north of *le Mote* and later in the 16th century the site fell within a 30-acre enclosure called *Hall Close*.

On free land of Lady Essex following Enclosure.

Med 74 TF 9075 1256 (*Quarent.* 9, HER 7290). Heavy soil, 66m OD (Fig.7.35). Moated site of Kirkhams manor house. Pottery found immediately around the site suggests it was occupied from the 12th to the 15th century. Limited metal detecting produced two copper alloy objects: a 13th or 14th-century spur buckle and a 14th-century strap-end.

The four arms of the moat, now for the most part dry, enclose a trapezoidal island measuring 60m east-west and 47m north-south. The eastern, western and southern arms are now between 12 and 14m wide and c.1.5m deep. The northern arm, which may have been altered by the survival along its whole length until recent times of a ditch or drain, is only c.9m wide.

The north-west corner of the island is taken up with a post-medieval pond. This is joined to the northern and western arms and is shown, in almost the same shape as at present, on the Enclosure map. Recent mechanical dredging revealed a filling of predominantly peaty soil with very few medieval finds. Water was supplied by a ditch flowing into the north-west corner, and it departed from the moat's north-east corner into an eastward flowing ditch. This system has been altered in recent years by works associated with the amalgamation of fields. The pond is normally quite full, suggesting that the high water-table was also partly responsible for the provision of water.

There is no surviving indication of an original access to the island, which is not raised above the level of the surrounding ground. The surface of the interior, largely covered by scrub, is carpeted, wherever the soil is bare, with mortar and medieval ceramic roof tile fragments and a few pieces of medieval brick. Mortared flints are more common towards the south-east. Close to the southern inner edge of the eastern arm of the moat a 4m-long and 0.5m-wide stretch of wall, constructed of mortared flint and medieval brick, is visible just above ground level. Immediately to the west of this a fragment of plain glazed medieval ceramic floor tile was recovered.

The adjacent areas of fields to the north have produced very few surface finds and show no obvious sign of soil discoloration. To the south and east, and to a lesser extent the west, the field surface carries patches of darker soil and yellowish clayey soil, as well as a profusion of medieval ceramic roof tile fragments and a moderate spread of medieval brick. Some indications of earthwork banks and ditches, aligned north-south and east-west, are visible in the area to the south and west of the site on RAF vertical aerial photographs taken in 1946. Potsherds are not very common in the immediate vicinity of the moat, but such material as has been found suggests a 12th-century starting date for the site's occupation, and an end in the 15th century.

Carthew found this site of sufficient interest to merit a description, although he was unaware that it was the site of the Kirkhams manor house, '.....a quadrangular moated area containing about half an acre of land, within which formerly stood some edifice called *Baron's Hall*. The exterior of the ditch had until lately a bank or mound following its course, except at the north-east angle, where there is a large pond or reservoir which supplies the ditches with water. The bank, however, has now been carried away and leveled, and the pond partially filled with earth. At the south-east corner of the quadrangle are traces of the foundation of the building; and on the opposite external side lies a mass of rubble marble, possibly the remains of the barbican or entrance gate, or whence a drawbridge sprung.

Whether the name Baron's Hall was derived from the Tonys, the early lords of Fransham, I cannot say. I should rather suppose the Tony manor-house was in the adjoining parish of Necton' (Carthew 1879, 236).

There is now no hint of the 'rubble marble'. It may have been limestone, for Carthew added a footnote to the effect that stonework from the building had been used in the construction of a base for the font in St Mary's church.

A discrete and particularly dense concentration of medieval roofing tiles occurs c.150m east of the site over an area of 22m east-west by 12m north-south, at TF 9095 1260. This may mark the site of a building or is possibly no more than a dump.

Information on the maintenance of the manor house and its surrounding buildings, as well as the tenancy of the manor buildings and the cropping of the surrounding lands, is available in a number of sources, particularly account rolls for various years and parts of years between 1373 and 1443. The first and only formal description of the site was made in 1502, almost half a century after its abandonment. In all, the evidence is discontinuous but quite rich, and is therefore presented in some detail.

In the earliest surviving account, for the period from 29 September 1373 to 8 June 1374, the west gate (*porta*) was repaired with two long staples, other doors (*ostia*) were mended, two louvers? (*ventilabr.*) were purchased, and a damaged kiln (*toral.*) was repaired with clay. Small amounts of work were also done on cleaning *le pond* (MS 13121). Payments were made to two smiths (*fabri*) for working in the lord's forge (*fabrica*) in the manor in 1417–8. In the same year Walter Brend, roofer, was paid 10s for repairing various defects in various buildings in the manor, and another roofer worked for two days on the visitors' (*extraneorum*) stable. John Cook, carpenter, spent 2½ days mending the bridge over the moat (MS 13135).

In 1402–3 barley was sown on 1 acre next to *le Conewer* (see description of 1502, below) and on 1 acre, ¾ acre and ¼ acre near there (MS 13127). In 1412–3 barley was growing on 15 acres at *Smithecroft*. This large acreage suggests that the land in question was in fact *Halcrofte* to the west. In 1413–4 barley was sown on 3 acres at *Smethecroft* and oats on 7 acres below the manor (MS 13133). In 1417–8 1 acre at *le Conyngerclos* was sown with oats (MS 13135).

In 1427–8 William Wyskard, bailiff of the lord Sir William Oldhalle, was in the second year of a 5-year lease of the easement (*aysiam*) of 'divers' buildings with a dovecot in the manor, of four closes next to the site of the manor, with 44 acres in several pieces between the manor and the church. His rent was £13 6s 8d (MS 13137, an incomplete and damaged entry). In 1429–30 he was in the fourth year of the lease (MS 13138). In 1431–2 Wyskard was in the first year of a 5-year lease of all the buildings outside the manor, the dovecot, with all lands, meadows, pastures and feedings of the Kirkhams manor, with the manor of Wilcoks and all lands etc. His rent was £15 6s 8d, of which £8s 13 4d was for Kirkhams and the rest for Wilcoks. The arrangement was laid out in the previous year's account roll and in an indenture, but neither survives (HRO 8185). In the roll for 1432–3 it is made clear that the lord was to carry out repairs and all other charges (*onera*) pertaining to the said manors during the term of the lease (MS 13096).

In 1427–8 two roofers, each with an assistant, worked on four guest rooms (*camer. extraneorum*), the towers? (*les Garits*) on the east with an adjacent *stoklo* (meaning?) in the manor of Kirkhams (MS 13137). In 1429–30 major repairs carried out by a thatcher and assistants on the barn, smithy, stables and pig-sty over nineteen days at a cost of 12s 8d, and 16s 4d was spent on the purchase and delivery of straw (*alb. stram.*). A carpenter spent one day putting new studs (*stothes*) in the barn for 4d, 4s were spent on daubing walls (*pariet.*) in the barn and other buildings, and 2d on 60 nails for fixing laths (MS 13138). A carpenter did further work on the barn in 1432–3, a thatcher and his assistants worked on the stable, kiln-house and pig-sty, 11s was spent on the purchase of straw and 6s on its transportation (MS 13096).

At a leet court held in October 1436 it was presented that William Wyscard had cut down, lopped (*shrudav.*), carried away and burnt many oaks and ash trees around the manor. He had also broken walls (*pariet.*) of the lord's buildings in various rooms with his pigs and placed these pigs in the said rooms.

In 1436–7 Walter Lexham and John Balyston, styled Sir William Oldhall's farmers, were in the first year of a 5-year lease of both Kirkhams and Wilcoks lands, for the same rent and conditions as in William Wyskard's lease, with the same terminology being used in the account roll (MS 13139). Account rolls also survive for the years 1437–8, 1438–9, 1439–40 and 1440–1. The bailiff during the first two years of the lease, between 1436 and 1438, was John Sowles, but between 1438 and 1441 William Wyskard was again in post (MS 13037, HRO 8179 and MS 13038–9).

A new roof was put on the barn at *Kirkhams* in 1436–7, and this, along with other works at both *Kirkhams* and *Wilcoks* and on three tenements in the lord's hands, required 2000 sheaves of sedge bought in Feltwell, 4000 in Oxborough and 1000 in West Bilney. Oat and barley straw, some of which was purchased in Necton and Bradenham, and some from the barn of Little Fransham parsonage, was mixed with the sedge. John Grene, carpenter, and his two assistants constructed the barn's new timber roof over sixteen days at a cost of 11s 8d, and their food cost a further 8s 3d. Another carpenter, John Base, was employed for fourteen days. Many payments were made for the carrying of thatch, clay, laths and timber (MS 13139).

In 1437–8 John Grene worked for six days putting wooden supports in the north wall of the hall and trimming timber for the repair of the barn. He spent a further eighteen days at work on the barn. Daubing work was carried out on the barn in the same year. John Large spent four days making hedges (*haie.*) on either side of the drawbridge over the moat, and two men spent two days taking an old oak timber from the wall of the barn and taking into the manor for use as firewood (MS 13037). In 1438–9 three cartloads of sedge were brought from Oxborough and six cartloads of straw were purchased for roofing repairs at the great barn called *Kyrkhams*, and its east end was repaired (HRO 8179). In 1439–40 carpenters worked on *le Garett* and the door of the barn. Thatching was carried out on the buttery? (*buttr.*), *le gestchaumbr* and the stable by Thomas Stalworthy (MS 13038). He did further work on the kilnhouse and the malthouse in the following year (MS 13039).

In 1442–3 William Wyskard was in the second year of a 5-year lease. In his account roll he was styled farmer and bailiff of Sir William Oldhall (and was also messor for both Kirkhams and Wilcoks manors). His rent was £16. The words used in the description of the lease were similar to those of 1431–2 (all buildings outside the moat etc., lands etc. pertaining to each manor), but wards, marriages, reliefs, escheats and *extraction.* of wood and underwood were added. Rents from three Kirkhams customary tenements (Med 11A, 65 and 71) in the lord's hands were excepted and reserved to the lord. The tenant was to keep in repair etc. all buildings, walls, hedges and closes at his own expense, and he was to undertake and pay all other duties and charges owed by the manors (MS 13140).

In 1442–3 Thomas Stalworthy and two others paid 2s 6d for parts of an old piece of timber from the stable in the manor. The walls of the pig-sty were rebuilt in the same year, and payments were made for the transportation of clay and its tempering with straw. A long wall of the stable was also repaired, as was the bridge over the moat, with timber taken from *Wilcoks* and *Ellinghams*. Two men were paid 3d halfpenny per perch for digging a ditch and making a hedge on the bank on either side of the *le Entre* next to the manor, over a total length of 54 perches (MS 13140). After 1442–3 the account rolls cease.

In 1444 William Wyskard was amerced at the leet court because, without the permission of his fellow farmers [of the manor] he had taken a shutter (*tabul.*) from a window in the barn and carried it to a room within the lord's moat. He had kept it there and had claimed that it had been stolen.

In a rental of demesne lands for 1446–7 William Wyskard was listed as holding for a term of 5 years ending at Michaelmas 1447 lands comprising the site (*scitus*) of the manor with a garden and outbuildings (*domibus*), a 20-acre close on the south of the great barn, a close on the north of the manor, 23½ acres in the croft of the manor in two pieces (*Halcrofte* and land to the east), 10 acres in *Redeclos*, 20 acres in *Milleclos* and 8 acres of meadow in *le Raweyn* (MS 13142). In 1448 Richerus Wyskard was amerced at the manor court for doing damage to the lord's manor with his animals in *le moote* and on the bridge there.

It is likely that decline set in after the site was leased out in 1446–7, but that it gathered momentum after Sir William Oldhall, who was much embroiled in politics, lost all his possessions in 1452 after being indicted in the King's Bench. A Yorkist with considerable holdings in Norfolk and elsewhere, in the late 1440s he had begun to build a major castellated residence at Hunsdon in Hertfordshire (Roskell 1961). This venture may have further reduced his enthusiasm for the upkeep of his house in Little Fransham.

In *c.*1449, amongst lands formerly held by William Wyskard, were an enclosure called *le Smethycloos* to the south of the manor, held at farm by Manser Fouche for a rent of 5s, and a great close to the north of the manor, held at farm by Richerus Wyskard for 12s rent (MS 13142). In May 1449 Manser Fouch was amerced at the manor court for breaking and taking away the hedge around *Smethyclos* and in November Elianor Fouche, his servant, was amerced for the same. In 1450 the lord granted to John Cosyn and Christine his wife as hereditary copyhold for 4d annual rent a small sheep-rearing paddock below the house of the lord. This was to be of 12 hurdles or 14 at lambing time.

On 11 March 1454, at the first court of Walter Gorge esq. and Mary his wife (son-in-law and daughter of the disgraced William Oldhall), the homage was ordered to find out who had pruned and cut down wood and underwood in the lord's manor and in other closes belonging to the manor, and who had entered the manor and illegally carried away divers goods and chattels. At a leet court held on the same day the lord of the manor was urged to clean a watercourse at *Smethybrigge*. This probably led from the south side of *Smithyclos* onto the common.

On 31 March 1456, at Oldhall's first court after his re-entry, following a two year period when his son-in-law and daughter had been lords, the jury stated that the king's escetors had carried away various items from the manor: three ?lead pipes (*plumb.*) worth 34s 4d, 6s 8d and 2s; a lead trough (*trowe plumbat.*) worth 4s; divers lead from *les Goters*, a door from the counting house and a pair of old doors, worth 2s; a pair of *Gathenars* from the *Clekegate* (meanings?) on the bridge, worth 3s; eight other doors worth 1s; and a screen (*spere*) standing in the hall, worth 6s 4d. It was also said that Walter Gorge had carried away, as firewood, some oak branches intended for the repair of the manor. At the same court three men were said to have purchased trees in *Smethyclos* from Geoffrey Pouly: William Kede of Necton, six ash worth 6s 8d; Robert Mendham of Sporle, three ash worth 2s; Richard Clerk of Necton, two ash, two oaks and other wood worth 6s 8d. John Crudde was said to have cut down 300 oaks worth 10s at *le Conynger* (see below, description of 1502), and to have pruned a great oak on the manor site (*infra cit. Manerii*), worth 6s 8d. Brother John White had cut down two ash trees at *Conyger Dyke*, value 12d. John Yevan had cut down one oak worth 20d in *le Conyger* and had carried it away. He had also pruned four ash and two oak trees in the hedge (*super fossat.*) of *le Conyger*, value 3s. The rector of Little Fransham had cut down one oak there, one ash for rafters (*pro le Raftre*) and one oak for the belfry? (*le 1 par de Barfreys*), value 2s.

The manor house is probably mentioned in a royal pardon granted to Walter Gorge (Gorgies), knight, in 1460, in which he was released from debts to his father-in-law William Oldhall, knight. While Gorge was farmer of Little Fransham rectory Oldhall had attacked him there with a knife and Gorge's wife had intervened. Father-in-law then took son-in-law to his manor and forced him to take an oath to submit etc. (Cal. Pat. Rol. 1910, 541). William Oldhall died in November 1460 (Roskell 1961, 111). It is likely that the manor house went into rapid decline at about this time, although its precise date of abandonment is not known. In 1463 the ruckus in the rectory had not been not forgotten by the Gorges who sued, for damages of £100, two gentlemen, William Lexham late of London and Richard Wryght late of Saham Toney, for breaking into their close and home in Little Fransham on 23 December 1460, assaulting Mary and putting her in fear of her life (Mackman and Stevens 2010).

In 1474 John Hanke and John Dabbe were amerced at the manor court for breaking fences or hedges (*cepes*) around the site of the manor (*circa situm maner.*) without permission. Richerus Wyskard held at farm *Northclos* for a term of 5 years from 1476, rent 10s (MS 13141) and he was holding at farm a close behind (*aretro*) the hall in *c*.1484 for the same rent (MS 13162). William Gurre [rector of Little Fransham] held at farm, for a term of 5 years from 1476, 20½ acres for a rent of 16s. No name or further description of this land was given in this rental, but if in one piece it was probably the southern part of *Halclose* (MS 13141).

The extent of 1502 started with a description of the site of the manor and its surrounds, but no acreages were given (MS 13155). A damaged, incomplete and rough, but contemporary copy of the extent gives acreages (MS 13167). When known these are added below in [ ], as are any other details only in this copy. All the following lands, parcels and closes were enclosed by a ditch around the manor.

The manor of Little Fransham with water called *le Mote* surrounding a parcel of land formerly called *le Forine Court* (i.e. outer) and the site of the manor.

Parcel of land [½ acre] formerly called *le Okesyards* towards the south.

A close called *le Smethyclose* adjoining said parcel.

Two parcels of land called *le Okeyard* and *les Conyngers* [2 acres, or 2 acres + ?, at the west end of *Smethyclose*].

Unum Entre (perhaps a gatehouse).

Two parcels of land lying at the north end of the former two and west of *le Mote*, of which one was called *le Litill Estyards* [½ acre] and the other ...... [2 acres].

A close with a pightle lying north of *le Mote* containing [10 acres of pasture].

A pightle called *le Pynfold yard*.

A parcel of pasture [2½ acres] called *le Gret Gardyn* lying east of *le Mote*.

In *c*.1510 the site of the manor with its surrounding lands (*visum manerii cum omnibus inclus. super eumdem manerium penden.*) contained 39 acres and 14 perches (MS 13162). In 1566 these were described as pasture, 'The site which the manor house sometyme was in a close called Hall Close which close cont. by estimac. XXX acres'. In 1577 the site of the manor with all closes belonging and previously annexed to the manor and now called Hall Close contained 39 acres 1 rood and 25 perches. In 1605 *Halclose* was pasture, containing 30 acres by estimation and 33 acres 1 rood and 30 perches as surveyed by William Hayward. It lay between *Drovelane* and the common on the east, the common on the south, *Halcrofte* and *Caprede* on the west and *Barnardes moore* on the north.

On free land of Lady Essex at Enclosure. The Enclosure map depicts the moat quite accurately.

Med 75 TF 9078 1198 (*Quarent.* 11, HER 25668). Medium soil, 70m OD (Fig. 7.39). This site was first occupied in the 11th century (LS 18). A scatter of medieval and post-medieval sherds suggests that an occupation site lies close by, almost certainly to the north and north-east to judge from their distribution. The western edge of Cannons Green lies *c*.30m to the east. The area to the north is covered by farm buildings and a house, north-west of which is a substantial east-west moat-like feature, a pond *c*.8m wide and 55m long. This is shown on the Enclosure map. The house and buildings are on the site of a customary tenement of Cannons manor. This consisted of a messuage built with 2 acres in the croft, lying between land of the lord of Little Fransham on the west and the common pasture on the east, and butting north on the king's highway. A rent of 1s 8d due in 1370 from Vincent Fisor, who had freehold property in *Quarent.* 11 (MS 13089A) and the same due from the widow of William Muryell in *c.*1507–10 (CUL Dd VIII 42) must have been for this tenement, as this sum was cited as the rent in 1577. Both William Muryell and Robert Dabbe, a later tenant who died in 1552, also held Med 71 until 1527. In 1664 and 1666 the house of Widow Powley / Pawley had two hearths (Frankel and Seaman 1983, 61; Seaman 1991, 28). The tenurial descent has been traced from 1546 until Enclosure.

A Cannons copyhold close with a house, containing 3 roods and 18 perches, of Hamond Alpe esq. following Enclosure.

Med 76 TF 9076 1124 (*Quarent.* 15, HER 28886). Heavy soil, 79m OD (Figs 7.39 and 7.41). Concentration of 13th to 19th-century sherds. The medieval material is concentrated at the field's edge, and clearly much of the site lies under pasture to the east. A spread of post-medieval and later sherds along with 18th and 19th-century building material extends westwards. This site can be identified with a customary holding of Kirkhams manor, although the evidence of a charter of 1316/7 suggests it had been a Wilcoks freehold. Throughout its tenurial history the property was described in several ways, with a curiously variable acreage, but there is little doubt that only one holding was involved.

In a deed of 1316/7 a son [name missing] of Roger le Strange of Little Fransham granted to Henry le Strange and his son William of the same place, the homage etc. of Richard Coltinge of the same and 2½d rent for a messuage and 10 acres, lying between Roger Sewale's land on the west and the common pasture on the east (MC 360/49, 713X6). The low rent shows this was a freehold and the presence of William le Strange indicates it became part of Wilcoks manor. The common was *Coltinges green* which lay in the south-west corner of *Quarent.* 16. Richard Coltynge was a taxpayer in 1327 and 1332.

Stephen Coltyng was a taxpayer in 1379 and 1381. In 1384 William Coltyns held a messuage with 1 acre in the croft and ½ acre with a messuage in the same croft, for the low annual rent of 1d and 1 hen, with 1 autumn boon-work. In 1405 Geoffrey Tussenolf's widow Joanna quitclaimed all rights in 2¼ acres with a messuage once of Stephen Coltyng to Roger Grene. The property was mentioned in a perambulation of Necton in *c.*1427, as a certain tenement of Roger Grene, on the left and north as one proceeds eastwards along the Necton parish boundary, with *Neketonwode* on the right and south (MS 13177). Roger Grene had died in 1439, having surrendered 1¾ acres to the use of his children Emma and Paul. In 1443 Paul Grene and his sister Emma were tenants. The holding was described as in 1384 and given abuttals: in one piece, butting south on the common way below *Neketonwode,* lying between land of the lord on the east and a customary messuage and land of Sparhamhalle manor on the west. In 1445 the Grenes conveyed a messuage with 2 acres in the croft once of Geoffrey Tussenol to John Cosyn and his wife Christine, and in 1467 property of the same description passed to Nicholas Cosyn and his wife. In 1473 he paid a fine of 2s for the right to place boundaries in *Woderowefeld* between his land and that of the lord and that of Sparham manor, and the common way, i.e. on the east, west and south sides of his croft. In 1476 Cosyn paid another fine for licence to place a boundary at the north end of *Grenescroft,* although in the previous year he had surrendered the property, now described as 1½ acres of soiled land of the tenement Tossenol, to Richerus Wyskard, an important landholder in Little Fransham. Members of the Wyskard family were tenants throughout the 16th century.

Occupation may have ceased after 1476, as implied by the description of 1502, a toft and three half acres lying together enclosed by hedges and ditches. On several occasions between 1558 and 1578 the property was described as 2½ acres of soiled land in a close called *Wodroweclose,* and there was no reference to a messuage (MS 13169, MS 13158, MS 13104 and MS 13106). A ½-acre piece at the southern end was separated from the rest in 1596 (MS 13212). By 1599 this contained a newly built cottage (*superinde ex novo edificat.* SRO E3/10/9.16). The cottage and ½ acre were held by Bridget Whiskard widow according to a gloss of 1627/8 in a rental of 1618 (MS 13153), but the next reference in court proceedings is not until 1697. The property cannot be identified in either the 1664 or 1666 Hearth Tax assessment (Frankel and Seaman 1983, 61; Seaman 1991, 28), although throughout the 18th century it was described as built. In 1786 Samuel Jennings, a bricklayer of North Tuddenham, was admitted.

A Kirkhams and Wilcoks copyhold messuage and ½ acre was awarded to Samuel Jennis, innkeeper of North Tuddenham, at Enclosure, a building being depicted on the Enclosure map. At a court of 1818 Samuel Jennings alias Jennis was again described as a bricklayer.

Med 77 TF 9066 1125 (*Quarent.* 15, HER 28886). Heavy soil, 79m OD (Figs 7.39 and 7.41). Concentration of 13th to 19th-century sherds with 18th and 19th-century building material, 30m north-south x 25m east-west, on the east edge of *Woodrowgreen* common pasture. This can be identified with a messuage of the tenement Benendict Heveds, a customary holding of Sparhams manor in 1385/6. The tenement amounted to 11 acres with a messuage containing 1¼ acres. Later sources show that the messuage lay next to a 2-acre croft and that the other elements, comprising 4¾ acres, lay in eight parcels: ¾ acre in *Quarent.* 8, ¼ acre and ¾ acre in *Quarent.* 11, ½ acre, ¾ acre and ¾ acre in *Quarent.* 12, ½ acre in *Quarent.* 28, and ½ acre in *Quarent.* 29. Three other acres probably lay in *Quarent.* 11, but their tenurial history cannot be followed beyond 1531.

In 1485 the messuage and croft had been alienated without licence and were seized into the lord's hands. The messuage was described as built in 1487, and according to abuttals of 1572 it and 1¼ acres lay next to the common pasture next to *Necton Wood* on the west and butted south in part on the same common and in part on the king's highway next to *Necton Wood.* To the east lay a close of John Wyscard (i.e. Med 76) and to the north was the 2-acre croft.

By 1657 the southern part of the 1¼ acres was separated from the remainder and was normally described as a house or messuage with ½ acre. A barn just to the north of this was mentioned in 1656, while the remainder of the 1¼ acres and the 2-acre croft contained a house from 1613 (see Med 78). In 1664 and 1666 the house of

Widow Goodson, the messuage with ½ acre, contained one hearth (Frankel and Seaman 1983, 61; Seaman 1991, 28). By 1685 the property was again said to contain 1¼ acres. Thereafter the descent of the tenure can be followed to Enclosure, when it was held by one Anne Girdlestone.

Inexplicably this site, or at least the southern part of the 1¼ acres, was considered following Enclosure as 1 messuage with ¼ acre copyhold of Kirkhams and Wilcoks manor held by Isaac Powley. His holding and Anne Girdlestone's had been swapped. The 'true' site of Powley's tenement was further east, at TF 9087 1124.

Med 78 TF 9066 1132 (*Quarent.* 15, HER 28886). Heavy soil, 78m OD (Figs 7.39 and 7.41). Concentration of 13th to 18th-century sherds, 40m north-south x 25m east-west. This site, on the eastern edge of *Woodrowgreen*, lay in the croft of the tenement Benedict Heveds, a customary holding of Sparhams manor (see Med 77). The somewhat curious way in which in the late 15th century the messuage containing 1¼ acres was itemised separately from the 2-acre croft might suggest that at some earlier date there had been two distinct houses here. The distribution of sherds certainly showed two discrete concentrations. In 1613 this property was descried as newly built, and it had been combined with 1 acre of the tenement Dagonettes to the north (Med 79). This was the house of Richard Goodson which in 1664 and 1666 contained two hearths (Frankel and Seaman 1983, 61; Seaman 1991, 28). In 1731 it fell into the hands of Philip Alpe gent., a major landholder and by this time 'some of the Edifices were let downe and pulled downe from off the Copyhold contrary to the Customs of the Manner…'. Hamond Alpe was admitted in 1768.

On free land of Hamond Alpe esq. following Enclosure. No building was shown on the Enclosure map.

Med 79 TF 9062 1140 (*Quarent.* 15, HER 25564). Medium-heavy soil, 78m OD (Figs 7.39 and 7.41). Concentration of 13th to 18th-century sherds with a small amount of ?18th-century building material, 30m x 30m, on the northern edge of *Woodrowgreen*. This can be identified with a messuage and 1¾ acres of the tenement Hotche once of Dagnet, a customary holding of Sparhams manor in 1385/6. In 1335 ½ rood of customary land at *Dagonits croftisend* was conveyed at a Kirkhams manor court. For much of the time after 1485, when it was described as 1¾ acres with a messuage once Dagonetts, this tenement was associated in land transactions with the tenement Benedict Heveds (see Med 77 and 78).

In 1572 a tenement called *Dagonettes* once built and now decayed contained 1¾ acres and was given abuttals: between 2 acres of the tenement Benedict Heveds (i.e. the croft thereof) on the east, a tenement of Little Fransham manor held by William Powley (Med 80) on the west, butting south on the common pasture below *Necton Woode*. In 1586 a parcel of 1½ roods, divided off by a fence and boundary and now built, was granted by the tenant, John Harwyn, to Thomas and Robert Wyskard. Margery Lamberd was to have for her life the occupancy of a shed there (*unius domus vocat. A Shudde*). By 1611 it is clear that there were two houses here, on 1-acre and ½-acre plots. The former had been amalgamated with the northern part of Med 78 and thereafter they were regarded as one. The tenancy of the ½-acre holding has been traced up to Enclosure. It was described either as a house (*domus*) or cottage with an adjoining garden or hempland. The house of Edward Shene contained two hearths in 1664 and 1666 (Frankel and Seaman 1983, 61; Seaman 1991, 28). The tenement name (*Daganetts*) was last used in 1629. In 1758 Hamond Alpe failed to attend court for admittance to 'a piece of ground whereon a messuage formerly stood called the Orchard', which Mary West widow had surrendered to his use, out of court, in 1747. He was admitted in 1759.

On free land of Hamond Alpe esq. following Enclosure. No building is shown on the Enclosure map.

Med 80 TF 9052 1130 (*Quarent.* 15, HER 25564). Heavy soil, 77m OD (Figs 7.39 and 7.41). Concentration of 13th to 16th-century sherds, 30m x 30m. In 1384 Roger Knot, who had been a taxpayer in 1379 and 1381, held a Kirkhams customary messuage and 5½ acres once of Walter Cope. Walter Cope was listed as a juror at a leet court in 1328, and his last appearance at a Kirkhams court was in 1348. He was clearly a man of some substance, being assessed at 2s 6d for the Lay Subsidy of 1327 and at 4s in 1332. In 1443 the tenement was described in four pieces, 2 acres in Woodrowfield with ¾ acre at the southern end (*Quarent.* 15), ¾ acre in Middlefurlong (*Quarent.* 12), and the messuage with 2 acres in the adjoining croft. These last lay between lands of Sparhams manor (*Sparhamhalle*) to the east and west and butted south on a common. The messuage was described as built in 1508, 1511, 1539/40 and 1587 (MS 13055, MS 13067, MS 13102, MS 13104 and MS 13416). The lands were often said to be of the tenement Knots, Roger Knots or Roger Kinots in the 16th century.

According to the 1605 rental, the tenement had been acquired in 30 Elizabeth I (almost certainly 1588, a year for which there are no court proceedings) by Richard Beckham on the surrender of Nicholas Powley. The abuttals given in 1605 serve to locate this messuage accurately: in a close called *Godfries*, Richard Beckham's ground of the tenement Godfries (Med 81) to the west, *Wodrowgreen* in part to the east, butting south on the same green. Beckham's son Richard was admitted in 1616 to the reversion, to follow on his mother's death, of a messuage built with 5 acres of land and meadow, parcel of the tenement Roger Kynotte (MS 13415). Settlement had probably been abandoned by then, and in 1677, on the admittance of Robert Alpe after the death of Philip Alpe of Saham Toney gent., the property was described as 2 roods (*recte* acres) of land formerly of Nicholas Powley. Philip Alpe gent. was admitted to the same (still described as 2 roods) in 1702, as were his widow Alice in 1705, Hamond Alpe gent. in 1740 and his son Hamond Alpe esq. in 1768 (MC 1850/1–3, 858X9 and MC 1850/4–5, 858X8).

On free land of Hamond Alpe esq. following Enclosure. No building is shown on the Enclosure map.

Med 81 TF 9047 1130 (*Quarent.* 15, HER 25564). Heavy soil, 77m OD (Figs 7.39 and 7.41). Concentration of 13th and 14th-century sherds with a small number of 15th and 16th-century sherds, 40m east-west x 30m north-south. In 1385/6 a Sparhams customary holding, 11½ acres of the tenement Godfry, was not stated to contain a messuage. From 1492 until 1595 the tenants of a messuage or tenement and 6 acres were consistently the same as those who held Med 80. On several occasions before 1535 8 rather 6 acres were listed with the messuage, the extra 2 acres being Sparhams soiled land, apparently lying in the same area. The remainder of the tenement lay in three parcels: ½ acre in *Quarent.* 11, 2 acres in *Quarent.* 18 and 3 acres in *Quarent.* 27. By the time all three parcels had appeared in the documentary record they had tenurial histories quite distinct from that of the messuage or tenement and 6 acres. No abuttals for the messuage and its associated lands were entered in court proceedings, but its location is clear from the abuttals of Med 80. A messuage was described as built in 1493, but subsequently it was a tenement rather than a messuage that was so described. The tenant, Robert Whytte was amerced for non-repair of a barn here in 1531 as was Helen Powley widow in 1586. In 1594 the tenant, John Brymley was amerced for totally ruining the roof of a building (*domus*) called 'An haiehouse and stalle' and was separately fined for non-repair of the roof and walls of his barn. At the same court the tenement was seized into the lord's hands because Brymley had defaulted on suit of court. The lord of Sparhams manor was Richard Beckham, the tenant of Med 80. After 1595 there was no further reference to this part of the tenement Godfrey.

The archaeological and the documentary evidence both point towards a lack of domestic occupation on this site in the 15th and 16th centuries. The tenants (or occupiers) of Med 80 lived there and used this site as part of a farm complex, both set within a close which in 1605 was called *Godfries*. The presence of non-domestic agricultural buildings ensured that the description 'built' was still appropriate.

On free land of Hamond Alpe esq. following Enclosure. No building is shown on the Enclosure map.

Med 82 TF 9035 1132 (*Quarent.* 15, HER 25556). Heavy soil, 75m OD (Figs 7.39 and 7.41). Concentration of 13th and 14th-century sherds, 50m x 20m, aligned south-west to north-east, on the northern edge of *Woodrowgreen*. Five acres with a messuage in one piece, freehold of Wilcoks manor were held by Roger Grene (glossed 'Will. Dey') in *c*.1420, for 3d annual rent. Grene's dwelling house was probably Med 76. This piece lay between Roger's lands to the east and west and butted north on land of John Sevepens. In *c*.1395 Margaret Bolt had paid 5d halfpenny rent for unspecified lands. The difference in rent might be explained by messor's account rolls for 1409–10, 1414–6 and 1420–1 (MS 13132, MS 13134 and MS 13136) in which deductions of 2d were made for 2 acres late Alice Bolt's which were in the lord's hands. William Dey / atte Broke was tenant in *c*.1483, *c*.1488 and *c*.1494 to judge from three short Wilcoks rentals (MS 13143, MS 13175 and MS 13162). In 1502 William Broke (frequently alias Dey) held a free messuage and 5 acres called *le Wodrowe* which butted south on *Woderowe more*. In 1605 William Daie alias Brookes held a free tenement and 5 acres enclosed called *Woodroweclose* for a joint rent of 3d with two freeholds comprising 2¾ acres and a messuage in *quarents.* 4 and 5. No reference to a messuage built has been found. This piece was not singled out in the will of William Brooke alias Dey, which was proved in 1605, although his other two freeholds were (ANW 189 Sawyer). However, in the will of Henry Dye alias Brook, proved in 1628, a free tenement and land called *Woodrowhouse and Close* was left to his wife Thomazin for life (ANW 326 1626–9). In 1714 three daughters and co-heirs of the late William Dey acknowledged that they held 3 acres in Little Fransham for an annual rent of 2d (MC 1850/3, 858X9). Between 1780 and 1792 the rent paid by Hamond Alpe esq. for a tenement and land late Dyes was 2d (MS 13165 and MC 969/8, 858X7).

On free land of Hamond Alpe esq. following Enclosure. No building is shown on the Enclosure map.

Med 83 TF 9005 1135 (*Quarent.* 15, HER 25556). Medium-heavy soil, 76m OD (Figs 7.39 and 7.41). Concentration of 13th to 15th-century sherds, 40m north-south x 20m east-west, on the northern edge of *Woodrowgreen*. This site can be identified with 3½ acres enclosed in one piece called *Brayesclos*, freehold of Wilcoks manor, held by Geoffrey Bray in *c*.1420. Walter Le Bray / Bray was a taxpayer in 1327 and 1332, as was Roger Bray in 1379 and 1381. Geoffrey Bray's annual rent was 8d halfpenny in *c*.1395. In *c*.1420 he paid 7d for *Brayesclos* and John Sevepens paid 1d halfpenny for 1 acre once of Geoffrey Bray in *Chownesfurlong* (*Quarent.* 11). In 1406 John Croupius was amerced at a Little Fransham leet court for keeping a close called *Brayes* closed when it should have been open. By 1429 Geoffrey Bray had died seized of a free messuage and 4 acres, and his son John, aged 15, was said to be mentally unsound (*fatuus natural.*). The holding was seized into the lord's hands. In 1436 it was presented at the leet court that the lord of the manor had not scoured a watercourse at *Brayesyerd*. John Bray, son and heir of Geoffrey, was of age (and presumably sound of mind) when he paid a relief of 9d for his father's lands, 3½ acres enclosed called *Brayesclos* and 1 acre once of John Sevepens. John Bray had died in 1455, seized of a free void messuage and 4½ acres. His brother John [sic] swore fealty and paid 9d relief. In the next year John was amerced at the leet court for failing to scour a watercourse at *Brayesclos*, while at the same sitting of the manor court Robert Bray was distrained for default of suit of court. Tenants of the lands or tenement Brayes were unnamed in *c*.1483 (MS 13143), Robert Constabil in *c*.1487 (MS 13175) and Nicholas Mynne in *c*.1494 (MS 13162).

In 1502 a freehold toft and 3½ acres in a croft called *Brayes* enclosed with ditches were held for a rent of 7d halfpenny by Nicholas Mynne. Richard Beckham held a toft and 3½ acres at the south end of a close called *Braies* lying next to *Wilcocks* (see Med 85) for the same rent in 1605. He also held the 1 acre called *Braies* in *Quarent.* 11. In 1677 Robert Alpe swore fealty for the same which he held for the same rent, as did Philip Alpe in 1702 (MC 1850/1–2, 858X9).

In a parcel of 5 acres 1 rood and 38 perches held by Lady Essex for Hamond Alpe esq. following Enclosure. No building is shown on the Enclosure map.

Med 84 TF 9010 1144 (*Quarent.* 15, HER 25556). Medium soil, 77m OD (Figs 7.39 and 7.41). Weak concentration of discoloured 12th to early 13th-century sherds, predominantly oxidised and partly under- and overfired, probably representing pottery production. The sherds were spread over an area *c*.15m across on the north-east edge of an unusually square pit which is now ploughed over. It is very likely that part of the concentration has been removed by the digging of the pit that is depicted on the Enclosure map as a miniature moat-like feature *c*.35m square. This site may possibly be identified with a Kirkhams customary messuage and 3 acres of the tenement Thomas Clerkes or Coyse held by Walter Grene in 1384. He had been admitted in 1370 and held it in 1374 when this tenement and the tenement Hobbyslond, which was in the lord's hands, had been elected to the office of messor. Walter Grene was a taxpayer in 1379 and 1381. Glosses in the 1384 rental indicate that John Ballyston and Nicholas Mynne were later tenants. The former held in 1443, when the messuage with 3 acres in the adjoining croft were said to butt on the common pasture to the south. Thomas Wryghte was tenant in c.1460 (MS 13144), and he was elected to the office of messor in 1464 as the tenant of the tenement Roger Knots (Med 80) and of the tenement Essylins which contained 3 acres. No earlier reference to the latter tenement name has been found, nor has anyone of this name been noted, apart from a Nicholas Eslyn who occurred in a court roll of as late as 1459. Robert Constabill, who took up Thomas Wryghte's lands in 1480 and held a messuage once of Roger Grene in c.1487, conveyed 3 acres with a void messuage to Nicholas Mynne and his wife in 1492.

In 1502 Nicholas Mynne held 3 acres called *Estlens*. Three acres with a void messuage called *Esstelyns* lay in *Brayes Close* in 1542 (MS 13162). A similar description was given in 1575 when the land was said to butt on *Woodrow more* to the south (MS 13104). In 1605 this was held by Richard Beckham as 3 acres with a void messuage of the tenement Esl'ms at the north end of *Braies close*, with *Woodrowclose* (Med 82) to the east and *Wilcocks* (see Med 85) to the west. The piece lay together with 1 acre of soiled land called *Cavesacre*. This had been held by Roger Knot in 1384 when it lay in *Coysicroft* and was once of Roger Coyse. It shared common tenants with the above 3 acres and messuage into the 17th century, and was designated, somewhat surprisingly, as soiled land for the first time in as late as 1492. In 1616 Richard Beckham junior was admitted to the reversion, to follow on his mother's death, of both these pieces of land, 3 acres with a void messuage of the tenement Eslinges in *Brayes Close* and 1 soiled acre called *Coyves* in the same close (MS 13415). Both pieces were to come to Alpe family later in the 17th century. In 1677, when they were next described, 2 additional acres of uncertain origin had appeared: two pieces called *Bruiles* and *Brayes* containing 6 acres and lying next to the common called *le Ling alias Woodrowe more*. This description was to be repeated with odd changes of nomenclature, *Brimlowes and Brayes* lying near the common called *Leringe alias Woodrough Moore* in 1705, *Le Ring otherwise Woodrough Moore* in 1740 and 1767.

This site is unusual in that the messuage, if indeed the archaeological fits the documentary evidence, was placed c.130m back from the common pasture. Presumably the 3-acre croft extended south from the messuage to the common edge and passed by the east side of Med 83.

In a parcel of 5 acres 1 rood and 38 perches held by Lady Essex for Hamond Alpe esq. following Enclosure. No building is shown on the Enclosure map.

Med 85 TF 8989 1153 (*Quarent.* 14, HER 24771). Medium soil, 77m OD (Figs 7.39 and 7.41). Concentration of 12th, 13th and ?14th-century sherds, 40m north-south x 25m east-west, on the eastern edge of a common pasture, the *common lynge* in 1605. Limited metal-detecting produced a farthing of Henry III, a 13th-century buckle late and a 15th-century Tournai jetton.

This site lay within a large close of demesne of Kirkhams and Wilcoks manor known as *Wylkoks clos* in 1402–3 (MS 13127). Of the four settlements falling within this close and within *Wilcocks pightles* (see Med 86–8), this one is the most likely site of the manor house of Wilcocks on the evidence of a perambulation of the bounds of Necton parish in 1427 (MS 13177). After describing a route along a way towards the east with *Neketon Wode* on the right and the common pasture of Little Fransham on the left, the witness arrived at a certain built-up place (*locum edificat.*) called *Wylcokys* on the left-hand side and on the north in Little Fransham parish, and a stile called *Walsinghamstyle* on the right in Necton. This itinerary does not fit the other three sites in the area.

A messuage cited in a release of 1338 may perhaps be identified with this site. John son of William Atterode of Little Fransham quitclaimed all rights etc. in a messuage and 5 acres in the croft, a toft and other lands, rents and services to William son of Henry le Strange of the same place. The messuage lay next to a common pasture on the west and to the toft on the north. The latter lay on the south side of a common (MC 360/68, 713X6). William atte Rod was a taxpayer in 1327

Some information on the maintenance of a barn, dovecot and other buildings that stood at *Wilcoks* in the earlier 15th century can be found in Kirkhams and Wilcoks bailiffs' account rolls. These contain no indication that there was any domestic occupation here during this period.

The barn at *Wylkoks* yielded 21 quarters of barley in 1402–3, and a crop was sown on 9½ acres in *Wylkoks clos* in the same year (MS 13127). The barn yielded 25 quarters 5 bushels of peas, 83 quarters 6 bushels of barley and 33 quarters 2 bushels of oats in 1412–3. Further amounts of crops from the barn at *Wylcoks* were given for 1413–4 and in the same year 1 quarter and 4 bushels of barley were used to feed pigeons kept in a certain building during the repair of the dovecot at *Wylcoks* (MS 13133).

In 1417–8 1s 6d were paid for the cleaning of a bridge (*pont.*) around the dovecot at *Wylcoks*, and 10s farm rent for the dovecot was received from Roger Catour. A pair of large gates or doors (*magnarum portarum*) at *Wylcoks* were sold to the parson of Little Fransham for 9s 6d. Crops were again recorded from the barn at Wylcoks, and Isabell Catour, wife of Roger and dairymaid (*daya*), paid 12s 5d as a farm rent for thirty cows and a bull at *Wylcoks* (MS 13135). In 1427–8 John Yevan was in the second year of a 5-year lease of Wilcoks manor. That year carpentry repairs were carried out on a cowshed at *Wylcoks* (MS 13137). In the following year the walls of the dovecot were repaired and re-daubed. A sum of 24s 8d was paid for the making of 330 perches of new hedge (*haia*) for a new pasture enclosure and for the cutting of underwood there. Nine pence were paid for the making of a new watering-hole (*adaquaro*) and 9d were expended on three locks? (*fecherlokes*) for the gates or doors of the manor of *Wylcoks* and the said new enclosure. In the same year the farmer, John Yevan, was unwell, and so he retained the farm of only 8½ acres and the dovecot out of the 132½ acres that he had previously held. Five other men held 42½ acres and there was no income from the remainder (83 acres) because it was pastured with lord's beasts of chase (MS 13138).

William Carter was amerced for placing sheep hides (*pell.*) on the lords' bridge in *Wilkocks cloos* in 1429. In 1436–7 daubing was carried out on buildings at *Wylcoks*. Work was carried out by John Grey, thatcher (*Reder*), on the dovecot. Wattling in the latter and in the barn was repaired (MS 13139). Divers old pieces of timber from a certain old building at the manor of *Wylcoks* were sold to John Yevan for 8d in 1437–8, and in the same year 10d was paid for the dragging of straw for the roofing of a building there (MS 13037). In 1439–40, 105 roods of ditch were dug, cleaned and scoured around one close near the common at *Wylcoks*. Willow, ash and oak trees along the same ditch, at *Wylcoks clos*, were lopped and cut down, and a length of 103 perches was hedged anew. In addition, 260 faggots were cut and made on a certain ditch or bank (*fossat.*) at *Wylcoks* (MS 13038).

William Gelder, roofer, was paid 2s for six days work on the east part of the barn of *Wylcoks* in 1440–1 (MS 13039), and in 1442–3 Richard and Geoffrey Maunde were paid for cutting timber at *Wylcoks* for the repair of the bridge over the moat at *Kirkhams* (MS 13140). In the absence of any bailiff's account rolls after 1442–3 no further information on the fate of the buildings at *Wilcoks* has been recovered.

Wylcokys was described as demesne pasture in a court roll of 1443. Richerus Wyskard was granted *Wylkocks clos* and *Butty acre* (in *quarent* 11) in 1483, as hereditary copyhold, for a new annual rent of 20s 6d. In 1502 Thomas Wyskard's fee farm rent for *Wilcokkes close* was 20s. He died in 1538 and according to an Inquisition Post Mortem held in 1546 he had held a close called *Wylcocks* at hereditary fee farm for 20s 6d rent (TNA C 142/72/46). In *c.*1555 the farm rent paid by John Wyskard son of Thomas for *Wylcokks* was 20s. It is not known when this hereditary tenure came to an end. *Wilcoks* contained 24 acres of demesne pasture in 1566, and 20 acres 3 roods and 11 perches in 1577. In 1605 the jurors estimated that it amounted to 24 acres but William Hayward's survey showed that it contained 12¼ acres of pasture and 8 acres 1 rood and 10 perches of wood and 'bushshes'.

On free land of Lady Essex following Enclosure. No building is shown on the Enclosure map.

Med 86 TF 8996 1163 (*Quarent.* 14, HER 24770). Medium-heavy soil, 76m OD (Figs 7.39 and 7.40). Concentration of 12th, 13th and ?14th-century sherds, 50m east-west x 25m north-south on the south-east edge of a common pasture. This site lies immediately behind and south of a modern farmhouse called the Manor and north-east of a pair of pits, within what were described in 1577 as three arable closes of Kirkhams and Wilcoks demesne called *Wilcokks crofts* containing 5½ acres. These three comprised 6 acres of pasture and were called *Wilcocks pightles* in 1605. This as well as Med 87 and 88 can be identified with these three pightles. That the pightles were not singled out and described before 1577 is probably because they had previously been regarded as part of *Wilcoks close* to the south.

Despite the late arrival of the three pightles in the documentary record, several 13th and 14th-century charters were probably concerned with them. This suggestion is based on the location of the moor (common pasture) to the north. Two deeds of *c.*1273–90 concern two parts of a messuage held by Nicholas and John, sons of Bartholomew the clerk of Little Fransham, and granted respectively to John de Caly and William de Sapy. The moor lay to the north and the messuage of Alice Swengeden to the east (MC 360/29, 713X6 and NRS 12710, 27F4). This messuage in two parts is probably the same as a messuage and 3 acres conveyed on 13 June 1333 by John son of William Atterode of Little Fransham to William le Estrange. It lay between *Swengedenscroft* on the east and the messuage held by John's mother for life on the west and butted south on land of William le Strange. The messuage of John's mother Margaret with 3 acres adjoining was conveyed by the same deed (MC 360/63, 713X6). She announced her son's grant of the messuage to le Strange in a deed of declaration on the following day (MC 360/68, 713X6). In 1338 John quitclaimed all rights etc. in the same messuage, now described as half a messuage with 2½ acres and held by his mother for life, to William son of Henry le Strange (MC 360/67, 713X6). Interests in a toft, along with other lands, rents and services, were quitclaimed by John son of William Atterode to William le Strange and recorded in two deeds of 1333 and 1338 (MC 360/62 and 68, 713X6). Despite variations in acreages, the above properties approximate to 2 messuages, a toft and 6 acres.

At a Wilcoks manor court in 1401 John Wavyonn, servant of John Croupius parson of Little Fransham, was amerced for harvesting grass in a close of the lord next to *Swyngdewes* and taking it away without permission.

On free land of Lady Essex following Enclosure. No building is shown on the Enclosure map.

Med 87 TF 8999 1173 (*Quarent.* 14, HER 25559). Medium-heavy soil, 75m OD (Figs 7.39 and 7.40). Concentration of 13th and 14th-century sherds, 30m north-south and 20m east-west, on the south-east edge of a common pasture, within one of three closes called *Wilcokks crofts* in 1577. See Med 86.

Med 88 TF 9004 1175 (*Quarent.* 14, HER 25559). Medium-heavy soil, 74m OD (Figs 7.39 and 7.40). Concentration of 12th and 13th-century sherds, 25m north-south x 20 east-west, on the south edge of a common pasture, within one of three closes called *Wilcokkes crofts* in 1577. See Med 86.

Med 89 TF 8986 1178 (*Quarent.* 5, HER 24759). Medium-heavy soil, 75m OD (Figs 7.31 and 7.32). Concentration of 13th and 14th-century sherds, 25m east-west x 20m north-south on the north edge of a common pasture. Immediately to the west, at the eastern end of the adjacent field, twenty medieval sherds were recovered from an area of little more than 3m². This site, along with Med 90, lay within three small yards called *Sheppeards Yerds* containing 2½ acres and butting on the *common linge* to the west and south in 1605. A charter of *c.*1273–90 recorded the grant by Alexander le Strange of Little Fransham to Henry le Strange of the same, for an annual rent of a clove of garlic, of three properties: a small messuage, a sheep-house (*domus bercaria*) above the messuage, and an empty plot (*placia vacua*) between the sheep-house and the common pasture (MC 360/18, 713X6). This site might well be the empty plot, although the presence of 14th-century pottery shows it was to be reoccupied.

A messor's account roll of Kirkhams manor for 1392–3 lists Geoffrey Tussenol as paying 1s rent to the lord of Kirkhams for pasturage in *Shephousyerd* (MS 13123). Four bushels of beans were sown on 1 acre in *le Shepehouseyerd* in 1400–1 (MS 13126), and 'dredge' (a mixture of barley and oats) was sown on 1¼ acres in 1402–3 (MS 13127). In 1411 Margery wife of John son of John Wilkynson junior was amerced at a Kirkhams manor court for cutting the lord's grass (*herbag.*) at *Shephousyerd*. Wheat was sown on 2 acres at *Shephousyerdes* in 1412–13 (MS 13133).

In 1427–8 Thomas Rous's farm rent for 2 acres in the shepherd's close (*in inclaus. bercar.*) was 4s (MS 13137). In 1429–30 Thomas Reve's rent was the same for 2 acres in *le Schephousclos* and Reve, a shepherd (*bercar.*) was paid 6s 8d for guarding the lord's sheep (MS 13138). *Shephousyard* appeared in a rental of demesne lands for 1446–7. It was leased to Henry Hokeryng, tenant of the nearest Kirkhams customary messuage to the east (MS 13142). It was presented at a manor court held in 1450 that Geoffrey London had cut down wood and underwood in a number of named pieces of demesne including *Schepehose yerdis*.

In 1482 three yards or gardens (*ort.*) called *Shepehousyards* were granted out as copyhold to Richard Fletcher and his heirs, and in 1485 they passed to Nicholas Mynne and his wife. In 1502, still held by Mynne, they contained 2½ acres and were described as three *virgates*, the unique occurrence of this term in a Fransham document (MS 13053). Richard Beckham was tenant in 1605, and his son Richard was admitted in 1616 (MS 13415).

With Med 90 on Kirkhams and Wilcoks copyhold land of John Allison following Enclosure. No building is shown on the Enclosure map.

Med 90 TF 8985 1188 (*Quarent.* 5, HER 23899). Medium-heavy soil, 75m OD (Figs 7.31 and 7.32). Concentration of 12th and 13th-century sherds, 40m east-west x 25m north-south. A few late Thetford-type and Grimston-Thetford ware sherds might suggest that this site began in the 11th century. It sits *c*.90m back from the north edge of the common and is separated from Med 89 by a small watercourse draining eastwards. If this site is to be identified with the small messuage granted by Alexander le Strange to Henry Le Strange (see Med 89), then perhaps it was to be abandoned in favour of the vacant plot, Med 89, which could be seen as an encroachment on the common, especially if the watercourse had until then formed the northern boundary of the common.

Med 92 TF 9106 1192 (*Quarent.* 28, HER 24767). Medium-heavy soil, 69m OD (Fig. 7.47). Concentration of 13th and 14th-century sherds, 35m north-south x 20m east-west, close to the east edge of Cannons Green common pasture. An 11th and 12th-century site (LS 19) lying *c*.50m to the east may have been a predecessor, but discontinuity in occupation during the late 12th and ?early 13th centuries may suggest that they were tenurially distinct. Med 92 lay at the west end of *Jekkes*, which was demesne of Kirkhams manor in 1402–3 when peas were sown there (MS 13127). The place name may be derived from the family name Jok, which first occurs in a charter of *c*.1273–90 (MC 360/21, 713X6). Near to this site, as well as eastwards on the margins of *Eastendmoor* were the lands and tenements of Edmund Jocke and Hamond Jocke, customary holdings of Sparhams manor (see Med 67 and 97).

Kirkhams and Wilcoks demesne called *Jekkes* contained 9 acres in 1446–7 (MS 13142). Nine acres of demesne land and meadow lay in *Millfield* with a grove at one end and a church way called *Jekkespath* to the north in 1502. The acreage had increased to 10 in 1532–3 (HRO 8186). Seven acres of arable lay in *Millfield* with *Jekkes grove* on the west in 1566. *Jecks pece* contained 7 acres, 1 rood and 16 perches in 1577, with a piece of meadow at the east end and *Jecks grove* at the west end. In 1605 *Jeckespeece* consisted of 7 acres of arable. There was a small parcel of 20 perches in the south west corner. In the north-west corner lay *Jecksgrove*, a pasture pightle of ¾ acres.

Jeckesgrove, in which this site probably lay, was first named in 1433, at a manor court when the lord's bailiff, William Wyskard, was amerced for not fencing it off, thus allowing animals to destroy the coppiced underwood (*virgul.*) growing there. Robert Bucke was paid 3½d per perch for digging and scouring a ditch on the west of *Jeckesgrove*, and for cutting timber growing on the ditch's bank, for a length of 21 perches (MS 13140). Underwood was stolen from *Jekkysgrove* in 1460. In the later 15th and throughout the 16th century this was a *grovetta*. In 1502, 1566 and 1577 it was said to contain ¾ acre. In 1603 *Jecks grove* was described as a pightle newly converted from wood to pasture and containing ½ acre and 16 poles (MS 13279).

On Cannons copyhold land of Hamond Alpe esq. following Enclosure. No building is shown on the Enclosure map.

Med 93 TF 9277 1190 (Area O, HER 25546). Medium-heavy soil, 64m. OD (Figs 7.19 and 7.27). Concentration of 13th to 15th-century sherds, 35m x 35m This may be identified with a messuage and 9 acres with pasture, once of Geoffrey son of William de Southwood, freehold of Great Fransham manor and held by Thomas Futche in *c*.1400. Both William and Geoffrey de Suthwod were taxpayers in 1327 and 1332, and again in 1337. William de Southwood had died in 1349 seized of a messuage and 7 acres, leaving an underaged son, Geoffrey, as heir. The rental of *c*.1400 did not specify that this land lay in *Southwoodfield*. However, it is likely to have been near Futche's other messuage (Med 62). This is corroborated by a gloss in one version of the rental stating that it was then (probably in the 1540s) held by Robert Hogan and called *Wardes Close* (MS 13084 Book B). For Hogan and Ward see Med 62. Abuttals in the rental of *c*.1400 are not very helpful: between Futche's land on the north and of William Priour on the south, butting east on a common way. At the same time Priour held 9 acres of land and 1 of pasture, freehold of Great Fransham, and all in *Southwoodfield*. Three of his four parcels butted on Futche's lands. In 1456 John Colyn was amerced at a leet court for allowing branches to overhang the way next to the messuage called *Southwodes* and for not scouring his ditch near the same (MS 13051). To judge from similarities of rents, this holding, probably with Med 62, may be the same as a free tenement called *Futches* held by Henry Mynne in 1573 and 1579 (MS 13079) and a free tenement once of Collens held by Richard Beckham in 1595.

On free land of Matthew Nelson esq. following Enclosure.

Med 94 TF 9042 1205 (*Quarent.* 11, HER 25571). Heavy soil, 70m OD (Fig. 7.39). Concentration of 13th to late 16th or early 17th-century sherds, 40m east-west x 20m north-south, on the south edge of a common pasture. Although this site can confidently be identified with 2 acres of the tenement Segars, freehold of Kirkhams and Wilcoks manor and held by Richard Beckham in 1605, both the earlier and later histories of the site and its associated lands are exceptionally confused, involving several changes of tenure between free, customary and leasehold.

Throughout the start of the story there are some tenuous links. In 1332 Nicholas de Bedingtone swore fealty at a Kirkhams manor court and showed his charter for 17 acres and a windmill that he had bought from Ralph Bottler. Bedingtone did not appear in a long list of freeholders distrained to swear fealty in 1336, but Robert de Waltone, Mary his wife and Petronilla his mother were included. In 1337 it was said that Robert de Walton held certain lands for a rent of 2s 10d. This rent had been granted to John de Kirkham and Margaret his wife by Ralph de Bagethorp. Adam, Roger and John Syger were mentioned in plea cases at a manor court held on 4 February 1346. At the same court (the first of John le Strange, lord of Kirkhams) it was presented that Roger Syger had died seized of 17 acres with a messuage that he had held of the lord for an annual rent of 2s 10d. Adam Syger clerk (*cappel.*) swore fealty and paid a relief of the same amount. In 1347 John Scramige and Mabel his wife swore fealty for 7 acres of free land that they had purchased from Adam Syger clerk. In March 1363 a messuage and 7 acres once of Adam Syger were granted as a customary holding to William son of Nicholas Jordan (see Med 71). Presumably half of Adam's original 17-acre property had fallen into the lord's hands and thus became bond land.

John Sygor / Syger was a taxpayer in 1379 and 1381. Two parcels were granted as customary holdings in October 1391: John Smyth received 2¾ acres and 4 perches with a messuage once Sygeres, and John Syger 1¾ acres in *Woderowefeld* once of Roger Syger. Both properties were to be held for what appear to have been 'new' money rents and work services. Relevant entries in the supplement to the 1384 Kirkhams rental both use the term 'by copy' (*per copiam*), its earliest occurrence in a Fransham document. Nothing more is known of the second parcel. The first was in the lord's hands between 1398 and 1408 (MS 13125 and MS 13131). It was said to be once of Roger Syger in 1409 when granted out as customary land to Adam Drowry, webster, and his wife, and was called the tenement Smethes when leased at farm in 1429. Thereafter its fate is also unknown.

Edmund de Oldhalle was amerced at a Little Fransham leet court in 1395 for not repairing a bridge at *Sygeres*. To judge from the abuttal this property was held by Henry Ram in 1443. In 1452 Richerus Wyskard was amerced at a leet court and ordered to remove a style with which he had blocked a common church path near his messuage. At a leet court held in 1455 it was presented that in the year before Wyskard had blocked the common church path next to *Segers* with hedges.

In his will, proved in 1493, Richerus Wyscard left his cottage called *Sygers* with lands belonging to his wife with reversion to his son Thomas (ANW 235 Fuller alias Roper). In 1502 Thomas held a messuage and 8½ acres (n.b. half of 17) called *Seggers* in six parcels in *Woodrowfield*, for 6d rent. A free messuage built with 2 acres in the croft was held by John Crispe in 1557 jointly with his wife Faith, a daughter of Thomas Wiscard (MS 13169). In 1595 Robert Davies held a messuage and 8½ acres called *Segars*, rent 6d (MS 13211), and in the following year he conveyed these in an exchange with Richard Beckham, who held for an annual rent of 5d (MS 13212). A copy of an indenture for this exchange, which involved 3 extra acres including *Braies Acre* (see Med 83), gave detailed abuttals for each piece which correlate well with those of 1502 (MS 13268). Inexplicably only 2 acres of the tenement Segars butting north on *the moare* were listed in the 1605 survey, although the rent remained at 5d.

In 1615 Alice Beckham widow was amerced at the manor court for not scouring her ditch at *le Gate apud Siggars*. Alice died in 1626, and at some stage thereafter this land became copyhold of Kirkhams and Wilcoks. In 1696 Edward Swift, son of William Swift rector of Little Fransham (ob. 1687) was admitted to 6 acres in close called *Seigoos*. In 1697 when Swift conveyed them to William Large gent. of Swaffham they were in a close called *Leagers* [sic]. In 1722 this scribal error was corrected when Susanna Large was admitted to six pieces of land in a close called *Seagers Field* and then surrendered them to the use of Philip and Alice Alpe. The misspelling returned in 1740 on the admission of Hamond Alpe gent. to several pieces of land in a close called *Leagers Field* containing 6 acres and was repeated when his son Hamond was admitted in 1768.

On Cannons copyhold of Hamond Alpe esq. following Enclosure. No building is shown on the Enclosure map.

Med 95 TF 9213 1433 (Area D, HER 28881). Heavy soil, 71m OD (Figs 7.14 and 7.15). Concentration of 12th and 13th-century sherds, 30m x 30m, near the Wendling parish boundary. Although there is no supporting documentary evidence, it is probable that this site was a Great Fransham customary messuage that, following an approximately 4-acre encroachment on the common pasture severing *Elverycsmore* to the west from *Hey Green* to the south, moved southwards to the edge of the latter, at TF 9214 1424, a site now under grass. The putative encroachment is largely covered by the degraded remains of ridge-and-furrow aligned east-west (Fig. 7.15). By the time relevant written sources become available, the messuage was already in its new position. The following summary of the tenurial history refers to this later messuage, although Med 95 remained within land of the associated tenement.

In July 1349 a messuage and 16 acres of which John Kigeman had died seized without heir was taken into the hands of the lord of Great Fransham manor. This may have been a freehold. In September that year a messuage and 16 acres once of Roger 'Thoonoks' (probably a late 16th-century mistranscription of Kinnoks) were granted out as a customary holding to William Gibbe. In 1384 Agnes widow of William Gybbe held at farm for her life a messuage and half of her late husband's land. In 1391 the same land was let at farm for a term of ten years to Roger Henke and his wife Agnes [?the widow Gybbe]. In 1396

John Maunfras junior took out a 4-year lease on 1½ acres of the tenement Gibbes with 5½ acres at *Kynnokscroft*. In 1397 the tenement of William Gybbes containing 24 acres was elected to the office of messor, but it was in the lord's hands.

The extent of *c*.1430 listed three elements of the tenement Gybb comprising only 9 acres: a 1-acre close once built, lying next to land of the prior of Castle Acre on the east and butting south on the common pasture; 1 acre lying between lands of the prior east and west, and butting north on the same; 7 acres in one piece between land of the prior east and of Edmund Reeve clerk (i.e. of Ellinghams manor) west, butting south on the common way called *Gybbeslane*. According to a farm rental of about the same date Simon Large held 7½ acres with an adjoining close at 4d per acre (MS 13073). A messuage called *Gybbys* was described as once built in 1454 when it was granted out as copyhold to William Large, his wife, Simon his son and his heirs, along with other lands including Med 96 (MS 13049).

In 1553 Gilbert Whiskard was the copyhold tenant of the 9 acres, and his rent was still 8s. The 1-acre close was said to be 'somtime edifyed'. It was soon to be built once again. By 1569 his rent had increased to 20s for the "ferm of a tent. with appurtenancies called Gibbys atte highe'. In 1570 he paid the same for the farm rent 'of his howse' (MS 13077). In another rental of 1570 his rent was the same for a tenement called *Gibbes at Hey Greene*. At various times between 1573 and 1582 Whiskard's farm rent was said to be for his 'howse' called *Gybbes* (MS 13079). He was in fact a sub-tenant, the copyhold remaining in the hands of the Larges and then the Mynnes: in 1573 Margaret wife of Edward Mynne of East Lexham was admitted to a messuage called *Gibbes* with a 6½ croft on the death of her uncle William Large. She surrendered the holding to the use of Nicholas Mynne gent., one of the lords of Great Fransham (MS 13062). It was to remain in Mynne's portion of manor after 1603. Before Enclosure only two subsequent glimpses at the history of this property are possible. In 1668 Amy Spencer was amerced for keeping her customary messuage called *Gybbs* in disrepair, and in 1669 Daniel Spencer son and heir of John Spencer was admitted to a messuage built called *Gybbys* with an adjoining 6½-acre croft (MC 1847/1, 741X2).

Both Med 95 and the site of the later messuage were on Great Fransham copyhold land of Henry Bensley following Enclosure. Four buildings are shown on the Enclosure map on the site of the later messuage. A small 19th-century barn still stands.

Med 96 TF 9174 1441 (Area D, HER 28889). Heavy soil, 70m OD (Fig. 7.14). A settlement site lying nearby to the east on permanent grassland is inferred from the finding of twenty medieval sherds in spoil from the recutting of *c*.20m length of north-south ditch. This contrasts with a sparse scatter of sherds in an arable field to the west and with fifteen sherds recovered from the upcast of an adjacent ditch running westwards for over 200m following the north edge of *Elverycsmore* common pasture. Conditions for seeing pottery were not good along either stretch of ditch. The only archaeological features noted in the sides of the ditches were land-drains and several recent disturbances associated with the Second World War airbase (RAF Wendling) of which this field was part.

The tenement(s) Piggis and Cokerelys was let at farm to Robert Clement for a term of 5 years in 1370. A messuage and 12 acres were granted by the lord of Great Fransham to Richard de Holt and his heirs, for an annual fee farm rent of 4s, in 1395. In *c*.1400 de Holt's rent remained the same and his lands were listed in six pieces: 8 acres in one piece next to the lord's land on the east, butting north on the field of Beeston (there was no reference to a messuage) The other five, all of 1 acre or less, were in Area F and were no longer associated with the 8-acre piece by *c*.1430. A 9-acre close called *Pigges* and afterwards *Holtes*, butting south on the common pasture, was listed amongst Great Fransham demesne in *c*.1430. According to a farm rental of about the same date Thomas Fynche held at farm 9 acres at *Pygges*, for 4½d per acre per annum (MS 13073). In 1454 a messuage lying next to *Elvereds* called *Pygges* contained 9 acres enclosed. It was granted out with other lands (see Med 95) as copyhold to William Large, his wife, son and heirs (MS 13049). In 1490 Thomas Heyward had a messuage called *Holtis* (MS 13052).

In 1537 John Large held a customary messuage called *Ellreds alias Pygges* containing 9 acres enclosed for an annual rent of 5s (MS 13075), but in another rental of the same year Richard de Holt was anachronistically entered as tenant of 12 acres of customary land (MS 13074). Land of Ellingham manor is consistently abutted to the west from *c*.1430. Useful abuttals were given in 1538: the common pasture of Great Fransham called *Elverycs Moore* to the south, and *Geldars Close* to the north (MS 13056). 'Gelders' is written on the Enclosure Award map just above the parish boundary with Beeston at TF 919 146. The tenurial history of the piece has been traced down to 1595 when it was called *Pygges* and held by John Bayley for 5s rent. His will, proved three years later, instructed his executor to sell all his free and customary properties in Great Fransham (ANW 32 Lyncolne). As this land was to remain with Nicholas Mynne's portion of Great Fransham manor after 1603, its tenurial descent is unknown.

In 1668 George Large, who held a tenement called *Everids alias Piggs* with 9 acres, had cut down and sold eleven oak and ash trees growing on his customary land. His land was confiscated, and he had to pay 60s for readmittance in the following year (MC 1847/1, 741X2).

On Great Fransham copyhold of Robert Bear following Enclosure. According to the award he had held 1 messuage and 9 acres, copyhold of Great Fransham manor. The enclosure map depicts a building in a position now covered with 19th-century farm buildings just to the west of where a 19th-century farmhouse now stands. Careful searches in the gardens of this house, which lies 130m east of the ditch which produced the sherds representing Med 96, failed to recover any medieval finds.

Med 97 TF 9154 1198 (*Quarent*. 18, HER 28876). Heavy soil, 62m OD. (Figs 7.44 and 7.55). Concentration of 13th to 19th-century sherds with 18th and 19th-century building material in dark humic soil set within a (now ploughed) enclosure, butting east on *Eastendmoor* common pasture. Ditches are visible as slight earthworks in the ploughsoil on the west, north and south sides. Immediately to the west an area of chalky clay soil is coincident with an elongated north-south pit shown on the Enclosure map. To the south of this the site of two buildings shown on the map is marked by a slight spread of 18th and 19th-century bricks and tiles. The map depicts another building within the enclosure near its north-east corner. This site can be identified with two customary holdings of Sparhams manor.

The first, the southern part, was a parcel of 12 acres with a messuage and a cottage which were once of Hamond Jocke in 1385/6. In 1504 Margery widow of Silvester Boore died seized of a messuage built and a cottage with 9 acres of the tenement Jokes. Three acres built were split off from the rest in 1514 (see Med 67). Thereafter the remainder was known as the tenement late of John Bore, and until 1546 was associated with 7 acres. From 1546 it was usually called simply the tenement Bores with 2 acres and was often said to be built. Perhaps it can be equated with the cottage of 1385/6. From 1581 it was normally described as a tenement with adjoining garden or yard (*ortum*) containing together 2 acres. Abuttals were given on only one occasion, in 1578: between the common called *Estendmore* and the common way on the south, and land of John Harwyn (the tenant of both the northern and southern parts at the time) to the north, butting west on land of the said John and on the common way, and east on the common of Little Fransham. In 1623 the upper parts of the tenement were burnt (an unusual entry in a court roll). Thereafter there was no further mention of a standing building. In 1659 the tenement Bores was said (in English) to have an adjoining yard, and in 1699 and subsequently an adjoining croft. The tenurial history has been traced down to Enclosure, and the tenants were always different from those who held the northern part. After 1728 tenants were not Fransham residents, Anthony Franklin, a miller of Necton, his son James in 1731, the latter's widow in 1740 and Thomas Forby of Stoke Ferry in 1771. William Stratton of Swaffham was admitted in 1773 and his daughter-in-law Alice Stratton in 1806.

The second holding to be included in this site, and forming the northern part, was a parcel of 5 acres once of Edmund Jocke and held by Margery Jocke in 1385/6. Land of Edmund Jok had been abutted in a charter of 1361 (MC 360/75, 713X6). Edmund Joke was a taxpayer in 1332, as was Margaret Jook in 1381. In 1507 this property was described as 5 acres with a messuage of the tenement Jookis. The tenurial history of these 5 acres is very complex. By the 1570s seven parcels, all between *Eastendmoor* and *Cannons Green*, can be distinguished. The relevant parcel here was described in 1561 as a tenement built called *Jocks* with 2½ acres and was given abuttals: between land of Faith Wyskard (the tenant of Med 68) to the north, and late of Richard Collyn now held by John Harwyn (a former and the contemporary tenant of the southern part of this site) to the south, butting east on the common pasture of Little Fransham. Abuttals given in 1599 confirm the location: land of Robert Hunt (the tenant of Med 68) to the north, butting west on the common way called the *Packwaie*. In 1581 1 acre of this 2½ acre holding was described as meadow, and from then on followed a separate tenurial descent. That of the messuage and 1½ acres, described as a garden or yard (*ortum*), and from 1740 in English as an orchard, has been traced to Enclosure, with the messuage continuously standing from 1504, when its thatching was in disrepair. The messuage was recorded as standing (*edificat.*) in 1648 when the eastern part was occupied by a sub-tenant. It was not listed in the 1664 Hearth Tax returns (Frankel and Seaman 1983, 61), but in 1666 James Dey's house, the southern part contained one hearth (Seaman 1991, 28). In 1670–3 the two occupiers of the northern part, Elizabeth Newman and Jane Purle widows, were exempted from the Hearth Tax (TNA E 179/338/422, E 179/335/890, E 179/336/535 and E 179/337/344).

On the eve of Enclosure Alice Stratton was tenant of the southern part and John Baly (styled as of Litcham in 1799) held the northern. After the Award both parts were on the Sparhams copyhold allotment of Alice Stratton, while John Baly's Sparham copyhold was partly on what had been *Eastendmoor* and partly on a former Wilcoks freehold messuage and croft (Med 68).

Med 98 TF 9090 1212 (*Quarent.* 10, HER 29218). Medium-heavy soil, 67m OD. (Figs 7.36 and 7.37). Concentration of 13th and 14th-century pottery, 20m x 20m, on the west edge of Cannons Green. There is no documentary evidence for a settlement here. A pightle of Kirkhams and Wilcoks demesne, which in 1605 contained 2 acres and 20 perches, lay next to the common on the east and south. Another pightle (½ acre) lay to the north, and one other (containing Med 100 and perhaps Med 101) to the west. This piece may have been one of two pightles leased out for 5 years to William Gurr in 1476 (MS 13141). It was pasture in 1577 and *c.*1609 (MS 13160).

On free land of Lady Essex following Enclosure.

Med 99 TF 9085 1226 (*Quarent.* 10, HER 29218 and 29217). Medium-heavy soil, 66m OD. (Figs 7.36 and 7.37). Slight concentration of 12th to 14th-century sherds, 40m north-south x 30m east-west. A small number of late Thetford-type and Grimston Thetford sherds suggest that occupation on this site might have begun in the late 11th century. It lay on demesne of Kirkhams and Wilcoks manor in what was described as a pightle of pasture and called *Dovehouseyard* in 1605. It contained 2 acres and 25 perches and butted on the common to the east and north. In 1393 John Smyth's cow damaged barley of the lord of Kirkhams in *Dufhouscroft*. Ninety-three pigeons from the dovecot were sold to various persons for 2s 7d in 1401–2, and the building was under repair in 1436–7 (MS 13126 and MS 13139). It stood *c.*300m south of the Kirkhams manor house.

In 1427–8 Alice Huberd paid 4s farm rent for a close called *Dofhousyerd* which lay next to her tenement (MS 13137). This was Med 71, which lay to the south-east on the far side of *Cannons Green* in *Quarent.* 27. At a manor court held in October 1437 John Sewles [bailiff of William Oldhall, lord of the manor] was amerced, after a presentment by the Kirkhams jury, for not clearing away manure lying around the dovecote, in accordance with an agreement made between him and the lord before the previous Easter. No income was received from the dovecote or from pasturing animals in the lord's pasture there in 1436–7, because it was held at farm by Walter Lexham, one of the two farmers of Kirkhams and Wilcoks manors (MS 13139).

Dovehouseyard was leased out in the 1440s, 1470s and 1480s. In 1491 a 2-acre pightle called *Doffehowesyerd* became copyhold, with the tenant, John Stalworthy, owing an annual rent of 1s 8d. By 1532–3 John Lacy held *Doffus yard* (HRO 8186) and in 1554 he had died seized of 2 customary acres called *Dowehouseclose* (MS 13169). It was not listed amongst tenanted lands or as demesne in 1566. By 1577 it was once again demesne.

On free land of Lady Essex following Enclosure.

Med 100 TF 9080 1203 (*Quarent.* 10, HER 29217). Medium-heavy soil, 70m OD. (Figs 7.36–7.38). Concentration of 13th and 14th-century sherds, 50m east-west x 30m north-south. Five medieval coins were recovered by metal-detecting here and/or on Med 101 and 102 (Henry II or Richard I, John or Henry III, Henry III, Edward I and illegible 14th-century). A coin of Elizabeth I and a Norwich token of 1667 were also found.

A pightle of 1 acre 10 perches, Kirkhams and Wilcoks demesne in 1605, lay between another pightle (containing Med 98) on the east, *Chowneslane* on the south and *Arrowsmithsclose* (see Med 102) on the north and west. This may have been one of two pightles leased out in 1476 (see Med 98).

Very strong linear soil marks, visible on Ordnance Survey air photographs taken in 1971, suggest that the fields had then only recently been taken into arable (Fig. 7.38). This site and Med 101 were bounded on the north by a single ditch that is cut by a pit, now ploughed over. It appears that the two sites were contained within one rectangular enclosure. Within this, incomplete lengths of seven north-south ditches are discernible. These are probably a combination of recent drainage and medieval subdivision.

In common with the other settlement sites in this *Quarent.*, the tenurial history of this one is entirely obscure. However, two pieces of written evidence may possibly be relevant. They refer to land which, if not in this *Quarent.*, is otherwise unidentifiable. In 1316 Henry le Strange of Little Fransham granted to his son William 7 acres there, lying between the common pasture on the east and land of Henry's villein Henry Sewal on the west, butting north on land of Thomas Tarkeys and south on the common pasture. An endorsement reads *tr. q. vocat.* [land called] *Prestiscroft* (MC 360/48, 713X6). Henry le Strange was lord of Kirkhams (Blake 1952, 269). In *c.*1420 Walter Pouly held freely of Wilcoks manor 5 acres with a parcel of a messuage and a barn built, in one piece called *Prestysbythe*. The name of one later tenant, John Wyot, who appeared in court rolls and land transactions between 1457 and 1467, was written above that of Walter Pouly. No later references to this land have been found.

On free land of Lady Essex following Enclosure.

Med 101 TF 9072 1205 (*Quarent.* 10, HER 29217). Medium-heavy soil, 70m OD. (Figs 7.36–7.38). Concentration of 13th and 14th-century sherds, 30m x 30m on the north-east side of a medieval road. It is uncertain whether this site fell within the same pightle as Med 100, or whether it should be included in another piece of demesne, *Arrowsmithsclose*, which lay to the north and west (see Med 102). The former is more likely in view of the air photographic evidence (see Med 100). If the very uncertain evidence cited for Med 101 is to be believed then this site was occupied by Henry Sewal, a Kirkhams villein, in 1316.

On free land of Lady Essex following Enclosure.

Med 102 TF 9056 1211 (*Quarent.* 10, HER 29217). Medium soil, 70m OD. (Figs 7.36 and 7.37). Concentration of 11th and 12th-century sherds, 30m x 30m, on the east edge of the junction between a medieval road and a common pasture (see LS 17). This site was at the west end of *Arrowsmithsclose*, a pasture close of Kirkhams and Wilcoks demesne which contained 12½ acres and 30 perches in 1605. It lay next to the common on the north and west, *Chowneslane* in part on the south, and a pightle (containing Med 100 and probably Med 101) on the south and east.

Bailiffs' account rolls contain no reference to the cropping of this close in the early 15th century. In 1429–30 John Taylor held at farm a pightle in *Narowsmythclos* for an annual rent of 1s 4d (MS 13138). One Henry Arwesmyth had been paid for ploughing on Kirkhams land in 1401–2 (MS 13126), but the surname has been not found in other sources. In 1435 the pigs of William Maunfras did damage in a close called *Arwesmethes*. In 1439 the rector of Ovington broke down fences around the lord's close called the same. In 1446–7 Henry Warde paid a rent of 12s 6d for a pightle called *Arwesmethes yerd* with 2 acres in the adjoining croft and 17½ acres in various pieces in *Millfield* (MS 13142). Its size was given as 10 acres in 1485 when it was leased to Richerus Wyskard for a 20-year term, at 9s per annum. John Wyskard senior and his son John took out a 30-year lease in 1512, at the same rent (MS 13102). In 1566 it consisted of 9 acres of pasture and in 1577 *Harrowsmythes close* contained 15½ acres and 20 perches.

Whatever may have been the origin of this close's name, it was to be forgotten in the post-medieval period. In 1526 it was called *Herry Smethes* close, in 1560 *Henr Smythes* and in 1564 *Harry Smythes close* (MS 13251, MS 13105 and MS 13104). A ditch in *Henry Smiths lane* was unscoured in 1673, and in 1683 William Powley and Anthony Bunting were ordered to 'scowre and cleanse their Dykes against a certein close of Henry Smith wch annoys the Churchway' (MC 1850/1, 858X9).

On free land of Lady Essex following Enclosure.

Med 103 TF 9096 1128 (*Quarent.* 16, HER 29222). Heavy soil, 78m OD (Fig. 7.42). Concentration of discoloured, predominantly oxidised, under- and overfired 12th to early 13th-century sherds, 20m in diameter. This is the debris from a small-scale and probably short-lived period of pottery production. A greater quantity of 'normal' medieval sherds (including Grimston ware) was spread in and around the concentration than elsewhere in this field, suggesting there had been contemporary and subsequent domestic occupation in the same place. The site, lying on the east edge of a common pasture called *Coltinges Green* in 1566, was within an 8-close of Cannons manor customary land called *the Rudde* in the 16th century. There is no documentary evidence to indicate that there was a settlement site here in the Middle Ages.

Med 105 TF 9195 1166 (*Quarent.* 29, HER 30220). Heavy soil, 63m OD. (Figs 7.48 and 7.50). Concentration of 13th and 14th-century sherds in a 22m-wide arable strip along the west edge of a permanent pasture containing rather indistinct earthworks which must also have been damaged by tillage at some stage. Ditches on the east and north sides of the sherd concentration form an enclosure measuring 60m north-south and 25m east-west and lying lengthways along the east edge of *Eastendmoor* common pasture, with its south end butting a sunken road which was called *Maryoneslane* in 1392. The east edge of the common is followed by a north-flowing stream immediately west of a hedge. Rather more pottery was recovered from the southern half of the enclosure than from the northern.

A cottage and 1 acre of the tenement Jourden[v] were held by Marion Soutere as a customary holding of Kirkhams manor in 1384. The rent of ½d was *de increment*, indicating that this was a soiled holding. The property was also held freely of Wilcoks.

Marion Soutere had died in 1394 seized of 1 acre of soiled land with a cottage once Jurdons, her heir being her son John de Schortwode, who had been a taxpayer in 1379 and 1381. He did not attend court for admission and the property was taken into the lord's hands. In 1395 the Kirkhams jury said that John and his son William had occupied it, and a writ was issued. The short Wilcoks rental of *c*.1395 listed John Shortwod's rent as 1¼d. This same holding was also entered in the Wilcoks rental of *c*.1420 as a messuage and 1 acre, freehold of Wilcoks and soiled of Kirkhams. The tenant was William atte Brook and the rent was 1¼d. A cottage with 1¼ acres of soiled land once of Marion Sowter were listed in the Kirkhams rental of 1443, with Walter at Brook as tenant and the rent ½d. The cottage lay between Walter Lexham's messuage on the north and the king's highway on the south and butted west on the common pasture. The 1¼ acres were in three pieces: ½ acre lay to the east of the cottage, and of the other two pieces one, and probably both, were in *Eastfield*. In 1451 Richard Necoll was amerced for cutting down wood growing on (*super*) the cottage. In 1452 the property was described as a messuage once built containing at the most ½ rood, when it was surrendered, along with 1 acre of soiled land called *Marionys*, by Walter at Brook to the use of Walter Lexham and his wife. In 1462 the cottage was to be void. The tenurial history has been followed to 1578, the last reference to the former cottage occurring in 1511 (MS 13102), after which only the 1¼ acres of soiled land are mentioned.

The final tenant was Robert Harlewyn, whose Kirkhams and Wilcoks lands were seized into the lord's hands in 1578 because he had been convicted of a felony, the lord taking permanent possession in 1580 (MS 13106 and MS 13416). These lands included Med 106. See Med 116 for details of the crime. In 1600 and 1603 George Stalworthy paid 8d for the farm rent of *herwyns* and *harwins* (MS 13148–9). The land was described as two pightles of demesne pasture in 1605. One contained 1¾ acre and 15 perches and lay between *Marions Lane* on the south and John Stalworthy's copyhold on the north and butted west on *Eastendmoor*. The other contained 2 roods and 30 perches and was at the east end of the former.

On Kirkhams and Wilcoks copyhold of Anne Griggs following Enclosure. No building is shown on the Enclosure map.

Med 106 TF 9195 1171 (*Quarent.* 29, HER 30220). Heavy soil, 62m OD. (Figs 7.48 and 7.50). Concentration of 13th and 14th-century sherds in a 22m-wide arable strip towards the north-west corner of a field of permanent pasture. Earthwork ditches survive on the north, south and east sides of an enclosure measuring 18m north-south by 52m east-west and abutting the east edge of *Eastendmoor* common pasture. The west end of the southern ditch forms the northern ditch of the enclosure containing Med 105. Within the enclosure at its west end there are slight indications of a house platform. A freehold of Wilcoks manor.

Simon Caton was amerced at the leet court for not scouring a watercourse at *Souteslane* in 1379 and for obstructing the road at *Maryoneslane* with underwood in 1392. He is probably to be identified with someone of this name, styled *faber* (smith) who paid Poll Tax in Wendling in 1379. Edmund Edyman held 1½ acres formerly built with a messuage, freehold of Wilcoks manor in *c*.1420. The property lay between land of William Brook (the tenant of Med 105) on the south and land of Thomas Stalworthy (Med 117) on the north and butted west on the common pasture. The rent, 5½d, was the same as that which Edmund Sawher (alias Edyman) had paid for unspecified lands in *c*.1395. He had also held a built messuage in *Quarent.* 17 on the western side of *Eastendmoor* (property no.4, **pp48–9***). John Camplion was amerced at the leet court for not scouring a watercourse at *Catons* in 1429. After an undocumented gap of almost sixty years this holding appeared in a charter grant of 1486 (MS 13235) as a messuage once built with an adjoining croft once Catones containing 1½ acres. The tenurial descent has been followed from this point until 1578. The property was conveyed by charter twice in 1520, in March and April. It was described as once built in one document (*quondam edificat.*), and as void (*vacuum*) and once of Cottons in the other (MS 13249–50). The conveyance in March was also recorded in an indenture (BL Add Ch 71048). A fourth charter recorded its conveyance in 1527 (MS 13252), and a fifth in 1549 (MC 2334/1, 958X1). Abuttals given in these documents indicate that this land was to the north of Med 105. It butted to the south not only on other land but also on the common way and must therefore have 'wrapped around' the east side of Med 105.

In 1560 on the death of the tenant, Robert Harwen, the rent was cited as 6d (MS 13105), but by the time Robert son of Robert swore fealty in 1575 the rent was only 3d (MS 13104). In 1577 it was still described a void messuage with 1½ acres, and the joint rent for this and another free acre in *Eastfield* was a mere 2d (MS 13104). Like Med 105, it was seized into the lord's hands in 1578 on account of the tenant's felony and became part of the demesne of Kirkhams and Wilcoks manor (MS 13106).

On Kirkhams and Wilcoks copyhold of Anne Griggs following Enclosure. No building is shown on the Enclosure map.

Med 107 TF 9162 1312 (Area G, HER 20742). Medium-heavy soil, 57m OD (Fig. 7.14). Concentration of 12th and 13th-century sherds, 30m east-west x 20m north-south, on the western edge of *Eastendmoor* common pasture. In tenurial terms this site is particularly interesting being both a freehold of Great Fransham and a customary holding of Kirkhams manor.

Richard Heyhe was distrained, along with other free tenants, to swear fealty to the lord of Kirkhams in 1336. Richard Le Heghe was a Great Fransham taxpayer in 1332. In 1372 the lord of Kirkhams granted a messuage with adjoining croft containing ½ acre in Great Fransham once of Richard le Heye to Robert Wattys for life to hold by customary tenure, for a rent of 2 hens, and 2 days of reaping in autumn. John Fuller was the next tenant and was probably admitted in 1375/6 (court roll missing). He was a taxpayer in 1379. According to additions made in c.1391 to the Kirkhams rental of 1384, the property was held by John Fuller as ½ acre and a parcel of one toft, rent and services as above, plus 1d. Fuller had died by 1398–9 (MS 13125). In the Great Fransham rental of c.1400 a free messuage with a headland (*forera*) was held for a rent of 1d farthing by Edmund Oldhall [lord of Kirkhams manor] once of Peter le Strange and once of Richard le Heye by the right of his wife Christine. It butted east on the common pasture of Great Fransham. At a Kirkhams manor court held in 1410 the property was described as ½ acre of customary land in Great Fransham, and in 1411 as a toft with a ½-acre croft once of Agnes Fuller. In 1443 Robert Droury [a Great Fransham man] held ½ acre with a parcel of a toft once of Richard Heyghe and afterwards of John Fuller, for the same rent and services as in c.1391. The tenurial descent can be followed, with a few gaps, from 1443. The latest evidence that the holding was still considered as a freehold of Great Fransham manor was in a short rental of 1537 (MS 13074): Edmund Oldhall now Giles Capell [lord of Kirkhams] held a messuage once of Richard Hey for an annual rent of 1¼d, a note adding that it was also a Kirkhams customary holding (*Will. Large sen. ten. nat. per copiam de manerio de Fr. Parva*). The will of William Large the elder of Great Fransham was proved in 1541 (ANW 175 Athowe).

In 1605 the property was described as ½ acre of copyhold in Great Fransham, with parcel of a toft once of John Fullers. 'It hath a tenent new builte upon it'. The annual rent was 7d. This amount was paid by one John Crowdson in 1618, and a gloss of 1627/8 stated it was paid by Simon Allen (MS 13153). There follows an interruption in the story after which the property had shrunk. In 1674 Thomas Brock had died, having held for life a messuage or tenement and ¼ acre called a hempland in Great Fransham, formerly of Thomas Beale, lying next to the common pasture on the east. His son John Brock was admitted, and the annual rent had also shrunk, to 3d. Thomas Case, tanner of Great Fransham and a major landholder, was admitted in 1743, Brock having died 'several years since' (he had been buried at Great Fransham in 1699). The property was to remain with Case's descendants into the 19th century.

To the south of this site a pair of 19th-century cottages now sit within a hedged close. This is of a different shape to that shown on the Enclosure map and the 1928 edition OS 1:2500 scale map. Portions of the northern and western parts of the earlier close are now within the surrounding arable and have produced 16th to 20th-century sherds. The former cottage garden is shown by the usual dark garden-type soil, and its edges are marked by a pronounced upward scarp into the arable field proper to the west and north. The medieval site sits on the top of the scarp to the north. The former enclosure contained a building following Enclosure and was copyhold of Kirkhams and Wilcoks, held by Thomas Henry Case. At a court held in 1807 following the Enclosure Act he was said to stand admitted to a messuage and ¼ acre of copyhold. The messuage lay on 1 rood and 3 perches of land, and in lieu of common rights he was allotted a further 1 acre and 27 perches of former common on the south side.

It would seem therefore that the medieval site was on the southern headland of a north-south furlong in *Henfield* and that it had ceased to be occupied for many years before it entered the documentary record in the later 14th century. At the end of the 16th century a rectangular encroachment of slightly more than ½ acre was made onto the common from the west and north for the re-establishment of the tenement 'new builte' in 1605, and finally another chunk, of more than 1 acre, was detached from the former common in 1807.

Med 108 TF 9160 1288 (Area G, HER 20639). Medium soil, 60m OD (Fig. 7.14). The site is now inaccessible beneath buildings and is inferred from 11th-century and later sherds (see LS 15) found in an arable field immediately to the west. It was a customary holding of Great Fransham manor in c.1400 consisting of a messuage once of Roger Browne held by Katherine Rad for the annual rent of 1d and 1 hen, and 3 autumn boon-works. It lay next to the common pasture on the east and butted south on the same. This common was *Eastendmoor*. The 15th-century tenurial descent is a blank. His rent total shows that Thomas Ringold was tenant of this and other copyhold lands in 1511/2. He conveyed all of them to John Bryde in 1529. When Bryde showed his copy at a manor court held in 1544 this property was described as a cottage built called *Cookes* lying at *Pystile* (MS 13056). Five acres of customary land called *Pysecroft* lay in *Henfield* to the north-west.

In 1603 the holding passed into the Capell portion of Great Fransham manor and was held until at least 1609 by Christopher Hodgskyn (MS 13082). At the end of a gap in surviving manor court records the property reappeared in 1670 as a tenement or cottage with ¼ acre. By 1677 it was described as a messuage or tenement with a hempland (*linario*) containing 1½ roods. In 1713 Edward Wacey of Longham became tenant (MC 969/1, 858X7), and sometime after 1726 during another gap in surviving court proceedings, he sold the holding to Thomas Case, tanner of Great Fransham. It was specified in Case's will, proved in 1761, as a house and land purchased from Edward Wacey, and was left to Thomas' third son Edward (ANW W55.303 1761).

At a manor court held in 1807 after the Enclosure Act, Anne wife of Clement Overton, claimed to be entitled, by virtue of a marriage settlement with her late husband Edward Case, to a messuage and 1½ roods, to which Thomas Henry Case then stood admitted. Anne Overton was then admitted to a copyhold at TF 9018 1287 some 1.4km to the west, for and in lieu of the land she had claimed (MC 969/2, 858X7). The real successor to this holding was the magnificent Hyde Hall (Pevsner and Wilson 1991, 367) built on the western edge of the common in the 1770s by Edward Case, the copyhold tenant and then husband of Anne. Hyde Hall was the freehold of Anne Overton following Enclosure.

Med 109 TF 8989 1300 (Area M, HER 21618). Light to medium soil, 73m OD (Fig. 7.24). A small number of late 15th- and 16th-century sherds was recovered amongst a mass of late 17th to 20th-century sherds and building material in a matrix of dark grey garden soil, over an area of 40m x 40m in the angle between the *Greenway* on the north and a medieval road leading towards Little Fransham on the east. This site can be equated with the 'newe howse ther att the chyrch gate' which John Crudde, a lord of Great Fransham manor, left to his servant

Margaret for life with reversion to his son Nicholas in his will, written in 1499 and proved in 1500 (NCC 43–5 Wight). This may also be the same as a yard or garden (*ortum*) near Great Fransham church, enclosed within a ditch and with a building (*domus*) on it, which Nicholas Mynne of Little Fransham reserved to himself in a charter of 1509 granting lands to the trustees of the Necton Town charity (PD 143/77). These lands had been granted by John Crudde in 1491 to his wife, Nicholas Mynne and four others, to follow the uses of his will (MS 424). The tenurial status of the land on which this house stood is uncertain, and nothing is known of the site's history after 1509.

On freehold of Mr Buck following Enclosure. A building is shown on the Enclosure map. A house stood on the site until *c*.1960.

Med 111 TF 9155 1457 (Area D, HER 28889). Heavy soil, 72m OD (Fig. 7.14). Concentration of 13th and 14th-century sherds 20m in diameter, on the east edge of a common pasture called *Elverycsmore* and adjacent to the Beeston parish boundary, in a field named *Dimers* on a map of 1831 (MC 52/65, 505X8), but *Divers* (sic) on the Enclosure map. A freehold of Ellinghams manor.

A Robert Dymes of Beeston was amerced at the Mills-on-the-Moor leet court in 1469 and 1471, as was Agnes Smyth alias Dymes in 1472. *Dymesclos*, which seems to have extended into Beeston, was named in 1480–3 (MS 13048). A close called *Great Dynnes* was said to be demesne at an Ellinghams manor court held in 1587. The will of John Large, butcher of Little Fransham, proved in 1651, referred to lands in Beeston and Great Fransham called *Great Dinnes* that he had purchased from John Beckham of Narford (ANW 461 1651). Beckham had been lord of Ellinghams until 1648. *Dimes Closes* in Beeston and Great Fransham were also named in the will of John Halcott, a London lawyer, which was written in 1681 (ANW 290 1683–4, MR/RO309). In 1754 Matthew Halcott acknowledged at an Ellinghams manor court that he held free lands in Great Fransham called *Dines*, and he had held lands in Beeston and Great Fransham according to his will, proved in 1770 (ANW W52.58 1770).

On free land of J.G. Booty following Enclosure. No building is shown on the Enclosure map.

Med 112 TF 9209 1401 (Area D, HER 33589). Heavy soil, 70m OD. (Figs 7.14 and 7.15). Two distinct holdings, neither subjected to survey by fieldwalking, lay within an area of permanent grass and farm buildings on the western edge of *Hey Green*. On the north a messuage with 1 acre of the tenement *Kynnokes*, once of Edmund Hey, was held by Reginald Pope as customary land of Great Fransham manor in *c*.1400, for an annual rent of 7d. John Kinnok / Kynnoks was a taxpayer in 1327 and 1332, and again in 1337. In 1346 1 acre of customary land purchased by Richard Kynnock was seized into the lord's hands and at the same court Adam Kynnock was distrained to show his charter for 1½ roods of free land. In 1349 Adam Kynott had died seized of a messuage, 2 acres and ½ rood, leaving his brother Richard as heir. Richard Kynott, a villein (*nativus*) of the lord, was granted 1 acre of demesne on a 5-year lease in 1365, and in 1368 Edmund le Heye senior was said to have pulled down a building (*domus*) on the tenement *Kynotts*, to the value of half a mark. John Kynnoc was a taxpayer in 1381. In 1397 1 acre of soiled land with a messuage was surrendered by Edmund Heyes senior and Reginald Pope was admitted. In *c*.1400 the property was next to Pope's messuage on the south and butted west on pasture of the prior of Castle Acre. One acre with a cottage was surrendered by Pope in 1401 and Simon and Alice Large were admitted. After a gap in the remainder of the 15th and the beginning of the 16th century, the tenurial history resumes in 1537 (MS 13074–5). In 1553 a messuage with 1 acre of the tenement *Kynockes* sometime Edmund Hay were copyhold, the tenant being 'Reginald Pope nowe Henry Skott' (MS 13077). After this time the rent was subsumed under that due for the property immediately to the south, Richard Burgess paying a joint rent of 1s 5d in 1595.

The property survives under grass as a degraded rectangular enclosure containing *c*.480m^2 and surrounded on the north and west by ditches, on the south by a scarp and on the east by a pond on the common edge. One medieval sherd was recovered from a molehill within the enclosure and another immediately to the north.

The southern property was also held by Reginald Pope in *c*.1400 as a messuage, a portion of a messuage and 1 acre, freehold of Great Fransham manor, once of Edmund Hey, lying next to the lord's land called *Haddocks* on the south and butting east on the common, called *le Heygrene* in one version of the rental (MS 13084 Book B). Pope also held 1½ acres of free land and paid a joint annual rent of 10d. A Thomas le Heye was a taxpayer in 1337. Hamon de Sengham swore fealty to the lord of Great Fransham in 1343 and died in 1349 seized of a messuage, 1 acre and ½ rood, with Edmund son of John Heigh as his heir. Edmund was underaged and the land remained in the lord's hands, as did 3 acres to which he was heir on the death of his sister Agnes le Heigh. For Edmund Heye see Med 55. Edmund was a taxpayer in 1379. The tenurial history of this land during the 15th century is also unknown. By 1511 it was held by Robert Crowe, tenant of the property to the north. William Bennett, who held both in the 1560s, was amerced for not scouring ditches in his close next to the common way called *Heighgrengate* in 1564 and next to *Heighgrenemore* in 1565 (MS 13061). Both properties were held by the same men throughout the 16th century, with the latest evidence of tenure being in a rental of 1595. In 1603 they remained in the portion of Great Fransham manor held by Nicholas Mynne esq. and as a consequence nothing is known of their later history. In a typically misleading way the Enclosure Award cut across the true tenurial history of both holdings: they fell within an allotment to Abel Brereton of 2 acres, copyhold of the Capel portion of Great Fransham manor (Mills on the Moor with Great Fransham). Brereton, who was of Brinton in Norfolk, had held copyhold land of this manor which actually lay *c*.750m to the south-west.

The 19th-century farmhouse and outbuildings on the site of Abel Brereton's allotment were demolished in 1998. No significant archaeological evidence was recovered from observations of the groundworks for new buildings in the same area. Topsoil was extremely thin over very heavy natural clay with a high water table. Only post-medieval sherds were recovered. However, minor below-ground disturbances immediately to the west of the former farm buildings, at TF 9208 1402, yielded 39 sherds of the 13th to the 16th centuries. This suggests either that during the post-medieval period there was an encroachment eastward onto the common, or that intense use of the area of the buildings, as stockyards etc., had eradicated all traces of medieval occupation. The latter is more likely.

Med 113 TF 9165 1342 to 9170 1320 (Area E, HER 21624–5, 28875 and 28892). Medium to heavy soil, 56–58m OD (Figs 7.14 and 7.16). An area on the eastern edge of *Doesgate* and *Eastendmoor* is now covered by farm buildings, a bungalow, permanent grass with earthworks, a railway embankment and a plantation. Within the area there is documentary evidence of varying quality for a row of six settlement sites which, for brevity, have been allotted a single entry. A minor aura of Late Saxon sherds shows that occupation began in the 11th, or perhaps the 10th century (LS 11). Earthworks survive in a pasture field north of a railway embankment. A very pronounced house platform, in part destroyed by a modern bungalow and garden, lies at the east end of a toft and north of a bank which does not extend as far west as a scarp marking the edge of *Eastendmoor*. South of the bank a rectangular toft has no internal features and is edged by ditches to the east and south. The next toft on the south has a shallow pit near the north-west corner on the west side of a slight bank. Its southern and eastern sides are marked by ditches, and the line of the southern ditch protrudes as a bulbous terminal beyond the eastern. At the southern end there are slight indications of another toft which lies largely beneath the railway embankment. South of this a triangular piece of scrubland, now a plantation, contains a continuance of the common edge scarp and is edged on the south by an open ditch. The documented properties will be summarised from north to south. All lay within the southern half of a block of free land (23 acres 3 roods and 12 perches) held by Rev. Baily Wallis following Enclosure. Four buildings are depicted on the Enclosure map at the northern end of the row and a single building at the south end. The same number of buildings appear on the 1838 Tithe map. One of the northern four and that to the south were dwelling houses (DN/TA 189). The site of the latter lies under the embankment.

1. In *c*.1400 1 enclosed acre of Great Fransham manor customary land was held by John de Poketon. It butted west on the common pasture and lay on the north side of de Poketon's messuage and land. John Peketone was a taxpayer in 1379. By 1537, when John Large was tenant, a bake house stood there (MS 13075) and in 1560 the tenant was ordered to repair it (MS 13059). The messuage of John de Poketon, which had 1 acre in the croft, was also a Great Fransham customary holding. It butted west on the common pasture and lay north of another of his messuages. In 1553 the common pasture was named as *Fendersmore* (MS 13077). In the 16th century this land and that to the north were held by the same tenants. In 1603 a 'cottage customarye' and 1 acre passed into the Capel portion of Great Fransham manor and its tenurial descent can be followed, with some gaps, down to Enclosure. Following the Act land containing this holding was allotted to Rev. Baily Wallis, who did not hold lands of the Capel portion, and in 1812 Abel Brereton of Brinton, the real tenant, was admitted to lands elsewhere in Great Fransham (Med 112).

2. A free messuage with 1¼ acres in the croft was first listed in the detailed Kirkhams rental of 1443 when it was described as once of Alice daughter of Henry Kynnok and was held by William Ryngolf for an annual rent of 2d. Its location is far from certain, and the abuttals, between land of the prior of West Acre north and of Great Fransham manor south, are of no help. In *c*.1460 and *c*.1487 the tenant was William Large who paid a rent of 1½d. In 1502 William Large senior held 1 acre once of William Ryngolf for 1d rent. It lay next to his messuage between the prior of West Acre's land north and his own land south. No later reference to this property has been found.

3. One of John de Poketon's other messuages was a freehold of Kirkhams manor. In 1384 he held, for an annual rent of 3d, a messuage and 1 acre of the fee of Roger le Strange and in the croft once of Ralph Heyie, which butted west on the common and lay to the south of a toft and land of Agnes de Fransham [lord of Great Fransham manor]. At a Kirkhams manor court held in 1333 William son of Roger le Strange was distrained to show how he had entered the lord's fee. In June 1336 the tenant of the lands of Roger le Strange was distrained to swear fealty, as was William son of Roger in July. In *c*.1375 Edmund de Poketon held a messuage and 1 acre once of Richard le Heigh for 3d rent and John Poketon held the same in *c*.1395. In a messor's account roll for 1403–4 an allowance of 3d was made on the rent arrears of John Bekyrton because the rent could not be collected (*eo quod null. modo potest levar.*, MS 13128). In the 15th and earlier 16th centuries the property was held by various members of the Large family, tenants of lands to the north. In a charter grant of 1505 the messuage, with 1 acre adjoining, was described as built (MC 2755/4/1, 1004X2).

4. In 1548 John Large held ¼ acre of Rougholme customary land which lay between lands of Robert Howell east and south and the common on the west (TNA SC 12/3/22). This piece was the same as a customary cottage built lying next to *Jantes Stile* in *Estende* in Great Fransham which was held by Alice Large widow in 1552, for an annual rent of 1d (TNA SC 12/3/23). It was amongst Rougholme lands which became part of the possessions of Richard Hoo in 1548, along with the ex-Wendling Abbey manors of Northendhall and Guntons. At a manor court held in 1552, court proceedings of 1444 and 1470 relating to the tenure of the piece were quoted. In 1553 the cottage was described as once built. A bake house on the property was in total disrepair in 1559 and 1560 (TNA SC 2/192/96). One Thomas Complin had been admitted to a decayed tenement lying next to *Janckstyle* in *Eastend* in 1591 and surrendered the same to the use of Henry Bayley in 1615. The tenurial descent of the property, invariably described as decayed or void, can be followed to Enclosure. In 1753 it passed, as a customary holding, into the hands of Charles and John Bailey, lords of the manors of Ellinghams and Rougholme (EVL 595 and 596).

Two acres called *Kayds closse* or *Cadescloos* and late of Robert Crowe, copyhold of Rougholme manor, were held by Robert Howell in 1548 and 1552 for an annual rent of 11d (TNA SC 12/3/23 and SC 12/3/22). This land lay between the cottage on the north and no.5 to the south but did not extend west to the common edge. It came within the fee of Richard Hoo in 1552. In 1645 John Spencer became tenant and in 1653 he also acquired the cottage. Thereafter both properties were held by the same people.

5. A messuage built and 1½ acres, freehold of Ellinghams manor, one of Richard Holte and later of William Cadde, were held by Robert Hovell for 1d annual rent in *c.*1550. The property lay between the messuage and land of Thomas Cadde south and north, the land of Thomas Harlewyn east and the common pasture west. At the same time Hovell also held a parcel of a freehold messuage, late of William Cadde and afterwards of Thomas Cadde, for 1d rent (KIM 1/8/16). William Cade's fixed rent due to Ellinghams manor in 1440–1 and 1442–3 had been cited as 1s 4d (MS 13039 and MS 13140). Robert Hovell of Wendling died in 1567, leaving lands in Great Fransham to his wife for life with reversion to his son Thomas (NCC 30 Bunne). At two Ellinghams manor courts held in 1582 it was ordered that a customary messuage built with 1½ acres in the croft of the tenement Doyes, of which Robert Hovell had died seized fourteen years earlier, be taken into the lord's hands, following illegal occupation by Thomas Jewell. The north end of the messuage was said to have fallen down. There was considerable confusion as to both the tenurial status and location of the property. It lay next to the common pasture on the west and was certainly of customary tenure when granted to Adam Bosom gent. at the second court held in 1582. Like Robert Hovell, Bosom was of Wendling, and died in 1612 (ANW 97 Dewpleet). In 1669 Daniel Spencer, tenant of nos 4 and 5, was admitted, on the death of his father John, to a messuage built called *Cadds Barne* with 1½ acres in the croft. Thereafter the tenurial descent was the same as those of nos 4 and 5.

6. The final property in the row, a freehold pightle of Cannons manor, was that with the most obscure documentary coverage. Thomas Drewry's rent in *c.*1507–10 was 1d (CUL Dd VIII 42). There were close connections between the Drewry and Crowe families. In 1548 the tenant of land late of Robert Crowe was amerced for default of suit of court, as was Robert Hovell tenant of the same land in 1549 and in 1551–5. Thomas Jewell was frequently amerced for the same between 1576 and 1589. In 1582 no.6 was said to lie next to a void messuage and free croft late of Robert Hovell now of Thomas Jewell on the south. It was presented at a Cannons manor court in 1592 that Thomas Jewell had died seized of various free lands and tenements which he had held for 1d rent. In 1596 Thomas Hovell swore fealty for a pightle of free land which he held for 1d rent. It lay in *Harwynes felde* in Great Fransham next to land of John Blomfeld late Large's. Hogan Jewell was amerced for default in 1597, as was Thomas Hovell in 1602, and the tenant of land late of Thomas Hovell in 1612–15. Edmund Brockinnge, who had married Thomas' widow Alice, swore fealty for a piece of land in Great Fransham in 1616. Alice Alyeard, late wife of Edmund Browning, had died seized of the same piece in 1625 and her eldest son Hogan Hovell was distrained to swear fealty. In 1628 Huggan and Nicholas Hovell had sold free land which they had held for 1d rent to William Willymot. He was last amerced for default in 1633, and his copyhold rent was cited as 1d in 1649. No further reference to the property has been found.

Med 114 TF 9150 1330 to 9160 1330 (Area G, HER 20791, 30219 and 31011). Medium to heavy soil, 56m OD (Fig. 7.14). Most of this area, which lies under a railway embankment, buildings, a plantation and lawns, was not available for fieldwalking. One patch, at TF 9157 1332 and measuring 40m north-south by 26m east-west, was examined under poor conditions after the removal of an orchard. Twenty-five medieval sherds were recovered from the southern half (HER 31011). To the east and west of here only a few pieces of post-medieval pottery were found in a flower bed and in a field under very poor conditions. However, documentary evidence is available for four medieval settlements here, between meadow, pasture and common pasture to the north, *Henfield* to the south and *Eastendmoor* to the east. The evidence is somewhat lacking in topographical accuracy, but the four properties will be described from west to east.

1. In *c.*1430 a ¾-acre close of Great Fransham demesne was described as once built and as lying in *Henfield* at (*apud*) the Chapel, i.e. St Katherine's chapel which must have stood to the west. The close was not situated immediately south of low-lying ground, pasture or meadow because land of one Thomas Southwood lay to the north. Southwood was described as a clerk (*capell.*) in one version of the extent (MS 13084 Book A). By 1537 the close was held by customary tenure for an annual rent of 4d when it passed from William Large senior to John Warner, and there was no reference to a former building (MS 13056 and MS 13075). The next tenant was Richard Constable who was admitted in 1542 and died in 1544. Thomas Burston and his wife were admitted on the surrender of Constable's son in 1544 (MS 13056). It was named as *Chappel close* in the will of Thomas Burston, husbandman of Beeston-next-Mileham, which was proved in 1568 (NCC 88 Ponder). In 1591 and 1595 ¾ acre of customary land was held by Thomas Ede for 4d rent. Thereafter the tenurial descent is unknown, although in 1658 John Spencer bequeathed a 3-acre enclosure called *Chapell Close* to his son Daniel (TNA PROB 11/274/546). It had been purchased from Mr Hastnet, who must have been Samuel Harsnett esq., lord of Great Fransham manor at this time (Carthew 1879, 160). The northern part of *Henfield* was named *Chapel Close* on the 1839 Tithe map (DN/TA 189).

2. A free messuage, once of Agnes Clement, was held of Great Fransham manor by John Fuller in *c.*1400. It lay next to the common pasture on the west and butted north on the same common. For John Fuller see Med 107. Thomas and Hugh Clement were taxpayers in 1332. Hugh Clements had died in 1349 seized of a messuage and 1¾ acres. Leaving an underaged son Robert as heir. A gloss in the rental of *c.*1400 gives the name Etheldr. Taylor as a subsequent tenant. In *c.*1430 no.1 butted east on the messuage of Robert Taylor. Members of the Taylor alias Droury family occur frequently in Great Fransham documents throughout the 15th century. At 1511 William Large junior was said to have purchased a messuage built and certain free lands from Robert Droury. In his will, proved in 1516, William Large son of Robert left his 'place, lond free & bond' to the disposal of his executors (NCC 102 Spyrlynge). In 1527 William Large senior, who had been a witness to this will, was tenant (MS 13074 and MS 13075), and in the same year the property was acquired by John Warner (MS 13056). For the remainder of the 16th century this messuage and no.1 were held by the same tenants, but thereafter their tenurial history is not known.

3. A free messuage, once of Peter Geney, was held of the prior of Castle Acre by Mancer Large in *c*.1400. The prior held of the lord of Great Fransham in pure and perpetual alms and Large's annual rent payable to the lord of Great Fransham was ½d. This messuage was not given abuttals in any document, and it has been located by reference to various lands held by tenants in *Henfield*.

The messuage can be, very tentatively, identified with one messuage that features in five undated deeds in the Castle Acre cartulary (BL Harley MS 2110 f92 and 94). Gilbert de Fransham granted to Isabel wife of Reginald son of Adelwald of Fransham and to Reginald's son Thomas, the messuage of Reginald with 8 acres in his toft, 4ac in *Tullescroft* and 1 acre in *Caulinge*, to hold for the rent of a gilt spur or 6d. Thomas son of Reginald granted to Castle Acre priory, with the assent of his two sons, all that he held in Fransham of Gilbert de Fransham, arable and non-arable lands with a messuage and all buildings belonging, as well as rents due to him from three tenants. Thomas' gift was confirmed in two deeds by his sons, Roger and Reginald, and in another by Gilbert de Fransham knight. If the identification of Reginald's messuage with that held by Mancer Large is correct, then most of the other lands must have become disassociated from it during the 13th or 14th centuries. The 4 acres in *Tullescroft* may be the same as 4 acres at *Ladismer* (Area K) and once of Roger Knott, which in *c*.1400 were held by Mancer Large for 4d rent. In 1369 Simon [Fincham] rector of Great Fransham and Thomas his chaplain were distrained to show title and swear fealty for 4 acres once of Peter Giney and for which a rent of 4½d was payable. The extra halfpenny may have been for the messuage. The two properties continued to be held by the same tenants throughout the 16th century.

The messuage once of Mancer Large was held by John Futche between 1537 and 1553 (MS 13074–6 and MS 13077), and it is probably the same as the messuage of John Large which lay to the north of *Pysecroft* according to one version of the extent of *c*.1430 (MS 11352). In 1560 Thomas Stalworthy was distrained to swear fealty for freehold lands late of John Futche (MS 13059), and in 1575 Henry Mynne paid free rent late Storyes, i.e. Stalworthy's. By 1581 John Ranson was tenant, the rent having risen to ¾d (MS 13079). Robert Burges paid ½d free rent late Futches in 1591. In an indenture lease of 1603 *Pyes Croft* was said to butt north on the messuage of Richard Burges, once Large's (MS 13278).

After the beginning of the 17th century no details of tenure under Great Fransham manor are known, but it is likely that the messuage, never described more specifically than as 'certain free lands', occurs in court proceedings, beginning in 1623, of the manor of Herringshall and Dikewood in Wendling, the post-dissolution successor of the Castle Acre manor (MC 2104/1–4, 920X9). Interestingly these court books show that the tenurial descent down to Enclosure to have been identical to that of 6¼ acres of Ellinghams customary land in two pieces at *Medowe Close ende* (Area C). In 1623 Robert Powly clerk was amerced for default of suit of court and in 1626 it was presented that he held certain land late of Richard Burgis for 10d annual rent, but whether he held by free or customary tenure was not known. At the time of Enclosure, the tenant was Abel Brereton, but Herringshall and Dikewood manor was not involved in Great Fransham Enclosure proceedings, and lands allotted to Brereton were not on this site.

4. The most easterly messuage in the group of four was a Great Fransham freehold. John Spirling was a taxpayer in 1327 and 1332. In 1343 Margaret Spirling was distrained for default of suit of court, and a note added that John Spirling now held [the property] on her behalf (*modo tenuret...pro eadem*). John swore fealty at the same court and died in 1349, seized of a messuage and 3 acres, leaving his underaged son Richard as heir. The latter, or someone with the same name, held a messuage, 3¾ acres in six pieces and 1 acre of meadow in *c*.1400 for an annual rent of 10d. The messuage butted east on the common pasture of Great Fransham.

Richard Spirling also held 5 acres in *Spyrling croft*, freehold of the Sparhams manor, in 1385/6. This must relate closely to the 7 acres and 1 acre of meadow that had been held by Thomas de Eston, Matilda Ale and John Spyrling of John le Bretun, lord of Sparhams, in *c*.1279 (Table 6.2 no.27).

All or part of the Spirling holding is probably the same as a tenement called *Shyrlynges* that was left by William Maschale to his wife Aveline for her life, with reversion to Aveline daughter of John Blyford, in his will proved in 1439 (NCC 76 Doke). Thomas Harlwyn of Great Fransham may have been tenant later in the 15th century. In his will, proved in 1482, he left all his possessions to his wife and Robert his son (NCC 91A Caston). In the same year a leet court jury ordered a boundary to be made between the lands of Robert Droury and John Cade at *Spyrlyngescroft* (MS 13048). In 1493 Nicholas Mynne [of Little Fransham] swore fealty at a Sparhams manor court for 5 acres in Great Fransham, once of William Mascall, that he had purchased from John Cade.

Nicholas Mynne was tenant of the Great Fransham holding in 1511 to judge from the rent that he paid (MS 13056). All bar the 1 acre of meadow was held by Edward Mynne in 1537 (MS 13074 and MS 13075). He was to acquire the greater part of the lordship of Great Fransham in 1538, and to hold his first court in 1539 (MS 13056). In his will, proved in 1543, he left his tenement called *Spirlings* with all lands in Great Fransham 'sometime Harlewins, Larges and Brondes', to his son Henry. In Edward's Inquisition Post Mortem the property was described as a messuage built and 3 acres in the croft adjoining called *Spirlyngs* (TNA C 142/70/6).

Henry Mynne, who was to be lord of Great Fransham manor between 1547 and 1566, sold various Great Fransham free lands to John Harydance in 1544. In the same year Harydance swore fealty for, *inter alia*, a messuage and 3¾ acres once of Richard Spyrlynge, which he held for 10d rent (MS 13056). By 1553 Walter Harydance was tenant of not much more than the messuage, paying only 2d rent 'the one penny is for the mese and the other for the backehowse close within the garden'. However, his rent total suggests that he held the 3¾ acres as well (MS 13077).

In 1570 Simon Allen paid £17 farm rent for the tenement Spirlinges. In 1581–2 John Mase paid the same (MS 13079) at a time when Nicholas, the underaged son of Henry Mynne, was lord of Great Fransham and in the wardship of Andrew Clark gent., his step father. At this time many tenanted lands had been engrossed by the lord and were leased out at rents which were astronomical in comparison with those that had been charged for ancient freeholds and copyholds. It is certain, though, that much more than a messuage and 3¾ acres were involved in the above lease. A late 16th-century gloss against one version of the rental of *c*.1400 reads 'Mr Mynne wold have 40a[cres] belong to this mess late Spirlyngs' (MS 13084 Book B).

The tenurial history of the Spirlings messuage falters after the 1580s, but the name was still current in 1674 when leet court proceedings referred to a common footway from *Eastend* to the parish church running through several lands called *Spurlings* and *Katherine Mead* (MC 969/1, 858X7). Abuttals for Med 107 given in the will, proved in 1699, of John Brock blacksmith of Great Fransham, indicate that Brock's dwelling house must have been on or about the site of the Spirlings messuage. He left to his wife Sarah with reversion to his son John the houses [plural] in which he lived, with shop, outhouses, meadow, hempland, outyard and outhouses. The same property, which must have included all or some of the other three messuages to the west, was the messuage or tenement called *Harwins* with 30 acres of pasture, meadow and arable in Great Fransham that was itemised in a draft marriage settlement of 1761 between Thomas Case of King's Lynn gent. and Martha Mallet of Dunton (Salmon A).

The tenurial descent of the 5 acres of Sparhams freehold closely followed that of the messuage, and can be traced throughout amercements for default, oaths of fealty and entries in rentals: Nicholas Mynne down to 1625, Robert Freeman 1676–86, his heirs 1689, Thomas Case in the right of his wife daughter of Freeman 1694–1735, Thomas Case senior 1758, Edward Case 1762, his son Edward 1782–3, and his son Thomas Henry 1783–99.

Following Enclosure Rev. Baily Wallis held a freehold block containing 8 acres 3 roods 37 perches on either side of the stream at the northern end of *Henfield*. This must have included the sites of two or three of the above messuages. The main part of northern *Henfield*, 15 acres 1 rood 22 perches, was the freehold of Thomas Henry Case. The north-east corner including a house and part of the enclosed common, was a freehold of William Sizeling containing 1 acre 3 roods and 24 perches (and the site of Spirlings messuage). Fortunately, two deeds of feoffment show that the house had then only recently left the ownership of Thomas Henry Case. In 1801 he had conveyed a messuage or cottage with yard or garden and grass pightle or enclosure adjoining, butting on the common pasture north and east, to Elizabeth Drew widow of Little Fransham, and in 1806 she had sold the same to William Sizeling pedlar of Hilborough (Salmon F and G).

Med 115 TF 9233 1241 (adjacent to Area O, HER 30217). Heavy soil, 53m OD (Figs 7.19 and 7.26). Concentration of 13th-century pottery, 35m north-south by 25m east-west, lying 10m south of a stream in Wendling parish immediately against the boundary with Great Fransham and near the northern end of *Southwoodfield*. Until the 1950s a small field to the west in Great Fransham was separated from the site by a hedge, while the boundary to the south was physically unmarked by the early 19th century, with the Enclosure map showing an enclosure called *Wrangle Acre* straddling the division between the parishes.

In *c*.1430 2 acres called *Ravenes*, with 2 acres in the croft where once there was a messuage, were part of the demesne of Great Fransham manor. The land lay in *Southwoodfield* in Great Fransham, west of the land of *Echerards* and east of the common way leading from *Southwood* to *Pynkesmedow* and north of 2 acres of the same tenement. The latter piece had *Hulverhegge lane* on its west side and a common path from East Dereham on the south. Two more acres of the same tenement butted north on a common path leading from Great Fransham to East Dereham market and lay east of land of Henry Ram.

Four acres and a messuage called *Ravensyard* were farmed out to Thomas Fulcher for five years in 1369. In 1374 Fulcher took out a lease (term not stated) on two messuages with a building (*due mess. cum un. domo super*) and six acres which once were Ravenes, along with *Emesaker* and 1 acre next to land of John de Shortwode, for a rent of 2 quarters of barley. An enclosure and 6 acres of the tenement Ravenes were farmed out to Thomas Fulcher in 1382 during the lifetime of the lord, for the same rent.

The site lies remarkably close to the present course of a stream, which cannot have strayed very far from its medieval position. A bridge carrying a north-south lane over the watercourse just to the north was known as *Weston Brygge* in 1370. Despite its low-lying location, this area was probably not meadow in the medieval period because a thin sprinkling of medieval sherds occurs to the east, west and north. A pronounced east-west headland bank *c*.60m south of the site must mark the northern edge of *Southwoodfield* proper.

At Enclosure of Great Fransham on free land of Matthew Nelson esq., and following the Enclosure of Wendling in 1815 on free land of J. Nelson (C/Sca 2/323).

Med 116 TF 9180 1235 (*Quarent.* 19, HER 31013; Pl. 7.14). Medium/heavy soil, 60m OD (Fig. 7.20). Archaeological evidence for a medieval settlement site is minimal. The area is covered by a house and permanent grass. Two medieval sherds were recovered from a short and shallow water-pipe trench east of the house. A half-groat of Edward III (1351–2) and two joining pieces of a 13th-century circular lead seal matrix were recovered during metal-detecting in the field to the south at TF 9173 1230 (L132, HER 20821). The matrix is inscribed + S : PAVLI : [?D]o : d'FRAVSAM

Documentary evidence for a settlement site in the medieval period is slight and very confusing, while there is no doubt that a substantial house stood here in the 16th century, in Little Fransham parish, at the north-west corner of *Eastendmoor* and adjacent to the Great Fransham boundary.

Thomas Wiskard (Wyskard), a prominent landholder in both Franshams, with properties in Longham, West Bradenham and Scarning, died in 1538. It has not proved possible confidently to identify this site with any of the properties listed in his Inquisition Post Mortem, which is of variable reliability on matters of manorial allegiance (TNA C 142/72/46). The most likely candidate is a messuage in Little Fransham said to be held of the heir of Walter de Fransham as of his manor of Great Fransham, although no messuage in Little Fransham owed allegiance to this manor and nothing is known of Walter. Perhaps William de Fransham was intended. No reference to this property has been noted in Great Fransham manorial sources. If it had been subordinate to that manor, the link must have been severed at an early stage. It can probably be identified with a messuage in Little Fransham, once of John Anyell[vi], entered on a list of *c.*1555 of the possessions of John Wyskard, son and heir of Thomas. Two enclosed acres lay on the east side of the messuage and another 2 acres in the croft on the north. A number of small pieces of free land held by Wyskard and listed in *c.*1555 are absent from any rental. They can be recognised in abuttals by their owner's names, those of Wyskard, his father or his successors. They lay in *quarents.* 19, 20, 23 and 26.

John Wiskard became a civil servant and a man of some wealth. Thomas' assessment in the Lay Subsidy of 1524–5 is illegible. John's movable assets were set at £10, apparently the third highest Little Fransham, after Nicholas Mynne and his father (TNA E 179/150/213). He was buried in 1593, having died at about the age of 100 according to the Little Fransham parish register. In his will, proved in the same year, John Wiscarde gent., 'one of the Queene her maiesties Eschequer', left his capital messuage in Little Fransham to his wife with remainder to his grandson Robert Davye (NCC 83 Clearke)[vii]. Some idea of Wiskard's wealth can be obtained from a robbery committed at his Little Fransham house in 1578, when £200 and plate were stolen by two Little Fransham men described as 'hoopmakers', John Harlewyn and Robert Harlewyn alias Rudd. They were pardoned on the petition of Wiborrowe, John's wife. 'Many others' had taken part in the deed (Cal. Pat. Rol. 1982, 427, no.2844). This crime led to Robert Harlewyn losing lands he had held of Kirkhams and Wilcoks manor (Med 105 and 106).

The location of the house of Robert Davye gent. is given in an indenture of 1598 whereby the lord of Kirkhams and Wilcoks granted him four pieces of Little Fransham common on a 100-year lease. Precise measurements give a total of 134 perches of land on the north and west edges of a common, with one piece lying 'right over against the porche of the hale of the messuage' (MS 13265). In 1605 the size of Davye's purpresture [land taken from the common] was given as only 1 rood, 'being the south parte of a litle square yarde now walled in before his capitall mess: by Eastendmoare on the south east and west'.

The Wiskard / Davy house was clearly substantial as can be seen from elements listed in four probate inventories:

- John Whiskarde late of her Majesty's Exchequer gent., July 1593, parlour, hall, buttery, little buttery, kitchen, brew house, dairy, parlour chamber, hall chamber, maids' chamber, men's chamber, yards and stable (DN/INV 10/245).

- John Wiskard gent., December 1593, parlour, parlour chamber, hall chamber, buttery chamber, kitchen, buttery, little buttery, mill house, brew house, stables, store house, servants' chambers (n.b. hall and dairy omitted; DN/INV 11/713).

- Robert Davye gent., September 1639, hall, parlour, kitchen, pantry and cellar, hall chamber, parlour chamber, 'in the false rufe [i.e. garret] over the parlor', living chamber, pantry chamber, long gallery chamber, dairy, dairy chamber, bake house, brew house, chamber over the last two, yard and outhouses (DN/INV 46/105).

- Dorothy Davie widow, October 1667, parlour, parlour chamber, hall, pantry and entry, buttery, kitchen, kitchen chamber, pantry chamber, hall chamber, porch chamber, gallery chamber, dairy, barn, old dairy, and yard (DN/INV 52B/27).

The large size of this building is indicated by the Hearth Tax returns for 1664 and 1666, when the house of Mrs Davy widow had seven hearths. This was the highest figure in the parish, with only one other house (Little Fransham Old Hall in *Quarent.* 13) having as many (Frankel and Seaman 1983, 61 and Seaman 1991, 28).

The tenurial history can be followed with reasonable confidence up to Enclosure. Hamond Davy, worstead-weaver of Swaffham, in his will proved in 1676, instructed his wife and executor to sell his house in Little Fransham (ANF 194.1675). The house, like other lands of Hamond Davy, must have passed to Henry Large. He died in 1705 leaving all Little Fransham properties to his wife Frances (ANW 176.1705–6). To judge from how she disposed of her copyhold lands, she must have sold the house in 1710/11 to Joseph Wilking, blacksmith of Little Fransham. Likewise, it can be assumed that Wilking conveyed the house, as he did all his copyholds, to Thomas Case junior of King's Lynn gent. in 1757. It is listed in Case's marriage settlement of 1761 as a messuage or tenement with yard, garden and orchard in Little Fransham occupied by Edward Case, with 20 acres associated (Salmon A). Subsequent owners would have been Edward Case gent., tanner of Great Fransham and Thomas Henry Case of the same, gent. In 1801 the latter conveyed several properties by lease and release to William Watlin farmer of Little Fransham. They included a dwelling house with yard, garden and buildings in Little Fransham formerly of Joseph Wilkin (Salmon C and D).

After Enclosure William Watling held the house as freehold, and most of his allotment lay on what had been the northern end of *Eastendmoor*. The Enclosure map depicts one small building aligned north-south and two ponds, as well another building to the south-east just within the enclosed common. The present house, of 19th-century clay lump construction, lies to the south of its predecessor and is aligned east-west, with agricultural buildings nearby on the former common.

Med 117 TF 9196 1177 (*Quarent.* 29, HER 30218). Heavy soil, 62m OD (Figs 7.48 and 7.50). A rectangular tree and shrub-covered close containing 0.16 acre (0.065 hectare) is bordered by wet ditches on the north, south and east, and on the west by a stream, that marks the edge of *Eastendmoor* common pasture. Seven medieval sherds were found on several small patches of bare soil.

In *c.*1420 Thomas Stalworthy held freely of Wilcoks manor a void messuage with 4¼ acres in five pieces in *Eastfield* for an annual rent of 1s. Of these, the messuage and ¾ acre in two pieces were also soiled of Kirkhams manor. The messuage butted west on the common pasture and a close of Edmund Edyman (Med 106) lay to the south. His rent total suggests that John Shortwode, who had held Med 105, was tenant of these lands in *c.*1395. The messuage and ¾ acre of soiled land were listed in 1443 as 1 ac in three pieces in *Eastfield* held by Thomas Stalworthy.

One rood, parcel of 1 acre of soiled land, was held by John Stalworthy in 1502. It was described as a pightle butting west on the common pasture and lying between land of William Colyn on one side (Med 106) and land of

Nicholas Mynne and John Stalworthy (lands called Wyotts, the Kirkhams customary tenements Edildes and Renggis) on the other. In 1605 this was merely a 'parcell' butting west on the common and no acreage was given.

On Kirkhams and Wilcoks copyhold of Anne Griggs following Enclosure. The 0.16-acre close is not depicted on the Enclosure map.

Endnotes

i The fifty-five medieval coins comprise one Stephen, two Henry II, one Henry II or John, one Richard I, three John, one John or Henry III, seven Henry III, one Alexander III of Scotland (1250–80), eleven Edward I, three Edward II, twelve Edward III, one Robert II of Scotland (1371–90), one Richard II, three Venetian *soldini* of Doge Michael Stener (1400–13), one Henry V, three Edward IV, two 14th or 15th century, and one Henry VII.
ii The Cistercian Abbey at Robertsbridge, Sussex was founded in 1176. No good link has been made between the de Fransham family and Robertsbridge. A very tentative one might lie in the de Plaiz family from which Great Fransham manor was held and which did have Sussex connections. The seal matrix, now in Norwich Castle Museum (acc.no. NWHCM 2008.481), is illustrated in Clayton 2009. See also https://www.artfund.org/supporting-museums/art-weve-helped-buy/artwork/10402/robertsbridge-seal-matrix
iii In *c*.1427 a house (*mansum*) called *Rycheres* was said to lie in Necton parish somewhere nearby, east of which the parish boundary continued to *Rycherus Faldegate* (MS 13177). A *porta caduta* called *Richerfaldegate / Richerysfaldegate* in 1462 and 1463 probably lay on the boundary to the south of Med 65.
iv The couple were to have 12 feet wide ingress and egress to the croft and to a stable on the south side of the house. Stalworthie was to occupy the bakehouse where he would make for them 6 combs of barley into malt each year. They would be able to bake bread in the bakehouse oven and grind malt at the querns there. Stalworthie would carry out all repairs and pay the 20d annual rent. He was to pay off the purchase price at £1 each Michaelmas.
v There were many people called Jordan or Jurdan in Little Fransham before the Black Death. This property is the only one said to be of the tenement Jourdon in 1384. See properties 1–6 on the east side of *Eastendmoor* in *Quarent*. 29 for places called *Jurdones*, *Jordonys* and *Jurdons croft*. In 1327 Bartholomew son of John Jordan surrendered a Kirkhams customary building plot measuring 40 x 40 feet to his son. Bartholomew Jordan was a taxpayer that year. In 1328 probably the same person, with the sobriquet *albus* ('the white') died leaving an impressive array of property: one sixth of a customary messuage and 1½ acres, a free messuage and 5¾ acres with his three sons as heirs, ½ acre of customary land, 1½ acres held freely and jointly with his wife, a customary ½ rood with a cottage, ¾ acre once of [illeg.] of Bradenham, and finally a free messuage, 4 acres and 1½ acres held jointly with his wife. Earlier in 1328 another Bartholomew Jordan, son of Nicholas, had died seized of a messuage and 4¼ acres, of which 1½ were of customary tenure. Three sons were admitted. Two Jordons, Adam and John, were taxpayers in 1332. John Jordan was titled *mercator* (merchant) in 1336. There were many land transactions, grants and inheritances involving Jordans in the 1330s and 1340s. At the latest pre-Black Death Kirkhams manor court with extant records (held in October 1348), Adam and John Jordan swore fealty for parcels of the tenement Hotches, and the jury presented that Hamon Jordan lived in Swaffham and John Jordan and his sons Henry, Thomas and Adam, as well as Nicholas Jordan, all lived in Attleborough. After 1349 few members of the family remained. The tenement Jordan, whose acreage was never given, was last elected to messor duties in 1361. The last Jordan, Peter son of William, tenant of Med 71, was dead or had left Little Fransham by 1391–2.
vi The earliest reference to a member of the Anyell family of Little Fransham is of 1244 when John Aygnel / Aignel was involved in a lawsuit with Constance widow of Godfrey de Fransham over 2½ acres there (Brand 1999, 306, no. 1480). John Anyell / Amiel of Little Fransham was a party or a witness to five charters antedating *c*.1273 (MC 360/6 and 14–5; BL/O/T3.2; BL Add Ch 71036). Bartholomew, son of the same, was a grantor in *c*.1273–90 (MC 360/32). Another of the same or similar name occurs in seven charters of 1333–8 (MC 360/62–8), and Agnes, widow of the same, was a grantor in 1348 (MC 360/71). John Aniel does not appear in the Lay Subsidy assessment roll for 1327 but was assessed at 20d in 1332. For this surname see also Med 11, 25 and 27.
vii Davye's father, Robert Davye gent. of Stanfield had married Katherine daughter of John Wyskard (Rye 1891, 95 and 326; Carthew 1879, 397).

Appendix 3. Documents relating to 'Rougham and Fransham' Manor

1202 Final Concord (Dodwell 1952, 129–30, no.295; Rye 1881, 78–9, no.96)
William Peus and his brother Fulcho settled 11 acres in Frawesham on Margaret de Cressingham.

1265–73 Charter grant and release (TNA E 40/10572 and E 40/12118))
Grant by William le Butelyer in free alms of homage and service of two tenants, Hamon son of Avice and John Kynnock, in Fransham and 2s 11½d rent to Wendling Abbey. Release by Olive widow of William le Buteler of 3s rent in Fransham, her dower given by her husband, to Wendling Abbey. The grant is endorsed '*pro Tenement. Kynnokkys*'.
    Carthew (1877, 243) considered that le Butiler / de Boteler was an alternative name for de Cressingham.

1273/4 Hundred Roll (Illingworth and Caley eds 1812, 434 and 540)
William de Brisingham, William Burel and Clement de Cressingham claimed franchises in Rougham. Clement le Butiller, William de Brysingham and Robert Burel, heirs of William le Butiller, did the same.

***c*.1279** Feodary (MS 11352 T134D, see Table 6.2)
Geoffrey de Marscall held a manor (17 and 18) of William de Bressyngham and Alexander le Strange who held of John de Warenne. Three free tenants held of Geoffrey (19–21).

1292 Two charter grants (NRO NRS 6762 and NRS 6902)
Grant by Roger son of Nicholas le Hauwil / Auwl de Laxfield [Suffolk] to Thomas son of John de Rougham and Sara his wife of rents, homage and service of eleven named free tenants in Rougham and two in Fransham (Hamon son of Avice and Godfrey de Hockering), and four named villeins with their broods (two specified as of Rougham), for a payment of 20 marks and a rent of 1 rose, with a rent of 1 pound of cumin to the capital lord of the fee.

1293 Final Concord (TNA CP 25/1/160/116.645)
Roger son of Nicholas de Hauvill conveyed to Thomas son of John de Rougham and Sara his wife 20s rent in Rougham and Fransham, homage and service of John son of William and Richard son of John and all their tenements.

1293–1304 Charter (Holkham Hall, Longham bundle 1, 20)
Grant by Sara widow of Thomas son of John de Rougham in free alms of the homage and service of two tenants (Richard son of Hamo of Little Fransham and Godfrey de Hockering) with their tenements in Little Fransham and 26d rent to Wendling Abbey.

1302 Feudal Aids (1904, 416)
Heirs of William le Boteler with their tenants and parceners held 1 knight's fee in Rougham and Fransham of the heirs of Henry de Skegeton of John de Gatesdene of Earl Warenne of the King, of which Ralph le Mareschal held a quarter of Roger Extraneus [*i.e.* le Strange] and his parceners of John de Gatesdene of Earl Warenne of the King.

1316 *Nomina Villarum* (Blake 1952, 269; Feudal Aids 1904, 453–4)
Lords in Great Fransham: Geoffrey de Fransham and Alice le Mareschall.
Lords in Rougham: Richard atte Grene, Fulco de Brysyngham (*cf.* William de Bressyngham in *c*.1279), John de Cressyngham, John Hunte and Alice de Rougham.

1325 Inquisition post mortem (Cal. Inq. Post Mort. 1910, no.518)
John de Cressingham and parceners held 1 knight's fee in Rougham and Fransham of Aymer de Valence, Earl of Pembroke.

1332 and 1337 Lay Subsidies (TNA E 179/149/9 and E 179/238/111)
Alice Maschald / Mareschal was assessed at 6 shillings / 3 shillings under Great Fransham, on both occasions the second highest figure, after Geoffrey de Fransham.

1346 Feudal Aids (1904, 539)
John atte Grene and John de Doune and parceners held 1 knight's fee in Rougham and Fransham of Edward de Warenne of heirs of John de Gatesdene of Earl Warenne, of which Alice Mareschal held a quarter of John Extraneus and his parceners of heirs of John de Gatesdene of Earl Warenne of the King.

1375 Inquisition post mortem (Cal. Inq. Post Mort. 1952, no.86)
John de Cressyngham and parceners held 1 knight's fee in Rougham and Fransham of Elizabeth Countess of Athol.

1377 Inquisition post mortem (Cal. Inq. Post Mort. 1970, no.73)
[blank] and parceners held 1 knight's fee in Reynham [sic] and Fransham of David Earl of Athol.

1391 Inquisition post mortem (Cal. Inq. Post Mort. 1974, no.1052)
John de Cressyngham and parceners held 1 knight's fee in Reynham [sic] and Fransham of David Earl of Athol.

1401–2 Feudal Aids (1904, 634)
Ralph Bedyngham, John Yelverton and Edward Hunte clerk held 1 knight's fee in Rougham and Fransham as in 1346, of which Thomas Mascal held a quarter as in 1346.

1428 Feudal Aids (1904, 595)
William Yelverton and William Bedyngham held 1 knight's fee in Rougham and Fransham of the heirs of Henry de Skegeton, of which Ralph le Mareschall held a quarter of heirs of Roger Extraneus.
    See Carthew 1877, 238–47 for some detailed and rather muddling genealogy.
    The Fransham element of this manor seems to have become part of East Lexham manor by the 16th century.

Appendix 4. Unlocated Place Names in Medieval Deeds

MC 360/1 etc = NRO MC 360/1–78, 713X6
Fr, GFr and LFr = Fransham, Great and Little Fransham
A piece of land = *pecia*, 'a common term used to describe….one or more strips' (Hassall and Beauroy 1993, 52)

Benecroft   2 acres in the field of Fr, probably GFr, before c.1273 (MC 360/14)

Berewenesaker   1 acre of arable in LFr, before c.1273 (MC 360/3)

Butteslond   piece of land probably in GFr, before 1265 (TNA E 40/10684)

Chyttelwong   2 acres in LFr, before c.1273 (MC 360/13)

Coldhamcroft   ½ acre in LFr, 29/12/1318 (MC 360/51)

Delewenesacre   piece of land in LFr, c.1273–90 (MC 360/25)

Fyweacrys   land probably in LFr, early 14th century (MC 360/39)

Goldincroft   2 acres in LFr, c.1273–90 (MC 360/17)

Har'Aker   piece of land in LFr, c.1273–90 (HRO M/155)

Harviis aker   1 acre probably in LFr, 7/11/1297 (TNA E 40/10519)

Hichescroft   piece of land in LFr, 27/6/1323 (MC 360/55)

Hosyherslond   land abutted in LFr, 69/1333 (MC 360/65)

Kalvecroft   ½ acre in LFr, c.1273–90 (MC 360/32)

Le Kerrs   probably in LFr, 7/11/1297 (TNA E 40/10519)

Kyngesgate   road in LFr, 28/5/1312 (BL Add Ch 14669)

Leticecroift   piece of land in LFr, before c.1273 (MC 360/13)

Litelkroft   in LFr, before c.1273 (MC 360/9)

Okiistoift   piece of land in LFr, before c.1273 (MC 360/13)

Potekinesaker   meadow probably in GFr, before 1265 (TNA E 40/8885)

Poteriscroft   1 acre in LFr, c.1273–90 (TNA WARD 2/53/179/15)

Potersecroft   1 acre in Fr or perhaps Wendling, mid 13th century (TNA WARD 2/53/179/10)

Potterescrof'   piece of land in LFr, before 1290 (MC 360/34)

Potters Lund   with croft adjoining, probably in LFr, 7/11/1297 (TNA E 40/10519)

Princescroft   messuage and 4 acres in LFr, before c.1273 (MC 360/5)

Rewaldesaker   meadow probably in GFr, before 1265 (TNA E 40/8885)

Wodegate   road abutted in LFr, 29/6/1351 (MC 360/73)

Ywerthlond   furlong (*cultura*) in GFr, 13/11/1311 (TNA E 40/10528)

Appendix 5. References to Fald Gates up to 1526

Great Fransham

All amercements at Mills at Moor leet courts except those marked GFr, Great Fransham

1369 blocked watercourse at *Kattesfaldegate* (GFr MS 13034)
1449 branches overhanging common way at *Odesfalgate* (MS 13048)
1450 unscoured ditch on south side of *Medowys Faldgate* at meadow of Great Fransham manor (MS 13048)
1450 unscoured ditch at and on both sides of *Emmesfaldgate* (MS 13048)
1452 non-repair of *porta caduta* at *Emmysfaldgate* (MS 13048
1454 unscoured ditch at *Hallekarre Faldgate* (GFr MS 13049)
1455 unscoured ditch and watercourse and *porta caduta* unrepaired at *Emmies Faldgate* (MS 13048)
1455 unscoured ditch at *Emmysfaldgate* (GFr MS 13049)
1456 *porta caduta* of John Crudde broken by John Maunde at *le Scalemedowys* (MS 13051)
1463 *porta caduta* broken by Ethelred Taylour's horse that entered the field etc. (MS 13048)
1465 non-repair of porta caduta versus Heryngshawewong (MS 13048)
1468 non-repair of common way at *Medowefaldgate* (MS 13048)
1471 Geoffrey Wyrre's boys opened a *porta caduta* allowing animals into field (MS 13048)
1473 John Colyn kept part of *Wardysmor* common closed with a *porta caduta* all year (MS 13048)
1473 William Yevan kept two *portae cadutae subtus Kewaldeshaugh* [entry probably incomplete] (MS 13048)
1474 unscoured watercourse at *Emmesfaldgate* (MS 13048)
1477 unscoured watercourse at *Pratts Faldgate* (MS 13048)
1478 unscoured ditch at *Emesfaldgate* (MS 13048)
1480 unscoured watercourse at *Skeetes faldgate* (MS 13048)
1489 unscoured ditch at *Emmesfaldgate* (MS 13052)
1490 unscoured ditch at *Sowdes Falgate* (MS 13052)
1492 unscoured ditch at *Odes Falgate* (MS 13052)
1494 unscoured watercourse at *Emmesfalgate* (MS 13052)
1495 unscoured ditch at *Emmesfalgate* (MS 13167)
1496 non-maintenance of fence (*custod. defenc.*) at *Medowfalgate* (MS 13167)
1498 unscoured watercourse at *Emmesfaldegate* (GFr MS 13035)
1508 unscoured watercourse next to *porta caduta* called *Wardes Faldgate* (MS 13067)
1502 tenants and inhabitants sufficiently to fix all *portae cadutae* within eight days (GFr MS 13035)
1508 insufficiently repaired *porta caduta* next to messuage late of Robert Parker (MS 13067)
1521 non-repair of *porta caduta* next to Edmund Pratt's messuage (MS 13068)
1523 non-repair of *porta caduta* next to Edmund Pratt's messuage at end of lane there (MS 13167)
1526 insufficiently repaired *porta caduta* next to *Maundesclose* at *Halwoodlane* (GFr MS 13056)
1544 *porta caduta* called *Meadow falgate* broken by Christopher Crowe of Wendling (MS 13056)

Little Fransham

*c.***1427** *Rycherus Faldegate* (Necton perambulation MS 13177)
1439 watercourse blocked with an ash tree at *Maryonesfaldgate* (MS 13097)
1440 tree still in ditch at *Maryones faldgate* (MS 13097)
1447 no fence against common at *Marionesfaldgate* (MS 13097)
1448 unscoured watercourse at *Maryonesfaldgate* (MS 13097)
1450 branches overhanging common way and *le Market Mere* at *Marionesfaldgate* next to *Ulnesmedowe* (MS 13097)
1450 unscoured watercourse at *Mariones Faldegate* (MS 13097)
1462 unscoured watercourse at *Richerfaldegate* (MS 13099)
1463 water from ditch diverting king's highway at *Cosynesfaldegate* (MS 13099)
1463 *porta caduta* called *Richerysfaldgate* to be made by communal effort and not by Nicholas Cosyn alone (MS 13099)
1465 blocked watercourse at *Mantildes Faldgate* (MS 13099)
1467 unscoured ditch at *Rechers Faldegate* (MS 13099)
1471 two *portae cadutae* erected in the common way at *Coltynges* by Thomas Wryght, against custom etc. (MS 13099)
1492 *porta caduta* kept closed by William Maunde jun. throughout common shack time (MS 13100)
1508 unscoured ditch at *Buntyngesfalgate* (MS 13100)
1508 *porta caduta* at *Skalemedow* [in Great Fransham] blocked by stile (MS 13100)
1517 unscoured ditch near *Buntynges falgate* (MS 13103)
1518 unscoured ditch at *Buntyngesfalgate* (MS 13103)
1519 unscoured ditch at *Buntyngesfaldgate* (MS 13103)
1520 unscoured watercourse at *Chanonsffaldegate* (MS 13103)
1521 unscoured watercourse at *Canones falgate* (MS 13103)
1526 order to erect two *portae cadutae* at both ends of the common path in *Ulnesmedowe* (MS 13103)

Appendix 6. Gazetteer of Post-Medieval Sites

This gazetteer lists post-medieval sites for which there is some archaeological evidence. The introduction to each entry begins with the national grid reference. This is followed by the Area letter (for Great Fransham) or *Quarent.* number (for Little Fransham), the Norfolk Historic Environment Record (HER) number, soil type and, finally, height above Ordnance datum. Where possible, a summary of the tenurial history down to the Enclosure Act of 1807 is given. Frequently cited documents are not individually referenced. They are listed in Chapter 7 *Documentary references*. Site locations are shown on Fig. 9.1.

PM 1 TF 9163 1433 (Area C, G337, HER 20783). Heavy soil, 71m OD. Concentration of late 16th to early 18th-century sherds with abundant post-medieval building material, 40m east-west x 20m north-south, butting north on *Elverycsmore* in the same way as Med 44 and 45. There is no clear pottery evidence for medieval settlement, although a low medieval sherd count might possibly be explained by the very dark garden-type soil which is coincident with the concentration of finds.

At a Mills-on-the-Moor leet court in 1565 John Tompson of Mileham was amerced for encroaching on the King's highway next to *Elyngham moore* with his ditches and for not scouring them (MS 13061). He, a yeoman, was the plaintiff in a chancery case of 1558 or later. Having acquired 'about one year past' a 'close of pasture grownde' in Great Fransham containing 10 acres from Richard Turnor of Castle Rising, he claimed that the defendants, Thomas Stalworthie and Dorothy his wife had retained the deeds and had entered the premises and attempted to expel him (TNA C 3/177/25). In his will proved in 1570, John Thompson, again styled a yeoman of Mileham, left all his lands in Beeston and Fransham to his son John who had not yet reached the age of 14 (ANW 33 Busbye).

In 1582 John Tompson, who had a newly built tenement, was amerced at a Mills-on-the-Moor leet court for commoning illegally on the common of Great Fransham (MS 13063 and MS 13065). In 1583 he was amerced again, this time as holder of a newly built cottage (MS 13064). At an Ellinghams manor court held in 1582 the heirs of John Thompson were distrained to swear fealty for a freehold 10-acre close lying in two *quarentinae* next to *Ellinghams Close*. Tompson himself was distrained once more in 1592, and in 1595 the tenant of lands late of John Tompson was amerced for default of suit of court. The tenant was named as Richard Kett in 1597 and 1600 (MC 1847/1, 741X2). There are no later records of this property. Although there was no reference to a dwelling thereon at any Ellinghams court, the identification of Tompson's newly built cottage of 1582 with this site seems reasonable in view of the proximity of *Ellinghams Close*. Between 1575 and 1591 he also held a Great Fransham customary tenement (Med 113 no.1) in Area E (MS 13062 and MS 13079). John Tompson was buried at Great Fransham in 1595. The jury reported in 1597 that some years previously Thompson had alienated divers free lands (rent 1s) to Richard Kett, who was distrained. Kett did fealty in 1598 for a free enclosure containing 10 acres lying over the length of two *quarentinae*. He was distrained to do fealty in 1600. However, at a Milles-on-the-Moor leet court held in 1597, a Jeremy Shilling had been amerced for default of suit of court on account of lands late John Tompson (MS 13167).

The Enclosure map does not show a building. A parcel of 1 acre 1 rood and 16 perches which included this site was awarded at Enclosure to Hamond Alpe esq. as copyhold of the manor of Ellingham Curtlings etc., in lieu of common rights.

PM 2 TF 9050 1283 (Area M, G216, HER 20643). Heavy soil, 62m OD. Concentration of ?late 16th and 17th to 19th-century sherds and building material on the north edge of *Barnards Moor* common pasture next to the parish boundary with Little Fransham. This is one of only two entirely post-medieval sites to be located in the survey. In the late medieval period it would have been within the furlong on the south side of *Southgateway alias Greenway*, but on which documented parcel of land it lay is unknown.

One Simon Allen may perhaps have been the first inhabitant of this house. Like John Tompson, probable tenant of PM 1, he was amerced for illegally commoning in 1582 and 1583, as holder of a newly-built tenement or cottage (MS 13063–5). He (surnamed Alleyn) had first appeared at a Mills-on-the-Moor court in 1569, amerced for not maintaining the common drain next to the tenement in which he lived, and was fined for commoning before the end of autumn at a Great Fransham leet court in the same year. In 1573 he was amerced at the same time as John Tompson for not scouring a ditch near *Claypittemore*, probably in Area C. He paid farm rent for the (ancient) free tenement of Spirlings and other lands of Great Fransham manor in 1570, 1573 and 1575. By 1582 another person held Spirlings (MS 13079). In 1580, 1582, 1587 and 1589 Allen was amerced at the Little Fransham leet court for pasturing on *Barnards Moor*, a common straddling the boundary between the Franshams and very close to this house (MS 13416 and MS 13205). In 1591 he paid a free rent of 5d, a rent that cannot be identified in earlier sources (MS 13062). An acre of freehold conveyed in a charter of 1594 lay in *le Chirchefeild apud le Sallowedich* and butted north on *le Grenewaie* and south on land late of Simon Allen (MS 13268). His name does not appear in later Great Fransham documents.

Following Enclosure, the site contained two buildings and lay within a small parcel at the southern end of a narrow plot of 1 acre, 3 roods and 2 perches, freehold of Rev. Baily Wallis. One building within a small enclosure is depicted on the 1838 Tithe map (DN/TA 189), but on the 1st edition of the Ordnance Survey 1:2500 scale map the site is void and lies at the south-east corner of a large field.

PM 3 TF 9092 1129 (*Quarent.* 16, L86, HER 29222). Heavy soil, 78m OD. Concentration of late 16th to 19th-century sherds, with very little 18th and 19th-century building material, 40m x 25m, at the north end of a common pasture called *Coltinges Green* in 1566 (MS 13158). It lies within an 8-acre close called the *Rudde*, copyhold of Cannons manor in 1542, and contained 9 acres in 1543. In 1589 ½ acre, with a house (*domus*) now built and marked out from the remainder by a hedge and ditch, was split off and thereafter held separately. In 1613 a small building (*domicil.*) with a parcel of land containing 20 feet in the south-west corner of the ½ acre was individually conveyed to a widow and her daughter for their lives, but the property was not mentioned in any subsequent court proceedings. In 1659 abuttals for 2 acres in the south part of the main close show that it lay next to *Coultings Lane* on the west, and the whole close was said to be next to the same lane on the west in 1669. The will (proved in 1662) of William Copper, a tenant of the ½-acre piece with the house, mentions 'ingate' and 'outgate' to the common on the south side of the property, as well as a house in which Anne Turner lived and which stood on a piece of ground 'dooled out'. This may have been the 20-feet plot mentioned above, or perhaps another sub-division (ANW 51 1662/3, MF/RO 330). The main property was the house of Edward Buddle, which contained one hearth according to the 1664 and 1666 Hearth Tax lists (Frankel and Seaman 1983, 61; Seaman 1991, 28). The other dwelling(s) were not taxed. In 1670 Edward Buddwell [Buddle] was exempted from the Hearth Tax, as were Edmund Budwell and Elizabeth Cooper widow. It is possible that Edmund Budwell lived elsewhere, perhaps in the nearby Kirkhams and Wilcocks customary cottage on the west edge of *Coltinges Green*. By 1705 all had been acquired by Philip Alpe, a major landholder in Little Fransham.

Following Enclosure, the site fell within a large block of Sparhams manor copyhold allotted to Hamond Alpe esq. A close of about the same dimensions as the sherd concentration is shown with a building in its north-east corner on the Enclosure Award map but is absent from the 1839 Tithe map (DN/TA 168). The site is still visible as a slight rise in an arable field.

PM 4 TF 9175 1361 (Area E, G266, HER 20750). Heavy soil, 61m OD. A very large quantity of potsherds of the late 17th to 19th centuries was collected by the prehistorian Dr Frances Healy in the 1980s while gardening at the rear of her house which sits on heavy soil on the former east edge of a common pasture, *Doesgate/Fendersmoor*. Medieval sherds were very sparse. Similar post-medieval material was collected during fieldwalking in the east part of the former garden, which has been incorporated within an arable field. The standing building consists of a pair of 19th-century cottages. No documentary evidence has been found.

Following Enclosure, a house here was the freehold of Abel Brereton, who owned a block of land to the north-east.

PM 5 TF 8982 1347 (Area K, G110, HER 30840). Heavy soil, 65m OD. A mutilated timber-framed house of *c.*1600 lies on the south-west corner of *West End moor*. No documentary evidence has been found. It is likely that the site is not medieval in origin but was established on the headland at the north end of the open field lying on the north side of the *Whiteway*. Seven medieval and ten post-medieval sherds were recovered during renovation works in 1995.

Following Enclosure on free land of Edward Wellingham.

Bibliography

Primary sources

Estimated dates for undated deeds are given in square brackets.

Norfolk Record Office, Norwich
Within the texts of chapters 5–7 and appendices 2–6 the standard prefix NRO has been omitted from the catalogue references of all cited documents.

In all citations of documents whose catalogue references begin with MS, box code suffices have been omitted. For example, MS 13084 40A3 appears as MS 13084.

No reference is made in the brief descriptions below to matters concerning other manors and other places included in some documents.

ANW/15/1.18
Great Fransham Glebe Terrier, 1635

ANW/15/1.46
Little Fransham Glebe Terrier, 1635

ANW/15/2.61
Great Fransham Glebe Terrier, 1613

ANW/15/2.135
Little Fransham Glebe Terrier, 1613

BL/MA 42
Manor court book of Wendling Nuper Abbis, 1588–1607 with list of tenements liable to perform the office of messor, c.1570

BL/O/T3.2
Undated charter grant [thirteenth century]

BL/O/U3/1
Undated charter grant [mid thirteenth century]

BRA 925/3/1–3
Deeds, 1779–1820

C/Ca 1/22
Copy of Great and Little Fransham Enclosure map, drawn in 1833, approximate scale 1 inch : 6 chains

C/S 3 Box 4
Norwich Quarter Sessions records, 1555–6

C/Sca 1/5
Norfolk Enrolled Deeds 1628–41

C/Sca 2/122
Enclosure Award for Great Fransham, Little Fransham and North Pickenham, 1807, with map of the Franshams by John Browne of Norwich, 1805, scale 1 inch : 6 chains

C/Sca 2/187
Enclosure map of Beeston next Mileham by John Glegg and Robert Chasteney of Norwich, 1814, scale 1 inch : 9 chains

C/Sca 2/323
Enclosure map of Wendling by Benjamin Lock of Holt, 1815, scale 1 inch : 6 chains

DN/FCB 2/1
Faculty to sell two of three bells of St Mary's church, Little Fransham, 1742

DN/FCB 4/2
Faculty to demolish the south aisle of All Saints' church, Great Fransham, to sell lead from the roof and to build a new nave south wall, 1801

DN/FCB 5/1
Faculty to demolish Little Fransham rectory and to build a new house on a different site, 1804

DN/FCP 7/7
Petition for faculty to demolish the south aisle of All Saints' church, Great Fransham, to sell lead from the roof and to build a new nave south wall, 1801

DN/FCP 8/1
Petition for faculty to demolish Little Fransham rectory and to build a new house, with plans of old and proposed new buildings, 1804

DN/TA 168
Tithe Apportionment for Little Fransham, 1839, with map by W.G. Bircham of Fakenham, 1839

DN/TA 189
Tithe Apportionment for Great Fransham, 1839, with map by W.G. Bircham of Fakenham, 1838

DN/TER/68/4
Great Fransham Glebe Terriers, beginning in 1677

DN/TER/68/5
Little Fransham Glebe Terriers, beginning in 1633

EVL 595 and 596
Court book of the manors of Northendhall, Scarning Parva, Guntons and Rougholme ex part Hoo, 1615–1760 and 1764–1839

EVL 599 and 601–4
Short rentals of the manors of Northendhall, Scarning Parva, Guntons and Rougholme ex part Hoo, 1710–59, 1745–70 and 1775–8

FX 110/1
Photocopy of agreement between the rector and township of Little Fransham re tithes and ancient customs, 1648

Hansell Stevenson 13/07/1972 36–39, and 41–42
Six court books of Cannons, Little Fransham and Sparhams or Sparham Hall, Little Fransham: Cannons 1541–1820 and Sparhams 1485–1826; with a short rental of 1649 for both in Book B (37)

Hansell Stevenson 13/07/1972 46
Rental book of Cannons and Sparhams, 1765–99

Hansell Stevenson 13/07/1972
Court papers including short rentals of Cannons and Sparhams, 1686, 1689, 1699 and 1731–5 (uncatalogued)

Hood, Vores and Allwood 14/03/1980, Box 56
Indenture of bargain and sale, 1553

KIM 1/8/12
Bailiff's account rolls, East Lexham manor, 1555–61

KIM 1/8/14
Extent of East Lexham manor, 1496/7

KIM 1/8/15
Early seventeenth-century copy an undated mid-sixteenth-century terrier or dragge of East Lexham.

KIM 1/8/16
Book containing early seventeenth-century copies of an undated rental of lands of East Lexham manor in Great Fransham and elsewhere [c.1550] and of an undated mid-sixteenth-century terrier or dragge of East Lexham; and brief East Lexham manor court roll extracts, 1451/2–1501/2

KIM 1/8/18
Short rental, East Lexham manor, 1727

LEST/GA 7
Bailiff's account roll, manor of Rougholme in Gressenhall, 1441–2

LEST/NK 1
Undated release [*ante* 1259]

MC 52/65, 505X8
Map of the estate in Beeston and Great Fransham of J.G. Booty deceased, 1831

MC 125/10, 600X1
Field book of Kempstone, 1495/6

MC 360/1–78, 713X6
Seventy-eight deeds (charter grants and releases) relating to properties in Little Fransham, and in a few cases in Great Fransham, comprising forty-one undated [mid-thirteenth to fourteenth century], and thirty-seven of 1286–1361 almost all relating to properties of the Le Strange family and therefore associated with the manors of Kirkhams and Wilcoks

MC 969/1, 858X7
Manor court rolls, Great Fransham (Capell portion) and leet court rolls, Mills-on-the-Moor, 1670–84, 1689–1703 and 1709–26

MC 969/2, 858X7
Court book of Great Fransham manor (Capell portion) and Mills-on-the-Moor leet, 1787–1873 and 1956–9

MC 969/8, 858X7
Short rentals, Kirkhams and Wilcoks and Great Fransham (Capell portion), 1780–92

MC 1122/5, 805X8
Charter grant, 1539

MC 1683/22b, 821X4
Final concord, 1664

MC 1683/27, 821X4
Final concord, 1695

MC 1812/49, 838X5
List of tenanted lands of East Lexham manor with tenurial histories, early seventeenth century

MC 1847/1, 741X2
Court Book containing manor courts of Ellinghams cum Rustyns (or Ellinghams Rustins cum Curtlins) in Great Fransham, 1576, 1582, 1587, 1592–3, 1595–7, 1600, 1638, 1640; manor courts of parcel of the Chapel of St Nicholas at Rougholme, 1638 and 1640; manor courts of Great Fransham [ex-Mynne, non-Capell, portion], 1668–70, 1674 and 1676; combined manor courts of Ellinghams etc. and Rougholme, 1668–70, 1674, 1676, 1683, 1686, 1690, 1694, 1697, 1705, 1711, 1714, 1718, 1727, 1742, 1749, 1754–5, 1766, 1805–6, 1812, 1833 and 1839; memorandum re certain copyholds by Roger Lestrange, 1676

MC 1850/1–3, 858X9
Manor and leet court rolls, Kirkhams and Wilcoks, 1670–84, 1689–1705, 1709–26

MC 1850/4–5, 858X8
Manor and leet court books, Kirkhams and Wilcoks, 1727–90, 1791–1852

MC 2104/1–2104/4, 920X9
Four manor court books, Herringshall and Dikewood in Wendling, 1623–1840

MC 2104/6, 920X9
Rental book, Herringshall and Dikewood in Wendling, 1750–1851

MC 2234/14, 943X1
Undated charter grant [mid thirteenth century]

MC 2334/1, 958X1
Charter grant, 1549

MC 2755/4/1, 1004X2
Charter grant, 1505

MC 3115/1/1–18, 1037X4
Deeds relating to Little Fransham properties of the Allison/Allanson family, acquired by Edmund Senkler, 1478–1761

Mills and Reeve 12/03/70 Mason Necton deeds
Very large collection of medieval and post-medieval deeds, copies of court rolls etc. relating to holdings of the Mason family in Necton and elsewhere (uncatalogued)

MR 28, 240X6
Manor court rolls of Rougholme in Gressenhall, 1504–9, 1516–21, 1523, 1528, 1530 and 1534 [rolls of 1428/9–1430/31 contain nothing of relevance to Fransham]. As PRO/SC2/192/95

MR 255A, 242X2
Indenture of bargain and sale, 1552

MS 424, T131D
Copies of various documents concerning Necton Town charity lands, with a schedule of deeds, compiled on 23 August 1786: charter grants of 1462, 1468, 1489, 1491, 1542, and 1552/3; indenture of 1509; Great Fransham rectory manor court roll extracts of 1510, 1548 and 1558; rental for lands etc. owing rents to the capital messuage of Blyfords in Great Fransham, 1550; deeds of enfeoffment re lands in Great Fransham, 1572–1770

MS 1890, 2B7
Undated extract of rental, Drayton Hall manor [early fifteenth century]

MS 2691, 3B2
Extract of rental, Drayton Hall manor, 1470/1

MS 3802, 8A2
Undated charter grant [1265–73]

MS 3808, 8A2
Indenture leading to the uses of a deed, 1351

MS 3809, 40A3
Undated charter grant [*c.*1273–90]

MS 3813, 8A3
Revenue roll of Wendling Abbey, 1269

MS 4129–30, 4E
Manor and leet court books of manor of Wendling Nuper Abbis, 1646–1708 and 1712–60

MS 11352
Late sixteenth-century book of Richard Beckham containing copies of two versions of an undated extent of Great Fransham [*c.*1430], copies of two versions of an undated Great Fransham rental [*c.*1400], a copy of a Great Fransham feodary [*c.*1279], very short extracts from Great Fransham manor and leet court rolls from seventeen years between 1272–3 and 1338–9

MS 12832, 31E5
Book of manor and leet court extracts of East Lexham, 1377–1609 [little relevant to Fransham], four sheets of extracts of the same, 1625–50, bundle of court verdicts of the same, memoranda and lists of those bound to attend leet courts, 1646–81

MS 12835–12837, 31E5
Short rentals of manors of East Lexham and Lexham Rouses, 1790–3, 1797–1802, 1803–10

MS 13034, 40A1
Extracts of manor and leet court rolls, Great Fransham, 1330–1, 1334–5, 1337–40, 1343, 1346, 1349, 1353, 1355, 1357, 1362, 1364–75

MS 13035, 40A1
Copy of manor and leet court rolls, Great Fransham, 1498 and 1502–3

MS 13037–9, 40A1
Account rolls of Sir William Oldhall's farmers, bailiff and messor, Fransham [Kirkhams and Wilcoks with part of Great Fransham], 1437–8, 1439–40, 1440–1

MS 13042, 40A2
Manor court rolls, Great Fransham rectory, 1324, 1335, 1339, 1344, 1377 and 1381/2; fragment of a rental possibly of Little Fransham [Kirkhams] freeholds in Great Fransham [first half of the fourteenth century]; charter grant [thirteenth century]; charter grant, 1316

MS 13043, 40A2
Extracts of manor and leet court rolls, Great Fransham, 1381–97

MS 13044, 40A2
Extracts of manor and leet court rolls, Great Fransham, 1397 and 1398 [fragment joining end of MS 13043 40A2

MS 13045, 40A2
Extracts of manor and leet court rolls, Great Fransham, 1398–9

MS 13046, 40A2
Extracts of manor and leet court rolls, Great Fransham, 1399–1405 and 1413

MS 13047, 40A2
Leet court roll, Little Fransham, 1425; leet court roll, Mills-on-the-Moor, 1425

MS 13048, 40A2
Leet court rolls, Mills-on-the-Moor, 1431–5, 1437, 1439–44, 1447–52, 1455, 1458–75 and 1477–86. Copy of undated short rental of Great Fransham [c.1500–1520]

MS 13049, 40A2
Manor and leet court rolls, Great Fransham, 1454–5

MS 13051, 40A2
Leet court roll, Mills-on-the-Moor, 1455–7

MS 13052, 40A2
Leet court rolls, Mills-on-the-Moor, 1487–90, 1492, 1494 and 1503

MS 13053, 40A2
Manor court roll and two versions of a rental of Little Fransham [Kirkhams and Wilcoks] of Sir William Capell and his cofeoffees, 10 June 1502

MS 13054, 40A2
Leet court roll, Mills-on-the-Moor, 1501–2

MS 13055, 40A2
Leet court roll, Mills-on-the-Moor, 1509

MS 13056, 40A2
Copies of various short rentals, Great Fransham, of fixed and farm rents 1510–2, of farm rents 1511 (three copies), of customary rents 1511, of customary rents undated (two copies), of free rents undated [early sixteenth century], of demesne meadows undated [early sixteenth century], of fixed and farm rents 1515/6; copies of manor and leet court rolls, Great Fransham, 1511, 1525–6, 1537–40, 1544, 1546–9; copies of leet court rolls, Mills-on-the-Moor, 1544–7

MS 13058, 40A2
Copy of manor and leet court roll, Great Fransham, 1557 and 1558

MS 13059, 40A2
Copy of manor and leet court roll, Great Fransham and leet court roll, Mills-on-the-Moor, 1560

MS 13061, 40A2
Leet court roll, Mills-on-the-Moor, 1563–9

MS 13062, 40A2
Extracts of manor and leet court rolls, Great Fransham, 1569, 1573–4; short rental, Great Fransham, 1591

MS 13063–4, 40A2
Copies of leet court rolls, Mills-on-the-Moor, 1582 and 1583

MS 13065, 40A2
Leet court roll, Mills-on-the-Moor, 1582

MS 13066, 40A2
Extract of leet roll, Mills-on-the-Moor, 1400

MS 13067, 40A2
Extracts of manor and leet court rolls, Little Fransham [Kirkhams and Wilcoks], 1508 and 1511; extracts of leet court rolls, Mills-on-the-Moor, 1498, 1504, 1508, 1511–2

MS 13068, 40A2
Extracts of leet court rolls, Mills-on-the-Moor, 1524 and 1528

MS 13071, 40A3
Copy of undated rental, Great Fransham [c.1400]

MS 13072, 40A3
Undated rental, Great Fransham [c.1400]

MS 13073, 40A3
Undated rental of farm rents, Great Fransham [c.1430]

MS 13074, 40A3
Short rental, Great Fransham, 1537

MS 13075, 40A3
Short rental of fixed and farm rents, Great Fransham, 1537

MS 13076, 40A3
Short rental of fixed and farm rents with list of meadows, Great Fransham, 1547/8

MS 13077, 40A3
Rental, list of meadows, brief rental of farm rents, Great Fransham, 1553; short rentals, Great Fransham, 1553, 1555, 1569–70

MS 13078, 40A3
Pedigree of the de Fransham family [sixteenth century], undated list of Great Fransham lands held by Robert Crowe [of Wendling, ob. 1541], lists of Great Fransham meadows, their tenants and their rents 1557/8, undated copy of part of a short rental, Great Fransham [1470s or 1480s]

MS 13079, 40A3
Short rentals of fixed and farm rents, Great Fransham, 1570, 1573, 1575, 1581–2

MS 13080–3, 40A3
Short rentals of fixed and farm rents, Great Fransham (Capell portion), 1603, 1604, 1609, 1614

MS 13084, 40A3
Survey book of demesne and other lands of Nicholas Mynne gent., Great Fransham, with short rental of fixed rents, 1595; six sixteenth-century survey books (A–F) of Great Fransham, each containing a copy of an undated extent [c.1430] in two slightly different versions (version 1 in A, C, and E, version 2 in B, D and F), each containing a copy of an undated rental [c.1400], three (A, D and E) containing incomplete copies of an undated feodary [c.1279], one (E) containing very short extracts of fourteen court rolls between 1335 and 1366

MS 13085, 40A3
Undated notes re a case between Andrew Clarke and Henry Mynne concerning 7 acres of Great Fransham demesne [late 1570s or 1580s]; three undated lists of Great Fransham demesne lands and other lands in the parish with their acreages and annual rents [probably 1590s]

MS 13089, 40A3
Notes re Great Fransham demesne and customary lands prepared for a case in Chancery between Sir Arthur Capell and Nicholas Mynne gent., titled "Papers of no great valewe lefte at the viewe of the evedense in January 1600"

MS 13089A, 40A3
Undated short rental of Cannons manor [c.1370]

MS 13090, 40A4
Manor court roll, Little Fransham [Kirkhams], 1327–8, with leet court of 1328

MS 13091, 40A4
Manor court rolls, Little Fransham [Kirkhams], 1328–48

MS 13092, 40A4
Manor court rolls, Little Fransham [Kirkhams], 1351–77, with leet courts of 1366, 1372, 1373, 1374 and 1376

MS 13093, 40A4
Manor court rolls, Little Fransham [Kirkhams], 1377–80 and 1391–5, with leet courts of 1377, 1379, 1380 and 1391–5

MS 13094, 40A4
Manor court rolls, late William le Strange, Wilcoks, 1399–1405; manor court rolls, Little Fransham, Kirkhams, 1405–11 with leet courts of 1406–8

MS 13095, 40A4
Leet court rolls, Little Fransham, 1422–3 with list of suitors to the leet, 1423

MS 13096, 40A4
Account roll of Sir William Oldhall's farmer and bailiff, Little Fransham [Kirkhams and Wilcoks with part of Great Fransham], 1432–3

MS 13097, 40A4
Manor and leet court rolls, Little Fransham [Kirkhams and Wilcoks], 1426–61

MS 13098, 40A4
Manor court rolls, Little Fransham, Kirkhams, 1422–4 and Kirkhams and Wilcoks, 1462–3

MS 13099, 40A4
Manor and leet court rolls, Little Fransham [Kirkhams and Wilcoks], 1462–85

MS 13100, 40A4
Manor and leet court rolls, Little Fransham [Kirkhams and Wilcoks], 1486–97 and 1508

MS 13101, 40A4
Paper copy of manor court roll and rental, Little Fransham [Kirkhams and Wilcoks], 1502 (as MS 13053, 40A2)

MS 13102, 40A4
Manor and leet court rolls, Little Fransham [Kirkhams and Wilcoks], 1511–5; leet court rolls, Mills-on-the-Moor, 1512, 1514

MS 13103, 40A4
Manor and leet court rolls, Little Fransham [Kirkhams and Wilcoks], 1517–27 and 1541

MS 13104, 40A5
Manor and leet court book, Little Fransham [Kirkhams and Wilcoks], 1555 and 1564–77, with an undated extract (deleted) from a Cannons manor court [probably 1569]

MS 13105–6, 40A5
Manor and leet court rolls, Little Fransham [Kirkhams and Wilcoks], 1560, 1578

MS 13113, 40A5
Extract of manor court roll, Little Fransham [Kirkhams and Wilcoks], 1527

MS 13117, 40A5
Extracts of manor and leet court rolls, Little Fransham [Kirkhams and Wilcoks], 1530–3

MS 13121, 40A5
Account roll of the bailiff of Peter Strange [Kirkhams], 1373–4

MS 13122–3, 40A5
Messor's account rolls, Little Fransham [Kirkhams], 1383–4, 1391–2, 1392–3

MS 13124, 40A5
Account roll of the bailiff (*serviens*) of Edmund de Oldhalle, Little Fransham [Kirkhams], 1394–5

MS 13125, 40A5
Messor's account roll, Little Fransham [Kirkhams], 1398–9, 1399–1400

MS 13126–7, 40A5
Bailiff's account rolls, Little Fransham [Kirkhams], 1401–2, 1402–3

MS 13128, 40A5
Messor's account roll, Little Fransham [Kirkhams], 1403–4

MS 13129, 40A5
Messor's account roll, manor late of William le Straunge, Wilcoks, 1404–5, 1405–6

MS 13130–1, 40A5
Messor's account rolls, Little Fransham [Kirkhams], 1405–6, 1406–7

MS 13132, 40A5
Messor's account roll, Wilcoks, 1409–10

MS 13133, 40A5
Bailiff's account roll of produce of the grange, Kirkhams and Wilcoks, 1412–3, 1413–4

MS 13134, 40A5
Messor's account roll, Wilcoks, 1414–5, 1415–6

MS 13135, 40A5
Bailiff's account roll, Little Fransham Kirkhams, 1417–8

MS 13136, 40A5
Messor's account roll, Wilcoks, 1420–1

MS 13137, 40A5
Bailiff's account roll, Little Fransham [Kirkhams and Wilcoks with part of Great Fransham], 1427–8

MS 13138, 40A5
Account roll of Sir William Oldhall's bailiff, Little Fransham [Kirkhams and Wilcoks with part of Great Fransham], 1429–30

MS 13139–40, 40A5
Account rolls of Sir William Oldhall's farmers, bailiff and messor, Little Fransham [Kirkhams and Wilcoks with part of Great Fransham], 1436–7, 1442–3

MS 13141, 40 A5
Rental of Little Fransham [Kirkhams and Wilcoks] farm rents for lands let on a 5-year lease from Michaelmas 1476; Kirkhams and Wilcoks messors' account rolls, one undated, 1469–70, 1470–1, 1471–2, 1472–3, and 1476–7

MS 13142, 40A5
Damaged and incomplete extract of rental of farm rents for [Kirkhams and Wilcoks] demesne lands, 1446–7, and undated rental of farm rents for demesne lands formerly held by William Wyskard [*c.*1449]

MS 13143, 40A5
Undated short rental of Wilcoks [*c.*1483]

MS 13144, 40A5
Undated short rental of Kirkhams [*c.*1460]

MS 13145, 40A5
Rental of Kirkhams (of Sir William Oldhall) 29 September 1443
741X2
MS 13146, 40A6
Sixteenth-century paper copy of Kirkhams rental, 29 September 1443

MS 13147–50, 40A6
Short rentals of Kirkhams and Wilcoks, 1597, 1600, 1603 and 1604

MS 13151–2, 40A6
Short rentals of Kirkhams and Wilcoks, 1613

MS 13153, 40A6
Short rental of Kirkhams and Wilcoks fixed and lease rents, 11 March 1618

MS 13154, 40A6
Rental of Wilcoks, date missing, Henry V [*c.*1420]

MS 13155, 40A6
Extent of Kirkhams and Wilcoks, of Sir William Capell and his cofeoffees, 3 August 1502, no acreages given

MS 13156, 40A6
Extent on parchment of Kirkhams and Wilcoks, of Henry Capell esq., 5 March 1577

MS 13157, 40A6
Extent on paper of Kirkhams and Wilcoks, of Henry Capell esq., 5 March 1577

MS 13158, 40A6
Survey book [damaged, with fragments missing] of Kirkhams and Wilcoks, 2–4 September 1566, containing extent, rental of customary tenants, and short rental of freeholders

MS 13159, 40A6
Survey book of Little Fransham Kirkhams and Wilcoks, of Sir Arthur Capell, 12 April 1605, containing extent and rental (the cover is made from an indenture lease of 3 pieces of Great Fransham demesne, 1595)

MS 13160, 40A6
Undated rental of Kirkhams and Wilcoks lease rents, with valuations per acre of demesne lands [c.1609]

MS 13162, 40A6
Bundle catalogued as 'Notes re commons in Little Fransham' and containing: several paper sheets with notes and brief manor court roll extracts re dispute over lordship of manor and soil of Little Fransham between Sir Arthur Capell and Richard Beckham senior, gent. in 1595; late sixteenth-century copy of undated rental of Kirkhams and Wilcoks [1484]; undated short rental of Wilcoks [c.1494]; undated rental of Kirkhams and Wilcoks [c.1530]; updated copy of rental of Kirkhams and Wilcoks [1502]; extract (concerning one surrender) of manor court roll of Kirkhams and Wilcoks, 1542; two versions, in paper book and on parchment, of incomplete undated extent of Kirkhams and Wilcoks [c.1510]; late sixteenth-century copy of rental of the manor of Sparham Hall in Little Fransham, Great Dunham, Little Dunham and Holme Hale 1385/6

MS 13165, 40A7
Rentals, Kirkhams and Wilcoks and Great Fransham (Capell portion), 1780s

MS 13166, 40A7
Copy of manor court roll and rental, 1502 (as MS 13053 40A2) and of manor and leet court roll, 1504, Kirkhams and Wilcoks; copy of manor court rolls, Great Fransham, 1502 and 1504

MS 13167, 40A7
Damaged copy of extent of Kirkhams and Wilcoks, 1502 (as MS 13155 40A6, but with acreages); manor and leet court roll, Kirkhams and Wilcoks, 1515–6; leet court rolls, Mills-on-the-Moor, 1495–7, 1502, 1515, 1519–20, 1523–4, 1527, 1531, date missing [1540s], 1597

MS 13169, 40A7
Manor and leet court book, Kirkhams and Wilcoks, 1548–58; Mills-on-the-Moor, 1550–5, 1557–8

MS 13170, 40A7
Extracts of manor court rolls, Great Fransham (Capell portion), 1605/6, 1607, 1611, and of manor and leet court, Kirkhams and Wilcoks, 1611

MS 13173, 40A7
Rental, Kirkhams and Wilcoks, 1655

MS 13175, 40A7
Six undated rentals: short rental of free tenants of Sir Peter le Straunge in Little Fransham, Great Fransham and Necton, with list of other tenants paying farm and customary rents [Kirkhams] [c.1375]; short rental of rents received by William Wyskard, bailiff [of the lord of Kirkhams and Wilcoks], from tenants of Ellinghams manor, tenants in Great Fransham and from others in Scarning [mid fifteenth century]; short rental of Kirkhams, [c.1487]; incomplete short rental of lands of Kirkhams in Great Fransham and of fee simple lands in Scarning [late fifteenth century]; copy of rental of lands of Kirkhams in Great Fransham [c.1395]; short rental of Wilcoks [c.1487]

MS 13176, 40A7
Rental of Lady Emma le Strange [Kirkhams] for her free and customary tenants in Little Fransham, Great Fransham and Necton, 6 October 1384

MS 13177, 40A7
Depositions in an ecclesiastical case between the rector of [Great] Fransham and the vicar of Necton re tithes due on Pylwode, [heading missing, but dated 1427 on the evidence of one witness who referred to an event of 30 years before, in 1397]

MS 13205–14, 40B3
Manor and leet court rolls, Kirkhams and Wilcoks, 1589–98

MS 13219, 40A7
Undated short rental of William Straunge [Wilcoks] [c.1395]

MS 13221, 40A7
Writ commissioning an Inquest for a case in Chancery between Sir Arthur Capell and Nicholas Mynne gent., with a set of interrogatories, 1598

MS 13223, 40 B4
Final concord, 1347 (joins TNA CP 25/1/165/159.760)

MS 13227, 40B4
Charter grant, 1429

MS 13234, 40B4
Indenture lease, 1485

MS 13235, 40B4
Charter grant, 1486

MS 13249–50, 40B4
Charter grants, 1520

MS 13251, 40B4
Indenture sale of timber and underwood growing in [various parts of the demesne of Kirkhams and Wilcoks] Little Fransham, 1526

MS 13252, 40B4
Charter grant, 1527

MS 13253, 40B4
Indenture lease, 1532

MS 13255, 40B4
Indenture of bargain and sale, 1538

MS 13256–7, 40B4
Indenture leases, 1543 and 1555

MS 13260–1, 40 B4
Charter grants, 1578 and 1590

MS 13265, 40B4
Indenture lease, 1598

MS 13268, 40B4
Copies of charters and of indentures of exchange, 1594 and 1596

MS 13270–1, 40B4
Indenture leases, 1598

MS 13274, 40C2 to MS 13323, 40C2
Fifty indenture leases, 1601–1631

MS 13326, 40C2
Indenture lease, 1637

MS 13328, 40C2
Indenture lease, 1739

MS 13337, 40C2
Indenture lease, 1761

MS 13390, 40B7
Papers re case between Sir Arthur Capell and Nicholas Mynne gent., 1597–9

MS 13391, 40B7
Royal writ commissioning the hearing and determining of a case between Sir Arthur Capell and Nicholas Mynne gent., 1598

MS 13392, 40B7
Decree in Chancery re a case between Sir Arthur Capell and Nicholas Mynne gent., 1601

MS 13393, 40B7
Decree in Chancery re a case between Sir Arthur Capell and Nicholas Mynne gent., 1602 [as TNA C 78/128/4]

MS 13409, 40C1
Copies of two charter grants, 1480 and 1501

MS 13413, 40C1
Bond re land in Great Fransham stocked with rabbits, 1461

MS 13415, 40C3
Manor and leet court book, Kirkhams and Wilcoks and Mills-on-the-Moor, 1610–6

MS 13416, 40C3
Manor and leet court book, Kirkhams and Wilcoks, 1580, 1582 and 1586–7

MS 21063, 34F
Extracts of manor court rolls of Herringshall and Dikewood in Wendling, 1623–1790

NNAS, G1/7
Wendling Abbey sacrist's rental, 1386/7

NRS 1730, 10F6
Copy of a Recovery re the manor of Ellinghams, Curtelys and Rustyns, 1588

NRS 3828–3838, 13E4
Eleven deeds re a property in Great Fransham, 1682–1757

NRS 6762 and 6902
Two charter grants, 1292 (microfilm)

NRS 11288, 26B2
Leet and manor court book, West Bradenham, 1499–1506

NRS 12175, 27B6
Copy of an indenture of conveyance, 1769

NRS 12346, 27C5
Leet and manor court book, West Bradenham, 1496

NRS 12710, 37F4
Undated charter grant [c.1273–90]

NRS 24133–4, 119X
Manor court books, Wendling Nuper Abbis, 1761–1811 and 1814–69

NRS 24136 119X
Rental of demesne and tenanted lands, Wendling, 1777

PD 143/46–7
Necton churchwardens' accounts, 1536–99 and 1657–92

PD 143/48
Necton churchwardens' accounts, 1693–1735

PD 143/76
Rental of lands late of William Mascale of Great Fransham, 1434/5

PD 143/77
Indenture grant, 1509

PD 143/79
Copies of Great Fransham Rectory manor court rolls, 1510, 1548 and 1558

PD 143/82
Indenture grant at farm, 1598

PD 299/47–54
Eight court books of West Bradenham manor, 1625–1797

PD 299/59
Rentals of West Bradenham manor, 1750–1797

PD 682/1
Parish register, Little Fransham, 1538–1730

PD 683/1
Parish register, Great Fransham, 1558–1716

PHI/126, 577X1
Undated release [1331/2 or slightly later]

Traf 710, 92X5
Grant of custody and wardship, 1569

WAL 314, 272X4
Copy of decree in Chancery, 1657

WIS 11, 163X1
Court roll extracts of Kempstone manor, 1359–1413, and depositions re bounds of Kempstone foldcourse.

All **wills**, except those proved in the Prerogative Court of Canterbury and accessible in the National Archives (TNA PROB), are held in Norfolk Record Office, and were proved either in the Norwich Consistory Court (NCC) or in the Archdeaconries of Norwich (ANW) or Norfolk (ANF).

All **probate inventories** (DN/INV) cited in the text are held in Norfolk Record Office.

The British Library

BL Add MS 10621
Receipt book of Hempton Priory, 1501/2

BL Add MS 61900
Cartulary of Creake Abbey

BL Add Ch 6192
Charter grant [*ante c.*1310]

BL Add Ch 6193
Indenture lease, 1609

BL Add Ch 14669
Charter grant, 1312

BL Add Ch 39413 and 39414
Final concord (joining documents) re manors of Ellinghams, Curteleyes and Rustyns, 1588

BL Add Ch 66654
Charter grant, 1390

BL Add Ch 71036
Undated charter grant [13th century]

BL Add Ch 71037
Receipt, 1345

BL Add Ch 71038
Release, 1352

BL Add Ch 71039
Indenture, 1354

BL Add Ch 71040
Charter grant, 1359

BL Add Ch 71046
Indenture leading the uses of a deed, 1409

BL Add Ch 71048
Indenture grant, 1520

BL Add Ch 71050
Indenture lease, 1613

BL Harley MS 2110
Cartulary of Castle Acre Priory

Cambridge University Library, Cambridge

CUL Dd VIII 42
Undated rental book of West Acre Priory [early sixteenth century]

Christ Church Oxford Library

3d.2.1
Court Book of Wendling Nuper Abbis and other manors, 1550–8

MS Estates 53
Rental of 1558 or slightly earlier and many later documents relating to the manor of Wendling Nuper Abbis

Essex Record Office, Chelmsford

A8173
Cartulary of Sir William Capel, 1515

Hertfordshire Archives and Local Studies, Hertford

HRO M/155
Undated charter grant, *c*.1273–*c*.1290

HRO 8179
Account roll of Sir William Oldhall's farmers, bailiff and messor, Kirkhams and Wilcoks with part of Great Fransham, 1438–9

HRO 8181
Fragment of court book, 1538–40

HRO 8182
Charter grant, 1598

HRO 8184
Charter grant, 1318

HRO 8185
Account roll of Sir William Oldhall's farmer and bailiff, Kirkhams and Wilcoks with part of Great Fransham, 1431–2

HRO 8186
Paper book of short rentals of the 'Lordshyppe off Lityll Fransham', Kirkhams and Wilcoks, 1532/3, 1538–42

HRO 10652
Manor and leet court book, Kirkhams and Wilcoks, 1680–88

Holkham Hall

Davidson, Holkham 953
Manor and leet court roll, West Bradenham, 1609

Davidson, Tittleshall 68
Field book of Beeston, 1550–51

Longham Bundle 1, 20
Undated charter grant [1293–1304]

Longham Bundle 3, 34
Late fifteenth-century copy of rental of Great Fransham rectory manor, 1343; extract of rental of Wendling Abbey manor, 1446–7; extract of rental of Guntons manor, 1481/2

Longham Bundle 8, 401
Notes re wood sold at Great Fransham, 1564

Tittleshall Register Books 29
Extract of Herringshall in Wendling (Heryngsaugh) manor court roll, 1557

Tittleshall Register Rolls 39
Account of properties of West Acre Priory taken by the Bishop's bailiff, 1435

Tittleshall Register Rolls 43
Account of bailiff of West Acre Priory, 1457

Tittleshall Register Rolls 78
Account of bailiff of West Acre Priory, 1505

Tittleshall Register Rolls 147
Rental of West Acre Priory [date missing, early sixteenth century, pre-Dissolution]

The National Archives (formerly the Public Record Office), Kew

TNA C 1/864/44–6
Pleadings in a case in Chancery between Ralph Orrell and Thomas Chester, 1533–8

TNA C 3/177/25
Pleadings in a case in Chancery between John Tompson and Thomas and Dorothy Stalworthie, 1558–79

TNA C 21/M18/12
Depositions in a case in Chancery between Edward Mynn and Elizabeth Shipdham, *c*.1645

TNA C 66/999
Grant of concealed monastic lands, Patent Roll, 1564

TNA C 66/1091/22
Licence to alienate lands formerly of Hempton Priory, Patent Roll, 1572

TNA C 78/128/4
Decree in Chancery re a case between Sir Arthur Capell and Nicholas Mynne gent., 1602 [as MS 13393 40B7]

TNA C 132/31/3
Inquisition post mortem, Roger de Tony, 1264

TNA C 133/118/13
Inquisition post mortem, John Lestraunge, 1305

TNA C 142/70/6
Inquisition post mortem, Edward Mynne, 1543

TNA C 142/72/46
Inquisition post mortem, Thomas Wyskard, 1546

TNA C 142/85/18
Inquisition post mortem, Nicholas Mynne, 1547

TNA C 142/165/147
Inquisition post mortem, Edward Mynne, 1573

TNA C 143/94/18
Licence ad quod damnum, for alienation in mortmain, 1313

TNA C 143/390/2
Inquisition ad quod damnum, grant to Peter Le Strange of right to hold a weekly market and annual fair in Little Fransham, 1377

TNA C 143/442/2
Inquisition ad quod damnum, grant to Geoffrey de Fransham to divert a road in Great Fransham, 1410

TNA C 260/53/5
List of temporalities of West Acre Priory, 1342

TNA CP 25/1/156/57.595
Final concord, 1234

TNA CP 25/1/157/69.882
Final concord, 1244

TNA CP 25/1/157/82.1212
Final concord, 1254

TNA CP 25/1/159/109.174
Final concord, 1280

TNA CP 25/1/160/116.645
Final concord, 1293

TNA CP 25/1/164/158.737
Final concord, 1346

TNA CP 25/1/165/159.760
Final concord, 1347

TNA CP 25/1/167/170.1331
Final concord, 1368

TNA CP 25/1/168/177.73
Final concord, 1382

TNA CP 25/1/168/183.54
Final concord, 1405

TNA CP 25/1/283/16.446
Final concord, 1268

TNA E 36/98
Bailiff's account with rental of Scarning (Northendhall, Guntons and Rougholme) ex part Hoo, 1558

TNA E 40/8506
Undated charter grant [*ante* 1265]

TNA E 40/8769
Charter grant, 1253

TNA E 40/8885
Undated charter grant [*ante* 1265]

TNA E 40/8979
Undated release [mid 13th century]

TNA E 40/10111
Charter grant, 1327

TNA E 40/10463
Undated charter grant [1265–73]

TNA E 40/10496
Charter grant, 1316

TNA E 40/10516
Release, 1316

TNA E 40/10519
Indenture of agreement, 1297

TNA E 40/10528
Charter grant, 1311

TNA E 40/10539
Undated charter grant, mid 13th century

TNA E 40/10540
Undated charter grant [*ante* 1265]

TNA E 40/10571–3
Three undated charter grants [1265–73]

TNA E 40/10574 and E 40/10575
Two charter grants, 1299

TNA E 40/10610
Indenture of grant in fee farm, 1303

TNA E 40/10684
Undated charter grant [*ante* 1265]

TNA E 40/10712
Undated charter grant [*ante* 1265]

TNA E 40/10919
Release, 1292

TNA E 40/11038
Undated charter grant [1265–73]

TNA E 40/12003
Undated charter grant [*ante* 1265]

TNA E 40/12118
Undated release [1265–73]

TNA E 40/12124
Undated release [mid 13th century]

TNA E 40/14712
Loose sheet from a manor court book [of Northendhall, 1549]

TNA E 42/216
Undated release [mid 13th century]

TNA E 138/3/84
Grant of farm of lands of Hempton Priory, 1544

TNA E 150/659/7
Inquisition post mortem, Henry Mynne, 1567

TNA E 179/149/7
Lay Subsidy assessment rolls, 1327

TNA E 179/149/9
Lay Subsidy assessment rolls, 1332

TNA E 179/149/53
Poll Tax assessment rolls, 1379 and 1381

TNA E 179/238/111
Lay Subsidy assessment rolls, 1337

TNA E 179/150/213
Lay Subsidy assessment rolls, 1524/5

TNA E 179/150/310
Lay Subsidy assessment rolls, 1543

TNA E 179/151/317
Lay Subsidy assessment rolls, 1544

TNA E 179/335/890, E 179/336/535, E 179/337/344 and E 179/338/422
Hearth Tax exemption lists, Little Fransham, 1570–3

TNA E 318/3/84
Particulars of sale of Crown lands, 1544

TNA JUST 1/1258A
Assize roll, 1281/2–1283/4

TNA JUST 1/1258B
Assize roll, 1284/5

TNA LR 14/570 and LR 14/571
Two undated charter grants [mid 13th century]

TNA SC 2/192/95
Manor court rolls of Rougholme in Gressenhall, 1504–9, 1516–21, 1523, 1528, 1530 and 1534 [rolls of 1428/9–1430/31 contain nothing of relevance to Fransham]. As NRO MR 28 240X6

TNA SC 2/192/96
Manor court book of Northendhall and Rougholme ex part Hoo, 1548–68

TNA SC 2/192/102
Manor court roll of Herringshall and Dikewood in Wendling, 1559

TNA SC 2/193/3
Manor court roll of Herringshall and Dikewood in Wendling, 1608–9

TNA SC 2/193/4
Manor court book of Herringshall and Dikewood in Wendling, and West Bradenham, 1619–20

TNA SC 2/194/21
Manor court roll of Wendling Abbey, 1465–67

TNA SC 2/194/22–3
Manor court rolls of Wendling Abbey, Northendhall and Guntons, 1513 and 1515–17

TNA SC 8/343/16168
Incomplete and undated petition to the King from Gressenhall and Great Fransham for relief from taxation [*c*.1336]

TNA SC 11/473
Undated short rental of Wendling Abbey lands in Great and Little Fransham and elsewhere [*c*.1540]

TNA SC 11/476
Incomplete copy of an undated short rental of lands of the chapel of St Nicholas at Rougholme in Great Fransham and elsewhere [late fifteenth century]

TNA SC 11/478
Undated short rental of Northendhall and Guntons manors [mid sixteenth century]

TNA SC 11/483
Short rental of fixed and farm rents of manors of Richard Hoo, 1557

TNA SC 11/485 and SC 11/486
Short rental of fixed and farm rents of manors of Richard Hoo, 1558 and 1559

TNA SC 12/3/22
Rental of lands of the chapel of St Nicholas at Rougholme, 1548

TNA SC 12/3/23
Rental of the possessions of Richard Hoo in Great and Little Fransham and elsewhere, the manors of Northendhall, Scarning Parva, Guntons and part of Rougholme, 1549 with amendments of 1552

TNA SC 12/3/24
Undated rental of the possessions of Richard Hoo, rough copy, partly rearranged, of TNA SC12/3/23

TNA SP 23/73
Papers of the Committee for the Compounding of Delinquents 1649

TNA WARD 2/52/177/91
Undated charter grant [13th century]

TNA WARD 2/53/179/10
Undated charter grant [mid 13th century]

TNA WARD 2/53/179/15
Undated charter grant [*ante* 1290]

Raynham Hall

RAW Norfolk manorial, T–W
Manor and leet court rolls, Wendling Abbey, 1513–21

Suffolk Record Office (Bury St Edmunds)

SRO E3/10/9.16
Manor and leet court book, Kirkhams and Wilcoks, 1599

Thetford Borough Archive, Thetford

TBA T/C1/10
Book containing copies of deeds relating to the estate of Sir Richard Fulmerston, sixteenth and early seventeenth century

University of Chicago Library, Chicago

Norfolk Collection of Misc. English Deeds Box III Folder 20
Release, 1678

University of Nottingham Library

Mi D 3617/1
Undated charter grant [mid thirteenth century]

Documents in the possession of C. Gardner esq. of South Creake, Norfolk

Gardner A
Indenture lease, 1568

Gardner BB
Lease, 1719

Gardner F
Charter grant, 1472

Gardner G
Release, 1495

Gardner H
Charter grant, 1507

Gardner L
Charter grant, 1570

Documents in the possession of N.E. Salmon Ltd. of Great Fransham

Salmon A
Copy of draft of marriage settlement, 1761

Salmon C and D
Lease and release, 1801

Salmon F
Feoffment, 1801

Salmon G
Feoffment, 1806

Document in private possession

Priv. Pos. 1
Court Book of Great Fransham Rectory manor 1671–1856, including records of manor courts and courts leet of Great Fransham manor (ex-Mynne non-Capell portion) for 1671, 1674 and 1675 (titled, incorrectly, as Rougholme and Ellinghams etc.)

Secondary sources

Åberg, N. 1926 — *The Anglo-Saxons in England* (Stockholm)

Albone, J.E. 2016 — *Roman Roads in the Changing Landscape of Eastern England c.AD410–1850* (PhD thesis, University of East Anglia)

Allen, M.J. 1991 — 'Analysing the Landscape: a Geographical Approach to Archaeological Problems', in Schofield (ed.) 1991, 39–57

Allison, K.J. 1955 — 'The Lost Villages of Norfolk', *Norfolk Archaeol.* 31, 116–62

Allison, K.J. 1957 — 'The Sheep-Corn Husbandry of Norfolk in the Sixteenth and Seventeenth Centuries', *Agric. Hist. Rev.* 5, 12–30

Anderson, S, Breen, A.M., Caruth, J. and Gill, D. 1996 — 'The Late Medieval Pottery Industry on the North Suffolk Border', *Medieval Ceramics* 20, 1–12

Andrews, P. 1992 — 'Middle Saxon Norfolk: evidence for settlement, 650–850', *The Annual* (Norfolk Archaeol. Hist. Res. Group) 13–28

Arnold, C.J. 1984 — *Roman Britain to Saxon England* (London)

Arnold, C.J. 1988 — *An archaeology of the early Anglo-Saxon kingdoms* (London)

Arnold, C.J. and Wardle, P. 1981 — 'Early medieval settlement patterns in England', *Medieval Archaeol.* 25, 145–9

Ashley, S. 2006 — 'Recent finds of Anglo-Norman 'High-Status' objects from Norfolk', *Norfolk Archaeol.* 45, 105–8

Ashley, S. and Marsden, A. (eds) 2014 — *Landscapes and Artefacts: Studies in East Anglian Archaeology Presented to Andrew Rogerson* (Oxford), 189–97

Ashley, S. and Penn, K. 2012 — ''Contained the bones of Horses': an Early Anglo-Saxon cemetery at Sporle with Palgrave', *Norfolk Archaeol.* 46, 281–310

Ashwin, T. 1996 — 'Excavation of an Iron Age site at Silfield, Wymondham, Norfolk, 1992–3', *Norfolk Archaeol.* 42, 241–82

Ashwin, T. 1999 — 'Studying Iron Age Settlement in Norfolk' in Davies and Williamson (eds) 1999, 100–24

Ashwin, T. and Davison, A. 2005 — *An Historical Atlas of Norfolk*, 3rd edition (Chichester)

Ashwin, T. and Flitcroft, M. 1999 — 'The Launditch and its setting: excavations at the Launditch, Beeston with Bittering, and Iron Age features and finds from its vicinity', *Norfolk Archaeol.* 43, 217–56

Astill, G. and Grant, A. (eds) 1988 — *The Countryside of Medieval England* (Oxford)

Aston, M. 1985 — *Interpreting the Landscape* (London)

Aston, M., Austin, D. and Dyer, C. (eds) 1989 — *The Rural Settlements of Medieval England: studies dedicated to M.W. Beresford and J.G. Hurst* (Oxford)

Atkin, M. 1978 — 'Viking race-courses? The distribution of *Skeið* place-name elements in northern England', *J. English Place-Names Soc.* 10, 26–39

Atkin, M., Ayers, B. and Jennings, S. 1983 — 'Thetford-type ware production in Norwich', *East Anglian Archaeol.* 17, 61–97

Ayscough, S. and Caley, J. (eds) 1802 — *Taxatio Ecclesiastica Angliae et Walliae auctoritate Papae Nicholai IV circa 1291* (London)

Bailey, M. 1989 — *A marginal economy? East Anglian Breckland in the Later Middle Ages* (Cambridge)

Bailey, M. 2002 — *The English Manor c.1200–c.1500* (Manchester)

Barfield, L. and Hodder, M. 1987 — 'Burnt Mounds as saunas, and the prehistory of bathing', *Antiquity* 61, 370–79

Barney, J.M. 2000 — 'Building a fortune: Philip Case attorney, 1712–1792', *Norfolk Archaeol.* 43, 441–56

Barnes, G. and Williamson, T. 2006 — *Hedgerow History: Ecology, History and Landscape Character* (Macclesfield)

Barnes, G. and Williamson, T. 2015 — *Rethinking Ancient Woodland: the archaeology and history of woods in Norfolk* (Hatfield)

Barringer, C. (ed.) 1984 — *Aspects of East Anglian Prehistory 20 years after Rainbird Clarke* (Norwich)

Barringer, C. 2005a — 'Heaths and Commons' in Ashwin and Davison (eds) 2005, 84–5

Barringer, C. 2005b — 'Norfolk Hundreds' in Ashwin and Davison (eds) 2005, 96–7

Batcock, N. 1991 — *The Ruined and Disused Churches of Norfolk*, East Anglian Archaeol. 51

Bedingfield, A.L. (ed.) 1966 — *A Cartulary of Creake Abbey*, Norfolk Record Soc. 35

Bennett, H.S. 1937 — *Life on the English Manor: a Study of Peasant Conditions 1150–1400* (Cambridge)

Bennett, K. 1983 — 'Devensian late-glacial and Flandrian vegetational history at Hockham Mere, Norfolk, England', *New Phytologist* 95, 457–87

Beresford, G. 2009 — *Caldecote: the development and desertion of a Hertfordshire village* Soc. Medieval Archaeol. Monog. Ser. 28

Bigmore, P. 1982 — 'Villages and Towns' in Cantor (ed.) 1982, 154–92

Blair, J. 2018 — *Building Anglo-Saxon England* (Princeton)

Blake, W.J. 1952 — 'Norfolk Manorial Lords in 1316, Part II', *Norfolk Archaeol.* 30, 263–86

Blinkhorn, P. 2012 — *The Ipswich Ware Project: ceramics, trade and society in Middle Saxon England*, Medieval Pottery Res. Group Occas. Pap. 7 (Dorchester)

Blomefield, F. 1807 — *An Essay towards a Topographical History of the County of Norfolk* Volume 6, continued by C. Parkin (London)

Blomefield, F. 1808 — *An Essay towards a Topographical History of the County of Norfolk* Volume 9, continued by C. Parkin (London)

Blomefield, F. 1809 — *An Essay towards a Topographical History of the County of Norfolk* Volume 10, continued by C. Parkin (London)

Boyle, M. 2008 — 'An Archaeological Evaluation and Historic Building Recording at Lane Farm, Main Road, Little Fransham, Norfolk' NAU Archaeology Report 1954

Brand, P. (ed.) 1999 — *Curia Regis Rolls of Henry III preserved in the Public Record Office, Volume XVIII 27 to 30 Henry III (1243–1245)* (Woodbridge and London)

Brindle, T. 2014	*The Portable Antiquities Scheme and Roman Britain*, Brit. Museum Res. Pub. 196	Cal. Inq. Post Mort. 2010	*Calendar of Inquisitions Post Mortem and other analogous documents preserved in the Public Record Office Vol. XXIV 11–15 Henry VI* (Woodbridge and London)
Brown, P. (ed.) 1984	*Domesday Book: Norfolk* (Chichester)		
Brown, R., Teague, S, Loe, L., Sudds, B. and Popescu, E. 2020	*Excavations at Stoke Quay, Ipswich: Southern Gipeswic and the parish of St Augustine*, East Anglian Archaeol. 172	Cal. Pat. Rol. 1893	*Calendar of the Patent Rolls preserved in the Public Record Office Edward I Vol II AD 1381–1292* (London)
		Cal. Pat. Rol. 1906	*Calendar of the Patent Rolls preserved in the Public Record Office Henry III Vol. III AD 1232–1247* (London)
Brown, T. and Foard, G. 1998	'The Saxon landscape: a regional perspective' in Everson, P. and Williamson, T. (eds) *The archaeology of landscape: studies presented to Christopher Taylor*, 67–94 (Manchester)	Cal. Pat. Rol. 1908	*Calendar of the Patent Rolls preserved in the Public Record Office Henry III Vol. IV AD 1247–1258* (London)
Brudenell. M. 2018	*Late Bronze Age to Middle Iron Age*, Regional Research Framework Review. Available http://eaareports.org.uk/algao-east/regional-research-framework-review/. Accessed 15 April 2021	Cal. Pat. Rol. 1910	*Calendar of the Patent Rolls preserved in the Public Record Office Henry VI Vol. VI AD 1452–1461* (London)
Bryant, T.H. 1903	*Norfolk Churches. The Hundred of Launditch* (Norwich Mercury Series, Norwich)	Cal. Pat. Rol. 1925	*Calendar of the patent Rolls preserved in the Public Record Office Edward VI Vol. III AD 1549–1551* (London)
Butler, L. and Wade-Martins, P. 1989	*The Deserted Medieval Village of Thuxton, Norfolk*, East Anglian Archaeol. 46	Cal. Pat. Rol. 1939	*Calendar of the patent Rolls preserved in the Public Record Office Philip and Mary Vol. IV AD 1557–1558* (London)
Cal. Close Rol. 1898	*Calendar of the Close Rolls preserved in the Public Record Office Edward III Vol. II AD 1330–1333* (London)	Cal. Pat. Rol. 1948	*Calendar of the Patent Rolls preserved in the Public Record Office Elizabeth Vol. II 1560–1563* (London)
Cal. Close Rol. 1900	*Calendar of the Close Rolls preserved in the Public Record Office Edward I Vol. I AD 1272–1279* (London)	Cal. Pat. Rol. 1982	*Calendar of the Patent Rolls preserved in the Public Record Office Elizabeth I Vol. VII 1575–1578* (London)
Cal. Close Rol. 1905	*Calendar of the Close Rolls preserved in the Public Record Office Edward III Vol. VIII AD 1346–1349* (London)	Caley, J. and Hunter, J. (eds) 1817	*Valor Ecclesiasticus temp. Henry VIII auctoritate regia institutus* III (London)
Cal. Close Rol. 1908	*Calendar of the Close Rolls preserved in the Public Record Office Edward I Vol. V AD 1302–1307* (London)	Caley, J., Ellis, H. and Bandinel, B. (eds) 1825 and 1830	*Monasticon Anglicanum* Vols.5 and 6 (London)
Cal. Fine Rol. 1921	*Calendar of the Fine Rolls preserved in the Public Record Office, Vol. VI, Edward III AD 1347–1336* (London)	Cam, H.M. 1930	*The Hundred and the Hundred Rolls* (London)
Cal. Inq. Misc. 1916	*Calendar of Inquisitions Miscellaneous (Chancery) preserved in the Public Record Office Vol. II* (London)	Campbell, B.M.S. 1980	'Population Change and the Genesis of Commonfields on a Norfolk Manor', *Econ. Hist. Rev.* 33, 174–92
Cal. Inq. Post Mort. 1906	*Calendar of Inquisitions Post Mortem and other analogous documents preserved in the Public Record Office Vol. II Edward I* (London)	Campbell, B.M.S. 1981a	'Commonfield Origins — the Regional Dimension' in Rowley, T. (ed.) *The Origins of Open-Field Agriculture*, 112–29 (London)
Cal. Inq. Post Mort. 1909	*Calendar of Inquisitions Post Mortem and other analogous documents preserved in the Public Record Office Vol. VII Edward III* (London)	Campbell, B.M.S. 1981b	'The extent and layout of Commonfields in Eastern Norfolk', *Norfolk Archaeol.* 38, 5–32
Cal. Inq. Post Mort. 1910	*Calendar of Inquisitions Post Mortem and other analogous documents preserved in the Public Record Office Vol. VI Edward II* (London)	Campbell, B.M.S. 1986	'The complexity of manorial structure in medieval Norfolk', *Norfolk Archaeol.* 39, 215–62
Cal. Inq. Post Mort. 1921	*Calendar of Inquisitions Post Mortem and other analogous documents preserved in the Public Record Office Vol. X Edward III* (London)	Campbell, B.M.S. 2000	*English Seigniorial Agriculture 1250–1450* (Cambridge)
		Cantor, L. (ed.) 1982	*The English Medieval Landscape* (London)
Cal. Inq. Post Mort. 1952	*Calendar of Inquisitions Post Mortem and other analogous documents preserved in the Public Record Office Vol. XIV Edward III* (London)	Carthew, G.A. 1877–9	*The Hundred of Launditch and Deanery of Brisley in the County of Norfolk* Vols I–III (London)
Cal. Inq. Post Mort. 1970	*Calendar of Inquisitions Post Mortem and other analogous documents preserved in the Public Record Office Vol. XV 1–7 Richard II* (London)	Carthew, G.A. 1883	*A History topographical, archaeological, genealogical and biographical of the parishes of West and East Bradenham with those of Necton and Holme Hale in the County of Norfolk* (Norwich)
Cal. Inq. Post Mort. 1974	*Calendar of Inquisitions Post Mortem and other analogous documents preserved in the Public Record Office Vol. XVI 7–15 Richard II* (London)	Carver, M. 1989	'Kingship and material culture in early Anglo-Saxon East Anglia' in Bassett, S. (ed), *The Origins of Anglo-Saxon kingdoms* (London)

Cautley, H.M. 1949 — *Norfolk Churches* (Ipswich)

Cavill, P. 2018 — *A New Dictionary of English Field-Names* (Nottingham)

Census Office 1831 — *Comparative Account of the Population of Great Britain in the Years 1801, 1811, 1821 and 1831* (London)

Cherry, J. 1991 — 'Pottery and Tile' in Blair, J. and Ramsay, N. (eds) *English Medieval Industries: Craftsmen, Techniques, Products*, 189–209 (London)

Cherry, J.F., Gamble, G. and Shennan, S. (eds) 1978 — *Sampling in Contemporary British Archaeology*, Brit. Archaeol. Rep. Brit. Ser. 50 (Oxford)

Chester-Kadwell, M. 2009 — *Early Anglo-Saxon Communities in the Landscape of Norfolk: Cemeteries* Brit. Archaeol. Rep. Brit. Ser. 481 (Oxford)

Christie, N. and Stamper, P. (eds) 2012 — *Medieval Rural Settlement: Britain and Ireland, AD 800–1600* (Oxford)

Clapham, A.W. 1930 — *English Romanesque Architecture before the Conquest* (Oxford)

Clark, J.G.D. and Fell, C.I. 1953 — 'The Early Iron Age at Micklemoor Hill, West Harling, Norfolk, and its pottery', *Proc. Prehist. Soc.* 19 (1), 1–40

Clark, J.G.D. and Higgs, E.S. 1960 — 'Flint Industry', in Clark, J.G.D., 'Excavations at the Neolithic Site at Hurst Fen, Mildenhall, Suffolk (1954, 1957 and 1958)', *Proc. Prehist. Soc.* 26, 202–45

Clark, R.H. and Schofield, A.J. 1991 — 'By Experiment and Calibration: an Integrated Approach to Archaeology of the Ploughsoil', in Schofield (ed.) 1991, 93–105

Clarke, D.L. 1970 — *Beaker Pottery of Great Britain and Ireland* (Cambridge)

Clarke, H. 1970 — 'Excavations on a kiln site at Grimston, Pott Row, Norfolk', *Norfolk Archaeol.* 35, 79–95

Clarke, H. and Carter, A. 1977 — *Excavations in King's Lynn 1963–70*, Soc. Medieval Archaeol. Monog. Ser. 7

Clarke, R.R. 1939 — 'The Iron Age in Norfolk and Suffolk', *Archaeol. J.* 96, 1–113

Clarke, R.R. 1960 — *East Anglia* (London)

Clarke, R.R. and Clarke, W.G. 1937 — *In Breckland Wilds*, 2nd edition (Cambridge)

Clay, P. 2007 — 'Claylands Revisited: the Prehistory of W.G. Hoskins's Midlands Plain' in Fleming, A. and Hingley, R. (eds) 2007, 70–82

Clayton, P. 2009 — 'The Art Fund and Antiquities', *Minerva* 20 (5), 38–9

Cobbett, W. 2001 — *Rural Rides* (edited by I. Dyck, London)

Colvin, H.M. 1951 — *The White Canons of England* (Oxford)

Corbett, W. and Dent, D. 1993 — 'The Soil Landscapes', in Wade-Martins (ed.) 1993, 18–9

Corbett, W.J. 1897 — 'Elizabethan village surveys', *Trans. Royal Hist. Soc.* 11, 67–87

Cox, B. 1973 — 'The significance of the distribution of English place-names in -HAM in the Midlands and East Anglia', *J. English Place-Name Soc.* 5, 15–73

Cox, J.C. 1906 — 'The religious houses of Norfolk' in Doubleday, H.A. and Page, W. (eds) *The Victoria History of the County of Norfolk*, Vol 2 (London), 315–460

Craster, H.H.E. 1909 — *A History of Northumberland Volume IX* (Newcastle-upon-Tyne)

Crawley, P. and Sillwood, R. 2010 — 'An Archaeological Excavation at All Saints' Church, Great Fransham, Norfolk', *NAU Archaeology Report* 1438

Crook, D. (ed.) 2002 — *Curia Regis Rolls of Henry III preserved in the Public Record Office, Volume XIX 33 to 34 Henry III (1249–1250)* (London)

Crowther, D. and Pryor, F. 1985 — 'The Surface (field-walking) Survey', in Pryor, F. et al., *The Fenland Project, No.1: Archaeology and Environment in the Lower Welland Valley*, East Anglian Archaeol. 27, 44–53

Dallas, C. 1992 — 'Post-Roman Pottery', in Rogerson, A. and Lawson, A., 'The Earthwork Enclosure at Tasburgh', *East Anglian Archaeol.* 54, 31–58

Dallas, C. 1993 — *Excavations in Thetford by B.K. Davison between 1964 and 1970*, East Anglian Archaeol. 62

Dallas, C. 1994 — 'Pottery', in Ayers, B.S., *Excavations at Fishergate, Norwich, 1985*, East Anglian Archaeol. 68, 19–29

Darby, H.C. 1971 — *The Domesday Geography of Eastern England*, 3rd edition (Cambridge)

Darby, H.C. 1987 — 'Domesday Book and the Geographer' in Holt, J.C. (ed.) *Domesday Studies*, 101–19 (Woodbridge)

Davenport, F.G. 1906 — *The Economic Development of a Norfolk Manor 1086–1565* (Cambridge)

Davies, G. 2010 — 'Early Medieval 'rural centres' and West Norfolk: a growing picture of diversity, complexity and changing lifestyles, 600–1150 AD', *Medieval Archaeol.* 54, 89–122

Davies, J.A. 1996 — 'Where Eagles Dare: the Iron Age of Norfolk', *Proc. Prehist. Soc.* 62, 63-92

Davies, J.A. and Gregory, T. 1991 — 'Coinage from a Civitas: a Survey of the Roman coins found in Norfolk and their contribution to the Archaeology of the Civitas Icenorum', *Britannia* 22, 65–101

Davies, J.A. and Williamson, T. 1999 — *Land of the Iceni: the Iron Age in Northern East Anglia* (Norwich)

Davison, A. 1980 — 'West Harling: a village and its disappearance', *Norfolk Archaeol.* 37, 295–306

Davison, A. 1982 — 'Petygards and the medieval hamlet of Cotes', *East Anglian Archaeol.* 14, 102–7

Davison, A. 1983 — 'The distribution of medieval settlement in West Harling', *Norfolk Archaeol.* 38, 329–36

Davison, A. 1987 — 'Little Hockham', *Norfolk Archaeol.* 40, 84–93

Davison, A. 1988 — *Six Deserted Villages in Norfolk*, East Anglian Archaeol. 44

Davison, A. 1990 — *The Evolution of Settlement in Three Parishes in South-East Norfolk*, East Anglian Archaeol. 49

Davison, A. 1991 — 'Great Hockham — a Village which has Moved?', *Norfolk Archaeol.* 41, 145–61

Davison A. 1992 — 'The Documentary Evidence' in Dallas, C. *Excavations in Thetford by B.K. Davison between*

	1964 and 1970, East Anglian Archaeol. 62, 194–217	Ekwall, E. 1960	*The Concise Oxford Dictionary of English Place-names*, 4th edition (London)
Davison, A. 1993	'Chapter 1. The Changing Pattern of Settlement in a Breckland Parish', in Davison, A., Green, B. and Milligan, B. *Illington: A Study of a Breckland Parish and its Anglo-Saxon Cemetery*, East Anglian Archaeol. 63, 1–10	Evans, D.H. and Carter, A. 1985	'Excavations on 31–51 Pottergate (Site 149N)' in Atkin, M., Carter, A. and Evans, D.H., *Excavations in Norwich 1971–1978*, East Anglian Archaeol. 26, 9–84
Davison, A. 1994a	'The Survey of Hales, Loddon and Heckingham' in Parker Pearson and Schadla-Hall (eds) 1994, 15–20	Faden, W. 1797	*Map of Norfolk*, reprinted with an introduction by J.C. Barringer, Norfolk Record Soc. 42 (1975)
		Fairclough, J. and Hardy, M. 2004	*Thornham and the Waveney Valley: an historic landscape explored* (Great Dunham)
Davison, A. 1994b	'The field archaeology of Bodney and the Stanta Extension', *Norfolk Archaeol.* 42, 57–79	Farmer, D.H. 1987	*Oxford Dictionary of Saints*, 2nd edition (Oxford)
Davison, A. 1995	'The field archaeology of the Mannington and Wolterton estates', *Norfolk Archaeol.* 42, 160–184	Farnhill, K. 2001	*Guilds and the Parish Community in Late Medieval East Anglia, c.1470–1550* (Woodbridge)
Davison, A. 2003	'The archaeology of the parish of West Acre Part 1: field survey evidence', *Norfolk Archaeol.* 44, 202–221	Fawcett, R. 1980	'A group of churches by the architect of Great Walsingham', *Norfolk Archaeol.* 37, 277–94
Davison, A. 2007	'Investigations at Godwick and Beeston St Andrew', *Norfolk Archaeol.* 45, 141–54	Fenwick, C.C. (ed.) 2001	*The Poll Taxes of 1377, 1379 and 1381* (London)
		Fernie, E. 1983	*The Architecture of the Anglo-Saxons* (London)
Davison, A. and Cushion, B. 2004	'The archaeology of the parish of West Acre Part 2: the documentary background', *Norfolk Archaeol.* 44, 456–481	Feudal Aids 1904	*Inquisitions and Assessments relating to Feudal Aids, with other Analogous Documents preserved in the Public Record Office, AD 1284–1431 Vol. III Kent to Norfolk* (London)
Davison, A. with Cushion, B. 1999	'The archaeology of the Hargham estate', *Norfolk Archaeol.* 43, 257–274	Fisher, E.A. 1962	*The Greater Anglo-Saxon Churches* (London)
Dodwell, B. (ed.) 1952	*Feet of Fines for the County of Norfolk for the tenth year of the reign of King Richard the First, 1198–99, and for the first four years of the reign of King John, 1199–1202*, Pipe Roll Soc. Volume 65 (new series 27 for the year 1950)	Fleming, A. and Hingley, R. (eds) 2007	*Prehistoric and Roman Landscapes* (Macclesfield)
		Fleming, F. 2016	*A Persistence of Place: a Study of Continuity and Regionality in the Roman and Early Medieval Settlement Patterns of Norfolk, Kent and Somerset*, Brit. Archaeol. Rep. Brit. Ser. 626 (Oxford)
Douglas, D.C. 1927	*The Social Structure of Medieval East Anglia* (Oxford)
Dowell, S. 1965	*A History of Taxation and Taxes in England from the Earliest Times to the Present Day*, 3rd edition (London)	Foard, G. 1980	'The recovery of archaeological information by systematic fieldwalking: research in Northamptonshire and Bedfordshire', in Hayfield (ed.) 1980, 34–40
Drury, P.J. 1993	'Ceramic Building Materials' in Margeson, S. *Norwich Households: The Medieval and Post-Medieval Finds from Norwich Survey Excavations 1971–1978*, East Anglian Archaeol. 58, 163–7	Fowler, C.T. (ed.) 1922	*Curia Regis Rolls of the reigns of Richard I and John preserved in the Public Record Office, Volume I Richard I to 2 John* (London)
Drury, P.J. and Rodwell, W. 1980	'Settlement in the later Iron Age and Roman periods' in Buckley, D.G. (ed.), *Archaeology in Essex to AD 1500*, Counc. Brit. Archaeol. Res. Rep. 34	Fowler, C.T. (ed.) 1955	*Curia Regis Rolls of Henry III preserved in the Public Record Office, Volume XI 7 to 9 Henry III* (London)
Dyer, C. 1990	Short review of Davison 1988, *Medieval Archaeol.* 34, 298–9	Fowler, C. (ed.) 1959	*Curia Regis Rolls of Henry III preserved in the Public Record Office, Volume XIII 11 to 14 Henry III (1227–1230)* (London)
Dyer, C. 1991	*Hanbury: Settlement and Society in a Woodland Landscape* (Leicester)	Fowler, P.J. 1976	'Agriculture and rural settlement', in Wilson, D.M. (ed.) 1976, 23–48
Dymond, D. 1985	*The Norfolk Landscape* (London)	Frankel, M.S. and Seaman, P.J. 1983	'The Norfolk Hearth Tax Assessment, Michaelmas 1664', *Norfolk Genealogy* 15
Dymond, D. (ed.) 1995	*The Register of Thetford Priory Part 1, 1482–1517*, Norfolk Record Soc. 59
Dymond, D. (ed.) 1996	*The Register of Thetford Priory Part 2, 1518–1540*, Norfolk Record Soc. 60	Frieman, C.J. 2015	'Making a point: re-evaluating British flint daggers in their cultural and technological contexts', in Frieman, C.J. and Eriksen, B.V. (eds) *Flint Daggers in Prehistoric Europe* (Oxford)
Dymond, D. 2002	'The Parson's Glebe: Stable, Expanding or Shrinking?' in Harper-Bill, C., Rawcliffe, C. and Wilson, R.G. (eds) *East Anglia's History: Studies in honour of Norman Scarfe*, 73–91 (Woodbridge)	Fulford, M. 1990	'The Landscape of Roman Britain: a Review', *Landscape Hist.* 12, 25–31
Dymond, D.P. 1968	'The Suffolk Landscape' in Munby, L. (ed.) *East Anglian Studies*, 17–47	Gaffney, C., Gaffney, V. and Tingle, M. 1985	'Settlement, Economy or Behaviour? Micro-regional Land Use Models and the Interpretation of Surface Artefact Patterns', in Haselgrove, Millett and Smith (eds) 1985, 95–107

Gaffney, V. and Tingle, M. 1989 — *The Maddle Farm Project*, Brit. Archaeol. Rep. Brit. Ser. 200 (Oxford)

Gairdner, J. (ed.) 1891 — *Letters and Papers, Foreign and Domestic, Henry VIII, Volume 12 Part 2* (London)

Gardiner, J. (ed.) 1993a — *Flatlands and Wetlands: Current Themes in East Anglian Archaeology*, East Anglian Archaeol. 50

Gardiner, J. 1993b — 'The flint assemblage' in Davies, J.A., 'Excavation of an Iron Age pit group at London Road, Thetford', *Norfolk Archaeol.* 41, 441–61

Gardiner, J. and Williamson, T. 1993 — 'Archaeologies of a Region', in Gardiner (ed.) 1993a, 171–81

Gardiner, M. and Rippon, S. (eds) 2007 — *Medieval Landscapes* (Macclesfield)

Gerrard, C. 1997 — 'Misplaced faith? Medieval pottery and fieldwalking', *Medieval Ceramics* 21, 61–72

Gerrard, C. with Aston, M. 2007 — *The Shapwick Project, Somerset. A rural landscape explored* Soc. Medieval Archaeol. Monog. Ser. 25

Gibson, A.M. 1982 — *Beaker Domestic Sites part i*, Brit. Archaeol. Rep. Brit. Ser. 107 (i) (Oxford)

Gilchrist, R. and Reynolds, A. (eds) 2009 — *Reflections: 50 years of Medieval Archaeology, 1957–2007*, Soc. Medieval Archaeol. Monog. Ser. 30

Giles, J.A. 1853 — *Matthew Paris's English History from the year 1235 to 1273* (London)

Glasscock, R.E. 1975 (ed.) — *The Lay Subsidy of 1334* (London)

Godwin, H. 1968 — 'Studies in the post-glacial history of British vegetation 15. Organic deposits of Old Buckenham Mere, Norfolk', *New Phytologist* 67, 95–107

Gray, H.L. 1915 — *English Field Systems* (Cambridge, Massachusetts)

Green, H.S. 1980 — *The Flint Arrowheads of the British Isles*, Brit. Archaeol. Rep. Brit. Ser. 75 (Oxford)

Greenway, D.E. 1982 — 'A newly discovered fragment of the Hundred Rolls of 1279–80', *J. Soc. Archivists* 7, 73–7

Gregory, T. 1982 — 'Romano-British Settlement in West Norfolk and on the Norfolk Fen Edge' in Miles, D. (ed.), *The Romano-British Countryside*, Brit. Archeol. Rep. Brit. Ser. 103.2, 351–76 (Oxford)

Gregory, T. 1992 — *Excavations in Thetford, 1980–1982, Fison Way Volume One*, East Anglian Archaeol. 53

Gribbin, J.A. 2001 — *The Premonstratensian Order in Late Medieval England* (Woodbridge)

Gurney, D. 1993 — 'The Roman Period' in Wade-Martins (ed.) 1993, 34–5

Gurney, D. 1995 — 'Small towns and villages in Roman Norfolk. The evidence of surface and metal-detector finds' in Brown, A.E. (ed.) *Roman Small Towns in England and Beyond*, Oxbow Monog. 52, 53–67 (Oxford)

Gurney, D. 1998 — *Roman Burials in Norfolk*, East Anglian Archaeol. Occ. Pap. 4

Gurney, D. 2005 — 'Roman Norfolk' in Ashwin and Davison (eds) 2005, 28–9

Hall, D. 1982 — *Medieval Fields* (Aylesbury)

Hall, D.N. 1985 — 'Late Saxon Topography and Early Medieval Estates' in Hooke, D. (ed.) *Medieval Villages: a Review of Current Work*, 61–9 (Oxford)

Hall, D. 1988 — 'The Late Saxon Countryside: Villages and their Fields' in Hooke, D. (ed.) 1988, 99–122

Hallam, H.E. (ed.) 1988 — *The Agrarian History of England and Wales Vol. II, 1042–1350* (Cambridge)

Hamerow, H. 1993 — *Excavations at Mucking Volume 2: the Anglo-Saxon settlement* English Heritage Archaeol. Rep. 21 (London)

Hamerow, H. 2012 — *Rural Settlements and Society in Anglo-Saxon England* (Oxford)

Harding, D.W. 1974 — *The Iron Age in Lowland Britain* (London)

Hardy, M.J. 1985 — 'Mendham' and 'Metfield', *Proc. Suffolk Inst. Archaeol.* 36, 47–8

Hardy, M.J. with Martin, E.A. 1986 — 'South Elmham St Cross' and 'South Elmham St James', *Proc. Suffolk Inst. Archaeol.* 36, 147–50

Hardy, M.J. with Martin, E.A. 1987 — 'South Elmham St Margaret' and 'South Elmham All Saints and St Nicholas', *Proc. Suffolk Inst. Archaeol.* 36, 232–5

Hardy, M. with Martin, E. 1988 — 'South Elmham St Michael and St Peter', *Proc. Suffolk Inst. Archaeol.* 36, 315–7

Hardy, M. with Martin, E. 1989 — 'Flixton', *Proc. Suffolk Inst. Archaeol.* 37, 66–9

Harper-Bill, C. (ed.) 1990 — *English Episcopal Acta 6: Norwich 1070–1214* (Oxford)

Harper-Bill, C. (ed.) 2007 — *English Episcopal Acta 32: Norwich 1244–1266* (Oxford)

Harvey, P.D.A. 1989 — 'Initiative and Authority in Settlement Change', in Aston, Austin and Dyer (eds) 1989, 31–43

Hart, C. 1992 — *The Danelaw* (London)

Haselgrove, C., Millett, M. and Smith, I. 1985 (eds) — *Archaeology from the ploughsoil: studies in the collection and interpretation of field survey data* (Sheffield)

Haselgrove, C. 1985 — 'Inference from Ploughsoil Artefact Samples', in Haselgrove, Millett and Smith (eds) 1985, 7–29

Hassall, W. and Beauroy, J. (eds) 1993 — *Lordship and Landscape in Norfolk, 1250–1350; Early Records of Holkham* (London)

Hatcher, J. 1977 — *Plague, Population and the English Economy 1348–1530* (London)

Hawes, T. 2001 — *The Inhabitants of Norfolk in the Fourteenth Century: the Lay Subsidies of 1327 and 1332 preserved in the Public Record Office* (Norwich)

Hawkes, S.C. and Dunning, G.C. 1961 — 'Soldiers and settlers in Britain, fourth to fifth century: with a catalogue of animal-ornamented buckles and related belt-fittings', *Medieval Archaeol.* 5, 1–70

Hayes, P.P. 1991 — 'Models for the Distribution of Pottery around Former Agricultural Settlements', in Schofield (ed.) 1991, 81–92

Hayfield, C. 1980 — 'Wharram Percy Parish Survey', in Hayfield, C. (ed.) *Fieldwalking as a method of archaeological research* (London)

Hayfield, C. 1987 — *An Archaeological Survey of the Parish of Wharram Percy, East Yorkshire, 1. The Evolution*

	of the Roman Landscape, Brit. Archaeol. Rep. Brit. Ser. 172 (Oxford)	Hoggett, R. 2010	*The Archaeology of the East Anglian Conversion* (Woodbridge)
Healy, F.M.A. 1980	*The Neolithic in Norfolk* (Unpublished PhD thesis, Institute of Archaeology, Univ. London)	Homans, G.C. 1941	*English Villagers of the Thirteenth Century* (Harvard)
Healy, F. 1984	'Farming and field monuments: the Neolithic in Norfolk' in Barringer (ed) 1984, 77–140	Hooke, D. 1988	'Regional Variation in Southern and Central England in the Anglo-Saxon Period and its Relationship to Land-Units and Settlement' in Hooke (ed.) 1988, 123–51
Healy, F. 1991	'Appendix 1. Lithics and Pre-Iron Age Pottery' in Silvester 1991, 116–39	Hooke, D. (ed.) 1988	*Anglo-Saxon Settlements* (Oxford)
Hector, L.C. (ed.) 1979	*Curia Regis Rolls of Henry III preserved in the Public Record Office, Volume XVI 21 to 26 Henry III (1237–1242)* (London)	Hooke, D. 1989	'Early Medieval Estate and Settlement Patterns: The Documentary Evidence', in Aston, Austin and Dyer (eds) 1989, 9–30
Heslop, T.A. 2014	'Great Dunham church and its eleventh-century context' in Ashley and Marsden (eds) 2014, 189–97	Hooke, D. 2012	'"*Wealdbæra & Swina Mæst*': Wood pasture in Early Medieval England' in Turner and Silvester (eds) 2012, 32–49
Hesse, M. 2000	'Domesday land measures in Suffolk', *Landscape Hist.* 22, 21–36	Hoskins, W.G. 1955	*The Making of the English Landscape* (London)
Higham, N. 1990	'Settlement, land use and Domesday ploughlands', *Landscape Hist.* 12, 33–44	Hoskins, W.G. and Stamp, D.L. 1963	*The Common Lands of England and Wales* (London)
Hills, C. 1993	'Who were the East Anglians?', in Gardiner (ed.) 1993a, 14–23	Hudson, W. 1895	'The Assessment of the Townships of the County of Norfolk for the King's tenths and fifteenths, as settled in 1334', *Norfolk Archaeol.* 12, 243–97
Hills, C. 2017	'The Anglo-Saxon migration to Britain: an archaeological perspective" in Meller, H, Daim, F., Krause, J. and Risch, R. (eds) *Migration and Integration from Prehistory to the Middle Ages*, 239–53 (Halle (Salle))	Hudson, W. 1910	'The 'Norwich Taxation' of 1254, so far as relates to the Diocese of Norwich', *Norfolk Archaeol.* 17, 46–157
Hills, C. and Wade-Martins, P. 1976	'The Anglo-Saxon cemetery at The Paddocks, Swaffham', *East Anglian Archaeol.* 2, 1–44	Hunn, J.R. 1994	*Reconstruction and Measurement of Landscape Change: A study of six parishes in the St Albans area*, Brit. Archaeol. Rep. Brit. Ser. 236 (Oxford)
Hills, C.M. 1977	*The Anglo-Saxon cemetery at Spong Hill, North Elmham Part I: Catalogue of Cremations*, East Anglian Archaeol. 6	Hurst, J.G. 1957	'Saxo-Norman pottery in East Anglia, Part II. Thetford ware; with an account of Middle Saxon Ipswich ware', *Proc. Cambridge Antiq. Soc.* 50, 29–60
Hills, C. and Penn, K. 1981	*The Anglo-Saxon cemetery at Spong Hill, North Elmham, Part II: Catalogue of Cremations*, East Anglian Archaeol. 11	Hurst, J.G. 1959	'Middle Saxon Pottery' in Dunning, G.C. *et al.* 'Anglo-Saxon pottery: a symposium', *Medieval Archaeol.* 3, 13–31
Hills, C., Penn, K. and Rickett, R. 1984	*The Anglo-Saxon cemetery at Spong Hill, North Elmham Part III: Catalogue of Inhumations*, East Anglian Archaeol. 21	Hurst, J.G. 1962–3	'White Castle and the dating of medieval pottery', *Medieval Archaeol.* 6–7, 135–55
Hills, C., Penn, K. and Rickett, R. 1987	*The Anglo-Saxon cemetery at Spong Hill, North Elmham Part IV: Catalogue of Cremations*, East Anglian Archaeol. 34	Hurst, J.G. 1963	'Excavations at Barn Road, Norwich, 1954–55', *Norfolk Archaeol.* 33, 131–79
Hills, C., Penn, K. and Rickett, R. 1994	*The Anglo-Saxon cemetery at Spong Hill, North Elmham Part V: Catalogue of Cremations*, East Anglian Archaeol. 67	Hurst, J.G. 1976	'The Pottery' in Wilson, D.M. (ed.) 1976, 283–348
Hingley, R. 2007	'The Roman Landscape of Britain: From Hoskins to Today' in Fleming, A. and Hingley, R. (eds) 2007, 101–12	Illingworth, W. and Caley, J. (eds) 1812	*Rotuli Hundredorum Temp. Henry III and Edward I in Turr. Lond' et in Curia Receptae Scaccarii Westm. asservati* Vol. 1 (Record Commission, London)
HMC 1914	*Report on Manuscripts in various Collections Vol. VII* (Historical Manuscripts Commission)	Jacobi, R. 1984	'The Mesolithic of Northern East Anglia and Contemporary Territories' in Barringer (ed.) 1984, 43–76
Hodder, M.A. 1992	'Continuity and Discontinuity in the Landscape: Roman to Medieval in Sutton Chase', *Medieval Archaeol.* 36, 178–82	Jennings, S. 1981	*Eighteen centuries of pottery from Norwich*, East Anglian Archaeol. 13
Hodge, C.A.H., Burton, R.G.O., Corbett, W.M., Evans, R. and Seale, R.S. 1984	*Soils and their use in Eastern England*, Soil Survey of England and Wales Bull. 13 (Harpenden)	Jennings, S. and Rogerson, A. 1994	'The distribution of Grimston Ware in East Anglia and beyond' in Leah 1994, 116–9
		Jessop, A. 1888	'The condition of the Archdeaconry of Norwich in 1603', *Norfolk Archaeol.* 10, 1–49
Hodges, R. 1989	*The Anglo-Saxon Achievement: Archaeology and the Beginnings of English Society* (London)	Joby, R. 2005a and b	'Railways' and 'Early Roads and Turnpikes' in Ashwin and Davison (eds) 2005, 152–5

Jones, G. 1979 — 'Multiple estates and early settlement' in Sawyer, P. (ed.) *English Medieval Settlement* (London), 9–34

Jones, R. 2004 — 'Signatures in the Soil: the use of pottery in manure scatters in the identification of medieval arable farming regimes', *Archaeol. J.* 161, 159–188

Jones, R. 2010 — 'Contrasting patterns of village and hamlet desertion in England' in Dyer, C. and Jones, R. (eds) *Deserted Villages Revisited* (Hatfield)

Jones, R. and Hooke, D. 2012 — 'Methodological Approaches to medieval Rural Settlements and Landscapes' in Christie and Stamper (eds) 2012, 31–42

Jones, R. and Page, M. 2006 — *Medieval Villages in an English Landscape* (Macclesfield)

Johnson, C. 1906a — 'Introduction to the Norfolk Domesday' in Page 1906, 1–37

Johnson, C. 1906b — 'The Danegeld in Norfolk' in Page 1906, 204–11

Jope, E.M. 1952 — 'Excavations in the City of Norwich, 1948', *Norfolk Archaeol.* 30, 287–323

Jurkowski, M., Smith, C.L. and Crook, D. 1998 — *Lay Taxes in England and Wales 1188–1688* (Kew)

Jurkowski, M. and Ramsay, N. with Renton, S. (eds) 2007 — *English Monastic Estates, 1066–1540: A list of manors, churches and chapels* List and Index Soc. Special Series Vol 41 (Kew)

Kerridge, E. 1969 — *Agrarian Problems in the Sixteenth Century and after* (London)

Kilmurry, K. 1980 — *The Pottery Industry of Stamford, Lincolnshire, AD 850–1250*, Brit. Archaeol. Rep. Brit. Ser. 84 (Oxford)

Knowles, D. and Hadcock, R.N. 1971 — *Medieval Religious Houses, England and Wales*, 2nd edition (London)

Latham, R.E. 1965 — *Revised Medieval Latin Word-List from British and Irish Sources* (London)

Lawson, A. 1978 — 'The Investigation of a Mesolithic and Later Site at Banham', *East Anglian Archaeol.* 8, 9–18

Lawson, A. 1980 — 'The Evidence for Later Bronze Age Settlement and Burial in Norfolk' in Barrett, J. and Bradley, R. (eds), *Settlement and Society in the British Later Bronze Age*, Part ii, Brit. Archaeol. Rep. Brit. Ser. 83 (ii), 271–94 (Oxford)

Lawson, A.J. 1983 — *The Archaeology of Witton, near North Walsham, Norfolk*, East Anglian Archaeol. 18

Lawson, A. 1984 — 'The Bronze Age in East Anglia with Particular Reference to Norfolk' in Barringer (ed.) 1984, 141–77

Leah, M. 1994 — *The Late Saxon and Medieval Pottery Industry of Grimston, Norfolk: Excavations 1962–92*, East Anglian Archaeol. 64

Leah, M.D. and Flitcroft, M. 1993 — 'Archaeological surveys at Park Farm, Snettisham and Courtyard Farm, Ringstead', *Norfolk Archaeol.* 41, 462–81

Leeds, E.T. and Pocock, M. 1971 — 'A survey of the Anglo-Saxon cruciform brooches of florid type', *Medieval Archaeol.* 15, 13–36

le Patourel, H.E.J. 1968 — 'Documentary evidence and the Medieval Pottery Industry', *Medieval Archaeol.* 12, 101–26

Le Strange, H. 1916 — *Le Strange Records* (London)

L'Estrange, J. 1874 — *The Church Bells of Norfolk where, when and by whom they were made: with the inscriptions on all the bells in the county* (Norwich)

Letters, S. with Fernandes, M., Keene, D. and Myhill, O. 2003 — *Gazetteer of Markets and Fairs in England and Wales to 1516*, List and Index Soc. Special Series Vol 32 (Kew)

Lewis, C. 2007 — 'New avenues for the investigation of currently occupied medieval rural settlement: preliminary observations from the Higher Education Field Academy', *Medieval Archaeol.* 51, 133–63

Lewis, J.M. 1957 — 'The Launditch: a Norfolk linear earthwork', *Norfolk Archaeol.* 31, 419–26

Liddiard, R. 2000 — *'Landscapes of Lordship': Norman Castles and the Countryside in Medieval Norfolk, 1066–1200*, Brit. Archaeol. Rep. Brit. Ser. 309 (Oxford)

Little, A. 1994 — 'The pottery from Sites 22954 and 24054', in Leah 1994, 84–100

Longcroft, A. 2006 — 'The Hearth Tax and Historic Housing Stocks: a case study from Norfolk', in Barnwell, P.S. and Airs, M. (eds) *Houses and the Hearth Tax: the later Stuart house and society*, 62–73, Counc. Brit. Archaeol. Res. Rep. 150

Loyd, L.C. and Stenton, D.M. 1950 — *Sir Christopher Hatton's Book of Seals to which is appended a select list of the works of Frank Merry Stenton* (Oxford)

Luard, H.R. (ed.) 1880 — *Matthaei Parisiensis. Monachi Santi Albani, Chronica Majora Vol. V AD 1248 to AD 1259* (London)

Lucy, S., Tipper, J. and Dickens, A. 2009 — *The Anglo-Saxon Settlement and Cemetery at Bloodmoor Hill, Carlton Colville, Suffolk*, East Anglian Archaeol. 131

Mabey, R. 1996 — *Flora Britannica* (London)

Mackman, J. and Stevens, M. 2010 — 'CP40/807: Hilary term 1463', in *Court of Common Pleas: the National Archives, CP40 1399–1500* (London, 2010), British History Online Available: http://www.british-history.ac.uk/no-series/common-pleas/1399-1500/hilary-term-1463. Accessed 10 December 2018

Macnair, A. and Williamson, T. 2010 — *William Faden and Norfolk's 18th-Century Landscape* (Oxford)

MAFF 1972 — *Provisional Agricultural Land Classification of England and Wales, Map sheet 125* (Ministry of Agriculture, Fisheries and Food)

MAFF 1977 — *Agricultural Land Classification Map of England and Wales. Explanatory Note* (Ministry of Agriculture, Fisheries and Food)

Margary, I. 1973 — *Roman Roads in Britain*, 3rd edition, (London)

Martin, E. 2012 — 'Norfolk, Suffolk and Essex: Medieval Rural Settlement in 'Greater East Anglia'' in Christie and Stamper (eds) 2012, 225–48

Martin, E. and Satchell, M. 2008 — *Wheare most Inclosures be East Anglian Fields: History, Morphology and Management*, East Anglian Archaeol. 124

McCarthy, M.R. and Brooks, C.M. 1988 — *Medieval Pottery in Britain AD 900–1600* (Leicester)

McKerracher, M. 2018 — *Farming Transformed in Anglo-Saxon England: Agriculture in the Long Eighth Century* (Oxford)

McKinley, J.I. 1994	*The Anglo-Saxon Cemetery at Spong Hill, North Elmham Part VII: The Cremations*, East Anglian Archaeol. 69	Oosthuizen, S. 2013	*Transition and Transformation in Anglo-Saxon England: archaeology, common rights and landscape* (London)
Meaney, A. 1964	*A Gazetteer of Early Anglo-Saxon Burial Sites* (London)	Page, W. (ed.) 1906	*The Victoria History of the County of Norfolk* (London)
Mellor, M. 1976	'The Pottery' in Rogerson, A., 'Excavations at Fullers Hill, Great Yarmouth', *East Anglian Archaeol.* 2, 169–96	Palgrave, F. (ed.) 1835	*Rotuli Curiae Regis: rolls and records of the court held before the King's justiciars or justices* Vol 1 (Record Commission, London)
Messent, C.J.W. 1936	*The Parish Churches of Norfolk and Norwich* (Norwich)	Parker Pearson, M. and Schadla-Hall, R.T. (eds) 1994	*Looking at the Land: archaeological landscapes in Eastern England* (Leicester)
Miles, D. 1989	'The Romano-British Countryside' in Todd, M. (ed.), *Research in Roman Britain 1960–89*, Britannia Monog. Ser. 11	Pat. Rol. 1901	*Patent Rolls of the reign of Henry III preserved in the Public Record Office* (London)
Millett, M. 1990	*The Romanisation of Britain: an essay in archaeological interpretation* (Cambridge)	Patten, J. 1979	'Population distribution in Norfolk and Suffolk during the sixteenth and seventeenth centuries' in Patten, J. (ed.) *Pre-industrial England* (Folkestone)
Milligan, B. 1982	'Pottery', in Coad, J.G. and Streeten, A.D.F., 'Excavations at Castle Acre Castle, Norfolk, 1972–7', *Archaeol. J.* 139, 199–227	Peglar, S., Fritz, S. and Birks, H. 1989	'Vegetation and land use history at Diss, Norfolk', *J. Ecol.* 77, 203–22
Milligan, B. 1987	'Pottery', in Coad, J.G., Streeten, A.D.F. and Warmington, R., 'Excavations at Castle Acre Castle, Norfolk, 1975–1982: The Bridge, Lime Kilns and Eastern Gatehouse', *Archaeol. J.* 144, 286–93	Penn, K. 2005	'Early Saxon Settlement' in Ashwin and Davison (eds) 2005, 30–1
		Pestell, T. 2004	*Landscapes of Monastic Foundation; the establishment of religious houses in East Anglia c.650–1200* (Woodbridge)
Milligan, B. 1997	'[The Pottery] Saxo-Norman, medieval and later', in Morley, B. and Gurney, D., *Castle Rising Castle, Norfolk*, East Anglian Archaeol. 81, 112–22	Pevsner, N. and Wilson, B. 1999	*The Buildings of England: Norfolk 2, North-West and South* (London)
Mills, A.D. 2011	*A Dictionary of British Place Names* (Oxford)	Pickering, D. 1763	*The Statutes at Large, from the First Year of Queen Mary to the Thirty-fifth Year of Queen Elizabeth inclusive* (Cambridge)
Mills, J. and Palmer, R. 2007	*Populating Clay Landscapes* (Stroud)	Raban, S. 2004	*A Second Domesday? The Hundred Rolls of 1279–80* (Oxford)
Mills, N. 1985	'Sample Bias, Regional Analysis and Fieldwalking in British Archaeology', in Haselgrove, Millet and Smith (eds) 1985, 39–47	Rackham, O. 1976	*Trees and Woodland in the British Landscape* (London)
Moorhouse, S. 1983	'The Medieval Pottery Research Group', in Hinton, D.A. (ed.), *25 Years of Medieval Archaeology*, 102–16 (Sheffield)	Rackham, O. 1986a	'The Ancient Woods of Norfolk', *Trans. Norfolk Norwich Naturalist's Soc.* 27, 161–77
Morris, R. 1983	*The church in British archaeology*, Counc. Brit. Archaeol. Res. Rep. 47	Rackham, O. 1986b	*The History of the Countryside* (London)
Morris, R. 1989	*Churches in the Landscape* (London)	Reaney, P.H. and Wilson, R.M. 1991	*A Dictionary of English Surnames* 3rd edition (London)
Mortlock, D.P. and Roberts, C.V. 1985	*The Popular Guide to Norfolk Churches 3: West and South-West Norfolk* (Cambridge)	Reynolds, A. 2009	'Meaningful Landscapes: An Early Medieval Perspective' in Gilchrist and Reynolds 2009, 409–34
Newman, J. 1992	'The Late Roman and Anglo-Saxon Settlement Pattern in the Sandlings of Suffolk', in Carver, M.O.H. (ed.) *The Age of Sutton Hoo* (Woodbridge) 25–38	Rickett, R. 1995	*The Anglo-Saxon Cemetery at Spong Hill, North Elmham, Part VII: The Iron Age, Roman and Early Saxon Settlements*, East Anglian Archaeol. 73
Newman, J. 1994	'East Anglian Kingdom Pilot Survey', in Parker Pearson and Schadla-Hall 1994, 10–5	Rippon, S. 2007	'Emerging Regional Variation in Historic Landscape Character: The Possible Significance of the 'Long Eighth Century' in Gardiner and Rippon 2007, 105–21
Nicol, A (ed.) 1991	*Curia Regis Rolls of Henry III preserved in the Public Record Office, Volume XVII 26 to 27 Henry III (1242–1243)* (London)	Rippon, S. 2008	*Beyond the Medieval Village the diversification of landscape character in Southern Britain* (Oxford)
Noddle, B. 1980	'Identification and Interpretation of the Mammal Bones', in Wade-Martins 1980a, 377–409	Rippon, S. 2009	'Understanding the medieval landscape' in Gilchrist and Reynolds 2009, 227–54
O'Drisceoil, D.A. 1988	'Burnt Mounds: cooking or bathing?', *Antiquity* 62, 671–80	Rippon, S., Smart, C. and Pears, B. 2015	*The Fields of Britannia: Continuity and Change in the Late Roman and Early Medieval Landscape* (Oxford)
Oosthuizen, S. 1993	'Saxon Commons in South Cambridgeshire', *Proc. Cambridge Antiq. Soc.* 82, 93–100	Roberts, B.K. 1977	*Rural Settlement in Britain* (Folkestone)

Roberts, B.K. and Wrathmell, S. 2000 — *An Atlas of Rural Settlement in England* (London)

Robinson, B. 1981 — *Hunters to First Farmers* (Fakenham)

Robinson, B. and Gregory, T. 1987 — *Celtic Fire and Roman Rule* (North Walsham)

Rodwell, W.J and Rodwell, K.A. 1986 — *Rivenhall: investigations of a villa, church, and village, 1950–1977*, Counc. Brit. Archaeol. Res. Rep. 55

Rogerson, A. 1988 — 'Appendix 1: The Medieval Pottery', in Silvester 1988, 174–5

Rogerson, A. 1995 — *Fransham: an archaeological and historical study of a parish on the Norfolk boulder clay* (PhD thesis, University of East Anglia)

Rogerson, A. 1996 — 'Rural Settlement c.400–1200' in Margeson, S., Ayers, B. and Heywood, S. (eds) *A Festival of Norfolk Archaeology*, 58–64 (Norwich)

Rogerson, A. 1999 — 'Arable and Pasture in Two Norfolk Parishes: Barton Bendish and Fransham in the Iron Age' in Davies and Williamson (eds) 1999, 125–31

Rogerson, A. 2003 — 'Six Middle Anglo-Saxon Sites in West Norfolk' in Pestell, T. and Ulmschneider, K. *Markets in Early Medieval Europe*, 110–21 (Macclesfield)

Rogerson, A. and Adams, N. 1978 — 'A Saxo-Norman Pottery Kiln at Bircham', *East Anglian Archaeol.* 8, 33–44

Rogerson, A. and Ashley, S.J. 1985 — 'A medieval pottery production site at Blackborough End, Middleton', *Norfolk Archaeol.* 39, 181–9

Rogerson, A. and Dallas, C. 1984 — *Excavations in Thetford 1948–59 and 1973–80*, East Anglian Archaeol. 22

Rogerson, A. and Silvester, R. 1986 — 'Middle Saxon occupation at Hay Green, Terrington St Clement', *Norfolk Archaeol.* 39, 320–22

Rogerson, A. with Davison, A. 1997 — 'An archaeological and historical survey of the parish of Barton Bendish, Norfolk' in Rogerson, A., Davison, A., Pritchard, D. and Silvester, R. *Barton Bendish and Caldecote: fieldwork in south-west Norfolk*, East Anglian Archaeol. 80, 1–42

Rose, G. and Illingworth, W. (eds) 1811 — *Placitorum in domo capitulari Westmonasteriensis asservatorum abbreviatio, Richard I –Edward II* (London)

Roskell, J.S. 1961 — 'Sir William Oldhall, Speaker in the Parliament of 1450–1', *Nottingham Medieval Studies* 5, 87–112

Rowlands, M.J. 1976 — *The Production and Distribution of Metalwork in the Middle Bronze Age in Southern Britain*, Brit. Archaeol. Rep. Brit. Ser. 31 (Oxford)

Rutledge, E. and Rutledge, P. 1978 — 'King's Lynn and Great Yarmouth: two thirteenth-century surveys', *Norfolk Archaeol.* 37, 92–114

Rutledge, P. 1990 — 'Colkirk: a North Norfolk settlement pattern', *Norfolk Archaeol.* 41, 15–34

Rutledge, P. 2003 — 'Colkirk settlement pattern: a reappraisal and a question', *Norfolk Archaeol.* 44, 331–34

Rye, W. (ed.) 1881 — *Pedes Finium, or Fines relating to the County of Norfolk* (Norwich)

Rye, W. (ed.) 1891 — *The Visitacion of Norffolk*, Pub. Harleian Soc. 32

Rye, W. 1901 — 'The "Land Buyers' Society"', *Norfolk Archaeol.* 15, 1–3

Sawyer, P.H. 1983 — 'English Archaeology before the Conquest: a historian's view', in Hinton, D.A. (ed.), *25 Years of Medieval Archaeology*, 44–7 (Sheffield)

Sawyer, P. 1985 — '1066–1086: A Tenurial Revolution?', in Sawyer, P. (ed.) *Domesday Book: a reassessment* (London)

Schofield, A.J. 1989 — 'Understanding early medieval pottery distributions: cautionary tales and their implications for further research', *Antiquity* 63, 460–70

Schofield, A.J. (ed.) 1991 — *Interpreting Artefact Scatters: contributions to ploughzone archaeology* (Oxford)

Scull, C.J. 1992 — 'Before Sutton Hoo: structures of power and society in early East Anglia' in Carver, M.O.H. (ed.) *The Age of Sutton Hoo* (Woodbridge), 3–23

Scull, C. 2009 — *Early medieval (late 5th–early 8th centuries AD) cemeteries at Boss Hall and Buttermarket, Ipswich, Suffolk*, Soc. Medieval Archaeol. Monog. Ser. 27

Seaman, P. 1991 — 'Norfolk and Norwich Hearth Tax Assessment, Lady Day 1666', *Norfolk Genealogy 20*

Sheail, J. 1968 — *The Regional Distribution of Wealth in England as indicated in the 1524–25 lay subsidy returns* (Unpublished PhD thesis, Univ. London)

Shennan, S. 1985 — *Experiments in the Collection and Analysis of Archaeological Survey data: the East Hampshire Survey* (Sheffield)

Shepherd Popescu, E. 2009 — *Norwich Castle: Excavations and Historical Survey, 1987–98 Part 1: Anglo-Saxon to c.1345*, East Anglian Archaeol. 132

Silvester, R.J. 1988 — *The Fenland Project Number 3: Marshland and the Nar Valley*, East Anglian Archaeol. 45

Silvester, R.J. 1991 — *The Fenland Project Number 4: The Wissey Embayment and the Fen Causeway, Norfolk*, East Anglian Archaeol. 52

Silvester, R.J. 1993 — 'The addition of more-or-less undifferentiated dots to a distribution map? The Fenland Project in retrospect', in Gardiner (ed.) 1993a, 24–39

Simms, R. 1978 — 'Man and vegetation in Norfolk' in Limbrey, S. and Evans, J.G. (eds), *The Effect of Man on the Landscape; the Lowland Zone*, Counc. Brit. Archaeol. Res. Rep. 21

Skipper, K. and Williamson, T. 2005 — 'Late Saxon Social Structure' in Ashwin and Davison (eds) 2005, 40–1

Smith, A., Allen, A., Brindle, T. and Fulford, M. 2016 — *The Rural Settlement of Roman Britain*, Britannia Monog. Ser. 29

Smith, A.H. 1956a and b — *English Place-Name Elements Parts I and II* (Cambridge)

Soil Survey 1973 — *Soils of Norfolk, 1:100,000 scale map* (Harpenden)

Soil Survey 1983 — *Soils of England and Wales: map sheet 4, Eastern England, 1:250,000 scale* (Harpenden)

Spufford, M. 1974 — *Contrasting Communities: English Villagers in the Sixteenth and Seventeenth Centuries* (Cambridge)

Stamper, P. 1988 — 'Woods and Parks' in Astill and Grant (eds) 1988, 128–48

Steane, J.M. 1985 — *The archaeology of medieval England and Wales* (London)

Taylor, C.C. 1983 — *Village and Farmstead. A History of Rural Settlement in England* (London)

Taylor, C.C. 1992 — 'Medieval Rural Settlement: changing perceptions', *Landscape Hist.* 14, 5–17

Taylor, H.M. and Taylor, J. 1965 — *Anglo-Saxon Architecture* (Cambridge)

Taylor, J. 2007 — *An Atlas of Roman Rural Settlement in England*, Counc. Brit. Archaeol. Res. Rep. 151

Taylor, R. 1821 — *Index Monasticus; or the abbeys and other monasteries, alien priories, friaries, colleges, collegiate churches, and hospitals, with their dependencies, formerly established in the Diocese of Norwich and the ancient Kingdom of East Anglia* (London)

Thirsk, J. 1967 — 'The Farming Regions of England', in Thirsk, J. (ed.), *The Agrarian History of England and Wales* Vol. IV, 1500–1640, 1–112 (Cambridge)

Thomas, G. 2003 — *Late Anglo-Saxon and Viking Age strap-ends 750–1100*, Finds Research Group AD 700–1700 Datasheet 32

Thornton, M. 2012 — 'Lord's Man or Community Servant? The Role, Status and Allegiance of Village Haywards in Fifteenth-Century Northamptonshire' in Turner and Silvester (eds) 2012, 213–24

Tingle, M. 1991 — *The Vale of the White Horse Survey*, Brit. Archaeol. Rep. Brit. Ser. 218 (Oxford)

Tompkins, M. 2012 — 'Counting Houses: Using the Housing Structure of a Late Medieval Manor to Illuminate Population, Landholding and Occupational Structure' in Turner and Silvester (eds) 2012, 225–38

Turner, S. and Silvester, B. (eds) 2012 — *Life in Medieval Landscapes, People and Places in the Middle Ages: Papers in Memory of H.S.A. Fox* (Oxford)

Tylecote, R.F. and Owles, E. 1960 — 'A second-century iron smelting site at Ashwicken, Norfolk', *Norfolk Archaeol.* 32, 142–62

Vince, A. 2005 — 'Ceramic petrology and the study of Anglo-Saxon and Later Medieval ceramics', *Medieval Archaeol.* 49, 219–45

Vincent, N. 1993 — 'The foundation of Westacre Priory (1102 x 1126)', *Norfolk Archaeol.* 41, 490–4

Vincent, N. 2001 — 'The Wonderful Will of William of Wendling (d. 1270)', *Nottingham Medieval Studies* 45, 68–96

Wade, K. 1976 — 'Excavations at Langhale, Kirstead', *East Anglian Archaeol.* 2, 101–27

Wade, K. 1980 — 'The Pottery' in Wade-Martins 1980a, 413–77

Wade, K. 1983 — 'The Early Anglo-Saxon Period' in Lawson 1983, 50–69

Wade, K. 2009 — 'Pottery vessels' in Scull 2009, 109

Wade-Martins, P. 1971 — *The Development of the Landscape and Human Settlement in West Norfolk from 350–1650 AD, with particular reference to the Launditch Hundred* (Unpublished PhD thesis, Univ. Leicester)

Wade-Martins, P. 1974 — 'The linear earthworks of West Norfolk', *Norfolk Archaeol.* 36, 23–38

Wade-Martins, P. 1980a — *Excavations in North Elmham Park 1967–1972*, East Anglian Archaeol. 9

Wade-Martins, P. 1980b — *Village Sites in Launditch Hundred*, East Anglian Archaeol. 10

Wade-Martins, P. 1989 — 'The Archaeology of Medieval Rural Settlement in East Anglia', in Aston, Austin and Dyer (eds) 1989, 149–65

Wade-Martins, P. (ed.) 1993 — *An Historical Atlas of Norfolk* (Norwich)

Wade-Martins, P. 2016 — 'The date of the West Norfolk linear earthworks — an unresolved debate', *Norfolk Archaeol.* 47, 329–33

Wade-Martins, S., Williamson, T. and Silvester, R.J., 2005 — 'Norfolk Agriculture 1500–1750; Drainage of the Fens', in Ashwin and Davison 2005, 115–17

Wade Martins, S. and Williamson, T. 1999 — *Roots of Change: Farming and the Landscape in East Anglia, c.1700–1870* (Exeter)

Walton Rogers, P. 2013 — *Tyttel's Halh: the Anglo-Saxon Cemetery at Tittleshall, Norfolk. The Archaeology of the Bacton to King's Lynn Gas Pipeline, Volume 2*, East Anglian Archaeol. 150 (Lincoln)

Warner, P. 1983 — 'Origins: the example of green-side settlement in East Suffolk', *Medieval Village Research Group Annual Rep.*

Warner, P. 1986 — 'Shared churchyards, freemen church builders and the development of parishes in eleventh-century East Anglia', *Landscape Hist.* 8, 39–52

Warner, P. 1987 — *Greens, Commons and Clayland Colonisation: The Origins and Development of Green-side Settlement in East Suffolk* (Leicester)

Watts, V. (ed.) 2004 — *The Cambridge Dictionary of English Place-Names* (Cambridge)

Welch, M.G. 1985 — 'Rural settlement patterns in the Early and Middle Anglo-Saxon periods', *Landscape Hist.* 7, 13–25

Welldon Finn, R. 1967 — *Domesday Studies: the Eastern Counties* (London)

West, S. 1985 — *West Stow The Anglo-Saxon Village*, East Anglian Archaeol. 24

West, S. 1999 — 'The Early Anglo-Saxon period' in Dymond, D. and Martin, E. (eds) *An Historical Atlas of Suffolk*, 44–5, 3rd edition (Ipswich)

West, S.E. 1963 — 'Excavations at Cox Lane (1958) and at the Town Defences Shire Hall Yard, Ipswich (1959)', *Proc. Suffolk Inst. Archaeol.* 29, 233–303

West, S.E. and McLaughlin, A. 1998 — *Towards a Landscape History of Walsham le Willows, Suffolk*, East Anglian Archaeology 85

White, W. 1845 — *History, Gazetteer and Directory of the County of Norfolk and the City and County of the City of Norwich* (Sheffield, reprinted 1969)

Whiteman, A. 1986 — *The Compton Census of 1676: a critical edition*, Rec. Social and Econ. Hist. n.s. X (London)

Whyte, N. 2009 — *Inhabiting the Landscape: Place, Custom and Memory, 1500–1800* (Oxford)

Wilkinson, T.J. 1982 — 'The Definition of Ancient Manured Zones by Means of Extensive Sherd-Sampling Techniques', *World Archaeol.* 9, 323–33

Wilkinson, T.J. 1989	'Extensive Sherd Scatters and Land-Use Intensity: Some Recent Results', *World Archaeol.* 16, 31–46	Williamson, T. 2014	'The Franshams in context: isolated churches and common edge drift' in Ashley and Marsden (eds) 2014, 167–79
Willard, J.F. 1934	*Parliamentary Taxes on Personal Property 1290 to 1334* (Cambridge, Mass.)	Williamson, T. and Bellamy, L. 1987	*Property and Landscape* (London)
Williamson, T.M. 1984	'The Roman Countryside: Settlement and Agriculture in NW Essex', *Britannia* 15, 225–30	Williamson, T. and Skipper, K. 2005	'Late Saxon Population Densities' in Ashwin and Davison (eds) 2005, 38–9
Williamson, T. 1987	'Early co-axial field systems on the East Anglian boulder clays', *Proc. Prehist. Soc.* 53, 419–31	Wilson, D.M. (ed.) 1976	*The Archaeology of Anglo-Saxon England* (Cambridge)
Williamson, T. 1988	'Settlement Chronology and Regional Landscapes: The Evidence from the Claylands of East Anglia and Essex' in Hooke (ed.) 1988, 153–75	Witney, K.P. 1982	*The Kingdom of Kent* (London)
		Woodward, H.R. 1884	'The Scenery of Norfolk', *Trans. Norfolk Norwich Naturalists' Soc.* 3, 439–66
Williamson, T. 1993	*The origins of Norfolk* (Manchester)	Woodward, P.J. 1978	'Flint Distribution, Ring Ditches and Bronze Age Settlement Patterns in the Great Ouse Valley. The problem, a field survey technique and some preliminary results', *Archaeol. J.* 135, 32–56
Williamson, T. 1994	'Site, Settlement, Landscape: some reflections on fieldwalking in Eastern England' in Parker Pearson and Schadla-Hall (eds) 1994, 5–9		
		Wright, D.W. 2015	*'Middle Saxon' Settlement and Society* (Oxford)
Williamson, T. 2003	*Shaping Medieval Landscapes: Settlement, Society, Environment* (Macclesfield)	Wymer, J.J. (ed.) 1977	*Gazetteer of Mesolithic Sites in England and Wales*, Counc. Brit. Archaeol. Res. Rep. 20
Williamson, T. 2005a	'Soil Landscapes' in Ashwin and Davison 2005, 8–9	Wymer, J. 1984	'East Anglian Palaeolithic Sites and their settings' in Barringer (ed.) 1984, 31–42
Williamson, T. 2005b	'Place-name Patterns' in Ashwin and Davison 2005, 34–5	Wymer, J. 1985	*The Palaeolithic Sites of East Anglia* (Norwich)
Williamson, T. 2007a	'The Distribution of 'Woodland' and 'Champion' Landscapes in Medieval England' in Gardiner and Rippon (eds) 2007, 89–104	Yaxley, D. 2003	*A Researcher's Glossary of words found in historical documents of East Anglia* (Guist Bottom)
Williamson, T. 2007b	*Rabbits, Warrens and Archaeology* (Stroud)	Yaxley, D. 2005	'The Communicant Returns of 1603', in Ashwin and Davison (eds) 2005, 105–6
Williamson, T. 2008	*Sutton Hoo and its Landscape: The Context of Monuments* (Oxford)	Young, A. 1804	*General View of the Agriculture of the County of Norfolk* (London)
Williamson, T. 2013	*Environment, Society and Landscape in Early Medieval England: Time and Topography* (Woodbridge)	Youngs, F.A. 1979	*Guide to the Local Administrative Units of England Volume I: Southern England* (London)

Index

Page numbers in *italics* denote illustrations. Places are in Norfolk unless indicated otherwise.

The following abbreviations have been used in this index: C – century; d. – died; *fl.* – *floruit*; GF – Great Fransham; jnr – junior; LF – Little Fransham; snr – senior.

A47 1, 194, *194*
Abbys rode (*Abrode*) 105
Acre, Robert de 106
Aethelgyth 64
Agges (Aggys)
    Edmund 203
    Joanna 203
    Richard 213
Aggs (*Agges*; *Agses*) (tenement) 203
Agrave field 117
agriculture
    Roman 32, 33, *34*, 35
    early–middle Saxon 44, 50
    late Saxon–early Norman 53, 63, 67–8, 193
    medieval 173–4
    post-medieval 184–5
Alanson (Alansone; Allanson)
    John (d.1631) 212
    John (*fl.*1638) 212
    Martha 212
    Robert 212
    Thomas 152, 212
    see also Allenson; Allison
Albert, Roger 73, 196
Le Alderker 99, 197
Ale, Matilda 73, 196, 234
Aleby, Thomas de 113
Alexander, rector of Great Fransham 85
Allen (Alleyn)
    Simon (C16) 183, 234, 241
    Simon (C17) 230
    Stephen 208
Allens close 135
Allenson
    Agnes 204
    Edmund 183, 204
    Nicholas 204
    see also Alanson; Allison
Alleyn *see* Allen
Allison (Alyson)
    Widow – 179
    Alice 212
    John (d.1555) 212
    John (d.1632) 152
    John (C18–19) 212, 224
    Robert (*fl.*1664–6) 179
    Robert (C17–18) 212
    Thomas (d.1607) 212
    Thomas (*fl.*1664–6) 179, 213
    William 151
    see also Alanson; Allenson
Alpe family 222
    Alice 220, 225
    Hamond esq. 190–1, 219, 220, 221, 222, 224, 225, 241, 242
    Hamond gent. 212, 220, 225
    Philip 220, 221, 225, 242
    Richard 200
    Robert 220, 221
Alyeard, Alice 233
Alyson *see* Allison
Amielles Lane (*Aniels lane*) 133, 136
Andrews, Bartholomew and Margaret 215
Anger
    Alexander 132
    Geoffrey 132
Angeville, Richard and wife 128
Anguishe, Thomas 210
animal bone 28, 33, 48
Antingham, William 201

Anyell (Anyel)
    Bartholomew 158
    David 135, 204, 205
    John 236
    Robert 199
Anyell grove 133, 185, 186, 199
Anyellysclos (*Anyel*; *Anyelys*) 133, 134
arrowheads, Neolithic–Bronze Age 15, *15*
Arrowsmith (Arwesmyth), Henry 228
Arrowsmithclose (*Narowsmythclos*) 143, 228
Ashley
    Thomas 179
    William 179
Ashwood 210
Askew, William 184
assarting 168
Asshill (Asshyll)
    John 201
    Thomas 204
Astellsyard 197
Astelsdyke 197
Attcheys, Roger and wife 215
Atterode *see* Rode
Aula *see* Hall
Avelynnescroft 103
axes
    Neolithic 15–16, 16–17, *17*
    Bronze Age 21–3
    see also hand-axe

Bacon, Stephen 111
Baconesgrene (*Bakonsmore*) 111, 206, 207
Bagethorp, Ralph de 225
Bailey (Baley; Bayly)
    Charles 232
    George 183
    John (brother of Thomas jnr) 183
    John (d.1676 carpenter) 183
    John (*fl.*1753) 232
    Thomas (d.1670, butcher) 183
    Thomas (nephew of Thomas) 183
    see also Baly; Bayley
Baldwin, Richard son of Roger 85
Bale 157
Balepiece (*Balepeece*) 157, 158
Baly, John 213, 227
Balyston (Ballyston), John 217, 222
Bardolf (Bardolph)
    Agnes 84
    Hugh 84
    Isabel 84
    Thomas 84
    William 73, 84
    William jnr 195
Barghmyllefeld 136
Barghmyllehill 134–5
Barker, James 201
Barnards Moor (*Barnaldesmore*; *Barnardismor*; *Bernarsmor*)
    common pasture 127, 168, 182, 241
    depiction on 1833 map 94
    settlements 126, 141, 183, 241
    woodland 68
barns 198, 217, 219
Baron's Hall 216
Barsham, Alan de 146
Barton, John 117
Barton Bendish 24, 61
Base
    Joanna 143
    John (*fl.*1400–1) 156
    John, carpenter (*fl.*1436–7) 217
Bastard, Mary 179
Bate, Christina daughter of Hugh 146
Bathe, John de 158
Bathescroft (*Bathe*; *Bathelond*) 157–8

Baxter, Thomas 187
Bayesbolle medowe 123
Bayfeld (*Bayfeild*; *Bayfeldyard*; *Bayfeldcroft*) 140, 182
Bayley
  Henry 188, 232
  John (C16) 208
  John (C18) 226
Baynard, Ralph 64
Baysboll (Bayesbolle) (tenement) 78, 111, 112
Baysboll (Bayboll), Ralph 73, 78, 195, 196
Baysboll brygge (*Baisbollesbridge*; *Baybolsbrigg*; *Baysebollysbrigge*) 29, 123
bead, Roman 30
Beale, Thomas 230
Bear, Robert 226
Beaufour (Bellafago), Ralph de 63, 83
Beaumont, Eleanor de 83
Beck, Sarah 199
Beckerton (Bekyrton)
  John 232
  William 188
Beckham
  Alice 225
  Henry 207
  John 231
  Richard snr 111, 146, 147, 182, 184, 187, 206, 207, 220, 221, 222, 224, 225
  Richard jnr 187, 220, 222, 224
  Walter 188
Bedingtone, Nicholas de 225
Bedyngham
  Ralph 238
  William 238
Beeston 66, 73, 76, 178
Beeston, Ralph de 78, 123
Beeston with Bittering, compared
  Saxon period 39, 45, 47
  late Saxon–early Norman period 53
  medieval period 70, 71, 173
Beetley 71, 72
Bekyrton *see* Beckerton
belt fitting, medieval 212
belt mounts
  late Roman *42*, 43
  Saxon *43*
Bemond *see* Beumond
Benecroft 239
Benedick, Henry 135
Benedict Heved (tenement) 141, 145, 146, 149, 158, 162, 172, 219, 220
Bennett (Benett), William 208, 231
Bensley, Henry 226
Berewenesaker 239
Bernham, John 146; *see also* Burnham
Bertelotesride 141
Beston
  Thomas de 118
  William son of Augustine de 73, 195
Bette, Adam 73, 74, 196
Bettes (Betys), John 162
Bettes (Betys) (alias Sowde)
  Isabelle 131
  Nicholas 131, 132
Beumond (Bemond)
  Godfrey de 83
  Joan 83
Bilacre 127
Bilney (Bilneie; Bylney)
  Agnes 102
  Clement 102
  Henry de 73, 74, 102, 196
  John 102
  William de 74, 102
Birch, Robert 202
Bird stile (*Byrds style*) 117
Birdes croft 116, 117
Birdes field (*Byrds Feald*) 116, 117
Birds acre 116
Black Death 71, 167, 173
Blacks 152
Blak, William 152
Blog, John 151, 211–12
Bloggs (tenement) 151, 211–12

Blomfield, John 233
Blunkall, Widow – 179
Blyford
  Agnes 202
  Aveline 234
  John 77, 121, 190, 202
Blyfords manor
  description 77
  holdings 169, 170, 190
    Area B 103, 104, 105, 106, 200, 202
    Area C 109
    Area E 115, 116, 209
    Area F 117
    Area G 118
    Area H 119, 121, 209
    Area J 121, 123
Bochelylond 146
Bocher, John 214
Boketonlond 162
Boles (Bolys) (tenement) 135, 171
Bolesyerd 135
Bolt
  Alice 221
  Margaret 221
Bond Closse 211
Bond Pightle 211
Bondeswood 81
book clasp, medieval 126, *127*
Boor (Boore; Bore)
  John 162, 227
  Margery 227
  Silvester 212, 227
  see also Bour
Booty, J.G. 231
Bore *see* Boor
Bores (tenement) 227
Bosom (Bosome)
  Adam 209, 233
  John 209
boss/knob, Roman 28
Boter, Geoffrey 212
Boters/Boteres 152, 212
Boterscroft (*Butcherscroft*) 152, 212
Bottler, Ralph 225; *see also* Buteler
Bour (Boure)
  John 123
  John att 210
bracelet, Roman 32
Brackiscroftesende 128
Bradenham 27, 47, 64, 66, 67; *see also* East Bradenham; West Bradenham
Braies acre 145, 225
Brake (Brakke)
  Geoffrey 207
  John 109
Brakes (*Brakkes*; *Brakkys*) 77, 109, 128, 129
Brakes (Bracks; Brakkes) (tenement) 128
Brancaster more 99
Brande (Bronde) family 172
  Robert 135
  Simon 116, 135
Brandes (tenement) 172
Brandes close 126
Brandonsland 126
brass, memorial 124, 194
Bray
  Geoffrey 221
  Hugh 146
  John 221
  Robert 221
  Roger 221
  Sara 146
  Walter 221
Brayes (*Braies*) 221
Brayes (Braies) (tenement) 145, 149, 221
Brayes Close (*Braies close*; *Brayesclos*) 221, 222
Brenchmere pitt 154
Brend, Walter 216
Brereton, Abel 208, 231, 232, 234, 242
Bressyngham (Brisingham; Brysyngham)
  Fulco de 238

William de 73, 77, 195, 238
Breton (Bretoun)
   Edmund le 81
   Elizabeth 81
   John le 73, 76, 81, 83, 196, 234
Bretton, John, clerk 187
bricks
   medieval 89, 197, 216
   post-medieval 200, 203
brickworks, Roman 27
Bride, John 209
Briggemeadowe 202
Brimlowes 222
Brisingham *see* Bressyngham
Brisley 71, 72
Broad half acre 202
Brock (Brocke)
   John 183, 230, 235
   John jnr 235
   Sarah 235
   Thomas 183, 230
   Thomas jnr 183
Brockinnge
   Alice 233
   Edmund 233
Broke *see* Brook
Bromehill Priory 83
Bronde *see* Brande
Brondesclose 135
brooches
   Roman 29, 30, 32
   Saxon 40, 41, *41*, *42–3*, 43, 49
   medieval *102*, 197, 212
Brook (Brooke; Broke)
   John (alias Daye) 187, 188
   Thomazin 221
   Walter at 158, 229
   William 212, 221, 229
   William (alias Dey) 221
Brookes, William 221
Brounesmer/Brounismere Pytt 154
Browne (Broun)
   Alexander 135
   Edmund 200
   Margaret 105
   Roger 230
Browning, Edmund 233
Brownsgrene (*Brounesgrene*; *Brownsmore*)
   common pasture 103
   road to 56, 105
   settlements 57, 104, 167, 169, 200
Brownslane 200
Bruiles 222
Bryde, John 230
Brydes (Brydes; Byrddes; Byrdys) (tenement) 116, 152, 163
Brygmedowe (*Brigmedow*; *Briggemeadowe*; *Brigges medowe*) 121
Brymley, John 221
Brysyngham *see* Bressyngham
Buck (Bucke)
   Mr – 231
   Robert 224
bucket binding, Saxon 41
buckles
   Roman 43
   late Saxon 62, *62*
   medieval *102*, 103, *105*, 197, 200, 212, 213, 216, 222
Bucles (tenement) 152
Buddle (Buddwell)
   Edmund 242
   Edward 179, 242
Bules (*Boles*; *Bolys*; *Bules*) (tenement) 134, 135
Bullefield/Bullesfield (*Bolesfeld*; *Boolesfeld*; *Bullysfeld*) 56, 134–5, 136, 168, 171, 174
Bullesgrove (*Bullys grove*) 135, 185, 186
Bullock, Dorothy 207
Bullsmead 162, 190
Bunn, John 183
Bunting
   Anthony 179, 214, 228
   Deborah 200

Buntyngesfaldgate 162
Buntyngs 162
Burel, William 238
Burgess (Burges; Burgis)
   Richard 231, 234
   Robert 234
Burnham, John 210; *see also* Bernham
burnt mounds 20
Burston (Byrston), Thomas 208, 233
Bury St Edmunds Abbey (Suffolk) 64, 84
Buscall, Matthew 215
Bushshie close (*le Bushe close*) 163, 189
Bustelond (*Buskelond*) 125
Butchers (tenement) 212
Buteler (Butelyer; Butiller; Butiler; Boteler)
   Clement 238
   Olive 238
   William 238
   see also Bottler
Butteslond 239
button-and-loop fastener, Iron Age 25
Buttyacre (*Bottylond*) 145, 149, 223
Buttys 145
Byketon (Bycketon), Ralph de 73, 77, 196
Bylney *see* Bilney
Byrston *see* Burston

Cacy *see* Casy
Cadds Barne 233
Cade (Cadde)
   John 234
   Thomas 123, 208, 233
   William 116, 123, 199, 208, 233
Cadescloose (*Kayds closse*) 117, 232
de Cailly (Cali; Caly; Caylii)
   Adam 78
   Joanna 140
   John 140, 223
   Osbert 78
   Thomas 80
Calibutt (Calybutt), John 109, 111, 186, 206, 207
Camplion, John 229
Cannon, John 201; *see also* Canon
Cannons Green 145, 157, 167, 168, 170, 215, 224
Cannons Lane 146
Cannons manor
   documentary evidence 81–2, 94, 177, 178
   holdings 167, 168–9, 170
      Area B 105
      Area E 115, 233
      Area F 117
      Area G 118
      Quarent. 3 134
      Quarent. 6 140–1
      Quarent. 8 141
      Quarent. 11 143, 145, 146, 218, 219
      Quarent. 13 147
      Quarent. 16 149–50, 182, 186, 228, 241
      Quarent. 17 152, 213
      Quarent. 18 153
      Quarent. 23 155
      Quarent. 25 157
      Quarent. 29 211
   manor house 146, 168
Cannons Moor 58, 214
Cannons Pightle 149–50
Canon, John 111; *see also* Cannon
Canonsclos 149
Canonysrode 149
Capell (Capel)
   Sir Arthur 175, 186–9, 198
   Sir Arthur jnr 189
   Sir Giles 82, 147, 149, 185, 186, 230
   Henry (C14) 203
   Henry (C16) 147
   William, Earl of Essex 189
Cappe, Hugh 157, 158, 214
Cappes (tenement) 141, 182, 214–15
Cappesride 141
Caprede 141

Carter
  John 136
  William 223
Case family 189
  Edward (*fl*.1770) 230
  Edward (*fl*.1761), tanner 189, 230, 236
  Edward snr (*fl*.1762) 235, 236
  Edward jnr (*fl*.1782–3) 235
  Thomas snr (*fl*.1758) 189, 230, 235
  Thomas jnr 235, 236
  Thomas Henry 210, 230, 235, 236
Castle Acre 39, 63, 89
Castle Acre Priory
  documentary evidence 83–4
  holdings in Fransham 72, 74, 77, 167, 177
    Area D 114
    Area F 116, 117
    Area G 234
    Area O 131
Casy (Cacy)
  John 199
  Roger 136, 171, 199
Casys (*Cases*; *Casies*; *Cassys*) 133, 185
Casys (Cassys; Casyes) (tenement) 172, 199
Catislond 128
Caton, Simon 229
Catons 229
Catour
  Isabell 222
  Roger 222
Caulinge 234
Cavesacre 222
Cawston, Margaret de 153
cemeteries, Saxon 39, 40, 43, 45, 192
ceramic building material
  Roman 28, 29, 30, 35
  medieval 89, *90*, 99, 197, 198, 216
  post-medieval 200, 203
Chancellend close 138
chapel of St Katherine 117, 183, 233
le Chapelmedowe (*Chaplemedowys*) 123
Chapelrode 113
Chapilyards 117
Chapman
  Edmund 188
  Edward 213, 214
  John 179
  William 136
Chappel close 118, 233
Chappell House (*Chappell hurn*) 183
Charlepoynts (tenement) 117
Charlepoynts, Richard 117
Charwin, Guichard de 85
the Checker (*Chekyr*; *Chequers*) 184, 214
Checker, John att 157
Cheslond 111
Childes Pictell 116
Chirche mere (*Chirchemer*) 156, 159
Chokett, Henry 163
Chounes (*Chownes*) 145, 146, 185, 186
Chounescroft 145
Chouneslane (*Chewneslane*; *Chowneslane*) 142, 143, 145, 228
Chownesfurlong (*Chewnesfurlong*) 145, 146, 221
Christemesse (Cristemesse)
  Roger 172
  Walter 172
church of All Saints
  description 124, *125*
  floor tiles 89
  location 45, 168
  payment to 84
  Saxon finds 49
  valuations, C13 85
Church Farm 57, 202, 203
church path 143, 149, 157, 158
church of St Mary
  description 138–9, *140*
  floor tiles 89
  location 168
  Saxon finds 49
  valuations, C13 85
Church Way (*Churchway*) (GF) 124, 126
Church Way (LF) 56
Churcheman
  John 81
  Margaret 81
  Ralph 81
Churchfield (*Chirchfeld*) (LF) 56, 134, 141–2, 168, 174, 215
Churchfield (*Church Field*; *Chirchfeild*; *Chyrchefeyld*) (GF) 124, 126, 184, 241
Churchgate (*Chyrchgate*) 138
Chyleyspyghtell 116
Chyttelwong 239
Clackthornes (*Clackthorndes*; *Clackesthornes*; *Clackthorns*; *Clakethornes*; *Clakthornes*) 118
Clare, William de 214
Clares (tenement) 214
Clark (Clarke)
  Andrew 234
  Robert 187
  Thomas 82
  see also Clerk
Clawthorns (*Clack*; *Cleath hornes*; *Cloathhans*) 118
Claxton, William 179
Claypittemore 241
Clement
  Agnes 233
  George and Edmund 110–11, 186
  Hugh 233
  Robert 226, 233
  Roger son of William son of Henry 76
  Thomas 233
  William 73, 76, 196
  William son of Henry 76
Clerk
  Adam 165–6
  Matilda 166
  Richard 218
  Roger 165–6
  Thomas 165–6
  see also Clark
Clerkes/Coyse, Thomas 222
Clifford (Clyfford), Roger 73, 81, 196
Clober, Turstan 207
Clyfford *see* Clifford
Cockertons 106
Coddelingescroft 105
Codling, John 201
coin blank, Iron Age 25
coins
  Iron Age 25
  Roman 29, 30, 31, 32, 35
  Saxon 57, 62
  medieval 197, 211, 212, 222, 228, 235
  post-medieval 198, 211, 213
Coke (Cook; Kooc)
  John (*fl*.1417–18) 216
  John (d.1442) 77, 128
Cokerelys (tenement) 226
Colbiclos 105
Coldhamcroft 239
Colkirk 44, 71
Collen *see* Colyn
Collenge
  Grace 204
  Henry 203
  Matilda 203
  Robert 203, 204
Colling *see* Colyn
Collysyarde 114
Colmanscroft (*Colemanscroft*) 147, 185
Coltinge (Coltynge; Coltyns)
  Richard 219
  Stephen 149, 219
  William 149, 219
Coltinges green 149, 219, 241, 242
Coltings (*Coltinges*; *Coltyngs*; *Coltyngges*) 149, 182–3
Columbel (Columbell)
  John 73, 195, 196
  Roger son of William 205

Walter 205
Colyn (Collen; Colling; Collyn)
  Adam 99
  John (C15) 129, 131, 224
  John snr (C16) 203, 204, 205
  Matilda 203
  Richard 227
  Robert 204
  William 203, 236
Colynespytt (*Colins pitt*) 99, 197
Colyngswong 124
common fields *see* open fields
common lynge 133, 135–6, 199, 222
common pastures
  discussion 68–9, 184–5
  enclosure 193
  location *88*, 94
  pottery 91
  settlements 167, 168, 169, 170
    Area A 99, *100*
    Area B 103, 104, *104*, 105, 106
    Area C *108*, 109
    Area D *112*, 113–14
    Area E *112*, 115
    Area H 118, *119*
    Area O *119*, 128, 129–31
    Quarents. 5–6 135, *136*, 138
    Quarent. 11 143, *145*
    Quarent. 17 150, *150*
    Quarent. 18 153, *153*
    Quarent. 19 *153*, 154
    Quarent. 27 157, *158*
    Quarent. 29 158, *159*
common way 100
Complin, Thomas 232
Compton Census 178–9
le Conewer 216
Constable (Constabil)
  Richard 233
  Robert 221, 222
le Conynger (*le Conyger*) 86, 100, 103, 218
le Conyngerclos 216
Conyngerlond (*Conynglond*; *Cuniver*) 91, 103, 104, 105, 200
Coo, William 146
Cook *see* Coke; *see also* Wadelow
Cookes 230
Cook's Meadows 204
Cooks (tenement) 106
Cooper, Elizabeth 242; *see also* Couper
Cope, Walter 220
Copper, William 242
Copysclos 132–3
Corbel, Walter 124
Cornebelys 123
Cornell (Cornwell) (alias Wryght)
  Mother – 183
  Edward 183, 210
  John 183
  Thomas 183, 210
Cornubells (tenement) 205
Cortelylane 106, 199
Costyne, William 187, 188
Cosyn
  John and Christine 217–18, 219
  Nicholas and wife 219
Coultings Lane 242
Couper
  John 134
  Margaret 188
  William 199
  see also Cooper
Coupers (tenement) 199
Coyse
  Roger 222
  Thomas 222
Coysicroft 222
Coyves 222
Crane's Corner 169
Creake Abbey 84
Cressingham
  Clement de 238
  John de 238
  Margaret de 238
Cricke
  Lettice 188
  Thomas 188
Crispe (Cryspe)
  Faith 213, 225
  John 213, 225
Cristmasse (tenement) 116, 153, 154, 155
the Crofts 153, 154
le Crosse pasture 123
Croupius (Croupus; Crupes), John
  holdings 76
    Area C 206, 208
    Area J 123
    Area M 127
    Quarent. 2 134
    Quarent. 5 135
    Quarent. 6 138, 139
    Quarent. 11 221
    Quarent. 13 147
    Quarent. 27 158
  servant of 223
Crowdson, John 230
Crowe
  Christopher 117
  Robert 190, 201, 231, 232, 233
  Thomas 215
Crowes Close 190
Crowe's Hall 127
Crudde family 199
  John (?) 111, 190, 205
  John (*fl.*1395) 147
  John (*fl.*1400) 124, 205
  John (*fl.*1404), servants of 101
  John (*fl.*1427–68) 99, 102, 198–9, 202, 218
  John (d.1499) 205, 206, 212, 230–1
    servant of 230–1
  John (*fl.*1537) 198
  Nicholas 231
  William, servant of 156
  see also Curd
Cruddes (tenement) 102
Cryspe *see* Crispe
Curd (Curde), John 102, 205, 207; *see also* Crudde
Curds Croft 186, 198
Curds Green (*Cruddes*; *Cruddes Green*; *Cruddesgrene*)
  Area A 99, 102, 103, 198
  disappearance of 94
  settlements 167, 169, 170
Curds Hall 102, 182
Curtlys (Curtelyns) (tenement) 199
Curtlys (*Curtileys*) 177, 202
Cushing (Cushinge), Samuel 185, 204
Cycestre, Christopher de 207

Dabbe
  John 182, 218
  Robert 215, 219
dagger, Neolithic 16, *17*
Daginotis croftisend 149, 220
Dagnet 149
Dagonetts (tenement) 149, 220
Daie *see* Dey
Dames (Danes; Daines)
  Richard 201
  Richard jnr 201–2
  Robert 201–2
  see also Deymes; Dymes
Danger, Robert 179, 212
Danyell cloos 133
Davies, Robert 225
Davy (Davey; Davye)
  Widow – 179
  Dorothy 236
  Hamond 236
  Robert 187, 188, 189, 212, 236
Debil furlong 109
Delewenesacre 239

demesne lands
    Kirkhams and Wilcoks manors 80–1
    post-medieval 185–9
Denby, Thomas 102, 133–4, 147
Denbysgrene 102
Dene
    Agnes 205
    Stephen 205
Dennis
    Edward 204
    John 183
Denry, Mr – 183
Denyes
    Edward 204
    John 204
deserted settlements 165, 169, 173, 182, 193
Dewes 115, 117
Dey (Daie; Deye; Dye)
    Christina le 142
    Henry (alias Brook) 221
    James 179, 227
    William (alias Pulter) (C16) 82
    William (atte Broke) (C17) 221
Deymes, Henry 206; *see also* Dames
Dikewood 83, 115, 167
Dikewood manor 83–4
Dillington 83
Dimers 231
disc, gold, Iron Age 25
documentary evidence
    common pastures 94
    Domesday survey 62–7
    manorial structure 72–86
    population and wealth 70–2
    post-medieval 175–8
    use of 11, 94, 193
Doesgate (*Kynnoks Lane*; *Kenoxe lane/Layn*)
    Area C 109, 111
    Area D 115
    Area E 115, 208, 232, 242
    Area F 117
    settlements 169
Dokett, Christopher 203
Doukys *see* Duke
Doune, John de 238
dovecots 80, 143, 147, 216, 222, 223, 227
Dovehouseyard 143, 227
Dowesmedow 162
Doyes (tenement) 233
Drayton Hall manor 83
dress fitting, medieval 211
Drew, Elizabeth 235
Drewry, Thomas 233
Drosier, John 197, 198, 199
Droury *see* Taylor
Drovelane (*Drovieslane*; *Drouteslane*) 142
Drowry
    Adam 225
    Thomas 123
Duke (Doukys)
    Henry 209
    Richard 103
Dukes (*Dewks*; *Dukks*; *Dusks*) 209
Dulls gat 208
Dunger, Robert 212
Dunham 64, 66, 67; *see also* Great Dunham; Little Dunham
Dunham Close 186
Dunham Croft (*Dunhamlond*) 99, 103, 197
Dunninge (tenement) 159
Dunynge (Dymyng), John 208
Dunyngs 214
Dye *see* Dey
Dykewood House 84
Dymes (Daynes)
    Robert 231
    Thomas 201
    see also Dames
Dymesclos 114, 186, 231
Dynnshtund/Dynghaund medowe 123

East Bilney 71
East Bradenham 47, 53, 173, 178
East Dereham 63, 70, 83
East Lexham 63, 67, 70, 71, 76, 83
East Lexham manor
    documentary evidence 76, 77, 175–7, 238
    holdings 167, 169
        Area B 103, 104, 106, 199, 200
        Area C 109, 110, 186, 205, 205–6, 207
        Area D 114
        Area G 117
        Area J 121, 123
        Area O 128
Eastendmoor
    Area E 115, 232
    Area G 229
    Area H 118, 120, 121, 209, 210
    Quarent. 17 150–3, 211, 212
    Quarent. 18 213, 214
    Quarent. 29 158, 211, 228–9
    settlements
        late Saxon 57, 167
        medieval 167, 168, 169, 170, 184
        post-medieval *161*, 236
    Sparhams manor rights 81
Eastfield 161–3, 185, 189, 212, 214, 229, 236
Eastfield Close 190
Eastmillfield (*Estmyllefeld*) 154, 215
Ebotesyerd 147
Echard, William 132
Echerard, Gilbert 132
Echyld, Nicholas 214
Ede
    John and wife 154
    Thomas 233
Edild (Edildes; Edyld) (tenement) 162, 171, 214, 237
Edild (Edilles; Edlides; Edyld) family
    Agnes 214
    John 214
    Nicholas 171
    Robert 160, 171, 214
Edildescroft 214
Edmund son of Payne 64
Edyman (alias Sawher), Edmund 229, 236
Ellingham House 207
Ellingham way 123
Ellinghams field/close 109, 115, 172, 241
Ellinghams manor
    description/documentary evidence 76–7, 175–7
    holdings 167, 190
        Area B 203
        Area C 109, 111, 206, 241
        Area D 114, 208, 231
        Area E 115, 233
        Area H 119, 209, 210
        Area J 123
        Area M 127
        Area O 131
        Quarent. 19 154
    manor house 109, 207
Ellinghams meadow 55, 121–3, 127
Elmedon, George 210
Elvereds 226
Elverycsmore 113, 114, 115, 225, 226, 231
Elvys 162
Elyngham, Thomas de 76
Elyngham grene 111
Elynghams more 111, 241
Elynghams Wode 109, 167
Elyot, Simon 157
Elys grove 185
Emmesfaldgate (*Emmies Faldgate*; *Emmysfaldgate*) 86, 129
Emmestile (*Emesaker*) 129, 235
enclosure
    ditched, Roman 28, *28*, 33
    medieval 129, 170, 174, 193
    post-medieval 189–90, 190–1, 193
Enclosure Award maps 1, *2–3*, *92–3*, 94, *137*
Ernesslane (*Ernneslane*) 133, 198, 199
Erny

Cecilia 198
John 198
Ernyesyard 102, 198
Ernys 198
Ernys croft (*Ernescroft*) 186, 198
Escherclos (*Escherdclos*) 119, 132, 210
Eslyn, Nicholas 222
Essex
   Earl of 183, 185
   Lady 209, 214, 218, 221, 222, 223, 227, 228
Esshe yard 210
Essylins (Eslings; Esl'ms) (tenement) 222
Estende 151
Estfeld 124
Estlens (*Esstelyns*) 222
Estmer 142
Estmerewong 142
Eston, Thomas de 73, 196, 234
Estune, Thomas de 172
Eudo son of Clamahoc 63
Evan, William 201
Everids alias Piggs (*Ellreds alias Pygges*) 226

Faber, William son of Walter 116
fair, Little Fransham 80
fald gates 109, 132, 174, 184, 240
Fastolf
   Elizabeth 134
   Isabelle 134
Fawkes 214
Fenbridge (*Fennbrigge*; *Forthbridge*) 118, 127
Fender, Godfrey 101
Fenders (*Fendors*) 114, 115, 117
Fenders Close 111
Fendersmoor (*Fendoures mor*)
   Area C 109, 111
   Area E 115, 232, 242
   Area F 117
   Settlements 167, 169
Fendours (alias Maunfras), John 152
feodary, Great Fransham 72–4, *73*, 195–6
Ferres, Hermer de 64, 66
fieldwalking 7, *8*, 9
Finch *see* Fynch
Fincham (Fyncham), Simon 117, 131, 234
finger-rings, Saxon 62
Fingh, Bartholomew 158
fire-bar, Roman 30
Fisher (Fysher; Fissor; Fisor)
   Alice daughter of Vincent 143
   Eustace 143, 201
   John 143
   John of Scarning 162
   Margery 143
   Petronilla 142
   Vincent 142, 143, 219
Fisherbrigg 143
fitting/fob, Iron Age 25, *25*
Fitz Alan family 83
   Richard 83
Fitz Alexander, William 80
Flatlond 162
Flegge, John 201
Fletcher, Richard 224
flint
   Palaeolithic 13, *13*
   Mesolithic 13
   Neolithic–early Bronze Age 15–18, *15*, *16*, *17*, *18*, 19
   later Bronze Age–Iron Age 21
   see also arrowheads; axes; dagger; hand-axe; pick; pot-boiler sites
floor tiles, medieval 89, 216
Flynt
   John 201
   Margaret 201
Flyntes (tenement) 124, 201
foldcourse system 91
Foliot family 76
   Jordan 73, 76, 195, 196
   Sir Richard 195
Forby, Thomas 227

forge 182, 184
Forncett 171
Forthbridge see Fenbridge
Forthmeadow (*Forthemedowe*) 125, 127
Fouche
   Elianor 217
   Manser 217
Fowne (Foun), William 147
Fox, Widow 179
Francheville family 83
Franklin
   Anthony 227
   James 227
Fransham family 83
   Agnes de (C12) 74
   Agnes de (C14) 76, 111, 232
   Geoffrey de (*fl.*1316–32) 74, 238
   Geoffrey de (d.1414) 74, 76, 86, 99, 123, 124, 127, 175, 194, 198
   Gilbert de (C13) 84–85, 234
   Gilbert de (*fl.*1343–57) 71, 103, 124, 201
   Henry son of William 118
   Isabel wife of Reginald son of Adelward 234
   Joan 86
   Matilda daughter of Bonde 84
   Philip son of Odo 116
   Ralph son of Roger 84
   Reginald 234
   Roger de (C13) 84, 85
   Roger son of Gilbert de 83
   Roger son of Thomas 114, 234
   Thomas 200, 234
   William de (*fl.*1279–80) 72, 73, 74, 76, 82, 84, 103, 118, 119, 129, 195, 196
Fransham Lyng 105, 199
Fransham parish
   boundaries 1–6, *5*
   location *xii*, 1, *5*
   place name 37
   study area 1–6, *2–5*
      choice of 6–7
   village sign *194*
   see also Great Fransham; Little Fransham; survey
Fransham/Wendling land-unit 1–5, 37, 50–1, *50*
Frederic 62, 63, 64
Freeman, Robert 235
Frœndi 37
Froesham (Fravesham), Gilbert de 83
Frydaywell 152
Fuche, Thomas 129
Fueche *see* Futch
Fulcher, Thomas 235
Fuller
   Agnes 230
   John 229–30, 233
Futch (Fueche; Futche)
   John 203, 208, 234
   Thomas (*fl.*1400) 211, 224
   Thomas (d.1504) 201, 208
Futches (tenement) 204, 224
Futter
   Alice 207
   John 206
   Richard 111, 207
Fylippes (tenement) 152
Fynch (Fynche)
   Alexander 129, 131
   John 116
   Thomas 226
Fyncham *see* Fincham
Fynches 186
Fynches modo Petyfers 116
Fynchesclos 149
Fysher *see* Fisher
Fyweacrys (*fyveacres*) 120, 154, 239

Galt, Fucher 83
Gardener, Juetta (Inotte) 143
Gateley 70, 71, 72
Gateley, Ralph de 84
Gatesdene, John de 238
Gaude

Geoffrey 140
William 140
Gaudes (*Guadesyard*) 140
geld payments 66
Geldars Close 226
Gelder, William 223
Gelewiygescroft 114
Geney (Giney), Peter 234
Geoffrey son of Gilbert 73, 195
geology 1
Gernyshil 152
Gibbe (Gibbes; Gibbs; Gybbe; Gybbes)
   Agnes 225
   Nicholas 212
   William 172, 225, 226
Gibbes (Gybbes) (tenement) 172, 226
Gilbert 62, 64, 74
Giney *see* Geney
girdle hangers, Saxon 41, *43*
Girdlestone, Anne 220
Glas, John 123
glebe *see* Great Fransham glebe; Little Fransham glebe
Gleymesford, John 136, 171, 199
Godards 146
Goddards (tenement) 146
Goddards lane 150
Godfreston, William 135
Godfrey (Godefrey)
   William (alias Smyth) 203, 204
   William jnr 135, 149
Godfrey son of John of Little Fransham 141
Godfries close 220, 221
Godfry; Godfrey, Godfries (tenement) 145, 149, 154, 158, 220–1
Godwick 71, 72, 178
Goggles Lane (*Cannons*; *Coltings*; *Goddards Lane*) 146
Golder, Nicholas 200
Goldincroft 239
Goodson
   Widow – 179, 220
   John 179, 215
   Richard 179, 220
Gorge (Gorges)
   Sir Edmund 81, 185
   Mary 218
   Walter 103, 218
Gotte
   Geoffrey 141
   Humphrey 140
   Olive 72, 140
Gottespightel 140
Grandimonte, Aymo de 85–6
grange 82, 150, *150*
Great Bittering 71, 173
Great Clos (*Grete Clos*) 205
Great Dunham
   church of St Andrew 54
   compared
      Roman period 27, 35
      Saxon period 39, 45–7, 50
      late Saxon–early Norman period 53, 54
      medieval period 71, 173
      post-medieval period 178
Great Dynnes 231
Great Fransham glebe
   documentary evidence 85, 94
   Enclosure, effect of 191
   holdings
      Area B 104, 186
      Area C 109
      Area J 121
      Area K 124
      Area L 124, 125, 205
      Area M 126
Great Fransham manor
   documentary evidence 72–6, *73*, 94, 167, 173, 175, 189, 195–6
   holdings 169, 170, 171, 172
      Area A 99–100, 102, 186
      Area B 103, 104, 105, 106, 201, 203, 204, 205
      Area C 109, 111, 112, 184, 186, 206, 207, 208
      Area D 113, 114, 115, 208, 225, 226, 231
      Area E 115, 209, 232
      Area F 116, 117
      Area G 117, 118, 183, 229, 230, 233, 234
      Area H 118, 121, 210
      Area J 123
      Area K 124
      Area M 126
      Area N 127
      Area O 129, 131, 132, 210, 211, 224, 235
      Quarent. 1 132
      Quarent. 2 134
      Quarent. 19 154, 235–6
   manor house 76, 99–100, 168, 197–8
Great Fransham parish
   boundaries 5–6
   land divisions, medieval 94–7, *98*
   manorial structure 72–86
   merger with Little Fransham 1
   population and wealth
      medieval 70–2, 173
      post-medieval 178–9
   settlements, medieval
      distribution and chronology 167, 168
      manorial allegiance and tenure 168, 169, 170
   survey results
      late Saxon–early Norman 53, 55, 56–8, 61, 67
      medieval 99–32
Great Fransham rectory 61, 67, 106, *106*, 168, 182, 205
Great Fransham Rectory manor
   documentary evidence 85, 177
   holdings 170
      Area B 106, 204
      Area C 109, 190
      Area F 117
      Area G 118
      Area H 119, 209, 210
      Area K 124
      Area L 125
      Area M 126
      Quarent. 2 134
Great Millclose (*Great Milclose*; *Gretemylleclos*) 155–6
Great Palgrave 39
Great Watering 161, 162
Greate New close 198
Green (Grene)
   Emma 219
   John, carpenter 217
   John atte 238
   Paul 219
   Richard atte 238
   Roger 156, 219, 221, 222
   Walter 222
Greengate 132
Greenhood (Grenehode), William 118, 154, 208
Greenway (*Greneway*)/*Southgateway* 168, 184
   Area M 126, 127, 183
   Area N 127
   origins 40, 55
   Quarent. 4 134
   Quarent. 7 141
   Quarent. 29 162, 163
Grenescroft 219
Gressenhall
   compared
      Saxon period 37, 45
      late Saxon–early Norman period 54
      medieval period 70, 71, 173
      post-medieval period 178
   Domesday evidence 63, 64, 66, 67, 76
   pottery production 172
   see also Rougholme
Gressenhall, Alexander son of Adam 169, 206
Grey, John 223
Griggs
   Anne 212, 229, 237
   Money 214
Grimston 91
Grope Acre 126
Gropelond 126, 190
the Grove 154, 186

Gryffyn, William 204
guild of St Katherine 117, 183
Gunton, Matthew de 85
Guntons manor
   documentary evidence 78, 85, 177, 189
   holdings 170
      Area E 116, 232
      Area F 117
      Area H 119, 210
      Area J 123
      Area O 128, 131
      Quarent. 4 135
      Quarent. 7 141
      Quarent. 25 157
      Quarent. 29 161, 162, 163
Gurnayes 111, 207
Gurnaysacre 111
Gurr (Gurre), William 218, 227
Guybon, Thomas 200
Gybbe/Gybbes *see* Gibbe
Gybbeslane 226

Haddock (Haddok)
   John 111, 118, 209
   John jnr 209
   Reginald 73, 196
Haddocks (*Haddokks*) 209, 231
Haddokes pightell 111, 184, 209
Halcott
   John 231
   Matthew 231
Haleyweythorp 84
Halfthesheld 127
Hall (Aula; Halle)
   Agnes atte 172
   John de 102
   Thomas 102
   William de 73, 102, 195
Hall Close (*Halclose*) (LF) 56, 142, 189, 215, 218
Halleclos (GF) 100
Hallecroft (*Halcroft*) (GF) 56, 103–4, 200–1
Hallecroft (LF) 138, 142, 216, 217
Hallekarre faldgate 99
Halleker 99, 197
Halleker lane 99
Hallesrod 105
Hallwood (*Hallewood*; *Halrode*) 99, 186, 197
Hallwood meadowe 197
Halwoodlane 198
Hammond, John 203; *see also* Hamond
Hamo son of Richard 73, 196
Hamond, John 184; *see also* Hammond
Hamondescroft 135
hand-axe, Palaeolithic 13, *13*
Hanke
   John 218
   Roger 132
Har'Aker 239
Haraldes (*Harhalds*) 123, 197
Haraldisaker 99
Haringeshag 83
Harlewyn (Harlwyn)
   John 236
   Paul 131
   Robert 229, 234, 236
   Thomas 119, 233, 234
harness fittings
   Iron Age 25, *25*
   medieval 126, *127*, 197
harness mounts, Iron Age 25
harness pendants, medieval *102*, 197
Harold 63, 64, 68
Harold (Harrold)
   Aveline 101, 197
   Beatrice 197
   James 202
Haroldscroft (*Haraldscroft*) 99, 197
Harry Smythes close (*Herry Smethes close*) 228
Harsnett, Samuel 183, 233
harvest shack time 173, 174

Harviis aker 239
Harwen (Harwyn)
   John 182, 220, 227
   Robert 229
   Robert jnr 229
Harwynes (*Harwins*) 116, 235
Harwyns field (*Harwynes felde*) 57, 233
Harwynsmedowe 131
Harydance
   John 118, 209, 234
   Walter 234
Hastelisdiche 197
Hastell, John 197
Hastings (tenement) 158
Hastings family 76
   Edward 77, 202
Hastyngeslane 158
Haut, Roger 132
Hauwil (Auwl; Hauvill), Roger son of Nicholas 238
Hawebushes 105
Hawke, John 182
Hayward, William 97, 143, 146, 149, 157, 185, 223
Headacre 127
Hearth Taxes 178, 179, *180–1*
Hebydlond 120
Hecham, Adam son of John de 129
heckle tooth, Saxon 48
Heddingham, honour of 102
Heighgrenemore 231
Heighgrengate 231
le hemplond 147
Hempton Priory 84, 152, 158, 163
Henfield (*Henfeld*; *Henne Feld*) 117, 118, 168, 230, 233, 234, 235
Henke, Roger and Agnes 225
Henry Smiths lane 228
Henson, William 187, 212
Herningshawe (*Herningsawe*) 113, 114, 167, 168, 207
Herringshall 115
Herringshall and Dikewood manor 177, 234
Herringshall manor 83–84
Herveus son of Juliana 74
Heryngshawewong 115
Hevedlond 151
Hey (Hay; Heigh; Heye; Heyghe; Heyie) family 114
   Agnes 231
   Edmund snr 209, 231
   Edmund son of John 208, 231
   John le 115–16
   Ralph 232
   Richard 115, 116, 229, 230, 232
   Simon 115
   Thomas le 163, 231
Hey Green 113–15, 167, 168, 169, 208, 225, 231
Heycalling 117
Heygate 121
Heylott
   Cristina 213
   William 213
Heyward, Thomas 226
Hichescroft 239
Hicke, Adam 183
High Green Farm *frontispiece*
Hill Farm 207
Hillyacre 127
Hirnclose 154
Hobbes (Hobbys)
   Katherine 136
   Margaret 136
   Richard 136
Hobbyscroft 146
Hobbyslond (tenement) 146, 222
Hoberds (tenement) 140, 172
Hoche, John 150, 211
Hoches 150
Hochesfield (*Hochisfeld*) 151–2, 174, 211, 212, 214, 215
Hockering (Hockryng; Hokeringe)
   Adam 119
   Avice 238
   Geoffrey de 118
   Godfrey de (C13) 73, 119, 196, 238

Godfrey de (C14) 154
Hamon de 119, 238
Henry 136, 224
Hockering manor 83
Hodgskyn, Christopher 230
Hoe 70, 71, 72
Hogan (Hoogan)
   Robert 131, 163, 177, 211, 224
   Thomas 131, 163
Hoggesmedowe 123
Hokeringe *see* Hockering
Hokerynge (tenement) 119
Holkam, Burghall manor 171
Holme Hale 13
Holt (Holte), Richard de 226, 233
Holtes (*Holtis*) 226
Home Farm 57
Homes, Thomas 203
Hoo, Richard 78, 177, 190, 232
hooked tag, Saxon 49
Horningtoft 71
Hosyer (tenement) 129
Hosyer, Vincent 214
Hosyherslond 239
Hotche (Hoches; Hotches) (tenement) 149, 150–1, 152, 211, 220
Hovell *see* Howell
Hoverd, Robert 205
Howard
  Amy 202
  Elizabeth 202
  Mary 202
  Sarah 202
  Thomas, Duke of Norfolk 83
Howell (Hovell)
  Alice 233
  Hogan 233
  John 187
  Nicholas 233
  Robert 232, 233
  Thomas 233
Howes, Thomas 82
Howfield (*Howefield*; *Hewefeld*) 123–4, 190
Howlond 124
Hoyp, Ralph 154
Hoywicks (tenement) 207
Huberd (Hubert)
  Alice 227
  Robert 205
  Robert jnr 205
  William (C14) 135, 136
  William (d.1427) 172
Huberdseslaneshende (*Hoberdslanesende*) 134, 136
Huberdslane (*Hoberdlane*; *Hooberdislane*; *Huberslane*) 56, 134, 135, 140, 182
Hubert son of Hugh of Castle Acre 157
Hugh, parson 85
Hugh, villein 157–8, 169
Hulbys 162
Hulls 163
Hullsmedowe (*Hulls Meadow*; *Hulvesmedow*) 162, 190
Hulverhegge 132
Hulverhegge lane 235
Hulverstreet 131–2
Hunson, Mary 213
Hunt (Hunte)
  Edward 238
  John 238
  Robert 213, 227
Hyde Hall 230

Inquisitions Post Mortem 177
ironworking sites, Roman 30, 31, *31*, 32, 33, 192; *see also* forge
Isaacs close 99
Isaak, Thomas 99
Isakes (*Isack*) 99

Jaggs (*Jagges*; *Jaggescroft*) 149, 186
Jantes Stile 232
Jeckesgrove 158, 185, 186, 224
Jekkes (*Jeckespeece*) 158, 182, 224

Jekkespath (*Jecks mere*) 158, 224
Jenior, John 119, 129
Jennings (Jennis), Samuel 219
jettons
  medieval 197, 222
  post-medieval 198
Jewell
  Hogan 233
  Thomas 233
Jocke (Jok; Joke; Jook) family 224
  Edmund 153, 154, 155, 157, 224, 227
  Hamond 152, 153, 158, 211, 213, 224, 227
  Margery 227
Jocks/Jokes/Jookis (tenement) 152, 211, 213, 227
John of Little Fransham 75
John, servant of William Crudde 156
John son of Bartholomew 223
John son of Simon 169, 206
Johnson (Jonsone)
  Bernard 189
  Henry 212
  John 201
Jok (Joke) *see* Jocke
Jokeslane 157
Jonesyard 200
Jook *see* Jocke
Jordan (Jurdan; Jurdon)
  Adam 165, 171
  Bartholomew son of John 165
  Cecilia 165
  Nicholas 160, 161
  Peter son of William 215
  William 159, 214, 215, 225
Jordans (Jourden; Jurdon) (tenement) 159, 161, 172, 229
Jowettesbrygge 143
Jownesfurlong 145
Junyor, Thomas 129, 131
Jurdan (Jurdon) *see* Jordan
Jurdones (*Jordonys*) 160, 174
Jurdons croft 161

Kalvecroft 239
Katherine daughter of Roger 172
Katherine Mead 235
Kattesfaldegate 132
Kaulynges 57, 116, 209
Kayds closse see Cadescloos
Kaysescrofte 199
Kede, William 218
Kempstone
  church of St Paul 53
  compared
    Roman period 27
    Saxon period 37–9, 45, 50
    late Saxon–early Norman period 53
    medieval period 71, 173
    post-medieval period 178
  Domesday evidence 64, 66, 67, 76
  Great Fransham manor tenement 76
Kempstonhall 86
Kenellhawgh Woode 205
Kenting, John 117
Kenyshawewaie 121, 123
Kerbusk 134, 136
Kerlane 99
Kerlanesende 99
le Kerrs (*le Ker*) 99, 239
Kett, Richard 241
key, medieval *102*, 197
Kigeman, John 225
King *see* Kyng
Kingscroft (*Kingescroft*; *Kynggescroft*) 116, 117, 177
Kinots *see* Knot
Kinwalds 109, 205, 206
Kirkham
  John de 225
  Margaret 225
Kirkhams manor
  documentary evidence 74, *75*, 78–80, *79*, 94, 167, 173, 174
  holdings 168, 169, 170, 171–2

Area C 111–12, 205
Area E 115, 232
Area G 118, 229–30
Area J 123
Area M 126–7
Area O 128, 210
Quarent. 1 132, 133, 199
Quarent. 2 133, 134, 198, 199
Quarent. 3 134
Quarent. 5 135, 136, 224
Quarent. 6 139–40, 182
Quarent. 8 141–2
Quarent. 9 142, 168, 215–18
Quarent. 10 143
Quarent. 11 143, 145, 146, 225
Quarent. 12 146
Quarent. 13 146, 182
Quarent. 15 149, 219, 220, 222
Quarent. 16 149
Quarent. 17 151, 152–3, 211, 212
Quarent. 18 153, 214
Quarent. 19 154
Quarent. 20 154
Quarent. 21 154
Quarent. 22 155
Quarent. 24 155, 156
Quarent. 27 157, 182, 215
Quarent. 28 158, 224
Quarent. 29 158, 159, 162, 189, 229, 236
manor house 80, 142, *142, 143,* 165, 168, 215–18
Kirkhams and Wilcoks manor
demesne lands 80–1, 185–9
documentary evidence 177, 178, 184
enclosure 189
holdings 170, 174
Area H 120, 210
Area J 121, 123
Area N 127
Area O 210
Quarent. 3 134
Quarent. 4 135
Quarent. 5 135, 224
Quarent. 6 139, 140
Quarent. 7 141
Quarent. 10 142, 227, 228
Quarent. 11 145, 146, 225
Quarent. 13 147
Quarent. 14 222, 223
Quarent. 15 149, 182, 219, 220
Quarent. 16 149
Quarent. 17 152, 211, 212
Quarent. 18 154, 214
Quarent. 19 154, 189, 236
Quarent. 22 155
Quarent. 23 155, 189
Quarent. 25 157, 215
Quarent. 26 157
Quarent. 27 215
Quarent. 28 158, 224
Quarent. 29 161, 162, 163, 189, 211, 229, 237
Kirtling 64, 66
knife, Saxon 48
knife/rapier, Bronze Age 21
Knights/Knyghts (tenement) 146
Knightsrod (*Knytrod*) 132, 168
Knightwodd (*Knyghtwode*) 185, 205
Knightwood Lane 205
knob *see* boss/knob
Knot (Knots; Knott; Kinots; Kynotte), Roger 146, 149, 172, 220, 222, 234
Knots (tenement) 172, 220, 222
Knyght (Knyt)
David 146
Henry 146, 172
Roger 171
Knyvet, Sir John 82
Kooc *see* Coke
Kyneswaldeshaugh (*Kenwaldeshalle*; *Kewaldeshaugh*; *Kinwaldyshaghe*; *Kinwalsawe*; *Kynwaldshawe*) 109, 123, 167, 174, 186, 205, 206
Kyng, Ralph 141
Kyngesgate 239

Kyngesway 156
Kynnockersmore 114
Kynnockkshalfacre 124
Kynnocks 111, 114
Kynnockscroft 226
Kynnokes (Kynnokks) (tenement) 111, 115, 172, 231, 238
Kynnokes (Kinnok; Kynnoc; Kynnock; Kynnoks; Kynott)
Adam 231
Alice daughter of Henry 232
Avice 238
Hamon 238
John 231, 238
Richard 111, 231
Roger (Thoonoks) 225
see also Knot
Kynnoks Lane see Doesgate
Kynwelshaweclose 77, 109
Kyrketon, Ralph de 206

Lacy, John 227
Ladismedowe 123
Ladymerelond/Ladismerwong/Ladiscroft 55, 125, 127
Ladymerpytt 125
Ladymoorclose/Ladimer 125
Ladymoorefeild 124
Ladysmere (*Ladismer*; *Ladysmeer*) 125, 234
Lalle, Thomas 172
Lamberd, Margery 220
Lamp land 126, 190
land tenure 168–70, 193; *see also* tenemental system
land-use 193
Domesday evidence 63, 67–9
medieval 99, 173–4
post-medieval 186
Langton (Langeton), Walter de, Bishop of Chester 83
Large (Lardge) family 202, 208, 232, 233
Agnes widow of William 208
Alice 231, 232
Frances 236
George 226
George snr 179, 214
George jnr 179, 213
George son of Henry 188
Henry (*fl.*1607) 187
Henry (*fl.*1666) 179
Henry (d.1705) 236
John (*fl.*1437–8) 217
John (*fl.*1537) 209, 226, 232, 234
John (*fl.*1566) 215
John (d.1651), butcher 231
John (*fl.*1664–6), butcher 179, 215
Mancer 234
Nicholas 201
Peter 179, 215
Prudence 182
Robert 209
Simon 226, 231
Susanna 225
Thomas (*fl.*1462) 202
Thomas (*fl.*1607) 188
Thomas jnr (*fl.*1607) 188
Walter 188
William (*fl.*1365) 160
William (*fl.*1454–87) 208, 226, 232
William snr (d.1541) 123, 230, 232, 233
William jnr (*fl.*1511) 233
William (*fl.*1664/6) 179
William (*fl.*1697), gent. of Swaffham 225
Launditch 23, 37
Launditch Hundred 1, 5, 6, 70, 71
Lawdy, Ralph 115, 209
Lay Subsidies 70, 71, 72, 94, 178
Leagers Field 225
Leath *see* Leith
Leche
Cecilia 111
Geoffrey 111, 207
John 198
William 111, 199
Lee (Leigh), Walter 213

Leffeyn (Leffen)
  Hamon 208
  Robert 208
  Thomas 208
Leigh *see* Lee
Leith (Leath)
  Cook 202, 205
  Edward 202
Lenne
  Matilda 207
  Reginald de 207
Leticecroift 239
Lewes (Sussex) 62, 63, 195
Lexham
  Walter 147, 217, 227, 229
  William 218
Lingeclose 135–6
Ling's End Farm 135
Litcham 67, 71
Litelkroft 239
Little Bittering 178
Little Dunham
  compared
    Mesolithic period 13–15
    Roman period 27
    Saxon period 39, 45, 47, 50
    late Saxon–early Norman period 53
    medieval period 71, 173
    post-medieval period 178
  manor 50, 99
Little Fransham glebe
  documentary evidence 85–6, 94
  Enclosure, effect of 191
  holdings 168, 184
    Area J 123
    Area L 125
    Area M 126
    Quarent. 3 134
    Quarent. 4 135
    Quarent. 5 136
    Quarent. 6 138, 141
    Quarent. 7 141
    Quarent. 8 142
    Quarent. 9 142
    Quarent. 11 145
    Quarent. 12 146
    Quarent. 20 154
    Quarent. 25 157
Little Fransham Old Hall 27, 146, 236
Little Fransham parish
  boundaries 5–6
  land divisions, medieval 94–7, *98*
  manorial structure 72–86
  market and fair 80
  merger with Great Fransham 1
  population and wealth
    medieval 70–2, 173
    post-medieval 178–9
  settlements, medieval
    distribution and chronology 167–8
    manorial allegiance and tenure 168–9, 170
    survey results
      late Saxon–early Norman 53, 56, 58–62, 67
      medieval 132–63
Little Fransham rectory 138, *138*, *139*, 182, 185
Little Millclose (*Litillemylleclos*; *Litilmelfeld*; *Parva Millecloos*) 157
Little Scarning manor 177
Logan, John le 78
London
  Geoffrey 224
  Richard of 200
long acre (GF) 128, 189
long acre (LF) 145
Longclos (*le Long closse*) 134, 158
Longham
  compared 37, 47, 53, 71, 173
  Domesday evidence 64, 66
Longmeadow (*Longmedowe*) 134, 135
le Lounde (*Lound*) 58, 145, 154
Lower Farm 161, *161*, 189

le Lund 120, 154, 174
Lyle
  Cristiana 213
  Walter 213
Lylmannescroft (*Lollemanescroft*) 82, 149
le Lyng (*Ling*) 135, 167, 222
Lyttylmore 109, 111, 113, 205, 206

Mabbesyerd 147
Maceon, John 209
Maddy, John 105
Magna Mille Cloos 61
Magotesclos 140
Malaysel, Geoffrey 85
Malby
  Elizabeth 204
  John 204
Mallet, Martha 235
Mandeville, Richard de 73
Manor Close 100, 198
Manor Pightle 150
manorial structure 72–4
  Barony of Rye 83
  Bromehill Priory 83
  Castle Acre Priory 83–4
  Creake Abbey 84
  Great Fransham manor 74–6
  Great Fransham Rectory glebe and manor 85
  Hempton Priory 84
  Little Fransham glebe 85–6
  Mileham manor 83
  Milles atte Mor leet 86
  Pentney Priory 84
  Rougham/Fransham part of de Warenne fee 76
    Blyfords 77
    East Lexham 77
    Ellinghams 76–7
    Mascales 77
    Rougholme 77–8
  Thetford Priory 84
  de Tosny manors in Little Fransham 78
    Cannons 81–2
    Kirkhams 78–81, *79*
    Sparhams 81
    West Bradenham 82
    Wilcoks 80–1
  Wendling Abbey 84–5
Marche, Adam 211
Marches 211
market, Little Fransham 80
Marscall (Marescal; Mareschall; Marscall; Marschall) *see* Mascall
le Marketmere (*Market meare*) 161, 162, 163
Martenet, William 138
Martinet (Martynet)
  Alice 152
  Walter 152
  William 152
Maryoneselane (*Maryones lane*) 158, 161, 162, 229
Maryonesfaldgate 158, 162
Mascall (Marescal; Mareschall; Marscall; Marschall; Mascale; Maschale; Maschald; Maskall; Maskell) family 83
  Agnes 195
  Alice (*fl.*1279–80) 73, 195
  Alice (*fl.*1332/7) 238
  Aveline 234
  Edward 206
  Geoffrey de 72, 73, 77, 195, 238
  Gilbert le 128
  John 83
  Ralph 238
  Thomas (*fl.*1346) 238
  Thomas (*fl.*1370–1406) 121, 128, 203, 204
  Thomas (*fl.*1442–3) 77, 128
  William (C12) 103
  William (*fl.*1362) 206
  William (*fl.*1430–9) 77, 94, 104, 105, 106, 109, 113, 118, 121, 123, 124, 126, 190, 202, 234
Mascalls 'manor' 77, 128
Mascallyng 103, 104, 200, 205
Mase, John 234

Mason, William 197, 198, 205
Matilda daughter of Laurence 169, 206
Matilda daughter of Odo 172
Maunde family 147
   Geoffrey 174, 223
   Joanna 136
   John snr and jnr 102, 136, 154, 157, 171, 214
   Richard 140, 142, 198, 214, 223
Maundesclose 136, 198
Maundsacre 147
Maunfras
   John 152
   John jnr 156, 226
   William 228
Mawby, John 204
Mayken
   Henry 116
   Robert 116
   Thomas 116
Maynard, John 124, 204
Meadowhouse 111
meadows
   Roman 33
   Domesday evidence 63, 67
   medieval 121–3, 127, 128, *128*, 134, 153
   pottery 91
Meadowscroftsend 111
Mechill, John 86, 129
Medowclos (*Medowe Close end*) 131, 234
Medowecroft 111, 112
Medowfalgate (*Medowys Faldgate*) 112, 123
Mendham, Robert 118, 218
Menewood 115
Menewood stye (*Manhoode stye*) 117
Menewoodwaye 115
Meriell 215
Merielles alias Wennes (tenement) 215
Meryell
   Alexander 73, 196
   William 215
Meschalismore 103, 109, 200
messors 171–2
metal-detected evidence 7–9
Michel, Thomas 187
Michills 163
Middlefurlong 55, 124–5, 146, 168, 174, 220
Middleton, Blackborough End 172
Midland and Great Northern Joint railway 1
Mileham 39, 66, 71, 76
Mileham manor 83, 205
military metalwork, late Roman 41–3, *42*
Mill Field (GF) 184; *see also Millfield*
Millane 156
Milleclos (*Mylclose*) 155, 156, 157, 217
Millegate 135
Miller (Myller; Myllers)
   John 201
   Laurence de 85
   Richard 201
   William 187, 188
Miller Lane 201
Millers Close 201
Millers (*Myllers*) 201
Millerslond 135
Milles atte Mor leet
   amercements 116, 123, 241
   description 86
   documentary evidence 175
   holdings 201, 202, 231
   leased to Nicholas Mynne and John Stalworthy 81
   origins 50–1
   site of 103, 200
Millfield (LF)
   boundaries 174
   description 153–5, 157–8, 162, 214, 215, 224, 228
   enclosure 189
   mill 184
   pottery 58, 91
   Quarents. 185
Millrod 103

Mills 103
mills 62, 63, 67, 135; *see also* windmills
moated sites
   Cannons manor house 150
   Great Fransham rectory 106, *106*, 182
   Herringshall manor house 84
   Kirkhams manor house 142, *142*, *143*, 215–18
   Little Fransham rectory 138, *138*, 182
Moltysyarde 114
Monioye, John 147
Morhae 113
Morley (Morlee) family 83
   Robert de 83
mortar, cosmetic, Roman 30
Mounte Joyes 147
Mountjoy, – 213
mounts
   Roman 28, 31
   medieval *102*, 197
   see also belt mounts; harness mounts; scabbard mount; stirrup-strap mounts
Mucking (Essex) 43
Mugelles thre rodes 117
Mundeforde, Osbert de 204
Mundevile (Amoundevill; Amundevill)
   Maud 83
   Richard de 83, 196
Mundham, Cecilia 199
Munsell, William 179
Muryell, William and widow 219
Musterdyard 132
Mydyfurlong 162
le Myllefurlond 154
Myllehill 155
Myller *see* Miller
Myllers see Millers
Myllers *see* Miller
Mynne (Minn; Myn; Mynn; Mynns)
   Edward (d.1543) 145, 146, 147, 152, 162, 163, 185–6, 205, 209, 213, 234
   Edward (d.1572) 135, 147, 186
   Edward (*fl*.1627) 200
   Henry 186, 204, 224, 234
   John (*fl*.1532) 186
   John (*fl*.1607–11) 183, 188
   John (d.1651) 210
   John (*fl*.1664/6) 179
   Margaret wife of Edward 226
   Matilda 146, 162
   Nicholas (*c*.1459–1530) 81, 145, 162, 183, 185, 190, 202, 221, 222, 224, 231, 234, 237
   Nicholas (d.1528) 172
   Nicholas (d.1546) 147, 186, 205
   Nicholas (*fl*.1555) 186
   Nicholas (1561–1631) 99, 175, 186–9, 197, 198, 199, 200, 205, 226, 231, 234–5
   Nicholas (*fl*.1610). of East Lexham 190, 205–6
   Randolph 179
   William (*fl*.1558) of London 200
   William (*fl*.1664–6) 179, 214
Necoll *see* Nicholls
Necton
   adjunct 133, 199
   compared
      Palaeolithic period 13
      Roman period 27
      Saxon period 37, 45
      late Saxon–early Norman 53
      medieval period 70, 72, 173
      post-medieval period 178
   Domesday evidence 63, 64, 66, 67, 68
   Kirkhams manor tenements 78
   manor 68, 78, 82
Necton Town Estate
   history and description 77, 190
   holdings 109, 126, 200, 202, 203, 205, 206
Necton Wood (*Neketone wode*; *Neketonwode*) 149, 167, 168
Nekyr, Thomas 116
Nel, Robert 154
Nelson
   J. 235
   Matthew 211, 225, 235

Nephew, Roger 172
Nerford, Sir Robert and Alice de 84
Netherclose 205
Netherhennefelde (*Netherhenfeld*) 118
Nethiroxmer 157, 215
Neve, John 212
Neves 212
Neweclose 135
Neweshepowscroft 100
Newman, Elizabeth 227
Nicholas son of Bartholomew 223
Nicholls (Necoll; Nicoll; Nycholls; Nycoll; Nycolles)
   Elizabeth 211
   John (d.1559) 211
   John snr 152, 162, 163
   John jnr 212
   Richard (*fl*.1443–51) 152, 162, 163, 229
Nomansmere 126
Nomina Villarum 72, 74, 83
Norman
   Alice 157, 205
   John 73, 76, 157, 196, 204, 205
   Roger 205
Normannscroft 106, 202
North Elmham, compared
   Saxon period 37, 39, 44, 48, 54
   medieval period 71
   post-medieval period 178
North Meadows 121–3
North Mille Cloos 156
North Pickenham 39
Northclos 215, 218
Northendhall manor
   documentary evidence 78, 85, 177
   holdings 189
      Area C 111
      Area D 114, 232
      Area E 116
      Area F 116
      Area H 119
      Area O 128, 131
      Quarent. 4 135
      Quarent. 7 141
      Quarent. 25 157
      Quarent. 29 161
Northfeld 154
Norwich, pottery 48–9
Norwich, John of 200
Nowlys, Alexander 151
nucleation 192–3
Nycholls; Nycoll; Nycolles *see* Nicholls
Nycolls croft 152
Nyneacres (*le Nineacres*) 106

Oateclose 99
Odesfalgate 118
Odeslane 118, 119, 154, 155, 156
Okiistoift 239
Old Close 153
Oldhall
   Christine 230
   Edmund 76, 80, 118, 123, 126, 210, 225, 230
   William de (d.1460) 76, 77, 83, 86, 123, 128, 216, 217, 218
Olvis 162
open fields
   description
      Area C 109
      Area F 116
      Area G 117
      Area H 118
      Area K 123–4
      Area M 126
      Area O 128
      Quarent. 2 133
      Quarent. 4 134
      Quarent. 7 141
      Quarent. 8 141–2
      Quarent. 11 143
      Quarent. 12 146
      Quarent. 18 153
      Quarent. 19 154
      Quarent. 20 154
      Quarent. 22 154
      Quarent. 23 155
      Quarent. 25 157
      Quarent. 26 157
      Quarent. 28 158
      Quarent. 29 158
   discussion 68, 173–4, 184–5, 193
   pottery 91
Osmund 64
Osmund the merchant 114
Osyers (Osyeres) (tenement) 120, 214
Overhenfeld 118
Overoxmer 157
Overton
   Anne 210, 230
   Clement 230
Owles, Richard 187
Oxborough, William son of Ralph of 172
Oxford (Oxon), Christ Church 85, 177
Oxford, earl of 102
Oxmedowe/Oxlesowemead 109, 123, 132
Oxmere (*Oxemere*; *Oxmeare*; *Oxmerecloos*; *Oxmerewong*) 157, 215
Oxwick 71
Oxwick family
   John de (C12) 207
   John de (C14) 207
   Richard de 73, 196
Oxwicks (tenement) 207
oysters, Roman 28

pack ways
   GF 121
   LF 56
      Quarent. 3 134
      Quarent. 5 135
      Quarent. 7 141
      Quarent. 18 153, 214, 227
      Quarent. 19 154
      Quarent. 20 154
      Quarent. 27 158
      Quarent. 29 163
Padlocks Close 131
palstave chisel, Bronze Age 21, *21*
papal bull seals 197
parish registers 178
le Parke 77
Parker
   Agnes 205
   Robert 205
   Thomas 205
Parkin *see* Perkins
Parle
   Ralph 172, 204
   Roger 204
Parles 203, 204
Parlisyard 203
Parnaldesyards 112
le Parrock (*Le Parok*) 131
Parse, Roger 203
Parson, John 120–1
Parsones 209
Parsonscroft 106
Passur, Matilda 207
pastures *see* common pastures
Pattesley 71, 72
Paul Ulfes 162, 211
Pauli (Pauly; Pawley) *see* Powley
Payne 64
   daughter of 64
Peckingham 146
Peddars Way 27
Pekehams (tenement) 172
Peketone, John 232
Pekylbrygge 174
Pellesmeer 162
Pellis 162
Pellislond 162
Pellisrode 162

pendant, Bronze Age 23, *23*
Pentney Priory
    documentary evidence 73, 74, 84, 85, 195
    holdings in Fransham
        Area C 109, 111, 207
        Area H 121
        Area J 123
        Area N 127
Peretre close 186
Perkins (Parkin), Henry 13
Person, John 209
Peryscroft 152
Petrie Clos 205
Petyfere, Nicholas 116
Petyfers 116
Peus
    Fulcho 238
    William 238
Philip, prior of Castle Acre 117
Philip, John, clerk 123, 126, 127, 206, 207, 208
Phillipps acre 123, 124
Phillips
    Agnes 183
    William 183
pick, Neolithic 15, *16*
Piers (Pers; Petrus; Perters; Persses; Persys; Perys; Parsones) (tenement) 152
Pigges (*Pygges*) 226
Piggis (tenement) 226
Pilewood Covert 103
Pillwood (*Pilewude*; *Pilwude*; *Pylwod*)
    fieldwalking 7
    Fransham lands 5, 73, 74, 195
    land-use 168, 186
    in Necton 103
    origins 68
pin, spiral-headed, Iron Age 25
Pittacre 123
Playce (Plaiz; Playz)
    Alice de 73, 74, 195, 196
    Sir Hugh de 83
    Ralph de 73, 195
plough-teams, Domesday 63, 65, 67–8
Plowright, William 179, 215
Podyngwong 163, 190
Poketon
    Edmund de 232
    John de 127, 232
Poley *see* Powley
Poll Tax assessments 71–2, 94
Pomfrettes 117
Pomfrey, John and Margaret 163
Pope
    John 131, 214
    Reginald 231
Popes close (*Popys clos*) 129
population
    Domesday evidence 63, 66
    medieval 70–2, 165
    post-medieval 178–9
    present day 1, 193
pot-boiler sites *14*, 19–21, 68
Potekinesaker 172, 239
Potters lund 172, 239
Potterscroft (*Poteriscroft*) (LF) 61, 156, 172–3, 239
Potterscrofte (*Pottercroft*) (GF) 103, 172–3, 198
pottery
    Beaker 15, 17–19
    Iron Age 23–5, 28, 30, 32
    Roman *26*, 28–30, *31*–2, *33*
    early Saxon *38*, 39–41, 44
    middle Saxon 45, *46*, 47–9
    late Saxon–early Norman *52*, 53, 54–5, 56–61, 61–2, 67–8
        Early Medieval ware 54–5, 56, 57, 58
        St Neots-type ware 54, 56, 57
        Stamford ware 54
        Thetford-type ware 53, 54–5, 56–61
    medieval 89–91, 109, *111*
        distribution between settlements 91
        Grimston ware 91
    post-medieval 175

pottery industry 172–3
pottery production sites
    late Saxon–early Norman
        LS 14 58, 193
        LS 20 58–61, *59–60*, 193
    medieval
        discussion 165
        Med 8 103, 198
        Med 36 109, *111*, 206
        Med 43 110, 207
        Med 84 149, 170, 221–2
        Med 103 149, 167, 228
Pouly *see* Powley
Powell, Thomas 212
Powley (Pauli; Pauly; Pawley; Poley; Poulie; Pouly) family 212, 213
    Widow – 179, 219
    Agnes 187
    Alexander 213
    Geoffrey 212, 214, 218
    George 213
    Helen 221
    Isaac 220
    Jane 213
    John (*fl.*1379–86) 159, 210, 211
    John (d.1604) 213
    John (*fl.*1621) 188
    John (*fl.*1664/6) 179, 182
    Margaret 213
    Nicholas 184, 220
    Peter (*fl.*1699) 213
    Peter (*fl.*1780–92) 212, 213
    Ralph 183–4, 213
    Robert 234
    Thomas (*fl.*1353–64) 160, 211
    Thomas (*fl.*1420) 213
    Thomas (*fl.*1604) 213
    Walter 159, 161, 214, 228
    William (*fl.*1572) 220
    William (*fl.*1598–1603, son of Ralph) 184, 187
    William (*fl.*1666) 179, 213
    William (*fl.*1683) 228
Pratt family 209
    Beatrice 209
    Edmund 119, 209, 210
    Edmund jnr 209
    Margaret 209–10
    Thomas 210
    William jnr 115
Pratts Faldgate 119
Presmedwe 118
Prestiscroft 228
Princescroft 239
Prior (Priour), William 131, 224
probate inventories 177–8
processional way 116
Pryowrsys rod de Westacre 105
Puddyngs wong 163
Pulter, William 82
Pumfret, John 206
Purle, Jane 227
purse bar 211
Pygelsaker 141
Pykelesdyke 141
Pykelsbrygge 141
Pykenham, John de 146, 172
Pykenhams (tenement) 146, 182
Pynkesmedow 131
Pynne
    Alexander 200
    Thomas 200, 201
    William 200
Pysecroft 118, 230, 234
Pystile 230
Pyt half acre 202
Pytecok, Thomas 215
Pytlond 125
Pytylacre 141

Quinmillrod 103
Qwynes; Quinnys (tenement) 206

Rad, Katherine 230; *see also* Rode
Ralleson, Thomas 208, 209
Ralph son of Henry son of William of Little Fransham 118, 172
Ralph Guader, Earl 63
Ram (Ramme), Henry 129, 132, 147, 235
Ranson
    Gilbert 182, 187
    John 234
rapier *see* knife/rapier
Rareyniscroft 128–9
Rasthyens, Robert 128
Ravenes (tenement) 132, 235
Ravensyard 131, 235
Rawen (*Rawyn*; *Raweyn*; *Raweyne*) 155–6, 217
Rawlenysbrygge 210
Rawlings (Rawlenis; Rawlyns) (tenement) 128, 210
le Rawynmede 125, 127, 156
Rayner
    Dorothy 183
    Katherine 183
razor, Iron Age 25, *25*
le Rede see Ryde
Redeclos 141, 217
Redemedow (*le Redmedwe*) 153, 215
Reeve (Reve)
    Edmund 76, 206, 226
    John 212
    Thomas 199, 224
Renge, Henry 160
Renges (Renggis; Rengs) (tenement) 160, 162, 214, 237
Renges (*Rengys*) 160–1
Rengyscroft 162
Reve *see* Reeve
Rewaldesaker 239
Reynold the priest 64
Richard 64
Richard son of Hamon 118, 238
Richers, Roger 151
ridge-and-furrow *frontispiece*, 113–14, 225
ring-ditch 15
Ringold (Ringolde; Ringolles; Ringolls; Ryngolde; Ryngolf; Ryngolfs)
    Adam 119, 160, 209
    John 162
    Nicholas 209
    Petronilla 162
    Thomas 230
    William 209, 232
    William (now Fynch) 208
Ringstead
    Agnes 161
    Alexander de 161
roads
    Roman 27, 29, 35, 192
    Saxon 40, 45, 47
    medieval *88*
    present day 1, 194, *194*
Robert son of John the reeve 154
Roberts (Robynson), Robert 179, 182, 187
Robynscroft acre 106
Robynsyard 106
    Rode (Atterode; Rod)
    John son of William 135, 222, 223
    Margaret 135, 223
    William 140, 222
le Rode (*Rudde*) 149–50, 167, 168, 213, 228, 241
Rodland (Rodeland), John 129, 152
Roger son of Fuka 118
Roger son of William son of Baldwin 169
roof tiles, medieval 89, *90*, 197, 198, 216
Roome, Robert 212
Rougham 62, 63–6, 71, 76, 238
Rougham family
    Alice de 238
    John son of William 238
    Richard son of John 238
    Sara 238
    Thomas son of John de 238
Rougholme, chapel of St Nicholas 77, 123, 169, 177
Rougholme manor
    documentary evidence 177

holdings 77–8, 169, 170
    Area B 104, 106, 200, 203
    Area C 109, 111, 190
    Area D 113, 115, 208
    Area E 115, 116, 208, 232
    Area F 117
    Area H 119, 210
    Area J 121, 123, 190
    Area K 124
round barrow 103
Rous, Thomas 174, 224
Rowlands 210
Rudd, Thomas 212
Rudlondes (tenement) 152
Runacre/Ronacre 119
Rusteng (Rusteyn)
    Henry 206
    William 206
Rusteyn (Rusteyns) (tenement) 177, 206
Ruston family 201
    Edmund 188
le Ryde/Rede 141
Le Rydepit (*Redepyt*; *Rudpytte*) 142
Rye, Barony of 83
Rye, Hubert de 83
Ryngolf (Ryngolde; Ryngolfs) *see* Ringold

St Katerines Gappe 155
St Katherine's Meadow 55, 127, *128*
St Katherine's well 127
St Omero, Robert de 161
St Thomas (Sancto Thoma), Robert de 141, 161
Saldygges aker (*Saldyngesakre*) 125
Sale, William de la 85
le Salowdyke 134
Sammes (Sammys)
    Andrew 187, 188, 203, 204
    Christian 203
    Luke 203
    William 203, 205
Sapy (Sappe)
    Thomas de 80
    William de 80, 154, 223
Sarysmer 125
Sawlepit 162
Sawler (alias Edyman), Edmund 152
scabbard chapes, medieval 125, *125*, 197
scabbard mount, Iron Age 25, *25*, 28
Scalam, Robert son of Roger ad 133
Scalemedowe see Skathemedowe
Scales, Robert son of Robert of 74
Scarning
    compared
        Roman period 27
        Mesolithic period 13
        Saxon period 37, 45
        late Saxon–early Norman period 54
        medieval period 70, 71, 72, 173
        post-medieval period 178
    Domesday evidence 62, 64, 66, 74
    Great Fransham manor lands 76
    Scarning Hall manor 74
Scarning, River 6
Scarning (Skarning; Skernynge) family
    Agnes 161
    Avelina 206
    Henry de 210
    Henry son of Peter de 140
    Roger de 206
    Roger son of Thomas de 85
    Simon de 85
    Thomas 161, 172
Scathilcroft see Skathemedowe
Sconings, John 207
Scott (Skott), Henry 231
Scramige, John and Mabel 225
seal matrices, medieval *102*, 103, 155, 197, 235
Seel, John 209
Sefepens *see* Sevepens
Segars (*Sygers*) 143–5, 145–6, 225

Sel, Isabelle 109
Selysaker 109
Sengham *see* Shengham
Senkler
   Charles 211, 212
   Edmund 212
Serviant (Seriaunt), John 152
settlements
   definition 9–11, *10*
   Iron Age 24–5
settlements, Roman *26*, 32–5, *34*
   RB 1 28, *28*, 32, 33, 35
   RB 2 28–9, 32, 33, 35
   RB 3 29, 32, 33, 35
   RB 4 29, 32
   RB 5 29–30, 32, 33, 35
   RB 6 30, 32, 33, 35
   RB 7 30, 32, 35
   RB 8 30–1, 33, 35
   RB 9 31, 32, 33
   RB 10 31–2, *31*, 33, 35
   RB 11 32, 35
settlements, early Saxon *38*, 43–5
   ES 1 40, *41*, 44, 45
   ES 2 40, *41*, 44
   ES 3 40, 44
   ES 4 40–1, 44
   ES 5 41, 44
   ES 6 41–3, *41*, 45
settlements, middle Saxon *46*, 49–51, *50*
   MS 1 47–50, *47*, 51, 192–3
settlements, late Saxon–early Norman *52*, 61–2, 67–8, *166*
   LS 1 55, 67, 169, 193
   LS 2 56, 67, 169, 193
   LS 3 56
   LS 4 56
   LS 5 56–7
   LS 6 57
   LS 7 57
   LS 8 57, 67
   LS 9 57, 67
   LS 10 57, 67
   LS 11 57
   LS 12 57
   LS 13 57
   LS 14 58, 193
   LS 15 58
   LS 16 58, 67
   LS 17 58
   LS 18 58
   LS 19 58, 67
   LS 20 58–61, *59–60*, 193
settlements, medieval
   allocation of site numbers 94
   discussion 70, 193
      chronology, manorial allegiance and tenure 168–70
      distribution 167–8
      late medieval decline 173
      numbers and population 165–6, *166*
      tenemental system 171–2
   distribution *88*
   listed 95–7
   locating 89–91
   Med 1 99, 167, 197
   Med 2 99, 167, 197
   Med 3 99, 197
   Med 4 99, *101*, 197
   Med 5 99, *101*, 168, 197–8
   Med 6 102, 198
   Med 7 103, 198
   Med 8 103, 198
   Med 9 133, *133*, 198
   Med 10 133, *133*, 198–9
   Med 11 133, *133*, 199
   Med 11A 133, 199, 217
   Med 12 133, *133*, 199
   Med 13 104, 199
   Med 14 103, 199–200
   Med 15 103, *105*, 167, 177, 200
   Med 15A 104, 167, 200
   Med 16 103, 165, 200
   Med 17 103, 182, 200
   Med 18 103–4, 200–1
   Med 19 104, *105*, 170, 182, 201–2
   Med 20 104, 165, 169, 202
   Med 21 106, *106*, 182, 190, 202–3
   Med 22 106, *107*, 203
   Med 23 *107*, 182, 203
   Med 23A 106, 165, 182, 203
   Med 24 106, *107*, 203–4
   Med 25 106, *107*, 204
   Med 25A 106, 165, 182, 204
   Med 26 106, *107*, 204
   Med 27 106, *107*, 182, 204–5
   Med 28 106, *107*, 205
   Med 29 106, *107*, 205
   Med 30 124, 168, 205
   Med 31 109, 205
   Med 32 109, 205
   Med 33 109, *110*, 205–6
   Med 34 109, *110*, 206
   Med 35 109, *110*, *111*, 206
   Med 36 109, *110*, *111*, 206
   Med 37 109–10, *110*, 206
   Med 38 109–10, *110*, 206–7
   Med 39 109–10, *110*, 207
   Med 40 109–10, *110*, 182, 207
   Med 41 109–10, *110*, 207
   Med 42 109–10, *110*, 207
   Med 43 110, *110*, 207
   Med 44 109–10, 207
   Med 45 111, 208
   Med 47 115, 124, 208
   Med 49 115, 208
   Med 50 115, 182, 208
   Med 53 112, 208–9
   Med 54 115, *115*, 209
   Med 55 115, *115*, 209
   Med 56 115, *116*, 121, 209
   Med 57 119, *120*, 131, 209–10
   Med 58 118–19, 121, 210
   Med 59 119, 210
   Med 60 *120*, 121, 154, 167, 210
   Med 61 128, 210
   Med 62 *130*, 131, 167, 170, 211
   Med 63 *159*, 163, 165, 167, 211
   Med 64 158, *159*, 211
   Med 65 150, *151*, 211, 217
   Med 65A 151, *151*, 211–12
   Med 66 *151*, 152, 182, 212
   Med 66A 152, 212
   Med 67 *151*, 182, 184, 213
   Med 68 153, *153*, 182, 213
   Med 69 *120*, 153, 170, 182, 213–14
   Med 70 157, 182, 214–15
   Med 71 155, 157, 172, 182, 215, 217
   Med 72 157, 215
   Med 73 142, 165, 168, 215
   Med 74 142, *142*, *143*, 165, 168, 215–18
   Med 75 145, 182, 218–19
   Med 76 *148*, 149, 182, 219
   Med 77 *148*, 149, 167, 172, 182, 183, 219–20
   Med 78 *148*, 149, 167, 182, 183, 220
   Med 79 *148*, 149, 167, 182, 220
   Med 80 *148*, 149, 167, 182, 220
   Med 81 *148*, 149, 167, 220–1
   Med 82 *148*, 149, 167, 221
   Med 83 145, *148*, 149, 167, 221
   Med 84 *148*, 149, 170, 221–2
   Med 85 *148*, 167, 168, 170, 222–3
   Med 86 147, *147*, 167, 223
   Med 87 23, 147, *147*, 223
   Med 88 147, *147*, 167, 223
   Med 89 136, *138*, 223–4
   Med 90 136, *138*, 168, 224
   Med 92 158, 224
   Med 93 *130*, 131, 167, 170, 224–5
   Med 94 143–5, 182, 225
   Med 95 113, 225–6
   Med 96 113, 114, 117, 226

Med 97 153, *153*, 182, 226–7
Med 98 142, 143, *144*, 227
Med 99 142–3, *144*, 227–8
Med 100 142, 143, *144*, 170, 228
Med 101 142, 143, *144*, 228
Med 102 142, 143, *144*, 165, 228
Med 103 149, 167, 228
Med 105 158–9, *160*, 228–9
Med 106 159, *160*, 229
Med 107 118, 170, 229–30
Med 108 118, 170, 182, 230
Med 109 126, 182, 230–1
Med 111 113, 114, 231
Med 112 *113*, 114, 165, 182, 231–2
Med 113 115, 165, 167, 182, 193, 232–3
Med 114 117–18, 165, 182, 193, 233–5
Med 115 131, 165, 235
Med 116 154, *155*, 165, 182, 210, 235–6
Med 117 159, *160*, 165, 236–7
settlements, post-medieval 175, *176*, 179–84
   PM 1 182, 183, 241
   PM 2 182, 183, 241
   PM 3 182, 241–2
   PM 4 182, 242
   PM 5 182, 242
Sevenpens meadow/Sepensmedowe 121
Sevepens (Sefepens; Sevenpens)
   Adam 204
   Isabelle 204
   John (*fl*.1385–1400) 146, 204
   John (*fl*.1420) 152, 212, 221
   Richard 146–7
   Richard jnr 147
Sewale (Sewal; Seweles; Sules)
   Adam 201
   Alexander 152
   Geoffrey 157, 214
   Henry (*fl*.1316) 228
   Henry (*fl*.1400) 208
   John (*fl*.1353) 214
   John (*fl*.1400) 201
   John (*fl*.1437) 227
   Nicholas 172, 201
   Roger 219
   see also Sowles
Sewles (tenement) 56, 124, 125, 126
Sewlesclose (*Solleys close*; *Sowlisclosse*) 56, 104–5, 201
Sextons lond 120, 121, 131
Sharpin, Edward 213
Sheene (Shene)
   Edward 179, 220
   Richard 201
   William 179
le Sheld (*Scheld*; *Scheld medowe*) 127
Sheldeds halfacre 134
Sheldesendes 127
Shengham (Sengham), Hamon de 208, 231
Shepehousefield 91, 105, 174, 200
Shepehowscroft 105, 135, 200
Shephousyerd (*Sheppeards Yerds*) 136, 223, 224
Sheryngton, Thomas 103
Shilling, Jeremy 241
Shinkin (Shinquin)
   John 184
   John jnr 184
Shokete, Henry 163
Short (Schort; Shorte)
   William (C14) 127, 131, 208
   William (C15) 115
Shortcalling 117
Shortes 116
Shortwood (Schortwode)
   John 131, 210, 229, 235, 236
   Walter de 157
   William 161, 229
Shyrlynges 234
Simpson, Mr – 13
site definition 9–11, *10*
Sizeling, William 235
Skarning (Skernynge) *see* Scarning

Skathemedowe (*Scalemedowys*; *Scathilcroft*; *Skalemedowe*; *Skathell*; *Skathil*; *Skayth*) 101–2, 126
Skeetes faldgate 208
Skegeton, Henry de 238
Skepper, Henry 198
Skeppers grove/close (*Shepperds grove*) 198
Sket, Geoffrey 208
Sketesfeld 116
Sketts (*Sketes*) 208
Skott *see* Scott
Skynner, Richard 184
Skythclosse 208
slag, Roman 30, 31, *31*, 32
Smethes (tenement) 225
Smethybrigge 218
Smith *see* Smyth
Smithecroft (*Smethycloos*; *Smethecroft*; *Smythecroft*; *Smythiecroft*) 159, 216, 217, 218
Smyth (Smith)
   Agnes 214
   Agnes (alias Dymes) 231
   Christina 152
   Henry 228
   John (*fl*.1391, 1393) 225, 227
   John (*fl*.1420) 147
   Margaret 159, 214
   Margery 214
   William 152
Snape (*Snapespiece*) 100, 101, 126
soils 1, *4*
Sokelyngacr 155
Soreharte (*Sorhert*) 162
Soudes (*Sowdsclose*) 162
Souldan, John 187
Soutere (Sowter), Marion 158, 162, 229
Souters (tenement) 214
Souteslane 229
South Greenhoe Hundred 5
Southfield 189
Southgate 124
Southgateway see Greenway (*Greneway*)/*Southgateway*
Southmeadow 127
Southwodedike 162
Southwodes 224
Southwong (*Sowdewonge*; *Sowdsclose*) 73, 129, 131, 162, 195
Southwood (*Sudvude*; *Suthwode*) 83, 129, 131
Southwood (Sudwode; Suthwood) family 167
   Geoffrey de 73, 129, 161, 195
   Geoffrey son of William de 131, 224
   Isabelle 131
   John de 121, 129, 210
   Nicholas 129
   Sibil de 211
   Thomas 233
   Walter de 73, 131, 195
   William de 161, 224
   William son of Walter de 131
Southwoodbushes 131
Southwoodfield
   description 128–32
   pottery 91
   settlements 167, 168, 170, 211, 224, 235
Southwoodlane (*Southwoodgate*) 131, 162
Southwoodmoor (*Southwode green*) 94, 129, 167, 168, 170
Sowdes Falgate 131
Sowdismore (*Sowds more*) 131
Sowerlond 131
Sowles 201
Sowles, John 217
Sowlesmedowe 123
Sparham 53, 173
Sparham Hall 81
Sparhamhalle (tenement) 159
Sparhams manor
   documentary evidence 81, 94, 177, 178
   holdings 168, 170, 171, 172
      Area E 115, 116, 209
      Area G 118, 234–5
      Area H 119
      Area O 128

Quarent. 7 141
Quarent. 11 143, 145, 146
Quarent. 12 146
Quarent. 13 146, 147
Quarent. 15 149, 219, 220–1
Quarent. 16 242
Quarent. 17 152, 212, 213
Quarent. 18 153–4, 213, 227
Quarent. 19 154
Quarent. 20 154
Quarent. 22 155
Quarent. 23 155
Quarent. 24 156
Quarent. 26 157
Quarent. 27 157, 158, 182, 214, 215
Quarent. 28 158, 182, 224
Quarent. 29 158, 159, 162, 189, 211
manor house 146
Sparle, Beatrice daughter of Agnes de 132
spearhead, Bronze Age 21, *21*
Spencer
   Amy 226
   Daniel 118, 226, 233
   John 118, 226, 232, 233
spindle whorl, not dated 48
Spirling (Spyrling)
   John 73, 196, 234
   Margaret 234
   Richard 234
Spirlinges (tenement) 234–5, 241
Sponer
   Elot 208
   Emma 208
   Hamon 208
   John 208
Spooners 208
Sporle with Palgrave, cemetery 39
spur buckle, medieval 216
spur fragments, medieval 197
Spurnn, Thomas 146
Spyrling *see* Spirling
Spyrling croft (*Spurlings*) 234, 235
Stalonde (Stalonn), John 140
Stalworthy (Stallworthie; Stalworthie) family 189, 214, 215
   Dorothy 241
   George 161, 189, 229
   John (*fl.*1476–1502) 81, 185, 210, 227, 236–7
   John (*fl.*1513) 161
   John snr (*fl.*1532–56) 161–2, 189, 214
   John jnr (*fl.*1566–75) 151
   John (*fl.*1605) 229
   John (*fl.*1611) 189
   John (*fl.*1664/6) 179
   Richard 214, 215
   Thomas (*fl.*1420) 229, 236
   Thomas (*fl.*1439–40) 217
   Thomas (*fl.*1443) 161, 236
   Thomas (*fl.*1462) 174
   Thomas (*fl.*1558–60) 234, 241
   William 151, 211
Stanfield 71
Stanford (Standford)
   Henry 200, 203, 204, 205
   John 204
   Samuel 204
   Thomas 204
Steade, William 201
steelyard weights, Roman 29, 30
Steeplend Close (*Steplendclose*) 56, 139, 140
Stewart
   David, Earl of Athol 238
   Elizabeth, Countess of Athol 238
Stigand 64
stirrup terminals, late Saxon 62, *62*
stirrup-strap mounts, late Saxon 58, 62
Stonegate (*Stone Lane*; *Stonweye*) 123
Stowe
   Edward de 140
   Thomas de 135, 149
Le Strange family 94

Alexander 73, 77, 195, 196, 223, 224, 238
Emma 78, 80, 81, 156, 172–3
Geoffrey 158
Henry (*fl.*1273–90) 157, 223, 224
Henry (*fl.*1316/17) 78, 80, 120, 157, 158, 169, 219, 228
John le (*fl.*1279–80) 73, 78, 132, 157, 169, 195, 196, 210
John le (*fl.*1346) 225, 238
Sir Nicholas 177
Sir Peter 118, 126, 210
Peter 80, 230
Robert son of Roger 75
Roger le (*fl.*1243) 78, 132, 169
Roger (*fl.*pre-1302) 238
Roger (*fl.*1316–36) 219, 232
William son of Henry (*fl.*1318–48) 80, 124, 126, 135, 140, 141, 157, 158, 219, 222, 223, 228
William son of Roger (*fl.*1333) 232
William (*fl.*1355–9) 101, 138, 147
strap-ends
   Roman 43
   Saxon 41, *43*, 48, *48*, 49, 62
   medieval 216
Stratton
   Alice 227
   William 227
de Stutevill family 76
   Robert 84
   Robert son of William 84
   William 77–8, 85, 113
Sudwode *see* Southwood
Suengeden *see* Swengeden
sunken ways 103, 120, 158, 229
survey
   description
      Palaeolithic *12*, 13, 192
      Mesolithic *12*, 13–15, 192
      Neolithic–early Bronze Age *14*, 15–21, 192
      later Bronze Age *14*, 21–3, 192
      Iron Age *22*, 23–5, 192
      Roman
         discussion 32–5, *34*, 192
         local background 27–8
         survey evidence *26*, 28–32
      early Saxon
         discussion 43–5, 192
         local background 37–9
         survey evidence *38*, 39–43
      middle Saxon
         discussion 49–51, *50*, 192–3
         local background 45–7
         survey evidence *46*, 47–9
      late Saxon–early Norman
         compared with surrounding vills 66–7
         discussion 67–9, 193
         Domesday evidence 62–6
         local background 53–4
         summary 61–2
         survey evidence *52*, 54–61
      medieval period
         land divisions 94–7, *98*
         overview
            agrarian organisation, land-use and landscape change 173–4
            late medieval decline 173
            pottery industry 172–3
            settlement chronology, manorial allegiance and tenure 168–70
            settlement distribution 167–8
            settlement numbers and population 165–6, *166*
            settlements 193
            tenemental system 171–2
         pottery 89–91
         survey evidence
            Area A 99–103, *100*
            Area B 103–106, *104*, *107*
            Area C *108*, 109–13
            Area D *112*, 113–15
            Area E *112*, 115–16
            Area F *112*, 116–17
            Area G *112*, 117–18
            Area H 118–21, *119*
            Area J 121–3, *121*

Area K *122*, 123–4
Area L *122*, 124–5
Area M 126–7, *126*
Area N *121*, 127, *128*
Area O *119*, 128–32
Quarent. 1 132–3, *132*
Quarent. 2 *132*, 133–4
Quarent. 3 134, *134*
Quarent. 4 134–5, *134*
Quarent. 5 135–6, *136*, *137*
Quarent. 6 *136*, *137*, 138–41
Quarent. 7 141, *141*
Quarent. 8 141–2, *141*
Quarent. 9 142, *142*
Quarent. 10 142–3, *143*
Quarent. 11 *137*, 143–6, *145*
Quarent. 12 *137*, *145*, 146
Quarent. 13 *145*, 146–7
Quarent. 14 *145*, 147
Quarent. 15 *145*, 149
Quarent. 16 149–50, *150*
Quarent. 17 150–3, *150*
Quarent. 18 153–4, *153*
Quarent. 19 *153*, 154, *155*, *156*
Quarent. 20 *153*, 154
Quarent. 21 154, *156*
Quarent. 22 154–5, *156*
Quarent. 23 155, *156*
Quarent. 24 155–6, *156*
Quarent. 25 *156*, 157
Quarent. 26 *156*, 157
Quarent. 27 157–8, *158*
Quarent. 28 158, *158*
Quarent. 29 158–63, *159*
post-medieval period
archaeological evidence 175, *176*
common pastures and fields 184–5
demesne lands 185–9
documentary evidence 175–8
enclosure 189–90, *190–1*
population 178–9
settlement 179–84
methods 7–9, *8*
postscript 192–4
Surwdewongys 129
suspension ring, Saxon 41
Suthwood *see* Southwood
Sutton, Constantine son of Geoffrey de 82
Swaffham 39
Swankescroft 132
Swanton Morley
Beaufour possessions 63, 83
population 70, 71, 72, 178
Swengeden (Suengeden), Alice 147, 223
Swengendenscroft 147, 223
Swift
Edward 225
William 225
Swingden (tenement) 147
Swingdons 147
Sydemedow 127
Syger (Sygger; Sygor)
Adam 215, 225
John 135, 146, 225
Nicholas 199
Roger 225

Tarkeys (Turkeys)
Hawys 141
John 152
John jnr 152, 212
Thomas 228
Thomas jnr 152
Tarkeys (tenement) 152
Taylor
Etheldr. 233
Joane 212
John 228
Robert 230, 233, 234
Taylor (alias Droury) family 233

tenemental system 171–2
tenements 76, 77, 78, 81, 169, 171–2; *see also* individual tenements by name
Tenmark (Tenmarke), Edmund 134, 136
Tharrolde, Henry 189; *see also* Thurrold
Thetford Priory 84
thimbles, post-medieval 211
Thomas, chaplain 234
Thomas son of Osbert 73, 195
Thomas son of Walter 73, 196
Thomas
William 126–7
William jnr 126
Thomas Clerkes (tenement) 166, 222
Thomeys *see* Tomeys
Thompson, Ambrose 210; *see also* Tompson
Thoonoks, Roger 225
Thorold *see* Thurrold
Thorpe, Walter 73, 84
Thurrold (Thurrolde; Thorold)
Cecily 187
Nicholas 188
William 202, 205
see also Tharrolde
Thyrlyngges Dokeland 127
tiles *see* ceramic building material; floor tiles; roof tiles
Tittleshall 39, 63, 71, 76
Toftes, Roger de 74–6, 102, 103, 173, 198
Toftgate 111, 123, 207, 208
Toftgateway 29
Tokelys (tenement) 152
tokens, post-medieval 228
Toki 62, 63, 64
Toly (Tolie; Tolye) family 200
Henry 190, 200, 201
Margaret 200
Robert 210
Thomas 200
Tolyes close (*Toolys close*) 201
Tomeys (Thomeys), William 126, 127, 208
Tompson
John 109, 183, 241
John jnr 241
see also Thompson
Tony (Tonie) family 216
Ralph de 73, 78, 81, 195, 196
Tosny family 82, 168, 169
Ralph de (1086) 62, 63, 64, 66, 67
Ralph de (C13) 85
Robert 85
Roger de 78, 80, 81
Tossenol (tenement) 219
Totefacs; Totfayts (tenement) 206, 207
Townesendclose 135
Tuddenham, Sir Thomas 82
Tukele (tenement) 152
Tullboye, Beatrice 160
Tullescroft 234
Turkeys *see* Tarkeys
Turner (Turnor)
Anne 242
Nicholas 187
Paul 182
Richard 241
Tuskenol *see* Tussenolf
Tuskenolnysines 136
Tussenolf (Tuskenol; Tuskenolf; Tussenoll)
Geoffrey son of Roger 136, 199, 219, 224
Johanna 199, 219
Roger 136
William 136, 199
Tussenoll (tenement) 172, 199
tweezers, Saxon 41, 58, 62

Ulfe, Paul 163, 211
Ulfes 162
Ulvesmedowe (*Hullsmedowe*; *Hulvesmedow*; *Ulnesmeadowe*) 162, 163, 190, 211
Unggers 120

Valence, Aymer de, Earl of Pembroke 238
Vaux, Robert de 84
Vergons, William 103
vessels, cast, medieval–post-medieval 197

Wacey, Edward 230
Wadelow (alias Cooke)
   Dorothy 183
   Richard 183
Waderowfeld 146
Walcot, Sir Walter de 85
Walker, Samuel 202
Wallis, Revd Baily 206, 207, 208, 210, 232, 235, 241
Walsham le Willows (Suffolk) 44
Waltone
   Mary 225
   Petronilla 225
   Robert de 225
Ward (Warde)
   Henry 158, 228
   John and Isabelle 136, 199
   Nicholas 129–31, 211
Wardes alias Tussenolf (tenement) 199
Wardes Close 224
Wardes Faldgate 131
Wardesgrene (*Wardysmor*) 129–31, 211
Warenne
   Edward de 238
   John de, Earl of Surrey 73, 74, 195, 196, 238
   William de I 62–3, 64, 67
   William de II 83
   William de III 84
Warner, John 233
warrens 100–1, 103
water supply 1, 6
Watlin, William 210, 236
Watling, William 210
Watson, George 215
Wattys, Robert 229
Wavyonn, John 223
wealth, medieval 70–2
Weasenham 63, 71, 76
Weasenham (Wesenham), Richard de 136
Webster, Adam 156
Wellacre (*Wellemedow*) 127
Wellingham 71
Wellingham, Edward 200, 201, 202, 242
Welnetham, Johanna widow of Alexander de 80
Wen *see* Wenne
Wendham, Henry de 115, 116
Wendling
   abbey *see* Wendling Abbey
   airbase 226
   compared
      Mesolithic period 13
      Roman period 27
      Saxon period 37, 45
      late Saxon–early Norman period 54
      medieval period 70, 71, 173
      post-medieval period 178
   Domesday evidence 64, 66, 67
   Great Fransham manor lands 76
   manor 84; *see also* Wendling Nuper Abbis manor
   see also Fransham/Wendling land-unit
Wendling Abbey
   documentary evidence 84–5, 195, 196, 238
   founder 114
   holdings in Fransham 72, 73, 74, 77, 177
      Area C 111
      Area D 114
      Area E 116
      Area F 117
      Area G 118
      Area H 119, 120
      Area N 127
      Area O 128–9, 131, 132, 211
      Quarent. 1 132–3
      Quarent. 13 146
      Quarent. 21 154
      Quarent. 29 161, 162

   holdings in Wendling 81
Wendling family
   Fulcher son of Alfar 183
   Henry de 116
   Laurence son of Elfer 117
   Leffei son of Lewin 117
   Leiffein son of William 117
   William de 84, 85, 129, 131
   William son of Leftheyn (Leftheine) 118, 172
   William son of William 114
Wendling Nuper Abbis manor 85, 117, 131, 177
Wenne (Wen)
   John 117
   Nicholas 215
Wesenham *see* Weasenham
West, Mary 220
West Acre 39
West Acre Priory
   holdings in Fransham 73, 74, 81–2, 169, 195
      Area B 105
      Area F 117
      Quarent. 16 149
      Quarent. 18 153
West Bradenham
   compared
      Saxon period 39, 45, 50
      late Saxon–early Norman period 53
      medieval period 72, 173
      post-medieval period 178
   manor
      holdings in Fransham 82, 170
      Quarent. 17 151, 152, 211, 212
      Quarent. 29 162–3
West Common 121
West End meadow 121
West End Moor
   road connecting to Brounesgrene 200
   settlements
      late Saxon–early Norman 56, 57, 169
      medieval 167, 168, 169
         Area A 203, 204, 205
         Area B 104, 106, 202
      post-medieval 242
West Lexham 71
West Stow (Suffolk) 43, 44
Westfield 133–4, 147, 168, 174, 199
Weston
   Aveline de 209
   John de 131, 209
   Robert de 73, 74, 195
Weston Brygge 131, 235
Westrode (*Westrade*) 132–3
Whinburgh, Elizabeth widow of Ostelin 210
Whinn Common 185
Whippescrofte 106
Whiskard *see* Wyscard
Whissonsett 71
Whistede, Katherine de 203
White (Whyte; Whytte)
   Brother John 218
   Robert 221
Whitemill Brook 6
Whiteway (*Whyghtlye*) 168
   Area A 99–100, 102, 197, 202, 203, 204
   Area B 106
   Area G 118
   Area K 123
   Area L 125
   Area N 127
   origins 40, 47, 55
Whitlok, John 151
Whynnes moore (*Whinny Green*) 109, 205
Whynnesfeld 109
Whynnys (tenement) 206
Whyte (Whytte) *see* White
Wichereslond 113
Wicklewood 200
Wicklewood, William of 200
Wilcocks pightiles 223
Wilcokks crofts 147, 223

Wilcoks 147, 185, 186, 222–3
Wilcoks manor
   documentary evidence 74, 75, 80–1, 94
   holdings 168, 170, 171, 172
     Area H 120
     Quarent. 1 132–3
     Quarent. 2 133–4
     Quarent. 3 134–5
     Quarent. 5 135, 136
     Quarent. 6 140, 182
     Quarent. 10 143
     Quarent. 11 145, 221
     Quarent. 12 146
     Quarent. 13 147
     Quarent. 14 147, 222–3
     Quarent. 15 149, 183, 219, 221
     Quarent. 17 151, 152, 212
     Quarent. 18 153, 213, 214, 227
     Quarent. 21 154
     Quarent. 22 155
     Quarent. 25 157
     Quarent. 27 157
     Quarent. 28 158
     Quarent. 29 158, 159, 162, 163, 189, 190, 229, 236
   manor house 147, 168, 170, 222
Wilcoks (Wilcokks) (tenement) 171
Wilking (Wilkin), Joseph 236
Wilkins close 135, 210
Wilkinson (Wylkenson) (tenement) 145, 146, 149, 171, 172
Wilkinson (Wilkenessson; Wylkynesson)
   John 133, 145, 171, 172
   John jnr 140, 172
   Margery 224
William I 64, 66
William Blak and Wylkynson (tenement) 172
William the chaplain, son of Ralph son of Henry of Little Fransham 157
William Fitz John 73
William in the Medowe 112, 208
William *ad Pratum* 111, 208
William son of Godfrey 135
William son of John 83, 196
Williamson, John son of William 140
Willori 124
Willow Farm 154
wills 177
Willymot, William 233
Wilps, John 157
Wilton, John de 136
Wimer *see* Wymer
Windmillrode 103
windmills
   GF manor in Area B 86, 103, 195, 200
   Kirkhams manor in *Quarent.* 24 155–6, 225
   Wilcoks manor in *Quarent.* 4 80
   post-medieval in Area M 183–4
Wiscard *see* Wyskard
Witton 44
Wodebarres 152
Wodegate 239
Wolsey, Cardinal Thomas 85, 177
wood-pasture 68, 69, 99, 167, 186
woodland
   Roman 33
   Saxon 44, 49
   Domesday evidence 63, 66–7, 68
   medieval 74, 110–11, 115, 129, 168, 170
     pottery 91
     Quarent. 2 133
     Quarent. 11 143

     Quarent. 16 149
     Quarent. 28 158
   post-medieval 185–9
Woodrow 149, 221
Woodrow (Woodrowe)
   Christine 203
   John 179
   Simon 188, 203
Woodrowclose 221, 222
Woodrowfield
   pottery 91
   Quarent. 11 143, 172, 215, 225
   Quarent. 12 146, 172
   Quarent. 15 149, 166, 172, 182, 219
Woodrowgreen 149, 167, 168, 170, 220, 221
Woodrowhouse and Close (tenement) 221
Woodrowmore 221, 222
Wrangle Acre 235
Wrendham, Henry 115
Wrenglond 158
Wright (Wryght)
   Widow – 179
   Richard 218
   Thomas 213, 222
wrist-clasps, Saxon 41, *43*
Wroo, John 210
Wryght *see* Wright
Wyates (Wyotts) (tenement) 162, 237
Wylkenswong 133
Wylkoks clos 185, 222
Wylkynsclos 135
Wyllers, John 203
Wylmondheithe 103, 105, 167, 199
Wymer the Dapifer 63, 64, 76, 77
Wymer, Thomas 76, 201
Wymers; Wymer; Wymerys (tenement) 56, 76, 123, 172, 201
le Wyndemyllecote 155
Wyndhams 115
Wyot, John 162, 174, 214, 228
Wyskard (Whiskard; Wiscard) family 219
   Anne 212
   Bridget 219
   Faith 227
   Gilbert 226
   John (*fl.*1496) 171
   John snr (*fl.*1512) 228
   John jnr (*fl.*1512) 228
   John of LF (*fl.*1539) 163
   John, gent. (*c.*1493–1593), son of Thomas 115–16, 134, 208–9, 212, 219, 223, 236
   Richerus 174, 217, 218, 219, 223, 225, 228
   Robert 182, 220
   Thomas (*fl.*1509) 190, 202
   Thomas (d.1538) 116, 185, 208, 212, 223, 225, 235, 236
   Thomas (*fl.c*1557) 213
   Thomas (*fl.*1586) 220
   Wilborrowe 236
   William 80–1, 82, 86, 142, 216–17, 224
Wyton, John 172

Yelverton
   John 238
   Nicholas 131
   Sir William 202, 238
Yelvertons close 131
Yevan, John 109, 218, 222, 223
Yool, Thomas 156
Younge, Dorothy 202
Ywerthlond 239

East Anglian Archaeology

is a serial publication sponsored by ALGAO EE and English Heritage. It is the main vehicle for publishing final reports on archaeological excavations and surveys in the region. For information about titles in the series, visit **https://eaareports.org.uk**. Reports can be obtained from:
Oxbow Books, **https://www.oxbowbooks.com/oxbow/eaa**
or directly from the organisation publishing a particular volume.

Reports available so far:

No.1,	1975	Suffolk: various papers
No.2,	1976	Norfolk: various papers
No.3,	1977	Suffolk: various papers
No.4,	1976	Norfolk: Late Saxon town of Thetford
No.5,	1977	Norfolk: various papers on Roman sites
No.6,	1977	Norfolk: Spong Hill Anglo-Saxon cemetery, Part I
No.7,	1978	Norfolk: Bergh Apton Anglo-Saxon cemetery
No.8,	1978	Norfolk: various papers
No.9,	1980	Norfolk: North Elmham Park
No.10,	1980	Norfolk: village sites in Launditch Hundred
No.11,	1981	Norfolk: Spong Hill, Part II: Catalogue of Cremations
No.12,	1981	The barrows of East Anglia
No.13,	1981	Norwich: Eighteen centuries of pottery from Norwich
No.14,	1982	Norfolk: various papers
No.15,	1982	Norwich: Excavations in Norwich 1971–1978; Part I
No.16,	1982	Norfolk: Beaker domestic sites in the Fen-edge and East Anglia
No.17,	1983	Norfolk: Waterfront excavations and Thetford-type Ware production, Norwich
No.18,	1983	Norfolk: The archaeology of Witton
No.19,	1983	Norfolk: Two post-medieval earthenware pottery groups from Fulmodeston
No.20,	1983	Norfolk: Burgh Castle: excavation by Charles Green, 1958–61
No.21,	1984	Norfolk: Spong Hill, Part III: Catalogue of Inhumations
No.22,	1984	Norfolk: Excavations in Thetford, 1948–59 and 1973–80
No.23,	1985	Norfolk: Excavations at Brancaster 1974 and 1977
No.24,	1985	Suffolk: West Stow, the Anglo-Saxon village
No.25,	1985	Essex: Excavations by Mr H.P.Cooper on the Roman site at Hill Farm, Gestingthorpe, Essex
No.26,	1985	Norwich: Excavations in Norwich 1971–78; Part II
No.27,	1985	Cambridgeshire: The Fenland Project No.1: Archaeology and Environment in the Lower Welland Valley
No.28,	1985	Norfolk: Excavations within the north-east bailey of Norwich Castle, 1978
No.29,	1986	Norfolk: Barrow excavations in Norfolk, 1950–82
No.30,	1986	Norfolk: Excavations at Thornham, Warham, Wighton and Caistor St Edmund, Norfolk
No.31,	1986	Norfolk: Settlement, religion and industry on the Fen-edge; three Romano-British sites in Norfolk
No.32,	1987	Norfolk: Three Norman Churches in Norfolk
No.33,	1987	Essex: Excavation of a Cropmark Enclosure Complex at Woodham Walter, Essex, 1976 and An Assessment of Excavated Enclosures in Essex
No.34,	1987	Norfolk: Spong Hill, Part IV: Catalogue of Cremations
No.35,	1987	Cambridgeshire: The Fenland Project No.2: Fenland Landscapes and Settlement, Peterborough–March
No.36,	1987	Norfolk: The Anglo-Saxon Cemetery at Morningthorpe
No.37,	1987	Norfolk: Excavations at St Martin-at-Palace Plain, Norwich, 1981
No.38,	1988	Suffolk: The Anglo-Saxon Cemetery at Westgarth Gardens, Bury St Edmunds
No.39,	1988	Norfolk: Spong Hill, Part VI: Occupation during the 7th–2nd millennia BC
No.40,	1988	Suffolk: Burgh: The Iron Age and Roman Enclosure
No.41,	1988	Essex: Excavations at Great Dunmow, Essex: a Romano-British small town in the Trinovantian Civitas
No.42,	1988	Essex: Archaeology and Environment in South Essex, Rescue Archaeology along the Gray's By-pass 1979–80
No.43,	1988	Essex: Excavation at the North Ring, Mucking, Essex: A Late Bronze Age Enclosure
No.44,	1988	Norfolk: Six Deserted Villages in Norfolk
No.45,	1988	Norfolk: The Fenland Project No. 3: Marshland and the Nar Valley, Norfolk
No.46,	1989	Norfolk: The Deserted Medieval Village of Thuxton
No.47,	1989	Suffolk: West Stow: Early Anglo-Saxon Animal Husbandry
No.48,	1989	Suffolk: West Stow, Suffolk: The Prehistoric and Romano-British Occupations
No.49,	1990	Norfolk: The Evolution of Settlement in Three Parishes in South-East Norfolk
No.50,	1993	Proceedings of the Flatlands and Wetlands Conference
No.51,	1991	Norfolk: The Ruined and Disused Churches of Norfolk
No.52,	1991	Norfolk: The Fenland Project No. 4, The Wissey Embayment and Fen Causeway
No.53,	1992	Norfolk: Excavations in Thetford, 1980–82, Fison Way
No.54,	1992	Norfolk: The Iron Age Forts of Norfolk
No.55,	1992	Lincolnshire: The Fenland Project No.5: Lincolnshire Survey, The South-West Fens
No.56,	1992	Cambridgeshire: The Fenland Project No.6: The South-Western Cambridgeshire Fens
No.57,	1993	Norfolk and Lincolnshire: Excavations at Redgate Hill Hunstanton; and Tattershall Thorpe
No.58,	1993	Norwich: Households: The Medieval and Post-Medieval Finds from Norwich Survey Excavations 1971–1978
No.59,	1993	Fenland: The South-West Fen Dyke Survey Project 1982–86
No.60,	1993	Norfolk: Caister-on-Sea: Excavations by Charles Green, 1951–55
No.61,	1993	Fenland: The Fenland Project No.7: Excavations in Peterborough and the Lower Welland Valley 1960–1969
No.62,	1993	Norfolk: Excavations in Thetford by B.K. Davison, between 1964 and 1970
No.63,	1993	Norfolk: Illington: A Study of a Breckland Parish and its Anglo-Saxon Cemetery
No.64,	1994	Norfolk: The Late Saxon and Medieval Pottery Industry of Grimston: Excavations 1962–92
No.65,	1993	Suffolk: Settlements on Hill-tops: Seven Prehistoric Sites in Suffolk
No.66,	1993	Lincolnshire: The Fenland Project No.8: Lincolnshire Survey, the Northern Fen-Edge
No.67,	1994	Norfolk: Spong Hill, Part V: Catalogue of Cremations
No.68,	1994	Norfolk: Excavations at Fishergate, Norwich 1985
No.69,	1994	Norfolk: Spong Hill, Part VIII: The Cremations
No.70,	1994	Fenland: The Fenland Project No.9: Flandrian Environmental Change in Fenland
No.71,	1995	Essex: The Archaeology of the Essex Coast Vol.I: The Hullbridge Survey Project
No.72,	1995	Norfolk: Excavations at Redcastle Furze, Thetford, 1988–9
No.73,	1995	Norfolk: Spong Hill, Part VII: Iron Age, Roman and Early Saxon Settlement
No.74,	1995	Norfolk: A Late Neolithic, Saxon and Medieval Site at Middle Harling
No.75,	1995	Essex: North Shoebury: Settlement and Economy in South-east Essex 1500–AD1500
No.76,	1996	Nene Valley: Orton Hall Farm: A Roman and Early Anglo-Saxon Farmstead
No.77,	1996	Norfolk: Barrow Excavations in Norfolk, 1984–88
No.78,	1996	Norfolk:The Fenland Project No.11: The Wissey Embayment: Evidence for pre-Iron Age Occupation
No.79,	1996	Cambridgeshire: The Fenland Project No.10: Cambridgeshire Survey, the Isle of Ely and Wisbech
No.80,	1997	Norfolk: Barton Bendish and Caldecote: fieldwork in south-west Norfolk
No.81,	1997	Norfolk: Castle Rising Castle
No.82,	1998	Essex: Archaeology and the Landscape in the Lower Blackwater Valley
No.83,	1998	Essex: Excavations south of Chignall Roman Villa 1977–81
No.84,	1998	Suffolk: A Corpus of Anglo-Saxon Material
No.85,	1998	Suffolk: Towards a Landscape History of Walsham le Willows
No.86,	1998	Essex: Excavations at the Orsett 'Cock' Enclosure
No.87,	1999	Norfolk: Excavations in Thetford, North of the River, 1989–90
No.88,	1999	Essex: Excavations at Ivy Chimneys, Witham 1978–83
No.89,	1999	Lincolnshire: Salterns: Excavations at Helpringham, Holbeach St Johns and Bicker Haven
No.90,	1999	Essex:The Archaeology of Ardleigh, Excavations 1955–80
No.91,	2000	Norfolk: Excavations on the Norwich Southern Bypass, 1989–91 Part I Bixley, Caistor St Edmund, Trowse
No.92,	2000	Norfolk: Excavations on the Norwich Southern Bypass, 1989–91 Part II Harford Farm Anglo-Saxon Cemetery
No.93,	2001	Norfolk: Excavations on the Snettisham Bypass, 1989
No.94,	2001	Lincolnshire: Excavations at Billingborough, 1975–8
No.95,	2001	Suffolk: Snape Anglo-Saxon Cemetery: Excavations and Surveys
No.96,	2001	Norfolk: Two Medieval Churches in Norfolk
No.97,	2001	Nene Valley: Monument 97, Orton Longueville

No.98,	2002	Essex: Excavations at Little Oakley, 1951–78
No.99,	2002	Norfolk: Excavations at Melford Meadows, Brettenham, 1994
No.100,	2002	Norwich: Excavations in Norwich 1971–78, Part III
No.101,	2002	Norfolk: Medieval Armorial Horse Furniture in Norfolk
No.102,	2002	Norfolk: Baconsthorpe Castle, Excavations and Finds, 1951–1972
No.103,	2003	Cambridgeshire: Excavations at the Wardy Hill Ringwork, Coveney, Ely
No.104,	2003	Norfolk: Earthworks of Norfolk
No.105	2003	Essex: Excavations at Great Holts Farm, 1992–4
No.106	2004	Suffolk: Romano-British Settlement at Hacheston
No.107	2004	Essex: Excavations at Stansted Airport, 1986–91
No.108,	2004	Norfolk: Excavations at Mill Lane, Thetford, 1995
No.109,	2005	Fenland: Archaeology and Environment of the Etton Landscape
No.110,	2005	Cambridgeshire: Saxon and Medieval Settlement at West Fen Road, Ely
No.111,	2005	Essex: Early Anglo-Saxon Cemetery and Later Saxon Settlement at Springfield Lyons
No.112,	2005	Norfolk: Dragon Hall, King Street, Norwich
No.113,	2006	Norfolk: Excavations at Kilverstone
No.114,	2006	Cambridgeshire: Waterfront Archaeology in Ely
No.115,	2006	Essex: Medieval Moated Manor by the Thames Estuary: Excavations at Southchurch Hall, Southend
No.116,	2006	Norfolk: Norwich Cathedral Refectory
No.117,	2007	Essex: Excavations at Lodge Farm, St Osyth
No.118,	2007	Essex: Late Iron Age Warrior Burial from Kelvedon
No.119,	2007	Norfolk: Aspects of Anglo-Saxon Inhumation Burial
No.120,	2007	Norfolk: Norwich Greyfriars: Pre-Conquest Town and Medieval Friary
No.121,	2007	Cambridgeshire: A Line Across Land: Fieldwork on the Isleham–Ely Pipeline 1993–4
No.122,	2008	Cambridgeshire: Ely Wares
No.123,	2008	Cambridgeshire: Farming on the Edge: Archaeological Evidence from the Clay Uplands west of Cambridge
No.124,	2008	*Wheare most Inclosures be*, East Anglian Fields: History, Morphology and Management
No.125,	2008	Bedfordshire: Life in the Loop: a Prehistoric and Romano-British Landscape at Biddenham
No.126,	2008	Essex: Early Neolithic Ring-ditch and Bronze Age Cemetery at Brightlingsea
No.127,	2008	Essex: Early Saxon Cemetery at Rayleigh
No.128,	2009	Hertfordshire: Four Millennia of Human Activity along the A505 Baldock Bypass
No.129,	2009	Norfolk: Criminals and Paupers: the Graveyard of St Margaret Fyebriggate *in combusto*, Norwich
No.130,	2009	Norfolk: A Medieval Cemetery at Mill Lane, Ormesby St Margaret
No.131,	2009	Suffolk: Anglo-Saxon Settlement and Cemetery at Bloodmoor Hill, Carlton Colville
No.132,	2009	Norfolk: Norwich Castle: Excavations and Historical Survey 1987–98 (Parts I–IV)
No.133,	2010	Norfolk: Life and Death on a Norwich Backstreet, AD900–1600: Excavations in St Faith's Lane
No.134,	2010	Norfolk: Farmers and Ironsmiths: Prehistoric, Roman and Anglo-Saxon Settlement beside Brandon Road, Thetford
No.135,	2011	Norfolk: Romano-British and Saxon Occupation at Billingford
No.136,	2011	Essex: Aerial Archaeology in Essex
No.137,	2011	Essex: The Roman Town of Great Chesterford
No.138,	2011	Bedfordshire: Farm and Forge: late Iron Age/Romano-British farmsteads at Marsh Leys, Kempston
No.139,	2011	Suffolk: The Anglo-Saxon Cemetery at Shrubland Hall Quarry, Coddenham
No.140,	2011	Norfolk: Archaeology of the Newland: Excavations in King's Lynn, 2003–5
No.141,	2011	Cambridgeshire: Life and Afterlife at Duxford: archaeology and history in a chalkland community
No.142,	2012	Cambridgeshire: *Extraordinary Inundations of the Sea*: Excavations at Market Mews, Wisbech
No.143,	2012	Middle Saxon Animal Husbandry in East Anglia
No.144,	2012	Essex: The Archaeology of the Essex Coast Vol.II: Excavations at the Prehistoric Site of the Stumble
No.145,	2012	Norfolk: Bacton to King's Lynn Gas Pipeline Vol.1: Prehistoric, Roman and Medieval Archaeology
No.146,	2012	Suffolk: Experimental Archaeology and Fire: a Burnt Reconstruction at West Stow Anglo-Saxon Village
No.147,	2012	Suffolk: Circles and Cemeteries: Excavations at Flixton Vol. I
No.148,	2012	Essex: Hedingham Ware: a medieval pottery industry in North Essex; its production and distribution
No.149,	2013	Essex: The Neolithic and Bronze Age Enclosures at Springfield Lyons
No.150,	2013	Norfolk: Tyttel's *Halh*: the Anglo-Saxon Cemetery at Tittleshall. The Archaeology of the Bacton to King's Lynn Gas Pipeline Vol.2
No.151,	2014	Suffolk: Staunch Meadow, Brandon: a High Status Middle Saxon Settlement on the Fen Edge
No.152,	2014	A Romano-British Settlement in the Waveney Valley: Excavations at Scole 1993–4
No.153,	2015	Peterborough: A Late Saxon Village and Medieval Manor: Excavations at Botolph Bridge, Orton Longueville
No.154,	2015	Essex: Heybridge, a Late Iron Age and Roman Settlement: Excavations at Elms Farm 1993–5 Vol. 1
No.155,	2015	Suffolk: Before Sutton Hoo: the prehistoric remains and Early Anglo-Saxon cemetery at Tranmer House, Bromeswell
No.156,	2016	Bedfordshire: Close to the Loop: landscape and settlement evolution beside the Biddenham Loop, west of Bedford
No.157,	2016	Cambridgeshire: Bronze Age Barrow, Early to Middle Iron Age Settlement and Burials, Early Anglo-Saxon Settlement at Harston Mill
No.158,	2016	Bedfordshire: Newnham: a Roman bath house and estate centre east of Bedford
No.159,	2016	Cambridgeshire: The Production and Distribution of Medieval Pottery in Cambridgeshire
No.160,	2016	Suffolk: A Late Iron-Age and Romano-British Farmstead at Cedars Park, Stowmarket
No.161,	2016	Suffolk: Medieval Dispersed Settlement on the Mid Suffolk Clay at Cedars Park, Stowmarket
No.162,	2017	Cambridgeshire: The Horningsea Roman Pottery Industry in Context
No.163,	2018	Nene Valley: Iron Age and Roman Settlement: Rescue Excavations at Lynch Farm 2, Orton Longueville, Peterborough
No.164,	2018	Suffolk: Excavations at Wixoe Roman Small Town
No.165,	2018	Cambridgeshire: Conquering the Claylands: Excavations at Love's Farm, St Neots
No.166,	2018	Norfolk: Late Bronze Age Hoards: new light on old finds
No.167,	2018	Norfolk: A Romano-British Industrial Site at East Winch
No.168,	2018	Cambridgeshire: Small Communities: Life in the Cam Valley in the Neolithic, Late Iron Age and Early Anglo-Saxon Periods. Excavations at Dernford Farm, Sawston
No.169,	2019	Suffolk: Iron Age Fortification Beside the River Lark: Excavations at Mildenhall
No.170,	2019	Cambridgeshire: Rectory Farm, Godmanchester: Excavations 1988–95, Neolithic monument to Roman villa farm
No.171,	2020	Norfolk: Three Bronze Age Weapon Assemblages
No.172,	2020	Suffolk: Excavations at Stoke Quay, Ipswich: Southern *Gipeswic* and the parish of St Augustine
No.173,	2020	Nene Valley: Prehistoric Burial Mounds in Orton Meadows, Peterborough
No.174,	2021	Suffolk: Provisioning Ipswich: Animal Remains from the Saxon and Medieval Town
No.175,	2021	Norfolk: Crownthorpe: a Boudican Hoard of Bronze Vessels from Early Roman Norfolk
No.176,	2022	Norfolk: Fransham: people and land in a central Norfolk parish